RULES AND NETWORKS

Titles in this Series

Rules and Networks

The Legal Culture of Global Business Transactions

Edited by

RICHARD P. APPELBAUM
WILLIAM L.F. FELSTINER
VOLKMAR GESSNER

Oñati International Series in Law and Society

A SERIES PUBLISHED FOR THE OÑATI INSTITUTE
FOR THE SOCIOLOGY OF LAW

·HART·
PUBLISHING
OXFORD – PORTLAND OREGON

Hart Publishing
Oxford and Portland, Oregon

Published in North America (US and Canada) by
Hart Publishing c/o
International Specialized Book Services
5804 NE Hassalo Street
Portland, Oregon
97213-3644
USA

© The Oñati I.I.S.L. 2001
First published 2001. Reprinted (hardback and paperback edition 2003).

Hart Publishing is a specialist legal publisher based in Oxford, England.
To order further copies of this book or to request a list of other
publications please write to:

Hart Publishing, Salter's Boatyard, Folly Bridge,
Abingdon Road, Oxford OX1 4LB
Telephone: +44 (0)1865 245533 or Fax: +44 (0)1865 794882
e-mail: mail@hartpub.co.uk
WEBSITE: http//www.hartpub.co.uk

British Library Cataloguing in Publication Data
Data Available
ISBN 1–84113–295–0 (cloth)
1–84113–296–9 (paper)

Typeset by Hope Services (Abingdon) Ltd.
Printed and bound in Great Britain on acid-free paper by
Biddles Ltd, www.biddles.co.uk

Series Editor's Foreword

Business transactions across national borders in contemporary life face both new challenges and those that have confronted domestic exchanges for centuries. Though there continues to be concern with problems of trust, predictability and dispute processing, there are new hurdles imposed by the speed and volume of business in the modern world. This book explores the roles that various institutions play in making international business transactions possible, institutions that partially substitute for national law and legal institutions in the case of domestic exchanges. In this effort, it focuses on the capacities and limitations of international law, the private law of business sectors (*lex mercatoria*), international law firms, and personal networks as well as highlighting the continuing relevance of national law. It is the first sustained effort to explore this territory simultaneously from the perspectives of legal reasoning, formal law, empirical sociology, economics and relational anthropology. The contributions to this book, by leading scholars in these fields, are an important first step in developing an interdisciplinary discourse on the globalisation of law.

The book is the product of a workshop held at the International Institute for the Sociology of Law (IISL) in Oñati, Spain. The IISL is a partnership between the Research Committee on the Sociology of Law and the Basque Government. For more than a decade it has conducted an international master's programme in the sociology of law and hosted hundreds of workshops devoted to sociolegal studies. It maintains an extensive sociolegal library open to scholars from any country and any relevant discipline. Detailed information about the IISL can be found at www.iisj.es. This book is the most recent publication in the Oñati International Series in Law and Society, a series that publishes the best manuscripts produced from Oñati workshops conducted in English. A similar series, Coleccion Oñati: Derecho Y Sociedad, is published in Spanish.

Eve Darian-Smith

Preface

This book addresses the theme of global business transactions from an inter disciplinary point of view. It grew out of research at the Center for European Legal Policy at the University of Bremen, Germany, and at the University of California, Santa Barbara, USA. The three editors all had strong interest in issues currently discussed in the area of the globalisation of law and convened to contribute their common socio-legal and empirical background to the debate. Together with other activities and publications a workshop was held at the International Institute for the Sociology of Law (IISL) in Oñati, Spain, in June 1999. The initial papers were heavily debated and discussed at the workshop, finally evolving into the chapters of this book. We are indebted to the Volkswagen Foundation for supporting the conference as part of Volkmar Gessner's project on "Global Legal Interaction," to Malen Gordoa Mendizabal and the Oñati Institute for providing excellent staff assistance and a highly supportive and lovely atmosphere for the conference, and to Diane Johnson for here tireless assistance in preparing the manuscripts. We also wish to acknowledge the helpful comments of two unknown reviewers for Hart Publishing, as well as the fine editorial support of Richard Hart, Jane Parker and Hannah Young at Hart. And finally, we wish to thank the authors of the chapters in this volume for providing stimulating discussion at the original conference, and responding to our suggestions for strengthening their final contributions.

Richard P Appelbaum
William L F Felstiner
Volkmar Gessner

Contents

List of Contributors

Richard P. Appelbaum is Professor of Sociology and Global & International Studies, and Director of the Institute for Social, Behavioral, and Economic Research at the University of California, Santa Barbara. His address is Department of Sociology, UCSB, Santa Barbara, CA 93106, USA. His e-mail address is appelbau@sscf.ucsb.edu.

Harry Arthurs is a University Professor of Law and Political Science, and President Emeritus, of York University. His address is Osgoode Hall Law School, York University, 4700 Keele Street, Toronto M3J 1P3, Canada. His e-mail address is harthurs@yorku.ca.

Wai-Keung Chung is a Ph.D. Candidate in the Department of Sociology at the University of Washington, Seattle. His address is Department of Sociology, University of Washington, Seattle, WA 98195, USA. His e-mail address is wchung@u.washington.edu.

Jerome A. Cohen is Professor of Law at New York University, Adjunct Senior Fellow at the Council on Foreign Relations and Of Counsel at the law firm of Paul, Weiss, Rifkind, Wharton & Garrison. His address is New York University School of Law, 40 Washington Square South, New York, NY 10012, USA. His e-mail address is jacohen@paulweiss.com.

Felix Dasser is Privatdozent at the University of Zurich for private law, conflicts of law and private comparative law. He is practising law at Homburger Rechtsanwälte, Zurich, specialising in international commercial arbitration. His address is Weinberg str. 56/58, 8006 Zurich, CH. His e-mail address is Felix.Dasser@homburger.ch.

Filip De Ly, LL.M (Harvard 1983) is professor of private international law and comparative law at the Faculty of Law of the Erasmus University Rotterdam. His address is POB 1738, 3000 DR Rotterdam, The Netherlands. His e-mail address is dely@frg.eur.nl.

William L. F. Felstiner is Distinguished Research Professor of Law at Cardiff University, and Scientific Director of the International Institute for the Sociology of Law at Onati, Spain. His address is IISL, 20560 Onati, Gipuzkoa, Spain. His e-mail address is felstine@sscf.ucsb.edu.

John Flood is Professor of Law and Sociology at the University of Westminster, London. His address is School of Law, University of Westminster, 4 Little Titchfield St., London W1W 7UW, UK. His e-mail address is J.A.Flood@wmin.ac.uk.

Franco Furger is Associate Research Professor at George Mason University's School of Public Policy. His address is School of Public Policy, MS 3C6, 4400 University Drive, Fairfax, VA, 22030–4444, USA. His e-mail address is ffurger@gmu.edu.

Volkmar Gessner is Professor of Private Law, Sociology of Law and Comparative Law at the University of Bremen. His address is Law Faculty, University of Bremen, 28334 Bremen, Germany. His e-mail is gessner@uni-bremen.de.

Gary G. Hamilton is Professor of Sociology, with a joint appointment in the Jackson School of International Studies. His address is Department of Sociology, University of Washington, Seattle, WA 98195, USA. His e-mail address is ggh@u.washington.edu.

Janet T. Landa is Professor of Economics at York University, Toronto, Canada, and Editor-in-Chief of *Journal of Bioeconomics*. Her address is Department of Economics, York University, 4700 Keele Street, Toronto, Ontario M3J 1P3, Canada. Her e-mail address is jlanda@yorku.ca.

Tai-Lok Lui is Associate Professor of Sociology at the Chinese University of Hong Kong. His address is Sociology Department, Chinese University of Hong Kong, Shatin, New Territories, Hong Kong. His e-mail address is tailoklui@cuhk.edu.hk.

Dieter Martiny is Professor of Private Law, Private International Law and Comparative Law at the University of Frankfurt/Oder. His address is Law Faculty, European University Viadrina, Große Scharrnstraße 59, 15230 Frankfurt (Oder), Germany. His e-mail address is martiny@euv-frankfurt-o.de, http://viadrina.euv-frankfurt-o.de/~intrecht/martiny.htm.

John K. M. Ohnesorge is an Assistant Professor at the University of Wisconsin Law School. His address is 975 Bascom Mall, University of Wisconsin Law School, Madison, WI 53706–1399, USA. His e-mail address is ohnesorg@law.harvard.edu.

Rogelio Perez Perdomo is Professor of Law and Business Ethics at the Instituto de Estudios Superiores de Administración in Cacacas, and Academic Director of the Stanford Program for International Legal Studies. His e-mail address is rperez3@leland.stanford.edu.

William E. Scheuerman is Associate Professor of Political Science at the University of Minnesota. His address is 1414 Social Sciences Building, Political Science, 267 19th Ave. South, Minneapolis, MN, 55455, USA. His e-mail address is scheuerm@polisci.umn.edu.

Richard Whitley is Professor of Organisational Sociology at Manchester Business School, University of Manchester. His address is Manchester Business School, Booth Street West, Manchester M15 6PB, UK. His e-mail address is Rwhitley@man.mbs.ac.uk.

Michael Zürn is Professor of International and Transnational Relations at the University of Bremen, and Co-Director of the Institute for Intercultural and International Relations (InIIS). His address is University of Bremen, InIIS, Postfach 3304040, 28334 Bremen, FRG. His e-mail address is mizuern@uni-bremen.de.

Introduction: The Legal Culture of Global Business Transactions

VOLKMAR GESSNER, RICHARD P. APPELBAUM,
WILLIAM L.F. FELSTINER

Abstract

Business transactions are embedded in an environment of culture, practice and rule. The construction and fate of business relationships within a nation-state may encounter differences in modes of negotiation, enforcement of contracts, and in dispute processing, but these conflicts are magnified many times over in cross-border transactions where nation-state control and support are weak or absent, and where the legal and legal-cultural backgrounds of participants may diverge considerably. This introductory chapter distinguishes and critiques four different approaches that attempt to minimise the effect of these magnified difficulties. Most prominent among international and comparative lawyers as well as international organisations is the creation of unified or harmonised law. Because the world economy in many sectors may be too complex to be governed by universal rules, we question the proposition that global legal convergence may be the immediate and inevitable result of increased global interaction. Rather, less formal mechanisms for achieving normative understanding and predictability in business dealings may also play an important role. Among those mechanisms lex mercatoria *and international arbitration have raised expectations in academic debates. But we believe that the practical relevance of global rules autonomously created by business communities is far from obvious. A third way of explaining the construction of global legal certainty is the work of mega law firms—mostly US and British. Their experience in cross-cultural negotiation, drafting contracts and making legal policy seems to support global interactions—at least very large ones. But small and medium-sized enterprises and consumers generally avoid the world of large international law firms. Finally, we discuss the practice of relational contracting. Cross-border obligations may be secured by the creation of trust and interdependence mechanisms, long-term business relationships and mediation procedures in case of breach. Relational contracts are common in many business communities. As the most prominent example we deal in some detail with the practice of* guanxi *in Chinese business circles, but even in that context limitations and exceptions are noted.*

INTERNATIONAL BUSINESS TRANSACTIONS, like everything, are heavily influenced by culture, practice and rule. The construction and fate of business relationships within a nation-state may encounter differences in the generation of norms and the processing of disputes, but these conflicts are magnified many times over in cross-border transactions where nation-state control and support are weak or absent. This book seeks different explanations of the ways in which business people and their legal advisers try to minimise the effect of these magnified difficulties. Since most explanations are dominated by North American and European legal scholarship and practice, a second concern of this book is to open up the discussion to competing explanatory frameworks. Specifically, we entertain the notion that global legal convergence may not be the immediate, inevitable result of increased global economic interaction. Rather, less formal mechanisms for achieving normative understanding and predictability in business dealings may also flourish.

To address our concerns, in June 1999 we convened a three-day workshop of scholars at the Oñati (Spain) International Institute for the Sociology of Law. This volume grew out of the resulting papers. At the outset we suggested four sources through which the international business community might be considered to have supplemented nation-state conflict prevention and dispute resolution institutions—an international legal order, the development of a private normative order based on common business practices (denominated the *lex mercatoria*), through the efforts and work product of internationalised law firms, and by means of extensive, thick personal relationships often referred to by their Chinese term *guanxi*.

Our discussion below elaborates on these themes. We begin by discussing the domination of a particular type of discourse concerning the relationship between modernity and law—one that emphasises the inevitable global triumph of convergent formal-rational legal systems as the key to understanding globalised business practices. We then turn to a more detailed discussion of the four approaches that structure this volume.

MODERNISATION AND LEGAL CONVERGENCE: ONE DISCOURSE—OR MANY?

Discourses about modernity, like modernity itself, originated in the West. The uniquely western marriage between scientific technology and industrial production assured not only the economic and political hegemony of European and North-American capitalism, but of European and North American theories about this hegemony as well. Indeed, the birth of modern social science in the eighteenth and nineteenth centuries was inextricably bound to the Enlightenment belief that history was now to be written as a single story—one of an inexorable, and increasingly global, march from tradition to a golden age of reason. Local particularisms would fall in the face of global universals, as the corrosive effects of modernisation dissolved every trace of local cultures and institutions.

This belief can be traced to the founding of sociology, where it remains a core assumption today. Comte (1975, originally 1830–1842), for example, called for a "social physics" that would enable sociologists to guide industrialists towards the development of a positivist utopia; Spencer (1860) argued that societies evolve from "incoherent homogeneity to coherent heterogeneity", in which rationally organised differences contributed to the common good. Durkheim (1964 [1893]) drew on the evolution of legal institutions as evidence for his notion that the solidarity achieved through the functional integration of highly specialised roles supersedes solidarity on the basis of communally shared beliefs and values. Tönnies (1963 [1887]) sought to demonstrate that modern cultures evolve from *Gemeinschaft* driven by tradition, habit, and instinct to *Gesellschaft* shaped by deliberation and reason. Henry Sumner Maine (1961) argued that a growing range of social relations change from a basis in status to one in contract.

It was, of course, Weber (1979 [1921]; 1946 [1919]) who provided the most influential and enduring formulation of the argument that the end-point of modernisation is a world organised according to rational principles. His painstakingly historical writings on the long-term Western secular trend towards legal-rational forms of social, economic and political organisation provided foundational thinking in economic sociology, political science and legal studies. These classical views became incorporated into a wide range of social thinking in the twentieth century: multilinear evolutionary theory in anthropology (Service, 1976; Sahlins and Service, 1960); Parsonian modernisation theory in sociology (Parsons, 1966; Levy, 1972); rational choice theory in economics (Becker, 1976, 1996).

The rapid acceleration of globalisation during the past quarter century has given new life to these ideas. As modern industrial capitalism has spread throughout the world, so too have discourses about the modern, rationally organised institutions that are assumed to accompany it. A global economy is seen as portending global institutional and cultural homogeneity, as western beliefs, values and institutions follow western corporations around the world.

This is a view widely shared across the spectrum of theories about the emerging world economy. The neoliberal belief in the rationalising effect of unfettered markets, for example, underpins the IMF's push towards open trade and the dismantling of state intervention in the economy. Such structural adjustment, it is argued, is necessary for the rule of law to triumph over "cronyism" and other market-distorting particularisms that arise when the presumably heavy hand of government impedes the rational choice of economic actors. At the other end of the spectrum, neo-Marxist world-systems theorists view the global extension of capitalism as an inevitable consequence of capitalism's systemic properties— a survival-of-the-fittest drive for accumulation and profit necessitating perpetual market expansion and new sources of ever cheaper labour. In the world-system view, each epoch is characterised by a primary economic power, whose economic dominance is reinforced by political and cultural hegemony. At the present time, the principal challenges to global US dominance are found in a united Europe, although the rise of East Asia (including China) is also heralded as possibly foretelling an economically polycentric world (Arrighi, 1996). Although world-systems theory does not directly address the rational-legal assumptions that underlie the contemporary world-system, it does imply that US hegemony—with Europe in close pursuit, and Asia only distantly emergent—includes the cultural and institutional foundations of US capitalism as well.

Within sociology, the framework that most directly addresses the question of institutional convergence is the so-called Stanford Institutionalist School, identified with the work of John Meyer, his colleagues and their students (McNeely, 1995; Scott and Meyer, 1994; Meyer, Boli, and Thomas, 1987; Meyer, Ramirez, and Boli, 1987). The institutionalists focus on the emergence of shared cultural understandings that accompany the global spread of common institutions. In their view, as globalisation leads to growing interdependence among countries, their institutions will increasingly come to resemble one another. By becoming part of a global economic and legal system, countries and organisations are pressured into playing by a common set of international rules and regulations. All the countries of the world are seen as eventually adopting similar laws and institutions, permitting them to interact freely and efficiently with one another. An institutional isomorphism will follow, as countries come to resemble one another in terms of their governments, education, law, and most other areas of life.

Obvious parallels exist with sociology of law and its study of legal institutions. To perceive the globalisation of law as a result of modernisation processes has most prominently been advocated by Friedman (1994, 1996). He points to universal convergence not only in areas like consumer behaviour and business styles but also in legal cultures. Contracts have a central position in a market economy, litigation is a consequence of increasing rights consciousness and lawyers play an active role in the production, the implementation and the enforcement of law. In the course of developments toward modernisation the differences between legal cultures will become less visible and less problematic for global exchanges. A strong argument for the "transnationalisation of the legal field" is also associated with the work of Yves Dezalay and Bryant Garth, who seek to show that a combination of global business hegemony and educational imperialism on the part of US law schools and corporate law firms is responsible for the global triumph of the North American legal model, particularly in the realm of international business law (Dezalay, 1990; Dezalay and Garth, 1996). The growing global influence of US legal services constitutes a motive force, and is the best indicator of the importance of the process of homogenisation of global economic space. The opening and expansion of the market in legal services has unleashed a process of homogenisation and interconnection between national legal systems which until now have strongly preserved their own identities. The breaking down of barriers favours the strongest performers—in this case, the great North American firms—and forces the others to align themselves on their model if they wish to survive (Dezalay, 1990: 283–5). Thus, whatever the analytic framework, a single verdict seems assured: the juggernaut of modernity remakes everything it touches in its own image (Giddens, 2000). Cultures and institutions the world over are transformed; the end of history will see the emergence of a single, institutionally homogeneous world (Fukuyama, 1992). A single future awaits us all.

Or does it? One challenge to modernity is obvious—the rejection of western economic, political and cultural hegemony associated with religious nationalisms around the world. From Afghani Taliban to Iranian mullahs, from Israeli Haredim to Indian Hindu nationalists, powerful religious movements opt for *jihad* over McWorld (Barber and Schultz, 1996; Juergensmeyer, 1994, 2000).

Other challenges to the Western version of modernity are less obvious, because they share modernity's embrace of untrammeled economic development, yet pose alternatives to its highly Western, rational-legal cultural-institutional framework. One challenge is the growing economic power of East Asia and China, which has historically been based on personal networks and relationships of mutual obligation (*guanxi*) rather than the rational-legal set of rules that formally governs business transactions in the West. Such highly particularistic networks and relationships are a direct organisational legacy of Chinese trading networks that date back more than a thousand years (Arrighi, 1994, 1996; Hui, 1995; Hamashita, 1994; Kawakatsu, 1986; Trocki, 1997). Moreover, they appear to have an affinity for the equally informal, personalistic forms of organisation associated with the new, flexible organisational forms that accompany post-Fordist regimes of accumulation (Harvey, 1996). Another challenge is found in the so-called *lex mercatoria*, which Filip De Ly, later in this volume, defines as "a set of rules finding their origins outside domestic legal systems and which are applicable to international business transactions [largely] composed of international sources of law and self-regulatory rules". The emergence of such a *lex mercatoria* also appears to pose a potential challenge to the hegemony of a legal-rational order based primarily in western-dominated political and juridical institutions.

Global economic decentring has not yet brought with it discursive decentring, at least not in terms of our understanding of the intersection of business and law. The present volume, and the conference out of which it grew, reflects our belief that the legal-cultural frameworks shaping the rapidly emerging global economy should not be viewed from exclusive legal and institutional standpoints and from universalistic models prevailing in Europe and North America. It is in hopes of addressing this question that the present volume is devoted.

EXPLAINING GLOBAL LEGAL CERTAINTY IN A RAPIDLY
GLOBALISING WORLD

Economic globalisation has opened the way to a rethinking of the ways in which
international business transactions are regulated and governed in order to avoid
normlessness and anarchy. As we have seen, one answer to the problem of governance lies in the assumption of institutional convergence—modernisation theories that herald the hegemony of western rational-legal institutions and values.
Such theories offer a compelling starting point, based on a long-term trend
towards rationalism, a global market economy, and increasingly contractual
forms of social relationships. But the empirical evidence is weak, particularly in
discourses concerning the globalisation of law. Even where modernisation
theories are able to explain a basic institutional convergence toward rationality
and secularism, the frequently used examples of globalising business, communication, tourism and entertainment cannot be easily generalised to legal developments. As Whitley (this volume) demonstrates, regulatory models and legal
cultural behaviours in the world remain highly diversified, even among societies
which otherwise have achieved a similar level of modernisation. Modern societies offer a highly diverse institutional context leading to different business
environments. There are differences in the extent states regulate the market,
intervene in the market or encourage corporatist forms of organisation. The
financial systems vary on a number of dimensions (like credit based or capital
market-based patterns) as do the norms governing trust and authority relations
(like contractual or communal forms of authority)—with considerable consequences for the respective business and legal cultures.

The persistence of legal diversity among nation-states is generally perceived
as an obstacle for global governance as well as for legal certainty in global transactions. Global governance refers to public law, the organisation of government–citizen relationships in matters like control over mergers and acquisitions,
unfair competition, free trade, environmental protection, labour standards and
human rights. Legal certainty refers to private law, the organisation of citizen-
–citizen relationships in such matters as contracts, debt-enforcement, torts,
inheritance, divorce and child support. The combination of conflicting public
law among nation-states and of conflicting private law in global business
exchanges and family relations makes it difficult to achieve legal solutions,
resulting, according to some scholars, in societal anarchy (Bull, 1995).

Yet we believe such anarchy is over-rated. Global actors clearly require some
form of institutional support if they are to survive in a generally inhospitable
global environment, and—even in the absence of global institutions—they find
it where it has always been: in national legal systems. In discussing the presumed
absence of global governance and legal certainty, globalisation theories of law
tend to disregard or underestimate the adaptive capacities of nation-states in
creating law and legal institutions suitable for the new global environment

(Hirst and Thompson, 1996). Even in an increasingly global economy, the largest part of law that organises, controls or supports cross-border social behaviour remains domestic law—a fact that economists and sociologists have only belatedly discovered. Nation-states are and will likely remain for the fore-seeable future the most important source of legal support and certainty, continuing to provide legal rules as well as the institutional frameworks needed to establish predictable contractual relations and to adjudicate international disputes. It is clearly time to bring the nation-state back into the globalisation discussion. Many domestic institutions are affected by the internationalisation of business and in particular by the "new economy", where distances seemingly disappear and where the location of the parties and the delivery or provision of services or information are ultimately a circumstantial, rather than an essential, element of the contractual relationship. Confronted with the uncertainties of multinational and global transactions and the problem of how to stabilise the law applicable to the global context, nation-states are active in coping with new situations such as the information economy in general and electronic commerce in particular (Nimmer, 2000).

Even prior to reliance on national legal systems as frameworks for resolving regional and global risks and uncertainties, other forms of institutional support are sought in civil society: family and kinship relationships, religious and ethnic communities, formal and informal economic associations. The diversity of legal and social institutions shaping the global business environment certainly increases its complexity, but at the same time prevents it from becoming an-archical.

In the present volume, we deal only with "rules and networks" that create or fail to create legal certainty in horizontal business relations across borders. With the exception of Furger's study on industry self-regulation, aspects of public global governance, trade regulation, consumer protection, taxation, money laundering and environmental protection are beyond the scope of the contributions assembled in this book. We concede that these issues of global governance are crucial and that they deserve the high degree of public atten-tion observable in media and academic writing. But our focus on global busi-ness cultures will also enhance a better understanding of current globalisation processes and eventually contribute to the governance debate. Within discus-sions of business cultures legal certainty is, of course, only one issue among many others (such as flexibility, responsiveness, creativity as elements of busi-ness environments). It is an issue of utmost importance in institutional eco-nomics where legal certainty is a means for reducing transaction costs (Wallis and North, 1986; North, 1990). Our choice for focusing on legal certainty is based on the assumption shared in sociological theory that all social inter-actions rely on some institutional support for mutual expectations. We were curious how this support is organised in a culture above the level of social units we are accustomed to calling societies, that is in an emerging culture eventu-ally developing into a world society.

We distinguish four distinct discourses about the way businesses are supported and structured in the global environment: one emphasises the importance of formal legal rules, a second emphasises autonomous rules in the form of business self-regulation (*lex mercatoria*), a third focuses on the decisive role of the legal profession itself in structuring business relationships and in bridging the gap between legal cultures, and a fourth emphasising the importance of tightly-knit, informal business networks, as exemplified in the *guanxi* relationships of Chinese business culture. These four discourses form a rough continuum, ranging from highly universalistic to highly particularistic normative solutions to the problem of co-ordination and regulation in global business cultures. We structured our workshop, and the present volume, around these four approaches, which we now take up in turn.

Legal Approaches

Legal approaches emphasising the role of formal legal institutions in fostering certainty in international and cross-border exchanges lie at the universalistic pole of the four discourses. These approaches, supported by most sociologists of law, follow from the insights of Max Weber: an increasingly globalising world is predicted to evolve universal rules, an independent judiciary, and a formal rational bureaucracy above the nation-state. Both nation-states and international organisations can be expected to generate public and private law, by means of international conventions accorded universal applicability. According to Bonell (1990) it is no longer possible to count the number of international conventions, uniform laws, codes and rules of conduct that attempt to regulate the most varied aspects of global dealings by means of uniform rulings. In the area of commercial law, the first objective is predictability and stability in international commercial relations and the reduction of legal risks. Unification efforts therefore have concentrated on contract law and the resolution of contractual disputes. Examples of prominent global or international legal institutions include (Stephan, 1999):

- The UN Commission on International Trade Law (UNCITRAL). This organisation embodies 36 official delegations representing national governments chosen on a rotating basis by the UN General Assembly. Since 1991 it has approved two conventions and four model laws, the most important convention being the UN Convention on Contracts for the International Sale of Goods.
- The International Institute for the Unification of Private Law (UNIDROIT). Previously a League of Nations institution, it became an independent international organisation in 1940. Its membership consists of 58 nations whose governments send representatives to periodic conferences. To date it has produced eight international conventions.

- The Hague Conference, which began work in 1893 but did not take on a permanent institutional character until 1955. It has 45 members. Since World War II it has promulgated 33 Conventions, some of which have achieved widespread adoption.
- At the regional level, the European Union and the Organisation of American States also draft multilateral conventions involving international commercial law and otherwise encourage unification and harmonisation of commercial law. Both have developed, *inter alia*, laws affecting carriage of goods by rail and intermodal transport and transnational private litigation.

Europe, with its long codification traditions, has been particularly keen on creating unified law. As the existing differences in public and private law are considered to function as non-tariff barriers, thereby distorting competition and adding to existing transaction costs, there is a common understanding that unification of law should be a high priority. This applies not only to public economic law, but to private law as well, particularly contracts and torts. Spurred on by a resolution of the European Parliament, a number of scholarly initiatives have launched an ambitious project to harmonise the civil law of all 15 member countries (Hartkamp *et al.*, 1998; Martiny, 1999).

But the number and reputation of these international lawmakers and scholarly writers does not mean that their work actually provides a realistic picture of developments in regulating global business. There are critical voices both within and outside the realm of legal discourses. Most drafters of uniform law are aware of the fact that, first, international conventions meet with very different implementation structures all over the world. The gap referred to in many studies in the sociology of law is far greater between international law and legal practice than between domestic law and legal practice (Bonell, 1990; Gessner, 1996; von Freyhold, 1996; Gessner and Budak, 1998; Budak, 1999; Gordon, 1998). A good test case is the practice of the UN Convention on Contracts for the International Sale of Goods, a convention currently in force in almost 50 nation-states. Bailey (1999) has studied its importance in the USA where the convention became part of domestic law in 1988 but is virtually unknown to US courts and practitioners. Global actors often circumvent legal institutions by legitimate means (for example, *lex mercatoria* contracts, discussed below) or illegitimate ones (mafia, money laundering, arms trafficking) (Santino, 1988). Secondly, domestic legal systems are mostly unable to recognise the specificities of a cross-border (as opposed to a domestic) case (David, 1972). And thirdly, interpretation differences of unified law are a common and easily predictable occurrence.

At the level of the nation-state, increasingly pluralistic and differentiated societies make it difficult to develop and implement highly general laws with universal applicability. And on the even more plural and differentiated global level, universal law might not only be inefficient but counterproductive: widely divergent values and methodological approaches to the interpretation and application of supposedly universal rules could well exacerbate insecurity and unpredictability as a result of conflicting interests. This may well be one of the reasons why hardly any convention truly reaches the goal of universality. Usually it is considered a success if a convention (like the UN Convention on Contracts for the International Sale of Goods) is ratified by 30 or 40 states.

Other criticisms of the legal discourse show unresolved and even irresolvable problems of legal globalisation. These problems include differentiation processes in global business cultures which run contrary to the ambition of making commercial law universal, highly diversified implementation processes that emerge in efforts at legal harmonisation (for example, European Community law: see Duina, 1999), and highly technocratic forms of law production among academics that result in less rather than more legal certainty (Stephan, 1999). We will briefly consider each of these in turn.

Differentiation processes that occur in global business cultures challenge the basic assumptions of legal unification, namely that a single global business culture is developing with similar interests, values and behavioural patterns. Santos (1995: 281; see also Teubner, 1997) observes rather the opposite: the emergence of a new form of plurality of legal orders, partial legal fields constituted by relatively unrelated and highly discrepant logics of regulation coexisting on the local, the state and the global levels. He perceives therefore uniform laws as very limited in scope and unable to account for the tremendous growth, in number, complexity and variety, of transnational contracts and other business transactions (Santos, 1995: 289). Based on similar observations of differentiation processes, Gessner (1996, 1998) questions the very idea of norm production for societal structures above the nation-state. The larger the social unit the less likely it is that normative expectations can be successfully integrated on the level of norms. Social exchanges across borders are based on lower, more specific expectation structures like social roles (a well known law firm, an arbiter, the London Commercial Court) or simply on personal relationships. The opportunities for steering global exchanges and for creating confidence among global actors then lie on institutions rather than on law, be it domestic, international or unified.

Another challenge to legal unification comes from empirical research on European Community law—an area of law that in legal discourse is always used as exemplary for its unification and harmonisation successes. An important instrument of harmonisation presumably consists of EU directives which are binding, as regards the result to be achieved, upon each Member State to which they are addressed, but which leave to the national authorities the choice of form and method (Article 189(3) EEC Treaty). In a recent comparative study of two directives Duina (1999) shows that Member States are far from complying with these obligations. They do comply if the *status quo* suffers none or only minor changes. But they fail either to transpose all of the directive's principles or to implement them after transposition into domestic law if there is major resistance among relevant domestic interest groups. The problem is the democratic deficit of EU legislative processes—and such a deficit can be observed in virtually all international institutions involved in the drafting of unified law. If social interests are not sufficiently articulated in the drafting stage they will obstruct the implementation process.

Finally, Stephan (1999) discusses the role of experts and interest groups in the drafting process of conventions of international commercial law. Each nation's leading specialists convene in realising the technocratic ideal of rules for the business community, having a relatively free hand to discover the common ground among differences in legal culture and economic development. National politicians and lobbyists do not participate, mostly only retaining the final say over accepting the completed instrument. In this late stage some interest groups will succeed in introducing changes protecting their specific clients. The overall result of this process is assumed to be sub-optimal (in comparison to domestic legislative processes and case law of domestic or arbitration courts). A similar critique is currently part of the "comitology" research agenda where mainly the technocratic preparation of EU law is under scrutiny (Joerges and Vos, 1999). Expert knowledge seems to be appropriate only as part of a political process but not as a substitute for it. Academic reasoning—in particular if it is, as in legal scholarship, not open to interdisciplinary discussions—creates less rather than more legal certainty.

The critique of the legal approach might well overlook some unified law that works and is universally accepted. Practitioners and researchers at times are not even aware of the fact that the domestic law they are dealing with is nothing but globalised law transformed into a national statute or administrative regulation. A German tort law might have been shaped by a directive of the European Union, while an Indian labour regulation regarding minimum age of joining the workforce might be nothing but the implementation of an international labour standard set by the child labour convention of the International Labour Organisation. The degree to which law is already universal tends therefore to be underestimated (Arthur's data, in this volume, may therefore have to be interpreted with caution).

Several chapters in this book testify to the incredibly wide range of formal rule systems designed to take up the slack in normative structures created when business transactions move beyond the boundaries of a single state. Most important to the international legal order are the range of institutions that Zürn describes as intergovernmental networks, international regimes, international organisations and supranational organisations. Zürn makes the important point that the growth in international governance structures, originating as they generally do with governments, demonstrates that states are not just passive witnesses to globalisation processes, but play an active role in the development of international institutions. Other chapters highlight the importance of international private law and of international conventions on conflict of laws or unification of law—both regimes continuously adapted to the needs of global business (Martiny)—and the growth of networks among national regulators or "transgovernmentalism". Martiny claims that the environment of global trans-actions consists of a mixture of different rules, international conventions, national legal rules and contracts. What remains to be theoretically and empir-ically specified is the extent and circumstances under which such legal regimes actually are effectively mobilised in practice.

But the opposite may also be true: the practical importance of global law may be overestimated. The fiercely defended monopoly of international and com-parative lawyers in creating an idealised picture of coherent and fair inter-national rule-making is currently challenged by social scientific research. Support and regulation of global business transactions through legal unification might prove to be an impasse. Martiny (this volume) at the end of his arguments in favour of a legal approach concedes that international conventions on legal unification do not have much value without more efforts of co-ordination, implementation and adaptation to the needs of international business, and asks for more supporting structures and self-regulation. Scheuerman (this volume) argues that given the "time-space compression" associated with globalisation (Harvey, 1996; Giddens, 1987, 1990), Fuller's (1964) insights about the possibil-ity of a mismatch between rapidly moving economic activities and more tradi-tional, stable forms of adjudication are more true today then when they were formulated 35 years ago: "[p]erhaps it was in part the relatively slow pace of tra-ditional forms of capitalism that helped give Weber's notion of an 'elective affin-ity' between capitalism and formal law real substance, whereas contemporary high-speed globalizing capitalism may be shedding much of its dependence on formal law" (see chapter by Scheuerman, 110). Scheuerman speculates that the "high-speed character of economic globalisation" may render some aspects of legalism obsolete, resulting in other, extra-legal approaches to resolving con-flict—including international commercial arbitration in which proceedings are secret and recourse to legal rules or precedent limited, fast-track arbitration, and the informality of particularistic relationships described below in the sec-tion on personal networks and *guanxi* relationships.

The "new economy" is the best example of a high speed economy that requires different tools for understanding the role of law and the appropriate approach to facilitate commerce as well as for structuring rules to avoid abuse in the new context (Nichols, 2000). The half life of products is less than a year, property rights are weakly protected, transaction costs are small and business relations are unstable (Siebert, 2000). "The online world entails a new level of automation in contracting, a different method of recording assent and the terms of a contract, and a different type of interaction between the provider and client than was true in the paper world" (Nimmer, 2000: 2). With the "new economy" a global business culture seems to have emerged which is universal in its trans-action patterns and therefore easier to operate than most other forms of global exchanges characterised by more diversity. Wiener (1999) treats the inter-national financial sector as a comparable universal business culture, but at the same time he gives evidence of the enormous problems for law to be developed and implemented universally. The "new economy" already faces similar problems (Cody, 1999; Modisett and Lott, 2000). Both areas of business activities demonstrate that observing the circumstances under which common cultures emerge and survive is a prerequisite for attempts at legal regulation.

The Law Merchant (*Lex Mercatoria*)

The discourse around the emerging law merchant (*lex mercatoria*), while also emphasising that relatively universalistic norms are emerging to govern global business transactions, claims to be closer to the perceived needs of the international business community than are legal approaches. As proponents of the law merchant approach point out, international legal practice—with active assistance of a number of law professors—has in an informal manner developed such a large number of contractual stipulations, standard contracts, commercial usages and customs, arbitral awards and rules formulated by the International Chamber of Commerce and by trade associations, that an almost entirely separate and self-sufficient body of law has come into existence. This body of law reportedly serves to keep international commercial disputes out of the courts, and thereby beyond the reach of domestic laws (see for example Berman and Kaufman, 1978; Berger, 1997). Although most state courts deny the law merchant legal standing, qualifying these rules only as commercial customs, it is claimed that sufficient sanctioning power is effected by arbitral tribunals, blacklisting, withdrawal of membership rights in trade associations and trading clubs, and forfeiture of reputation in the business community.

A major issue in the law merchant discourse is its legal qualification. If these rules are considered law arbitration tribunals and even state courts may enforce them. The problem is that there is no clearcut division between contractual stipulations (which can always be enforced as part of the unquestioned autonomy of contractual parties) and general rules (which need some more legitimation than contract). Is the reasoning in an arbitration award a sufficient legitimation? From a traditional legal point of view the answer is definitely negative. But things seem to change as the following example indicates: a recent book on the law of long-term international commercial transactions (Nassar, 1995) cites no fewer than 151 arbitration awards (plus 95 awards of the Iran–United States Claims Tribunal) and only 47 cases decided in state courts. It seems to be obvious from these numbers that, at least as regards the important area of contractual obligations in cases where long-term contracts break down or cause unforeseen damage to one of the contracting parties, the bulk of innovations comes from non-state actors and is considered—at least in the Common Law world—as a source of law.

Although not irrelevant, the legal standing of the law merchant is of minor importance for our more general perspective on the orientation and problem-solving capacity of this autonomous set of rules for global business transactions.

But the legal discourse also reveals: (a) that the law merchant is far from being universal, (b) that it is imperfect and incomplete and therefore cannot eliminate the need for a choice of law clause in an international contract, (c) that its identity is vague, (d) that there are no mandatory rules, (e) that, due to the lack of sufficient reasoning in many arbitral awards and the infrequent reporting of (mostly confidential) decisions, the state of the art is highly lacking in transparency, and (f) that the application of this body of rules is not tolerated in domestic courts and is exceptional even in arbitration (Bond, 1990; Maniruzzaman, 1999). Social-scientific studies which attempt to give an answer to the question of the problem-solving capacity of the law merchant provide a patchwork of theoretical and empirical insights, and seem generally positive as regards the acceptance and efficiency of this approach.

The economic analysis of law strongly supports what it calls "decentralised law-making", arguing that rather than proceeding from top to bottom (following an "imperative theory of law"), lawmaking is more efficient if it proceeds from bottom to top. Such analysis provides indirect support for the efficacy of the law merchant approach. Robert Cooter (1996), for example, has argued that the rules designed by parties in a decentralised market are more efficient than, and therefore preferable to, law enacted by a central power. Uniform centralised law and market laws of the parties' choice pose costs and offer benefits. Uniform laws are more predictable, reducing the parties' costs of information, uncertainty, and learning. In contrast, less predictable contractual norm-arrangements require parties to engage in continuous inventions, and to incur higher negotiation and enforcement costs. Uniform laws, however, increase the parties' costs by imposing one size on many transactions, regardless of parties' needs; by limiting experiments; and by delaying quick adaptation that is crucial in volatile situations. Centralised law reaches acceptance by a larger number of stakeholders with different, and perhaps conflicting, interests only by making—sometimes inadequate—compromises.

Suggestive within these economic approaches is Bernstein's (1992) analysis of the diamond trade where dealers and brokers "opt out of the legal system" by creating a completely autonomous normative community with merchant rules, blacklisting, reputational bonds and—as last resort—arbitration (see also Teubner 1997 for additional examples of law merchant communities). But the diamond trading merchants are a rather exceptional global tribe, due to very particular social, economic and even religious bonds. In general the autonomy of these communities seems to be overestimated due to persisting state law effects. This was convincingly demonstrated by Bernstein (1996) in another study where she observed the arbitration practice of the US National Grain and Feed Association. The arbitration awards never take notice of autonomous norms and usages of this trade and apply contract law strictly and even more formalistically than state courts. She develops an interesting hypothesis in explaining this observation: autonomous norms are used to preserve the relationship, whereas legal norms offer solutions for ending the relationship. The interplay of law merchant rules, private contracts, state law and uniform law has also been impressively demonstrated in the securitisation business, which, not unlike banking, bridges the gap between the demands for risk protection of borrowers and savers, but achieves this goal by different mechanisms (Frankel, 1998).

What is called self-regulation is often initiated by international regimes like the United Nations Code of Conduct on Transnational Corporations, the OECD Guidelines for Multinational Enterprises and similar principles elaborated by the ILO. Together with religious and environmental groups the AFL-CIO promoted "Maquiladora Standards of Conduct". But some corporations—well-known cases are Levi Strauss and Reebok—issued their own self-initiated and self-supervised codes of conduct in order to be shielded from legislative intervention, to deflect responsibilities from retailers to manufacturers and to ward off criticism and pressure by community groups (Compa and Darricarrère, 1996; Bonacich and Appelbaum, 2000: 303). In the United States, the Fair Labor Association—an offshoot of the White House's Apparel Industry Partnership—is a consortium of apparel manufacturers committed to self-regulation through internal monitoring in combination with outside monitors. In fact, a sizeable industry has arisen to provide such external monitors, including major accounting firms (for example, PriceWaterhouseCoopers) and firms created for just this purpose (for example, Calsafety Compliance). Studies of the effectiveness of self-regulation are not encouraging (BSR, IRRC, and O'Rourke, 2000; O'Rourke, 2000; Appelbaum, *et al.*, 2000). Furger (in this volume) now provides a comprehensive and critical picture of these issues of industry self-regulation. It seems important to note that self-regulation for the purpose of contract enforcement is a different matter from self-regulation aimed at protecting public goods. Whereas the former is fostered by the rule of reciprocity leading to utilitaristic co-operation (co-operative clusters discussed below), the latter is much more difficult to establish due to free-rider problems (Vanberg, 1987).

The assumed autonomy of globalised business has been interpreted by a systemic approach in sociological theory as a communicative process with closed circuit arbitration, "which has to judge the validity of the contracts, although its own validity is based on the very contract the validity of which it is supposed to be judging", and self-regulatory contracts "which regulate the future behaviour of the parties, but also 'secondary rules' which regulate the recognition of primary rules, their identification, their interpretation and the procedures for resolving conflicts" (Teubner, 1997: 17, 16). This type of "reflexive law" is assumed to be more flexible and more adaptive to continuously changing circumstances in the global economy. But conceding juridification and politicisation of the *lex mercatoria*—as Teubner does toward the end of his article (at 21 and 22)—can mean only that his assumption of autonomy is unconvincing.

Empirical research on law merchant rules and autonomous business communities is rare. Berger (2000) reports some preliminary results of a worldwide inquiry on the use of transnational commercial law in international legal practice. About one third of those addressees who provided the data used in the data entry (23 per cent of the sample) indicated that they were aware of some form of law merchant. But *lex mercatoria* rules are reported to be used mainly to interpret domestic law or supplement international uniform law. There seem to be little evidence in this study of any autonomous legal practice. The research published in Gessner and Budak (1998) observed almost nothing which can be defined as autonomous law production (at 11). Nor does a recent study of the London reinsurance market (Stammel, 1998) confirm theoretical assumptions of autonomy and reflexive law-making. Contractual disputes between insurance companies and reinsurance companies are—much to the surprise of the author herself—frequently taken to the London Commercial Court. The businesses involved in the reinsurance market seem to have grown in number over the size of a community that can be autonomously regulated. And the stakes in reinsurance disputes are frequently too high to leave the matter within informal procedures. Arbitration is important in this market but not more than in most other global markets.

The assumption of a qualitative superiority of arbitration also lacks empirical evidence. The London Commercial Court and also New York courts (von Freyhold, 1996; von Freyhold, Gessner and Olgiati, 1996) have developed a considerable competence in international matters. The quantitative importance of arbitration is challenged by data showing the impressive number of cross-border cases taken to state courts (60,000 cases annually in Germany alone: see Vial, 1998: 47). The amounts in dispute must be very high to lead to use of an arbitration tribunal. And arbitrators seem to be not so much innovative institutions of contractual self-validation and business self-regulation but are, according to Dezalay and Garth (1996), better characterised as a relatively small number of individuals—mostly (western) lawyers and law professors—who after discovering arbitration as a new lucrative business and as a means in the struggle for power and influence promote it as more flexible and more competent. In their characterisation the *lex mercatoria* was originally the province of European master academics and learned jurists who played important roles in the deliberations of the International Chamber of Commerce in Paris. Constituted of "general principles of international commerce", the *lex mercatoria* became salient and consequential in disputes between Western oil and construction companies and third world oil-producing countries during the four decades from the 1930s to the 1970s. It provided an escape for the companies which did not want their conflicts with the oil countries to be governed by local law and for the countries which did not want to have it appear that English, American or French law had been imposed upon them. To Dezalay and Garth, the *lex mercatoria* may have had its day. The increasing influence in international arbitration of American-style law firms wedded to American-style litigation practices and the growth of anti-dumping, anti-trust and bilateral trade agreements have led to a "relative decline of the *lex mercatoria*" (Dezalay and Garth, 1996: 90).

Several chapters in this book make glancing, and contradictory, references to *lex mercatoria*. Zürn suggests "that the *lex mercatoria* seems to have grown in importance in recent years", a view also noted by Arthurs. The most embryonic forms of *lex mercatoria* seem to be the private governance involved in industry self-regulation and standard-setting organisations described by Furger. The product testing, safety and environmental standards and certification processes that are the core of such efforts are potentially, thanks to information technologies, as available internationally as nationally. Furger points to the fact that they are subject to the same infirmities of stagnation and lack of credibility that have plagued national efforts. But some industry and business communities seem to be able to establish sufficient reputational bonds and soft control mechanisms in order to achieve non-state public regulation. This observation is strongly supported by a recent report of the European Commission on industry self-regulation on environmental protection (European Commission, 1996). Most EU Member States practise governmental restraint in politically highly controversial or technologically complicated areas, experiencing self-regulation to be more cost-efficient and more successful than legislative measures.

The two chapters in the book that are directly concerned with the *lex mercatoria* also take quite different tacks. De Ly believes that Dezalay and Garth's concentration on large, oil-related cases does not do justice to the potential for the *lex mercatoria* in more run-of-the-mill disputes. He outlines the arguments that have been made about the need for and legitimacy of the *lex mercatoria* and traces its transformation from a controversial academic theory to acceptance "as a fact of life", approved in effect by several national arbitration codes, enshrined in several international conventions and model laws, and fostered by the tendencies in international conventions to adopt "restatement-like" approaches to resolving cross-border disputes.

Although De Ly concludes that "the *lex mercatoria*, as . . . a autonomous legal system, is here to stay as a fact of life and . . . the question is more about the conditions . . . under which it should be applied", he also is guarded about the empirical support for his own position—"there is scant empirical evidence regarding the frequency and means of application of . . . usages and custom in international trade". The chapter by Dasser in good measure provides that very empirical evidence. Dasser argues that the *lex mercatoria* must mean something more than the recognition of trade usage in dispute resolution which is, after all, a ubiquitous practice in courts as well as arbitrations. To Dasser "the real question . . . [is] whether we may simply and *exclusively* apply rules that were developed for international business transactions outside the traditional framework of national laws and international conventions". Then he sets out to determine whether or not a *lex mercatoria* in this sense is actually used in international arbitrations. After extensive review of arbitration archives, Dasser concludes that very few awards are based on "a non-national legal system" and that those that were tend to be special cases of state contracts in the 1950s and 1960s or where the arbitrators were explicitly empowered to base decisions on equity rather than substantive legal rules.[1] The *lex mercatoria*, at least at the present time, seems to have far greater significance in the minds of legal scholars and sociologists of law than it does for the merchants themselves.

The Legal Profession

International law firms (ILFs) are heavily involved in capital markets, trade and direct investment across national borders. Their work frequently involves the construction of extensive contractual arrangements that are intended both to determine the behaviour of the contracting parties during the life of the relationship and to provide for the resolution of conflicts that may arise between them during it. It follows, therefore, that ILFs are strategically poised to help generate international law.

The notion that ILFs play a central role in providing support and legal certainty to business actors is a relatively new paradigm. It assumes, at least in its extreme version, that in a complex world of global economic exchanges any attempt at generalising expectations like unified law or *lex mercatoria* rules is doomed to failure. What is important, according to this literature, is the assistance of a creative law firm which structures and restructures the business environment needed for a specific business strategy. Contracts are drafted which are largely independent of any state law, corporations are created in forms previously unheard of, financial transactions avoid state control, tax heavens are discovered and gaps in the trade law system are exploited. The model for this kind of comprehensive lawyering is the US mega law firm, which is especially effective in generating an international legal framework reflecting the legal culture of its clients (Silver, 2000).

US lawyering is known as "legal entrepreneurialism", a proactive attitude in structuring, negotiating and drafting their client's deals, requiring an understanding of business, financial and managerial concepts and a commitment to their client's interests and goals. US lawyers' experience in business deals enables them to export complex transactions and adapt them to local legal systems, American pragmatism helps in approaching business and legal issues regardless of the applicable law. Since US lawyers are also involved in the preparation of legislation and administrative regulations, in lobbying and other forms of political advocacy such as public-interest lawyering, as well as creative litigation, their contribution to the production of law on the micro and the macro level can hardly be overestimated. Trubek *et al.* (1994) describe this "American mode of production of law" as a system at whose core are the large, multi-purpose, commercially-oriented law firms. These firms not only have exercised substantial influence on US legal culture but are currently

---

[1] At the conference, Ibrahim Shihata noted that the *lex mercatoria* was almost never mentioned as a source of law or otherwise in arbitrations at the International Centre for Settlement of Investment Disputes, of which he has been the Secretary General for many years.

extending their influence to other legal cultures and to global business and finance. The US "mega" law firm is prepared to develop the contractual regimes needed in cross-border transactions, and to operate in multiple jurisdictions. It advises corporate clients as well as governments, and is active in creating and remaking the emerging global order (Trubek *et al.*, 1994: 433). The elite New York law firms have participated in international finance, counselling in Eurodollar transactions, the issue of American Depositary Receipts, sovereign and international institutional borrowings, and international branches of foreign securities offerings. They have accumulated expertise with specialised transactions initiated by banking clients, and they use this expertise to market their services to foreign clients (Silver, 2000). The only serious competitors of US law firms in the international legal market-place are English law firms that merge and fuel their growth internally and organically in order to provide their clients with similar expertise (Flood, 1996). But they are lagging behind opening offices abroad and their innovative potential is less evident since they lack the US pro-active tradition. According to interviews carried out recently by Flood the primary purpose of City lawyers in the international market is to sell English law: "the idea is to capture foreign clients for UK law" (Flood, 1996: 191).

The empirical evidence for the thesis that global law follows the American mode of production by way of mega lawyering—and to a certain degree also by elite in-house lawyers who represent exceedingly powerful multinational business entities (Daly, 1997)—depends on the role these US lawyers play in global business affairs. Trubek *et al.* (1994: 428, 431) describe "the European legal field" as already being heavily Americanised. The new (American) entrants are lending support to the development of EC law and are pressing for the modernisation of domestic laws of the Member States, for the development of new approaches in lawyering and for a more business-oriented organisation of legal services. Whereas the latter observation seems indeed to describe an ongoing trend (Dezalay, 1990) the former overemphasises the influence of lawyers in general and of US lawyers in particular in the complex process of European law production. The same might be true for other world regions and certainly for those regions dominated by civil law legal reasoning where legislation and legal scholarship play the dominant role in law production—a role which cannot be easily dismissed by calling it "the Old European Model" (Trubek *et al.*, 1994).

The picture of creative global restructuring is also challenged by frequent complaints of practising lawyers—in fact mostly US lawyers—about their problems in dealing with international cases (Roorda, 1993; Mears, 1993; Owen and Loperena, 1995; Simon, 1996; Sunwolf, 1997; Mazzini, 1997; Baraban, 1998). They would not desperately try to understand foreign law, foreign negotiation styles, foreign court and administrative procedures and foreign legal behaviour and attitudes if they were able to create and impose their own way of contracting, negotiating and litigating all around the globe.

A number of chapters in this volume address the role of ILFs in the emerging international legal order. Some firms have served their clients for more than a century (Flood); in other cases, their relationship with their client is based on a single, contemporary transaction (Cohen). The extent to which these services reflect supranational dimensions varies from field to field; slight in the case of labour relations (Arthurs) while pervasive in capital markets work (Flood). ILFs are not confined to highly-industrialised economies, but are active wherever their clients are engaged in business and even play a role in nationalised industries in countries unsympathetic to US-style capitalism (Pérez Perdomo).

ILFs are extremely sensitive to the choice-of-law predicament that occurs if serious conflicts occur in their clients' international business transactions (Martiny, Cohen, Pérez Perdomo, Flood). One theme that runs through many chapters of this book is the re-emergent role played by national law in these circumstances. When parties from different nations contract to do business in third, fourth or more countries, a choice-of-law approach, left to its own devices, can be a nightmare (Martiny). Of course, frequently to choose a forum is to choose a normative order. English and New York courts chosen as arbiters in many specialised transactions apply English and New York law, and in fact were selected for that very reason (Flood). But in the more open case of institutionalised or *ad hoc* arbitration, particularly in the face of the questionable and even declining role of a *lex mercatoria* (see above), the most usual ILF response is to denominate the law of one state or another to apply in case of irresolvable conflict (Dasser).

Finally, to see the role of ILFs as limited to such formal aspects of international business transactions as contract formation and dispute resolution is seriously to shortchange their important influence. For that influence, as is seen in the chapters by Cohen and Flood, is largely predicated on the ILFs' enormous experience on a local level all over the world in knowing how to initiate, negotiate, establish, operate and coexist with businesses and business people from vastly different traditions, practices and cultures. In this sense they provide more expertise than structure (Pérez Perdomo), and expertise may be the less common commodity. Ultimately, of course, the expertise is situated in individuals rather than in firms, but the people with the expertise tend to be in ILFs (Cohen).

In the last analysis, the efforts of ILFs are generally directed toward leaving questions of who will decide conflicts and what rules they will employ as little to chance as possible (Dezalay and Garth, 1996). A great deal more empirical research will be required before it will be possible to specify the extent to which they actually constitute a unique structure that regulates contingencies in contractual relationships—one that is different or more extensive than that provided for intrastate business by national law.

Personal Networks and *Guanxi* Relationships

The fourth and final discourse concerning the emerging normative framework that governs global business transactions emphasises the importance of informal, personalistic extra-legal factors over formal-legal ones. On our continuum from universalism to particularism, this approach lies at the latter pole. Moreover, judging solely on the basis of number of adherents and variety of disciplines, relational approaches would have to be regarded as by far the most important solution to the problem: theoretical arguments and empirical support is found in sociology, psychology, anthropology, economics and law.

These approaches share the assumption that business in general is co-ordinated by mutual interest so as to guarantee relatively stable and/or profitable exchanges. Additional external assistance in legal or institutional forms is considered sometimes superfluous, sometimes detrimental but sometimes necessary as part of a complex governance structure of business relations.

Mutually profitable exchanges are co-ordinated in classical economics by price mechanisms: transactions are continued if the price is acceptable given the market conditions, and are discontinued if the commodity is traded at a lower price elsewhere. This basic assumption of price co-ordination is maintained also for international exchanges, although additional elements (such as transportation, delays, quality and warranties, currency exchanges, etc.) are considered to influence the decision to initiate and/or continue a business relationship (Kiedaisch, 1997; Mascarenhas, 1982). Transaction cost theories, the theory of relational contract and the theory of trust criticise this ideal-typical model as inadequate because it explains only discrete transactions which according to this literature are the exception rather than the rule: "[a] one-time purchase of unbranded gasoline out-of-town at an independent station paid for with cash approximates a discrete transaction" (Dwyer, Schurr and Oh, 1987: 12). In reality it can be observed that commodities are purchased frequently from the same provider transforming the discrete exchange in an anonymous market into a business relationship characterised by relational elements. The co-ordination of continued, complex and possibly long-term business transactions is understood as a social achievement and explained in terms of its economic, psychological and sociological preconditions.

In the late 1930s the economist (and eventual Nobel prizewinner) Ronald Coase criticised the exclusive focus on commodity prices in neoclassic microeconomic market models by emphasising the importance of transaction costs—that is, the costs of running the economic system. Market exchanges cannot be efficiently co-ordinated by price mechanisms in case of insecurity, for example if the costs of setting up, maintaining and monitoring the transactions are too high. Transaction costs, which arise out of concerns about opportunistic behaviour, are in part legal costs: the costs of negotiating and writing contracts, of monitoring contractual performance, of enforcing contractual promises, and of addressing breaches of contractual promises. Firms where the price mechanism is replaced by command structures are a more efficient solution in such cases (Coase, 1937): their hierarchical structure renders contractual negotiations and dispute resolution superfluous. Coase's sharp delineation of markets and hierarchies has gradually given way to the recognition of "hybrid" forms between the poles of price and authority, and of plural forms that mix price and authority control (Bradach and Eccles, 1989).

Oliver Williamson (1975, 1979, 1981, 1985) subsequently developed, on the basis of Coasean paradigms, a more refined model of co-ordination and governance of business exchanges. These are said to range from markets—where buyers and sellers bear no dependency relation with each other and where the identity of the parties is irrelevant, through relational contracts that is (i.e., "various forms of long-term contracting, reciprocal trading, regulation, franchising, and the like") (Williamson, 1991: 280)—to hierarchy (the Coasean firm with its cost avoiding command structures). Increased insecurity in complex economies, caused by limited information, limited rationality and by opportunism, leads to increasing transaction costs which make the price mechanism less efficient and relational and hierarchical models more efficient. Since the international business environment is more uncertain than the domestic business environment (Mascarenhas, 1982; Kiedaisch, 1997; Schmidtchen, 1995; Whitley, this volume), governance of economic transactions across borders moves away from control through prices to more cost-efficient devices—that is, from anonymous, "pure" market-based transactions to more socially integrated forms of co-ordination.

As a consequence of the Coase–Williamson critique of classical economics the social integration of business relations has become a major focus of research in various disciplines. Marketing and management research discusses innovative arrangements and determinants of long-term orientation in buyer–seller relationships, psychologists discover that trust yields economic benefits, anthropologists and sociologists observe Asian business networks based on family ties, and legal scholars recognise and acknowledge the importance of co-operative behaviour that goes beyond purely contractual obligations. It is interesting to note that most authors put the emphasis not on the "firm" model of risk- (and transaction cost-) avoidance in Coasean terms, but rather on hybrid forms which precede hierarchical structures on Williamson's continuum.

Current developments in the creation of transnational corporations and mergers of big national enterprises into global business units seem to indicate that "firms" rather than forms of social integration below the "firm" level are preferred in many globally active branches. But their cost effectiveness might be so obvious that researchers are more interested in showing the existence of other less dramatic models of business co-operation. From a socio-legal perspective it is also interesting to observe changing definitions of relational contracting. Whereas Williamson (1991: 269), in distinguishing between market, hybrid and hierarchy, maintained that "each generic form is supported and defined by a distinctive type of contract law", the bulk of the current discussion focuses on non-contractual governance structures, elaborating often on a seminal essay written by a legal sociologist (Macaulay, 1963).

Although the vast literature discussing relational structures between the "market" and the "firm" cannot be easily summarised in this introductory chapter, three closely connected themes deserve special attention: trust, networks and relational contracts. Trust is considered to be the central goal of non-legal business co-ordination mechanisms such as informal networks and relational agreements. Trust reflects a willingness to rely on an exchange partner under both favourable and difficult conditions. It lowers the transaction costs of information and control, facilitates long-term relationships and is an important component in the success of strategic alliances. Trust reduces complexity and is a more flexible relational bond than command and supervision in forms of vertical integration. It may be founded on belief, characteristic of the "premodern", or may be founded on mutual self-interest and functional interdependence, characteristic of the "modern" (Luhmann, 1979). In this "modern" sense trust is a commodity in which people invest resources for the purpose of building a reputation for honesty (Dasgupta, 1988). It is not only an interpersonal but also an interorganisational phenomenon. The institutional and contractual structures of international relations are often understood as "trust-building mechanisms".

Observers point to numerous examples to illustrate that firms develop close bonds with other firms through recurrent interactions. Familiarity through prior contacts, repeated ties and alliances engenders trust substituting to some degree for contractual safeguards (Gulati, 1995). The term "partnership" implies a sort of moral contract, a long-term commitment under mutual dependency, continuous exchange of information, exchange for improved performance and non-opportunistic adaptations in case of changing circumstances. As Lorenz (1988) has been able to demonstrate on the basis of his research in the French engineering industry trust can be created intentionally not necessarily by fostering bonds of friendship between the managers or salespersons, but by sacrificing short-term gains for the long-term benefits of mutual co-operation; by advance warnings in situations of crisis; and by measures to guarantee a constant level of work. The ability to achieve significant social control on the basis of impersonal trust has become a major research field in sociology (Shapiro, 1987) and economics (Kiedaisch, 1997), which have found that suitable business strategies for cost-avoidance through trust are frequently developed. In the present context it is important to note that interfirm relationships based on trust are observed more frequently among domestic partners than among firms of different nations (Gulati, 1995: 95, 105), and that as a consequence the relative importance of formal contractual arrangements is larger in international business transactions (Kiedaisch, 1997: 171–84).

This relative importance of formal written contracts in global trade does not necessarily indicate a strong influence of traditional contract law doctrines in this area. From Gottlieb's (1983) reinterpretation of the international system as a "relational society", to theoretical and empirical research around what has been labelled "regime theory" (Krasner, 1983), traditional legal approaches to explain behavioural patterns of nation-states, international governmental and non-governmental organisations as well as business actors are perceived as largely inadequate. The conduct of these actors is far removed from the demands of the formal legal order, and is mainly guided by relational practices. Gottlieb points to international loan agreements where enforcement is simply out of the question for the banks. Similarly most conventions under public international law are better characterised by a regime of autochthonous rules, procedures, precedents and practices that emerge out of a sustained relationship between two or more actors. Mediating systems are concerned with interactions over time. They discourage the assignment of exclusive weight to formal documents and to the original intentions of the parties.

These "relational" approaches in legal discourses are akin to (and mostly based on) Ian Macneil's critique of "classical" notions in contract law (Macneil, 1971, 1974, 1975, 1981), a critique which runs parallel to the critique that transaction cost economists and sociologists raise against the faceless buyer and seller myth of classical economics. In law as well as in economics it is considered misleading to base theoretical models on a "discrete exchange": "contractual relations, not discrete contract, always have and always will be the dominant form of exchange behaviour in society", generating a co-operative attitude which respects solidarity and reciprocity (Macneil, 1985: 451). Seven elements characterise relational transactions: (1) the relational exchange does not begin at a precise point in time and has no definite end; (2) the commencement is characterised by ongoing negotiations and the duration of the contract may remain indefinite; (3) the performance can and must often be measured and specified not at the commencement of the agreement but during the course of the contract; (4) the parties' planning refers not only to the exchange conditions but also to future interaction and performance; (5) the planning may be co-operative or unilateral; (6) unlike discrete transactions, the contractual relations cannot afford to neglect expectations resulting from ongoing interactions; and (7) in contrast to discrete transactions, with relational contracts there is no set, long-term power structure (Joerges, 1985). Campbell (1990), in his most elaborate analysis of Macneil's writings, points to the consequences of this approach for classical contract law in areas like contract formation, performance, variation, termination and application of remedies.

Although most authors in this debate seem to agree with basic assumptions of relational contract theory, its range in domestic and international business exchanges still needs to be established. The technical progress in easy and almost costless communication leaves room for discrete exchanges on spot markets, increases volatility of financial and commodity markets, and fosters rapid changes in business preferences and relations. Is it realistic to expect long-term relationships, co-operation, solidarity and reciprocity under these conditions? Lindenberg and de Vos (1985) believe the opposite to be true. They point to the widely accepted classical assumptions in sociological theory: namely, that from Maine to Tönnies to Weber, the movement is from particularistic solidarities based on social status, to a lack of ethical restrictions among strangers requiring contracts and formal legal institutions to limit the degree of plunder, pillage and cheating.

Two approaches lead out of this dilemma. The first approach distinguishes between transactional, contractual and relational forms of exchanges, claiming a right of existence and survival for all three of them under specific circumstances. The second introduces a cultural dimension, arguing that cultures vary in terms of the legitimacy they accord more relational forms of exchange. According to the latter approach, Asian cultures demonstrate an especially strong preference for relational business exchanges, both domestically and in cross-border transactions. This is accomplished, it is argued, by means of ethnically homogeneous cross-border networks found in most industrialised countries—for example, the role played throughout southeast Asia by the so-called Chinese business diaspora.

One example among many of the first approach is a continuum of exchange developed by Dwyer, Schurr, and Oh (1987) and Gundlach and Murphy (1993). One polar archetype on this continuum is the single, short-term exchange event encompassing a distinct beginning and ending where classic contract doctrine provides an efficient system of governance. The other extreme is the relational exchange over an extended time frame where modern contract law with its many adjustments to existing contract relationships like good faith or fiduciary standards provides only an insufficient and mostly inadequate solution for potential difficulties. Between these types—well-described in Macneil's writings—are contractual exchanges ranging from executory or open-ended contracts to joint ventures (similar to Williamson's hybrid forms). The authors emphasise the practical relevance of this intermediate type where legal as well as ethical rules (like trust, equity, responsibility, commitment) provide the governance structures.

A second approach is represented by psychologists who study general cultural dimensions (e.g., Hofstede, 1980, 1983) and in particular the influence of culture on the development of trust (e.g., Doney, Cannon and Mullen, 1998) in international business. The most relevant consideration appears to be the dimension of uncertainty avoidance—putatively a Western cultural trait that clearly influences how exchanges are secured and stabilised. People in high uncertainty avoidance cultures desire to establish clear rules about how one should behave, and then to live by these rules. In low uncertainty avoidance cultures one's life experience suggests that nothing is predictable. Attempts to organise the future are therefore considered futile. Still, empirical research indicates that all cultures develop trust relationships in business—but under different circumstances.

Cultural elements are emphasised by sociologists and anthropologists as well as psychologists. This is especially likely to be true among those who deal with Japanese or Chinese business networks, where trust is the predominant governance device. In securing trust, Japanese businesses seem to prefer relational contracts, while Chinese businesses emphasise hierarchical settings in family networks (almost like the "firm" in Coasean and Williamsonean understanding: see especially the chapter by Whitley in this volume). Japanese large enterprise groups known as *keiretsu* are conglomerates where business is kept as much as possible within the group, where contracting is preferential, stable, obligated, and where benevolence is a duty. Common characteristics of Japanese business and labour relations include a generalised dutifulness combined with a low level of individualistic self-assertion (Dore, 1983), a consensual negotiation style, and a sense for loyalty, harmony and order (Zhang and Kuroda, 1989; Rohlen, 1989).

The literature on Chinese business practices emphasises even more closely affiliated networks called *guanxi* tied by mutual obligation through feeling and sentiment, rather than purely instrumental calculation (Yang, 1994). In order to achieve this informal form of integration, based on mutual dependency and trust, business is often carried out on the basis of family relationships. Appelbaum (1998) speculates that this business style will survive westernisation and globalisation processes (but see Guthrie, 1998) and possibly even grow in importance globally, since it has an affinity for the more "flexible", informal forms of contracting that are increasingly important today. Chinese business relationships involve what Chung and Hamilton (this volume) refer to as *guanxi* logic: a mixture of normative, instrumental and affective elements, *guanxi* relationships "balance obligation and sanction, on the one hand, and flexibility and instrumentality, on the other hand". In this sense, *guanxi* pervades economic activity to a high degree, fostering a degree of co-operation and predictability, as well as adding a level of complexity to business dealings. For one thing, it fosters interfirm alliances based on personal relationships and obligations, rather than more formal connections among firms.

Guanxi relationships arguably facilitate cross-border business ties, particularly in situations of uncertainty. This argument was succinctly stated by Lee Kuan Yew, former President of Singapore, at the 1993 World Chinese Entrepreneurs' Convention in Hong Kong: "what ethnic Chinese from Hong Kong, Macao and Taiwan did was to demonstrate to a sceptical world that *guanxi* connections through the same language and culture can make up for a lack in the rule of law and transparency in rules and regulations" (cited in Ong, 1997: 181).

The cross-border business structure of today's East Asian NIEs, unified through the Chinese business diaspora, has emerged "as a leading agency of processes of capital accumulation in East Asia" (Arrighi, 1994: 9–10, drawing on Hui, 1995). The growing economic power of the Chinese business diaspora has greatly accelerated with the incorporation of China into the world economy, with some four-fifths of foreign investment in the PRC today originating in the overseas Chinese business community (Arrighi, 1994: 15). Some scholars argue that this provides a significant advantage to East Asia in the global economy. As Hsing (1998: 152) points out:

An estimated 51 million overseas Chinese in Asia created $US450 billion gross national product in 1990 (East Asia Analytical Unit, 1995). Worldwide, the overseas Chinese probably hold liquid assets (not including securities) worth $1.5–2 trillion (*The Economist*, 1992). The resources that the overseas Chinese command, and the transnational networks they create, potentially provide the technologies, information, and finance tools that China needs.

Or, in the even more triumphalist language of the Singapore Chinese Chamber of Commerce and Industry:

Today, there are some twenty-five million ethnic Chinese outside of China, the bulk of whom are concentrated around the fast-growing Pacific Rim. Individually and collectively, they are well-placed to play a key role in realizing the potential and promise of globalization, particularly in making the Pacific Century come true (cited in Nonini and Ong, 1997: 4).

In this volume, Chung and Hamilton would seem partly to concur, concluding that "legal rules and *guanxi* logic work hand-in-glove to make Chinese entrepreneurs the formidable businesspeople they have become" (342). In his chapter, Lui expands on these arguments, cautioning against reducing the notion of *guanxi* to purely economistic terms. Rather, he argues, *guanxi* entails much more than an instrumentalist and functionalist approach to understanding trust: it requires understanding the ways in which trust is earned, as well as the "map of social relations"; it is both tacit knowledge and institutionalised. Moreover, the obligations entailed in *guanxi* can backfire, introducing economically unhealthy particularisms into business dealings. In Lui's view, *guanxi* is emotional and moral, and is not "a governance structure capable of replacing contract and other legal regulations" (396).

In her chapter, Janet Tai Landa elaborates the Coasean model previously discussed. Based on her research on Hokkien-Chinese rubber traders in Singapore and West Malaysia, she argues that ethnically homogeneous middleman groups—specifically, Chinese merchants—make up for contract uncertainty and lack of business infrastructure, by means of particularistic relationships rooted in familiarity and trust. In her view, *guanxi* decreases with social distance—from near kinsmen to distant kinsmen, then to clansmen, fellow villagers, fellow Hokkiens, non-Hokkien Chinese, and eventually non-Chinese (the latter gulf is the largest). John Ohnesorge, in his response, questions the notion—implicit in Landa's analysis, although not explicitly addressed—that Chinese culture lacks emphasis on "contractual formality and law-like commercial norms" (see Ohnesorge, this volume). He argues that "the role of law in Chinese life has been systematically underestimated"; moreover, ethnically homogeneous trading networks may serve as a system of ethnic discrimination against outsiders, as much as a rational response to contract uncertainty. He also argues that Landa's notion that shared cultural norms provide "rules of the game" begs the question of specific procedural rules which address dispute resolution—rules which are necessary to provide predictability in business dealings.

The term *guanxi* is thus used in two rather distinct senses in the present volume, reflecting its treatment in the globalisation literature. On the one hand, the strong use of *guanxi* signifies sets of business relationships that operate according to norms of reciprocity—relationships that are based on personal connections grounded in pervasive cultural contexts, themselves rooted in kinship, clan or some other powerful ethno-regional commonalities (Lui, this volume). On the other hand, *guanxi* can be taken simply as a synonym for network(s) of personal relationships (Pérez Perdomo, this volume), common among business people the world over. It remains questionable whether either form of *guanxi* can by itself fill the normative void in international business transactions. As Landa shows in her chapter, among ethnic Chinese *guanxi* in the strong sense falls off steeply with social distance. In fact, since non-Chinese business people are not subject to the ethical and practical rewards and penalties embedded in Chinese culture that can be mobilised in case of conflict, *guanxi* in the strong sense is not likely to be a major factor when "Boeing comes to Beijing"—although this cultural gulf can be partly overcome by working through Chinese intermediaries (see also the chapter by Cohen).

Since the principle of reciprocity is fundamental to interactions between people, *guanxi* in the weak sense of attributing a significant portion of the organisation of business transactions to personal relationships is, of course, socially epidemic. Every culture probably has its own aphorism to capture the notion, from mutual back-scratching in America to one hand washing the other in Russia. That every contingency in business transactions is not incorporated in contract and that every breach does not become a conflict reflect the power of reciprocity and the pull of the long term to produce flexible adjustments between firms as conditions emerge or change. Moreover, Whitley (this volume) reminds us of both the important role that personal networks may play in the search for business partners as well as in the conduct of business affairs and of the institutional features that affect the role of personal relationships. In neither instance does *guanxi* in the weak sense fill the void when the ties of personal contacts and networks fail to produce acceptable closure.

A PLEA FOR INTERDISCIPLINARY RESEARCH

In preparing the Oñati conference we were, on the one hand, impressed by the high standards of disciplinary discourses about global transactions and, on the other hand, disappointed by the almost complete lack of communication between these discourses. When do legal scholars start to take notice of self-regulation, the creative lawyering of mega law firms or the different forms business people have developed in order to manage global exchanges? Is empirical research so alien to doctrinal thinking that there is no way of capitalising on social-scientific observations and insights? Even *lex mercatoria* approaches, which are quite akin to legal reasoning, have remained at the margin of the current unification of law debate. *Lex mercatoria* scholarship has a legal branch which does not neglect state law, but remains—despite its claim of kinship to business practice—in a legal world, for the most part contesting definitions and concepts like law, rule and custom and defending arbitration as a means of dispute resolution allegedly superior to litigation. Few data on its practical relevance and virtually no social-scientific theories about the social implications of self-regulation (legitimacy, democracy, public goods) have been produced. Sociological perspectives, on the other hand, tend to overstate self-regulatory efficiency and to underestimate the structural (in particular legal) environment of relatively autonomous global business communities. Empirical evidence for the self-reproduction of order in these communities is scarce. Research on the role of the legal profession in the global economy is institutionally blind, deals only incidentally with aspects of *lex mercatoria* rules and completely neglects the efforts of legislators and international organisations to structure international business relations. The insights of economic, sociological and anthropological relationism that business "contracts" can be established without the assistance of big western law firms remains, lamentably, outside the research ambit in this area of study. Last, but not least, the network approaches are in silent competition with these discourses. Because they are close to social reality in run-of-the-mill business dealings, they are little concerned with whether law, lawyers and courts play a role—at least in the background or "in the shadow". The simple dichotomy of formal contract versus informal relationship does not seem to do justice to the legal complexities found in international business transactions.

During our conference debates and in preparing this volume we have made some modest steps toward a better understanding of the relevance and interconnections of these diverse approaches. We leave it to readers and other researchers to take further steps in the direction of much needed interdisciplinarity.

REFERENCES

Appelbaum, Richard P. (1998), "The Future of Law in a Global Economy", *Social and Legal Studies* 7; 171–92.
—— Bonacich, Edna, Esbensjade, Jill, and Quan, Katie (2000), *Fighting Sweatshops: Problems of Enforcing Global Labor Standards* (Santa Barbara, Cal.: UCSB Institute for Social, Behavioral, and Economic Research Center for Global Studies).
Arrighi, Giovanni (1994), *The Long Twentieth Century* (London: Verso).
—— (1996), "The Rise of East Asia and the Withering Away of the Interstate System", *Journal of World-Systems Research* 2; 15.
Bailey, James E. (1999), "Facing the Truth: Seeing the Convention on Contracts for the International Sale of Goods as an Obstacle to a Uniform Law of International Sales", *Cornell International Law Journal* 32; 273.
Baraban, Cyntia L. (1998), "Inspiring Global Professionalism: Challenges and Opportunities for American Lawyers in China", *Indiana Law Journal* 73; 1247.

Barber, Benjamin, and Schulz, Andrea (1996), *Jihad vs. McWorld: How the Planet is Both Falling Apart and Coming Together* (New York: Ballantine Books).

Becker, Gary Stanley (1976), *The Economic Approach to Human Behavior* (Chicago, Ill.: University of Chicago Press).

—— (1996), *The Economic Way of Looking at Behavior: the Nobel Lecture* (Stanford, Cal.: Stanford University, The Hoover Institution, Essays in Public Policy No. 69).

Berger, Klaus Peter (1997), "The Lex Mercatoria Doctrine And The Unidroit Principles of International Commercial Contracts", *Law and Policy in International Business* 28; 923.

—— (2000), "The CENTRAL Enquiry on the Use of Transational Law in International Contract Law and Arbitration" *MEALEY's International Arbitration Report* (no. 9); 15.

Berman, Harold J., and Kaufman, Colin (1978), "The Law of International Commercial Transactions (Lex Mercatoria)", *Harvard International Law Journal* 19; 221.

Bernstein, Lisa (1992), "Opting Out of the Legal System: Extralegal Contractual Relations in the Diamond Trade", *Journal of Legal Studies* 21; 115–57.

—— (1996), "Merchant Law in a Merchant Court: Rethinking the Code's Search for Immanent Business Norms", *University of Pennsylvania Law Review* 144; 1765.

Bonacich, Edna, and Appelbaum, Richard P. (2000), *Behind the Label—Inequality in the Los Angeles Apparel Industry* (Berkeley, Cal.: University of California Press).

Bond, Stephen R. (1990), "How to Draft an Arbitration Clause (Revisited)", *ICC International Court of Arbitration Bulletin* (December).

Bonell, Michael Joachim (1990), International Uniform Law in Practice—Or Where the Real Trouble Begins, *American Journal of Comparative Law* 38; 865–888.

Bradach, Jeffrey L., and Eccles, Robert G. (1989), "Price, Authority, and Trust: From Ideal Types to Plural Forms", *Annual Review of Sociology* 15; 97.

BSR, IRRC, and O'Rourke, Dara (2000), *Independent University Initiative: Final Report* (San Francisco, Cal.; Washington, DC; Cambridge, Mass.: Business for Social Responsibility and Investor Responsibility Research Center (September).

Budak, Ali Cem (1999), *Making Foreign People Pay* (Aldershot: Dartmouth Ashgate).

Bull, Hedley (1995), *The Anarchical Society: A Study of Order in World Politics* (2d edn., New York: Columbia University Press,.

Campbell, David (1990), "The Social Theory of Relational Contract: Macneil as the Modern Proudhon", *International Journal of the Sociology of Law* 18; 75–95.

Coase, Ronald (1937), "The Nature of the Firm", *Economica* 4; 386.

Cody, Jonathan P. (1999), "Protecting Privacy Over The Internet: Has the Time Come to Abandon Self-Regulation?", *Catholic University Law Review* 48; 1183.

Compa, Lance A., and Hinchliffe Darricarrère, Tashia (1996), "Private Labor Rights Enforcement Through Corporate Codes of Conduct", in Lance A. Compa and Stephen F. Diamond (eds.), *Human Rights, Labor Rights, and International Trade* (Philadelphia, Penn.: University of Pennsylvenia Press).

Comte, Auguste (1975). *Auguste Comte and Positivism: The Essential Writings* (ed. Gertrude Lenzer, New York: Harper Torchbooks).

Cooter, Robert (1996), "Decentralized Law for a Complex Economy: The Structural Approach to Adjudicating the New Law Merchant", *University of Pennsylvania Law Review* 144; 1643.

Daly, Mary C. (1997), "The Cultural, Ethical, and Legal Challenges in Lawyering for a Global Organization: The Role of the General Counsel", *Emory Law Journal* 46; 1057–1111.

Dasgupta, Partha (1988), "Trust as a Commodity" in Diego Gambetta (ed.), *Trust— Making and Breaking Cooperative Relations* (Oxford: Basil Blackwell).

David, René (1972), "The International Unification of Private Law", *International Encyclopedia of Comparative Law* (Tübingen: Mohr (Paul Siebeck)), vol 2:3.

Dezalay, Yves (1990), "The Big Bang and the Law: The Internationalization and Restructuration of the Legal Field", *Theory, Culture & Society* 7; 279–93.

—— and Garth, Bryant (1996), *Dealing in Virtue: International Commercial Arbitration and the Construction of a Transnational Legal Order* (Chicago, Ill.: University of Chicago Press).

Doney, Particia M., Cannon, Joseph P., and Mullen, Michael R. (1998), "Understanding the Influence of National Culture on the Development of Trust", *Academy of Management Review* 23:3; 601–20.

Dore, Ronald (1983), "Goodwill and the Spirit of Market Capitalism", *The British Journal of Sociology* 24; 459–82.

Duina, Francesco G. (1999), *Harmonizing Europe—Nation States within the Common Market* (Albany, NY: State University of New York Press).

Durkheim, Emile (1964 (orig. 1893)), *The Division of Labor in Society* (New York: Free Press).

Dwyer, F. Robert, Schurr, Paul H. and Oh, S. Sejo (1987), "Developing Buyer-Seller Relationships", *Journal of Marketing* 51; 11–27.

East Asia Analytical Unit (1995), *Overseas Chinese Business Networks in Asia* (Department of Foreign Affairs and Trade, The Australian Government, Canberra, Australia).

Economist, The (1992), "The Overseas Chinese: A Driving Force", 18 July, 21–24.

European Commission (1996), KOM (96) 561.

Flood, John (1996), "Megalawyering in the Global Order: The Cultural, Social and Economic Transformation of Global Legal Practice", *International Journal of the Legal Profession* 3; 169–214.

Frankel, Tamar (1998), "Cross-Border Securitization: Without Law, But Not Lawless", *Duke Journal of Comparative & International Law* 8; 255.

Freyhold, Hanno von (1996), "Cross-Border Legal Interactions in New York Courts" in Volkmar Gessner (ed.), *Foreign Courts—Civil Litigation in Foreign Legal Cultures* (Aldershot: Dartmouth).

—— Gessner, Volkmar, and Olgiati, Vittorio (1996), "The Role of Courts in Global Legal Interaction", in Volkmar Gessner (ed.), *Foreign Courts—Civil Litigation in Foreign Legal Cultures* (Aldershot: Dartmouth).

Friedman, Lawrence M. (1994), "Is There a Modern Legal Culture?", *Ratio Iuris* 7; 117–31.

—— (1996), "Borders: On the Emerging Sociology of Transnational Law", *Stanford Journal of International Law* 32; 65–90.

Fukuyama, Francis (1992), *The End of History and the Last Man* (New York: Maxwell Macmillan).

Fuller, Lon (1964), *The Morality of Law* (New Haven, Conn.: Yale University Press).

Gessner, Volkmar (1996), "International Cases in German First Instance Courts" in Volkmar Gessner (ed.), *Foreign Courts—Civil Litigation in Foreign Legal Cultures* (Aldershot: Dartmouth).

Gessner, Volkmar (1998), "Globalization and Legal Certainty" in Volkmar Gessner and Ali Cem Budak (eds.), *Emerging Legal Certainty: Empirical Studies on the Globalization of Law* (Aldershot: Dartmouth).

Gessner, Volkmar and Budak, Ali Cem (eds.) (1998), *Emerging Legal Certainty: Empirical Studies on the Globalization of Law* (Aldershot: Dartmouth/Ashgate).

Giddens, Anthony (1987), *The Nation-State and Violence* (Stanford, Cal.: Stanford University Press),

—— (1990), *The Consequences of Modernity* (Stanford, Cal.: Stanford University Press).

—— (2000), *Runaway World: How Globalisation Is Reshaping Our Lives* (New York: Routledge).

Gordon, Michael Wallace (1998), "Some Thoughts on the Receptiveness of Contract Rules in the CISG and UNIDROIT", *American Journal of Comparative Law* 46; 361.

Gottlieb, Gidon (1983), "Relationism: Legal Theory for a Relational Society" 50 *University of Chicago Law Review*; 567.

Gulati, Ranjay (1995), "Does Familiarity Breed Trust? The Implications of Repeated Ties for Contractual Choice in Alliances", *Academy of Management Journal* 38; 85–112.

Gundlach, Gregory T., and Murphy, Patrick E. (1993), "Ethical and Legal Foundations of Relational Marketing Exchanges", *Journal of Marketing* 57; 35–46.

Guthrie, Douglas (1998), "The Declining Significance of Guanxi in China's Economic Transition", *The China Quaterly* 154; 255.

Hamashita, Takeshi (1994), "The Tribute Trade System and Modern Asia" in A. J. H. Latham and H. Kawakatsu (eds.), *Japanese Industrialization and the Asian Economy* (London; New York: Routledge).

Hartkamp, Arthur, Hesselink, Martijn, Hondius, Ewould, Joustra, Carla and du Perron, Edgar (eds.) (1998), *Towards a European Civil Code* (2d edn., Njmegen: Ars Aequi Libri).

Harvey, David (1996), *The Condition of Postmodernity: An Enquiry Into the Origins of Cultural Change* (Cambridge, Mass.: Blackwell).

Hirst, Paul, and Thompson, Graham (1996), *Globalization in Question, the International Economy and the Possibilities of Governance* (Cambridge: Polity Press International).

Hofstede, Geert (1980), *Culture's Consequences* (Beverly Hills, Cal.: Sage).

—— (1983), "The Cultural Relativity of Organizational Practices and Theories", *Journal of International Business Studies* 14:2; 75–89.

Hsing, You-tien (1998), *Making Capitalism in China: The Taiwan Connection* (New York: Oxford University Press).

Hui, Po-keung (1995), *Overseas Chinese Business Networks: East Asian Economic Development in Historical Perspective*, Ph.D. Dissertation, Department of Sociology, SUNY Binghamton.

Joerges, Christian (1985), "Relational Contract Theory in a Comparative Perspective: Tensions between Contract and Antitrust Law Principles in the Assessment of Contract Relations between Automobile Manufacturers and Their Dealers in Germany", *Wisconsin Law Review* 37; 581–613.

—— and Vos, Ellen (eds.) (1999), *EU Committees: Social Regulation, Law and Politics* (Oxford; Portland, Or.: Hart Publishing).

Juergensmeyer, Mark (1994), *The New Cold War? Religious Nationalism Confronts the Secular State* (Berkeley, Cal.: University of California Press).

—— (2000), *Terror in the Mind of God: The Global Rise of Religious Violence* (Berkeley, Cal.: University of California Press).

Kawakatsu, Heita (1986), "International Competitiveness in Cotton Goods in the Late Nineteenth Century: Britain versus India and East Asia" in W. Fischer, R. M. McInnis and J. Schneider (eds.), *The Emergence of a World Economy, 1500–1914* (Wiesbaden: Franz Steiner Verlag).

Kiedaisch, Ingo (1997), *Internationale Kunden-Lieferanten-Beziehungen* (Wiesbaden: Gabler).

Krasner, Stephen D. (ed.) (1983), *International Regimes* (Ithaca, NY; London: Cornell University Press).

Levy, Marion J. (1972), *Modernization: Latecomers and Survivors* (New York: Basic Books).

Lindenberg, Siegwart, and De Vos, Henk (1985), "The Limits of Solidarity: Relational Contracting in Perspective and Some Criticism of Traditional Sociology", *Zeitschrift für die gesamte Staatswissenschaft (Journal of Institutional and Theoretical Economics)* 141; 558–69.

Lorenz, Edward H. (1988), "Neither Friends nor Strangers: Informal Networks of Subcontracting in French Industry" in Diego Gambetta (ed.), *Trust—Making and Breaking Cooperative Relations* (New York: Basil Blackwell).

Luhmann, Niklas (1979), *Trust and Power* (Chichester: Wiley).

Macaulay, Stewart (1963), "Non-contractual Relations in Business: A Preliminary Study", *American Sociological Review* 28; 55–67.

Macneil, Ian R. (1971), *Contracts: Exchange Transactions and Relationships* (Mineola: Foundation Press).

—— (1974), "The Many Futures of Contract", *Southern California Law Review* 47; 691–896.

—— (1975), "A Primer of Contract Planning", *Southern California Law Review* 48; 627–704.

—— (1981), "Economic Analysis of Contractual Relations: Its Shortfalls and the Need for a 'Rich Classificatory Apparatus'", *Northwestern University Law Review* 75; 691–816.

—— (1985), "Reflections on Relational Contract", *Journal of Institutional and Theoretical Economics* 141; 541–46.

Maine, Sir Henry (1861), *Ancient Law* (London: Murray).

Maniruzzaman, Abul F. M. (1999), "The Lex Mercatoria and International Contracts: A Challenge for International Commercial Arbitration?", *American University International Law Review* 14; 657.

Martiny, Dieter (1999), "Europäisches Privatrecht—greifbar oder unerreichbar? in Dieter Martiny and Normann Wizleb (eds.), *Auf dem Wege zu einem Europäischen Zivilgesetzbuch* (Berlin: Springer).

Mascarenhas, Briance (1982), "Coping with Uncertainty in International Business", *Journal of International Business Studies* 13; 87–98.

Mazzini, Danielle (1997), "Stable International Contracts in Emerging Markets: An Endangered Species?, *Boston University International Law Journal* 15; 343.

McNeely, Connie (1995), *Constructing the Nation-State: International Organization and Prescriptive Action* (New York: Greenwood).

Mears, Rona R. (1993), "Contracting in Mexico: A Legal and Practical Guide to Negotiating and Drafting", *St. Mary's Law Journal* 24; 737.

Meyer, John W., Boli, John, and Thomas, George M. (1987), "Ontology and Rationalization in Western Cultural Account" in George M. Thomas, John W. Meyer

Francisco O. Ramirez and John Boli (eds.), *Institutional Structure: Constituting State, Society, and the Individual* (Newbury Park, Cal.: Sage).

Modisett, Jeffrey A., and Lott, Cindy M. (2000), "Cyberlaw And E-Commerce: A State Attorney General's Perspective", *Northwestern University Law Review* 94; 643.

Nassar, Nagla (1995), *Sanctity of Contracts Revisited: A Study in the Theory and Practice of Long-Term International Commercial Transactions* (Dordrecht; Boston; London: Martinus Nijhoff Publishers).

Nichols, Philip M. (2000), "Electronic Uncertainty Within the International Trade Regime", *American University International Law Review* 15; 1379.

Nimmer, Raymond T. (2000), "International Information Transactions: An Essay on Law in an Information Society", *Brooklyn Journal of International Law* 26; 5.

Nonini, Donald M., and Ong, Aihwa (1997), "Chinese Transnationalism as an Alternative Modernity" in Aibwa Ong and Donald M. Nonini (eds.), *Ungrounded Empires: The Cultural Politics of Modern Chinese Transnationalism* (New York: Routledge).

North, Douglass C. (1990), *Institutions, Institutional Change and Economic Performance* (Cambridge: Cambridge University Press).

Ong, Aihwa (1997), "Chinese Modernities: Narratives of Nation and of Capitalism" in Aihwa Ong and Donald M. Nonini (eds.), *Ungrounded Empires: The Cultural Politics of Modern Chinese Transnationalism* (New York: Routledge).

O'Rourke, Dara (2000), *Monitoring the Monitors: A Critique of PriceWaterhouseCoopers (PWC) Labor Monitoring* (Cambridge, Mass.: MIT Department of Urban Studies and Planning (September 28). (http://web.mit.edu/dorourke/www/PDF/pwc.pdf)

Owen, Michael L., and Loperena R. Carlos (1995), "The Mexican Legal System Offers Benefits as well as Pitfalls in Resolving Transborder Disputes", *Los Angeles Lawyer (October)*; 36–61.

Parsons, Talcott (1966), *Societies: Evolutionary and Comparative Perspectives* (Englewood Cliffs, NJ: Prentice Hall).

Rohlen, Thomas P. (1989), "Order in Japanese Society: Attachment, Authority, and Routine", *Journal of Japanese Studies* 15:1; 5–40.

Roorda, Peter (1993), "The Internationalization of the Practice of Law", *Wake Forest Law Review* 28; 141.

Sahlins, Marshall D., and Service, Elman R. (1960), *Evolution and Culture* (Ann Arbor, Mich.: University of Michigan Press).

Santino, Umberto (1988), "The Financial Mafia: The Illegal Accumulation of Wealth and the Financial-Industrial Complex", *Contemporary Crises* 12; 203–43.

Santos, Boaventura de Sousa (1992), "State, Law, and Community in the World System: An Introduction", *Social and Legal Studies* 1; 131–42.

—— (1995), *Toward a New Common Sense—Law, Science and Politics in the Paradigmatic Transition* (New York; London: Routledge).

Schmidtchen, Dieter (1995), "Territorialität des Rechts, Internationales Privatrecht und die privatautonome Regelung internationaler Sachverhalte", *Rabels Zeitschrift für ausländisches und Internationales Privatrecht* 59; 57–138.

Scott, W. Richard, and Meyer, John W. (1994), *Institutional Environments and Organizations: Structural Complexity and Individualism* (Newbury Park, Cal.: Sage).

Service, Elman (1975), *Origins of the State and Civilization: The Process of Cultural Evolution* (New York: Norton).

Shapiro, Susan P. (1987), "The Social Control of Impersonal Trust", *American Journal of Sociology* 93; 623–58.

Siebert, Horst (2000), *The New Economy—What is Really New?* (Kiel Institute of World Economics: Kiel Working Paper, No. 1000).

Silver, Carol (2000), "Globalization and the U.S. Market in Legal Services—Shifting Identities", *Law and Policy in International Business* 31; 1093.

Simon, Joel (1996), "Lost in Mexico", *California Lawyer (July)*; 41.

Spencer, Herbert (1860), *The Social Organism* (London: Greenwood Press).

Stammel, Christine (1998), *Waving the Gentlemen's Business Goodbye: From Global Deals to Global Disputes in the London Reinsurance Market* (Frankfurt am Main: Verlag Peter Lang).

Stephan, Paul B. (1999), "The Futility of Unification and Harmonization in International Commercial Law", *Virginia Journal of International Law* 39; 743.

Sunwolf (1997), "Communication between Legal Cultures: Strategies, Perceptions and Beliefs of American Lawyers Who Practice International Litigation", paper presented at the Oñati International Institute for the Sociology of Law, Workshop on Changing Legal Cultures II, April.

Teubner, Gunther (ed.) (1997), *Global Law without a State* (Aldershot: Dartmouth).

—— (1997), " 'Global Bukowina': Legal Pluralism in the World Society" in Gunther Teubner (ed.), *Global Law without a State* (Aldershort: Dartmouth).

Thomas, George M., Meyer, John W., Ramirez, Francisco O. and Boli, John (eds.) (1987), *Institutional Structure: Constituting State, Society, and the Individual* (Newbury Park, Cal.: Sage).

Tönnies, Ferdinand (1963 (orig. 1887)), *Community and Society (Gemeinschaft und Gesellschaft)* (New York: Harper & Row).

Trocki, Carl A. (1997), "Boundaries and Transgressions: Chinese Enterprise in Eighteenth- and Nineteenth-Century Southeast Asia" in Aihwa Ong and Donald M. Nonini (eds.), *Ungrounded Empires: The Cultural Politics of Modern Chinese Transnationalism* (New York: Routledge).

Trubek, David M., Dezalay, Yves, Buchanan, Ruth and Davis, John R. (1994), "Global Restructuring and the Law: Studies of the Internationalization of Legal Fields and the Creation of Transnational Arenas", *Case Western Reserve Law Review* 44; 407.

Vanberg, Victor (1987), "Markt, Organisation und Reziprozität" in Klaus Heinemann (ed.), *Soziologie wirtschaftlichen Handelns* (Sonderheft 28 der Kölner Zeitschrift für Soziologie und Sozialpsychologie, Opladen: Westdeutscher Verlag).

Vial, Enzo (1999), *Die Gerichtsstandswahl und der Zugang zum internationalen Zivilprozeß im deutsch-italienischen Rechtsverkehr* (Baden-Baden: Nomos).

Wallis, John Joseph, and North, Douglass C. (1986), "Measuring the Transaction Sector in the American Economy, 1870–1970" in Stanley L. Engerman and Robert E. Gallman (eds.), *Long Term Factors in American Economic Growth* (Chicago, Ill.: Univiversity of Chicago Press).

Weber, Max (1946 (orig. 1919)), in *From Max Weber: Essays in Sociology* (trans. and ed. Hans Gerth and C. Wright Mills, New York: Oxford University Press).

—— (1979 (orig. 1921)), *Economy and Society: An Outline of Interpretive Sociology*, 2 vols. (Berkeley, Cal.: University of California Press).

Wiener Jarrod (1999), *Globalization and the Harmonization of Law* (London: Pinter).

Williamson, Oliver (1975), *Markets and Hierarchies: Analysis and Antitrust Implications* (New York: The Free Press).

—— (1979), "Transaction-Cost Economies: The Governance of Contractual Relations", *Journal of Law and Economics* 22; 233–61.

Williamson, Oliver (1981), "The Economics of Organization: The Transaction-Cost Approach", *American Journal of Sociology* 87; 548.

—— (1985), *The Economic Institutions of Capitalism: Firms, Markets, Relational Contracting* (New York: The Free Press).

Williamson, Oliver (1991), "Comparative Economic Organization: The Analysis of Discrete Structural Alternatives", *Administrative Science Quarterly* 36; 269.

Yang, Mayfair Mei-hui (1994), *Gifts, Favors, and Banquets: The Art of Social Relationship in China* (Ithaca, NY: Cornell University Press).

Zhang, Danian, and Kuroda, Kenji (1989), "Beware of Japanese Negotiation Style: How to Negotiate with Japanese Companies", *Northwestern Journal of International Law and Business* 10; 195–212.

PART ONE

The New Global Environment of Business Transactions

1

Sovereignty and Law in a Denationalised World[1]

MICHAEL ZÜRN

Abstract

Whereas in the national constellation all dimensions of statehood converged in one political organisation—the nation-state—the postnational constellation will be characterised by a systematic diffusion of the dimensions of statehood to different levels of political organisations. Among other things, this new constellation of statehood will differ from the national constellation regarding the capacity to deliver the goods of governance such as security, legal certainty, social welfare and democratic decision-making. The post-national constellation of statehood will be capable of ensuring legal certainty for global business transactions. Much more questionable, however, is whether or not the post-national constellation will suffice for a normatively more ambitious notion of law as integrity to the same extent as this was possible in the national constellation. A dissolution of the unity of the rule of law and the democratic shaping of the law will thus be one fundamental dilemma of a post-national order.

T HE CLAIM THAT—in the words of the British political scientist Barry Buzan (1994: 97)—"states are steadily dissolving, leaving their societies increasingly exposed to the cultural, economic, and human dynamics" of the whole world, is put forward from a number of different perspectives. The Frenchman Jean-Marie Guéhenno (1994, 13) prophesies that an "imperial age" will follow the era of the sovereign nation-state "just as the Roman Empire succeeded the republic".[2] The German Tilmann Evers (1994: 125) already perceives within the present "European architecture" more similarities with the constitution of the Holy Roman Empire than with the concept of competing and co-operating nation-states. In the USA, too, political scientists such as James Rosenau (1990) and Mark Zacher (1992) diagnosed at the beginning of this decade the end of the system of sovereign nation-states. Claims about the diminishing role of the state

---

[1] I received valuable comments from the participants of the conference on "The Legal Culture of Global Business Transactions" held at the International Institute for the Sociology of Law, Oñati, Spain, 17–19 June, 1999, as well as from Jürgen Neyer, Dieter Wolf and Bernhard Zangl. Many thanks also to Vicki May for brushing up my English and to Peter Arnhold for assistance.
[2] All quotes from non-English texts are translated.

are also put forward in academic disciplines other than political science. Some economists—from the far left to neo-liberals—see the state as the pure servant of economic organisations with a rapidly diminishing autonomy (see for example Hirsch, 1995; Ohmae, 1993). The new role of supranational law-making and supranational courts has also brought legal scientists to question traditional notions of sovereignty (see for example Franck, 1992; Joerges, 1996).

Is sovereignty really in decline? If so, what does this mean for the future of law? In order to contribute toward answering these questions I shall proceed in four steps. In the first section, I want to develop a multi-dimensional notion of sovereignty that binds this concept to the national constellation, thereby demonstrating that it was the interplay of a number of dimensions of statehood, all of them converging in the nation-state, that made sovereignty possible.

With the sharp rise in the number of societal transactions crossing national borders, this national constellation experiences on the one hand a fundamental challenge which nation-states on the other hand politically respond to instead of just yielding to external pressures as hyper-globalists want to make us believe. In the second section, I shall sketch the challenges of and the political responses to "societal denationalisation" (a term I prefer to globalisation).

Societal denationalisation and political responses to it may eventually lead to a "post-national constellation" (Habermas, 1998). Although it is impossible to sketch this post-national constellation in detail today—its shape is by no means determined and is more likely to be the outcome of political struggles—I wish to point to some components of the new statehood on the basis of developments that will probably be of structural importance.

In the fourth and final section, I argue that this new constellation will be capable of ensuring legal certainty for global business transactions. Much more questionable, however, is whether or not the post-national constellation will suffice for a normatively more ambitious notion of law as integrity to the same extent as this was possible in the national constellation. A dissolution of the unity of the rule of law and the democratic shaping of the law will thus be the fundamental dilemma of a post-national order.

STATEHOOD IN THE NATIONAL CONSTELLATION

The normative basis for modern statehood is *recognition*. The most important component of this dimension is the principle of sovereignty, that is, "the supreme legal authority of the nation to give and enforce the law within a certain territory and, in consequence, independence from the authority of any other nation and equality with it under international law" (Morgenthau, 1967: 305). From a historical perspective, it was recognition as an international legal subject which ultimately made a political organisation a state. Although the concept of sovereignty already *de facto* prevailed to a significant degree from the fifteenth century on, it became formalised only through the Westphalian treaties. And it took 300 additional years before the world was completely compartmentalised into different sovereign states, each responsible for a certain territory, and before other powerful threats to the monopoly of force like pirates and mercenaries lost significance in transnational spaces like the open sea (Thomson, 1994).[3] Only later on, mainly in the nineteenth century with the rise of nationalism, was external recognition supplemented by internal recognition of the sovereign government as the legitimate and necessary organisational form of a political community that defined itself as a nation. The territorial state thus became a nation-state. Although the territorial state was able to build upon proto-national cultures and communities, at the same time it contributed to the rise of national identities through harmonisation policies and the symbolic representation of "imagined communities" (Anderson, 1991). As a result of this, the notion prevailed that national boundaries and the boundaries of the territorial state have to coincide (Gellner, 1991).

Recognition, however, would not have been able to prevail without a material basis, that is, the underlying *resources*. The process of the monopolisation of force ran parallel to the establishment of the principle of sovereignty. A royal monopoly of force prevailed as a result of fierce competition between different power-holders first in France and in England. This monopolisation of force was accompanied by a tax-raising monopoly through which, in turn, the monopoly of force could be defended against aggressors from inside and outside the controlled territory (Elias, 1976; Tilly, 1985; Giddens, 1985).

In the long run, internal and external recognition as well as the monopoly of force and the capacity to raise taxes needs to be supplemented by another dimension of statehood if it is to be sustainable: the *realisation of governance goals*. Perhaps the most fundamental dimension of modern statehood is the notion of an organisation that is public in character and thus exists to *deliver goods* for the people who are part of this organisation (see Reus-Smit, 1997; Teschke, 1998). The linkage of the definition of modern statehood with a minimum of public-interest orientation does not imply that the agents who act in the name of the state—the political administrative system or the political class (cf. Borchert and Golsch, 1995)—must be altruists. Of course, they are not, as is amply proven by endless tales of abuse of official authority by dignitaries in any number of states. Apart from the political class, though, the super-ordinate institutional structure also has a vested interest in the activities of its agents, that is the self-interest of the state (Offe, 1975). As a rule, the self-interest of the state was, among else, promoted by policies that served societal goals.

What, then, are those goals of governance? At first sight, we must agree with Dieter Grimm (1994: 771) that "every area of life open to human influence has

---

[3] Krasner (1993, 1999) is therefore clearly right when he emphasises that it is a strong oversimplification to see the Peace of Westphalia as a turning point in history. Sovereignty has been a contested concept for many centuries, before and since 1648, and never prevailed in a pure form. It thus seems premature to conclude from some observations about deviations from the principle of sovereignty that sovereignty is in decline.

also been the target of state activity". However, a second look reveals that in various academic disciplines and discourses—be they normative or empirical—there are, despite partially divergent terminology, surprisingly similar notions of the general goals of governance.[4] These different perspectives can be integrated using the following formula: Governance in complex societies must aim at: (1) reducing external and internal threats to the security of human beings and their environment (security); (2) guaranteeing a sufficient degree of legal certainty (rule of the law); (3) establishing a symbolic system of reference within which a sense of civil identity and participation in collective decision-making can develop (participation); and (4) encouraging economic growth and curbing social inequalities with a view to general material prosperity (social welfare).

These four objectives are "normative goods", as they are regarded by most people—at least in the Western world—as valuable and desirable; at the same time, they are "functional goods", as in the long run the non-attainability of one or more of these objectives may lead to political crisis.

Governance goals[5] have, however, changed in the course of history. In spite of revolutions, counter-revolutions and restoration, and in spite of devastating civil and international wars, the expansion of state activities and the size of the state apparatus took place in a more or less linear way. In early sixteenth century, at the beginning of the absolutist period in France, around 12,000 people—that is, 0.0006 per cent of the total population of around 20 million—were state servants (cf. Braudel, 1992: 549). This proportion grew to around 1.25 per cent in 1905 (i.e., 500,000 employees with a population of around 40 million; cf. Hobsbawm, 1992: 99) and to well over 20 per cent in 1980 (Bruder and Dose,

---

[4] Historical state theory refers to the "minimum activities of the state", which include warfare, state-building, the protection of individuals and the collection of taxes (Tilly 1990, chap. 4). Economic theory of the state regards internal and external protection and the provision of public goods as the central "duties of the state" (Smith 1776; see also North 1981). Legal theory discusses the "duties (functions) for regulating human co-existence in the relevant state" and identifies peace, liberty, social security, social integration and co-operation as these duties (Horn 1996, 22–25). Sociological theory established the classic distinction between civil (guaranteed individual liberties), political (participation in political power) and social (minimum social security) subjective rights—that is, legitimate demands on the state (Marshall 1950). In a more recent contribution, Giddens (1994, 246) discusses the reduction of force and violence, the challenging of arbitrary claims to power, the establishment of compensation for environmental damage and the struggle against poverty as fundamental political orientations. In political theory, Benhabib (1996, 67) identifies legitimacy, economic welfare and a collective identity as the "public goods" that must be provided in modern societies. Modern political economy identifies the political regulation of the market, the provision of a public infrastructure and socio-political adjustments as the "main functions" of the state within the "socio-economic sphere" (see Cerny 1996, 124–30; Majone 1996, 54).

[5] I use the term "governance goals" for two reasons. First, it should not hastily be concluded that the attainment of these goals depends purely on the existence of a state. If we are to consider the concept of governance beyond the nation-state, then we must analyse the above objectives separately from the state. In this respect terms such as "state functions", "state aims", "state objectives", etc., are unsatisfactory. Second, it is important to avoid teleological characterisations of the state or of governance (Kaufmann 1994, 17) without falling back on the argument that desirable and necessary state activities are completely historically and culturally contingent. The term "governance goals" is, I think, a better expression of the desirable middle position than, say, purpose or function (which sound like a teleological characterisation) or activities (which sound completely contingent).

1992: 277). Simultaneously, the goals of state activities were expanded. Only the post-World War II welfare states aimed at a full set of governance goals including security, legal certainty, democratic legitimacy and social welfare. Sicily under Frederick II was a precursor of this process of expanding state activities, beginning in the fourteenth century, progressing from an *absolutist territorial state* (an ideal type of which is represented by absolutist France under Louis XIV with security as the major goal of governance), to a *constitutional nation-state* (ideal type: England during the Regency period of the Hanoverians adding the rule of law as a goal of governance), and a *liberal-democratic state* (ideal type: the USA during the presidency of Woodrow Wilson which made broader participation in decision-making possible) to the *democratic welfare state* (ideal type: social-democratic Sweden adding social welfare as a goal of governance). Hence, governance goals are not static; they change, are discursively constructed, and in fact have increased in number.

Statehood can thus generally be defined as a three-dimensional political constellation: (1) a legitimate monopoly of force which is needed to maintain internal autonomy and which determines the size of its territory according to its ability to collect taxes (*resources*); (2) recognition by other states and—at least in principle—on the basis of minimum constitutional standards (*recognition*); and (3) a minimum degree of public-interest orientation (*realisation of governance goals*).

These three dimensions, in general, need not always converge in *one* political organisation. The *nation-state*, as a historically specific form of statehood, is characterised by the "national constellation" of all three dimensions of statehood converging in one political organisation—the nation-state—with each dimension supporting the other and thus being to some extent dependent on each other.[6]

Of course, there have been and still are so-called nation-states that do not qualify as such according to the above criteria. There have been states riven by civil war which were still acknowledged without question by other states (for example, the American Civil War). There have been states whose monopoly of force was exploited for private purposes without any direct danger to the monopoly of force or to the recognition of that state as such by other states (for instance, Rhodesia in the initial period of white minority government). And there are states with internal autonomy and a certain degree of public-interest orientation without broad international acceptance (for instance, Taiwan since Chiang Ching-kuo). However, these deviations have been perceived and discussed as deficits and problems for modern statehood in all such cases. The

---

[6] More thoughtful contributions to the current debate about the future of sovereignty also disaggregate the notion of sovereignty in order to be able to paint differentiated pictures about its development. See, for example, Lyons and Mastanduno (1995), Thomson (1995), Litfin (1997), Krasner (1999), Sørensen (1998). They often overlook, however, the interdependence between the different dimensions and thus often conclude in contradiction to hyper-globalists that the core of legal sovereignty remains unchanged.

nation-state as an *institution* has been characterised by the convergence of a monopoly of force, internal and external recognition and policies displaying a public-interest orientation in one political organisation, even if in specific cases this has only ever been an approximation—and sometimes not even that.

The nation-state as an institution has proved to be more successful than any alternative forms of political organisation that emerged since the Dark Ages such as empires, city-states and city-associations (like the Hanseatic League). One important reason for this success was a greater ability to provide goods for the society in question. Modern sovereign statehood thus became linked to the capacity of the state to govern effectively. Only later was the people's right to self-determination disconnected from the governing ability of the state. As late as 1916, the British government refused to give up its colonies at short notice with the argument that these countries lacked an effective state that was able to pursue the goals of governance. The British government was able to cite the League of Nations, which restricted the right to state-building by establishing criteria for the "capacity for independence". Only 14 years later did the United Nations pass a resolution that the right to self-determination did not depend on the existence of the ability to govern. "Inadequacy of political, economic, social or educational preparedness should never serve as a pretext for delaying independence".[7] Subsequently, "quasi-states" emerged, which owed their existence primarily to recognition and assistance by other states and international organisations, but which hardly confirmed the notion of modern statehood as conceived by the early state theorists Jean Bodin and Thomas Hobbes.[8] Put differently, legal sovereignty exists as a legal *de facto* concept independent of the effectiveness of the national capacity to govern. In this respect, Robert O. Keohane (1991: 5) is correct in stating that the "problem that international interdependence poses in the first instance for governments is not that it directly threatens their formal sovereignty or even their autonomy, but that it calls into questions their effectiveness". However, the qualifying "in the first instance" is of the utmost significance here. Formal sovereignty, in the absence of material resources and the capacity to govern, is always extremely precarious. A system of states, all of which only persist with the help of other states, is an untenable construction. The recognition of quasi-states by quasi-states is quasi-meaningless.

In sum, the institution of the modern state is characterised by the interplay of recognition, resources and the realisation of governance goals—the three Rs. These three dimensions are synergetic, and it is not sufficient to diagnose that the governing capacity of the nation-state decreases while formal sovereignty in the form of recognition by other states remains untouched. On the contrary, it is necessary to ask questions that take into account the interdependence of the three dimensions of modern statehood. How is the national constellation challenged through societal denationalisation (Section 2)? What

---

[7] Resolution 1514 (XV), 14.12.60.

[8] Jackson (1990) coined the term "quasi-states" for these organisations. See also Knieper (1991) and especially Sørensen (1997) on this issue.

could a post-national constellation look like (Section 3)? What does this mean for the goals of governance, that is security, the rule of law—which is the focus of this chapter in Section 4—legitimacy and social welfare?

CHALLENGES OF AND RESPONSES TO DENATIONALISATION

Is globalisation really taking place? If so, in what way does it challenge the national constellation of statehood? Although it is true that very fundamental transformation processes can be observed, the term "globalisation" goes too far. Eighty-four per cent of world trade is transacted between countries inhabited by approximately 28 per cent of the world population. This OECD focus is even more evident if one looks at direct investments. Over 91 per cent of all foreign direct investments between 1980 and 1991 went to OECD countries and the 10 most important threshold countries (Hirst and Thompson, 1996: 67).[9] Communication flows indicate a similar concentration in OECD countries. A world map showing the distribution of Internet connections is particularly informative. It shows that even within the OECD world there are clear gravitational centres the borders of which, however, do not coincide with national borders. Even in the USA there are only extensive networks along the two coastlines, which also include parts of Canada (see Beisheim *et al.*, 1999: 65). For this reason, I use the term denationalisation instead of globalisation. The term denationalisation refers to the classic works of Karl W. Deutsch (1969) and Eric Hobsbawm (1992) on nationalism. According to them, a nation is a political community sustained by intensified interactions, which stands in a mutually constitutive relationship to the nation-state and is thus an expression of the national constellation. Consequently, denationalisation is an indication of the weakening link between territorial states and their corresponding national societies.

Denationalisation can be defined as the extension of boundaries of social transactions and identities beyond national borders, without being necessarily global in scope. Even though the scope of most of these cross-border transactions is indeed not global, they still cause a problem for national governance simply because the social space to be governed is no longer national. The degree of denationalisation can be operationalised as the extent of cross-border transactions relative to transactions taking place within national borders. Social transactions are constituted by the exchange or common production of goods, services and capital (which make up the issue area of economy), threats (force), pollutants (environment), signs (communication) and persons (mobility). An empirical investigation carried out against the background of this conceptualisation shows that denationalisation is not a uniform, but rather a jagged,

---

[9] This figure counts only the most important coastal provinces of China as "threshold countries", but not the whole of China. If China as a whole were included its share in world trade would increase marginally but its population ratio would increase by 15%.

process that differs notably among issue areas, countries and over time.[10] Denationalisation, defined in terms of a growing significance of cross-border transactions, has been taking place in mild forms since the 1950s. Accelerated denationalisation first occurred in the 1960s with the massive deployment of nuclear weapons in the issue area of force. From the 1970s on, the growth of cross-border exchanges accelerated with respect to goods and capital, information, travel, migration and regional environmental risks. Surprisingly, however, the growth of many of these exchange processes levelled off for a few years in the 1980s. Veritable denationalisation thrusts, however, occurred in a number of very specific issue areas just as the growth in cross-border exchanges slowed down. The most notable developments took place with respect to global financial markets, global environmental dangers, the Internet and organised crime. The common feature of all these more recent developments is that they concern the integrated production of goods and bads, rather than the mere exchange of goods and bads across national borders.

Challenges

Denationalisation undermines the capacity of the nation-state to realise governance goals. For the national constellation of statehood is based on the *principle of congruence*, according to which effective governance depends upon the spatial congruence of political regulations with socially integrated areas.[11] Consequently, the shift of boundaries of socially integrated areas—i.e., the place where there is some critical reduction in the frequency of social transactions (see Deutsch, 1969: 99)—requires an adaptation of political institutions if regulations are to remain effective. One can distinguish four causal pathways through which long-standing national policies may be challenged as a result of denationalisation:

(1) Most national regulations affect international trade by having a protective impact. Thus, each national regulation that is not harmonised on the international level separates markets and creates a barrier for the efficient allocation of goods through the market. In a world in which the barriers between different markets are dissolving, R&D costs rise and product cycles shorten, larger markets and unhindered co-operation with other enterprises are seen as essential to remain competitive. To put it differently: in a denationalised world the "static efficiency costs of closure" increase (Frieden and Rogowski, 1996: 35). For instance, all over the world, car manufacturers import parts that amount to over 50 per cent of the overall value of the end product. If, due to tariffs, these imports are more expensive in one country than in another with a more liberal trade policy, the former manufacturer will be at a significant comparative

---

[10] In a research project funded by the German Research Association we developed 72 indicators to determine the extent of denationalisation in different issue areas and different OECD countries (see Beisheim *et al.* 1999). For a similar undertaking with similar results see Held *et al.* (1999).

[11] The principle is discussed in Held (1995, 16); Scharpf (1993); and Zürn (1996).

disadvantage and will press for liberalisation. As another example: the nationally organised and protected organisations for Post and Telecommunications (PTTs) experienced increasing pressures from the 1980s on, when multinational corporations wanted to reorganise their internal communication at the best possible value. To the extent that the relative proportion of communication costs increased, MNCs were no longer willing to accept and pay for the inefficiencies of national PTT companies. The MNCs finally succeeded with their demand for the dissolution of national monopolies in the telecommunication market. In general, economic integration will create further demands for overcoming the disadvantages of political segmentation to maximise the gains from economic exchange by harmonising national policies or by common rules that prohibit national intervention. These demands for market-making policies at the international level are due to *efficiency pressure* and express a desire for non-discrimination in the markets. To the extent that such demands for transnational market-making policies are fulfilled, they serve the governance goal of the *rule of law* within the economic sphere in that legal certainty about the absence of arbitrary discrimination increases.

(2) Political regulations may have little impact if they cover only a part of the relevant social space. A national regulation by Australia alone could do little to prevent rising cancer rates due to the depletion of atmospheric ozone. Along the same lines, Germany—for good reasons—has more severe restrictions on the distribution of racist propaganda material than many other countries. However, if someone residing in the USA feeds such material into the Internet, authorities in Germany cannot legally prohibit, let alone effectively prevent, these activities. Moreover, different national policies directed at an integrated social space may interfere with each other. The resulting drop in *efficacy of national policies* has given rise to a demand for the co-ordination of regulatory policies at the international level. The governance goal to reduce threats to the *security* of people and their environment is most often the underlying motive for these demands.

(3) The establishment of a regulation that does not apply to all social actors within an integrated social space can even be counter-productive. In particular, policies that create costs for the production of goods may turn out to be self-defeating in terms of competitiveness for the area to which the policy applies. In this vein, manufacturers' associations all over the industrialised world complain at every opportunity that the social and environmental costs of production are too high. According to them, wages, social policies, environmental regulations and corporate taxes need to be cut. Against this background, the widespread fear of a race to the bottom in national social and environmental standards is not surprising.[12] In the

---

[12] To be sure, at least for environmental regulations this fear seems to be unsubstantiated (see Héritier *et al.* 1994; Vogel 1995; Jänicke 1998). While there indeed seems to be a parallel drop in corporate taxes in most OECD countries, the question whether there is a downward convergence of national regulations is most contested with respect to social policies (see e.g. Garrett 1998).

national context, this discourse benefits especially those groups that do not favour cost-intensive market-correcting or redistributive policies. On the other hand, groups in favour of redistributive policies will demand the establishment of common redistributive or cost-intensive market-correcting policies at the international level to avoid the *race-to-the-bottom dynamics*. The governance goal that is behind those demands is mostly *social welfare*, especially those components of it that require re-distributive policies.

(4) Effective participation depends on spatial congruence between the rulers (the nation-*state*) and the ruled (the national *society*). Yet this notion becomes problematic as soon as the nature of the relevant community is contested, as happens in the course of societal denationalisation. The rise of cross-border transactions damages the normative dignity of political borders (Schmalz-Bruns, 1998: 372). If there is no *input congruence*, then a group affected by a decision but not participating in its making can be considered as being subject to foreign determination rather than self-determined. This new form of foreign determination tends to be symmetrical and is based on manifold externalities the result of which is that many political decisions have, if not unlimited, at least transboundary effects. The decisions of the British and German governments in the 1960s and 1970s, for example, not to implement certain environmental protection measures, led to acid lakes and high fish mortality in Scandinavia. Nevertheless, the Swedish fishermen were not in a position to participate in public will-formation and decision-making in Great Britain or Germany. Against this background, demands for the enlargement of moral and political communities, so that the *participation* (direct or indirect) of all those affected by such decisions, are put forward as a normative requirement in the age of denationalisation.

Responses

These challenges to the effectiveness of national policies in achieving governance goals do not directly translate into a weakened capacity of nation-states to deliver goods for society. The challenges are serious, yet the outcome is largely determined by political choices. Governments and other political organisations can respond to these challenges in a number of different ways. First, they may passively await the decline in effectiveness of national policies, partly because they favour the institutional *status quo*, partly because they can use the pretext of international pressure for domestic reforms.[13] Secondly, regionalist parties may push for decentralisation or even secession from nation-states in order to be able to respond as flexibly as possible in the new denationalised environment. The rise of the Lega Nord and the revival of the Scottish National Party as well the Parti Québecois can be related to economic and cultural denationalisation

---

[13] For this interpretation, see Moravcsik (1994) and Wolf (1997).

Table 1.1 Challenges of Denationalisation

Challenge to Effectiveness of National Policies	Type of Policy Mainly Affected/ Demanded[1]	Governance Goal Mainly Affected	Example
Efficiency	Regulative/market-making policy	Legal certainty	Protection of domestic goods
Efficacy	Regulative/ regulative policy	Security	Environmental regulations
Race-to-the-bottom	Re-distributive/ regulative policy[2]	Social Welfare	Unemployment policies
Input-incongruence	Distributive Policy[3]	Participation Channels	Industrial Risks

[1] The policy that is affected is at the national, the policy demand at the international level.

[2] It is most often sufficient to employ a regulative policy at the international level (e.g., minimum social standards) to retain redistributive policies at the national level.

[3] It is a distributive policy in as far as the distribution of participation rights and channels are concerned.

and thus be interpreted as a fragmented political response.[14] Thirdly, governments and other political organisations may aim for integrative political responses to denationalisation. The incongruence between national political regulations and denationalised areas of social transactions calls into question the very capacity of the nation-state to provide what made it the dominant political institution in the first place. In this predicament, governments may endeavour to regain control by establishing new international and transnational regimes, networks and organisations for the co-ordination and harmonisation of their policies, i.e., to establish governance beyond the nation-state.

In general terms, governance is distinct from anarchy—the unrestricted interplay of actors driven by self-interest—in that social actors recognise the existence of obligations and feel compelled, for whatever reason, to honour them by their behaviour. Governance refers to the governing of purposive systems of norms and rules. In this sense, "governance is order plus intentionality".[15] Modern governance has best been provided within the nation-state by a government claiming a monopoly of legitimate force and that thus ruled by hierarchical orders. Governance took the form of *governance by government*.

The form of governance has, however, to be distinguished from its function, i.e., the provision of goods which are considered worthy and desirable by most people. These goods can be provided by a government, but also by governance with or without governments. International governance, specifically, lacks a central

[14] See Zürn (1998, chap. 9) and Lange (1998).

[15] Rosenau (1992, 5). See also Kohler-Koch (1993); Mayer, Rittberger and Zürn (1993); Young (1994).

authority or a "world state" equipped with a legitimate monopoly over the use of force.[16] Thus, governance beyond the nation-state cannot take the form of governance by government, but rather it needs to be governance with governments, as in international institutions, or governance without government, as in transnational institutions. In spite of the absence of governance by government, governance beyond the nation-state has developed significantly over the last decades. The sum of all institutional arrangements beyond the nation-state makes up regional or global governance systems.[17] Moreover, the interplay of different forms of governance beyond the nation-state can produce political systems of a new quality, as attested by the European Multi-Level Governance System (see Marks *et al.*, 1996; Jachtenfuchs and Kohler-Koch, 1996).

1. Governance with governments

Governance with governments regulates state and non-state activities the effects of which extend beyond national borders. Central to international governance are *international regimes,* defined as social institutions consisting of agreed-upon and publicly announced principles, norms, rules, procedures and programmes that govern the interactions of actors in specific issue areas. As such, regimes contain specific regulations and give rise to recognised social practices in international society.[18] Regimes comprise both substantive and procedural rules and are thus distinct from mere *intergovernmental networks* which frequently include only informal, procedural rules. Such networks meet on a regular basis and may develop co-ordinated responses to specific situations, but they do not govern behaviour in a certain issue area for a prolonged period of time.[19] Other components of international governance are *international organisations* that are material entities and can be the infrastructure for both international regimes and intergovernmental networks.[20] In specific instances, international organisations may develop into *supranational institutions.* Supranational institutions develop rules that are considered superior to national law and involve servants who are independent of national governments. The most well known supranational institutions are the European Commission and the European Court of Justice.[21] The current development of the Dispute Settlement Body and the Appellate Body of

[16] See Young (1978) for arguments why a world state is neither possible nor desirable.

[17] The definition of global governance used by Rosenau (1995, 13) goes even further: "all systems of rule at all levels of human activity".

[18] See Krasner (1983, 3). See Rittberger (1993), and Levy, Young and Zürn (1995), for further elaboration on the definition of international regimes.

[19] The distinction between international regimes and international networks is similar to the one drawn by Mayntz (1996) between networks for the management of ad-hoc problems and institutions for the regulation of recurring problems.

[20] The formal term is International Governmental Organisations (IGOs), as opposed to transnational Non-Governmental Organisations (NGOs). The latter consist of any kind of professional association, like the International Political Science Association, and also of profit-seeking NGOs, that is multinational enterprises.

[21] See Joerges and Neyer (1997) and Bogdandy (1999) for a productive use of this term.

the World Trade Organisation points into the same direction. Finally, *constitutional principles* encompass notions of conduct such as sovereignty or reciprocity which are valid across all issue areas. Any of these components of international governance beyond the nation-state can be regional or global in scope.

A first measure for the extent of governance beyond the nation-state is the number of existing international governmental organisations (IGOs). Until the early 1980s this figure grew continuously to a total of 378, thus reflecting the permanent growth in the importance of cross-border transactions. In the late 1980s, as the growth of some cross-border transactions slowed down, the overall number of international organisations declined rapidly to fewer than 300. Only recently has the number of international organisations begun to increase again. Currently, the number of IGOs is still below the 1980 figure, unless IGO-emanations are included.[22]

The number of international organisations is only a very rough measure for the development of international governance. It is easily conceivable that a relatively constant number of IGOs has produced a higher regulatory output and thus strengthened international governance. For instance, the number of EU directives, regulations and decisions grew significantly until the 1980s, when IGO memberships of the G–7 countries had already begun to decline. The total number of directives, regulations and decisions increased from 36 in 1961 to 347 in 1970 and 627 in 1980. The number of EU rules has remained quite constant since then, with a temporary peak of almost 800 in 1986. It is noteworthy that the relative weight of EU legislation clearly increased in comparison to national legislation in Germany, France and Great Britain, where the yearly legislative output has remained more or less constant since the 1960s. Similarly, the number of new international environmental treaties and agreements has grown continuously since World War II. A very similar pattern applies to the development of new international economic treaties and agreements. Within the group of economic treaties and agreements, those which deal with issues of legal certainty are especially numerous. The most important attempts to harmonise international trade law take place in the UN Commission on International Trade Law (UNCITRAL), the International Institute for the Unification of Private Law (UNIDROIT) and the Hague Conferences on Private International Law (Bonell, 1990). The effectiveness of these instruments is contested and we know much less about them than about other international regimes (see the contribution by Martiny).

In the field of culture and communication, the regulatory output of existing international regimes, such as the ITU-based telecommunication regime, again shows steady growth until the 1980s.[23] This pattern differs only slightly in the

---

[22] Emanations include those organisations that have other IGOs' names in their titles, have been created by a provision in another IGO's charter, are a joint or internal IGO committee or an international centre or institute. See Shanks, Jacobson and Kaplan (1996, 597).

[23] See Zacher with Sutton (1996). In this field it is hard to assess the precise amount of regulatory output in the most recent period, since a de facto decline of ITU importance relative to other regulating agencies has taken place (see Genschel 1995).

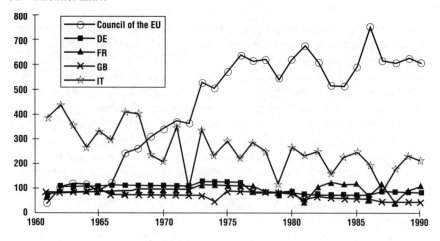

*Figure 1.1 Acts of the Council of the EU and Legislative Output in Germany,
France, Great Britain, and Italy*[1]

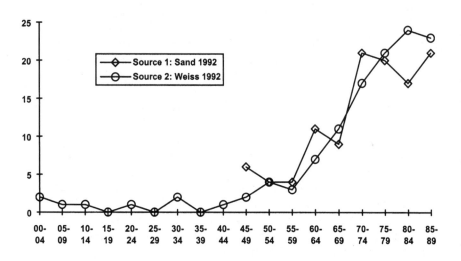

*Figure 1.2 Development of the Number of New International
Environmental Agreements (According to Two Different Sources)*

---

[1] The figures are taken from Beisheim *et al*. (1999, 325–64).

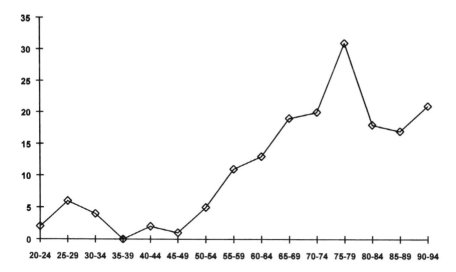

Figure 1.3 Development of the Number of New International Economic Treaties

field of international security. The regulatory output of the non-proliferation regime and the Security Council showed no clear pattern for a long time and were quite erratic. Since the end of the 1980s, however, the output of Security Council resolutions has grown dramatically.

2. Governance without governments

Although the role of governance without government has increased over the last two decades, it is arguably still less significant than governance with governments. To be sure, the number of transnational organisations has grown significantly over the last decades.[24] However, some of these organisations are standard-setting associations that work as part of a larger international institution set up by intergovernmental agreement, others are part of an issue-area specific policy network with national governments still in the position to accept or veto agreements. As Thomas Risse-Kappen puts it: "[t]he more regulated the inter-state relationship by co-operative international institutions in the particular issue area, the more transnational activities are expected to flourish" (Risse-Kappen, 1995: 30). Nevertheless, in some issue areas the role of transnational regimes, organisations and networks is remarkable.

The *lex mercatoria* may be a good example of a *transnational regime*.[25] It is a regime for the arbitration of conflicts in transnational business. Although its

[24] See the data of the Union of International Associations (UIA).
[25] Its character as a generically transnational regime is reflected in the legal debate on the extent to which this law can be regarded as autonomous from state law. See the contribution of De Ly in this volume.

roots are pre-modern, the *lex mercatoria* seems to have grown in importance in recent years (whereas its importance relative to intergovernmental institutions in this area[26] is contested). In some cases, parties to business transactions deliberately choose to settle disputes on the basis of the *lex mercatoria* instead of the nation-state-based system of "choice of law" (Dasser, 1991). Moreover, *lex mercatoria* norms used in arbitration panels are regularly backed by national courts, for the non-acceptor of arbitration awards loses most often in national courts. There are other important transnational regimes, for instance for the development of some of the technical standards related to the Internet such as the TCP/IP protocol. The Internet Engineering Task Force (IETF), a sub-organisation of the Internet Society (ISOC), developed the TCP/IP protocol. This issue network is open to all users and being on the mailing list constitutes membership. Decisions are made on the basis of discourses in different fora, which are regulated by a number of procedural rules. Ballots are held on the basis of a strongly qualified majority and after the new standard has demonstrated its effectiveness in practice. The decisions are then made public with the help of the mailing lists (see e.g. Hofmann, 1998).

One may further distinguish two types of *transnational organisations*. Some transnational organisations provide the organisational and infrastructural support for transnational regimes. The International Chamber of Commerce and the Internet Society (ISOC) are examples of about 600 such organisations (Shanks, Jacobsen and Kaplan, 1996: 596). In contrast, other transnational organisations aim at influencing international and transnational regimes by playing significant roles in different steps of the policy process (Beisheim/Zürn, 1999). They are often instrumental in the building of transnational concerns and in bringing issues onto the international agenda. In the fields of international environmental politics and human rights in particular, they collect and distribute information to raise an awareness in people and governments for environmental and human rights problems and potential solutions. Secondly, they influence the formulation of international policies by using the opportunities to participate in meetings organised by international organisations. Thirdly, NGOs play a paramount role in the implementation and verification of international rules by controlling and shaming states and governments. Amnesty International in the field of human rights regimes is a prime example. In most cases, credibility and perceived impartiality are the major sources of NGOs' influence. In these ways NGOs are able to exert some control on governments from outside the country, thus playing partially the role of a transnational civil society (see Keck and Sikkink, 1998; Risse *et al.*, 1999). Today, about 5,000 transnational organisations operate in the global environment carrying out these or similar functions.

Transnational organisations interact with each other and create networks that can be seen as the constituents of international and transnational policies. Against this background it comes as no surprise that in more recent analyses

---

[26] See the contribution of Martiny in this volume.

particular attention is paid to these transnational networks. In 1996, for instance, in the multi-level system of the European Union, there were 409 committees active in the implementation of General Council decisions and which in fact enjoy extensive interpretative freedom in their work (see Falke, 1996; Wessels, 1998). The committee members are mainly experts and representatives of concerned interest groups, as well as national civil servants who are usually selected by their governments. The quality and adequacy of these committees' decisions usually meet with approval (see Eichener, 1996; Joerges and Neyer, 1997). Particularly within the field of environmental politics, related developments can even be observed at the international level. After the admission of transnational non-governmental organisations (NGOs) to international negotiations, the latter received an impetus which distinguished them from conventional intergovernmental negotiations, while at the same time giving so-called epistemic communities a more prominent status (Adler and Haas, 1992; Princen and Finger, 1994). It is owing to these epistemic communities that, as opposed to simple bargaining, deliberative elements are at less of a disadvantage than is commonly the case, and that particular interests are relativised by public interests (see Gehring, 1995). In this sense one may speak of transnational sectoral publics and "sectoral *demoi*" (Abromeit and Schmidt, 1998).

This brief examination of the development of different types of institutions for governance beyond the nation-state, be they transnational, international or even supra-national, shows that governance beyond the nation-state has increased more or less in parallel to the growth of cross-border exchanges. From these findings we can draw two conclusions. First, governments and other political organisations do not merely sit back and watch denationalisation and the declining effectiveness of unilateral policies. One important response to the challenges described is—among others—the development of international institutions. Secondly, governance beyond the nation-state has now become a crucial factor that cannot be neglected in the analysis and understanding of the fulfilment of governance goals. The national constellation, that is the convergence of resources, recognition and the provision of governance goals into one political organisation—the nation-state—seems to be in a process of transformation into a post-national constellation.

THE NEW ARCHITECTURE OF STATEHOOD

Statehood in the national constellation has been characterised by the coincidence of the dimensions of statehood in *one* political organisation, that is the nation-state. The monopoly of force and the ability to collect taxes, the authority to recognise other states as such, and the capability to design and implement policies that show a certain degree of public-interest orientation could all be found at the nation-state level. The challenges of and responses to denationalisation seem, however, to have transformed this national constellation.

Nation-states experience increasing difficulties in designing unilateral policies that are of use in fulfilling the governance goals of security, legal certainty, legitimacy and social welfare *(the governance dimension)*. The incongruence of political and social spaces leads systematically to challenges to the effectiveness of national policies (see Section 2). Governments and other political groups react to these unintended consequences of social change, that were largely encouraged by national policies. The primary response to this is the formation of international institutions that help to re-adjust political and social spaces and thus to regain the effectiveness of policies, either by directly regulating cross-border activities or, more often, prejudicing national decisions to a large extent. Hence, systems of interest mediation that are restricted to the nation-state lose importance, especially since those political actors such as national executives who play on both levels can use their privileged position for manipulation. A secondary response for political organisations therefore is to participate directly at the level of international institutions, which happens increasingly, as indicated by the rise of transnational organisations and transnational networks. In this sense, the formulation of policies for most of the issue areas affected by the challenges of denationalisation has been deferred to the international level.

Moreover, the conditions for external *recognition* as a legitimate state seem to be changing, too. Traditionally, recognition as a sovereign state, once attained, was in principle valid for eternity. Thomas M. Franck (1992: 50) has pointed out that a fundamental change is going on in this respect: "[w]e are witnessing a sea change in international law, as a result of which the legitimacy of each government someday will be measured definitely by international rules and processes" (see also Friedman, 1996). Through the development of international penalty law, the human rights regime and the rights of minorities a global order seems to be emerging which is indeed more than what we traditionally know as international law, and which is anchored in states as the subjects and objects of international rules. The recognition of a state increasingly depends upon its respect of the rights of individual freedom, that can now be claimed by individuals before the European Court of Justice and under special conditions even before the European Court of Human Rights. In extreme cases, the violation of human rights can be even regarded as a justification for intervention—the war in Kosovo can be seen as a case in point. These developments lead Soysal (1994) to reflect upon a notion of "personhood" which is independent of national citizenship. Moreover, the growing use of international observers at national elections indicates a trend towards making critical elections into global events (Rosenau, 1997: 259), and the concept of "good governance" is now also used for evaluations of national policies through international institutions like the World Bank (1997). In the light of these developments, it seems that the recognition of a state as such is now seen less as a one-shot constituting act, and increasingly as the result of a *permanent legitimacy control*. Moreover, the subject carrying out this control function is today less the international society of states, and increasingly an *emergent transnational society*. The authority which assigns sovereignty, that is the right to set the rules of a given territory or the "Kompetenz-Kompetenz", as it is called in German, seems to change as well as the criterion for this assignment. What has changed in world politics then is the "Kompetenz-Kompetenz-Kompetenz".

These developments should, however, by no means be regarded as indications of the end of the nation-state, that is the institution that still provides *the resources*. First, the developments described apply only to strongly denationalised issue areas, while others still follow the logic of the national constellation. Secondly, and more importantly, it is hard to see how the goals of governance can be achieved without the nation-state. The increasing inability of an institution to fulfil a function can be seen as an indicator of its impending extinction only if there are rival institutions which promise to fulfil that function more efficiently (Spruyt, 1994). The elimination of the problems relating to global financial markets, organised crime or global environmental risks is hardly conceivable without nation-states. Especially for the implementation of policies with the help of the monopoly of force and for the provision of resources for policies (based on the capability to raise taxes) the nation-state seems to be indispensable. It thus follows that the nation-state is not only here to stay, but there are also good reasons for welcoming this. However, if denationalisation continues, the nation-state will certainly not look the same in the twenty-first century as it did in its heyday after World War II.

In the post-national constellation, statehood will be constituted by the interplay of different levels and organisations, with each level and organisation unable to work unilaterally. Governance beyond the nation-state will be the result of a complex arrangement of governance by, with and without governments. In this post-national constellation nation-states will not give away their resources such as the monopoly of force or the privilege to collect taxes in a given territory. Hence, while the nation-state will play a significant role in governance beyond the nation-state, it will no longer be the primary political institution, but one among others. Not only will it defer policy formulation to international institutions, but the subjects delegating legitimacy and authority will also no longer be nation-states (externally) and national societies (internally), but, to a greater extent than ever before, transnational society. In the postnational constellation, statehood itself will become functionally differentiated and it is likely that the convergence of the dimensions of statehood in one political organisation will come to an end.

LAW BEYOND THE NATION-STATE

From a normative point of view, statehood in the post-national constellation needs to be evaluated by the extent to which it helps achieve the (discursively constructed) goals of governance. Will statehood in the post-national constellation succeed in providing security, the rule of law, legitimate decision-making and social welfare to the same extent as some of the nation-states did in the

OECD world after World War II? Is governance beyond the nation-state potentially capable of providing the goods? I have discussed these questions with respect to security, democratic legitimacy and social welfare elsewhere.[27] In the concluding section of this chapter I want to focus on the provision of law in a denationalised world.

Rule of Law

Governance is expected to establish the rule of law, and thus legal certainty. The rule of law is defined by norms that are public, relatively stable, consistent and prospective. According to liberal principles one could add the requirement of legal equality, that is, like cases are treated alike (see e.g., Böckenförde, 1969; Peters, 1991: chap. 4). The rule of law is a general principle applying to all kinds of issue areas, and its political meaning is closely related to the concept of limitation of state power and to human rights in general. In the present context, however, I shall focus on legal certainty in the economic sphere.

Legal certainty in the economic sphere has been a major means of increasing the efficiency of economic activities and exchanges and thus fostering economic growth and prosperity. According to Douglass North (1990), the rise and success of the nation-state are closely related to its continuous ability to establish legal certainty in the economic sphere and thus to increase economic efficiency. The liberal nation-state effectively achieved legal certainty in the economic sphere by establishing property rights, by guaranteeing the free movement of labour, goods and capital, by standardising weights, measures and education, and by drawing up necessary product regulations in a non-discriminatory way. In doing so, national economies with more or less uniform price levels emerged as transportation and communication costs decreased. In the course of economic denationalisation, these national regulations come under efficiency pressure, in turn creating a demand for the establishment of common rules that prohibit national policies or intervention to overcome the disadvantages of national segmentation. The question is whether or not the rise of these international institutions in some way matches the speed of economic denationalisation. If so, one may state that the predictability in the economic sphere increases systematically.[28]

Most existing international economic institutions arose in direct response to efficiency pressures. The development of the GATT regime is a case in point. The early GATT removed government intervention at the borders, that is tariffs on

[27] With respect to security see Zürn (1998, chap. 3) and Zangl and Zürn (1999), with respect to democracy Zürn (1998, chaps. 8 and 13) and Zürn (1999), with respect to social welfare Zürn (1998, chap. 4).

[28] In framing the issue this way, I clearly use a very lean notion of the "rule of law". The rise of legal certainty is limited to those who act on the global market as subjects, it may be accompanied by a decline of legal certainty for others. For another perspective on the rule of law see the contribution of William Scheuerman in this volume.

manufactured goods. Over time this increased the importance of non-tariff barriers, thus inducing demands for a new type of market-making regulation that focused on behind-the-border issues. The Tokyo Round of negotiations (1973–9) began to deal with non-tariff barriers such as anti-dumping measures, government subsidies, government procurement, and custom and licensing procedures. The results of the Uruguay Round (1986–94) are a major step forward in this respect. Above all, the section of the new WTO on the manufactured goods trade brought in new monitoring and dispute settlement procedures to deal more effectively with behind-the-border issues. The Dispute Settlement Body and the Appellate Body seem to develop towards a supranational institution, at least in relation to the "Agreement on the Application of Sanitary and Phytosanitary Measures" (see Victor, 1999), and thus to some extent resembles the supranational role of the European Court of Justice (Godt, 1998). Moreover, regulations on technical standards aim at introducing the principle of mutual recognition of national standards and, where necessary, some international harmonisation. GATT furthermore established an institutional framework for the services industry that resembles those of other sections of the new WTO, and the Trade-Related Aspects of International Property Rights (TRIPS) Agreement regulates an essential field in any market-making process. Finally, the Trade Related Investment Measures Agreement mainly contains regulations that facilitate FDIs but do little to control the conduct of MNCs. In sum, with the successful conclusion of the Uruguay Round, a regime has emerged that has enlarged its scope and has sharpened its organisational profile as well as its monitoring and enforcement mechanisms (see Kahler, 1995: 46).

Similar institutional developments have occurred at the regional level. The Single European Act was initially a market-making programme that, on the basis of the logic of mutual recognition, aimed at removing national barriers for economic exchange,[29] followed by a re-regulation that carefully maintained market integration. Both European market-making and its regulation have been ensured with the help of supranational institutions like the Commission and the European Court of Justice. Furthermore, "NAFTA's goals, like those in CUSTA [and other regional trade agreements, M.Z.] were largely a clearing away of obstacles to exchange, not the construction of a framework for policy co-ordination" (Kahler, 1995: 103). A common feature of all the more successful attempts is the establishment of relatively strong monitoring mechanisms to deal with the relevant behind-the-border issues.

In addition, cross-border contractual relations take place in a more predictable environment. The European and the UN conventions on the Law Applicable to Contractual Relations were both signed in 1980 and further developed since then. However, "choice of law rules" are to some extent replaced by genuinely global rules that apply directly to the affected parties. Although states are involved in drafting general conventions, the rules applied in cross-border

---

[29] Among others see the apt phrase "Market without a State": Joerges (1991).

contractual relations sometimes derive with the consent of national courts from the transnational *lex mercatoria* (see section 2).

At first sight, this quantitative rise in intergovernmental regulations to assure legal certainty in the transnational economic sphere does not seem to affect the national constellation in qualitative terms. The *constitutional principles* of the Westphalian system of sovereign states are intergovernmental in that governments mutually acknowledge each other as governments, thus laying the ground for international society (see Bull, 1977). A closer look, however, reveals three anomalies and the development of legal certainty *beyond* the nation-state. First, the rise of issue-area specific international regimes has moved parts of the governance dimension to the international level. The international recognition to govern in a given territory, which is constitutive for the Westphalian system, may not be confused with international governance, which is a much more recent development. Secondly, it is still true that from the early nineteenth century on—many see the Vienna Conference after the Napoleonic Wars as the starting point— international institutions assisted states in the realisation of governance goals. What is new about more recent developments regarding transnational legal certainty is not only the sheer amount of governance with governments, but also the types and objects of regulation. Traditional international institutions regulated interaction between states. The current development in the field of transnational legal certainty is different: the final target of these regulations is society and, in addition, new issues have been taken up. International institutions have thus changed in character. They aim increasingly to regulate the action not only of state actors but also of societal actors. Finally, to the extent that international governance covers more and more issue areas, it creates overlapping and colliding jurisdictions with other international or national regulations. Supranational bodies are a logical response to resolve these collisions. Moreover, the more international regimes address behind-the-border issues, which are especially difficult to monitor and have significant impacts on societal actors, the more the question of credibility of commitments arises. A logical way to increase the credibility of commitments is the development of supranational bodies that monitor regulations and resolve conflicts (see Moravcsik, 1998: 73–7). Supranational bodies such as the WTO Dispute Settlement Procedure, however are a clear deviation from traditional notions of interstate co-operation as part of the national constellation of statehood.

To be sure, legal certainty in the global economic sphere is still provided mainly on the basis of international agreements between states. Here, it is also definitely still lower than within most OECD countries. However, while legal certainty within national territories has remained more or less constant over the last few decades, an enhanced legal certainty for cross-border activities can be observed parallel to the rise of economic denationalisation. Hence, the provision of regulations that ensure legal certainty and make economic efficiency possible has been successfully internationalised. Those institutions strengthened the process of denationalisation initially, but themselves were further strengthened when denationalisation accelerated in the last decades. Rigorous information and monitoring mechanisms make these institutions very effective. It is in this field that international, transnational and even supranational institutions seem strongest. With respect to the governance good of legal certainty in the economic sphere, supply somehow meets demand.

Law as Integrity[30]

The rise of market-making international institutions is, at best, partially matched by market-correcting international institutions, that is international institutions that intervene in markets in order to avoid undesirable social outcomes. Especially international redistributive policies or international policies that protect social standards are rare (see Streeck, 1997; see also Arthurs, this volume). This mismatch certainly affects the overall provision of social welfare policies. While neo-liberals welcome the trend towards deregulation, others perceive it as a danger for the social standards of the modern welfare state. In this sense, the provision of legal certainty without doubt increases economic efficiency, but is not a purely technical matter, as it clearly affects distributive questions and is an issue of public debate. This brings in a thicker notion of law, one that is not reduced to formal issues, but also to issues of substantive rationality. Consequently the question arises whether governance in a post-national constellation is adequate for normatively more ambitious notions of law.

According to one more ambitious notion of law, law is distinct from other social norms by the manner in which norms are generated and applied. In this sense, regulations count as law where, first, they are produced in the context of a legitimising and normative process and, secondly, their application is marked by rational linkage to the objectives associated with the regulation and with general principles. In making and applying the law, then, general precepts of justice and fairness must play a recognisable part (Dworkin, 1986). In so far as law constitutes a genuinely argumentative social practice, the required precepts of justice and fairness can best be determined procedurally. In this sense, both the discourses justifying the law and those applying it must approximate the principles of rational discourse and, at the same time, include the addressees of the regulations and others affected. Accordingly, only those norms of action are endowed with the highest type of legal quality that fulfil two criteria: First, all those that may be affected can assent to the norm as participants in rational discourse and; secondly, the norms are supported by a secondary institutional apparatus of arbitration, rule-monitoring and norm-development which in turn approximates the principles of public rational discourse (Habermas, 1992).

A conception of law based on integrity of decision-making and application refers at the same time to a role of law that previously did not seem to be

---

[30] Parts of this section are drawn from Zürn and Wolf (1999).

required in international institutions. Law constitutes through its twofold binding—to rationality and the broad public—a linking element, and carries out a pivotal function between the normative framework of the social and political system on the one hand, and the life-world conditions of the regulation's addressees and others affected on the other. In the words of Jürgen Habermas (1992: 78): "[t]he law acts, as it were, as a transformer, ensuring in the first place that the network of socially integrative pan-societal communication does not break down. It is only in the language of law that normatively meaningful messages can circulate throughout society". Law hereby develops a socially integrative function of its own, by on the one hand facilitating a codification of normative claims on the life-world, while on the other remaining equally responsive to problem pressures from that life-world. This social integration comes about through a common language, and presupposes a direct linkage between the law and the individuals concerned. In the sense of integrity of decision making and application, law is an essential component for successful governance, and is at the same time, different from a formal understanding of "rule of the law".

The reference to this specific function of legal norms undermines the dualism of national and international spheres. Norms above and beyond national society can attain full legal quality where they are legally, socially and politically internalised by the regulation's addresses (Koh, 1997: 2645–58). Legally internalised means here that norms of conduct developed beyond the nation-state directly affect their addressees; politically internalised means that those affected by the regulations have actionable civil rights and direct participatory rights; socially internalised means that there is a political public that accompanies the processes of both making and applying the law.

With the partial exception of the EU, most international institutions are inadequate when this more ambitious concept of law is taken as a yardstick. *Legal internalisation* is based, above all, on two foundations that can be best illustrated by the EU: on the one hand, the direct effect associated with the supremacy of European law over national law and, on the other, the direct enforcing effect of ECJ case law through the preliminary ruling procedure of Article 234 EC (ex article 177). The former guarantees European law undoubted validity in all Member States, so that Community provisions have to be seen as an inseparable part of the body of law valid for the EU's citizens (Weiler, 1993). This form of legal internalisation cannot yet be found for international regulations, despite the calls and developments in this direction in relation to the WTO (see Petersmann, 1997).

Political internalisation requires an immutable allotment of individual, subjective rights. These subjective rights must first and foremost be *individually* actionable, that is, they must not be attributed to collectivities or communities, but must be cast as individual rights, thus ensuring that all those affected by a regulation have the same rights, and that the equality principle is thus realised and reciprocity thus guaranteed. Secondly, *direct* actionability of these rights by the individual is required. Only where any infringements of rights can be brought directly before the judicial bodies by those affected by the regulation can the individually allotted rights attain their effect. With the exception of the EU, and limited rights of individual action in human rights in the context of the Civil Covenant, the Race-Discrimination Convention and the Convention against Torture (see Liese, 1998), such recourse is excluded at the international and transnational levels. Therefore, those affected by regulation are dependent on the willingness or non-willingness of their governments (the executive) to guarantee their citizens the corresponding substantive rights. In addition to the "entrenchment" of individual, subjective rights of action, political participation must also be facilitated so as to do justice to the claim for political internalisation. Here again, Europe has made considerable efforts, especially with the directly elected European Parliament and the development of a unitary EU citizenship. Yet even in Europe, and much more so in international institutions, political participatory rights remain rudimentary beyond the nation-state.

The clearest shortfall, however, is the case of *social internalisation*. Social internalisation—that is the linkage of the norms to a public that accompanies both the rule-making and the rule-application processes—is based on two preconditions. The first one is that public decision-making should aim at a fair balancing of interests, ethical self-evidence and also the moral justification of regulations. The *deliberative* formation of a general political will at the transnational level is vital for the attainment by governance beyond the nation-state of a high level of legal quality. On the basis of "bargaining" alone, governance beyond the nation-state cannot be justified in legal theory; that also calls for "arguing".[31] Discourse and argumentation alone are, however, still not enough in order to secure the social internalisation of norms. The second precondition is that *all* potential addressees of the regulation and others affected must have a chance to take part in these discourses, so they must in this sense be public. Publicity, or public discourse, is crucial if the instrumentalisation of law for the purposes of gaining power is to be avoided. Publicity, and public discourse, averts the danger of a transformation of social power into administrative power. Instead, all social interests and claims must be brought into public discourse before conversion into valid law. Only this form of discursive lawmaking guarantees the uninterrupted legitimation of the decisions reached and enables the law so arrived at to perform its socially integrative function as well.

How, then, do the European and international institutions look with regard to social internalisation? First, one may state empirically that in view of the increasing economic and social relevance of European and international rulemaking, increasing numbers of social agents are turning to Brussels and other sites of international institutions as an important level of action, and adopting decisions reached there as a set framework for their own action (see Eising and Kohler-Koch, 1994). This interest-group access does not, however, seem to be in

---

[31] On this pair of terms, see Elster (1992, 1998) and Gehring (1996).

possession of sufficient links to a deliberative public, even though the European Community at least makes continual efforts to promote the European identity. Against this background, the extended network of committees (comitology) at the European and epistemic communities at the international level, which brings experts and lobbyists into the process of policy-formulation beyond the nation-state, is considered to be vital and a sign of a rising transnational public (see Joerges and Neyer, 1997).

In the light of the above legal-theoretical considerations, however, the practice of these forms of interest-mediation remains inadequate. The adequate involvement of the informal expert publics and/or regulatory addressees in no way makes up for the inadequate involvement of the broad general public, that is, all those affected by regulation. Clearly, in order for law to be able to bring its socially integrative power to bear, the relationship between expert publics and the broad public is essential. The broad public can be defined as the range of people that may be directly or indirectly affected by a proposed regulation, who—normatively speaking—in a democratic legal system must at least potentially be offered the possibility and opportunity of being involved in making and applying the law (see Peters, 1994: 45–47).[32] Sub-publics, by contrast, take shape on the basis of social differentiation and stratification (for example local milieus, social associations or political camps). They mainly group together as issue networks, in which the materially affected circles—often the addresses of regulation—come together formally or informally. "These sub-publics are fields of dense communication with porous edges. . . . This sort of structure enables a higher degree of active participation by comparison with an undifferentiated large public, but clearly involves the danger of fragmentation into specialised interest groups" (Peters, 1994: 56). Accordingly, the decisive question becomes whether and to what extent the periphery sees itself as being in a position to track down social integration issues and transport them into the political centre. The object is to institutionalise a legal public that goes beyond the existing expert culture. Only if, alongside the addressees of regulation, all others affected also have the possibility of involvement in norm-formation, so that the expert culture is subject to broader control, can the law fully bring its socially integrative power to bear.

In the absence of this socially integrative effect, two particular governance deficits arise: first, the subsystems become independent and thus may exploit their privileged position in a self-serving fashion or become victim to regulatory capture. The most obvious example of a lack of control mechanisms is the often-heard accusation of alleged corruption among members of the European

---

[32] It is not being asserted here that, empirically, the broad public always guarantees this basic condition. The features of publicity (equality and reciprocity, openness and adequate capacity as well as discursive structure) are scarcely fully and completely present even in the classic welfare states. The point here is rather the question whether at the various levels (European, international) there are systematic or structural reasons why a linkage between the legal system concerned and this sort of—ideally conceived—broad public is impossible.

Commission. Though the flood of accusations eventually grew to an unstoppable mass, Commission members were extraordinarily tardy in recognising their seriousness. In a political system with an educated political public, such a situation would be inconceivable. Secondly, in the absence of the socially integrative function of law, sectoral subsystems of governance beyond the nation-state may fail to co-ordinate with each other. As a consequence, the overall co-ordination of international institutions continues almost exclusively to be left to intergovernmental conferences that decide on an *ad hoc* basis. In sum, "transnational sectoral *demoi*" (Abromeit and Schmidt, 1998) are a decisive step towards democratising international institutions. They are not, however, enough to establish procedures that meet the requirements of regulations with high legal quality. Without a broad, active political public, social internalisation will remain underdeveloped.

To conclude, the post-national constellation seems to be capable of producing legal certainty for global business transactions to a significant extent. Although it is easy by comparison with established national standards to identify deficits in this respect, the trend towards growing legal certainty in the economic sphere is strong and runs more or less parallel to economic denationalisation. However, it is much more doubtful whether or not the post-national constellation will suffice for a normatively more ambitious notion of law as integrity to the same extent as this was *possible* in the national context. To be sure, public debates about the organisation of legal certainty in the economic sphere, that is about the economic constitution, have also been rare in national contexts. Yet they took place, at least from time to time: in the 1930s in the United States, after World War II in West Germany, in 1968 in France. In the transnational sphere, these debates are not likely to take place at all, because the social prerequisites are missing. A dissolution of the unity of a rule of law on the one hand and the democratic shaping of law on the other will thus be some of the fundamental dilemmas of a coming post-national order.

REFERENCES

Abromeit, Heidrun, and Schmidt, Thomas (1998), "Grenzprobleme der Demokratie" in B. Kohler-Koch (ed.), *Regieren in entgrenzten Räumen* (PVS-Sonderheft 29/1998) (Opladen: Westdeutscher Verlag).

Adler, Emanuel, and Haas, Peter M. (1992), "Conclusion: Epistemic Communities, World Order, and the Creation of a Reflective Research Program", *International Organization* 46; 367–90.

Anderson, Benedict (1991), *Imagined Communities: Reflections on the Origin and Spread of Nationalism* (rev. edn., London: Verso).

Beisheim, Marianne, and Zürn, Michael (1999), "Transnationale Nicht-Regierungsorganisationen. Eine Antwort auf die Globalisierung?" Ansgar Klein, Hans-Josef Legrand, Thomas Leif (eds.), *Neue Soziale Bewegungen—Impulse, Bilanzen und Perspektiven* (Opladen: Westdeutscher Verlag), 306–19.

Beisheim, Marianne, Dreher, Sabine, Walter, Gregor, Zangl, Bernhard, and Zürn, Michael (1999), *Im Zeitalter der Globalisierung? Thesen und Daten zur gesellschaftlichen und politischen Denationalisierung* (Baden-Baden: Nomos).

Benhabib, Seyla (1996), "Toward a Deliberative Model of Democratic Legitimacy" in Seyla Benhabib (ed.), *Democracy and Difference: Contesting the Boundaries of the Political* (Princeton, NJ: Princeton University Press).

Böckenförde, Ernst (1969), "Entstehung und Wandel des Rechtsstaatbegriffs" in H. Ehmke (ed.), *Festschrift für Adolf Arndt* (Frankfurt: Europäische Verlagsanstalt).

Bogdandy, Armin von (1999), *Supranationaler Föderalismus als Wirklichkeit und Idee einer Herrschaftsform: Zur Gestalt der Europäischen Union nach Amsterdam* (Baden-Baden: Nomos).

Bonell, Michael Joachim (1997), *An International Restatement of Contract Law: the UNIDROIT Principles of International Commercial Contracts* (2nd edn., Irvington-on-Hudson, NY: Transnational Publishers).

Borchert, Jens and Golsch, Lutz (1995), "Die politische Klasse in westlichen Demokratien: Rekrutierung, Karriereinteressen und institutioneller Wandel", *Politische Vierteljahresschrift* 36; 609–29.

Braudel, Fernand (1992), *The Wheels of Commerce*, vol. 2, *Civilization and Capitalism 15th–18th Century* (Berkeley, Cal.: University of California Press).

Bruder, Wolfgang, and Dose, Nicolai (1992), "Öffentliche Verwaltung" in M. Schmidt (ed.), *Lexikon der Politik, vol. 3, Die westlichen Länder* (Munich: Beck).

Bull, Hedley (1977), *The Anarchical Society. A Study of Order in World Politics* (Basingstoke; London: MacMillan).

Buzan, Barry (1994), "The Interdependence of Security and Economic Issues in the 'New World Order'" in R. Stubbs and G. R. D. Underhill (eds.), *Political Economy and the Changing Global Order* (London: St. Martins Press).

Cerny, Philip G. (1996), "What Next for the State?" in E. Kofman and G. Youngs (eds.), *Globalization: Theory and Practice* (London: Pinter).

Dasser, Felix (1991), "Lex Mercatoria: Werkzeug der Praktiker oder Spielzeug der Lehre?" *Schweizerische Zeitschrift für internationales und europäisches Recht* 3; 299–323.

Deutsch, Karl W. (1969), *Nationalism and its Alternatives* (New York: The Free Press).

Dworkin, Ronald (1986), *Law's Empire* (Cambridge, Mass.: Harvard University Press).

Eichener, Volker (1996), "Die Rückwirkungen der europäischen Integration auf nationale Politikmuster" in M. Jachtenfuchs and B. Kohler-Koch (eds.), *Europäische Integration* (Opladen: Leske & Budrich).

Eising, Rainer, and Kohler-Koch, Beate (1994), "Inflation und Zerfaserung: Trends der Interessenvermittlung in der Europäischen Gemeinschaft" in W. Streeck (ed.), *Staat und Verbände* (PVS-Sonderheft 25/1994) (Opladen: Westdeutscher Verlag).

Elias, Norbert (1976), *Über den Prozeß der Zivilisation. Soziogenetische und psycho-genetische Untersuchungen* (Frankfurt: Suhrkamp).

Elster, Jon (1992), "Arguing and Bargaining in the Federal Convention and the Assemblée Constituante" in R. Malnes and A. Underdal (eds.), *Rationality and Institutions: Essays in Honour of Knut Midgaard* (Oslo: Universitetsforlaget).

—— (1998), "Deliberation and Constitution Making" in J. Elster (ed.), *Deliberative Democracy* (Cambridge: Cambridge University Press).

Evers, Tilman (1994), "Supranationale Staatlichkeit am Beispiel der Europäischen Union: Civitas civitatum oder Monstrum?", *Leviathan* 22; 115–34.

Falke, Josef (1996), "Comitology and Other Committees: A Preliminary Empirical Assessment" in R. H. Pedler and G. F. Schaefer (eds.), *Shaping European Law and Policy: The Role of Committees and Comitology in the Political Process* (Maastricht: EIPA).

Franck, Thomas M. (1992), "The Emerging Right to Democratic Governance", *American Journal of International Law* 86; 46–91.

Frieden, Jeffry A., and Rogowski, Ronald (1996), "The Impact of the International Economy on National Policies: An Analytical Overview" in R. O. Keohane and H. V. Milner (eds.), *Internationalization and Domestic Politics* (Cambridge: Cambridge University Press).

Friedman, Lawrence (1996), "Borders: On the Emerging Sociology of International Law", *Stanford Journal of International Law* 32; 65–90.

Garrett, Geoffrey (1998), *Partisan Politics in the Global Economy* (Cambridge: Cambridge University Press).

Gehring, Thomas (1995), "Regieren im internationalen System: Verhandlungen, Normen und internationale Regime", *Politische Vierteljahresschrift* 36; 197–219.

—— (1996), "Arguing und Bargaining in internationalen Verhandlungen: Überlegungen am Beispiel des Ozonschutzregimes" in V. von Prittwitz (ed.), *Verhandeln und Argumentieren: Dialog, Interessen und Macht in der Umweltpolitik* (Opladen: Leske & Budrich).

Gellner, Ernest (1991), *Nations and Nationalism* (3rd edn., Ithaca: Cornell University Press).

Genschel, Philipp (1995), *Standards in der Informationstechnik: Institutionaller Wandel in der internationalen Standardisierung* (Frankfurt: Campus).

Giddens, Anthony (1985), *The National State and Violence* (Berkeley, Cal.: University of California Press).

—— (1994), *Beyond Left and Right: The Future of Radical Politics* (Cambridge: Polity Press).

Godt, Christine (1998), "Der Bericht des Appellate Body der WTO zum EG-Einfuhrverbot von Hormonfleisch. Risikoregulierung im Weltmarkt", *Europäisches Wirtschafts und Steuerrecht* 9; 202–9.

Grimm, Dieter (1994), "Staatsaufgaben—eine Bilanz" in D. Grimm (ed.), *Staatsaufgaben* (Baden-Baden: Nomos).

Guéhenno, Jean M. (1994), *Das Ende der Demokratie* (Munich: Artemis & Winkler).

Habermas, Jürgen (1992), *Faktizität und Geltung* (Frankfurt: Suhrkamp).

—— (1998), *Die postnationale Konstellation: Politische Essays* (Frankfurt: Suhrkamp).

Held, David (1995), *Democracy and the Global Order: From the Modern State to Cosmopolitical Governance* (Cambridge: Polity Press).

—— McGrew, Anthony, Goldblatt, David, and Perraton, Jonathan (1999), *Global Transformations: Politics, Economics and Culture* (Cambridge: Polity Press).

Héritier, Adrienne, Mingers, Susanne, Knill, Christoph and Becka, Martina (1994), *Die Veränderung von Staatlichkeit in Europa: Ein regulativer Wettbewerb: Deutschland, Großbritannien, Frankreich in der Europäischen Union* (Opladen: Leske & Budrich).

Hirsch, Joachim (1995), *Der nationale Wettbewerbsstaat: Staat, Demokratie Politik im globalen Kapitalismus* (Berlin; Amsterdam: Edition ID-Archiv).

Hirst, Paul, and Thompson, Grahame (1996), *Globalization in Question: The International Economy and the Possibilities of Governance* (Cambridge: Cambridge University Press).

Hobsbawm, Eric J. (1992), *Nations and Nationalism since 1780: Program, Myth, Reality* (2nd edn., Cambridge: Cambridge University Press).

Hofmann, Jeanette (1998), "Am Herzen der Dinge—Regierungsmacht im Internet" in W. von Gellner and F. von Korff (eds.), *Internet und Demokratie* (Baden-Baden: Nomos).

Horn, Norbert (1996), *Einführung in die Rechtswissenschaft und Rechtsphilosophie* (Heidelberg: Müller).

Jachtenfuchs, Markus, and Kohler-Koch, Beate (1996), "Regieren im dynamischen Mehrebenensystem" in M. Jachtenfuchs and B. Kohler-Koch (eds.), *Europäische Integration* (Opladen: Leske & Budrich).

Jackson, Robert H. (1990), *Quasi-States: Sovereignity, International Relations, and the Third World* (Cambridge: Cambridge University Press).

Jänicke, Martin (1998), "Umweltpolitik: Global am Ende oder am Ende global?" in U. Beck (ed.), *Perspektiven der Weltgesellschaft* (Frankfurt: Suhrkamp).

Joerges, Christian (1991), "Markt ohne Staat? Die Wirtschaftsverfassung der Gemeinschaft und die regulative Politik" in R. Wildenmann (ed.), *Staatswerdung Europas? Optionen für eine Europäische Union* (Baden-Baden: Nomos).

—— (1996), "Taking the Law Seriously: On Political Science and the Role of Law in the Process of European Integration", *European Law Journal* 2; 105–35.

—— and Neyer, Jürgen (1997), "Transforming Strategic Interaction Into Deliberative Problem-Solving: European Comitology in the Foodstuffs Sector", *Journal of European Public Policy* 4; 609–25.

Kahler, Miles (1995), *International Institutions and the Political Economy of Integration* (Washington, DC: The Brookings Institution).

Kaufmann, Franz-Xaver (1994), "Diskurse über Staatsaufgaben" in D. Grimm (ed.), *Staatsaufgaben* (Baden-Baden: Nomos).

Keck, Margaret E., and Sikkink, Kathryn (1998), *Activists Beyond Borders: Advocacy Networks in International Politics* (Ithaca, NY: Cornell University Press).

Keohane, Robert (1991), *Sovereignity, Interdependence and International Relations* (Working Paper 1. Cambridge, Mass.: CFIA).

Knieper, Rolf (1991), *Nationale Souveränität: Versuch über Ende und Anfang einer Weltordnung* (Frankfurt: Fischer).

Koh, Harold Hongju (1997), "Why Do Nations Obey International Law?", *Yale Law Journal* 106; 2599–659.

Kohler-Koch, Beate (1993), "Die Welt regieren ohne Weltregierung" in C. Böhet and G. Wewer (eds.), *Regieren im 21. Jahrhundert: Zwischen Globalisierung und Regionalisierung, Festgabe für Hans-Hermann Hartwich zum 65. Geburtstag* (Opladen: Leske & Budrich).

Krasner, Stephen D. (1983), "Structural Causes and Regime Consequences: Regimes as Intervening Variables" in S. D. Krasner (ed.), *International Regimes* (Ithaca, NY: Cornell University Press).

—— (1993), "Westphalia and All That" in J. Goldstein and R. O. Keohane (eds.), *Ideas and Foreign Policy* (Ithaca: Cornell University Press).

—— (1999), *Sovereignty: Organized Hypocrisy* (Princeton, NJ: Princeton University Press).

Lange, Niels (1998), *Zwischen Regionalismus und europäischer Integration: Wirtschaftsinteressen in regionalistischen Konflikten* (Baden-Baden: Nomos).

Levy, Marc A., Young, Oran R., and Zürn, Michael (1995), "The Study of International Regimes", *European Journal of International Relations* 1; 267–330.

Liese, Andrea (1998), "Menschenrechsschutz durch Nichtregierungsorganisationen", *Aus Politik und Zeitgeschichte* B 46–47; 36–42.

Litfin, Karen (1997), "Sovereignty in World Ecopolitics", *Mershon International Studies Review* 41; 167–204.

Lyons, Gene M., and Mastanduno, Michael (eds.) (1995), *Beyond Westphalia? State Sovereignty and International Intervention* (Baltimore, Mld.: Johns Hopkins University Press).

Majone, Giandomenico (ed.) (1996), *Regulating Europe* (London: Routledge).

Marks, Gary, Scharpf, Fritz W., Schmitter, Phillipe C., and Streeck, Wolfgang (eds.) (1996), *Governance in the European Union* (London: Sage).

Marshall, Thomas H. (1950), *Citizenship and Social Class* (London: Cambridge University Press).

Mayer, Peter, Rittberger, Volker, and Zürn, Michael (1993), "Regime Theory: State of the Art and Perspectives" in V. Rittberger and P. Mayer (eds.), *Regime Theory and International Relations* (Oxford: Oxford University Press).

Mayntz, Renate (1996), "Politische Steuerung: Aufstieg, Niedergang und Transformation einer Theorie" in K. von Beyme and C. Offe (eds.), *Politische Theorien in der Ära der Transformation* (PVS-Sonderheft 26/1995) (Opladen: Westdeutscher Verlag).

Moravcsik, Andrew (1994), *Why the European Community Strengthens the State: Domestic Politics and International Cooperation* (Working Paper Series 52, Cambridge: Harvard University, Center for European Studies).

—— (1998), *Choice for Europe: Social Purpose and State Power from Messina to Maastricht* (Ithaca, NY: Cornell University Press).

Morgenthau, Hans (1967), *Politics among Nations: The Struggle for Power and Peace* (New York: Alfred Knopf).

North, Douglass C. (1981), *Structure and Change in Economic History* (New York: Norton).

—— (1990), *Institutions, Institutional Change and Economic Performance* (Cambridge: Cambridge University Press).

Offe, Claus (1975) *Berufsbildungsreform. Eine Fallstudie über Reformpolitik* (Frankfurt: Suhrkamp).

Ohmae, Kenichi (1993), "The Rise of the Regional State", *Foreign Affairs* 72; 78–87.

Peters, Bernhard (1991), *Rationalität, Recht und Gesellschaft* (Frankfurt: Suhrkamp).

—— (1994), "Der Sinn von Öffentlichkeit" in F. Neidhardt (ed.), *Öffentlichkeit, öffentliche Meinung, soziale Bewegung* (Kölner Zeitschrift für Soziologie und Sozialpsychologie, Sonderheft 34) (Opladen: Westdeutscher Verlag).

Petersmann, Ernst-Ulrich (1997), "Darf die EG das Völkerrecht ignorieren?", *Europäische Zeitschrift für Wirtschaftsrecht* 8; 325–31.

Princen, Thomas, and Finger, Mathias (1994), *Environmental NGOs in World Politics. Linking the Local and the Global* (London: Routledge).

Reus-Smit, Christian (1997), "The Constitutional Structure of International Society and the Nature of Fundamental Institutions", *International Organization* 51; 555–89.

Risse, Thomas, Ropp, Stephen C., and Sikkink, Kathryn (eds.) (1999), *The Power of Human Rights. International Norms and Domestic Change* (Cambridge: Cambridge University Press).

Risse-Kappen, Thomas (1995), "Bringing Transnational Relations Back", in T. Risse-Kappen (ed.), Introduction *Bringing Transnational Relations Back In: Non-State Actors, Domestic Structures and International Institutions* (Cambridge: Cambridge University Press).

Rittberger, Volker, with the assistance of Mayer, Peter (ed.) (1993), *Regime Theory and International Relations* (Oxford: Oxford University Press).

Rosenau, James N. (1990), *Turbulence in World Politics: A Theory of Change and Continuity* (Princeton, NJ: Princeton University Press).

—— (1992), "Governance, Order, and Change in World Politics" in N. Rosenau and E. O. Czempiel (eds.), *Governance without Government: Order and Change in World Politics* (Cambridge: Lexington Press).

—— (1995), "Governance in the 21st Century", *Global Governance* 1; 13–43.

—— (1997), *Along the Domestic-Foreign Frontier: Exploring Governance in a Turbulent World* (Cambridge: Cambridge University Press).

Scharpf, Fritz W. (1993), "Legitimationsprobleme der Globalisierung: Regieren in Verhandlungssystemen" in C. Böhret and G. Wewer (eds.), *Regieren im 21. Jahrhundert: Zwischen Globalisierung und Regionalisierung, Festgabe für Hans-Hermann Hartwich zum 65. Geburtstag* (Opladen: Leske & Budrich).

Schmalz-Bruns, Rainer (1998), "Grenzerfahrungen und Grenzüberschreitungen: Demokratie im integrierten Europa" in B. Kohler-Koch (ed.), *Regieren in entgrenzten Räumen* (PVS-Sonderheft 29/1998) (Opladen: Westdeutscher Verlag).

Shanks, Cheryl, Jacobson, Harold K., and Kaplan, Jeffrey H. (1996), "Inertia and Change in the Constellation of International Governmental Organizations, 1981–1992", *International Organization* 50; 593–629.

Smith, Adam (1776), *Inquiry into the Nature and the Causes of the Wealth of Nations* (London: W. Strahan & T. Cadell).

Sørensen, Georg (1997), "An Analysis of Contemporary Statehood: Consequences for Conflict and Cooperation", *Review of International Studies* 23; 253–69.

—— (1998), "States are not 'Like Units': Types of State and Forms of Anarchy in the Present International System", *Journal of Political Philosophy* 6; 79–98.

Soysal, Yasemin Nuhoglu (1994), *Limits of Citizenship: Migrants and Postnational Membership in Europe* (Chicago, Ill.: University of Chicago Press).

Spruyt, Hendrik (1994), *The Sovereign State and its Competitors: The Analysis of Systems Change* (Princeton, NJ: Princeton University Press).

Streeck, Wolfgang (1997), "Öffentliche Gewalt jenseits des Nationalstaates? Das Beispiel der Europäischen Gemeinschaft" in W. Fricke (ed.), *Globalisierung und institutionelle Reform: Jahrbuch für Technik und Wirtschaft 1997* (Bonn: Dietz Verlag).

Teschke, Benno (1998), "Geopolitical Relations in the European Middle Ages", *Internatinal Organization* 52; 325–58.

Thomson, Janice E. (1994), *Mercenaries, Pirates, and Sovereigns: State-Building and Extraterritorial Violence in Early Modern Europe* (Princeton, NJ: Princeton University Press).

—— (1995), "State Sovereignty and International Relations: Bridging the Gap Between Theory and Empirical Research", *International Studies Quarterly* 39; 213–33.

Tilly, Charles (1985), "War Making and State Making as Organized Crime" in P. B. Evans, D. Rueschemeyer and T. Skocpol (eds.), *Bringing the State Back In* (Cambridge: Cambridge University Press).

—— (1990), *Coercion, Capital and European States, AD 990–1990* (Oxford: Blackwell).

Victor, David G. (1999), *Risk Management and the World Trading System: Regulating International Trade Distortions of National Sanitary and Phytosanitary Policies* (Unpublished paper, New York).

Vogel, David (1995), *Trading up: Consumer and Environmental Regulation in a Global Economy* (Cambridge, Mass.: Harvard University Press).

Weiler, Joseph H. H. (1993), "Journey to an Unknown Destination: A Retrospective and Prospective of the European Court of Justice in the Arena of Political Integration", *Journal of Common Market Studies* 31; 417–46.

Wessels, Wolfgang (1998), "Comitology: Fusion in Action; Politico-administrative Trends in the EU System", *Journal of European Public Policy* 5; 209–34.

Wolf, Klaus Dieter (1997), "Entdemokratisierung durch Selbstbindung in der Europäischen Union" in K. D. Wolf (ed.), *Projekt Europa im Übergang? Probleme, Modelle und Strategien des Regierens in der Europäischen Union* (Baden-Baden: Nomos).

World Bank (1997), *World Development Report 1997* (Washington, D.C.).

Young, Oran R. (1978), "Anarchy and Social Choice: Reflections on the International Polity", *World Politics* 31; 241–63.

—— (1994), *International Governance: Protecting the Environment in a Stateless Society* (Ithaca, NY: Cornell University Press).

Zacher, Mark W. (1992), "The Decaying Pillars of the Westphalian Temple: Implications for International Order and Governance" in J. N. Rosenau and E. O. Czempiel (eds.), *Governance Without Government: Order and Change in World Politics* (Cambridge: Lexington Press).

Zacher, Mark W., with Sutton, Brent A. (1996), *Governing Global Networks: International Regimes for Transportation and Communication* (Cambridge: Cambridge University Press).

Zangl, Bernhard, and Zürn, Michael (1999), "The Effects of Denationalisation on Security in the OECD World", *Global Society* 13; 139–61.

Zürn, Michael (1996), "Über den Staat und die Demokratie im europäischen Mehrebenensystem", *Politische Vierteljahresschrift* 37; 27–55.

—— (1998), *Regieren jenseits des Nationalstaates: Denationalisierung und Globalisierung als Chance* (Frankfurt: Suhrkamp).

—— (2000), "Democratic Governance Beyond the Nation State", *European Journal of International Relations* 6:2 (2000), 183–221.

—— and Wolf, Dieter (1999), "European Law and International Regimes: The Features of Law Beyond the Nation State", *European Law Journal* 5; 272–92.

2

The Institutional Structuring of Business Transactions

RICHARD WHITLEY

Abstract

Relative to many national and regional business environments, the international context for economic transactions is weakly institutionalised and standardised. This means that firms: (a) limit commitments to business partners from different kinds of business systems, and (b) manage cross-border transactional uncertainty in many different ways because of their varied institutional contexts. Three key areas of such uncertainty concern: (a) the search for competent and reliable business parterns, (b) the nature of agreements, and (c) control over business partner behaviour. Typically, firms vary in the extent to which they manage these risks through personal networks or more formal procedures, and in their reliance on collective standards and norms, as a result of differences in their national and regional business environments. These differences stem from the institutions governing the capital and labour markets, the development of skills and attitudes to trust and authority. Such institutional variations also affect the ways that firms manage cross-border transactions.

INTRODUCTION

THE GROWTH OF strategic alliances and other forms of inter-firm collaboration in North America and Europe towards the end of the twentieth century has led to a considerable increase in academic interest in the organisation of inter-firm relationships and how firms manage different kinds of co-operative agreements (see e.g. Child and Faulkner, 1998; Ebers, 1997; Lane and Bachmann, 1998; Nooteboom, 1999). More or less at the same time, the success of the Japanese economy in the 1980s and the rapid industrialisation of other East Asian economies in the post-war period have stimulated comparative analyses of different varieties of capitalism, especially of how firms share authority, knowledge and resources with each other in different institutional environments (see e.g. Gerlach, 1992; Hollingsworth *et al.*, 1994; Orru *et al.*, 1997; Whitley, 1992).

Both literatures have emphasised the limited importance of classical spot market contracting for business transactions and the critical role of trust and related institutional mechanisms for managing transactional uncertainties. While conceptions of the central issues in the analysis of business transactions, and approaches to dealing with them, remain quite diverse, not to say opposed, between transaction cost economists, organisational sociologists and management researchers, there is general agreement that there are a number of different ways in which transactions can be organised, and these are closely related to the prevailing institutional arrangements governing exchanges and managing uncertainty in market economies.

In the case of international business transactions, most of these institutional arrangements are less strongly established and coherent than are those within national and regional boundaries, even if we agree with Teubner (1997) that *lex mercatoria*, is becoming a form of global law without a state. As a result, firms are able to be much more idiosyncratic in their approach to dealing with business partners abroad than at home, especially those based in strongly institutionalised business cultures such as that of post-war Japan (see e.g. Clark, 1979; Fruin, 1992; Westney, 1996). This means that the variety of ways of managing cross-border transactions is greater than that of most domestic ones. Furthermore, the relative weakness of most institutions governing international transactions results in considerable uncertainty about the competence and reliability of most business partners so that transaction costs are, in general, greater than those in many domestic environments (Appelbaum, 1998). This, in turn, can inhibit commitments across borders and makes relational contracting, as described by Dore (1986) and Sako (1992) among others analysing inter-firm relations in Japan, more difficult to develop.

Thus, international transactions are less likely to be broad in scope of activities covered and deep in terms of mutual commitment than are those where institutional arrangements reduce uncertainty and encourage co-operation. However, we could expect some differences in how firms from different environments deal with these uncertainties so that distinctive patterns of international business transactions can be discerned amongst different kinds of firms based in varied types of economic co-ordination and control systems (Whitley, 1999). For example, it seems unlikely that owners of firms in many Southeast Asian economies, especially those from minority ethnic groups, will have the same trust in formal arbitration procedures and institutions as managers from more legalistic business contexts.

These sorts of differences, and their expected impact upon the organisation and control—or "governance" as discussed by, amongst others, Nooteboom (1999)—of international transactions, emphasise the importance of particular institutions and agencies in structuring business transactions in different economies and suggest it would be useful to identify the linkages between institutions and the governance of transactions. Accordingly, in this chapter I outline a framework for connecting differences in transaction governance to variations in key societal institutions. First, I shall identify the key aspects of transactions that generate uncertainty and suggest six ways in which these are managed differently in different business environments. Next, I shall summarise the main features of these environments that influence the prevalence of these alternatives and then suggest how they do so. Finally, I shall briefly consider the implications of this analysis for international business transactions.

THE MANAGEMENT OF UNCERTAINTY IN BUSINESS TRANSACTIONS

In the extensive literature on business transactions, and inter-firm relationships more generally, much attention has been paid to compliance and control issues. That is, how do firms and other business partners, such as unions and quangos, manage the risk of "opportunistic" behaviour by the other party, and what are the roles of different institutional arrangements such as contractual conventions and authority-sharing norms among industry groups, in structuring such practices? Rather less attention has been paid to how they decide that other organisations are competent to fulfil agreements, or how they make contact in the first place. Both of these aspects of transactions are, of course, crucial, and involve considerable uncertainty that is managed differently across varied institutional environments. Three broad areas of uncertainty in business transactions can then be summarised as: search, agreement and control, or, in Nooteboom's (1999: 17–18) terms: contact, contract and control.

Search involves finding business partners who are both able to carry out whatever is agreed to the required standards, and willing to do so at the agreed time and price. It therefore requires knowledge of the range and location of potential partners, and the terms upon which they are likely to agree to collaborate. Such knowledge can be largely personal and/or reputational based on personal networks, or may be available through more formal and impersonal means such as trade associations, bank references and competence certification and auditing agencies. In general, the more formal are such mechanisms for resolving uncertainties about capabilities and reliability, the wider the range of potential partners will be. The management of search uncertainty varies, then, in its *reliance on personal networks* or on more formal procedures.

A second aspect of search and selection processes concerns their reliance on collective standards and norms governing membership of the industry and associated groupings. In some countries, entry to and exit from industries are more difficult and regulated than in others so that the identity of firms available for particular kinds of transactions at any one time is more clearly demarcated and bounded than elsewhere (see e.g. Herrigel, 1994, 1996). In the cases of industrial districts and similarly co-ordinated economic systems, these collective controls are relatively informal, and sometimes based upon ascriptive characteristics such as ethnicity. In others, they are more formally established through licensing regulations and certification rules. In countries like Japan they may be both strongly institutionalised through social conventions and industry practices in a "society of industry" (Clark, 1979: 95–7) and officially recognised and repro-duced through state co-ordinated employment policies, recession cartels, technology development groups, etc. (Dore, 1986; Johnson, 1982; Lincoln and Nakata, 1997; Okimoto, 1989). In these kinds of highly co-ordinated business systems (Whitley, 1999: 41–4), search costs are much lower than where the col-lective organisation of industries is weaker, but of course they also limit the range of possible business partners and so reduce access to novel competences and knowledge (Kern, 1998). This aspect of search uncertainty management can be termed the extent of *reliance on collectively organised standards and norms*.

Together these two aspects of managing the uncertainties involved in search-ing for business partners distinguish four ideal types of strategies, summarised in Table 2.1. First, where search is predominantly personal and/or ascriptive and cannot rely on institutionalised collective standards, it is highly *idiosyncratic* and *ad hoc*. Secondly, higher levels of collective organisation that are rarely for-malised into written rules and procedures administered by bureaucratically structured agencies, such as those forming distinctive industrial districts with low entry and exit rates, lead to what might be termed *community* search strate-gies. Thirdly, more formalised and bureaucratically organised ways of ensuring competence and reliability when combined with weak collective organisation encourage *procedural* search, while the combination of formalised procedures with strong collective organisation generates *associative rule governed* search.

Much of the discussion about agreement costs has focused on how firms can and do use formal contracts to pre-empt opportunism and structure business transactions in a predictable manner, as distinct from more informal and per-sonal agreements. The extent to which business contracts specify performance standards and how to deal with unforeseen contingencies varies quite strongly between countries, reflecting variations in legal systems and prevailing business norms (see e.g. Deakin and Wilkinson, 1998). Agreements also vary in their expected longevity and the range of activities they cover, from single, highly spe-cific transactions between anonymous traders to long-term partnerships dealing with many different kinds of collaboration. More generally, business agree-ments can be distinguished in terms of the degree of mutual commitment and risk sharing between the parties, as opposed to their preference for arm's length

Table 2.1: Ideal Types of Search Strategies:

| | | Reliance on Personal Networks | |
		Low	High
Reliance on Collectively Organised Standards and Norms	Low	Procedural	Idiosyncratic and ad hoc
	High	Associative rule governed	Community

contracting and the maintenance of considerable flexibility and freedom of action.

A simple way of contrasting agreements, then, is to compare them along the following two dimensions. First, how formalised and codified they are, including the extent to which they incorporate performance standards, contingency clauses and dispute settlement procedures. This can be termed their degree of *codification*. Secondly, they vary in their scope and longevity, including their encouragement of knowledge and risk sharing. This dimension can be characterised as their *level of mutual commitment*. Combining these in dichotomous forms yields four ideal types of agreement, summarised in Table 2.2, which are more or less likely to be used in business transactions according to the prevailing institutional context. Informal agreements that are limited in scope and time range from the simple exchange of goods in street markets to *ad hoc* subcontracting arrangements, such as those described by Shieh (1992) in his account of the organisation of export industries in Taiwan, but are usually concerned with relatively simple and standardised goods and services where quality can be readily assessed and price is the dominant consideration. These can be called *informal market* agreements.

Table 2.2: Ideal Types of Business Agreement:

		Degree of Codification	
		Low	High
Level of Mutual Commitment	Low	Informal market	Formal market
	High	Partnerships	Codified partnerships

More extensive and continuing relationships can be combined with relatively informal and tacit agreements where the owners and managers involved have close personal ties and/or strong particularistic reasons for presuming a high degree of mutual dependence and identity of interests such that opportunism is improbable and/or dangerous. Kinship ties can provide a basis for such agreements, as can ethnicity more generally, but process-based trust derived from successive dealings is usually needed as well, as Humphrey and Schmitz (1998) point out. These kinds of agreements can be termed *partnerships*. Formal and codified agreements covering single or a limited series of transactions constitute the standard arm's length contracting transaction and so are considered *formal market* agreements.

Finally, formally structured and detailed contracts covering a range of activities on a continuing basis, such as those common on the European continent (Deakin and Wilkinson, 1998; Lane and Bachmann, 1996; Lane, 1997), can provide a stable basis for pursuing long-term collaboration, information and risk sharing etc., but also can limit flexibility and radical innovation. When they do function as effective means of regulating economic exchanges, such contracts can restrict the pursuit of short-term self-interest and so encourage investment in joint activities and the continuing improvement of collective capabilities. This kind of agreement can be labelled *codified partnerships*.

Control over the execution of agreements can be exercised in two ways. *Reputational* means of transaction control rely on firms' need to remain in good standing with past, present and future business partners for their survival. Often their reputation within the sector, region or country for competence and compliance is crucial for their ability to obtain orders and to be invited to join industry initiatives, share information and opportunities. Where such reputational controls are strong, the likelihood of opportunistic pursuit of short-term gains is limited so that firms within the community can engage in longer term and more uncertain collaboration with each other than would be prudent in less controlled circumstances. For these kinds of controls to be effective, information flow has to be fast and reliable and the identity of the major firms relatively stable. Thus, close proximity and high industry entry and exit barriers encourage the use of reputational controls.

The second means of execution control is, of course, *formal contracting* and the use of third party sanctions against non-compliance. This can vary quite considerably, depending on the efficacy of the legal system and the availability of alternative sanctions that are cheaper and quicker. In principle, then, modes and costs of control vary in terms of the strength and weakness of both reputational and contractual means of ensuring compliance, and are associated with distinct kinds of transactions, as summarised in Table 2.3.

Table 2.3: Ideal Types of Control Systems:

| | | Strength of Reputational Controls | |
		Weak	Strong
Contractual Controls	Weak	Informal Particularistic	Informal Network
	Strong	Formal Contractual	Formal Network

Where both are relatively weak, as in countries and markets with unpredictable and costly legal systems and a large, rapidly changing number of potential transactions, firms are unable to rely very much on third party guarantees and sanctions. This means that agreements become highly dependent upon process-based trust for their fulfilment and monitoring costs are quite high. In turn, this limits firms' willingness to invest in complex transactions involving high levels of uncertainty, and so reduces their ability to co-operate in non-standardised and innovative activities. Sometimes, of course, ascription-based networks, such as ethnic groupings, help to increase reputational control sufficiently to encourage owners to engage in more risky agreements, as the overseas Chinese networks in Pacific Asia illustrate, but these are rarely sufficient in the absence of performance- and process-based trust developed over a series of transactions (see e.g. Menkhoff, 1992). Such weak control systems tend to encourage *informal particularistic* means of managing transactions.

The combination of strong contractual control and reliance on formal sanctions through the legal systems with weak reputational control represents the sort of arm's length contracting described by Sako (1992) as characteristic of British firms' subcontracting arrangements. Here, sector identities and common interests are rather weak, with considerable fluidity in the set of leading firms and only a weakly institutionalised "industrial order" in Herrigel's sense (1994, 1996). As a result, controls over opportunism tend to be limited to the legal system. Given the expense and disruption of legal action, this means that firms are more exposed to short-term opportunism than where reputational control is greater, and so will be relatively reluctant to commit themselves to long-term collaborations. That said, being able to rely on the contractual system in this case does render compliance more predictable than in the previous situation and so enable rational investment calculations to be made about business partners. It is associated, then, with *formal contractual* control strategies.

Strong reputational control combined with weak reliance on contractual controls enables firms within the boundaries of the reputational community to enter into agreements fairly easily without too much concern about short-term opportunism. Furthermore, the lack of reliance on legal sanctions and formal contracts here enables considerable flexibility and adaptation to changed circumstances, as acclaimed in the term "flexible specialisation". This combination can be termed an *informal network* type of transaction management strategy.

Finally, the combination of strong reputational control with extensive reliance on detailed and standardised formal contracts generates considerable trust in the quality and reliability of business partners within the reputational grouping. It therefore encourages longer-term collaboration and a willingness to share risks in the pursuit of joint opportunities. However, the very strength of these combined control structures can lock firms into a reliance on a limited set of collaborators and restrict new firm entry. In the longer term this may inhibit radical innovation, especially in technologically dynamic industries. Such control strategies can be characterised as *formal network* ones.

This discussion of the various ways in which firms and their owners/managers deal with the uncertainties associated with business transactions has highlighted two more general contrasts in inter-firm relationships. First, they vary considerably in terms of their flexibility and commitment. Secondly, they differ in how they are managed between a reliance on predominantly personal, informal and particularistic ways of dealing with transactional uncertainty, on the one hand, in contrast to more formal, standardised and procedural mechanism, on the other hand. These two sets of differences reflect major variations in business practices and cultures that result from significant differences in patterns of industrialisation and dominant institutions. I now turn to a brief description of the key features of the business environments that are associated with these variations and will then suggest how these institutional differences help to explain contrasts in the ways that firms manage business transactions.

INSTITUTIONAL FEATURES AFFECTING INTER-FIRM RELATIONSHIPS

To understand why economies differ in the general prevalence of flexibility over commitment and particularism over formalisation, or *vice versa*, and the more specific use of the mechanisms for managing business transactions outlined above, we need to consider both the organisation of general patterns of social interaction and the dominant institutions associated more specifically with economic co-ordination and control. Particularly critical for inter-firm connections are those institutions encouraging horizontal linkages, authority sharing and lock-in effects between economic actors, as opposed to vertical dependence on central authorities and/or arm's length contracting. Also important are the agencies and social structures governing labour markets and their implications for competitive priorities.

These institutional features can be very broadly characterised and compared across market economies in terms of four major arenas: the state, the financial system, the skill development and control system, and dominant conventions governing trust and authority relations. These deal with both the kinds of resources—especially human ones—that are available to privately owned economic actors in any particular market economy, and the terms on which they are available, as well as, of course, with the sorts of people who become private property rights' owners. To some extent, the location of particular features in one of these "systems" is a matter of convenience. For example, the degree of state regulation of labour markets can be seen either as part of the overall level of state regulation of markets or as a specific feature of the training and occupational system. However, they do together summarise the aspects of the institutional context that impinge most on how firms deal with each other and other economic actors.

The State

Considering first the state, there are, of course, many features of state structures and policies that influence inter-firm relations but three summary ones are particularly significant. First, the overall cohesion, prestige and autonomy of the state executive and bureaucracy, sometimes referred to as the "strength" of the state *vis-à-vis* social interest groups, landed elites, etc., is often seen as a crucial differentiating feature of states in different capitalist societies. When combined with considerable state elite commitment to co-ordinate and control economic development, this results in high levels of *business dependence on the state*. Such dependence usually limits the development of horizontal networks and alliances between firms as they compete for state support.

Some states, such as those in many Anglo-Saxon societies, have neither the wish to, nor the capability of, actively co-ordinating economic processes. Others, like perhaps the post-1950s Japanese, pursue "developmental" (Johnson, 1982; Okimoto, 1989) policies but do not commit large resources to sharing private sector investment risks or dominate private sector decision-making (Samuels, 1987), while a few do both, such as the post-1961 South Korean state (Amsden, 1989; Wade, 1990), and perhaps the post-war French state (Hart, 1992). Clearly, where the state is both "strong" and actively involved in directing the flow of capital and other resources, then private firms have to invest considerable resources in managing relations with the executive and bureaucracy.

A second significant feature of political systems is the extent to which the state encourages the establishment of important intermediary economic associations between individuals, firms and the state. This can be summarised as the degree of *state encouragement of, and delegation to, intermediaries*. Some European states, for instance, appear unable to tolerate such groupings while others, like the German and Austrian, seem positively to encourage their formation and to develop quite strong corporatist forms of intra- and inter-sectoral organisation. Clearly, interfirm co-operation, alliances and cartelisation will be easier in the latter sets of states than in the former.

Thirdly, there are significant differences in the extent to which states directly or indirectly regulate market boundaries, entry and exit, as well as set constraints on the activities of economic actors. They are here termed the extent of *formal segmentation of markets*. In many countries, for instance, states regulate which sorts of organisations can offer financial services and how they can sell them, as well as where they can do so. Similarly, licenses to undertake certain trades are often issued by national and local state agencies only when appropriate skill certificates have been acquired. In other countries, such powers are sometimes delegated to industry associations and quasi-statutory bodies. Product, capital and labour markets, then, are variously regulated and segmented across states, and this affects the intensity of competition, mobility of resources and flexibility of firms.

Financial Systems

Financial systems also vary on a number of dimensions, but the critical feature here deals with the processes by which capital is made available and priced. In particular, is it allocated by capital markets through competition between investment portfolio holders and managers, so that lenders and users remain relatively remote from one another, or is it provided by some set of intermediaries which deal directly with firms and become locked into their particular success? *Capital market based financial systems,* as characterised by Zysman (1983), mobilise and distribute capital largely through large and liquid markets which trade and price financial claims through the usual commodity market processes. Because many, if not most, investors and fund managers deal in portfolios of shares that can be readily traded on secondary and tertiary markets, they are only weakly committed to the growth of any single firm they own shares in. As a result, they have only a relatively short-term and narrow interest in its fortunes. This encourages a strong market for corporate control in capital market financial systems as ownership rights are easily traded and owners have little incentive to retain shares when offered considerable price premiums for them by acquisitive predators.

Credit based financial systems, on the other hand, typically have weak and fairly illiquid or thin capital markets, which play only a minor role in mobilising and pricing investment funds. The dominant institutions here are either large, "universal" banks as in Germany or a combination of commercial banks and long-term credit banks co-ordinated by state agencies and ministries, as in France, Japan and some other countries (Cox, 1986). Because of capital shortages during high growth periods, and/or state control of interest rates to support economic development, demand for investment funds often exceeds supply to a considerable degree in these systems. As a result, banks and/or the state allocate capital through administrative processes to particular sectors and activities, such as export industries or the heavy manufacturing sector. Since shares are not easily traded, owners, bankers and trust managers become locked into particular borrowers' fates and so have to be more involved in decision making and the detailed evaluation of investment plans than they do in capital market based systems.

This, in turn, means that they have to deal with a considerable amount of information about their customers' businesses and develop considerable expertise in them. Once that expertise has been developed by financial intermediaries, they have a vested interest in using it to provide new services and play a more active role in firms' growth planning. They thus become even more committed to particular enterprises and develop a common community of fate with them. Although a number of financial systems do not fit neatly into this broad dichotomy, such as that of the Netherlands (Iterson and Olie, 1992), this basic contrast between two major kinds of financial systems has strong implications for the ways in which firms deal with each other and share risks.

Skill Development and Control Systems

Considering, third, the system for developing and controlling skills, there are two broad and interrelated sets of institutions. First, there is the system that develops and certifies competencies and skills: the education and training system. Secondly, there are the institutions that control the terms on which the owners of those skills sell them in labour markets and how those markets are organised. In comparing education and training systems, two aspects are especially important: first, the extent to which practical skills are jointly organised and certified by employers, unions and state agencies; secondly, the degree of integration of practical learning in firms with formal learning in educational institutions. In their comparison of work organisation and control practices in France and Germany, Marc Maurice and his colleagues (1986) drew a contrast between unitary and generalist education systems, such as the French and Japanese, and dual, specialist ones, such as the German and some other Continental European ones.

In the former, children are successively filtered by academic examinations in the general educational system and only "failures" enter state practical training organisations, which are often poorly funded and have low social prestige. In the latter, practical skill training integrates theory and practice, as well as employers, unions and state education, and is seen as a different, but not greatly inferior, form of education from the grammar school system leading to university entrance. The "dual" or specialist training system, at least in Germany, combines some elements of traditional apprenticeship with college-based formal instruction and is co-operatively managed by representatives of labour, capital and the state. In analysing variations in the organisation of inter-firm relations, the critical aspect of such training systems is their encouragement of collaboration and continuing contact between firms in the management of skill certification and development.

There are three critical features of the organisation and control of labour markets: first, the extent to which the availability of skills and capabilities are controlled by trade unions and professional associations; secondly, how such associations are organised; thirdly, the way that bargaining is structured. Together these affect the fluidity and flexibility of labour markets and therefore employers' competitive strategies in terms of their ability to move in and out of industries. This in turn influences the membership of industries and the strength of their boundaries. These features also affect the extent to which employers have to work together in negotiating with the unions, especially the centralisation of bargaining. Generally, the stronger the unions are, the more they are organised on the basis of industrial sectors and the more bargaining is centralised between strong employers' associations and union federations, the more firms have to work together and the more important industry boundaries become. These three features of the skill development and control system can then be integrated into a single dimension of the *extent of corporatist co-ordination of training and negotiation*.

Norms and Values Governing Trust and Authority Relationships

Considering finally the norms governing trust and authority relations, these are crucial because they structure exchange relationships between business partners and between employers and employees. They also affect the development of collective identities and prevalent modes of eliciting compliance and commitment within authority systems. Variations in these conventions result in significant differences in the ways that firms deal with each other and other organisations.

How trust is granted and guaranteed in an economy especially affects the level of interfirm co-operation and tendency to delegate control over resources. While there are significant variations in how competence, contractual and goodwill forms of trust (Sako, 1992) are developed in different cultures, the key feature here is the strength of formal social institutions generating and guaranteeing trust between relative strangers. In particular, the extent to which property rights' owners and the economic actors they control feel able to rely on impersonal institutionalised procedures when making business commitments is a crucial factor in the establishment of collaborative relations within and between firms. It also affects the perception and management of risk (Zucker, 1986). Where such procedures are weak or judged unreliable, personal and particularistic connections become especially important in organising exchange relationships (Fafchamps, 1996; Menkhoff, 1992; Redding, 1990).

Superordinate-subordinate relations are typically governed by a number of different norms and rules, as Eckstein and Gurr (1975) have shown, so that a considerable variety of authority patterns has developed across cultures and political systems. One far-reaching distinction can be drawn between *formal* and *paternalist* political cultures. The former (a) restrict superordinate discretion through formal rules and procedures to a fairly narrow range of issues and actions, (b) acknowledge the independent and autonomous status of subordinates as individuals able to make rational decisions, and (c) involve subordinates in the choice of superordinates and in decision-making to some extent. The latter typically treat subordinates as children who cannot be expected to know their own best interests and act accordingly (Beetham, 1991; Iribarne, 1989).

Paternalism in turn can be divided into two major kinds: *remote* and *reciprocal*. Remote paternalism implies a high degree of social and moral distance between leaders and their followers with little direct reciprocity expected of superordinates in return for subordinates' deference. Common and shared interests are rarely invoked as the basis for compliance and superiors often claim a moral superiority which requires no further justifications, as in the virtuocracies of Confucian China and Korea (Jacobs, 1985; Pye, 1985; Silin, 1976). Reciprocal paternalism, on the other hand, involves much closer links between superordinates and subordinates, with reciprocal services expected of superiors through direct patronage and a strong belief in both leaders and led sharing a common community of fate, as in modern Japan (Haley, 1992; Iwata, 1992; Rohlen, 1974).

Formal authority can also be further subdivided into a number of different kinds, but perhaps the most significant contrast is between *contractual* and *communal* forms of authority. This distinction focuses on the extent to which authority rests upon widespread and diffuse appeals to common interests as opposed to highly specific and narrow agreements between discrete and separate contractors. Communal forms of authority imply relatively high levels of mutual trust and commitment, with shared understandings of priorities and interests, and often rely on expertise as a key quality of superordinates, while contractual authority tends to presume more adversarial relationships and a dominant pursuit of self-interest. The former seems to have become institutionalised in some Scandinavian and continental European countries, while the latter is found more in Anglo-Saxon societies (Lodge and Vogel, 1987).

These features of institutional structures are quite interrelated. For example, societies in which strong states play a major role in co-ordinating economic development and share risks with the private sector tend not to develop strong intermediary associations. Employers' associations and labour unions are, then, usually weak in such countries. Market regulation and segmentation, on the other hand, are often considerable since this is a major way in which state agencies co-ordinate development. These kinds of states tend to be associated with credit-based rather than capital market-based financial systems for two reasons: first, because they are typical of late industrialising economies where capital is scarce and more readily mobilised through the banking system, and, secondly, because it is easier for the state to influence economic development through the financial system when it is dominated by banks rather than capital markets (Zysman, 1983).

This combination of features can be characterised as a *dirigiste* type of business environment in which business development is highly dependent on the state and political risks are at least as important to firms' owners and managers as market risks. Typically this high level of vertical dependence is associated with the weak development of formal institutions such as the legal system and paternalist authority patterns, as in post-war South Korea (Jacobs, 1985; Kim, 1997; Woo, 1991). It leads to the establishment of a particular kind of economic co-ordination and control system, or business system that combines strong owner-control with considerable vertical integration and weak inter-firm linkages. Firms here tend to be large and diversified as the state pursues a variety of goals.

Where the state is less directly involved in the economy through ownership and/or credit allocation, and co-ordinates economic development with more independent industry associations, business is more autonomous. In these *state-guided* environments, intermediary associations are often encouraged by state agencies to take on co-ordinating and regulating functions. As Lincoln and Nakata (1997: 46) describe the "Japanese-style regulatory strategy", this sort of state "brings together private sector players and government bureaucrats in an effort to ascertain 'best practice' and encourage early buy-in and adoption by leading firms. Such consensus building legitimates the innovation and facilitates its spread." Market segmentation is often an important means of pursuing state policies in these business environments, and has certainly been critical to the state's ability to influence the credit-based financial system in post-war Japan

(Calder, 1993; Clark, 1979; Hidaka, 1997). Such delegation to private associations does not always extend to organised labour in these kinds of societies, and certainly has not done so in Japan where the prevailing political culture has been paternalist rather than contractual or communitarian. Firms in these kinds of business environments are highly embedded in networks and alliances within and across sectors, accordingly they can be characterised as allied hierarchies (Whitley, 1999: 77).

Conversely, low levels of state risk-sharing and economic co-ordination are often combined with capital market-based financial systems in what might be termed *arm's length* or differentiated business environments. In these contexts, institutional arenas and elites are organised quite separately from each other according to their own particular logics. Social relationships tend to be regulated by formal rules and procedures that treat actors as discrete individuals pursuing their separate interests, as exemplified by classical contracting. Authority and trust relations are here governed by formal institutions that limit mutual obligations to contractually specified duties. Collaboration between employers, unions and other groups is difficult to establish in such societies because collective actors are typically adversarial in their relations with each other, and training systems tend to be fragmented. As a result these sorts of business environments encourage quite high levels of ownership integration of economic activities through large units of financial control combining a variety of resources, but a low extent of alliance integration. Firms are here relatively isolated from each other and rarely share risks or opportunities.

On the other hand, in more corporatist societies where strong intermediary associations, including unions, have developed, often with state support, they tend to be involved in regulating market entry and exit. They typically engage in bargaining and negotiation with each other on a continuing basis with strongly institutionalised procedures limiting opportunistic behaviour. Such procedures depend on considerable trust between social partners and widespread beliefs in their joint dependence on co-operation for gaining group objectives. Commitment to relatively impersonal associations and an institutionalised ability to mobilise loyalties to collective goals beyond purely personal ones are important features of these kinds of societies. When combined with strong public training systems that are jointly managed by employers and unions with state agencies, as in many Continental European countries, these institutional features are conducive to continuing collaboration between economic actors. Accordingly, we can term them *collaborative* business environments in which labour organisations are formally incorporated into policy development processes and firms co-operate with each other on a variety of issues (Whitley, 1999: 76–7). A subset of this kind is found in some European regions such as Northern Italy and West Jutland. Here, the crucial institutions are stronger at the local and regional level than nationally, and so encourage co-operation and collaboration between members of industrial districts and occupational communities. They can be called *locally collaborative* institutional contexts.

Finally, cultures where trust in formal institutions is low and loyalties are focused on the immediate family rather than more impersonal collectivities limit the growth of intermediary associations and the development of exchange relationships governed by formal procedures. Capital markets are unlikely to be significant sources of investment funds in such societies and the largely personal nature of authority relationships will restrict the development of strong labour unions. Social relationships in these cultures tend to be highly personal and particularistic, and so can be described as *particularistic* business environments. Economic co-ordination in these business environments is limited and highly focused around owner-controlled firms that pursue highly opportunistic strategies (Whitley, 1999: 75–6).

In very broad terms, these different kinds of business environments encourage contrasting ways of managing business transactions. Particularistic, arm's length and *dirigiste* societies, for example, discourage extensive risk-sharing and mutual commitment between firms because of their low institutional support for lock-in arrangements and goodwill trust. Conversely collaborative and state-guided ones encourage such behaviour through the establishment of strong intermediaries and close links between banks and firms. The high levels of uncertainty in particularistic and *dirigiste* political economies likewise limit trust in formal institutions and the ability of codified rules to control agreements. They therefore inhibit reliance on formal contracting and encourage greater use of personal networks and obligations than is usual in the other types of business environments. I now discuss these linkages between institutional features, types of business environments and variations in the management of business transactions in more detail.

INSTITUTIONAL FEATURES, BUSINESS ENVIRONMENTS AND THE MANAGEMENT OF BUSINESS TRANSACTIONS

First of all I shall discuss how differences in the ways in which owners and managers deal with the uncertainties of search, agreement and control in transactions are connected to different institutional features. Subsequently, I will summarise the implications of this analysis for the sorts of transactions that are likely to be prevalent in the five major kinds of business environments just outlined. In Table 2.4, I present the most important positive and negative connections between the different ways of managing business transactions and particular features of the state, financial system, labour system and normative conventions.

Considering first search processes, the extent to which firms rely on personal networks in looking for reliable business partners is strongly related to their trust in formal institutions and prevalent authority relationships. Where owners and managers do not trust the legal system, or formal procedures for certifying competence, and the political culture is paternalist rather than rule-governed,

Table 2.4: Connections Between Institutions and Ways of Managing Uncertainty in Business Transactions: The Management of Business Transactions

INSTITUTIONAL FEATURES	Search		Agreement		Control	
	Personal Networks	Collective Standards	Codification	Commitment	Reputation	Contract
Business dependence on state elites	+	−		−	−	−
Strong intermediary associations	−	+	+	+	+	
Formal segmentation of markets	−	+	+	+	+	
Capital market based financial system	−	−	+			+
Credit based financial system		+		+	+	
Corporatist co-ordination of training and bargaining	−	+	+	+	+	
Low Trust in formal institutions	+		−	−		−
Paternalist authority	+	−	−			−
Contractarian authority	−		+	−	−	+
Communal authority		+		+	+	

business dealings are likely to rely greatly on personal contacts and reputations. In general, formal credentials and referencing systems are not considered trustworthy in countries where the state is omnipresent and unwilling to grant autonomy to intermediary agencies and political elites do not subject themselves to formal rules. Conversely, strong formal institutions and established procedures for dealing with credit assessment and negotiations enable companies to go beyond personal networks when searching for business partners.

Similarly, reliance on collective standards and norms for finding and trusting business partners, especially their competence, will be much greater in societies with strong intermediary associations, high levels of market segmentation and corporatist training and negotiation systems. This arises as a result of relatively stable industry membership, frequent interaction between firms and the development of distinctive industry cultures in these kinds of societies. It will also be encouraged by credit-based financial systems that lock banks into the destinies of their corporate clients because they learn more about them, their markets and capabilities, and so are able to act as knowledgeable guides to business partners. Clearly, the converse can be expected when intermediary associations are few and weak, as well as when prevalent norms and financial arrangements facilitate the market for corporate control and rapid changes in ownership and restructuring of industries and firms.

Turning to the nature of agreements in different contexts, these are more likely to be codified when formal procedures and institutions in general are regarded as reliable and contractual agreements offer a fairly good indication of what will be done. Thus, in societies with relatively autonomous and effective legal institutions governing a wide range of social relationships and where formal rule-governed procedures are generally used to generate predictable behaviour, business transactions will be more organised through codified agreements than where these institutional arrangements are absent. These conditions also enable capital markets to function effectively and markets to be formally segmented so that these institutional features are also associated with codified agreements. Additionally, the formalisation of corporatist arrangements, especially those involving labour organisations, represents the extension of rules and codified procedures to a wide range of economic relationships. Consequently, countries where this has become institutionalised are also likely to have quite codified business agreements. Conversely, weak formal institutions and/or the subservience of the legal system to state agencies and elites discourage reliance on codified agreements and are likely to result in more personal, tacit and informal understandings between business partners.

Commitment and risk sharing are closely associated with lock-in and mutual dependence so that institutions limiting "exit" from business relationships encourage longer-term agreements and greater commitment than if they facilitate it through, for example, a highly liquid market for corporate control. Market segmentation and the establishment of strong sectoral associations limit industry entry and exit, as do corporatist arrangements for co-ordinating training and bargaining activities where unions are both strong and based on industries. Together with close bank–firm connections derived from credit-based financial systems that lock banks and other providers of capital into the destinies of their major clients, these institutional arrangements encourage voice rather than exit strategies for dealing with uncertainty and risk, as well as longer term co-operative endeavours in general.

Conversely, market economies that enable firms to buy and sell business units in different industries easily, and thus readily change their identities and capabilities, have relatively low entry and exit barriers to sectors and thus encourage

greater turnover amongst the leading firms and their owners in any one industry. This in turn increases the uncertainty involved in entering into long-term
commitments with business partners, and so reduces the likelihood that such
agreements will be widespread. High levels of business dependence on the state,
as well as weak formal institutions, also inhibit firms' willingness to make
substantial commitments to each other because they increase the risks involved
and the overall level of uncertainty in the business environment. Generally,
dominant, especially predatory, states, and/or antagonistic and anomic business
contexts encourage highly flexible and short-term strategies rather than
commitment-based ones, as Fafchamp's (1996) discussion of contracting in
Ghana illustrates.

Similar points apply to the role of reputational and contractual control over
agreement execution. Reputational control is much more effective when
information flows freely and quickly between business partners that know each
other and cannot easily exit from relationships and locations. Thus, stable
industry boundaries and membership, close physical proximity and high
information flow density all facilitate reputational control. As Menkhoff (1992:
280–1) points out: "[b]usinessmen who are embedded in the local web of recurrent social interactions and who have a general reputation for probity are easier
to monitor than foreigners . . . in Chinese business communities where intense
face-to-face communication networks exist (obviously the case in Singapore)
and where the exit option is not feasible or very costly, gossip spreads very
quickly about anyone who breaks his *xinyong* (trustworthiness) or his promise
. . . negative sanctions include the withdrawal of credit by a creditor, resort creditors to the courts to bankrupt the offending party or excluding the offending
party from future transactions".

In contrast, high mobility in and out of industries and geographical locations,
limited and/or slow information flows, and low levels of collective identity and
organisation restrict the effectiveness of reputational control and make agreements very dependent on direct personal ties and process-based trust. This is
often the case in many developing countries or where radical institutional
change has resulted in the breakdown of traditional means of ensuring compliance, as in many former state socialist societies (Fafchamps, 1996; Humphrey
and Schmitz, 1998; Whitley *et al.*, 1996). Reputational control in any case needs
to be buttressed by performance monitoring and the development of trust
between business partners, and is rarely relied upon on its own, especially in situations of considerable uncertainty. This is especially so for reputational communities based on ascriptive characteristics where, as Menkhoff (1992)
emphasises, it would be foolhardy and naïve to assume that relatives and fellow
villagers are never opportunistic.

It would be a mistake, then, to counterpose reputational control mechanisms
with more formal contractual ones as strict alternatives to each other. Rather
they can, and often do, reinforce one another, as in many corporatist societies
where strong sectoral associations and unions limit entry and exit, and thus

facilitate reputational control, in combination with strong legal—not to say legalistic—frameworks and standardised contracting procedures that are widely relied upon. Control over agreement execution is here quite high because both reputational and contractual controls are effective, and transactional uncertainties are more limited than in societies where dominant institutions encourage either one or the other means of control, or of course neither.

In general, strong and reliable formal institutions, especially of course the legal system, encourage the use of contractual control, but, as many writers have pointed out, this is less effective when uncertainty over both what is being exchanged and its value to the user is high. This is typically the case in transactions involving innovative goods and services and/or when their use is dependent on highly tacit knowledge. Even in the most contractarian and arm's length business environment, then, the performance of business partners and expectations of future collaborations are important components of effective control mechanisms, and the reputations of business partners are crucial to the execution of trans- actions involving novel objects. Conversely, where formal institutions are unreli- able and subject to idiosyncratic and personal influence, contracts will either not be very common or else will be used ritualistically. High levels of business depend- ence on the state similarly discourages the use of contractual controls because the legal system is usually subject to state elite manipulation if not outright direction, and so is unreliable as a means of resolving disputes, in these sorts of societies.

These connections between particular features of the institutional environ- ment of business transactions and different ways in which they are managed suggest that different combinations of institutions, such as those summarised in the five types of business environment mentioned above, will be associated with particular kinds of search strategies, agreements and transaction control strate- gies. Particularistic business environments, for instance, encourage firms' own- ers and managers to engage in idiosyncratic and *ad hoc* search strategies that depend greatly on personal knowledge and contacts. The lack of reliable formal institutions and of strong collective intermediaries limits mutual commitments and trust in contractual procedures so that agreements between business part- ners tend to be of the informal market kind, as is typical of many transactions between the overseas Chinese, especially across community boundaries (Menkhoff, 1992). For similar reasons, both contractual and reputational con- trols are often weak in these business environments so that transactions are usu- ally short-term and highly particularistic.

Where industry mobility is restricted and risk-sharing encouraged by state agencies, however, as is arguably the case in Taiwan's Hsinchu science park, reputational controls may be more effective than in the traditional export indus- tries of Taiwan. This will be more likely when there is a common technical cul- ture and educational background based on training in the same, or very similar, universities. These factors may help to account for the significant differences between parts of the electronics industry in Taiwan and more traditional ones (Hung and Whittington, 1997; Saxenian, 1998; Shieh, 1992).

Arm's length environments on the other hand have stronger formal institutions for signalling competence, as well as for enforcing agreements through the courts. These encourage more impersonal and procedural search processes, as well as reliance on codified agreements and contractual control mechanisms. However, such societies do not encourage co-operation between firms and social groupings, and so long-term mutual commitments are risky. The limited institutionalisation of collective intermediaries in the economic sphere, coupled with easy entry to and exit from industries and commitments, likewise limit reputational control effectiveness and so transactions here tend to be low commitment contracts.

Both collaborative and state-guided societies are characterised by strong sectoral associations and market segmentation, together with powerful business peak associations and close business–state linkages. They also have significant lock-ins between capital providers and users. Reliance on collective standards and reputational controls for search strategies and transaction execution is therefore high in such market economies, and business partners are more willing to enter into long-term agreements than in arm's length or particularistic environments. However, they differ in terms of the significance and manner of state co-ordination and guidance of strategic decisions, and in the power and organisation of labour interests.

Collaborative institutional contexts are characterised by much greater labour representation in policy development and implementation, especially with regard to the training system and labour market management. In the case of post-war Germany, of course, this role has been considerably expanded by the formal entrenchment of labour representatives on the supervisory boards of companies and the incorporation of union federations in national policy discussions. This legal organisation of labour interests and regulation of labour relations both result from and expand the major role of the institutionally differentiated legal system, and formal procedures in general, in managing relationships between individuals and groups in these sorts of societies. This high level of formal regulation encourages firms to rely greatly on codified agreements and contractual controls in addition to reputational ones.

State-guided business environments in contrast are more centrally co-ordinated by state agencies, but these do not usually encourage the growth of strong union federations or involve them in policy development, let alone grant them formal powers in firms' decision-making processes. The legal system in many of these kinds of environments, such as that in Japan, is less autonomous and differentiated from the state administrative system (Hall, 1998; Upham, 1987; Wolferen, 1989) than in more collaborative ones. While, then, the important role of the state encourages formalisation of business transactions in these societies, the limited autonomy of legal institutions and their restricted role in regulating social relationships, especially corporatist arrangements, means that reliance on codified, formal procedures is, in general, limited. Co-operation here tends to be more flexible and less bound by standardised agreements than in collaborative societies, while state supported and powerful sectoral associations encourage widespread reliance on reputational controls. As a result, transactions in these environments are less governed by codified agreements and contractual sanctions.

Finally, *dirigiste* political economies increase vertical dependence at the expense of horizontal collaboration as firms compete for political support and risk-sharing. In this competition personal contacts with state elites are often crucial so that despite formal rules and procedures often being quite elaborate, obligations and trust are highly particularistic. The lack of a stable, independent legal framework for managing disputes and regulating agreements limits reliance on formal mechanisms as well as making strategic long-term decisions more difficult and liable to unpredictable state actions. Commitments between firms and reliance on collective organisations are therefore low in this kind of environment, as are the effectiveness of reputational controls, except for those based on state connections. In general, search strategies and control mechanisms are mediated by state agencies and networks in these societies.

THE MANAGEMENT OF INTERNATIONAL BUSINESS TRANSACTIONS

In broad terms, the organisation and management of cross-border transactions are less institutionalised and predictable than those within the national boundaries of most industrial capitalist societies because the key international institutions governing inter-firm relations are much less strongly established. This has two consequences. First, the uncertainties and risks involved in international transactions are greater than those within most countries, and, secondly, there are few institutional pressures to standardise search, agreement and control strategies between international business partners. In turn, these features of the international business environment result in process-based trust being particularly crucial in the management of business transactions as well as in a considerable variety of cross-border connections between firms from different business environments.

Reliance on process-based trust encourages firms to restrict their commitments to new business partners considerably and to make longer-term connections directly dependent upon performance. It also encourages them to continue to do business with suppliers, customers and agents that they already know rather than to risk resources and reputations with new firms, just as owners and managers do in highly particularistic domestic business environments (Fafchamps,, 1996). Indeed, many features of the international business environment are similar to national or regional particularistic ones.

In general, the collective organisation of leading firms in particular sectors is weak at the international level, although some capital intensive, high technology industries did co-operate extensively across borders before the internationalisation of anti-trust legislation (Arora *et al.*, 1999; Glimstedt, 2000; Djelic, 2000). Additionally, international legal institutions often apply only to transactions between firms from particular states. Formal certification mechanisms for evaluating the creditworthiness and/or competence of foreign firms do exist in the form of bank references, international standards and similar procedures, but again are often restricted in the range of countries they can be relied upon in, and are limited in their strength and continuity. They are also too costly for many firms in developing economies to access and use.

While international capital markets have grown in significance since the 1950s and 1960s, together with private regulatory agencies such as the debt ratings agencies, in many respects capital flows at the conclusion of the twentieth century are little more international than they were at its start and a truly global capital market has yet to become established (*Economist*, 1997; Hirst and Thompson, 1996; Kenworthy, 1997; Koechlin, 1995). Similarly, the institutions governing authority relationships and authority sharing between economic actors across national boundaries are limited in their scope and strength. As a result, market power and short-term classical contracting are more significant in cross-border transactions, including the commodity chains described by Gereffi (1966) and his colleagues, than in many industrial market economies.

This broad similarity to national particularistic business environments means that the prevalent ways of managing international business transactions involve considerable reliance on personal and informal networks, especially for smaller firms in peripheral economies (Fafchamps, 1996), and limited dependence on collectively organised standards. Similarly, codification of agreements and reliance on contractual controls are limited by the weakness of cross-national legal institutions and the costs and uncertainties of enforcing compliance in foreign jurisdictions. The lack of strong international institutions encouraging lock-in effects between businesses in different countries likewise limits the extent of mutual commitment in cross-border agreements, just as the limited barriers to entry and exit internationally—and practically non-existent corporatist arrangements—reduce the effectiveness of reputational control mechanisms. Overall, then, the bulk of international business transactions tend to involve low commitment and be quite particularistic.

This general picture may need to be modified for firms from different kinds of business environments engaging in transactions with firms located in particular kinds of institutional contexts, as well as by the growth of international regulation based predominantly on US models in the last few decades of the twentieth century (Braithwaite and Drahos, 2000). We might expect, for example, isolated firms from arm's length environments to manage their business risks in a similar kind of foreign environment in different ways from those deeply embedded in alliances and networks in their home economies. Considering first opportunistic firms from particularistic business environments, these seem likely to manage foreign business transactions in much the same way as domestic ones since many characteristics of the international business environment are the same. Distrust of unfamiliar and costly formal mechanisms for ensuring compliance in, say, arm's length societies will probably outweigh any benefits from relying on contracts that might emerge over time, at least for a number of years. Consequently, personal networks, process-based trust and short-term market contracting will be the dominant characteristics of the cross-border transactions of these kinds of firms.

Isolated firms from arm's length environments, on the other hand, will probably be strongly predisposed to rely on formal search and selection processes, codified agreements and contractual control mechanisms as they extend their domestic routines and conventions to international transactions. This is especially probable when they are trading with firms from similar contexts, such as the predominantly Anglo-Saxon societies. Elsewhere, though, such an approach is unlikely to be successful unless it is supported by considerable market power. Indeed, extensive reliance upon formal procedures may well be counter-productive in particularistic, state guided and *dirigiste* business environments where it often signifies distrust and low commitment. Cultivation of personal networks and the development of close and continuing relationships with state officials are more likely to be effective, but will be difficult to maintain in organisations where exit is often preferred to voice and managers frequently move between business units and roles.

Similar difficulties may be encountered by these kinds of companies when they seek to move beyond short-term contracting with firms in collaborative environments, although this does depend on the strength and autonomy of legal institutions and how strong are the lock-in relationships between firms in particular sectors. Generally, the stronger the local and/or national state's co-ordinating role, the more closely linked are firms within sectors, and the more effective are collective associations at representing sectoral interests, the more foreign firms will need to demonstrate their reliability and commitment to continuing business relationships if they are to develop long-term connections in these kinds of economies.

Firms from collaborative and state guided business environments are, of course, more used to working with each other, as well as with state agencies, sectoral associations and unions, in highly institutionalised contexts. This may lead to some initial difficulties for them when they engage in cross-border business transactions in a much more anomic and adversarial environment. In arm's length environments, however, they are able to rely on the formal apparatus of contract codification and enforcement to organise and police agreements, but commitments to particular business partners will be limited. Similarly to isolated firms, their ability to go beyond short-term contracting in highly co-ordinated economies will depend on their demonstrating commitments to their local business partners beyond immediate contractual obligations, and in particularistic environments with powerful states these kinds of firms will also have to adapt to the local business and political cultures if business transactions are to be based on more than market power.

State organised firms from *dirigiste* political economies can rely on their state supporters to enhance their market power and thereby manage quite high levels of risk and uncertainty in cross-border transactions, as the success of South Korean construction firms in the OPEC economies indicates. However, such close connections with state agencies may be less effective in developing longer term relationships with business partners abroad, especially in economies where such links are regarded with some suspicion. It also seems probably that firms used to focusing on vertical relationships with dominant state elites will find it difficult to adapt to business systems where horizontal collaboration is strongly institutionalised and social partnerships well entrenched.

These contrasting ways of dealing with the uncertainties of international business transactions by firms from different kinds of business environments emphasise the close connections between firm type and behaviour, domestic institutions and institutions in foreign economies. They also reflect the relative weakness of international institutions governing business relationships and the considerable differences in how owners and managers deal with each other more generally across market economies and institutional contexts. As long as these differences continue to be reproduced by variations in political systems, financial and labour systems and the norms governing trust and authority relationships at the national level, the organisation of international business transactions is most unlikely to become standardised around common norms and procedures. Rather, the ways in which these are managed will remain closely dependent upon the sorts of economic actors involved and their business environments. In addition it seems likely that market power, process based trust and particularistic networks will remain central.

REFERENCES

Amsden, Alice H. (1989), *Asia's Next Giant* (Oxford: Oxford University Press).

Appelbaum, Richard (1998), "The Future of Law in a Global Economy", *Social and Legal Studies* 7; 171–92.

Arora, A., Landau, R., and Rosenberg, N. (1999), "Dynamics of Comparative Advantage in the Chemical Industry", in D. C. Mowery and R. R. Nelson (eds.), *Sources of Industrial Leadership* (Cambridge: Cambridge University Press).

Beetham, David (1991), *The Legitimation of Power* (London: Macmillan).

Braithwaite, John, and Drahos, Peter (2000), *Global Business Regulation* (Cambridge: Cambridge University Press).

Calder, Kent E. (1993), *Strategic Capitalism: Private Business and Public Purpose in Japanese Industrial Finance* (Princeton, NJ: Princeton University Press).

Child, John, and Faulkner, David (1998), *Strategies of Cooperation: Managing Alliances, Networks and Joint Ventures* (Oxford: Oxford University Press).

Clark, Rodney (1979), *The Japanese Company* (New Haven, Conn.: Yale University Press).

Cox, Andrew (1986), "State, Finance and Industry in Comparative Perspective" in A. Cox (ed.), *State, Finance and Industry* (Brighton: Wheatsheaf).

Deakin, Simon, and Wilkinson, Frank (1998), "Contract Law and the Economics of Interorganizational Trust" in C. Lane and R. Bachmann (ed.), *Trust Within and Between Organizations: Conceptual Issues and Empirical Applications* (Oxford: Oxford University Press).

Djelic, Marie-Laure (2000), "The Origins, Workings and Limits of Globalization: Learning from Two Patterns of Cross-National Regulation" (Unpublished paper, ESSEC).

Dore, Ronald (1986), *Flexible Rigidities* (Stanford, Cal.: Stanford University Press).

Ebers, Mark (ed.) (1997), *The Formation of Inter-organizational Networks* (Oxford: Oxford University Press).

Eckstein, Harry, and Gurr, Ted R. (1975), *Patterns of Authority: A Structural Basis for Political Inquiry* (New York: J. Wiley).

Economist, (1997), "Capital Goes Global", 25 October, 139–40.

Fafchamps, Marcel (1996), "The Enforcement of Commercial Contracts in Ghana", *World Development* 24; 427–48.

Fruin, W. Mark (1992), *The Japanese Enterprise System* (Oxford: Oxford University Press).

Gereffi, Gary (1996), "Commodity Chains and Regional Divisions of Labour in East Asia", *Journal of Asian Business* 12; 75–112.

Gerlach, Michael (1992), *Alliance Capitalism* (Berkeley, Cal.: University of California).

Glimstedt, Henrik (2000), "Between National and International Governance: Geopolitics, Strategizing Actors and Sector Coordination in Electrical Engineering in the Interwar Era", (Unpublished paper. Stockholm: Stockholm School of Economics, Institute of International Business).

Haley, John Owen (1992), "Consensual Governance: A Study of Law, Culture and the Political Economy of Post-war Japan" in S. Kumon and H. Rosovsky (eds.), *The Political Economy of Japan*, vol. 3: *Culture and Social Dynamics* (Stanford, Cal.: Stanford University Press).

Hall, Ivan P. (1998), *Cartels of the Mind: Japan's Intellectual Closed Shop* (New York: W. W. Norton).

Hart, Jeffrey (1992), *Rival Capitalists: International Competitiveness in the United States, Japan, and Western Europe* (Ithaca, NY: Cornell University Press).

Herrigel, Gary (1994), "Industry as a Form of Order" in J. R. Hollingsworth, P. Schmitter and W. Streeck (eds.), *Governing Capitalist Economies* (Oxford: Oxford University Press).

—— (1996), *Industrial Constructions: The Sources of German Industrial Power* (Cambridge: Cambridge University Press).

Hidaka, Chikage (1997), "A Re-examination of Japan's Post-war Financing System" in E. Abe and T. Gourvish (eds.), *Japanese Success? British Failure? Comparisons in Business Performance Since 1945* (Oxford: Oxford University Press).

Hirst, Paul, and Thompson, Grahame (1996), *Globalisation in Question* (Oxford: Polity Press).

Hollingsworth, J. Rogers, Schmitter, Philippe, and Streeck, Wolfgang (eds.) (1994), *Governing Capitalist Economies* (Oxford: Oxford University Press).

Humphrey, John, and Schmitz, Hubert (1998), "Trust and Inter-firm Relations in Developing and Transition Economies", *Journal of Development Studies* 34; 32–61.

Hung, Shih-chang, and Whittington, Richard (1997), "Strategies and Institutions: A Pluralistic Account of Strategies in the Taiwanese Computer Industry", *Organization Studies* 18; 551–75.

Iribarne, Philippe d' (1989), *La Logique de l'Honneur* (Paris: Seuil).

Iterson, A. van, and Olie, R. (1992), "European Business Systems: the Dutch Case" in R. Whitley (ed.), *European Business Systems: Firms and Markets in their National Contexts* (London: Sage).

Iwata, R. (1992), "The Japanese Enterprise as a Unified Body of Employees: Origins and Development" in S. Kumon and H. Rosovsky (eds.), *The Political Economy of Japan*, vol. 3: *Social and Cultural Dynamics* (Stanford, Cal.: Stanford University Press).

Jacobs, Norman (1985), *The Korean Road to Modernization and Development* (Urbana, Ill.: University of Illinois Press).

Johnson, Chalmers (1982), *MITI and the Japanese Miracle* (Stanford, Cal.: Stanford University Press).

Kenworthy, L. (1997), "Globalization and Economic Convergence", *Competition and Change* 2; 1–64.

Kern, Horst (1998), "Lack of Trust, Surfeit of Trust: Some Causes of the Innovation Crisis in German Industry" in C. Lane and R. Bachmann (eds.), *Trust Within and Between Organizations* (Oxford: Oxford University Press).

Kim, Eun Mee (1997), *Big Business, Strong State: Collusion and Conflict in South Korean Development, 1960–1990* (Albany, NY: State University of New York Press).

Koechlin, T. (1995), "The Globalization of Investment", *Contemporary Economic Policy* 13; 92–100.

Lane, Christel (1997), "The Governance of Interfirm Relations in Britain and Germany: Societal or Dominance Effects", in R. Whitley and P. H. Kristensen (eds.), *Governance at Work: The Social Regulation of Economic Relations* (Oxford: Oxford University Press).

—— and Bachmann, Reinhard (1996), "The Social Constitution of Trust: Supplier Relations in Britain and Germany", *Organization Studies* 17; 365–95.

—— and —— (eds.) (1998), *Trust within and between Organizations: Conceptual Issues and Empirical Applications* (Oxford: Oxford University Press).

Lincoln, James R., and Nakata, Yoshifumi (1997), "The Transformation of the Japanese Employment Systems", *Work and Occupations* 24; 33–55.

Lodge, George C., and Vogel, Ezra F. (eds.) (1987), *Ideology and National Competitiveness* (Boston, Mass.: Harvard Business School Press).

Maurice, Marc, Sellier, François, and Silvestre, Jean-Jacques (1986), *The Social Foundations of Industrial Power* (trans. Arthur Goldhammer, Cambridge, Mass.: MIT Press).

Menkhoff, Thomas (1992), "Xinyong or How to Trust Trust? Chinese Non-Contractual Business Relations and Social Structure: The Singapore Case", *Internationales Asienforum* 23; 26–28.

Nooteboom, Bart (1999), *Inter-firm Alliances: Analysis and Design* (London: Routledge).

Okimoto, Daniel I. (1989), *Between MITI and the Market: Japanese Industrial Policy for High Technology* (Stanford, Cal.: Stanford University Press).

Orru, Marco, Biggart, Nicole, and Hamilton, Gary (1997), *The Economic Organization of East Asian Capitalism* (Thousand Oaks: Sage).

Pye, Lucian (1985), *Asian Power and Politics: The Cultural Dimensions of Authority* (Cambridge, Mass.: Harvard University Press).

Redding, S. Gordon (1990), *The Spirit of Chinese Capitalism* (Berlin: de Gruyter).

Rohlen, Thomas P. (1974), *For Harmony and Strength: Japanese White-collar Organisation in Anthropological Perspective* (University of California Press).

Sako, Mari (1992), *Prices, Quality and Trust: Inter-Firm Relations in Britain and Japan* (Cambridge: Cambridge University Press).

Samuels, Richard J. (1987), *The Business of the Japanese State* (Ithaca, NY: Cornell University Press).

Saxenian, AnnaLee (1998), "Silicon Valley's New Immigrant Entrepreneurs and their Asian Networks" (Presented to the International Conference on Business Transformation and Social Change in East Asia held at the Institute of East Asian Economies and Societies (TungHai University, Taiwan, 22–23 May).

Shieh, G. S. (1992), *"Boss" Island: The Subcontracting Network and Micro-Entrepreneurship in Taiwan's Development* (New York: Peter Lang).

Silin, Robert H. (1976), *Leadership and Values: The Organization of Large Scale Taiwanese Enterprises* (Cambridge, Mass.: Harvard University Press).

Teubner, Günther (1997), " 'Global Bukowina': Legal Pluralism in the World Society" in G. Teubner (ed.), *Global Law without a State* (Aldershot: Dartmouth).

Upham, Frank K. (1987), *Law and Social Change in Post-war Japan* (Cambridge, Mass.: Harvard University Press).

Wade, Robert (1990), *Governing the Market: Economic Theory and the Role of Government in East Asian Industrialisation* (Princeton, NJ: Princeton University Press).

Westney, D. Eleanor (1996), "The Japanese Business System: Key Features and Prospects for Changes", *Journal of Asian Business* 12; 21–50.

Whitley, Richard (1992), *Business Systems in East Asia: Firms, Markets and Societies* (London: Sage).

—— (1999), *Divergent Capitalisms: The Social Structuring and Change of Business Systems* (Oxford: Oxford University Press).

—— *et al.* (1996), "Trust and Contractual Relations in an Emerging Capitalist Economy: The Changing Trading Relationships of Ten Large Hungarian Enterprises", *Organization Studies* 17; 397–420.

Wolferen, Karel van (1989), *The Enigma of Japanese Power* (London: Macmillan).

Woo, Jung-En (1991), *Race to the Swift* (New York: Columbia University Press).

Zucker, L. (1986), "Production of Trust: Institutional Sources of Economic Structure, 1840–1920", *Research in Organisational Behaviour* 8; 53–111.

Zysman, John (1983), *Governments, Markets and Growth* (Ithaca, NY: Cornell University Press).

PART TWO

The Role of Legal Rules:
State Law and Unified Law

3

Global Law in Our High Speed Economy

WILLIAM E. SCHEUERMAN*

Abstract

Globalisation does not seem to be accompanied by the traditional liberal virtues of generality, clarity and prospectiveness. On the contrary, those areas of the law most closely tied to globalisation are amorphous and relatively irregular in character. This chapter suggests that the relative paucity of traditional liberal legal virtues in global economic law can be explained by reference to an economically-based process of "time-space" compression, which generates a reduced need among global economic actors for the "rule of law".

T HE ONGOING PROCESS of economic globalisation is accompanied by what Martin Shapiro has aptly described as the "globalization of law", according to which "the whole world [increasingly] lives under a single set of legal rules" (Shapiro, 1993: 37). The harmonisation and unification of some areas of international economic law seem to have accelerated in recent years, legal practice is increasingly transnational in scope, international business arbitration is flourishing, and a host of global economic institutions (most prominently, the World Trade Organisation) function to provide an emerging legal framework for global economic life.[1] At the same time, the "set of rules" constitutive of the globalisation of law often exhibits few of the virtues typically associated with traditional liberal conceptions of the rule of law. According to many studies, global law is deficient in the familiar liberal legal virtues of generality, publicity, prospectiveness, clarity, consistency and stability.[2] Crucial

---

* I would like to thank Volkmar Gessner for helpful criticisms of an earlier version of this chapter.

[1] For a conceptualisation of the idea of "international economic law," see Herdegen (1995: 1–8). International economic law includes different forms of what we traditionally have described as international private law, as well as public forms of international law crucial to globalisation (e.g. important legal features of the WTO and IMF).

[2] As Dieter Martiny notes in his contribution to this volume, such traditional legal virtues can be found in some important areas of global economic law. At the same time, they remain underdeveloped. For a survey of the literature on this point, see Scheuerman (1999b). Though by no means sharing my normative and political anxieties about this state of affairs, many of the essays collected in Teubner (1997) confirm the *empirical* thesis that traditional forms of law are relatively under-represented in the

features of international economic law remain, to a surprising extent, *soft law* disproportionately beneficial to the most privileged "global players" in the world economy (Cutler, 1999: 44); international arbitration is still relatively anti-formal and non-transparent in character (Carbonneau, 1990); the World Trade Organisation rests on a legal agreement that even today remains plagued by innumerable exceptional clauses (Jackson, 1997). In short, "global exchanges remain for the time being to a large extent insecure" (Gessner, 1998: 445), and one of the sources of this legal insecurity is probably the paucity of traditional liberal legal virtues within global business transactions.

From the perspective of an influential strand within modern liberalism, such legal weaknesses are likely to appear as little more than an atavistic leftover from the past, ultimately destined to diminish in significance as the intensification and integration of the global market economy proceeds. Liberal theorists from John Locke to Max Weber argued convincingly that market economies tend to rest on a system of legality characterised by a relatively substantial degree of formality, consistency, transparency and constancy; in Weber's famous phrase, an "elective affinity" obtains between modern capitalism and "formally rational administration and law" (Weber, 1978: 162; Kronman, 1983). Contemporary lawyers and policy advisors who insist on the necessity of an intimate relationship between the integration of the global economy and the likelihood of an increasingly formalistic set of contracts, property rights and legal norms are simply building on this indisputably rich intellectual legacy (Neate, 1995: 344–5; Sachs, 1995: 60–4), as do "rational choice" analysts who continue to emphasise the dependence of markets on traditional liberal legal devices (North and Weingast, 1989).[3]

The argument developed here pursues an alternative course. Although many reasons can be adduced to explain the idiosyncrasies of the present-day legal substructure of economic globalisation, the existing literature ignores what I take to be one of the main driving forces behind economic globalisation's relatively minimal reliance on classical liberal legal forms.[4] Traditional accounts of

arena of global economic law. This empirical trend meshes poorly with the political and normative preferences of many of the major political actors in the global economy (for example, those within the World Bank who fervently believe that market-style reforms and traditional rule of law virtues are simply two sides of the same coin). Alas, we would do well not to confuse our normative and political preferences with the empirical facts of global economic law. Although this is a complicated matter that I cannot address adequately here, I should also note that traditional liberal models of the rule of law typically see generality, clarity, prospectiveness, consistency and stability as inhering, though often in different ways, in both common law and civil law systems; common law systems often possess functional equivalents (e.g. the notion of a binding precedent) for the "formalistic" features of the civil law. In addition, the notion of the rule of law used here entails no commitment to an exaggerated legal formalism; the rule of law here is seen as compatible with some degree of indeterminacy within law, though assuredly not the "radical indeterminacy" attributed to it by some proponents of critical legal studies.

[3] For an incisive empirical and theoretical critique of the rational choice version of this approach, see Jayasuriya (1999). I should also note that some of the chapters in this volume, including those by Jerome Cohen and Michael Zürn, endorse the orthodox view that economic activity in capitalism relies on traditional rule of law virtues.

[4] One exception is Gessner (1994: 137–42), who has noted that the globalisation of law raises important questions about the time horizons of legal activity.

the relationship of formal law to capitalism typically obscure the manner in which capitalism constantly revolutionises the *pace* of economic activity, thereby generating increasingly *high-speed* forms of production and exchange. Capitalism's built-in drive to accelerate economic innovation and exchange ultimately poses a profound challenge to traditional forms of clear, general and stable law, which increasingly seem poorly suited to the dynamics of economic globalisation. The effectiveness of traditional legal devices inevitably becomes problematic precisely in those areas of the present-day economy undergoing globalisation, where the experiences of instantaneousness and simultaneity play an especially prominent role. In my view, we can hope to make sense of the main traits of the emerging system of global law only by acknowledging the existence of a mismatch between the *time horizons* of traditional modes of liberal law and of economic activity in the global economy.

LON FULLER—THEORIST OF GLOBALISATION?

Let us begin by recalling the American legal theorist Lon Fuller's (1964) neglected remarks on the nexus between law and economic activity in *The Morality of Law*. In accordance with influential strands in modern liberal jurisprudence, Fuller was committed to the view that private economic activity best takes places "within a framework set by the law", which Fuller defined in this context as a system in which "adjudication must act through openly declared rule or principle, and the grounds on which it acts must display some continuity through time" (Fuller, 1964: 171–2). A relatively stable system of legal norms, along with basic property rights and a functioning system of contracts, constitutes an indispensable basis for capitalism as long as legal norms (and "principles") possess a relatively substantial degree of those qualities making up what Fuller described as the "inner morality of law", including publicity, prospectiveness, clarity and consistency. Particularly if we bracket Fuller's own problematic commitment to natural law philosophy, on one level Fuller was saying nothing particularly controversial here.[5] Liberals have long argued that only a legal system exhibiting elements of Fuller's "inner morality of law" could best assure the minimum of predictability requisite to the successful operations of a capitalist market economy, and they have described many reasons why a stable framework of laws exhibiting such virtues could work effectively to buttress private property (Scheuerman, 1999c: 245–52).

---

[5] For the purposes of my discussion here, many of the longstanding disputes between legal positivists and natural lawyers are of secondary significance. I am primarily interested in the question why the globalisation of law seems so weak on traditional liberal legal virtues; of course, these virtues have been justified and interpreted in distinct ways by natural lawyers and positivists. For a positivist interpretation of the liberal rule of law, see Raz (1979: 210–29). My use of Fuller's comments on the relationship between law and economy entails hardly any commitment to his idiosyncratic brand of natural law theory.

Fuller was also in tune with the mainstream of modern liberalism when he insisted that certain forms of economic activity nonetheless "cannot and should not be conducted in accordance with anything resembling the internal morality of law". The operations of a firm are based on "one general principle, that of obtaining maximum return from limited resources", and this principle conflicts fundamentally with the underlying spirit of the "inner morality of law". The economic decisions of a corporate manager necessarily must be subject to quick reversal or alteration when novel conditions appear, whereas "the judge . . . acts upon those facts that are in advance deemed relevant. . . . His decision does not simply direct resources and energies; it declares rights, and rights to be meaningful must in some measure stand firm through changing circumstances" (Fuller, 1964: 171–2). Any attempt to determine wages and prices by legal means, and then allow courts to rule on wages and prices according to traditional forms of adjudication, is thus destined to "result in inefficiency, hypocrisy, moral confusion, and frustration" (Fuller, 1964: 173). When undertaking to deal in an unmediated manner with tasks of economic allocation, it soon becomes self-evident that "courts move too slowly to keep up with a rapidly changing economic scene" (Fuller, 1981: 112). Whereas a system of legality can successfully provide a *framework* for economic action, any attempt to expand the scope of adjudication to include activities *directly* concerned with the co-ordination or allocation of economic materials is doomed to fail. In short: some forms of economic activity can only be tightly harnessed to the inner morality of the law at the cost of generating both bad law and bad economics.

Though obviously critical of (primarily socialist) models of ambitious state economic planning, Fuller was no defender of economic *laissez-faire* either. His reflections merely seem to have suggested to him that attempts to regulate the externalities of the capitalist economy by means of governmental intervention often raise difficult questions of institutional design, since traditional legal devices are inappropriate to *some* forms of effective intervention in the economy (Fuller, 1964: 175). Many things could be said in defence of this position: Fuller was trying to avoid the Scylla of free market legal theory and its excessive hostility to state regulation of the economy, as well as the Charybdis of an exaggerated faith in the virtues of state economic planning that preferred to ignore its potential threats to classical notions of legality.

For now, however, my interest lies exclusively in Fuller's suggestive observations about the time horizons of economic activity and their implications for law. Fuller seems to have believed that we can delineate those economic areas where traditional legal instruments are likely to prove effective from those where they are destined to prove counter-productive in part according to the pace of change in the sphere of economic activity at hand. *Some* facets of economic life require "rapid" adaptation (for example, the day-to-day management of a firm), and thus an ambitious reliance on traditional formal legal devices may prove more of a hindrance than an aid there. Meanwhile, other facets of economic life are relatively constant and stable (for example, the entrepreneur's expectation that a particular set of time-consuming commercial transactions is likely to take place as promised), and there traditional legal devices (a system of stable contracts) can play an effective role in successfully buttressing economic interaction. Fuller's discussion also concludes with one further insightful observation. He noted that the distinction between "nonallocative" tasks (in part defined by their relative constancy) and "allocative" tasks (determined to some extent by their reliance on rapid, ever-changing action) could easily be blurred: "I do not mean to imply . . . that there are no gradations in the distinction between allocative and nonallocative tasks". In addition, the gradations between such economic tasks vary historically: "[t]asks that were only incidentally allocative may become more directly so with a change in circumstances" (Fuller, 1964: 174–5). By implication, the proper scope of adjudication may very well alter as both the character and *pace* of the activities at hand undergo change as well.

Why make so much of this relatively obscure facet of Fuller's legal thinking? If I am not mistaken, the ongoing process of economic globalisation places Fuller's remarks in a fresh light. One of the achievements of the recent social theory literature on globalisation has been to remind us that modern capitalism's underlying structural imperatives function incessantly to revolutionise the time horizons of economic activity. Economic globalisation is driven substantially by what Harvey (1989, 1996) has described as a "compression of time and space", according to which high-speed forms of economic production and interaction increasingly render national borders anachronistic.[6] When currency traders in Frankfurt can communicate instantaneously via computer with their peers in Singapore, or rapid-fire forms of communication suddenly make it profitable for corporate managers to undertake the production of different components of a single commodity (for example, an automobile[7]) simultaneously in many distant corners of the globe, it is hard to deny that the *phenomenological* horizons of economic activity are undergoing significant changes. Technological advances are working to undermine the distance between "there" and "here", while the high-speed pace of many facets of contemporary capitalism provides those of us living at the end of the twentieth century with a nervous sense of constantly "lagging behind" a world whose fast pace too often seems overwhelming and even debilitating (Reheis, 1998). As Harvey points out, modern capitalism is a:

revolutionary mode of production, always searching out new organisational forms, new technologies, new lifestyles, new modalities of production and exploitation and,

---

[6] The term "compression of time and space" is used by Harvey (1989, 1996), but Giddens (1987, 1990) has tried to capture a similar phenomenon with his notion of "distanciation", and Virilio (1986) has also devoted significant attention to the central importance of the increasingly high-speed character of contemporary social life. For a useful survey of the ongoing debate within social theory about this issue, see Urry's (1996) essay.

[7] The Ford Escort, for example, is made of components produced and assembled in 15 countries across three continents (Gereffi, Korzeniewicz, and Korzeniewicz, 1994: 1).

therefore, new objective social definitions of . . . time . . . The capacity to measure and divide time has been [constantly] revolutionized, first through production and the diffusion of increasingly accurate time pieces and subsequently through close attention to the speed and coordinating mechanisms of production (automation, robotisation) and the speed of movement of goods, people, information, messages, and the like (Harvey, 1996: 240–1).

Because the reduction of turnover time (in both production and distribution) is a key device for capitalists to improve profitability and compete effectively, "the history of capitalism has been characterized by a speed-up in the pace of life . . ." (Harvey, 1989: 240). Especially during junctures in the economic cycle characterised by intense competition or a major downturn, those businesses able to exploit the economic advantages of a faster turnover time may prove successful in outracing their economic rivals. Technological innovations resulting from this competition—for example, the possibility of rapid-fire computerised economic transactions—mean that instantaneousness and simultaneity increasingly become constitutive features of business activity. Modern capitalism has *always* worked to reduce turnover time and thereby accelerate the course of material production and exchange; our historical predecessors also experienced the "speed-up" of economic activities—as well as an "annihilation of distance" deriving from it—generated by railroads, automobiles, wireless telegraphs, telephones and aeroplanes (Kern, 1983). Yet a relatively *recent* bout of innovation in information, communication and transportation technologies has resulted in intensified rates of commercial, technological and organisational innovation in the last 20 years. Capitalism's immanent drive to accelerate technological innovation has generated unprecedented possibilities in recent years for a general speed-up *within* many facets of economic life.[8]

Maybe Fuller's neglected reflections on the relationship between law and economic activity can help explain why so much global law meshes poorly with traditional liberal legal models. Particularly among the "global players" so prominent within the contemporary economy, new technologies dramatically heighten the experience of instantaneousness and simultaneity, and thereby place a "premium on 'smart' and innovative entrepreneurship, aided and abetted by all the accouterments of swift, decisive, and well-informed decision-making". Simultaneity and instantaneousness offer novel possibilities for "flexibility with respect to labour processes, labour markets, products, and patterns of consumption" that surely would have astonished earlier generations of entrepreneurs (Harvey, 1989: 157, 147), and transnational enterprises have proven especially adept at making use of these new technologies as well as exploiting their economic advantages. Especially in those sectors of the capitalist economy in which

---

[8] Harvey (1989) describes this development as a consequence of the shift from Fordist to post-Fordist models of flexible capitalist accumulation. I am less interested here in defending any *particular* economic interpretation of this shift, however, than in documenting its implications for law. For the purposes of this chapter, many different interpretations of the recent acceleration of time-space compression within capitalism could serve my purposes equally well.

globalisation is most intense, the immediate consequences of the most recent bout of time–space compression are particularly pronounced. For example, the globalisation of financial markets would be inconceivable without recent innovations in informational technology, as would a host of no less decisive facets of contemporary capitalism.[9] Sub-contracting, outsourcing, "small batch" and short production runs, "just-in-time" inventory flows and delivery systems: each of these economic innovations can be interpreted as part of a broader trend towards accelerating the pace of production and adapting ever more rapidly to quick-changing forms of consumption, and each has been made feasible in part by dramatic technological developments (for example, the possibility of instant data analysis) that make it possible for firms to minimise the economic significance of distance and time. The half-life of many products has been dramatically cut in recent decades (Harvey, 1989: 156; Schoenberger, 1994: 59), impacting on production to the extent that enterprises often exhibit "low equipment dedication" and economic facilities may require more or less constant rationalisation; the half-life of productive facilities is reduced as well. In turn, this is one reason why it often proves profitable to shift economic activities to new locations, thereby directly contributing to the increased mobility of capital constitutive of economic globalisation.

Of course, the bourgeois adage of "time is money" has always played a significant role in capitalism; from this perspective, nothing novel has occurred. Nonetheless, this "old" bourgeois adage seems to be taking on heightened significance amidst economic globalisation. To be sure, globalising capitalism contains many features that hardly seem to express an obsession with "the new, the fleeting, the ephemeral" (Harvey, 1989: 171). Multinational corporations rarely vanish overnight from the global stage to be replaced by new upstart firms; investors still need assurances from host states that their property rights are likely to remain secure down the road; businesses often have an economic interest in cultivating good long-term relations with exchange partners. Yet even those facets of contemporary capitalism exhibiting stability and a "long-term" orientation now operate in a broader economic environment in which speed and rapid-fire adaptation take on great importance. Multinational economic giants need to figure out how to accelerate production and maximise flexibility; foreign investors require enforceable contracts to protect their property, but they simultaneously operate from the assumption that they may be forced to shift their activities to another location within a relatively short span of time; the cultivation of cordial business relations with economic partners by no means detracts from the advantages generated by relatively speedy, unproblematic transactions and forms of dispute resolution likely to facilitate such transactions.

Recall again Fuller's perceptive remarks about the danger of a mismatch between "rapid" forms of economic activity and traditional forms of ("stable")

---

[9] For a detailed discussion of the implications of recent technological innovations in communication, information and transportation technology for economic globalisation see Castells (1996).

adjudication. Fuller suggested that attempts directly to co-ordinate economic activities by traditional legal means might suffer from this mismatch. Although the polemical thrust of Fuller's argument was directed primarily at statist models of economic planning, perhaps the dilemma Fuller described is more fundamental than he grasped. To the extent that contemporary manifestations of economic globalisation rest on a dramatic speed-up in the time horizons of economic activity, Fuller's comments about the historical variability of the limits of traditional forms of adjudication seem prescient indeed. There is no *a priori* reason to assume that the problem of a mismatch between the time horizons of traditional law and economic activity is limited to centrally planned economies, or to exclude the possibility that this mismatch can manifest itself in different arenas and to varying degrees within the history of capitalism as well; Fuller himself admitted as much by noting that the gradations between those tasks suited to adjudication and those unsuited to it varied over time within market economies. Perhaps it was in part the relatively slow pace of traditional forms of capitalism that helped give Weber's notion of an "elective affinity" between capitalism and formal law real substance, whereas contemporary high-speed globalising capitalism may be shedding much of its dependence on formal law (Scheuerman, 1999c). Most empirical studies suggest that globalisation relies on a minimum of enforceable contracts and property rights. Beyond that bare minimum, however, the course of global legal development remains in flux. Might we take the relatively anti-formal character and inconstancy of so much global economic law as a confirmation of Fuller's observation that traditional forms of liberal law are likely to prove inadequate in the context of a "rapidly changing economic scene"? Is it possible that the high-speed character of economic globalisation is rendering some traditional legal instruments increasingly problematic there as well?

Legal theorists have had relatively little to say about the significance of the time horizons of traditional models of legality, let alone the implications of the changing time horizons of economic activity for legality. But some of their reflections could be taken as a confirmation of my worries. From the ranks of legal positivism, Schauer (1988: 542) has noted that clear, general legal rules always necessarily "force the future into the categories of the past" in a manner that may soon render them anachronistic. Every rule codifies expectations drawn from past experience, and the past necessarily becomes a guide to the future. Given a relatively high degree of constancy and stability in a particular economic arena, few immediate problems are likely to result from "forcing the future" into a legal framework based on past experience. In those areas of the economy characterised by high-speed forms of economic action and incessant change, however, these problems are destined to become more serious. Formal rules may then prove ineffective. To his credit, the Marxist legal theorist Anthony Chase better acknowledges the significance of tensions between economic conditions (subject to constant change) and legal forms. But Chase conceives the process by which the legal system responds to the dynamism of the capitalist economy in a relatively traditional manner: "[l]aw is changed either *overtly* by statute or by courts openly advocating 'social policy' justifications for their decisions, or it is changed *covertly*, as when a court radically alters legal results but does so more or less artfully reinterpreting existing precedent" (Chase, 1997: 48–9). Chase thereby downplays the possibility that each of these traditional devices faces profound challenges in light of the increasingly rapid pace of the time-space compression presently motoring economic globalisation. Judges may simply fail to reinterpret precedent quickly enough to keep law in accordance with contemporary economic realities. Alternatively, to the extent that they strive for an accelerated mode of judicial decision-making they may find themselves forced to sacrifice traditional legal protections (for example, due process). The need for rapid-fire adjustments to an ever-changing global economy also seems to conflict at times with the procedural and deliberative presuppositions of a legitimate form of parliamentary rule making (Scheuerman, 1999a).

For their part, legal sociologists have long underscored the manner in which traditional forms of formal adjudication rest on a "marked orientation to the past": judges engage in "retroactively oriented reasoning" to the extent that they are primarily concerned with the establishment of past events (for example, guilt) (Nader, 1969: 87; Aubert, 1969: 287). But in the context of economic sectors in which existing rules may seem outdated even before they have made their way into the law books, continuity with the legal past may appear to be more of an impediment to successful economic activity than an enabling factor. When economic transactions require lightning-fire responses and enormous flexibility, traditional forms of stable general law are just as likely to prevent economic actors from adjusting nimbly to the dictates of the global market-place as they are likely to underpin such action. To an ever greater extent, traditional forms of stable general law soon seem like a "dead" leftover from a past fundamentally incongruent with contemporary economic realities.

HIGH-SPEED DISPUTE RESOLUTION IN A HIGH-SPEED ECONOMY

Only substantial empirical research can succeed either in confirming or disproving the thesis developed above, and many difficult questions remain unanswered. For example, *which* facets of economic globalisation have experienced exactly *what* manifestations of time–space compression, and how precisely is this process evinced by particular trends in specific areas of the law? For now, I can merely point in a tentative manner to aspects of the globalisation of law that might be taken as a preliminary empirical confirmation of my suspicion that the altered time horizons of contemporary economic activity are likely to have far-reaching implications for traditional liberal views of the nexus between law and capitalism. Notwithstanding the unavoidably limited scope of my empirical discussion here, striking features of the ongoing globalisation of law confirm my expectation that traditional forms of liberal law increasingly conflict with the high-speed character of economic globalisation.

No discussion of the globalisation of law can ignore the tendency to devolve "the authority to create and to enforce commercial norms to the private sphere through the increasing emphasis on merchant autonomy as the operative substantive norm and the increasing legitimacy of private arbitration" (Cutler, 1999: 28). This trend takes myriad concrete forms, but two of its most salient features are probably the following: first, businesses operating abroad now sometimes opt to resolve disputes with their business partners by means of arbitration and, secondly, the legal substructure of international business arbitration remains flexible and discretionary, characterised by a relative absence of liberal legal virtues such as generality, publicity, clarity and constancy. In international commercial arbitration:

> If a contract appears insufficiently explicit to furnish a direct statement of the parties' rights, duties, powers, and liberties, then the arbitrators will construct it and fill the gaps in it by recourse to their own knowledge of how commerce works in practice, and how commercial men [*sic*] in the relevant field express themselves . . . What is important is the arbitrator should keep constantly in mind that he is concerned with international commerce, with all the breadth of horizon, flexibility, and practicality of approach which that demands (Mustill, 1988: 118–19).[10]

Although international commercial arbitration appears to be undergoing a process of change in which its limited legalistic features have undoubtedly been fortified somewhat, it remains a system of dispute resolution in which confidentiality (and even secrecy) is far-reaching, and recourse to clear legal rules (or precedent) remains relatively limited (Cutler, 1995: 384; deVries, 1984; Dezalay and Garth, 1996; van den Berg, 1998). Nonetheless, arbitration services are booming today, and the relative enthusiasm evinced by "global players" for business arbitration seems to confirm the claim of one academic observer that "[f]ormalistic facades are not necessary to achieve the sensible results dictated by a commercial ethic" (Carbonneau, 1990: 13). A substantial body of literature also suggests that the reliance on international commercial arbitration is having a greater impact on *municipal* legal systems than first might seem obvious. Most national legal systems today not only are striving to free international arbitrators from many traditional legal restraints on their activities, but they also are tolerating an expanded use of arbitration devices at home as well (Hirschman, 1985; Lillich and Brower, 1994; McDermott, 1985–1986). Courts are finding it increasingly difficult to distinguish clearly between national and transnational forms of economic activity, and thus the role of arbitration in the realm of international business dispute resolution

---

[10] On the role of the *lex mercatoria* here see Dasser (1991), who has graciously helped me sort out some previous misunderstandings about the topic. I should add that the extent to which arbitration has become crucial to conflict resolution in the global economy remains a controversial empirical matter.

inevitably makes arbitration ever more pervasive even in those areas of the economy traditionally considered "domestic" in character (Carbonneau, 1987, 1989, 1994; Delaume, 1979).

The popularity of international business arbitration has many sources,[11] but one of them arguably confirms the theoretical diagnosis offered above. Arbitration's "procedural norms emphasize speed", and many global entrepreneurs evidently believe that the economic advantages to be gained by the fast-paced character of arbitration outweigh any of the disadvantages stemming from its informality (Cutler, 1995: 385; Cutler, 1999: 31). An omnipresent theme in the literature on business arbitration is the promise of *rapid-fire* forms of dispute resolution free of the relatively time-consuming technicalities and formalities of traditional adjudication. Much of the academic literature tends to accept this view as well: for example, Banaker (1998: 370) characteristically refers to the "relatively subtle and swift procedures" characteristic of international business arbitration. Revealingly, those touting the merits of international business arbitration typically worry that legalistic trends within its development threaten to undermine the relatively speedy character of arbitration and thereby destroy one of its main attractions to the global business community (van den Berg, 1998). Although it would be a mistake to exaggerate the degree to which arbitration has come to institutionalise time-consuming procedural refinements, it nonetheless is striking that arbitration now faces a whole range of competitors (including variants of mediation and conciliation geared towards the needs of business) united by one common denominator: each promises an *even faster* mode of conflict resolution than that provided by arbitration (Pollock, 1993; Singer, 1994). In turn, defenders of arbitration have responded with a panoply of reform proposals minimising its purportedly wasteful use of the precious commodity of time. In a telling development, arbitration's promoters now are busy promoting the virtues of what they describe as *fast-track arbitration*, premised on the possibility of a mode of "accelerated justice" in which entrepreneurs can expect quick answers even in the most difficult disputes (Rovine, 1994; Müller, 1998; Schneider, 1998).

Whether or not arbitration (or its rivals) *in fact* is as speedy as its enthusiasts and many academic commentators assert requires careful empirical scrutiny. But even if such claims turn out to be exaggerated, it still remains relevant for the purposes of the argument here that one of the main selling-points of arbitration is the *promise* of speed: in itself, this highlights a surprising trend,

---

[11] On one level, the growth of arbitration confirms Shklar's (1986: 16–17) observation that "the resort to arbitration under chamber of commerce auspices" has been a widely-held preference for business groups throughout the history of modern capitalism. "Capitalist entrepreneurs have their own interest in stability and calculability, but the excessive formalities of lawyers' law are [often] uncongenial to them" (*ibid.*). For an account of the complicated history of commercial arbitration in the USA that confirms Shklar's comment see Auerbach (1983). Of course, a major selling point for commercial arbitration throughout its history has *always* been the promise of a speedy resolution to business disputes. Nonetheless, we still need to explain why "lawyer's law" has become *especially* uncongenial to global business groups in contemporary capitalism.

namely the global business community's apparent readiness to sacrifice formal legal virtues for the promise (if not the reality) of "getting things done" at a rapid pace. One might also legitimately point out that we would do well to avoid exaggerating the overall significance of arbitration to globalisation; traditional forms of litigation clearly remain important to global business. Yet the theoretical argument developed here might also help explain why *some* forms of litigation increasingly seem favored by major "global players". An important body of research underlines what we might describe as an "Americanisation" of some forms of legal practice closely tied to globalisation: global firms often prefer to give their business to American-style corporate law firms, lawyers and academics head to the USA to gain exposure to American theories and modes of legal reasoning, and American forms of legal decision-making and legislation are widely imitated throughout the world (Dezalay, 1990; Wiegand, 1991). In light of the reduced formality characteristic of common law systems like the American one, this trend *potentially* supports my expectation that global business increasingly is hostile to legal formalism in part because of its (purportedly) time-consuming characteristics.[12]

Arbitration and its "accelerated" rivals share one additional feature attractive to business in the age of global time and space compression. The reduced emphasis on legal precedent and pre-existing standing rules here implies that legal continuity and stability mean less than in traditional forms of adjudication. Classical models of the relationship between capitalism and law would lead us to expect entrepreneurs to strive to overcome this state of affairs for the sake of assuring legal predictability. Nonetheless, the global business community generally seems satisfied with the extreme situation-specific focus of decision-making within arbitration and "alternative dispute resolution". Who can blame them, given a global economy in which speed and flexibility are so crucial to economic survival? Precisely this situation-specific focus renders both arbitration and its competitors less *past-oriented* than traditional modes of legal regulation, thereby minimising the impact of a legal past that increasingly seems irrelevant in the face of fast-moving economic trends. For their part, those aggressively marketing alternatives to traditional adjudication intuitively grasp this point as well, at least to the extent that they note the degree to which non-traditional forms of dispute resolution seem well-suited to situations in which the cultivation of long-term relations with business partners is of paramount significance. In scenarios of this type, litigation concerned first and foremost with assigning "guilt" to one party in reference to a past act may be less useful economically than a relatively quick compromise emphasising positive lessons to be learned for both sides for the sake of maintaining cordial ties in the future (Singer, 1994: 74–5).

In this vein, it is also striking that global businesses often have resisted even modest attempts by *formal* intergovernmental organisations (for example, the

---

[12] Needless to say, this comment raises a series of difficult empirical questions. There are enormous differences regarding speed, legal reasoning and efficiency, not only between civil and common law systems, but within particular common laws systems and their many different components.

United Nations or OECD) to establish binding rules for the regulation of multi-national corporations or international business taxation; these pivotal areas of global law remain porous and irregular in part because of the hostility of business to traditional forms of legal regulation there (Picciotto, 1992; Scheuerman, 1999b: 8–12).[13] Not surprisingly, much of this enmity is motivated by an economic interest in warding off redistribution and governmental intervention potentially hostile to business, but part of it also seems driven by an intuitive sense that traditional forms of legal regulation increasingly conflict with the dynamics of global time and space compression. Global businesses today occasionally favour harmonisation and unification within global law, but often *only* to the extent that such efforts provide maximum scope for business flexibility. In turn, such flexibility is now widely seen as conflicting with traditional liberal modes of clear, general, stable law. Thus, the International Institute for the Unification of Law's (UNIDROIT) *Principles of International Commercial Contracts* note that many previous "[e]fforts towards the international unification off law have hitherto taken the forms of binding instruments, such as supranational legislation or international conventions, or of model laws". UNIDROIT suggests that such traditional efforts are destined to fail, however, since they "often risk remaining little more than a dead letter"—in part because formal modes of intergovernmental political regulation so often seem to lag badly behind the ever-changing needs of global commerce.[14] In light of the growing significance of the problem of a time-lag between law and economic life, *soft* and potentially flexible modes of law better accord with the imperatives of contemporary economic life.

A fascinating literature on recent legal development in East Asia also provides supplementary empirical support for the thesis developed in the first section of this chapter. Whereas many commentators have argued that market reforms in China as well as the integration of East Asian economies into global networks of production and exchange should strengthen the move towards formal law there (Gregg, 1995), a number of recent studies instead underline the resilience of traditional and non-formal modes of decision-making and dispute resolution within Asian capitalism (Jayasuriya, 1997, 1999; Li, 1996). Formal law is *not* supplanting the "personal networks of mutual dependence and trust" that traditionally have been central to a style of business interaction in which familial connections and the cultivation of personal ties are of paramount importance (Jones, 1994: 197; Appelbaum, 1998). On the contrary, such traditional features of East Asian economic life seem to be flourishing, arguably in part because global time and space compression means that the economic advantages of non-formal decision-making can be exploited in novel and unprecedented ways. New informational and communications technologies generate:

---

[13] Harry Arthurs' excellent chapter on labour law in this volume also seems to confirm this claim.
[14] Cited in Cutler (1999: 43–4).

information diffusion and access sufficiently powerful as to reduce significantly the level of bureaucratic underpinning previously necessary for the achievement of efficient markets. Information technology transcends the physical time and space barriers to the choice of transactional modes. In doing so, it offers the best opportunity for China [and some other Asian countries] to integrate efficient modernization with its traditional preference for less codified and personalized transactions. The electronic village or commune, reflecting an ever-widening scatter of transactions in the culture-space as its inhabitants discover that the technology imposes few transactional restrictions, is potentially both *Gemeinschaft* and *Gesellschaft* at the same time.[15]

According to some of this scholarship, traditional forms of business interaction (for example, those based on what the Chinese describe as *guanxi*) mesh effectively with novel economic possibilities for instantaneousness and simultaneity provided by recent technological innovations. The resulting union of traditional forms of business interaction and advanced technology leaves Asian entrepreneurs well suited to grapple with the exigencies of a high-speed and constantly changing form of capitalism, in part because the mixture of informality and high-speed information and communication technologies on which they rely maximises possibilities for flexible forms of rapid-fire economic adaptation (Jones, 1994: 201–4; Smart, 1993: 397, 402).

CONCLUSIONS

Let me conclude with a brief comment on the broader implications of my claim that the altered time horizons of contemporary economic activity contain profound implications for the future of traditional liberal models of law within the global economy.

From one perspective, the diagnosis developed here merely confirms the anxieties of legal theorists who have suggested that the rapid pace of contemporary social development increasingly raises difficult questions about the extent to which traditional forms of legal regulation are likely to continue to function effectively (Luhmann, 1981: 73–89). For sure, global law is hardly the only arena where the time horizons of present-day social and economic activity may be challenging traditional forms of adjudication.[16] As I have tried to argue, the mis-

---

[15] M. Boisot and J. Child, cited in Jones (1994: 203).

[16] As Denninger (1988: 6–9) suggests, this problem manifests itself in many areas of the law, and it arguably is one of the root causes of the movement towards increasingly "flexible" forms of state regulation. The theoretical framework developed here may also help us better understand the *deformalisation* of private law noted by many commentators (Neumann, 1996), as well as the virtually universal trend within recent legislative bodies to *speed up* lawmaking (for example, by means of "fast-track" legislation). In short, the notion of time–space compression may prove to be a useful conceptual tool for making sense of many widely-noted trends at work within recent legal development. Elsewhere I have also tried to argue that we can make sense of the proliferation of executive-centered exceptional powers within contemporary liberal democracy (and their surprising ubiquity as an instrument of economic regulation) only by focusing on the dilemmas posed by global time and space compression (Scheuerman, 1999a; 2000).

match between high-speed economic activity and traditional forms of adjudication is particularly pronounced within global law in light of the striking employment there of forms of advanced technology that accelerate time–space compression. Nevertheless, to the extent that the acceleration of economic activity and the concomitant "shrinkage" of space is hardly limited to global economic practices, the dilemma that I described above is sure to impact on many other legal arenas as well.

One possible implication of the account provided here is that only an embrace of a radical variant of economic liberalism makes sense given the mismatch between traditional law and economic globalisation. Along libertarian lines, maybe we simply need to minimise state-backed legal activity in the economy altogether and abandon even the most cautious aspirations to regulate the emerging global economy. In light of the manifest pathologies of contemporary global capitalism, this option seems not only utopian but morally irresponsible as well. Many of the traditional normative defences of a legal system based on general, clear, prospective and stable norms remain as valid as ever, and the increasingly obvious pathologies of *neo-liberal* economic globalisation cry out for relatively ambitious forms of social and economic regulation.[17] For similar reasons, the *status quo* of global law remains unsatisfactory. Many facets of the existing system suffer from precisely those ills described by traditional liberal thinkers who rightly worried about legal systems based on non-transparent, private, and *ad hoc* forms of decision-making (Scheuerman, 1999b). Moreover, too many elements of the *status quo* suggest that existing global law chiefly serves the interests of the most privileged economic interests in the global economy (Cutler, 1995, 1999).

Yet how are we to grapple with the tasks at hand given the limits of traditional forms of adjudication? Does my diagnosis necessarily force us to embrace a *Kulturpessimismus* according to which the course of social and economic development inevitably renders our most noble legal ideas anachronistic? Perhaps we should simply join forces with those who believe that the "end of law" is near.

Given the abiding strengths of the ideal of the liberal model of law, that surely would be a mistake. By the same token, those of us committed to the normative core of liberal jurisprudence urgently need to consider how we can both maintain a proper fidelity to that tradition *and* develop forms of co-ordination and regulation properly suited to the dictates of a high-speed economy.[18] In the spirit of Lon Fuller, we need to acknowledge the strengths of the classical liberal legal virtues he described as constitutive of the "inner morality of law", while

---

[17] As I write this, the World Bank reports that 1.3 billion inhabitants of our planet presently try to survive on less than $1 (US) a day (an *increase* of 100,000 since 1993), and by 2000 the number is likely to have risen to 1.5 billion (Lewis, 1999). See Habermas (1998) for a spirited defence of the need for transnational social and economic regulations.

[18] Constructive suggestions along these lines can be found in important recent studies by Reinecke (1998) and Zürn (1998).

simultaneously recognising that alternative forms of state activity are occasionally better suited to the co-ordination of some facets of economic life. Needless to say, determining which features of the global economy can be effectively regulated by traditional forms of adjudication from those that cannot poses a harrowing set of intellectual and political challenges.

Writing in the heyday of the post-war regulatory and welfare state, Fuller himself noted that the task "of finding the most apt institutional design for governmental control over the economy has been acute for a long time. In the future this problem is, I think, bound to become more pressing and pervasive" (Fuller, 1964: 175). Amidst the contours of the ongoing process of economic globalisation, Fuller's anxious comment seems even more timely than it did in 1964.

REFERENCES

Appelbaum, Richard (1998), "The Future of Law in a Global Economy", *Social & Legal Studies* 7; 171–92.
Auerbach, Jerold (1983), *Justice Without Law* (Oxford: Oxford University Press).
Aubert, Vilhelm (1969), "Law as a Way of Resolving Conflicts: The Case of a Small Industrialized Society" in L. Nader (ed.), *Law in Culture and Society* (Berkeley, Cal.: University of California).
Banaker, Reza (1998), "Reflexive Legitimacy in International Arbitration" in V. Gessner and A. C. Budak (eds.), *Emerging Legal Certainty: Empirical Studies on the Globalization of Law* (Aldershot: Ashgate).
Carbonneau, Thomas (1987), "The Exuberant Pathway to Quixotic Internationalism: Assessing the Folly of *Mitsubushi*", *Vanderbilt Journal of International Law* 19; 265–98.
—— (1989), *Alternative Dispute Resolution: Melting the Lances and Dismounting the Steeds* (Urbana, Ill.: University of Illinois).
—— (1990), "The Remaking of Arbitration: Design and Destiny" in T. Carbonneau (ed.), *Lex Mercatoria and Arbitration* (Dobbs Ferry, NY: Transnational Juris Publications).
—— (1994), "National Law and the Judicialization of Arbitration: Manifest Destiny, Manifest Disregard, and Manifest Error" in R. Lillich and C. Brower (eds.), *International Arbitration in the 21st Century: Towards Judicialization and Uniformity?* (Irvington, NY: Transnational Publishers).
Castells, Manuel (1996), *The Rise of the Network Society* (Oxford: Blackwell).
Chase, Anthony (1997), *Law and History: The Evolution of the American Legal System* (New York: New Press).
Cutler, A. Claire (1995), "Global Capitalism and Liberal Myths: Dispute Settlement in Private International Trade Relations", *Millennium: Journal of International Studies* 24; 377–97.
—— (1999), "Public Meets Private: The International Unification and Harmonization of Private International Trade Law", *Global Society* 13; 25–48.
Dasser, Felix (1991), "Lex Mercatoria: Werkzeug der Praktiker oder Spielzeug der Lehre?", *Schweizerische Zeitschrift für internationales und europäisches Recht* 3; 299–322.

Delaume, G. R. (1979), "What is an International Contract?: An American and Gallic Dilemma", *The International and Comparative Law Quarterly* 258–318.

Denninger, Erhard (1988), "Der Präventions-Staat", *Kritische Justiz 21;* 1–15.

DeVries, Henry P. (1984), "International Commercial Arbitration: A Transnational View", *Journal of International Arbitration* 1; 7–20.

Dezalay, Yves (1990), "The Big Bang and the Law: The Internationalization and Restructuration of the Legal Field" in M. Featherstone (ed.), *Global Culture: Nationalism, Globalization, and Modernity* (London: Sage).

—— and Garth, Bryant G. (1996), *Dealing in Virtue: International Commercial Arbitration and the Construction of a Transnational Legal Order* (Chicago, Ill.: University of Chicago).

Fuller, Lon (1964), *The Morality of Law* (New Haven, Conn.: Yale University Press).

—— (1981), "The Forms and Limits of Adjudication" in K. I. Winston (ed.), *The Principles of Social Order* (Durham, NC: Duke University Press).

Gereffi, Gary, Korzeniewicz, Miguel, and Korzeniewicz, Roberto (1994), "Introduction: Global Commodity Chains", in G. Gereffi and M. Korzeniewicz (eds.), *Commodity Chains and Global Capitalism* (Westport, Conn.: Greenwood Press).

Gessner, Volkmar (1994), "Global Legal Interaction and Legal Cultures", *Ratio Juris* 7; 132–45.

—— (1998), "Globalization and Legal Certainty" in V. Gessner and A. C. Budak (eds.), *Emerging Legal Certainty: Empirical Studies on the Globalization of Law* (Aldershot: Dartmouth).

Giddens, Anthony (1987), *The Nation-State and Violence* (Stanford, Cal.: Stanford University Press).

—— (1990), *The Consequences of Modernity* (Stanford, Cal.: Stanford University Press).

Gregg, Benjamin (1995), "Law in China: The Tug of Tradition, The Push of Capitalism", *Review of Central and East European Law* 21; 65–86.

Habermas, Jürgen (1998), "Jenseits des Nationalstaates? Bemerkungen zu Folgeproblemen der wirtschaftlichen Globalisierung" in U. Beck (ed.), *Politik der Globalisierung* (Frankfurt: Suhrkamp).

Harvey, David (1989), *The Condition of Postmodernity* (Oxford: Blackwell).

—— (1996), *Justice, Nature and the Geography of Difference* (Oxford: Blackwell).

Herdegen, Matthias (1995), *Internationales Wirtschaftsrecht* (Munich: C. H. Beck).

Hirschman, Linda (1985), "The Second Arbitration Trilogy: The Federalization of Arbitration Law", *Virginia Law Quarterly* 71; 1305–78.

Jackson, John H. (1997), *The World Trading System: Law and Policy of International Economic Relations* (Cambridge, Mass.: MIT Press).

Jayasuriya, Kanishka (1997), "Franz Neumann on the Rule of Law and Capitalism: The East Asian Case", *Journal of the Asia Pacific Economy* 2; 355–77.

—— (1999), "Introduction: A Framework for the Analysis of Legal Institutions in East Asia" in K. Jayasuriya (ed.), *Law, Capitalism, and Power in Asia: The Rule of Law and Legal Institutions* (New York: Routledge).

Jones, Carol (1994), "Capitalism, Globalization and Rule of Law: An Alternative Trajectory of Legal Change in China", *Social & Legal Studies* 3; 195–214.

Kern, Stephen (1983), *The Culture of Time and Space, 1880–1918* (Cambridge, Mass.: Harvard University Press).

Kronman, Anthony T. (1983), *Max Weber* (Stanford, Cal.: Stanford University Press).

Lewis, Paul (1999), "World Bank Says Poverty is Increasing", *New York Times*, 3 June, C7.

Li, Jielli (1996), "The Structural Strains of China's Socio-Legal System: A Transition to Formal Legalism?", *International Journal of the Sociology of Law* 24; 41–59.

Lillich, Richard B., and Brower, Charles N. (eds.) (1994), *International Arbitration in the 21st Century: Towards Judicialization and Uniformity?* (Irvington, NY: Transnational Publishers).

Luhmann, Niklas (1981), *Ausdifferenzierung des Rechts. Beiträge zur Rechtssoziologie und Rechtstheorie* (Frankfurt: Suhrkamp).

McDermott, John T. (1985–1986), "Significant Developments in the United States Law Governing International Commercial Arbitration", *Connecticut Journal of International Law* 1; 111–50.

Müller, Eva (1998), "Fast Track-Arbitration: Meeting the Demands of the Next Millennium", *Journal of International Arbitration* 15; 5–18.

Mustill, Lord Justice (1988), "The New *Lex Mercatoria*: The First Twenty-Five Years", *Arbitration International* 4; 86–119.

Nader, Laura (1969), "Styles of Court Procedure: To Make the Balance", in L. Nader (ed.), *Law in Culture and Society* (Berkeley, Cal.: University of California).

Neate, Francis W. (1995), "The SBL [Section of Business Law] and the Rule of Law", *International Business Lawyer* 23; 344–5.

Neumann, Franz L. (1996), "The Change in the Function of Law in Modern Society", in W. E. Scheuerman (ed.), *The Rule of Law Under Siege: Selected Essays of Franz L. Neumann and Otto Kirchheimer* (Berkeley, Cal.: University of California).

North, Douglass C., and Weingast, Barry R. (1989), "Constitutions and Commitment: The Evolution of Institutions Governing Public Choice in Seventeenth-Century England", *Journal of Economic History* 49; 803–32.

Picciotto, Sol (1992), *International Business Taxation: A Study in the Internationalization of Business* (London: Weidenfeld & Nicolson).

Pollock, Ellen Joan (1993), "Arbitrator Finds Role Dwindling as Rivals Grow", *Wall Street Journal*, 28 April, B10.

Raz, Joseph (1979), *The Authority of Law. Essays in Law and Morality* (Oxford: Clarendon Press).

Reheis, Fritz (1998), *Die Kreativität der Langsamkeit. Neuer Wohlstand durch Entschleunigung* (Darmstadt: Wissenschaftliche Buchgesellschaft).

Reinecke, Wolfgang H. (1998), *Global Public Policy: Governing without Government?* (Washington, DC: Brookings Institute).

Rovine, Arthur W. (1994), "Fast-Track Arbitration: A Step Away From Judicialization of International Arbitration", in R. B. Lillich and C. N. Brower (eds.), *International Arbitration in the 21st Century: Towards Judicialization and Uniformity?* (Irvington, NY: Transnational Publishers).

Sachs, Jeffrey (1995), "Consolidating Capitalism", *Foreign Affairs* 98; 50–64.

Schauer, Frederick (1988), "Legal Formalism", *Yale Law Journal* 509–48.

Schneider, Michael (1998), "Combining Arbitration with Conciliation", in A. J. van den Berg (ed.), *International Dispute Resolution: Toward an International Arbitration Culture* (The Hague: Kluwer).

Scheuerman, William E. (1999a), "Globalization and Exceptional Powers: The Erosion of Liberal Democracy", *Radical Philosophy* 93; 14–23.

—— (1999b), "Economic Globalization and the Rule of Law", *Constellations* 6; 3–25.

—— (1999c), "Globalization and the Fate of Law", in D. Dyzenhaus (ed.), *Recrafting the Rule of Law* (Oxford: Hart).

—— (2000), "The Economic State of Emergency", *Cardozo Law Review* 21; 1869–94.

Schoenberger, Erica (1994), "Competition, Time, and Space in Industrial Change", in G. Gereffi and M. Korzeniewicz (eds.), *Commodity Chains and Global Capitalism* (Westport, Conn.: Greenwood Press).

Shapiro, Martin (1993), "The Globalization of Law", *Indiana Journal of Global and Legal Studies* 1; 37–64.

Shklar, Judith N. (1986), *Legalism: Law, Morals, and Political Trials* (Cambridge, Mass.: Harvard University Press).

Singer, Linda (1994), *Settling Disputes: Conflict Resolution in Business, Families, and the Legal System* (2nd edn., Boulder, Colo.: Westview).

Smart, Alan (1993), "Gifts, Bribes, and *Guanxi*: A Reconsideration of Bourdieu's Social Capital", *Cultural Anthropology* 8; 388–408.

Teubner, Gunther (ed.) (1997), *Global Law Without a State* (Aldershot: Dartmouth).

van den Berg, Albert Jan (ed.) (1998), *International Dispute Resolution: Towards an International Arbitration Culture* (The Hague: Kluwer).

Urry, John (1996), "The Sociology of Time and Space" in B. S. Turner (ed.), *The Blackwell Companion to Social Theory* (Oxford: Blackwell).

Virilio, Paul (1986), *Speed and Politics* (New York: Semiotext).

Weber, Max (1978), *Economy and Society* (trans. Gunther Roth and Claus Wittich, Berkeley, Cal.: University of California).

Wiegand, Wolfgang (1991), "The Reception of American Law in Europe", *American Journal of Comparative Law* 39; 229–48.

Zürn, Michael (1998), *Regieren jenseits des Nationalstaates* (Frankfurt: Suhrkamp).

4

Traditional Private and Commercial Law Rules under the Pressure of Global Transactions: The Role for an International Order

DIETER MARTINY*

Abstract

Business transactions involving different countries and foreign markets are more common than ever. In these cases different legal rules of international and national origin apply; a variety of legal infrastructures, techniques, habits and customs have to be taken into account. The range of ambiguities and uncertainty is greater than for comparable domestic transactions. Legal diversity is generally an obstacle to international trade, for example, the diversity of sales law for import and export. The parties face higher cost in getting legal services and conducting court or arbitration proceedings. Certainty and legal security are, if available at all, not easy to achieve. A legal approach can be used to try to find the best solution within the framework of the existing rules and make an effort to develop more appropriate rules. There is, however, a great diversity of situations in which legal regimes are mobilised in practice. The strategies of private parties differ according to the kind of transaction, the market situation, the level and the stage of their commercial activities.

In some transactions the parties share a common background so that legal and cultural differences do not make much difference. However, in most cases there is not such a close network of relations; they also have to rely on legal rules or at least trade customs and standard forms. In the field of international trade law, there are many efforts to develop guidelines and rules, which are more appropriate to international situations than national law. Governmental and private organisations develop model contracts and forms, which are widely used. However, the existing international structures often seem to be in appropriate. Adaptation and modernisation are time-consuming; international conventions are subject to the process of ratification, which is a very slow one.

* The author is grateful to Thomas Crofts, Sabine Hoffmann and Ulrich Thoelke for their assistance in preparing this chapter.

Therefore more flexible "general principles" of contract law are used increasingly.

Nevertheless, the sovereignty of the nation-state, national diversity of contract law and the territoriality of public law are still important factors. To a certain extent the parties still find answers in their national legal order and court or arbitration systems. Many states also adapt their domestic rules under the pressure of investors and international competition.

There are efforts to reduce the complexity of national conflict rules by unification. The goal of unification is, however, often not achieved due to the rarity of uniform conflicts rules and the different ratification success of international instruments. Uniform rules on international civil procedure are often complicated and, due to their limited sphere of application, of limited success. On the other had in some fields such as international sale of goods, uniform substantive rules exist which are applied on all continents. At least for smaller sales contracts uniform laws as the Convention on the International Sale of Goods seem to be helpful.

In fields where no uniform rules exist, the parties make efforts to remove this uncertainty and to avoid risks by recourse to such devices as choice of law clauses, jurisdiction and arbitration clauses. Their efforts to find solutions for disputes outside the traditional legal approach will often be unsuccessful. The legal approach is therefore often, despite its shortages, the only alternative.

O NE OF THE approaches that provides insight into international business practices is the so-called "legal approach". This approach emphasises the importance of international conventions that unify laws and create normative expectations that transcend borders (for example, through conventions governing international contracts, international transport law and law regulating cross-border litigation), the emergence of special jurisdictions for international cases and, in general, the creation of a global legal system based on rational-legal premises. However, legislative measures and law enforcement are only one aspect of the picture and it is not easy to isolate their influence from other means. Presumably, not many lawyers concerned with international trade law today will be so naïve as to believe in the mere force of international legal norms alone. Nevertheless, there are considerable activities in national and international legislation; therefore it is interesting to ask on what assumptions these are built and what kind of results are to be expected.

It is obvious that at the beginning of the twenty-first century many interesting developments in international trade and communication are going on. However, it is difficult to get to the core of the matter and to analyse to what extent new developments are in support of the legal approach. There seem to be few empirical studies dealing with the application of international conventions, uniform laws and other instruments in international trade and in court practice.[1] A lack of sufficient data means that it is difficult to make an assessment of the current practice and the attitudes of the parties and lawyers.[2] Therefore, a lot of empirical work is still to be done. It seems premature to make too many generalisations; for almost every example in a certain area of law, there can be found a counter-example seemingly proving the opposite. One reason for this is that the problems can be regarded on different levels and from different perspectives: in respect of international and supranational organisations, the nation-state, lawyers or the parties themselves. Each of these aspects is worth a detailed analysis of its own. However, here mainly the perspective of the international transaction and its performance is chosen. This can obviously only be the starting point because generally transactions of this kind are not simple contractual relations which can be isolated easily. Instead they have contacts with different markets and states, concern different contract partners and contents, use specific legal techniques, are often carried out at special places by specifically trained persons and contain other additional elements. Even a simple import of electronic consumer goods from East Asia to Europe or to the United States involves questions of sale of goods law, contracts of carriage, financing, security interests and insurance in different legal relationships (cf. von Ziegler, 2000). Therefore it is necessary to explore in detail the different fields, to look at the mechanisms and how they can be explained.

"THE LEGAL APPROACH"

In General

Legal certainty as a goal can—according to Gessner (1998)—be measured in various ways. In a vertical sense it concerns interactions between state institutions and citizens, whereas legal certainty in a horizontal sense has to do with relations between citizens themselves. To a certain degree the parties can themselves create the necessary degree of legal certainty, for example, by making contracts. The social institutions providing stable action patterns in legally relevant situations are the effects of rules, the activity of courts, legal professions and the existence of support structures. In a broad sense, this means that the rule of law is followed and that the expectations arising out of contractual promises are met.

It must, however, be stated at the outset that there seems to be no single legal approach. What legislators and single lawyers do, know and intend seems to be different in different societies and even within a single society. There are various

---

[1] But see von Freyhold (1996); Gessner (1996); Olgiati (1996).

[2] According to von Freyhold, Gessner and Olgiati (1996), some 100,000 to 200,000 international cases are filed annually in civil first instance courts in the Member States of the European Union. The International Chamber of Commerce reported in 1993 about 350 international cases, and the American Arbitration Association in 1991 about 300 cases. See Dezalay and Garth (1996: 7 n. 4).

actors involved in international transactions; one has to deal with different actors on different levels, with various legal sources, not to mention the social environment in which legal activities take place. Thus a legal approach is understood here in a broad sense as the use of mainly legal norms and techniques. The classical means in international relations are international treaties between states, activities of international agencies, national laws and contracts between private parties. All of them play a role for international transactions.

The Instruments

International Conventions

The different legal instruments and techniques fulfil specific purposes. International treaties and conventions have some advantages, especially the fact that they have a binding force according to international law. After ratification they should be implemented by the authorities and the courts of the Member States. Thus, a convention has a greater binding force than a simple contract between individual parties. There is a chance that the solution of the convention (for example, in respect of the validity of an agreement or of a liability clause) can be enforced in many states despite the fact that within the Member States there are different social and legal backgrounds. The knowledge of a convention may be greater than that of a special arrangement. A convention has to be published; there are handbooks, articles, court decisions that explain the rules of a convention. However, some treaties are successful whereas others are not.

National Law

The second category of legal regulations is national laws and especially national statutes. These are the product of a national legal order and—at least in continental Europe—still the most important legal source. For most legal questions, even today, there exists only national statute and case law. This is the basis for the activities of national administrative bodies and courts. Parties that are weak and are not able to develop or to enforce an individual solution for their problems can expect at least some protection of their interests. Rules of this kind are of a general nature and are legally binding. Nevertheless the respective national statutes often simply do not fit with international cases. They do not take in account a different social and economic background (for example, the relation between the rate of inflation and the interest rate for breach of contract) and are not flexible enough. Despite all efforts for uniformity and many convergence trends there is still a great legal diversity between national laws.

Other Rules

In addition to these different international and national sources of law, there is a wide range of unofficial uniform rules (cf. De Ly, 1998). They are not designed to have legislative force and take the form of standard forms or customs introduced by official bodies or by the parties themselves. Especially here, solutions reflecting the necessities of international trade are widespread. The application of these rules generally depends on an agreement of the parties or the discretion of arbitrators. Arbitration is not only another method of conflict resolution. Starting arbitration proceedings generally means that different rules can be applied. In other words, the world of international arbitration seems to be different from the daily routine of the state courts.

In principle, among the different legal norms and instruments there is a hierarchy with international law on the top. The formal organisation of international relations today reflects in many respects the concept of the nation–state of the nineteenth century. According to such a state-centred approach each state is, at least in theory, a sovereign state with its own laws and jurisdiction. International relations are a question of communication and transactions between different national systems. The states get in contact by means of their national agencies and by negotiating international treaties. The resulting conventions then have to be implemented. In practice, however, there is no clear distinction between these sources of law. There is a mixture between the rules of different origin in different fields of activity. In these fields several actors appear.

Fields of Activity

Although there is a danger of oversimplification, one can distinguish between three different fields of legislative and judicial activity: activities in private international law, classical approaches in substantive uniform law and approaches in international civil procedure.

Activities in Private International Law

Private international law settles, with the help of conflict of law rules, the question of which national law is to be applied. Rules of this kind nationalise international cases in so far as they generally declare the law of one country applicable. This law can be a domestic law or a foreign one. The oldest approaches in the era of the nation–state were mainly approaches in private international law. There are many differences in detail. However, the basic assumptions are that these rules are known, that they can be handled by the courts and that they can lead to some kind of co-ordination. At the level of the parties, it is assumed that they themselves are able to cope with this system. Each party is generally interested in the application of a law he is accustomed with.

There are, however, difficulties in the choice of law process that can occur on all levels. Since the national conflict rules diverge, it is often not clear which domestic law will apply in the end. The courts have difficulties with the application of foreign law and there seems to be a strong homeward trend (Gessner, 1996: 178ff., 204ff.). For the parties and the authorities the system of the international conventions is often obscure. And there are doubts whether national legislation is really able to develop appropriate rules that give answers to the needs of international trade. Therefore, today it is generally admitted that this system has its deficits (Koch, 1995). One answer to this is the development of uniform conflict rules, the other is the creation of uniform substantive rules. Uniform conflict rules were already developed at the end of the nineteenth century by means of international conventions. Today they are created also by international organisations such as the European Union (EU).

Activities in Uniform Law

At the end of the nineteenth century, approaches in substantive uniform law were also developed (see David, 1971). Substantive rules were developed, mainly in fields where transborder transactions frequently occurred, especially in intellectual property and transport law. The common method was the preparation of international treaties. Today there exist a lot of these conventions on an international level.

Especially within the European Union, many other efforts for unification or at least harmonisation of law were made. There is, however, a constant debate in respect of the needs and the arguments for a harmonisation of law. Only the main arguments can be outlined here (see in more detail Lebron, 1996). One purpose is the creation of an "interface" for international transactions between different legal orders. This is especially the case if the uniform rules are restricted to international cases between two jurisdictions with different rules. Another purpose is uniform reactions in respect of the regulations in other jurisdictions ("externalities"). The non-efficiency of a unilateral rule ("leakage" in relation to protective measures) plays an important role. Especially within the European Union, the promotion of fair competition is always an important argument. A relatively high common standard can prevent the imminent danger of a "race to the bottom". Since using different national rules for every market can be costly, economies of scale are also a factor. Finally, creating common rules and standards instead of differing national regulations can promote transparency.

International Civil Procedure

A field of its own is international civil procedure. Here it is especially difficult to co-ordinate national efforts. Voluntary agreements of the parties alone are not be sufficient. There must be a probability that they can also be enforced. The use of the power of the state makes it necessary to have a formal legal basis for court activities. Classical approaches in international civil procedure mainly concentrate on questions of judicial jurisdiction, mutual assistance in civil matters, recognition and enforcement of foreign judgments, and so on. Without a formal recognition of a foreign judgment, new domestic proceedings would be necessary.

Institutional Framework

As I have said, the various legal sources, instruments and techniques can only be distinguished only in theory. The implementation of the various norms and the actual behaviour of the legal staff is always important. For instance, a lack of information is a problem for ministries, other administrative bodies, courts, attorneys and the parties. Whether there is an international convention, a uniform EU regulation or a national statute to be applied sometimes is less important. It is already difficult enough to deal with cases that are apparently "different" from many domestic cases. A major obstacle seems to be that the domestic courts are national institutions that have difficulties in coping with the complexities and uncertainties of the international legal arena (cf. von Freyhold, Gessner and Olgiati, 1996). Therefore, a better implementation, and more training and flexibility are demanded almost universally in respect to international cases. In this chapter, I show that the legal approach is, despite its deficiencies, widely used. It is not easy, however, to identify the fields where this approach has success compared to other approaches.

RISE OF GLOBAL TRANSACTIONS

Originally, transnational contacts occurred in relatively few cases. Today, with the growth of international trade they have become more and more frequent. Modern forms of transport and of telecommunication make the world smaller. Individuals and corporations interact with relative ease across borders. Transnational migration movements affect many states. At least in some respects, one can observe the emergence of a world society not confined by national borders.

"Global transaction" as such is not a term with a clear meaning. A transaction concerning the whole world at the same time will be rare even today. However, activities, especially of multinational corporations, with effects in several countries or on several continents occur; for instance, the activities of a US enterprise can have effects in Asia, or the activities of an Asian enterprise in Europe. In such business transactions involving different countries and foreign markets, different legal rules of international and national origin apply; a variety of legal infrastructures, techniques, habits and customs have to be taken into account. Transactions with transnational contacts are more common in smaller countries (for example, Luxembourg, Switzerland); due to the smaller size of the market, contacts will more often have international aspects. At least in some respects, these jurisdictions are thus more open-minded than others.

One result of the increase of international cases is a growing need for the co-ordination and standardisation that has been felt by national and international actors. An increasing number of international conventions appear in multilateral treaties. A bilateral treaty dealing with civil or commercial law-related activities is becoming more and more of an exception. For this kind of development, the term internationalisation seems to be appropriate; one has to do with the co-operative activities of national actors (Walker and Fox, 1996). I prefer to distinguish between internationalisation and globalisation.

There are many definitions of globalisation and the impact of globalisation on law is far from clear (cf. Röhl and Magen, 1996; McGrew, 1998). However, globalisation should only be used to describe a process of denationalisation. Here the distinction of foreign and domestic becomes blurred; national boundaries become irrelevant (Walker and Fox, 1996). This tendency has effects on domestic rules; many former barriers have been removed (for example, foreign exchange rules). On the other hand, there is a rise in the creation of norms of international origin. For the parties this means that in some respects there are fewer norms to be followed than before. In others there are more, but of international origin.

Globalisation often means also that economic efficiency should be improved (Alston, 1997: 442ff.). By liberalisation and deregulation, the mechanisms of market economy should be strengthened and the interventionist influence of the states in at least some respects should be reduced. This also means that the field for private transactions becomes greater.

Regionalisation means that several countries form regions with a certain common structure. Especially in recent years, states have tried to establish bigger markets and to remove some of the former barriers. Examples are the activities of the European Union,[3] the North American Free Trade Agreement (NAFTA)[4] and also the recent project of a Common Market between Argentina, Brazil, Paraguay and Uruguay (MERCOSUR).[5] Within these geographical borders, the economies become more or less integrated and common legal norms are created. Within the region there is a greater degree of freedom for transactions; a nation-centred attitude has to be overcome. The economic areas extend transnationally, borders become less significant and contact with foreign systems grows. This is especially true for the so-called internal market of the European Union. Very important in this context is the application of the

---

[3] Treaty Establishing the European Community (EC Treaty), consolidated version (1998) 37 ILM. 79.
[4] North American Free Trade Agreement, 17 December 1993 (1993) 289 ILM 605. Cf. Garro (1998).
[5] The Common Market Between Argentina, Brazil, Paraguay and Uruguay, Treaty of Asunción of 26 March 1991 (1991) 30 ILM 1041.

principle of non-discrimination,[6] the realisation of a better market access, the removal of impediments and the harmonisation of rules (Cottier, 1997). Therefore in some respects the effects of globalisation and regionalisation are the same (cf. Oppermann, 1998). However, if the regional organisation creates new barriers in respect of the area outside, new obstacles will be created. This is sometimes the situation between the European Union and the USA.

The transformation that is taking place in the former socialist states also affects international trade. The former system of planned economy, trade monopolies and obligatory state arbitration has been overcome. Reforms in the field of international business law in these countries are also enabling them to take part in international developments.

TYPES OF GLOBAL TRANSACTIONS

Different Types of Transactions

Statements on global transactions always run the risk that they either are simple truisms or are too broad and therefore questionable. Therefore, it is useful to identify the special problems of these transactions and then to distinguish between different types of transactions. The first question in respect of the suitability of the legal approach is what makes a global transaction different from a domestic transaction? The answer is that it is different with regard to several factors: the expectations of the parties, technical difficulties, the legal and social environment, etc. Many factors, such as the language, economic environment, social habits may be different. The range of ambiguities and uncertainty is greater than for comparable domestic transactions (Schmidtchen, 1995). It is often difficult to ascertain which law applies and what is the exact content of legal obligations and norms (cf. Petzold, 1998). Due to national disparities, it is also more difficult to enforce claims. Therefore, special knowledge and experience are needed for the parties themselves, the lawyers, courts and administrative agencies. As a result, transaction costs are rising. As I show in this chapter, there are different reactions to this problem.

It would be a futile enterprise to try to develop a sort of a worldwide formula to explain all types of global transactions. The areas of interaction are numerous and there are quite different types of international transactions. However, some types of transactions and some of the mechanisms that have influence are commonly known. Investments, sale of goods, distribution of service, formation of an enterprise are some examples of transactions. However, a contract is the most common legal method of acting in international trade. The law affects, at least in theory, all stages of contractual relations beginning with advertising and negotiation, contract drafting, performance or non-performance, disputes, proceedings and sanctions. Each stage has its own difficulties.

---

[6] See Art. 12 (formerly Art. 6) EC Treaty.

In international transactions, there is a different degree of distance between the parties. In some kinds of transactions the two parties have their places of business in different jurisdictions, each strongly related to a national environment, whereas in others, the transactions actually take place in a third country, for example, for construction work in the third world. In these cases, a special arrangement between the parties will be easier to achieve than in a simple transborder transaction.

Transactions often take place within the framework of a national system of the same multinational corporation. One may suppose that different expectations can be resolved simply within the same corporation. However, there can be conflicting national mandatory rules[7] and it may not be easy to reconcile the interests of the multinational group as a whole with the individual interest of each affiliated corporation.

Transnational employment concerns millions of foreign workers. But only a relatively small minority of leading employees and officials of international organisations are subject to a really international regime. There is often a division between international managers working in a foreign country and the local labour force. The local labour force as such has no international ties. Also, in the case of migration, most immigrants simply enter a foreign labour market and are subject to the national rules on this market. Due to choice of law clauses and due to national conflict rules, these labour relations follow the rules of the market (cf. Kronke, 1980). The international dimension as such is widely ignored. Mainly questions of non-discrimination of foreigners remain on the level of national law. New conflicts and tensions arise in transnational labour relations in respect of the posting of workers to foreign countries. Here the working conditions based on more liberal rules of the sending state are often in conflict with the mandatory local law and the labour conditions of the foreign working place. A similar situation exists for the majority of consumers. They are faced with foreign goods and services only in their domestic market. Real international consumer transactions still occur only relatively rarely. If there are international consumer contracts the application of the domestic rules of the consumer is expected.

Specialised Markets

It seems necessary to draw a distinction between different kinds of markets. In international trade different business branches are affected, for instance, import and export of goods, transportation, communication and financial services. Each branch has its own specific rules. Uniform rules have been developed above all for activities that are transnational by nature, such as air or

---

[7] For instance, under German private international law, the law of the seat of the corporation is decisive, not the law of incorporation.

road transport. In Europe, for instance, there is a Convention on the International Carriage of Goods by Road (cmr)[8] that deals with road transport and is also widely applied by national courts. It is supplemented by national standard forms.

In many highly specialised markets, there seems to exist a common background of the parties so that legal and cultural differences do not make much difference (for example, in maritime law). Here a unification based on private preparatory work and the activities of non-governmental international organisations seems to be successful. The aim to find pragmatic solutions is not so endangered by national rivalry and prestige as in governmental negotiations (cf. von Ziegler, 2000: 875 ff.). For European cross-border transactions, the banks have created their own institutional network with their own rules. State law is almost completely excluded. There is a network of inter-bank agreements and procedures to which bank customers have to submit. Conflicts are generally solved by negotiation within this system. Only recently has the EU Commission tried to strengthen the rights of consumers (Frick, 1998). In other fields there are small homogeneous groups, diamond traders for instance, where there is effective social control. In these cases, legal norms seemingly do not play any role at all. Here the specialisation of the market, a long family tradition and common religious beliefs seem to guarantee a sufficient degree of stability (Bernstein, 1992; Gessner, 1998: 437ff.). This, however, is not the typical situation today in European external trade. Many firms get in contact with their foreign counterparts without such an informal network and a common background. Especially for these actors in more anonymous relations in international trade, international conventions, legal rules and court proceedings are a kind of safety net.

Subject Matter of the Transaction

The subject matter of the transaction also seems to play a role. Commercial contracts are law-related to differing degrees. If the product itself is defined by law, as in banking contracts and insurance contracts, there is often a greater readiness of the parties to accept national law, at least in the relationship between enterprise and customer. However, these national rules also are widely influenced or changed by customs or usages developed in international trade. The sector of financial services especially is shaped by transnational rules that are mostly the result of self-regulation (cf. De Ly, 1998: 61ff.).

In other fields, the activities as such are only in one stage predominantly transnational. Direct investment, for example, by means of setting up of a company or the acquisition of a foreign company, often means that the consequent business activities in the foreign market simply follow this law. Despite the

---

[8] Convention on the Contract for the International Carriage of Goods by Road (CMR) of 19 May 1956.

engagement of foreign capital employees, tenants or consumers have seemingly only to do with domestic practices. There can be a change if for instance managers try to introduce foreign labour practices. Then the domestic system has to decide whether its own familiar rules will be changed or whether the foreign techniques, for instance free hiring and firing, will be prevented.

The bigger the economic value involved in a contract, the more specific the contract tends to be. When important matters are at stake it is worth seeking legal advice, to go into great detail and to develop a specific solution if necessary. For example, for the construction of the Eurotunnel between France and the United Kingdom, a special contract was drafted that dealt in detail with the eventualities and provided for the simultaneous application of French and English law (Neate, 1996).

Long-term or Short-term Contracts

The drafting of international contracts is also different depending on whether one has to do with long-term or short-term contracts. Long-term contracts involve investments or long-term relations of the parties such as distribution contracts, whereas short-time relations of the parties are contracts such as single sales contracts. In a long-term transaction, there is often a greater awareness of the problems that could arise because of the long-term commitment and the risk of changes. More knowledge, more mutual trust and more individual solutions are typical results. Often there is a carefully drafted contract. In short-term contractual relations, there is often no individually drafted contract. At least in Germany, standard forms are widely used. For these relationships, international conventions with uniform rules seem to be helpful because they provide at least in part a set of rules.

Contracts with State Participation

Contracts with state participation is a special category. There are many international contracts, where the state or a state entity is a party to the contract. In these cases the contracts are often regarded as involving public law or international public law. Then the state influence is often strong enough to enforce the application of its own law at least in the state courts. Therefore, in bigger investment contracts or in contracts dealing with the exploitation of raw materials, the foreign private party may suspect that the state—which is contract partner and legislator at the same time—could change the rules of the game afterwards. Therefore, there is a strong tendency towards stabilisation clauses, to apply rules of international law and to agree on international institutional or *ad hoc* arbitration; the application of a national law and the jurisdiction of national courts are thus avoided. There are conventions like the Convention on the Settlement of Investment Disputes[9] that recognise this trend and provide arbitration. Of course, even in this kind of business several different types of contracts and clauses are common and are used with variations. So under the CSID, the law of the host state also has to be applied (Article 42).

THE CHANGING ROLE OF THE NATION–STATE

Sovereignty of the Nation–State, National Diversity

Another aspect that needs discussion is the changing role of the nation–state. The sovereignty of the nation–state and the territoriality of its public law are still important factors. States in general try to promote wealth, secure economic success, protect their national interests and industries and enforce their mandatory rules. National diversity of contract law means that these rules must be taken into account, at least if they are of a mandatory nature. Mandatory law (those legal rules that are not subject to contrary agreement by the parties) is one major area of concern in international trade. In some respects, there is a tendency to reduce the effects of these provisions.[10] In other fields these national rules are given extraterritorial effect and are also enforced abroad. This is especially true for international cartel law (price-fixing, abuse of dominant positions, merger control) and embargoes (cf. Basedow, 1984; Stern, 1997).

Today the role of the state is contested. There are changes in respect of the areas of private and state activities; the existence of global markets means a loss of national control. There are some indications that the role of the nation–state is declining (cf. Oppermann, 1998: 40ff.). But due to some contradictory developments, there is no uniform view on the influence of the state at present and in the future (Alston, 1997: 443ff.). One reason for this is that there is no fixed set of given state activities and it is difficult to decide where only an adaptation is taking place. Several tendencies seem to exist here.

In some fields there is a real liberalisation, a reduction of state control. To encourage the flow of capital and to facilitate transborder transactions, there has been a decline of exchange controls and other trade restrictions. Due to deregulation in the telecommunications, transport, insurance and banking sectors today, there are more international transactions and acquisition deals than ever. In other areas of international trade law it is no longer rules of national, but of international or European, origin which have to be applied. This seems to be the result of internationalisation and regionalisation. In many fields there are attempts to establish international controls instead of national regulations,

---

[9] (Washington) Convention on the Settlement of Investment Disputes between States and Nationals of other States, 18 March 1965, 475 UNTS 195. According to Blaurock (1998), more than 20 procedures have been submitted to the ICSID.

[10] E.g., the new German rules on commodity exchange (s. 61 *Börsengesetz* of 11 July 1989), [1989] I BGBl. 1412.

for example by the Washington Convention on International Trade in Endangered Species of Wild Fauna and Flora.[11] The establishment of an international control mechanism in respect of the delocalisation of capital markets is an open question. All these developments, however, should not distract from the fact that modern states are still making considerable efforts to cope with these problems and that private parties in the case of conflicts can find at least some kind of support in the domestic courts and legal systems.

Adaptation of Domestic Rules

Today it is widely accepted that legal rules formulated solely in terms of national entities, without taking into account transnational and global developments, will be ineffective or even counter-productive. Many states adapt their domestic rules under the pressure of investors and international competition. For instance, Germany (as many other states) has not only restructured its telecommunication sector, but also reformed other areas of law such as its national rules on arbitration, to bring them into correspondence with the UNCITRAL Model Law on Arbitration.[12] Traditional fields of protection such as consumer law, labour law, social standards and environmental protection often come under pressure from bigger markets (for example, social dumping); the problem of a globalisation of protection thus becomes more and more acute. One example of this is rules introducing a so-called second or "international" register for ships. The purpose of these registers is to combat the trend to flags of convenience by offering a lower standard in maritime labour conditions also under domestic law (see Basedow, 1990). Another example is states in the close neighbourhood of a strong regional organisation which are indirectly forced to adapt their national rules. There is, for instance, a certain Europeanisation of Swiss law even if Switzerland is not a member of the European Union (cf. Alston, 1997; Cottier, 1997).

The Contribution of International Organisations

Today there is a considerable contribution of many international organisations.[13] Some of them are sub-organisations of the United Nations, while others are created separately by an international treaty. International trade has been developed within the framework of international trade law, for example, the rules of the Geneva-based World Trade Organisation of 1994 (WTO).[14] The

---

[11] Convention on International Trade in Endangered Species of Wild Fauna and Flora, 3 March 1973 (1973) 12 ILM 1085.

[12] See s. 1025 *et seq*. German Code of Civil Procedure (1998) 37 ILM 790.

[13] See the list of the Max Planck Institute for foreign and international public law (Heidelberg), at <http://www.mpiv-hd.mpg.de/de/link/IntOrg.cfm>.

[14] See the official website of the WTO, at <http://www.wto.org/>.

work of the former GATT[15] and of the WTO has had in many areas the effect of a removal of barriers. It is true that a rising number of conventions have to be taken in account in international trade law (Cottier, 1997: 227ff.). However, these international conventions often are not self-executing; they are not themselves the basis for the activities of the parties and do not affect them directly.[16] Nevertheless, there are increasing areas of law where individual conduct of the parties is now the subject of international regulations (Weeramantry, 1998). Examples are the work of the United Nations Commission on International Trade Law (UNCITRAL) created in 1966[17] and the International Institute for the Unification of Private Law (UNIDROIT) set up in 1926,[18] an intergovernmental organisation. In international transactions many uniform printed forms are used; international sales of goods, contracts of carriage, factoring and leasing contracts follow to a large extent uniform rules.

We should not forget that these organisations can only to a certain degree act autonomously. They remain under the control of the member states, so that their activities are an expression of the growing internationalisation but not necessarily of a reduction of the functions of the nation–state. However, as bureaucratic organisations, international agencies do not always act effectively. Sometimes they mainly try to justify and secure their own existence. In some cases there is even a rivalry between the agencies and they draft rules for the same complex.[19]

Today there are also many international non-governmental organisations. Often they concentrate on the interests of certain professions and business branches (cf. Schoener, 1997). To a certain extent these organisations also prepare model laws, guidelines and rules that are more appropriate to international situations than national law. Especially the ICC in Paris developed many model contracts and standard forms of contract that are widely used in international trade.[20] In some branches, like the construction industry for international construction work, there exist other model contracts and widely-used standard forms.[21] It was accepted from the very beginning of systematic unification of law that this kind of self-regulation has to play a central role in international

---

[15] General Agreement on Tariffs and Trade, 30 October 1947, UNTS 55, 187. Cf. van Houtte (1995: 51ff.).

[16] There are three types of laws to be distinguished: laws relating to economic transactions (private law), laws regulating to such transactions in order to implement national economic policies and laws relating to the underlying order of the world economy (public international law). Cf. Behrens (1986).

[17] See the official website at <http://www.un.or.at/uncitral/>. Cf. van Houtte (1995: 42ff.).

[18] See the official website at <http://www.unidroit.org/>. Cf. van Houtte (1995: 45); Kronke (2000).

[19] E.g. in the field of products liability, see on the one hand the European Convention on Products Liability in Regard to Personal Injury and Death (1977) of the Council of Europe, and on the other hand the EC Products Liability Directive (1985). For criticism of the law-making process see Stephan (1999).

[20] See the official website at <http://www.iccwbo.org/>.

[21] Cf. Fédération Internationale des Ingénieurs-Conseils, Conditions of Contract (International) for Works of Civil Engineering Construction (FIDIC).

trade, especially in the areas of law where there are no mandatory rules. On the other hand, self-regulation would not be so effective without a set of basic rules laid down in international conventions.

In regional organisations such as the EU, there is a great interest in common stable rules. One major effect of EU law is the removal of national barriers. For instance, exchange controls and customs duty have been removed within the European Union. The freedom of establishment in other countries of the EU has given access to foreign markets; the free flow of capital across the national borders has been guaranteed.[22] This was a condition for the development of free trade within the community. However, much legislation still is necessary to remove the remaining restrictions.

In some fields there are uniform rules of community origin. These rules should give similar conditions for competition within the European market. One legal technique for the creation of uniform rules is treaties between the Member States of the European Union.[23] Another is regulations that are directly applicable. Especially in commercial and consumer law, there are numerous directives of the community which have no direct effect but must be transformed and implemented into domestic law.[24] However, even after such an approximation of laws, considerable differences among the respective laws of the Member States remain. With respect to countries outside the European Union, many protectionist trade restrictions remained and others were introduced. Also, in private international law discrimination persists. For example, the basis for extraordinary jurisdiction of the courts still exists.[25] In many fields of economic activity, new restrictions on a European level were introduced following the removal of national restrictions.

INTERNATIONALISATION AND UNIFORMITY

Choice of Law Rules

After a look at the different kinds of transactions, the main instruments and actors in this field, we must discuss how the growing internationalisation and globalisation are changing the traditional system. In most fields of law even today, different national rules of law are in force. If one does not want to apply only domestic law (the *lex fori*), then the courts need a legal basis for their deviation from their established rules in domestic cases.

In the law of contracts, party autonomy is the equivalent of the freedom of contract on the national level: "the best judges of the interests of the parties are the parties themselves" (Nygh, 1995: 294). With the help of a choice of law

---

[22] See Art. 56 ff. (formerly Art. 73b ff.) EC Treaty.
[23] See Art. 293 (formerly Art. 220) EC Treaty.
[24] See Art. 249 (formerly Art. 189) EC Treaty.
[25] See Art. 4(2) Brussels and Lugano Conventions.

clause, the parties can agree on which law shall apply. Thus, a party can successfully ensure that its own domestic law shall be applicable, for example, English or New York law. It is also possible that the parties make a compromise and stipulate that a "neutral" law (for example, Swiss law in an Egyptian–English contract) shall apply. If with a forum selection or an arbitration clause it is also secured that possible legal proceedings will follow familiar rules, then the risk of unpleasant surprises for the party is reduced. There are efforts to reduce the complexity of national conflict rules by unification, for example, by multilateral Hague conventions or EU conflict rules (Knöfel, 1998). However, the Hague Conference on Private International Law is only occasionally involved in the creation of international conventions in the field of international trade. Most influential are the European and UNCITRAL conventions. Such a treaty is the European (Rome) Convention on the Law Applicable to Contractual Obligations of 1980[26] dealing with international contracts and in force since 1991. A new Convention on the Law Applicable to Extra-contractual Obligations (Rome II) is on the agenda (Jayme, 1998).

However, the ideals of uniform private international law—a distribution of legal questions to different national laws and the prevention of "forum shopping"—are often not achieved. Even unified rules leave the possibility open of enforcing domestic mandatory rules.[27] Moreover, the effect of conflict rules is a very modest one. They are nothing more than tools to bridge the gap between the different systems and they are difficult to apply (cf. Koch, 1995; Gessner, 1998). Only a small part of the process of adjudication is unified; in all other respects diversity remains.

Uniform Substantive Rules

As already mentioned in some fields uniform substantive rules deal with the subject matter itself. In Germany for instance, more than 50 such conventions in commercial law are in force and numerous others are expected to be ratified in the near future (cf. Blaurock, 1998: 15). These conventions often exist in fields where a certain practice has already been established. Sometimes there also are attempts to find a common solution for relatively new phenomena and types of contracts, for example, for leasing and factoring contracts.[28] Such uniform rules are especially to be found in the international sale of goods, as in the Convention on the International Sale of Goods of 1980 (CISG)[29] that is applied on all continents. Member states include not only European states such as Spain or

[26] Convention on the Law Applicable to Contractual Obligations, 19 June 1980, [1980] OJ L266/1 (1980) 19 ILM 1492. See also Juenger (1994, 1997a). For the text see (1994) 34 ILM 732.
[27] See Art. 7(2) Rome Convention of 1980.
[28] Cf. Convention on International Factoring, 28 May 1985 (1988) 27 ILM 943.
[29] United Nations (UNCITRAL) Convention on Contracts for the International Sale of Goods, 11 April 1980 (1980) 19 ILM 671. Cf. Schlechtriem (1998).

Germany, but also the USA, Russia and China. At least within the German export industry, there was a strong opposition to the new law. One reason was that in some respects the results could be more favourable to the buyer. The other, more important, reason seemed to be the ignorance of the new rules and the fear that some unexpected results might occur. Even today, it is not clear how often the rules of the convention are opted out of (cf. Article 6 CISG). However, at least for smaller contracts and for parties only occasionally involved in international trade, such laws seem to be helpful. Model laws of international organisations also are implemented into national law. Another important aspect is that apart from the legislative acts mentioned above, there are rules that result directly from the practice of international trade. The existing uniform laws often expressly recognise the existence of these rules. For example, according to Article 9 CISG, it is presumed that the parties follow the international customs that have been established in international trade. However, until now many academic discussions have remained on a relatively abstract level such as the discussion of the European principles of contract law of the Lando commission of 1995 (Lando, 1992; Lando and Beale, 1995) and the UNIDROIT principles of international commercial contracts of 1994.[30] The creation of these rules which do not fall into one of the traditional categories of legal norms was a response to the "crisis of the unification movement in private law" (Basedow, 2000).

Regional uniform law within in the European Union has already been mentioned. There have been various activities, mainly by directives, to create some uniformity in commercial and consumer law. The impression of the result, however, is according to one expert an "almost chaotic picture" (Drobnig, 1996: 13). Today there is an extended debate on the creation of a European Civil Code on a more systematic basis (Hartkamp *et al.*, 1998; Sonnenberger, 1998; Drobnig, 1999; Martiny, 2000).

In areas of law where uniformity to a certain degree has been achieved, a higher degree of legal certainty and reliability exists also for the parties (Kronke, 2000). However, in general the effect of uniform law should not be over-estimated; duplication of norms and uncertainty are the price to be paid. A uniform interpretation is often not achieved. Uniform interpretation has been established only in some areas of law, as by the European Court of Justice. Uniform law concerns only relatively small areas of law. At the border of these rules, there is always the question whether the rules of uniform law can be extended to situations not regulated. If not, the rules of private international law apply. The critics of uniform law maintain also that the mechanisms of elaboration, ratification, adaptation and modernisation are time-consuming and too slow, that uniform law is too artificial and does not sufficiently take into account different legal cultures (Kötz, 1986; Legrand, 1996, 1997; Markesinis,

---

[30] See UNIDROIT (ed.) 1994, Principles of International Commercial Contracts. See also Berger (1995); Bonell (1995, 1996, and 1997).

1997). Some also argue that there should be more competition between legislators and that methods other than legislation could be more effective (cf. Eger, 1999; Dreher, 1999). Therefore, we realise today that softer measures than legislation can—at least in some respects—be more effective, for instance in the form of restatements of law that at a first stage mainly give an overview over the existing solutions (Berger, 1999: 373ff.). New European research projects have been started, for example, in the law of torts (cf. von Bar, 1996, 1998, 1999, 2000).

We have also realised the necessity of a transnational legal education, including the study of foreign law and of studying abroad as a prerequisite of more uniformity (Clark, 1998: 264ff.). These different approaches are not mutually exclusive but influence each other. For instance, the fact that there is already a considerable amount of uniform European legislation makes it easier for law students to study law abroad. This will again be another stimulus for integration.

Uniform Rules on International Civil Procedure

The rules of international civil procedure are in principle also norms of national origin. However, more and more uniform rules on international civil procedure are in force. The most important European treaty is the Brussels Convention on Jurisdiction and Enforcement of Judgements in Civil and Commercial Matters.[31] The Brussels Convention contains uniform rules on jurisdiction and enforcement of judgments. Its system was extended to the Member States of the European Free Trade Association (EFTA) by a "parallel" convention, the Lugano Convention,[32] which is very similar to the Brussels Convention as amended in 1989. Similar efforts are also made within the framework of MERCOSUR.[33] In western Europe, more than 90 per cent of the applications for the enforcement of a foreign money judgment can be based today on an international convention.[34] And despite some criticism and the fact that these conventions are not applied to such an extent as one might have expected (Gessner, 1997), they are regarded as successful.

There are also several international conventions in the field of international commercial arbitration, such as the UN Convention on International Commercial Arbitration of 1958.[35] This is one of the most successful international treaties, with nearly 120 states participating. Estimates that 90 per cent

---

[31] 27 September 1968; amended version, 26 May 1989 (San Sebastian) [1989] OJ L285/1.

[32] Convention on Jurisdiction and Enforcement of Judgments in Civil and Commercial Matters, 16 September 1988 [1988] OJ L319/9.

[33] Protocol of Buenos Aires on International Jurisdiction in Disputes Relating to Contracts of 5 August 1994 (1997) 36 ILM 1263. Cf. Pabst (1999); Samtleben (1999).

[34] Cf. for Germany Martiny (1984: No. 72).

[35] New York Convention on the Recognition and Enforcement of Foreign Arbitral Awards, 10 June 1958 (1959) 330 UNTS 38.

of all transnational commercial contracts contain an arbitration clause (Streit and Mangels, 1996), seem, however, to be too high. Nevertheless, international arbitration is a widely used alternative to litigation in national courts; it is mostly concentrated in the form of "institutional" arbitration in some central institutions such as the International Chamber of Commerce in Paris, the American Arbitration Association (AAA)[36] and national Chambers of commerce. Arbitral tribunals formed for contested cases and which follow the ICC Rules of Arbitration.[37] have especially been created in the framework of a (private) "Court of Arbitration"[38] of the ICC.[39] They can apply national law but also uniform rules or may develop rules of their own (cf. Blessing, 1997). The applicable rules try to give more flexibility and to reach quicker and easier results than proceedings in national courts (Banakar, 1998). It may well be, however, that some of the alleged advantages (expert decision, speed and low cost) are more myth than reality.[40] Arbitration at a neutral venue is nevertheless a practical solution if each party is unwilling to accept the jurisdiction of the courts of the other. The results of arbitration proceedings seem to be more accepted by the parties than judgments of state courts (cf. Streit and Mangels, 1996). However, there is much litigation concerning the enforcement of arbitral awards. The unsuccessful party often denies the validity of the arbitration agreement, alleges procedural defects and tries to prevent the enforcement of the award. This can lead to new lengthy, costly and unpredictable proceedings.

There are considerable efforts to improve the system of international conventions. A new worldwide Hague Convention on the Recognition and Enforcement of Judgments which will also deal with (direct) jurisdiction is being prepared (von Mehren, 1994; Juenger, 1998; Schack, 1998). Other Hague conventions[41] and European regulations[42] deal with special aspects such as service of process and taking of evidence abroad.[43]

The international rules are generally more adapted to the demands of international transactions and more liberal than the former national provisions. They improve the chances for successful international litigation, especially for recognition and enforcement. The risk for a party that his or her claims cannot be enforced in international cases is reduced. The rules of international

---

[36] See International Arbitration Rules, 1 April 1997.

[37] In force as from 1 January 1998 (1997) 36 ILM 1604.

[38] The court is, in fact, a committee made up of members nominated by the ICC National Committee.

[39] See also the London Court of International Arbitration Rules, 1 January 1998.

[40] See Ulmer (1986: 1335): "[i]nternational commercial arbitration is often complex, frustrating and expensive". Cf. also on advantages and disadvantages of arbitration van Houtte (1995: 410 ff.)

[41] Hague Convention on the service abroad of judicial and extrajudicial documents in civil or commercial matters, 15 November 1965, 658 UNTS 163. In a country like Germany, every year more than 70,000 applications for service are made. More than 50,000 of them concern states within the European Union.

[42] Council Regulation 1348/2000 of 29 May 2000 on the service in the Member States of judicial and extrajudicial documents in civil or commercial matters [2000] OJ L160/37.

[43] Convention on the taking of evidence abroad in civil or commercial matters, 17 March 1970 (1969) 8 ILM 37.

procedure are, however, complicated and, due to their limited sphere of application, of limited success. The basic problem is that, according to the philosophy of these conventions, an international level is often added to the existing national structures. However, lack of skills and experience can already block all efforts on the national level. National central agencies such as so-called transmitting and receiving agencies should be specialised in the field of international civil procedure. This construction sometimes simply does not work, due to inactivity, incapability or bureaucratic behaviour. There seem to be no sufficient incentives for better management. But even if these specialised national agencies communicate effectively with each other, difficulties remain. The procedure is necessarily more time-consuming than in domestic cases, and a party often has to overcome the difficulties of two systems (Budak, 1998: 28ff., 47ff.). Only recently within the European Union has a system with a direct transnational access for service of process been developed.[44] The Brussels Convention itself is under review.[45] However, despite all reforms, the main deficit remains that civil procedure follows the rules of the *lex fori* and that there basically are no common rules for the procedure itself. There are only some proposals for a unification of the European civil procedure systems (Storme, 1994; Juenger, 1997b) and some ideas for uniform rules especially for transnational litigation (see Taruffo, 1997).

Today conciliation and mediation are recommended more and more as an alternative to litigation and arbitration. A conciliator does not take an adjudicative role like an arbitrator; the parties have to agree to settle the dispute. International organisations like UNCITRAL[46] and the ICC[47] have drawn up their own conciliation rules. Whether these proceedings are already widespread is, however, doubtful.

Negative Factors

Together with increasing global market activities, there also seems to be a rise in the activities of multinational criminal gangs, corruptive practices[48] and drug trafficking. These are fields in which the rules of a market economy seem to be ineffective and co-ordinated state intervention is needed (cf. Alston, 1997: 439ff., 442). Money laundering is another field in which tougher international conventions and national rules try to control international transactions. Here, uniformity of protective rules and the creation of international agencies should counterbalance the effects of a liberalisation of trade. Uniformity has a certain

---

[44] See Council Regulation 1348/2000, n. 42 above.

[45] See [1998] OJ C33/3.

[46] UNCITRAL Conciliation Rules 1980. Cf. Carr (1996).

[47] Cf. Art. 1 ICC Rules of Optional Conciliation, 1 January 1998.

[48] See the Convention on Combating Bribery of Foreign Public Officials in International Business Transactions, 17 December 1997; OECD Recommendations, 23 May 1997 (1997) 36 ILM 1016.

chance in fields where the negative effects to be expected and that could be avoided would be so great that all would suffer.

THE STRATEGIES OF PRIVATE PARTIES

Different Parties and Strategies

Different Parties

From the preceding analysis it follows that the strategies of private parties will differ according to the kind of transaction, the market situation, the level and the stage of their commercial activities. It is generally agreed that the parties also in international relations in general will try to maintain business relations without taking legal norms into account (Banakar, 1998: 364ff.). Nevertheless the parties face different sets of rules. Very important is the law where a party has its place of business (cf. Oppermann, 1998). This is the domestic law that generally has the closest connection with the transaction; it can easily be enforced against the party.

The parties have to be aware of the disparities between different national laws already for negotiations, contract drafting and setting up of their business. As already mentioned, the knowledge of these rules, their content and their application may not easily be obtained. The ability to take advantage of globalisation is much greater for a powerful multinational corporation than for a medium-size enterprise (cf. Dezalay, 1990: 283ff.). The first one generally is a "repeat player" in international business, whereas the latter often is only a "one shotter" with little or no experience (cf. Gessner and Budak, 1998: 8). International conventions are often more accessible than unofficial self-regulated rules. It is doubtful, however, whether it makes a fundamental difference for the "one shotter" whether the rules are contained in conventions or in other sources of law. The problems of information and enforcement remain in any case.[49] However, similar techniques of improving their own situation for smaller parties also exist, as in the national context. For instance, there are private organisations dealing with the protection of the interests of German apartment owners in foreign countries[50]; associations of car drivers give advice on the consequences of traffic accidents abroad, and so forth.

Weaker Parties

In cases where the parties create for their relationship their own legal order, contract is the main mechanism. Despite the fact that there is protection in some fields, party autonomy is the corner stone of transnational business activities.[51]

---

[49] Cf. for consumer organisations Koch (1995: 340f.).
[50] E.g., the German–Swiss *"Schutzgemeinschaft für Auslandsgrundbesitz"*.
[51] Cf. Art. 3 Rome Convention 1980.

The attitude to protecting some groups that are considered to be the weaker party by special legislation can also be found on the international level. For instance, in the European rules on international contracts and international civil procedure, there are special provisions for consumer contracts (sales of moveables and certain services) and employment contracts. The reach of choice of law clauses is restricted for these groups. For a consumer under certain circumstances the law of his habitual residence is enforced,[52] for an employee the law of the place where he habitually carries out his work.[53] Rules on jurisdiction try to prevent that these rules are circumvented.[54]

This approach leads inevitably to difficulties because other rules of community law try to establish freedom of services and freedom of establishment.[55] Therefore, there is a constant struggle between the enforcement of protective and mandatory provisions and the normal rules guaranteeing party autonomy. Consumers and workers sometimes get support in the international field by their national organisations. However, the usual collective forms of actions often do not exist on an international level (Lakkis, 1999).

Consumer organisations generally act only at a national level. Only in some fields of trade union activities, as for transport workers, do there exist some forms of collective action. There are also some groups like creditors of maintenance claims—generally women and children—who are considered to be in such a weak position that only by massive state support will they have a chance of enforcing at least a part of their maintenance claims (Grotheer, 1998).

The Involvement of Lawyers

Since legal norms are mostly of national origin and legal services are concentrated on these systems; legal services in international cases are an exception and a special area of activity (cf. Banakar, 1998: 384ff.). As long as there are no difficulties to be expected, legal questions are not of great interest to businessmen. However, there is a growing need for consultation on foreign law and international rules. The information of the parties has to take into account different aspects. Therefore, law firms are more and more forced to have branches in several countries or to collaborate with other law firms in different countries (cf. Dezalay, 1990). Within the European Union the freedom of establishment of foreign lawyers is extended more and more (Foster, 1991; Jost, 1996). The changing body of norms, changing attitudes in business and the need to provide transnational legal service for a wide range of activities also change the profession (cf. Hau, 1999). There is especially a steady growth in the number of great transnational law firms. Within the branches of foreign law firms, there is often

---

[52] Art. 5 Rome Convention.
[53] Art. 6 Rome Convention.
[54] See Arts. 7 ff., 13 ff. Brussels and Lugano Conventions.
[55] See Art. 39 ff. (formerly Art. 48 ff.), Art. 49 ff. (formerly Art. 59 ff.) EC Treaty.

a mixture of lawyers coming from abroad and locally licensed lawyers (Clark, 1998: 264ff., 273ff.).

If a lawyer has been trained under a certain legal system, he or she will be inclined to use the concepts he knows and to apply them also in a foreign environment. Therefore, an investor often tries to import at least some of his or her own legal concepts. One of the tasks of a lawyer is a sort of translation of the foreign demand into the forms of the local law. One example is the influence of US-American techniques in contracts (Wiegand, 1996). If an investor realises that there are obstacles, then he will adapt his attitude and his techniques. A local lawyer—sometimes trained abroad—will examine whether the foreign demand can be satisfied by means of the local law.

The growing internationalisation and globalisation mean that there will be more pressure also on the formation and training of lawyers. However, today the majority of judges and lawyers only know their own domestic rules and practices (Taruffo, 1997: 457ff.; 1998). Another major deficit of the existing legal machinery of international conventions seems to be the lack of effective support structures for cross-border legal interaction (Gessner, 1998: 436ff., 442).

Limitation of Risks

One important goal in international trade is to limit risks. One example is the technique of a letter of credit (documentary credit) (cf. Carr, 1996; August, 1997). In international sales, the goods are in transit and the parties are located in different countries. For the seller there is the risk that the buyer will not pay and it will be difficult for him to obtain the price of the goods immediately; for the buyer there is the risk that he will get goods of poor quality or no goods at all. There are different types of letter of credit to overcome these difficulties. However, the basic technique of exchange is based on the fact that every party has its own bank that is specialised in foreign trade. The buyer is in contact with his bank. This bank, the issuing bank, will open a letter of credit for the seller. The seller in general too has a bank, its seller bank, the advising bank. When the seller ships the goods, he obtains documents and presents them to his bank. The bank will pay as soon as the stipulated documents can be presented and are approved. The buyer only pays to his domestic bank that is in contact with the seller bank.

What is interesting is that the parties can communicate without leaving their own sphere. Each party can use the channels it knows in its own banking system. However, there are uniform guidelines for letters of credit of the ICC which are widely used.[56] These guidelines, developed by an autonomous institution in form of self-regulation, are an instrument to arrange a transnational financial transaction and to overcome legal diversity (cf. von Ziegler, 2000).

[56] Uniform Customs and Practices for Documentary Credits. 1993 Revision, ICC Publication No. 400.

Legal Diversity and International Trade

There are some cases in which legal diversity is really a plus for the parties (or at least for one of them) and in which they take advantage of it. A famous example is the Delaware law of corporations. Delaware is the state of incorporation for nearly half of the top 500 corporations of the United States (cf. Koch, 1995: 339). Its law seems to be particularly suitable for companies. Sometimes also liability rules and security standards are lower abroad, for example, for the production of chemicals or the testing of pharmaceutical products in the developing world (cf. Siehr, 1995). It is also quite common to profit from a cheap labour force and from lower standards in social security in Latin America or Eastern Europe. Other examples are time-sharing contracts with less protection for the seller (cf. Rauscher, 1996) or even the export of dangerous waste into developing countries.

Tax evasion is an area where the parties are looking for contractual arrangements that will result in a reduction of taxes. Major law firms will advise their clients in this regard. This is true not only for tax havens, but also for company law and some other cases of deregulation and liability rules. In this respect, international conventions can introduce common standards and make some kinds of transactions less attractive. These are cases where, as already mentioned, often some arguments exist in favour for a harmonisation.

Legal diversity often seems to be an obstacle to international trade and a factor distorting competition, such as the diversity of sales law for import and export. Private parties make efforts to remove the resulting uncertainty and to avoid risks by recourse to such devices as choice of law clauses, forum selection and arbitration clauses. The choice of law clause tries to secure that a certain national law will apply. By a forum selection clause, a national forum is fixed. An arbitration agreement makes sure that an arbitration tribunal has to decide. This tribunal is often not forced to apply national law in such a strict manner as a national state court. A prominent example is, as already mentioned, arbitration by the ICC.

An internationalisation of contracts with the application of the principles of the new *lex mercatoria*, in combination with international arbitration, gives the parties the possibility to escape national laws (cf. De Ly, 1992; Berger, 1996; Lando, 1985; Mertens, 1997; Banakar, 1998: 374ff.). Such a solution is often used if no party can force the other to accept its laws and arbitrators have to decide. Despite some scepticism, national legislators accept these techniques more and more.[57] Awards of arbitration tribunals that apply these rules are recognised. However, the *lex mercatoria* is far from being a uniform and coherent set of rules. The application of this technique is time-consuming and, in general, only used in arbitration cases of a certain size. Whereas in the past the influence of the *lex mercatoria* was sometimes overestimated, we must

---

[57] Cf. s. 1051 German Code of Civil Procedure; Behrens (1993).

emphasise that today its rules are only tolerated by state law and the courts. Its main weakness remains the dependence on the consensus of the parties and the fragmentary, unsystematic and only partially public nature of its content (cf. also Gessner, 1998: 434ff.).

CONCLUSION

Due to better international communication, transport and the development of international trade, there is a tendency to more transnational transactions than ever. There are trends towards internationalisation, which means an increasing body of international law, and globalisation, which means a certain denationalisation in international transactions. There are tendencies of liberalisation but also signs of protection of national or regional interests and certain parties. Against this background of fragmentary and contradictory rules the commercial transactions take place. Because of the complexity, the parties face higher cost in getting legal services, and in conducting court and arbitration proceedings. Certainty and legal security are, if available at all, not easy to achieve. A legal approach should try to find the best solution within the framework of the existing rules and make an effort to develop more appropriate rules. This is not easy because several dimensions have to be taken into account.

The environment of global transactions consists of a mixture of different rules, international conventions, national legal rules and contracts. An analysis of this patchwork must therefore concentrate on these different levels. However, if one tries to look especially at the legal approach in the sense of treaty-making and unifying law, especially by international conventions and statutes, one can make some general observations.

The international conventions unifying not only choice of law but also substantive law have some advantages. They create more stable rules and their binding force gives a greater security than bare contracts of private parties. Due to their general nature, these rules can play a role in which no individual solutions could be developed. They can help parties that are not able to create a legal framework themselves. Also in the fields of law where mandatory state laws and national values are at stake, international conventions and uniform laws can lead to predictable results. Conventions and uniform rules often are the only method of overcoming national barriers under the condition of reciprocity of the states. International legislation secures a framework within which free trade, party autonomy and arbitration can grow. Even in the fields of law where party autonomy and arbitration dominate, the ultimate basis of enforcement is the power of the judiciary of states. Also, arbitration needs effective support by national and international rules. Therefore, one should not underestimate the necessity of fixed rules and overestimate the value of informal regulations.

The results of international conventions and uniform law often do not have, however, only positive effects. There are conventions like the CISG with an almost universal application. But in general the regional and subject matter scope of conventions is restricted. Uniform law is often neither applied nor interpreted in a uniform manner. Due to its unsystematic nature, uniform law is often not easily applied. The rules remain unknown or at least difficult to apply; the implementation at the level of the individual transaction is difficult. Often international conventions that have been ratified are inflexible.

One response to this is more flexible international "general principles" which must not undergo the process of international negotiations and national ratification but can be applied immediately in the case of dispute settlement. It remains to be seen, however, whether these principles will really lead to better results.

For a foreseeable future national law will still be the most important legal source and the framework for many transactions. It can certainly be assumed that the parties would prefer the application of rules of a real international *lex mercatoria* to inappropriate national norms. Where, however, despite all promises the application of these rules is—apart from already existing laws and standard forms—mainly restricted to single cases with costly arbitral procedures this seems not to be an attractive alternative for average cases.

Other objections must be made against the use of personal relationships and professional skills alone. This approach can generally work only where there are intense networks with personal dependence or in situations where mainly drafting and negotiation are needed. This is, especially in cases where disputes between parties of different countries arise, not the problem. Here the possibility of adjudication and the threat of legal enforcement are necessary even for arbitration and conciliation.

If one dares to use a picture to describe the basis of transnational transactions, the image of a bridge constructed of various materials comes to mind. Within this construction there are elements of different origin, density and quality: national, international and partly private. But they are all used to reach the goal of the commercial transaction. The elements of mutual exchange, trust and common economic purposes are certainly very valuable ingredients for every international transaction. But at least in the case of conflict and also for conflict avoidance the existence of some reliable pillars of legal norms is essential even for arbitration and conciliation.

The use of the legal approach is still inevitable. However, it seems that in the past the making of conventions as such may have been overestimated. Conventions as such are only abstract rules which must be implemented and applied in individual cases. If they do not work satisfactorily businessmen and lawyers look for other means outside the traditional framework of international legislation. Without more efforts of co-ordination, implementation and adaptation to the needs of international transactions, a strengthening of international conventions as such does not seem to be a solution which has much value. Bureaucratic and excessive regulation should be avoided.

We should ask instead whether the existing structures in support of the international legislation are appropriate and effective. There should be more emphasis on the creation of supporting structures and self-regulation. A strengthening of existing legal services, training of lawyers and a better handling of international cases in the courts can be more important than new provisions in the statute book. There are also a considerable number of uniform rules enacted by non-governmental organisations and many legal rules accept the existence of customs. Here also, better co-ordination between the different efforts could be helpful. The reliance on the legal approach should never exclude the use of other approaches.

REFERENCES

Alston, Philip (1997), "The Myopia of the Handmaidens: International Lawyers and Globalization", *European Journal of International Law* 3; 435–48.

August, Ray (1997), *International Business Law* (2nd edn., Upper Saddle River: Prentice Hall).

Banakar, Reza (1998), "Reflexive Legitimacy in International Arbitration" in V. Gessner and A. C. Budak (eds.), *Emerging Legal Certainty—Empirical Studies on the Globalization of Law* (Aldershot: Ashgate).

Bar, Christian von (1996), *Gemeineuropäisches Deliktsrecht* (Munich: Beck), I–II.

—— (1998), *The Common European Law of Torts* (Oxford: Clarendon), I.

—— (2000), *The Common European Law of Torts* (Oxford: Oxford University Press), ii.

Basedow, Jürgen (1984), "Private Law Effects of Foreign Export Controls—An International Case Report", *German Yearbook of International Law* 27; 109–41.

—— (1990), "Billigflaggen, Zweitregister und Kollisionsrecht in der Deutschen Schiffahrtspolitik", *Berichte der Deutschen Gesellschaft für Völkerrecht* 31; 75–120.

—— (2000), "Uniform law Conventions and the UNIDROIT Principles of International Commercial Contracts", *Uniform Law Review NS* 5; 129–139.

Behrens, Peter (1986), "Elemente eines Begriffs des Internationalen Wirtschaftsrechts", *Rabels Zeitschrift für ausländisches und internationales Privatrecht* 50; 483–507.

—— (1993), "Arbitration as an Instrument of Conflict Resolution in International Trade", in D. Friedmann and E.-J. Mestmäcker (eds.), *Conflict Resolution in International Trade* (Baden-Baden: Nomos).

Berger, Klaus Peter (1995), "Die UNIDROIT-Prinzipien für Internationale Handelsverträge—Indiz für ein autonomes Weltwirtschaftsrecht?", *Zeitschrift für vergleichende Rechtswissenschaft* 94; 217–36.

—— (1996), *Formalisierte oder "schleichende" Kodifizierung des transnationalen Wirtschaftsrechts—zu den methodischen und praktischen Grundlagen der lex mercatoria* (Berlin: de Gruyter).

—— (1999), "Einheitliche Rechtsstrukturen durch außergesetzliche Rechtsvereinheit-lichung", *Juristenzeitung* 54; 369–77.

Bernstein, Lisa (1992), "Opting Out of the Legal System: Extralegal Contractual Relations in the Diamond Industry", *Journal of Legal Studies* 21; 115–57.

Blaurock, Uwe (1998), "The Law of Transnational Commerce" in F. Ferrari (ed.), *The Unification of International Commercial Law* (Baden-Baden: Nomos).

Blessing, Marc (1997), "Mandatory Rules of Law versus Party Autonomy in International Arbitration", *Journal of International Arbitration* 14; 23–40.

Bonell, Michael Joachim (1994), *An International Restatement of Contract Law—the UNIDROIT Principles of International Commercial Contracts* (Irvington, NY: Transnational Juris).

—— (1995), *Un "codice" internazionale del diritto dei contratti* (Milan: Giuffrè).

—— (1996), "The UNIDROIT Principles of International Commercial Contracts and the Principles of European Contract Law—Same Rules for the Same Purposes", *Uniform Law Review/Revue de droit uniforme* 1 (NS); 229–46.

Budak, Ali Cem (1998), "Cross-border Debt Collection—Examples of Turkey and Germany" in V. Gessner and A. C. Budak (eds.), *Emerging Legal Certainty—Empirical Studies on the Globalization of Law* (Aldershot: Ashgate).

Carr, Indira (1996), *International Trade Law* (London: Cavendish).

Clark, David S. (1998), "Transnational Legal Practice: The Need for Global Law Schools", *The American Journal of Comparative Law* 46 (*Supplement*); 261–74.

Cottier, Thomas (1997), "Die Globalisierung des Rechts—Herausforderungen für Praxis, Ausbildung und Forschung", *Zeitschrift des Bernischen Juristen Vereins* 133; 217–41.

David, René (1971), "International Unification of Private Law" in *International Encyclopedia of Comparative Law* (New York: Oceana), II.

Dezalay, Yves (1990), "The Big Bang and the Law—The Internationalization and Restructuration of the Legal Field" in M. Featherstone (ed.), *Global Culture* (London: Sage Publications).

—— and Bryant, Garth (1996), *Dealing in Virtue: International Commercial Arbitration and the Construction of a Transnational Legal Order* (Chicago, Ill.: The University of Chicago Press).

Dreher, Meinrad (1999), "Wettbewerb oder Vereinheitlichung der Rechtsordnungen in Europa?", *Juristenzeitung* 54; 105–12.

Drobnig, Ulrich (1996), "Private Law in the European Union", *Forum Internationale* 22; 1–28.

—— (1999), "Europäisches Zivilgesetzbuch—Gründe und Grundgedanken", in D. Martiny and N. Witzleb (eds.), *Auf dem Wege zu einem Europäischen Zivilgesetzbuch* (Berlin: Springer).

Eger, Thomas (1999), "Harmonisierung von Rechtsregeln versus Institutionenwettbewerb in Europa", in D. Martiny and N. Witzleb (eds.), *Auf dem Wege zu einem Europäischen Zivilgesetzbuch* (Berlin: Springer).

Foster, Nigel (1991), "European Community Law and the Freedom of Lawyers in the United Kingdom and Germany", *International and Comparative Law Quarterly* 607–34.

von Freyhold, Hanno (1996), "Cross-Border Legal Interactions in New York Courts" in V. Gessner (ed.), *Foreign Courts—Civil Litigation in Foreign Legal Cultures* (Aldershot: Dartmouth).

—— Gessner, Volkmar, and Olgiati, Vittorio (1996), "The Role of Courts in Global Legal Interaction" in V. Gessner (ed.), *Foreign Courts—Civil Litigation in Foreign Legal Cultures* (Aldershot: Dartmouth).

Frick, Klaus (1998), "Third Cultures versus Regulators: Cross-border Legal Relations of Banks" in V. Gessner and A. C. Budak (eds.), *Emerging Legal Certainty—Empirical Studies on the Globalization of Law* (Aldershot: Ashgate).

Garro, Alejandro M. (1998), "Legal Framework for Regional Integration in the Americas: Inter-American Conventions and Beyond" in F. Ferrari (ed.), *The Unification of International Commercial Law* (Baden-Baden: Nomos).

Gessner, Volkmar (1996), "International Cases in German First Instance Courts" in V. Gessner (ed.), *Foreign Courts—Civil Litigation in Foreign Legal Cultures* (Aldershot: Dartmouth).

—— (1997), "Europas holprige Rechtswege—Die rechtskulturellen Schranken der Rechtsverfolgung im Binnenmarkt" in L. Krämer, H.-W. Micklitz and K. Tonner (eds.), *Law and Diffuse Interests in the European Legal Order—Recht und diffuse Interessen in der Europäischen Rechtsordnung—liber amicorum Norbert Reich* (Baden-Baden: Nomos).

—— (1998), "Globalization and Legal Certainty" in V. Gessner and A. C. Budak (eds.), *Emerging Legal Certainty—Empirical Studies on the Globalization of Law* (Aldershot: Ashgate).

Grotheer, Kirstin (1998), "Cross-border Maintenance Claims of Children" in V. Gessner and A. C. Budak (eds.), *Emerging Legal Certainty—Empirical Studies on the Globalization of Law* (Aldershot: Ashgate).

Hartkamp, Arthur, *et al.* (eds.) (1998), *Towards a European Civil Code* (2nd edn., Njmegen: Ars Aequi Libri).

Hau, Wolfgang (1999), "Globalisierungstendenzen der Rechtsberatungsmärkte—Rahmenbedingungen, Rechtstatsachen und Regelungsbedarf", *Jahrbuch Junger Zivilrechtswissenschaftler* 207–27.

van Houtte, Hans (1995), *The Law of International Trade* (London: Sweet & Maxwell).

Jayme, Erik (1998), "Entwurf eines Übereinkommens über das auf außervertragliche Schuldverhältnisse anzuwendende Recht-Tagung der Europäischen Gruppe für Internationales Privatrecht in Den Haag", *Praxis des Internationalen Privat- und Verfahrensrechts* 18; 140–1.

Jost, Fritz (1996), "Anwaltliche Tätigkeit in Europa—grenzenlos?" in P. Yessiou-Faltsi (ed.), *Recht in Europa—Festschrift für Hilmar Fenge* (Hamburg: Kovac).

Juenger, Friedrich K. (1994), "The Inter-American Convention on the Law Applicable to International Contracts: Some Highlights and Comparisons", *The American Journal of Comparative Law* 42; 381–93.

—— (1997a), "Contract Choice of Law in the Americas", *The American Journal of Comparative Law* 45; 196–208.

—— (1997b), "Some Comments on European Procedural Harmonization", *The American Journal of Comparative Law* 45; 931–37.

—— (1998), "A Hague Judgments Convention?", *Brooklyn Journal of International Law* 24; 111–23.

Kerameus, Konstantinos D. (1995), "Procedural Harmonization in Europe", *The American Journal of Comparative Law* 43; 401–16.

Knöfel, Susanne (1998), "EC Legislation on Conflict of Laws—Interactions and Incompatabilities between Conflict Rules", *International and Comparative Law Quarterly* 439–45.

Koch, Harald (1995), "Private International Law: A Soft Alternative to the Harmonisation of Private Law?", *European Review of Private Law* 3; 329–42.

Kötz, Hein (1986), "Rechtsvereinheitlichung: Nutzen, Kosten, Methoden, Ziele", *Rabels Zeitschrift für ausländisches und internationales Privatrecht* 50; 1–18.

Kronke, Herbert (1980), *Rechtstatsachen, kollisionsrechtliche Methodenentfaltung und Arbeitnehmerschutz im internationalen Arbeitsrecht* (Tübingen: Mohr).

—— (2000), "International Uniform Commercial Law Conventions: Advantages, Disadvantages, Criteria for Choice", *Uniform Law Review NS 5*; 13–21.

Lakkis, Panajotta (1999), "Globale Märkte—Globaler Rechtsschutz?—Grenzen des grenzübergreifenden kollektiven Rechtsschutzes für Verbraucher", *Jahrbuch Junger Zivilrechtswissenschaftler* 255–69.

Lando, Ole (1985), "The Lex Mercatoria in International Commercial Arbitration", *International and Comparative Law Quarterly* 747–68.

—— (1992), "Principles of European Contract Law—An Alternative to or a Precursor of European Legislation", *The American Journal of Comparative Law* 40; 573–85.

—— and Beale, Hugh (1995), *The Principles of European Contract Law* (Dordrecht: M. Nijhoff).

Lebron, David W. (1996), "Claims for Harmonization: A Theoretical Framework", *Canadian Business Law Journal* 27; 63–106.

Legrand, Pierre (1996), "Sens et non-sens d'un Code civil européen", *Revue internationale de droit comparé* 48; 779–812.

—— (1997), "Against a European Civil Code", *Modern Law Review* 60; 44–63.

De Ly, Filip (1992), *International Business Law and Lex Mercatoria* (Amsterdam: North Holland).

—— (1998), "Uniform Commercial Law and International Self-Regulation" in F. Ferrari (ed.), *The Unification of International Commercial Law* (Baden-Baden: Nomos).

Markesinis, Basil S. (1997), "Why a Code is Not the Best Way to Advance the Cause of European Legal Unity", *European Review of Private Law* 5; 519–24.

Martiny, Dieter (1984), *Handbuch des Internationalen Zivilverfahrensrechts Vol. III/1* (Tübingen: Mohr).

—— (1994), "Maintenance Obligations in the Conflict of Laws", *Recueil des cours* 247; 131–289.

—— (1999), "Europäisches Privatrecht—greifbar oder unerreichbar?" in D. Martiny and N. Witzleb (eds.), *Auf dem Wege zu einem Europäischen Zivilgesetzbuch* (Berlin: Springer).

McGrew, Anthony G. (1998), "Global Legal Interaction and Present-day Patterns of Globalization" in V. Gessner and A. C. Budak (eds.), *Emerging Legal Certainty—Empirical Studies on the Globalization of Law* (Aldershot: Ashgate).

von Mehren, Arthur T. (1994), "Recognition and Enforcement of Foreign Judgments: A New Approach for the Hague Conference?", *Law & Contemporary Problems* 57; 271–87.

Mertens, Hans-Joachim (1997), "Lex Mercatoria: A Self-applying System Beyond National Law?" in G. Teubner (ed.), *Global Law Without a State* (Aldershot: Dartmouth).

Nygh, Peter (1995), "The Reasonable Expectations of the Parties as a Guide to the Choice of Law in Contract and in Tort", *Recueil des cours* 251; 269–400.

Ogus, Anthony (1999), "Competition Between National Legal Systems: A Contribution of Economic Analysis to Comparative Law", *International and Comparative Law Quarterly* 404–18.

Olgiati, Vittorio (1996), "Cross-border Litigation in Italy" in V. Gessner (ed.), *Foreign Courts—Civil Litigation in Foreign Legal Cultures* (Aldershot: Dartmouth).

Oppermann, Thomas (1998), "The International Economic Order—Regionalization versus Globalization", *Law and State* 58; 36–50.

Pabst, Haroldo (1999), "Das internationale Zivilprozeßrecht des Mercosul", *Praxis des Internationalen Privat- und Verfahrensrecht* 19; 76–9.

Petzold, Andreas (1998), "Obtaining Information on Foreign Legal Systems" in V. Gessner and A. C. Budak (eds.), *Emerging Legal Certainty—Empirical Studies on the Globalization of Law* (Aldershot: Ashgate).

Rauscher, Thomas (1996), "Gran Canaria—Isle of Man—Was kommt danach", *Europäische Zeitschrift für Wirtschaftsrecht* 7; 650–3.

Röhl, Klaus, and Magen, Stefan (1996), "Die Rolle des Rechts im Prozeß der Globalisierung", *Zeitschrift für Rechtssoziologie* 17; 1–57.

Samtleben, Jürgen (1999), "Das Internationale Prozeß- und Privatrecht des MERCO-SUR", *Rabels Zeitschrift für ausländisches und internationales Privatrecht* 63; 1–69.

Schack, Haimo (1998), "Entscheidungszuständigkeiten in einem weltweiten Gerichtsstand- und Vollstreckungsübereinkommen", *Zeitschrift für Europäisches Privatrecht* 6; 931–56.

Schlechtriem, Peter (1998), *Commentary on the Convention on the International Sale of Goods of 1980 (CISG)* (Munich: Beck).

Schmidtchen, Dieter (1995), "Territorialität des Rechts, Internationales Privatrecht und die privatautonome Regelung internationaler Sachverhalte—Grundlagen eines interdisziplinären Forschungsprogramms", *Rabels Zeitschrift für ausländisches und internationales Privatrecht* 59; 56–112.

Schoener, Wendy (1997), "Non-governmental Organizations and Global Acitivism: Legal and Informal Approaches", *Indiana Journal of Global Legal Studies* 4; 537–69.

Siehr, Kurt (1995), "Internationales Recht der Produktehaftung" in A. K. Schnyder, H. Heiss and B. Rudisch (eds.), *Internationales Verbraucherschutzrecht* (Tübingen: Mohr).

Sonnenberger, Hans Jürgen (1998), "Der Ruf unserer Zeit nach einer europäischen Ordnung des Zivilrechts", *Juristenzeitung* 53; 982–91.

Stephan, Paul B. (1999), "The Futility of Unification and Harmonization in International Commercial Law", *Virginia Journal of International Law* 39; 743–97.

Stern, Brigitte (1997), "Can the United States set Rules for the World? A French View", *Journal of World Trade* 31; 5–26.

Storme, Marcel (ed.) (1994), *Rapprochement du droit judiciaire de l'Union Européenne—Approximation of Judiciary Law in the European Union* (Dordrecht: Nijhoff).

Streit, Manfred E., and Mangels, Antje (1996), "Privatautonomes Recht und grenzüber-schreitende Transaktionen", *ORDO—Jahrbuch für die Ordnung von Wirtschaft und Gesellschaft* 47; 73–100.

Taruffo, Michele (1997), "Drafting Rules for Transnational Litigation", *Zeitschrift für Zivilprozeß International* 2; 449–60.

—— (1998), "A Project of Rules for Transnational Litigation" in F. Ferrari (ed.), *The Unification of International Commercial Law* (Baden-Baden: Nomos).

Ulmer, Nicolas C. (1986), "Drafting the International Arbitration Clause", *The International Lawyer* 20; 1335–50.

Walker, Gordon R., and Fox, Mark A. (1996), "Globalization: An Analytical Framework", *Indiana Journal of Global Legal Studies* 3; 375–411.

Weeramantry, Christopher G. (1998), "Private International Law and Public International Law", *Rivista di diritto internazionale privato e processuale* 34; 313–24.

Wiegand, Wolfgang (1996), "Americanization of Law—Reception or Convergence?" in L. M. Friedman and H. N. Scheiber (eds.), *Legal Culture and the Legal Profession* (Boulder, Colo.: Westview Press).

Ziegler, Alexander von (2000), "Particularities of the Harmonisation and Unification of International Law of Trade and Commerce" in J. Basedow *et al.* (eds.), *Private Law in the International Arena—Liber Amicorum Kurt Siehr* (The Hague: T.M.C. Asser Press).

PART THREE

The Role of Autonomous Rules: The New Lex Mercatoria and Self-Regulation

5

Lex Mercatoria (New Law Merchant): Globalisation and International Self-regulation

FILIP DE LY

Abstract

Regulatory issues regarding globalisation of business transactions may also be tackled by means of self-regulation. This approach may be called the lex mercatoria *approach, referring to theories developed in the 1960s in relation to the growth of international trade after World War II. The chapter briefly discusses this approach and focuses on trends in the 1990s, including transaction cost analysis developed by law and economics scholars as well as sociological analyses developed to explain the impact of international self-regulation on international business transactions and structures including international commercial arbitration.*

THE *LEX MERCATORIA* APPROACH TO GLOBALISATION

INTERNATIONAL BUSINESS LAW traditionally was based on a paradigm of control by government regulation consisting of national rules. In an international setting, conflict rules had to determine which national rules were to be applied. These conflict rules are also to a large extent of national origin. Furthermore, jurisdiction rules determine whether a court in a certain country may have jurisdiction over an international case. This whole process of national rules of jurisdiction, national conflict rules and national substantive rules *nationalises* international adjudication. Under the traditional paradigm, there is one major correction which is that conflict rules determine not only whether the law of the country where the judge sits may be applicable but also under which circumstances foreign law may be applied. In this respect, the traditional perspective is not nationalistic in its assumptions. However, in practice one notes that often and in many countries a *homeward trend* may be noticed in the adjudication of international business disputes.[1]

---

[1] For empirical research, see Freyhold (1996: 128–33), and Gessner (1996: 178–85).

Unification of law by international or intergovernmental agencies such as
UNCITRAL, UNIDROIT or the Hague Conference on Private International
Law does not really challenge the traditional paradigm. Uniform rules adopted
by these agencies by means of international conventions and uniform or model
laws need incorporation in domestic laws or approval and ratification by
domestic institutions in order to be formally binding.[2] Thus, these instruments
of uniform law do not challenge the state control assumption of traditional legal
thinking. This assumption is, however, more at stake when these agencies adopt
model contracts, arbitration rules, legal guides or restatement-like codes.
Similarly, international conventions and uniform or model laws may also challenge the state control assumption of traditional thinking when these instruments are not applied directly but influence decision-making by virtue of the
quality of their contents (*persuasive authority*). In both cases, it seems to be artificial to explain the impact of international sources of business law by referring
to formal sources of domestic law such as endorsement by legislators or domestic courts. The same observation also applies even more vigorously to supranational law-making. The most prominent example is in this respect the
European Union where, by virtue of the 1957 Rome Treaty establishing the
European Economic Community (as amended), legislative powers have been
transferred to the institutions of the European Union which can make binding
legislation by means of regulations and directives. In this respect, one can hardly
support the proposition that the thousands of regulations and hundreds of
directives are adopted by virtue of a constitutional permit in all EU Member
States and, therefore, that EU law is an emanation of national law. From a
substantive point of view, EU law is much more to be seen as an independent
supranational legal order between the national and the international legal
orders based on support from the Member States but with its own institutions,
procedures, instruments and characteristics (such as pre-emption of domestic
law by directly applicable EU rules) aimed at finding appropriate solutions for
cross-border problems within the European Union.[3]

Under the traditional approach, scant attention is paid to rules or standards
which do not emanate from the official rule-making authorities or agencies
(international self-regulation or private governance). Contract clauses, general
conditions, standard terms, usages and customs or general principles of law

[2] This applies equally to the monistic and the dualistic methods of unification of substantive law.
In the first case, no distinction is made between domestic and international cases and the uniform
text is applicable to both domestic and international transactions (e.g., the uniform laws of Geneva
of the 1930s regarding bills of exchange and promissory notes and regarding cheques). Under the
dualistic method, the unification effort is limited—primarily for political reasons—to international
transactions (e.g., the 1980 Vienna Convention on the International Sale of Goods).

[3] For a more extensive discussion of these elements of national and uniform law, one may refer
to the contribution of Professor Martiny to this book. These elements are discussed in this chapter
to show the conceptional problems of this traditional approach which in part explain the emergence
of the debate regarding the *lex mercatoria*. Also, some general conclusions may be drawn from both
the traditional approach and the *lex mercatoria* approach in relation to the key issue as to finding
appropriate legal answers to globalisation.

were recognised but reduced to no more than party autonomy recognised by national law or downplayed to rather unimportant sources of law.

From the end of the 1950s, scholars began advocating views under which these traditional conceptions of international business law were questioned and challenged.[4] Their basic proposition was that national sources (primarily codes and statutes and case law) did not reflect the realities of international business life. Also, they argued that these national sources were to a large extent inappropriate to cope with the problems and needs of international trade. They claimed that a new system was required and that any such legal order was developing. Similar to the *ius gentium* in Roman law and the *law merchant* in English law prior to the eighteenth century, a *new law merchant* or *lex mercatoria* had emerged and was developing.[5] This *lex mercatoria* may be defined for the purposes of this analysis as a set of rules finding their origins outside domestic legal systems which is applicable to international business transactions. By and large, it is composed of international sources of law and self-regulatory rules.[6]

At this point, an important distinction is to be made between various conceptions of *lex mercatoria*. Basically, two different attitudes may be observed. The first approach was advocated by the late Professor Clive Schmitthoff who stressed the importance of international and self-regulatory rules in international business law. However, this did not result in the proposition that these rules constituted a legal system different from domestic legal systems. This theory was both pragmatic and substantive. It emphasised that—within the boundaries of national legal systems—many international instruments and self-regulatory rules were relevant and useful for resolving international business disputes. Thus, Schmitthoff's theory was looking to the substance of international business law and dispute resolution and found that not only statutory rules and cases decided by national courts should be taken into account but that one should also analyse international and self-regulatory rules and means of dispute settlement (De Ly, 1992: 209–10).

As such, his theory did not challenge the traditional paradigm of international business law but pragmatically tried to incorporate rules other than national-origin rules into the scope of international business law. This pragmatic and substantive approach may explain that his theory was not controversial and did not meet so much resistance.

This was different in relation to the *lex mercatoria* theory as developed by the late Professor Berthold Goldman who advocated that the *lex mercatoria* was an autonomous legal system of its own different and apart from national legal systems. Such a *transnational* legal order in his view had its own sources and rules

---

[4] The discussion in the following paras. is based on De Ly (1992). In order to avoid repetition, no further references will be made in footnotes to the legal developments prior to 1992.

[5] For the remainder of this chapter, the concept of *lex mercatoria* will be used as a synonym for that of the new law merchant.

[6] For the latter concept including spontaneous rules, articulated rules and mixed rules see De Ly (1998b: 60–1).

and arbitration as the preferred means of solving international business disputes. This theory is formal in the sense that it argues that the *lex mercatoria* as to its formal sources and structures is separate from domestic legal systems. Thus, solutions for international business problems are not sought within but outside domestic legal systems (De Ly, 1992: 210–15). The theory is also fundamental since it is an outright attack on domestic law as the basis for international business adjudication.[7] Thus, it challenges and disputes the traditional national state paradigm[8] of international business law and its underlying assumptions.[9]

Because of the fundamental nature of Goldman's theory, it was to become controversial. It was by and large supported in France and the French-speaking part of Belgium. It met with opposition in Germany, the Dutch speaking part of Belgium, England and the USA. In other countries such as Switzerland and The Netherlands the theory was received in a mixed way with proponents and adversaries keeping one another in balance (De Ly, 1992: 215–48). However, more recently[10] one generally may note that scholars and practitioners publishing on arbitration have been more willing to accept *lex mercatoria* as a fact of life[11] and that since the publication in 1992 of my book *International Business Law and Lex Mercatoria* scant severe criticism has been expressed of *lex mercatoria*.[12] One of the reasons is that proponents of international Restatements

[7] One element of this attack is that Goldman's theory gradually became more and more substantive (i.e., directly looking to the *better law* solution) thereby bypassing traditional conflict rules (which look to the proper law or the law most connected to the dispute). Since conflict rules traditionally provide for allocations between national legal systems, the theory was deemed either to formulate *transnational* conflict rules or to embark on a search for direct substantive solutions. The latter process did in fact occur.

[8] Compare this with a similar attack on the paradigm of the sovereign nation-state from the public international law side, where a neo-Grotian natural law-related attempt was made to establish a gradually developing world order on the basis of values of human solidarity and dignity: Falk (1975: 969–1021).

[9] A somewhat isolated view argues that not only the traditional paradigm but also the *lex mercatoria* paradigm have to be rejected and that international business law is now to be based on the paradigm of uniform law. Under that perspective, transnational and global problems require uniform solutions at the international level to be achieved through instruments of uniform law. See Randall and Norris (1993: 599–636).

[10] For recent books on the *lex mercatoria*, see Carbonneau (1998), Berger (1996).

[11] See Goldman (1993: 241–55); Osman (1992); Stein (1995); Rigaux (1989: I, 9–407); Juenger (1995: 487–501); Strenger (1992: 207–355); Mertens (1992: 219–42); Mertens (1997: 31–43); Kahn (1992: 413–27); Meyer (1994); Berger (1993: 281–8); Kappus (1994: 189–91); Van Delden (1992: 39–49); Humphreys (1992: 849–56); Gaillard (1993); Medwig (1993: 589–616); Rivkin (1993b: 67–84); Blaurock (1993: 247); Matray (1992: 207–33); Vandenput (1992: 1–33); Gaillard (1996: 570–90); Kessedjian (1995: 381–410); Selden (1995: 11–129); Jin (1996: 163–98); Goode (1997: 1–36); Lando (1997a: 567–84). In relation to public international law, see Booysen (1992: 196–211); Booysen (1995a: 245–57); Booysen (1995b). The *lex mercatoria* has also been discussed in a major French newspaper, see Plouvier (1992: 34).

[12] For exceptions critical of *lex mercatoria* based on arguments of lack of predictability and certainty, see Reisman (1992: 134–9) (emphasising the absence of political values in the theory); Behrens (1993: 13–38); Giardina (1992: 461–70); Wilkinson (1995: 103–15); Weinberg (1994: 227–54); Chukwumerije (1994: 110–17); Rivkin (1993a: 161–208). Compare Grundmann (1992: 43–70). For a somewhat sceptical note by a practitioner, see Level (1993: 32).

of Contract Law (such as the UNIDROIT Principles of International Commercial Contracts and the Principles of European Contract Law) have come to support the *lex mercatoria* with all their authority in order to promote the use of these Restatements (see below). Another reason is that national arbitration laws have increasingly been liberalised as to the law applicable to the merits (see below), thus opening the way for application of the *lex mercatoria*. This assessment of the acceptability of the *lex mercatoria*, however, is based on publications and it remains to be seen whether this position has been accepted by uniform law, national legislation, case law (both by domestic courts and arbitral tribunals) and practice.

As regards case law, the French Supreme Court in 1981 upheld arbitral awards based on *lex mercatoria* in the course of setting aside and enforcement proceedings[13] and the same can be said of an Italian Supreme Court case of 1982.[14] Otherwise, one notes that domestic courts hardly apply the *lex mercatoria*.[15] In international conventions and model laws the *lex mercatoria* was discussed as an issue but this did not materialise in tangible effects on the international instruments finally adopted until the 1990s (De Ly, 1992: 252–4). Recently, one has noticed some change in those instances where international instruments reflect the influence of the *lex mercatoria*. Apart from international conventions and other instruments of official unification of law, one also should note that other international instruments recently have taken positions which are relevant in relation to the application of *lex mercatoria* and more generally transnational standards in international trade. In this respect, reference should first be made to the 1992 Cairo Resolution of the International Law Association (hereafter referred to as "ILA") adopted by its Committee on International Commercial Arbitration at the occasion of the 65th ILA Conference held in Cairo in April 1992. Since the ILA is a private organisation, its recommendations do not constitute binding authority. However, this does not imply that they could not have persuasive force based upon the quality of the analyses leading to the recommendation. In order to analyse the

---

[13] See De Ly (1992: 255–8) on case law published before 1992 and add to this the *Compania Valenciana* v. *Primary Coal* case (Cour de Cassation, 10 July 1990 [1992] Clunet, 177, case note Berthold Goldman [1992] *RCDIP*, 113, case note Bruno Oppetit [1992], *Rev. Arb.* 457, case note Paul Lagarde) and the *Pakistan Atomic Energy Commission* v. *Société Générale pour les Techniques Nouvelles* case (Cour de Cassation, Première Chambre Civile, 7 January 1992, Arrêt no. 44, Pourvoi no. 87–19.319, CD-Rom Lexilaser [1992] *Rev. Arb.* 659 (abstract), case note D. Bureau).

[14] [1982] *Riv. Dir. Int. Priv. Proc.* 829, Y.B.Com.Arb. IX–1984, 418. For a discussion, see De Ly (1992: 258–9).

[15] *Contra* Lando (1997a: 573). Of course, there are some exceptions. For instance, in a judgment of 11 July 1991, the Commercial Court of Nantes ([1993] Clunet, 330, case note by Philippe Leboulanger), decided to apply general principles and usages of international trade and particularly the *lex mercatoria* to a commission and agency contract between a French contractor and a Saudi-Arabian intermediary. Also, in a Philippine case (*Bank of America NT & SA* v. *Court of Appeals*, 228 SCRA 357 (3rd 1993, Supreme Court) reported by Selden (1995: 125)), reference was made to the *lex mercatoria* to solve a letter of credit dispute by reference to the ICC Uniform Customs and Practice regarding Documentary Credits ("UCP"). For a similar Chinese case, see Wang (1996: 36–7), the *Wulhan jute bag* case. *Adde* De Ly (1992: 255, n. 245) reporting on a Zurich Court of Appeal case.

recommendation, one may distinguish between the two instances in which the use of transnational rules is encouraged. As far as application by arbitrators of transnational rules by virtue of an agreement between the parties is concerned, the recommendation complies with the law in many countries where the arbitrators first have to base their award on standards of adjudication chosen by the parties.[16] The ILA recommendation does not codify existing law but attempts to develop and establish the principle of absence of conflict of laws and substantive review in relation to the application of transnational rules by international commercial arbitrators. This process is negative in the sense that review by domestic courts is limited and self-restraint by these courts is being recommended. Then, it follows from the absence of such reviews that arbitrators have much more freedom and discretion to apply conflict and substantive rules which opens the way for application of transnational rules. Behind these efforts, one may find two liberal policies: one to free international commercial arbitration from domestic court intervention in the course of setting aside and enforcement and one to free the international commercial arbitral process from domestic conflict of laws and domestic substantive law. However, both elements are not necessarily intertwined.[17] One may for instance well argue for the absence of conflict of laws and substantive review and at the same time remain sceptical about the application of transnational law and try to find acceptable solutions within more traditional patterns.

As a second example, the World Intellectual Property Organisation (hereafter referred to as "WIPO") has adopted as from 1 October 1994 dispute settlement rules which parties may adopt, primarily but not necessarily with regard to intellectual and industrial property disputes. These rules are: (1) the WIPO Mediation Rules; (2) the WIPO Arbitration Rules; and (3) the WIPO Expedited Arbitration rules.[18] The WIPO scheme provides a new framework for institutional arbitration administered by the WIPO Arbitration Centre based in Geneva. For the purposes of our discussion, one should note that Article 59 of the WIPO Arbitration Rules provides that arbitral tribunals instituted under the WIPO Arbitration Rules should apply the rules of law they deem appropriate to the merits of the dispute. Thus, the WIPO Arbitration Rules (unlike Article 13(3) of the 1988 edition of the ICC Arbitration Rules and Article 33(1) of the UNCITRAL Arbitration Rules) permit arbitrators to adopt the direct approach. However, the recommended WIPO arbitration rules still assume that a national law will be chosen by the parties.[19]

In relation to the ICC, one also should note that the 1998 ICC Arbitration Rules amended the 1988 edition of the ICC Rules in relation to the law applicable to the merits. Under Article 13(3) of the 1988 Rules, the arbitrators had—in the absence

---

[16] Art. VII(1) 1961 Geneva European International Commercial Arbitration Convention; Art. 1496 French NCPC; Art. 1054 Dutch CCP; Art. 187(1) Swiss Private International Law Act; Art. 28 Uncitral Model Law and national arbitration laws based on the Model Law.

[17] See also Derains (1993: 56–7).

[18] XX Y. B. Com. Arb. 1995: 331–77.

[19] Conference on Rules for Institutional Arbitration and Mediation, Geneva, WIPO, 1995, Annex IV, 189–91.

of a choice of law provision in the contract—to apply the conflict rule which they considered appropriate. Article 17 (1) of the 1998 Arbitration Rules now provides that the arbitrators shall apply the *rules of law* which they determine to be appropriate. Under the new rule, arbitrators no longer have to follow a conflict rule but may take the direct approach to substantive rules, not necessarily of a domestic legal system. Here again, one notes the influence of the *lex mercatoria* and in particular of Article 1496 of the French New Code of Civil Procedure.[20] Similar developments can also be found in other arbitration rules such as the Arbitration Rules of the London Court of International Arbitration and Article 29 of the International Arbitration Rules of the American Arbitration Association.[21]

Finally, an important development took place in relation to the development of the *lex mercatoria* with the adoption of US-like *Restatements* of contract law at the European and international levels. At the international level, the UNIDROIT Governing Council adopted in 1994 the UNIDROIT Principles of International Commercial Contracts[22] which were subsequently published first in English and French and later in many other languages.[23] At the level of the European Union, a private commission chaired by the Danish professor Ole Lando has been active since 1980 and published in 1995 (Lando and Beale, 1995) a first part of *Principles of European Contract Law* (hereinafter referred to as "PECL" or "Principles").[24] Both the UNIDROIT Principles (the *red book*) and the PECL (the *blue book*) pursue various objectives.[25] They may serve as a model law for partial codification or harmonisation of contract law or for statutory reform in developed countries, countries in transition or developing countries. Also, they may—like the Restatements in the USA—provide persuasive authority for case law and scholarly developments in national legal systems and at the European Union level. Furthermore, they may be used in legal education regarding comparative and uniform law. Finally, international contract drafting practice and international dispute settlement (particularly international commercial arbitration) may benefit from these Restatement-like efforts. Since this contribution deals with the *lex mercatoria*, only the latter function of both Principles will be discussed.[26]

---

[20] See De Ly (1998c: 228–9).

[21] See Jin (1996: 181–2).

[22] Principles of International Commercial Contracts, Rome, Unidroit, 1994.

[23] For some of the earlier writings, see Bonell (1976: 413); Bonell (1988: 873–88); Bonell (1990: 865–88); Bonell (1992a: 274–89); Bonell (1992b: 617–34). See also Fontaine (1991: 25–40). See also the publication of the University of Miami School of Law colloquium reports in the *American Journal of Comparative Law* 1992: 617–728 (reports by Ulrich Drobnig on substantive validity, Marcel Fontaine on content and performance, Dieter Maskow on hardship and *force majeur*, M. P. Furmston on Breach of contract, and Denis Tallon on damages, exemption clauses and penalties); Van Houtte (1994); Hartkamp (1994b: 127–37); Hartkamp (1994: 37–50).

[24] For some publications on the Pecl, see Lando (1983: 653–9); Lando (1985: 17–21); Lando (1989: 555); Lando (1992: 261–73); Lando (1993: 157–70); Remien (1988: 105–22); Van Der Velden (1990: 2–28); Drobnig (1990: 1141–54); Drobnig (1993); Tallon (1993: 485–94); Hartkamp (1994a: 37–50).

[25] Principles, Introduction, pp. xvii-xix; see also Hartkamp (1994a: 40–3); Tallon (1993: 490–1).

[26] For a first discussion of this aspect in relation to the Unidroit Principles, see Lando (1994: 129–43).

An extensive analysis of both Principles falls outside the scope of this chapter. The purpose of mentioning these Principles here is to emphasise their relevance in relation to the development of the debate regarding the *lex mercatoria* since the mid-1990s when they were adopted. In this respect, reference may be made to the Bristol Conference of the International Academy of Comparative Law where the Unidroit Principles were the object of one of the sessions.[27] The general impression is that it is still too early to assess the impact in legal practice of the UNIDROIT Principles. On the other hand, scholars see many possible ways to apply the Principles directly or indirectly. However, national court cases invoking or applying the UNIDROIT Principles are still rare. Also, contract clauses incorporating the UNIDROIT Principles are hard to find. However, in international commercial arbitration, there are a limited number of arbitral awards where the arbitral tribunal applied or invoked the Unidroit Principles.[28] In relation to the *lex mercatoria*, it may be said that both the UNIDROIT Principles and the PECL constitute an important step in its process to maturity because they reduce the uncertainties in its application to a certain extent. By doing so, the traditional objection that the *lex mercatoria* is vague and incomplete is countered and the parties may argue their case and the arbitrators may decide the case with the red and/or blue books in their hands.

The general conclusion after 40 years of developments regarding the *lex mercatoria* is that its theory remains the subject of immense debate, sometimes confusion primarily among legal scholars.[29] The most important development in the 1990s is that the debate is to a certain extent not reduced to religion with believers and non-believers but acknowledges somewhat more that the *lex mercatoria*—as conceived by Goldman as a autonomous legal system[30]—is here to stay as a fact of life and that the question is more about the conditions and circumstances under which it should be applied. That debate is by and large limited to international commercial arbitrations administered by international arbitration institutions. In that respect, the scope of the debate is rather limited. First, adjudication by national courts on the basis of national law, uniform law and self-regulation is hardly affected. Secondly, arbitration in specific branches of trade (for example, maritime arbitration or commodities arbitration) and arbitration by national arbitration centres remained also to a large extent unaffected by the theory because the dispute settlement in these cases is by and large determined by national legal rules and applicable international conventions and self-regulatory rules. Only the international

---

[27] The Unidroit Principles of International Commercial Contracts, Bonell (1999).

[28] For one instance where an ICC Arbitral Tribunal applied the Principles as the law applicable to the contract see De Ly (1999).

[29] The drawback of this assessment is that hardly any research is done in relation to alternative theories such as unilateral and direct methods, comparative conflict and substantive methods and domestic methods (on these methods, see De Ly (1992: 291–313)). For an example, see the *tronc commun* theory of Rubino-Sammartano (1993: 59–65).

[30] As was indicated before, the Schmitthoff conception of *lex mercatoria* does not raise substantial conceptual and practical problems.

arbitration cases handled by international arbitration centres such as the ICC were affected by the debate. There, international instruments and national statutes regarding arbitration, arbitration rules and arbitral and national case law were exposed to the practical consequences of an intrinsically academic debate. From a legal sociological perspective it is, however, difficult to find hard empirical evidence regarding the application of the *lex mercatoria* in arbitration practice. One reason is confidentiality. Even if awards are published, they may not represent a fair view of general arbitration practice. The other is legal reasoning by arbitration tribunals which may use different arguments to support conclusions. Alternative reasoning may reflect compromises in arbitral deliberations or may strengthen the persuasive authority of awards *vis-à-vis* losing parties. At the same time it is more difficult to interpret awards invoking *lex mercatoria*.

ANALYSIS OF THE *LEX MERCATORIA* APPROACH TO GLOBALISATION

The previous section was to a large extent descriptive and did not assess questions such as whether a new legal system apart from national, supranational and international legal systems was desirable or whether the third approach meets the needs of international business. This section will look to the *lex mercatoria* from the policy perspective. In this respect, one first may look to the debate from the angle of legal philosophy. The proponents of Goldman's conception have in this respect invoked three bases on which the *lex mercatoria* could be defended. First, Goldman himself in one short publication referred to natural law as the basis for the *lex mercatoria* (Goldman, 1956: 115–16). As such, a universal law merchant would exist based on reason. This argument is not new since it was also developed by the French comparatist Edouard Lambert in relation to uniform law. The common basis for these theories on universalism (De Ly, 1998a: 44) is a belief in rationalism as a unifying factor. The history of uniform law has proven that such a conception is overly ambitious, irrealistic and naïve. However, it is a recurrent theme in uniform law because in the European Union similar beliefs explain why there is a regional movement towards a European Civil Code, a new *ius commune* or a common core of European law (De Ly, 1998a: 44–5). In relation to the *lex mercatoria*, its universal aspirations have come under attack from the perspective of developing countries which reject legal rules to which they have not agreed and in whose formation they were not involved.[31] In this respect, one may also question whether globalisation actually is occurring or whether we see much more denationalisation and regional forms of internationalisation. If the latter were the case, there would be a lesser need for a universal *lex mercatoria*. Apart from the practical problems and implications, a natural law theory remains problematic because it does not address the

---

[31] See Jin's (1996: 181) recent article in which he speaks about a *North Atlantic lex mercatoria*.

question what reason would dictate for international business transactions. Furthermore, it hides value judgements about what is desirable in international trade where different cultures may provide different answers.

Faced with these problems, the proponents of the *lex mercatoria* quickly attempted to base its existence as a separate legal order on a sociological legal theory developed by the French scholar of public international law Georges Scelle. Under that theory, legal rules may be developed by sufficiently organised groups in society who have their own mechanisms (for example, arbitration, blacklisting or exclusion) of enforcing these rules. For international business transactions, the *société internationale des marchands* would develop its own rules outside the scope and often the reach of domestic law. Philippe Kahn had noticed that development in relation to international sales contracts but also on the international capital markets for eurobonds (Kahn, 1961: 2, 15; Kahn, 1973: 224–5). Also this foundation was shortlived. It was severely critised by Paul Lagarde who argued that this basis could not support the universal and general ambitions of the *lex mercatoria* because there is no single international business community but many subcommunities depending on the branch of trade concerned and the organisation of that branch. Consequently, not one single *lex mercatoria* but many *leges mercatoriae* exist. Moreover, the business community is often not homogeneously organised (for example, fast growing industries) or the degree of participation of businessmen in branch organisations may be low. Therefore, there are rather islands of self-regulation than one sea of uniformity (Lagarde, 1982: 135–6, 138–9). This intuitive assessment which was not empirically proven apparently was so forceful that this basis for the *lex mercatoria* was also abandoned.

Finally, the justification for the *lex mercatoria* was sought in Santi Romano's legal theory of *legal pluralism*. According to this theory, not only the state but any community may create legal rules. This theory may for instance help to explain religious law, tribal law or customary law. This basis for the *lex mercatoria* was first invoked by Professor François Rigaux of Belgium (among other things in relation to transnational activities of multinational companies escaping by their size and impact as well as by the availability of alternatives from the realm of national states[32]) and was later endorsed by Philippe Kahn to reconcile his views on the *lex mercatoria* with the movement in the 1970s towards a New International Economic Order (Kahn, 1982: 104–7). Also, Eric Loquin invoked legal pluralism to explain why the application of anational legal rules in international commercial arbitration had led to the development of the *lex mercatoria* as an autonomous anational legal system.[33] The theory of legal pluralism has the advantage that it explains that legal rules may also be developed by other

---

[32] Rigaux (1977a: 3–4, 344–5, 399, 413, 423 and 437–8); Rigaux (1997b: 108–11 and 114–15); Rigaux (1979: 291, 293 and 371); Rigaux and Vander Elst (1982: 231).

[33] Loquin (1986: 73–5 and 113–19). In this regard, Loquin uses the expression of anational rules or system as a synonym for transnational.

institutions than state-controlled institutions.[34] To that extent, it explains the existence of massive self-regulation. However, in relation to the *lex mercatoria*, it does not contain a normative element. As such, all groups in society may create legal rules including the mafia and organised crime. Also, the theory of legal pluralism does not address the issue of the relationship between these different legal systems. They may well be in harmony or co-ordinate with one another but instances will occur where conflicts arise that must be settled by instituting a priority rule. Finally, these legal systems may compete with one another, which also should be the subject of further analysis.

Both the sociological theory and the theory of legal pluralism focus on spontaneous or articulated forms of self-regulation by the business community or segments thereof. International trade—or to use a more recent term globalisation of business—may require regulation at the global or supranational level in which there is a role for the activities, role and responsibilities of the business communities. However, one may wonder whether this cannot be explained within the traditional national state paradigm of international business law. Put in another way, the preceding three legal bases for the autonomous conception of the *lex mercatoria* cannot solve the controversial nature of the theory and, therefore, stagnation is present.

A fourth philosophical basis which may be found somewhat implicitly in scholarly writings on the *lex mercatoria* is legal realism. It has already been emphasised that developments in the 1990s gradually accept *lex mercatoria* as a fact of life because arbitrators just apply it in arbitration cases notwithstanding controversy and objections from academic circles. The third approach to the *lex mercatoria* takes that into account when accepting arbitral adjudication on the basis of non-national rules and developing the *lex mercatoria* more as a method than as a system. On the other hand, legal realism as such cannot in itself find a legitimate basis for arbitral adjudication. For that reason, the third approach formally anchors the *lex mercatoria* as a method into national law while emphasising at the same time its substantive international character.

Apart from the legal philosophical perspective, one may also approach the *lex mercatoria* from the point of view of law and economics.[35] This angle is rather new but deserves to be mentioned here although only some four recent publications have been found in this respect. As regards the law and economics approach, one may distinguish between the empirical and the normative dimensions. Regarding the *lex mercatoria*, I am not aware of empirical studies on the economic costs and benefits of transnational legal rules developed by the business community. Also, I am not aware either of any such research regarding the economic effects of official harmonisation or unification.[36] Thus, one is left with normative propositions regarding these economic effects. First, there are three

---

[34] One should note that this proposition extends the traditional concept of objective right beyond the law-making authority of state institutions.

[35] For an early example see Benson (1987).

[36] Schmidtchen (1995: 72–3) refers in this regard to Amelung (1991: 716–32).

articles of Professor Cooter of Berkeley where he makes his case for *de-centralised law-making* starting from within society (bottom up) and against centralised law (top down) (Cooter, 1994: 215–31; 1996a: 341–64; 1996b: 1643–96). Of course, the *lex mercatoria* fits very well within any such perspective. However, Professor Cooter's analysis is not limited to international business and applies generally to both domestic and international transactions. Henceforth, it is difficult to draw any conclusions from his articles regarding the theory of the *lex mercatoria*.

The gap left by Cooter's analysis has been filled by German scholars who have applied law and economics analysis to international commercial transactions (see Schmidtchen, 1995: 56–112). Under this analysis, legal systems (national legal systems or EU law) should provide for private law rules guaranteeing possessive and transactional security.[37] The former is related to property law where legal rights should be protected against interference from third parties. For the debate regarding the *lex mercatoria*, transactional security is much more important. It requires that commercial transactions are protected by national or EU rules providing the conditions and means for enforcing contractual promises. In that respect, there is an intrinsic difference between national and international transactions because the latter by their very nature involve higher transactions costs in relation to enforcing contractual obligations. International transactions involve *per se* problems of international civil procedure (for example, jurisdiction, enforcement, evidence, law applicable to the procedure, service of process) and of conflict of laws which increase transaction costs. For instance, one has to spend more money suing abroad, obtaining evidence, doing research in and collecting information on foreign procedural and substantive rules, retaining foreign counsel and attorneys, for translation and communication purposes and enforcing abroad. All these factors also imply that time is lost.[38] Furthermore, there is a risk of bias on the part of local courts or that local courts manipulate conflict rules inorder to be able to apply local law (*homeward trend*).[39] The risk of increased transaction costs in international commercial transactions may be controlled or minimised in a number of ways including uniform private international law or uniform substantive law including self-regulatory rules eventually enforced through international commercial arbitration (Schmidtchen, 1995: 100–3, 107–11).

In general, one might infer from the foregoing that some law and economics analysts support self-regulation as an efficient process provided it is based on incentives producing these self-regulatory rules which make businessmen comply with these rules (Cooter, 1994: 226–7). In other words, from the outset self-regulation is a serious option for economically efficient law-making, especially in international commercial transactions. Of course, economic considerations

[37] Schmidtchen (1995: 69), citing Kronman (1985: 4–32).
[38] Expenses and time costs are reduced to a certain extent if uniform private international rules exist. Schmidtchen (1995: 76–7).
[39] On all these elements, see Schmidtchen (1995: 75–90); see also Gessner (1996a: 19–21).

alone cannot give final answers to the question of choices between different regulatory instruments and different degrees of regulation because cultural and social factors may also influence the choice process.

Finally, there is the thought-provoking article of Professor Procaccia (Jerusalem) who argues against the *lex mercatoria* and implicitly questions the analyses of the German law and economics scholars referred to above.[40] In this article, the question is not so much whether or not and to what extent self-regulation is efficient but whether the *lex mercatoria* (i.e., the law merchant) should remain as it was in the Middle Ages and until the eigthteenth century (i.e., diffuse and diverse) or whether an attempt should be made to promote uniformity through statutory codification or international unification. Professor Procaccia's analysis argues for diversity and against harmonisation. Although the main argument for harmonisation is reduction in transaction costs, diversity also has its advantages. In an environment where different legal rules or systems must compete with one another in order to be chosen—directly or indirectly—by economic operators, regulatory competition for contract law rules will ultimately lead to a *race to the top* where the parties will tend to choose the better contract law in order to optimalise the process of contracting (Procaccia, 1998: 89–91). Also, states have an indirect interest in adopting better contract rules than those of other states because they can win invisible earnings on the market for statutory products through the legal and other services rendered in connection thereto (Procaccia, 1998: 92). Under such a system of statutory competition, parties have choices and will choose efficient solutions. Uniform law on the other hand does not by necessity generate efficient contract rules and, therefore, may not provide efficient solutions because alternatives have disappeared. Furthermore, efficiency of rules is based on social and cultural factors too and uniformity reduces party choice regarding the most efficient solution in a given social and cultural context. Hence, uniform law does not necessarily produce efficient results and may involve higher transaction costs than under a system of diversity where there is statutory competition (Procaccia, 1998: 92–4).

The foregoing analysis has become familiar since the beginning of the 1990s in uniform law theory in relation to harmonisation of law within the European Union. In that period harmonisation was achieved in the financial services sector through the principle of reciprocal recognition of regulatory rules and standards.[41] Under the home control principle,[42] banks, insurance companies and investment services firms could operate throughout the European Union with one licence issued by the supervisory authorities of the home country of the financial institution (single licence system). It was hoped and to a large extent achieved that regulatory competition between the supervisory systems of the

---

[40] Procaccia (1998: 87–95). One should note that Professor Procaccia primarily defines the *lex mercatoria* not as international self-regulation but as the English law merchant.

[41] This method rests on the assumption of equivalent regulations between home and host countries.

[42] Also called the principle of the state of origin (*Ursprungslandprinzip*).

Member States would harmonise financial supervision downwards (see De Ly, 1993: 27–34; Reich, 1992: 861–96).

If we apply the foregoing discussion to the *lex mercatoria*, one should make a difference between the different constitutive elements of the *lex mercatoria*. To the extent that one agrees that official unification is part of the *lex mercatoria*, Professor Procaccia's analysis legitimately raises the question whether international conventions and other instruments of official unification live up to their promise of transaction cost reduction or whether competition between national laws in the end could not do better (see also De Ly, 1998b: 65–7). As regards the spontaneously developed rules of *lex mercatoria* such as customs, usages, standard terms, general conditions or contractual clauses, there is already competition between traders and trade organizations bringing about the expected benefits except in cases of market deficiences, such as for instance oligopolistic markets or market distortions by cartels and other forms of restraint of trade. Finally, there are the articulated efforts by businesses and business organisations (such as the ICC) or by arbitrators (by creating arbitral case law) to create uniform self-regulatory rules where the Procaccia question also applies and where it is not self-evident that these efforts create the anticipated economic benefits.

From the foregoing, it is clear that law and economics may provide helpful although not all-encompassing insights into the mechanics of self-regulation and into the virtues and deficiencies of the *lex mercatoria*. However, this is only the beginning, and opposing views exist. Much more research is needed in order to be able to draw some normative conclusions on the basis of empirical materials.

A third non-positive law perspective with respect to the debate regarding the *lex mercatoria* has been given by sociologists of law. This new perspective does not concentrate on how the law is (black letter approach) but on how it operates (law in action). The focus is not only on rules but on how these rules operate and are observed if applied by the legal profession and courts (see Gessner, 1998: 433–44; Teubner, 1997: 3–28). Here again, a distinction may be drawn between the empirical and the normative approaches. To my limited knowledge, there is scant empirical evidence regarding the frequency and means of application of contract clauses,[43] general conditions, standard terms, self-regulatory

---

[43] For an exception see the activities of the *Groupe de Travail Contrats Internationaux* ("GTCI") which was chaired until 1992 by Professor Marcel Fontaine and since then by the writer of this chapter. The GTCI is a working group established in 1975 by Marcel Fontaine and consists of company lawyers, attorneys and legal academics. On the basis of contract clauses provided by its members, an analysis is made of international contract practice. For the topics analysed so far, see: (1) Les clauses de hardship, Aménagement conventionnel de l'imprévision dans les contrats à long terme/Hardship clauses, D.P.C.I. 1976, 7–88; (2) Les lettres d'intention dans la négociation des contrats internationaux, D.P.C.I. 1977, 73–122; (3) Les clauses de l'offre concurrente, du client le plus favorisé et la clause de premier refus dans les contrats internationaux, D.P.C.I. 1978, 185–220; (4) Les clauses de force majeure dans les contrats internationaux, D.P.C.I. 1979, 469–506; (5) Aspects juridiques des contrats de compensation, D.P.C.I. 1981, 179–223; (6) Les clauses pénales dans les contrats internationaux, D.P.C.I. 1982, 401–42; (7) Les obligations "survivant au contrat" dans les contrats internationaux, D.P.C.I. 1984, 1–27; (8) Les clauses limitatives et exonératoires de responsabilité et de garantie dans les contrats internationaux, R.D.A.I./I.B.L.J. 1985, 435–78; (9) La pratique du préambule dans les contrats internationaux, R.D.A.I./I.B.L.J. 1986, 343–69; (10) Best

rules,[44] usages and custom in international trade.[45] Also, it is difficult to make assessments of the use of official uniform law instruments in practice based on empirical data because to my knowledge these data are lacking. Although huge efforts are sometimes made to collect information regarding for instance CISG and other UNCITRAL texts,[46] the 1958 New York Convention, UNIDROIT texts or transportation conventions, these collections remain incomplete and show only reported cases on these instruments. Unreported cases often remain hidden and the collections do not form empirical evidence regarding the attitudes of parties and lawyers (including judges and arbitrators) towards uniform law. As regards arbitral case law, confidentiality often requires that awards are not published and, therefore, it is often difficult to draw representative conclusions from the published awards. Thus, a lot of empirical work is still to be done in order to collect information about the various forms and manifestations of international commercial self-regulation[47] and regarding their actual use in practice.

A different perspective is the normative approach. Here, one may first refer to Gessner's contribution in relation to an empirical study on international court litigation. In that contribution, Gessner offers a theoretical framework for globalisation based on two postulates: (1) the existence of a world society; and (2) the existence of social institutions (Gessner, 1996a: 15–18). Both postulates are useful from the policy point of view since they clarify whether and to what extent global law is desirable and attainable and emphasise the role of individuals and groups in any such process. In this respect, national state regulation does not contribute much to a world society and social institutions such as

---

efforts, reasonable care, due diligence et règles de l'art dans les contrats internationaux/"Best efforts", "reasonable care", "due diligence" and industry standards in international agreements, R.D.A.I./I.B.L.J. 1988, 983–1027; (11) Les clauses de confidentialité dans les contrats internationaux/Confidentiality clauses in international contracts, R.D.A.I./I.B.L.J. 1991, 3–94; (12) Les clauses de divorce dans les contrats de groupement d'entreprises internationaux/Divorce clauses in international joint venture contracts, R.D.A.I./I.B.L.J. 1995, 279–315; (13) Les clauses de cession dans les contrats commerciaux internationaux/Assignment clauses in international commercial contracts, R.D.A.I./I.B.L.J. 1996, 799–833; (14) Termination clauses in international contracts/Les clauses mettant fin aux contrats internationaux, R.D.A.I./I.B.L.J. 1997, 801–36; (15) Interpretation clauses in international contracts/Les clauses d'interprétation dans les contrats internationaux, R.D.A.I./I.B.L.J. 2000 (forthcoming). The first 11 reports were written by the Honorary Chairman of the GTCI, Professor Marcel Fontaine. 10 of these reports were compiled by Fontaine (1989).

[44] One of the exceptions is the application of the ICC's Uniform Custom and Practices regarding Documentary Credits (UCP 500), ICC Publication No. 500 (Paris, ICC Publishing, 1993). UCP 500 are used in the great majority of letter of credit cases because of their endorsement by banking associations in many countries and of the standard use of a *subject to UCP 500* clause in letters of credit, primarily through electronic banking systems such as SWIFT.

[45] For an exception with empirical information on cross-border debt collection in England, Germany and Turkey, on the London reinsurance market and on international bank retailing activities, see the respective contributions of Budak, Stammel and Frick in Gessner and Budak (1998: 17–53, 61–91 and 93–137). See also Flood and Skordaki (1997: 109–31).

[46] For instance UNCITRAL's CLOUT system (Case Law On UNCITRAL Texts), databases on CISG cases in Rome (Unilex, Professor Bonell), White Plains NY (Mr. Kritzer), Freiburg (Professor Schlechtriem), Geneva (Professor Will, see Will (1999)), ICCA's database on the New York Convention (published in the Y.B.Com.Arb.) and the UNIDROIT Newsletter.

[47] For a first preliminary list see De Ly (1998b: 61–4).

national courts and the national legal professions are equally not heavily involved in finding global answers to problems regarding national court litigation and to application of national conflict and substantive rules or of uniform law (Gessner, 1996a: 19–24). This is different in relation to self-regulation where especially large and medium-sized companies may benefit from any such rules.[48] These rules are primarily related to business law (*lex mercatoria*)[49] because a clear need and interest are present to establish self-regulatory rules.[50] However, the non-comprehensive nature of the *lex mercatoria* reduces its impact in practice because for that very reason businessmen do not internalise or observe its rules and, therefore, its existence is to be derived from the legal profession and particularly from the international arbitration community (Gessner, 1998: 435–9). Increased international economic integration, however, has not produced to the same extent social and cultural integration, even within the business community. Attitudes are still to a large extent national, leading to culture shocks, conflicts and clashes although sometimes manifestations of more universalism (universal culture) or intermediate cultural forms (third cultures) may be found.[51] Thus, sociolegal research should concentrate on describing the mix between national regulation and self-regulation and explaining the social and cultural factors which determine these complex regulatory processes.

The merits of Gessner's approach are that the debate regarding the appropriate solutions for global commercial law problems is not reduced to finding exclusive answers in national law, uniform law or self-regulation but that the answer is formulated in finding the proper mix between various types of regulation. Also, the mere economic approach to globalisation where regulation should follow economic integration is rejected and globalisation is seen not only as an economic but also as a social and cultural process which raises the questions of the relationship between these various factors.

[48] Small enterprises will be less frequent users of international self-regulation because they are generally less engaged in international trade. A different picture is presented in relation to multinational companies which create their intra-group procedures and rules (internalisation) and in that respect do not need self-regulation aimed at inter-company problems.

[49] Individuals acting in their private capacity for instance as consumers or in relation to family law problems have fewer incentives and less organisational muscle to develop self-regulatory rules.

[50] Gessner (1996a: 31–2). It is submitted that need and incentive alone are insufficient and that it is also required that the industry has the organisational infrastructure to develop these rules. See De Ly (1998b: 60) where three conditions are set: (1) market operators must sufficiently participate in the activities of the trade organisation; (2) the organisation must be sufficiently representative for the trade concerned; and (3) the organisation should have sufficient authority to have its rules accepted by its members.

[51] Gessner (1996a: 33–9). Gessner cited transnational legal practice and codes of conduct for multinational companies as examples of building a universal culture and the self-regulation of the diamond trade as an example of a third culture. I would prefer to characterise all three forms as examples of third cultures because codes of conduct were highly controversial between developed countries and developing countries and hardly any universal solution has been accepted. For instance, the OECD code of conduct is a OECD product and not a universal product and developing countries would argue that it does not go far enough in the regulation of the activities of multinational companies. Also, transnational legal practice is primarily a US and UK led race which hardly can claim universality.

A second socio-legal contribution to the debate regarding the *lex mercatoria* is Dezalay and Garth (1996). This fascinating and sometimes controversial book analyses the international arbitration community and is, therefore, highly relevant for the purposes of a discussion regarding the *lex mercatoria*.[52] In doing so, it focuses on the big arbitration cases (Dezalay and Garth, 1996: 11, 86), for example, the large oil arbitrations and the mega-construction disputes, resulting from decolonisation, the oil crises and the petrodollar megaprojects (Dezalay and Garth, 1996: 31). It distinguishes primarily between two generations of arbitrators: the grand old men and the new generation of arbitration technocrats. Both generations are characterised by *virtue*: expertise, neutrality and judgement (Dezalay and Garth, 1996: 8). However, there are striking differences between the two generations. The grand old men are arbitrators mostly from continental Europe and with academic backgrounds recruited for reasons of their prestige (both national and international) and social skills (Dezalay and Garth, 1996: 35–6).

Thus, they tend to have more eye for the broader including political ramifications of a case than for the technicalities. They are *legal artisans* doing arbitrations primarily for reasons of status (Dezalay and Garth, 1996: 36–7, 54). The younger generation of arbitration technocrats, on the other hand, are more US-style influenced litigators which focus more than the great old man on factual analyses, issues of evidence, case management, litigation strategies and contract clause interpretation. Also, the new generation runs its arbitration service business much more as an enterprise with management tools and the client's needs as the decisive criterion for decision-making whereas the older generation was more supply-driven, looking at the long-term developments of the industry (Dezalay and Garth, 1996: 195–6).

The new generation is led by some Paris-based offices of US law firms which found an offshore line of business in relation to ICC arbitrations.[53] The differences in approach became manifest in instances such as the involvement of the Secretariat of the ICC International Court of Arbitration in the arbitral process, the fact that arbitration is gradually moving to litigation and the declaration of independence where prospective arbitrators have to disclose their relationships not only with the parties but also with counsel representing clients (Dezalay and Garth, 1996: 38 and 48–9).

In this battle between two generations, Dezalay and Garth claim that the new generation seems to be winning. The market for international business conflicts has become more transparent and competition has increased, replacing the more corporatist allocation mechanisms of the grand old men's club. This has influenced not only the ICC scheme but also the London and AAA arbitration markets. Arbitration centres in other cities such as Cairo and Hong Kong as well

---

[52] The methodology of this research is both descriptive and empirical based on interviews.

[53] Dezalay and Garth (1996: 31, 36, 40, 54). To this, one may add the prominence of some big London-based law firms which more recently strengthened their arbitration departments or groups which are hardly described in Chap. 7 of the book.

as the CIETAC scheme in mainland China have also increased competition and challenged the monopoly of the Club.[54]

According to both authors, the *lex mercatoria* must also be understood against this background and its changing environment. Basically, their proposition is that the *lex mercatoria* is a product of the old generation[55] which is not endorsed by the technocrats because it is too vague, unpredictable and too much of an academic product. Consequently, its importance is decreasing and it maybe doomed to disappear (Dezalay and Garth, 1996: 39, 41–2, 85–91 and 107–10).

After this brief summary of *Dealing in Virtue*, one must assess its relevance regarding the debate on the *lex mercatoria*. First, it must be noted that, to my knowledge, it is the most important contribution to the *law in action* regarding the application and attitudes with respect to transnational legal rules in international commercial arbitration. It confirms the impression created by publications of arbitrators that there is a lot of controversy in the international commercial arbitration community on the existence and application of any such system or rules in international commercial arbitration. It confirms that some grand old men for reasons common to their generation believed in the ideals of transnational commercial law fostering the interests of international trade. It also confirms that many English and American arbitrators are quite reluctant, if not hostile, to the *lex mercatoria*. However, the characterisation in two classes where one class sees the *lex mercatoria* as a religion and the other one pays lip-service to it but basically does not consider it as a legitimate standard for arbitral adjudication, seems to oversimplify things and does not correspond to the detailed analysis set forth above. There are intermediate forms combining in mixed degrees elements of both the old and new generations' approaches.

Another criticism is related to the fact that *Dealing in Virtue* primarily deals with mega-arbitrations such as in the petroleum industry. Often, one is then faced with *state contracts* which give their own flavours and raise specific problems. In that respect, it is risky to generalise about other ICC cases or other arbitrations. As has been stated above, ICC cases are not representative of international commercial arbitration in general. Also, in ICC cases other than the mega-cases, the environment is different because the interests at stake are lower, which implies that arbitration clients may be less willing to pay for extensive common law style litigation. This argument may also be rephrased as follows. The analyses and conclusions of *Dealing in Virtue* may be valid for the niche market for mega-ICC or -ICSID arbitrations but may be questionable for the bottom and non top arbitration markets administered by these or other[56] institutions.

---

[54] Dezalay and Garth, chaps. 7, 8, 11 and 12. One might add more recent developments such as the WIPO Arbitration Scheme in Geneva.

[55] The role of Goldman in the development of the *lex mercatoria* has been discussed above. His influence is related to his activities in French public life and his involvement as a leading arbitrator and scholar as well as to his personality.

[56] Notably commodities arbitration, maritime arbitration or national arbitration centres.

These observations limit the relevance of *Dealing in Virtue* which, however, does not imply that we are not witnessing a fierce battle for the top arbitration market. However, it is unclear whether this battle is to be won by the large firms. They have the advantage of economies of scale and—to a certain extent—of economies of scope and are able to hire top talent for reasons of status, power and money. They have the disadvantage of high cost structures (overhead) and firm-wide profitability targets which must be reflected in price (hourly rates) and limits on selection of cases (only the big cases). For that reason, niche firms (boutiques) such as some Swiss firms may be serious competitors with price, personal service and full arbitration service advantages.

Finally, Banakar has raised the question of the sociological legitimacy of the growing autonomy of international commercial arbitration from municipal laws and the creation in that respect of rules of *lex mercatoria* (Banakar, 1998: 347–98). Banakar—following Max Weber—distinguishes between particular legitimacy where the application of rules of *lex mercatoria* may be legitimate provided there is a legal basis for any such application and procedural rules have been observed. For instance, application of *lex mercatoria* is legitimate if there is no choice of law provision in the contract, any such application is invoked by one of the parties during the arbitral proceedings and is not criticised by the law at the place of arbitration because this law does not impose the application of national law by virtue of local conflict rules. However, there is also the concept of general legitimation where the issue is much more whether application of the *lex mercatoria* is compatible with other standards and values in global and municipal societies. Here, Banakar argues that the arbitration community is too much self-centred and one-dimensional to be able to achieve general legitimation (Banakar, 1998: 355–61, 390–1) and therefore develops formal rather than substantive rules ("reflexive rationality"). However, one should note that in the theory regarding the *lex mercatoria* this very process of general legitimation has been discussed and that this issue was a reason for scholars or practictioners either to reject the theory or to incorporate these concerns by means of concepts such as transnational substantive rules or transnational public policy. In the practice of international arbitration, pragmatic attitudes prevail but there have been cases (for example, arbitrability of anti-trust law, arbitrability of state contract litigation, corruption issues) where arbitrators cannot avoid taking a clear position regarding sensitive issues thereby developing substantive legitimation for their award and for international commercial arbitration as a dispute settlement technique.

By way of conclusion, one might say that sociolegal research indicates that international businessmen and lawyers are aware of the regulatory challenges created by globalisation. One of their answers is international self-regulation including international arbitral adjudication processes leading to application of non-national rules. Thus, sociolegal research seems to confirm the desirability of international self-regulation. However, sociolegal research also indicates that there are differences of opinion regarding the extent to which this has been (see the difference of opinion regarding the acceptance by the new generation of the *lex mercatoria*) or may be achieved (see Gessner's cultural and social factors).

The preceding section discussed the desirability of a *lex mercatoria* approach to globalisation. This section deals with the legitimacy of any such effort. Five different but interrelated reasons may be given which explain the application of the *lex mercatoria* primarily in international commercial arbitration.

First, there are legal considerations which may bring about the application of the *lex mercatoria* by arbitrators. The argument most advanced is that national legal rules are not adapted to be applied in international trade and that, therefore, differentiation is in order (see also Goode, 1997: 30–1). The argument was primarily developed in the 1920s in French domestic law in some instances to liberalise international transactions from mandatory provisions of domestic law.[57] The 1981 French International Arbitration Act also opted for a *dualistic system* to distinguish between domestic and international arbitrations. This line of reasoning influenced Goldman and was used as an argument to support the existence of the *lex mercatoria*. Thus, *lex mercatoria* may be applied in international commercial arbitration instead of domestic law when the applicable domestic law is out-dated or ill-adapted to the needs of international trade by virtue of a choice by the parties or by virtue of a liberal provision in the arbitration law of the place of arbitration. However, one might also construe such a conclusion on the basis of a differentiation between international transactions and domestic transactions in the applicable domestic law. Any such considerations are akin to the *better law* approach in conflict of laws. The major problem with these approaches is that arbitrators need to justify why a given rule is better than the normally applicable domestic rule. Uniform law and comparative analysis may provide important persuasive arguments in any such process. The argument that domestic law is out-dated or by its very nature is unfit for international transactions has often been used but seems to be a postulate of the mercatorists which is often based on the belief that domestic law is too dirigistic and needs to be supplemented by more liberal rules for international transactions (see below) (see De Ly, 1992: 312). In my opinion, it needs to be proved in any given case.

A second example of a legal consideration is these cases where conflict of laws does not produce satisfactory results. These cases include situations where the contract cannot be localised properly because it is not related to the territory of any country (open sea, space), it is related to too many countries (plurilocalisation) or localisation could be arbitrary. The shortcomings of the conflict of laws may then be solved by reference to the *lex mercatoria* (Goode, 1997: 31).

[57] E.g., the abolition of the gold standard for bonds, the prohibition on arbitral clauses for merchants, the non-severability of arbitral clauses, the prohibition for the state to enter into arbitration agreements: see De Ly (1992: 293–4).

Secondly, application of the *lex mercatoria* can also be justified on practical considerations. For instance, proof of foreign law may be difficult in international litigation or arbitration. Different legal systems have developed different answers to this problem. In England, foreign law is treated as fact and absence of proving it triggers the application of English law. In other countries, judges and arbitrators may *ex officio* apply foreign law. In a third category of countries, judges and arbitrators are under an obligation to apply foreign law *ex officio* with exceptions for provisional relief or where it is impossible to apply foreign law because no information is available. In these cases, general principles of law may be applied instead of the *lex fori*—certainly in arbitration because there is often hardly any link with the place of arbitration but for that place—which opens prospects—for practical reasons—for the application of the *lex mercatoria* (Lando, 1997a: 582–3). This practical element also has its downside. If *lex mercatoria* is to be applied for these reasons, it may itself raise practical problems because the contents of the *lex mercatoria* are vague and require further research.

Thirdly, the *lex mercatoria* may be applied for psychological reasons in international commercial arbitration. Since arbitration is a private dispute settlement process, it involves private relationships between the arbitrators, the parties and the attorneys. Arguments based on *lex mercatoria* may be used to convince others that a given solution is reasonable and fair. Any such argument then serves as a tool to come to a certain conclusion. It reverses the logical order of an argument and cannot for that reason alone legitimate an arbitral award.[58] If used with other legitimate arguments, it is used as an *obiter dictum* to convince the parties that the conclusion reached also finds support in the *lex mercatoria*. Furthermore, it may have the psychological advantage of neutrality if the law of one of the parties otherwise should prevail over the law of the other party (Lando, 1997a: 579; Goode, 1997: 30). This psychological reason can be important in cases such as *state contracts* where there are delicate political considerations.

Another element of this psychological argument relates to the deliberations within arbitral tribunals, particularly with party-appointed arbitrators. Deliberations also may involve negotiations and compromise.[59] Arguments based on the *lex mercatoria* can be used to find unanimity or a majority within the arbitral tribunal. In that respect, they serve a useful tool to avoid deadlocks if the argument confirms an argument under domestic law or is substantiated by uniform law or comparative law research. In the case of party-appointed arbitrators who block the decision-making process because of bias or lack of intellectual independence from the appointing party, reliance on the *lex mercatoria* may give the other arbitrators an opportunity to agree or to find an additional argument for their majority award.

---

[58] Violation of logics is, however, not a reason to set aside arbitral awards because judicial review regarding substance and motivation is in most jurisdiction excluded.

[59] See in this respect Bredin (1982: 15–27) and the same author's ironical contribution on the *aequitas mercatorum* (1994: 109–18); as well as Reisman (1992: 68 and 95–6).

Fourthly, the emergence of and debate regarding the *lex mercatoria* can also be explained on the basis of developments in the legal profession. One may refer again to Dezalay and Garth's book which emphasises that an intellectual elite created the *lex mercatoria* as an autonomous legal system to provide international arbitration services with less competition from the local bars. Contrary to Dezalay and Garth, I would argue that the big law firms and the boutique firms, which in their terminology constitute the new generation, are also sympathetic to the *lex mercatoria* for the same competitive reasons as the old generation. Participants on the international market for arbitration services have an interest in endorsing and promoting the *lex mercatoria* because as a product of the market in which they operate they are seen by clients as having expertise regarding that product while the local bars do not have a similar expertise. They have a competitive advantage which to a certain extent protects their market position from new entrants or increases the entry costs for new entrants. This management element helps to explain the success of the *lex mercatoria*. The question is whether in itself its use in practice can be legitimised if any such use is self-centred on the part of the supply side of the market. However, if the demand side is satisfied with these services or has sufficient alternatives to go to other suppliers, one might argue that market mechanisms and competition should be able to play. The counter-argument is, of course, that arbitration services are not only demanded and offered on a market but also function as dispute resolution mechanisms where broader public interests are at stake (see Reisman, 1992: 142–6).

Finally, one cannot understand the *lex mercatoria* if one does not take its liberal[60] underpinnings into account. One of the basic thrusts and assumptions of many proponents of the *lex mercatoria* is that parties and arbitrators should be freed from government interference, at the least regarding the substance of the dispute (De Ly, 1998a: 45–7). However, a preference for a political ideology can hardly alone be a legitimate reason for application of standards of adjudication in international commercial arbitration (Goode, 1997: 31).

ASSESSMENT AND CONCLUSION

The *lex mercatoria* is one of the answers to problems raised by increasing international trade transactions after World War II. The intensified economic integration of the end of the 1980s and the 1990s is often called a process of economic globalisation but does not raise new issues for international business law. The *lex mercatoria* has at least three meanings: (1) a substantive and international conception proposed by Schmitthoff; (2) a legal system apart from national law; and (3) a method of judicial and arbitral adjudication. The third concept is to be preferred. The *lex mercatoria* as defined under (1) is generally

---

[60] As this expression is used in continental Europe.

accepted. As defined under (2), it is influential with scholars, national arbitration statutes and in ICC arbitrations but it has limited practical impact in other cases. Since (3) is a new theory, its impact is still unknown.

Legal philosophy may show various elements of the theory of the *lex mercatoria*: its universal ambitions, its support from the business community or its support from practitioners applying and creating its rules. Law and economics may show whether and to what extent the *lex mercatoria* may be an efficient way of international regulation but empirical data and normative consensus are still lacking. Legal sociology seems to give contradictory indications regarding businessmen's and practitioners' desire for and perceptions of transnational self-regulation replacing the traditional national state paradigm. It is still unclear to what extent different views are representative for worldwide or regional communities of businessmen and practitioners.

Apart from existence, acceptance and desirability of the *lex mercatoria*, there also is the question of its legitimacy in a national or transnational legal setting. In that respect, it has been argued that legitimacy solely based on liberal policies is risky if not unacceptable. Also, legitimacy cannot alone be based on the interests of the legal profession benefiting from providing arbitration services. Therefore, legitimacy is to be sought if the *lex mercatoria* can contribute to substantive or processual justice (see the legal considerations above) or serves the arbitral process's efficiency (see the practical and psychological considerations above).

REFERENCES

Amelung, Torsten (1991), "The Impact of Transaction Costs on the Directions of Trade—Empirical Evidence for Asia Pacific", *Journal of Institutional and Theoretical Economics 147 (4);* 716–32.

Banakar, Reza (1998), "Reflexive Legitimacy in International Arbitration", in Volkmar Gessner and Ali Cem Budak (eds.), *Emerging Legal Certainty:Empirical Studies on the Globalization of Law*, (Aldershot: Ashgate).

Behrens, Peter (1993), "Arbitration as an instrument of conflict resolution in international trade: its basis and limits", in Daniel Friedmann and Ernst-Joachim Mestmäcker (eds.), *Conflict Resolution in International Trade* (Baden-Baden: Nomos).

Benson, Bruce (1987), "The Spontaneous Evolution of Commercial Law: What the Other Invisible Hand is Doing!" (Unpublished paper,Tallahasee, Flo.: Florida State University).

Berger, Klaus Peter (1993), "*Lex mercatoria* in der internationalen Wirtschaftsschiedsgerichtsbarkeit: der Fall 'Compania Valenciana'" *Praxis des internationalen Privat- und Verfahrensrechts;* 281–88.

—— (1996), *Formalisierte oder "schleichende" Kodifizierung des transnationalen Wirtschaftsrechts: zu den methodischen und praktischen Grundlagen der lex mercatoria* (Berlin: de Gruyter). (Translated into English by Klaus Peter Berger as *Creeping Codification of the Lex Mercatoria* (The Hague: Kluwer Law International, 1999).)

Blaurock, Uwe (1993), "Übernationales Recht des internationalen Handels", *Zeitschrift für europäisches Privatrecht* 1; 247–67.

Bonell, Michael Joachim (1976), "The UNIDROIT Initiative for the Progressive Codification of International Law", *International and Comparative Law Quarterly* 25; 413.

—— (1988), "A 'Restatement' of Principles for International Commercial Contracts: An Academic Exercise or a Practical Need?", *Revue du droit des affaires internationales/International Business Law Journal* 7; 873–88.

—— (1990), "International Uniform Law in Practice—Or Where the Real Trouble Begins", *American Journal of Comparative Law* 38; 865–88.

—— (1992a), "Das UNIDROIT-Projekt für die Ausarbeitung von Regeln für internationale Handelsverträge", *Rabels Zeitschrift für ausländisches und internationales Privatrecht* 56; 274–89.

—— (1992b), "Unification of Law by Non-Legislative Means—The UNIDROIT Draft Principles for International Commercial Contracts" , *American Journal of Comparative Law* 40; 617–33.

—— (ed.) (1999), *The UNIDROIT Principles of International Commercial Contracts* (The Hague: Kluwer Law International).

Bortolotti, Fabio (1995), "Vers une nouvelle *lex mercatoria* de l'agence commerciale internationale? Le modèle de contrat d'agence de la CCI", *Revue du droit des affaires internationales/International Business Law Journal* n° 6 (1995); 685–98.

Booysen, Hercules (1992), "Die internationale *lex mercatoria*—Das Erfordernis ihrer Umgestaltung zu einer rechtswissenschaftlichen Synthese und ihr Verhältnis zum Völkerrecht", *Archiv des Völkerrechts* 30; 196–211.

—— (1995a), "Völkerrecht als Vertragsstatut internationaler privatrechtlicher Verträge", *Rabels Zeitschrift für ausländisches und internationales Privatrecht* 59; 245–57.

—— (1995b), *International Transactions and the International Law Merchant* (Pretoria: Interlegal).

Bredin, Jean Denis (1982), "La loi du juge", in *Le droit des relations économiques internationales;Etudes offertes à Berthold Goldman* (Paris: Librairies Techniques).

—— (1994), "A la recherche de l' 'aequitas mercatoria'" , in *Internationalisation du droit, Mélanges en l'honneur de Yvon Loussouarn* (Paris: Dalloz).

Budak, Ali Cem (1998), "Cross-Border Debt Collection: Examples of Turkey and Germany" in Volkmar Gessner and Ali Cem Budak (eds.), *Emerging Legal Certainty: Empirical Studies on the Globalization of Law* (Aldershot UK: Ashgate).

Bühler, Michael (1998), *The German Arbitration Act 1997: Text and Notes* (The Hague: Kluwer Law International).

Burman, Harold S. (1995), "International Conflict of Laws, the 1994 Inter-American Convention on the Law Applicable to International Contracts, and Trends for the 1990s" *Vanderbilt Journal of Transnational Law* 28; 367-87.

Carbonneau, Thomas (ed.), (1998), Lex Mercatoria *and Arbitration; A Discussion of the New Law Merchant* (rev. ed.) (The Hague: Kluwer Law International).

Chukwumerije, Okezie (1994), *Choice of Law in International Commercial Arbitration* (Westport, Conn.: Quorum Books).

Cooter, Robert D. (1994), "Structural Adjudication and the New Law Merchant: A Model for Decentralized Law", *International Review of Law and Economics* 14 ; 215–31.

—— (1996a), "The Structural Approach to Decentralized Law: A Theory of Games and Norms", in Richard Buxbaum, G. Hertig, Alain Hirsch, and Klaus Hopt (eds.) *European Economic and Business Law* (Berlin: de Gruyter).

—— (1996b), "Decentralized Law for a Complex Economy: The Structural Approach to Adjudicating the New Law Merchant", *University of Pennsylvania Law Review* 144 ; 1643–96.

Davidson, Fraser (1997), "The New Arbitration Act: A Model Law?" *Journal of Business Law* 1997; 101–29.

Derains, Yves (1993), "Intervention During the Discussion", in Emmanuel Gaillard (ed.), *Transnational Rules in International Commercial Arbitration* (Paris: ICC Publication).

Dezalay, Yves and Bryant G. Garth (1996), *Dealing in Virtue, International Commercial Arbitration and the Construction of a Transnational Legal Order* (Chicago: University of Chicago Press).

De Ly, Filip (1992), *International Business Law and* Lex Mercatoria (Amsterdam: T. M. C. Asser Instituut).

—— (1994), "Judicial Review of the Substance of Arbitral Awards" in Katharina Boele-Woelki et al. (eds.) *Comparability and Evaluation: Essays on Comparative Law, Private International Law and International Commercial Arbitration in Honour of Dimitra Kokkini-Iatridou* (Dordrecht: M. Nijhoff Publishers).

—— (1993), *Europese Gemeenschap en Privaatrecht* (Inaugural address Erasmus University, Zwolle, Tjeenk Willink).

—— (1998a), "*Lex Mercatoria* and Unification of Law in the European Union", in Arthur S. Hartkamp et al. (eds.), *Towards a European Civil Code*, 2nd edn. (The Hague: Kluwer Law International).

—— (1998b), "Uniform Commercial Law and International Self-Regulation", in Franco Ferrari (ed.), *The Unification of International Commercial Law* (Baden-Baden: Nomos).

—— (1998c), "The 1998 ICC Arbitration Rules", *International Arbitration Law Review*; 228–29.

—— (1999), "An Interim Report Regarding the Application of the UNIDROIT Principles of International Commercial Contracts in The Netherlands", in Michael J. Bonell (ed.) *The UNIDROIT Principles of International Commercial Contracts* (The Hague: Kluwer Law International).

Drobnig, Ulrich (1990), "Ein Vertragsrecht für Europa" in *Festschrift für Ernst Steindorff* (Berlin: de Gruyter) 1141–54.

Lande, Ole (1993), "Die Regeln des Europäischen Vertragsrechts", in Peter Christian Müller-Graff (ed.), *Gemeinsames Privatrecht in der Europäischen Gemeinschaft* (Baden-Baden: Nomos).

El-Ahdab, Abdul Hamid (1997), "The New Omani Arbitration Act in Civil and Commercial Matters", *Journal of International Arbitration* 14 ; 59–87.

Falk, R. (1975), "A New Paradigm for International Legal Studies: Prospects and Proposals", *Yale Law Journal* 85; 969–1021.

Flood, John and Eleni Skordadi (1997), "Normative Bricolage: Informal Rule-Making by Accountants and Lawyers in Mega-Insolvencies" in Gunther Teubner (ed.), *Global Law Without a State* (Aldershot: Dartmouth).

Fontaine, Marcel (1989), "Droit des contrats internationaux, Analyse et rédaction de clauses" (Paris: Forum Européen de la Communication).

Fontaine, Marcel (1991), "Les principes pour les contrats commerciaux internationaux élaborés par UNIDROIT", *Revue de droit international et de droit comparé* 68; 25-40.

Freyhold, Hanno von (1996), "Cross-Border Legal Interactions in New York Courts", in Volkmar Gessner (ed.), *Foreign Courts:Civil Litigation in Foreign Legal Cultures* (Aldershot: Dartmouth).

Frick, Klaus (1998), "Third Cultures versus Regulators: Cross-Border Legal Relations of Banks" in Volkmar Gessner and Ali Cem Budak (eds.), *Emerging Legal Certainty: Empirical Studies on the Globalization of Law* (Aldershot: Ashgate).

Gaillard, Emmanuel (ed.) (1993), *Transnational Rules in International Commercial Arbitration* (Paris: ICC Publication).

—— (1996), "Thirty Years of *Lex Mercatoria*: Towards the Discriminating Application of Transnational Rules" in Albert Jan Van den Berg (ed.), *Planning Efficient Arbitration Proceedings: The Law Applicable in International Arbitration* (The Hague: Kluwer Law International). (Also published as Trente ans de *Lex mercatoria*, Pour une application sélective de la méthode des principes généraux du droit, in *Clunet*, 1995, 5-30.)

Gessner, Volkmar (1996a), "The Institutional Framework of Cross-Border Interaction", in Volkmar Gessner (ed.), *Foreign Courts: Civil Litigation in Foreign Legal Cultures*, (Aldershot: Dartmouth).

—— (1996b), "International Cases in German First Instance Courts", in Volkmar Gessner (ed.), *Foreign Courts: Civil Litigation in Foreign Legal Cultures* (Aldershot: Dartmouth).

—— (1998), "Globalization and Legal Certainty", in Volkmar Gessner and Ali Cem Budak (eds.), *Emerging Legal Certainty: Empirical Studies on the Globalization of Law* (Aldershot: Ashgate).

Giardina, Andrea (1992), "La *lex mercatoria* e la certezza del diritto nei commerci e negli investimenti internazionali", *Rivista di diritto internazionale privato e processuale* 28; 461–70. (Also published in French as La *lex mercatoria* et la sécurité du commerce et des investissements internationaux, in *Nouveaux itinéraires en droit, Hommage à François Rigaux*, Brussels: Bruylant, 1993.)

Goldman, Berthold (1956), "Arbitrage international et droit commun des nations", *Revue de l'arbitrage* 1956 ; 115–16.

—— (1993), "Nouvelles réflexions sur la *Lex mercatoria*" in Christian Dominice et al. (eds.), *Etudes de droit international en l'honneur de Pierre Lalive* (Basle: Helbing & Lichtenhahn).

Goode, Roy (1997), "Usage and Its Reception in Transnational Commercial Law", *International and Comparative Law Quarterly* 46; 1–36. (Also published in Jacob S. Ziegel (ed.), *New Developments in International Commercial and Consumer Law: Proceedings of the 8th Biennial Conference of the International Academy of Commercial and Consumer Law* (Oxford: Hart, 1998.)

Grigera Naon, Horacio A. (1992), *Choice-of-Law Problems in International Commercial Arbitration* (Tübingen: J. C. B. Mohr).

Grundmann, S. (1992), "*Lex mercatoria* und Rechtsquellenlehre—insbesondere die Einheitlichen Richtlinien und Gebräuche für Dokumentenakkreditive", *Jahrbuch Junger Zivilrechtswissenschaftler 1991* (Stuttgart: Boorberg).

Harris, Bruce, Rowan Planterose, and Jonathan Tecks (1996), *The Arbitration Act 1996.* (London: Blackwell Science).

Hartkamp, Arthur S. (1994), "Principles of Contract Law", in Arthur S. Hartkamp (ed.), *Towards a European Civil Code* (Nijmegen: Ars Aequi Libri).

—— (1994), *The UNIDROIT Principles for International Commercial Contracts and the New Dutch Civil Code, CJHB* (Brunner-bundel) [Liber Amicorum Brunner]. (Deventer: Kluwer).

Humphreys, Gordon (1992), "La *lex mercatoria* en matière d'arbitrage international-quelques différences dans les optiques anglo-françaises", *Revue de droit des affaires internationales/International Business Law Journal*; 849–56.

Jafarian, Mansour and Mehrdad Rezaeian (1998), "The New Law on International Commercial Arbitration in Iran", *Journal of International Arbitration* 15 ; 31-52.

Jin, N. (1996), "The Status of *Lex Mercatoria* in International Commercial Arbitration", *The American Review of International Arbitration* 7; 181.

Juenger, Friedrich K. (1994), "The Inter-American Convention on the Law Applicable to International Contracts: Some Highlights and Comparisons" *American Journal of Comparative Law* 42; 381-394.

—— (1995), "American Conflicts Scholarship and the New Law Merchant" *Vanderbilt Journal of Transnational Law* 28; 487–501.

Kahn, Philippe (1961), *La vente commerciale internationale* (Paris: Sirey).

—— (1973), "*Lex mercatoria* et euro-obligations", in F. Fabricius (ed.) *Law and international trade, Festschrift für Clive M. Schmitthoff zum 70 Geburtstag* (Frankfurt: Athenäum Verlag).

—— (1982), "Droit international économique, droit du développement, *lex mercatoria*: concept unique ou pluralisme des ordres juridiques?" in *Le droit des relations économiques internationales: Etudes offertes à Berthold Goldman* (Paris: Librairies Techniques).

—— (1992), "La *lex mercatoria*: point de vue français après quarante ans de controverses" *McGill Law Journal* 37; 413-27.

Kappus, Andreas (1994), *Lex mercatoria* und internationale Handelsschieds-gerichtsbarkeit: Einheitliches Sach-und Prozessrecht für den Handelsstand" *Wirtschaft im Betrieb*; 189–91.

Kessedjian, Cathérine (1995), "Principe de la contradiction et arbitrage", *Revue de l'arbitrage* 1995; 381-410.

Koch, C. (1999), "The New Irish Arbitration Act of 1998", *Bulletin ASA* 17; 51-57.

Kronman, A.T. (1985), "Contract Law and the State of Nature", *Journal of Law, Economisc and Organizations* 1; 4-32.

Kurkela, Matti S. and Uoti, Petteri (1994), *Arbitration in Finland* (Helsinki: Finnish Lawyers' Publishing).

Kwatra, G. K. (1996), *The New Arbitration and Conciliation Law of India* (New Delhi: Indian Council of Arbitration).

Lagarde, Paul (1982), "Approche critique de la *lex mercatoria*. In *Le droit des relations économiques internationales: Etudes offertes à Berthold Goldman* (Paris: Librairies Techniques).

Lando, Ole (1983), "European Contract Law", *American Journal of Comparative Law* 31; 653-59.

—— (1985), "A Contract Law for Europe" *International Business Lawyer* 13; 17-21.

—— (1989a), "Principles of European Contract Law" , in Johan Erauw et al. (eds.) *Liber memorialis Francois Laurent 1810–1887* (Brussels: E. Story-Scientia).

Lando, Ole (1989b), "The Law Applicable to the Merits of the Dispute" in Petar Sarcevic (ed.), *Essays on International Commercial Arbitration* (London: Graham & Trotman).

—— (1992), "Principles of European Contract Law: An Alternative to or a Precursor of European Legislation?", *Rabels Zeitschrift für ausländisches und internationales Privatrecht*; 261-73. (Also published under same title in *American Journal of Comparative Law* 40 (3) (1992); 573-85; and as "Teaching a European Code of Contracts", in De Witt and Forder (ed.) *The Common Law of Europe and the Future of Legal Education* (Deventer: Kluwer, 1992).)

—— (1993), "Is Codification Needed in Europe? Principles of European Contract Law and the Relationship to Dutch Law", *European Review of Private Law* 1; 157-70.

—— (1994), "Assessing the Role of the UNIDROIT Principles in the Harmonization of Arbitration Law", *Tulane Journal of International and Comparative Law* 2; 129-43.

—— (1996-97), "Some Issues Relating to the Law Applicable to Contractual Obligations", *King's College Law Journal*; 62.

—— (1997a), "*Lex mercatoria* 1985-1996" *Festskrift till Stig Strömholm*; 567-84

—— (1997b), *The Harmonization of European Contract Law Through a Restatement of Principles* (University of Oxford, Centre for the Advanced Study of European and Comparative Law).

Lando, Ole, and Hugo Beale (eds.) (1995), "Commission on European Contract Law" in *The Principles of European Contract Law*, part I, Performance, Non-Performance and Remedies (Dordrecht: M. Nijhoff).

Level, Patrice (1993), "Quelle loi pour vos contrats dans l'Europe de 1993?" *La semaine juridique éd Etude, Supplément 5 Cahiers de Droit de l'Entreprise 1993* I; 15-32.

Loquin, Eric (1986), "L'application de règles anationales dans l'arbitrage commercial international" in Institute of International Business Law and Practice (ed.), *L'apport de la jurisprudence arbitrale* (Paris: ICC Publication).

Mayer, Pierre, (1989), "L'autonomie de l'arbitre international dans l'appréciation de sa propre compétence" *Recueil des cours de l'académie de droit international privé/Collected Courses of the Hague Academy of International Law* 217; V.

Medwig, M.T. (1993), "The New Law Merchant; Legal Rhetoric and Commercial Reality", *Law & Policy in International Business* 24; 589-616.

Mertens, Hans Joachim (1992), "Nichtlegislatorische Rechtsvereinheitlichung durch transnationales Wirtschaftsrecht und Rechtsbegriff", *Rabels Zeitschrift für ausländisches und internationales Privatrecht* 56; 219-42.

—— (1997), "A Self-Applying System Beyond National Law?" in Gunther Teubner (ed.), *Global Law Without a State* (Aldershot: Dartmouth).

Meyer, Rudolf (1994), *Bona fides und* lex mercatoria *in der europäischen Rechtstradition* (Göttingen: Wallstein Verlag).

Osman Falati (1992), *Les principes généraux de la* lex mercatoria (Paris: LGDJ).

Paulsson, Jan (1990), "La *lex mercatoria* dans l'arbitrage CCI" , *Revue de l'arbitrage* 1990 ; 55-100.

Plouvier, E (1992), "Perspectives droit, Les secrets de l'arbitrage, La 'loi des marchands'", *Le Monde*, 16 June, 34.

Procaccia, Uriel (1998), "The Case Against *Lex Mercatoria*", in Jacob S. Ziegel (ed.) *New Developments in International Commercial and Consumer Law*, Proceedings of the 8th Biennial Conference of the International Academy of Commercial and Consumer Law (Oxford: Hart).

Randall, K. and Norris, J. (1993), "A New Paradigm for International Business Transactions", *Washington University Law Quarterly*; 599-636.

Reich, Norbert (1992), "Competition Between Legal Orders; A New Paradigm of EC Law?" *Common Market Law Review;* 861-896.

Reisman, W. M. (1992), *Systems of Control in International Adjudication and Arbitration* (Durham: Duke University Press).

Remien, Oliver (1988), "Ansätze für ein Europäisches Vertragsrecht", *Zeitschrift für vergleichende Rechtswissenschaft* 87; 105-22.

Rigaux, François (1977), *Droit public et droit privé dans les relations internationales* (Paris: A. Pedone).

—— (1977), *Droit international privé*, I (Brussels: Larcier).

—— (1979), "Pour un autre ordre international", in *Droit économique*, 2 (Paris: A. Pedone).

—— (1989), "Les situations juridiques individuelles dans un système de relativité générale", *Recueil des cours de l'académie de droit international privé/Collected Courses of the Hague Academy of International Law* 213; 9-407.

Rigaux, François, and Raymond Vander Elst (1982), "Relations juridiques transnationales ou dialogue sur un autre droit" *Journal des tribunaux* 101; 231.

Rivkin, David, W. (1993a), "*Lex Mercatoria* and Force Majeure", in Emmanuel Gaillard (ed.) *Transnational Rules in International Commercial Arbitration* (Paris: ICC Publication).

—— (1993b), "Enforceability of Arbitral Awards Based on *Lex Mercatoria*" *Arbitration International* 9; 67-84.

Rubino-Sammartano, Mauro (1993), "The Channel Tunnel and the *Tronc Commun* Doctrine", *Journal of International Arbitration* 10 n° 3; 59-65.

Sanders, Pieter (1995), "Unity and Diversity in the Adoption of the Model Law", *Arbitration International* 14; 1-37.

—— (1999), *Quo Vadis Arbitration?: Sixty Years of Arbitration Practice: A Comparative Study* (The Hague: Kluwer International).

Schmidtchen, Dieter (1995), "Territorialität des Rechts, Internationales Privatrecht und die privatautonome Regelung internationaler Sachverhalte", *Rabels Zeitschrift für ausländisches und internationales Privatrecht* 59; 56-112.

Seifi, Jamal (1998), "The New International Commercial Arbitration Act of Iran" , *Journal of International Arbitration* 15 n° 2; 5-35.

Selden, B. S. (1995), "*Lex Mercatoria* in European and US Trade Practice: Time to Take a Closer Look", *Annual Survey International and Comparative Law* 111.

Stammel, Christine (1998), "Back to the Courtroom? Developments in the London Reinsurance Market", in Volkmar Gessner and Ali Cem Budak (eds.), *Emerging Legal Certainty: Empirical Studies on the Globalization of Law* (Aldershot: Ashgate).

Strenger, I. (1992), "La notion de *lex mercatoria* en droit du commerce international", 227 *Collected Courses of The Hague Academy of International Law*, 1991, II. (Dordrecht: Nijhoff).

Stein, Ursula (1995), Lex mercatoria, *Realität und Theorie* (Frankfurt: V. Klostermann).

Tallon, Dennis (1993), "Vers un droit européen de contrat?" in *Mélanges offerts à André Colomer* (Paris: Litec).

Teubner, Gunther (1997), "'Global Bukowina': Legal Pluralism in a World Society" in Gunther Teubner (ed.), *Global Law without a State* (Aldershot: Dartmouth).

Van Delden, Rob (1992), *De Lex Mercatoria, nog eens bekeken, in Tot persistit!* (Arnhem: Gouda Quint).

Vandenput, Tangui (1992), "La *lex mercatoria*", in Jacques Putzeys (ed.), *Les ventes internationales et les transports* (Louvain-la-Neuve: Bruylant).

Van Der Velden, Frans (1990), "Europa 1992 en het eenvormig privaatrecht" in Dimitra Kokkini-Iantridou and Willem Grosheide (eds.), *Molengrafica 1990* (Vermande: Lelystad).

Van Houtte, Hans (1994), *UNIDROIT principles of international commercial contracts and international commercial arbitration: their reciprocal relevance* (Report at seminar, Institute of International Business Law and Practice, Paris).

Wang, K (1996), "The Unification of the Dispute Resolution System in China" *Journal of International Arbitration*; 36-37.

Weinberg, K.S. (1994), "Equity in International Arbitration: How Fair is 'Fair'? A Study of *Lex Mercatoria* and Amiable Composition", *Boston University International Law Journal* 227-54.

Wilkinson, Vanessa L.D. (1995), "The New *Lex Mercatoria*, Reality or Academic Fantasy?", *Journal International Arbitration* 12 n°2; 103-15.

Will, Michael R. (1999), *1988–1998: 11 Years International Sales Law under CISG, the First 555 or So Decisions* (Geneva; Faculty of Law).

Williams, D. (1998), "New Zealand—The New Arbitration Act", *International Arbitration Law Review* 214-16.

Yu, H. L. (1998a), "A-National Principles in Taiwan", *International Arbitration Law Review* 217-19.

—— (1998b), "Some Thoughts on the Legal Status of A-National Principles in China", *International Arbitration Law Review* 185-87.

6

Lex Mercatoria—*Critical Comments on a Tricky Topic**

FELIX DASSER

Abstract

The author examines core issues concerning the notorious lex mercatoria. *The term is normally used in a way that does not focus on trade usages or other rules created by international businesspeople, as the term might suggest. It rather denotes a new conflict-of-law approach that dispenses with the application of a national law in favour of some vaguely defined international commercial standards. This revolutionary and often criticised approach is sometimes resorted to by international commercial arbitration tribunals, based either on a choice of law by the parties or their own choice of law analysis. Such awards are, however, statistically very rare. In the meantime, it appears well settled that such arbitral awards are generally recognised and enforced by national courts.*

I T SEEMS THAT everybody is talking about *lex mercatoria*. It is not just the talk of the town; it is the talk of the world. However, here we are already faced with the first problem: When we talk about "*lex mercatoria*", "new law merchant", "autonomous law of international commercial transactions" and the like, what exactly are we talking about? Are we talking about legal rules created *by* merchants, or legal rules created *for* merchants by academics, legislators, arbitrators and others? In practice, when lawyers talk about *lex mercatoria*, they normally mean a mixture of both, with emphasis on the second. Often, the mixture is ill-defined and rather casual, creating misunderstandings galore.

In my view, a crucial clue to an understanding of the *lex mercatoria* lies in its rather general definition as "(autonomous) law of international trade" or similar phrases which all contain the concept of internationality, of cross-border business. Taking a closer look, I find such a definition puzzling. After all, what exactly is the factual difference, from a *merchant's* perspective, between a domestic transaction and an international one in terms of trade usage? I take it that there is not much of a difference, if any.

---

* This chapter is a slightly extended version of an oral contribution at the workshop with added statistical data. Its purpose is to elaborate on certain points raised in the excellent chapter by my learned colleague Filip De Ly.

LEX MERCATORIA: NOT TRADE USAGES AS SUCH

What, then, explains why lawyers confine the *lex mercatoria* to an international context? In my view, the reason is that lawyers do not usually look at the *lex mercatoria* from a businessperson's perspective, but from a conflict-of-law perspective. Their question is not whether there are business usages concerning, for example, commodity trading. Of course these exist, and of course judges all over the world can apply them under basically any legal system if they want to. In view of the universally accepted principles of good faith and protection of reasonable party expectations it would be difficult to justify *not* applying them, subject to (rare) mandatory rules of law. There is no need for a special legal theory to justify their application, let alone a fancy Latin word (see for example Paulsson, 1990: 69 ff.; Mustill, 1987: 149, 157–8). On the other hand, such casual application of rules created by merchants is a worthy subject for the sociology of law, although gathering meaningful data would not be easy.

The traditional legal systems often contain even explicit references to trade usage. Well known examples are Article 9 of the United Nations Convention on the International Sale of Goods (CISG), Sections 1–205, 1–103 and 1–102 of the Uniform Commercial Code (UCC), or section 346 of the German Commercial Code (see Berman and Dasser, 1998: 53, 56–7). In addition, in some jurisdictions, businesspeople sit alongside professional judges on the bench in order to provide the necessary knowledge of pertinent trade usages. For example, the Zurich Commercial Court has a roster of "commercial" judges, that is, businesspeople of the various branches of the economy. Each panel consists of two professional judges and three commercial judges who are acquainted with the business concerned. They decide the cases based on their own knowledge of any pertinent trade usages without bothering about grand legal theories. In arbitration, this intentionally pragmatic approach is better formalised by the many arbitration laws and rules that require the arbitral tribunal to "take into account" relevant trade usages in any case, even if the law applicable to the substance of the dispute does not contain such a reference to trade usages.[1]

Such an emphasis on business expectations is a *sine qua non* for a smooth and fruitful development of international business. As a consequence, such emphasis cannot just be the job of a specific legal theory or legal order; it must be the aim for the law as such. The legal orders are indeed smoothing out their

---

[1] See e.g., Art. 28(4) UNCITRAL Model Law on International Commercial Arbitration (1985); Art. VII(1) European Convention on International Commercial Arbitration 1961; Art. 1496(2) French Code of Civil Procedure; Art. 17(2) ICC Rules of Arbitration 1998. Such a reference to trade usages sometimes serves as a basis for the application of the *lex mercatoria* as such, including general principles of law, such as in the ICC award no. 5314/88. There, one party requested the application of Massachusetts law, the other the *lex mercatoria*. In an interim decision, the arbitrator tried hard to please both parties by deciding that he would apply Massachusetts law, "supplemented if needed by the lex mercatoria"—whatever that means.

parochial rough edges and converging towards common legal principles and methodologies at increasing speed. Remember the time when there was an abyss between common law and civil law? Where is it today, except in the books for first-year law students?

THE *LEX MERCATORIA* AS A NEW CONFLICT-OF-LAW THEORY

The real question lurking behind the concept of *lex mercatoria* that focuses on *international* commerce is whether we have to apply any national law at all according to the traditional conflict-of-law concepts—or whether we may simply and *exclusively* apply rules that were developed for international business transactions outside the traditional framework of national laws and international conventions.[2]

For businesspeople, this is an increasingly academic question—trade usages will be applied anyway (see Goode, 1997: 8). For conflict-of-law scholars on the other hand, it is—or rather was—about legal anarchy. Thus, when Berthold Goldman (1964) suggested almost 40 years ago that there exists a *lex mercatoria* that could eventually become a legal order independent of national laws, he earned an expected outcry from legal purists that still echoes today.[3] Businesspeople, however, did not respond. They were not expected to; and they were not even informed. Even now, you can ask almost any businessperson what he or she thinks of the *lex mercatoria* or the autonomous legal order of international commerce, and you will earn a blank stare. Nevertheless, the great *lex mercatoria* debate was born. It raged throughout the 1970s and 1980s.

A FIELD STUDY OF ARBITRAL AWARDS

In the late 1980s, I started to investigate the topic. I was soon intrigued by the fierce academic dispute, which was aptly described by one participant as "trench warfare" (Lagarde, 1982: 125). I decided to take a different approach, based on empirical work and so less likely to draw ideological flak.

First, I looked at arbitration practice. After extensive international research in libraries and in the "field", I found fewer than 30 arbitral awards that were

---

[2] In the tradition of Clive Schmitthoff, some international conventions are sometimes supposed to be part of a *lex mercatoria*, such as the Vienna Sales Convention CISG (see, e.g., ICC awards no. 6149/90, 7331/94). However, if the convention in question is applicable anyway, according to the conflict-of-law rule applied by the arbitrator, it does not serve any practical purpose to stick a fancy label to it. If, on the other hand, the arbitrator cannot apply it under any reasonable conflict-of-law rule, it would be rather audacious if she applied it nonetheless as part of a *lex mercatoria*, not least since the CISG—as the most important convention—is still consciously shunned by many merchants and was never designed as a codification of existing trade practices. See also Goode (1997: 20–5).

[3] For an overview of the debate, see the chapter by Filip De Ly (in this book); Berger (1996: 29–108); Carbonneau (1998); and Dasser (1989: 42–73).

exclusively based on a non-national legal system that could somehow be packed under the notion of a *lex mercatoria* in an extremely broad sense of the term—including natural law, general principles applied by international tribunals, and the like. Another 15 awards referred to a non-national law including principles of public international law *in combination with* a national law. These somewhat over 40 awards cover a time-span of about 50 years (Dasser, 1989: 180–257).[4]

To what percentage of arbitral awards does this correspond? An absolutely marginal one, although the necessarily haphazard method of my research—given the secretiveness of arbitration—does not allow any precise calculation. I found that the concept of a non-national law, be it the *lex mercatoria* or something else, was virtually absent in the arbitration of trade associations, where the overwhelming majority of international commercial arbitration cases is decided. These tribunals invariably either apply national law or act as *amiables compositeurs* who decide *ex aequo et bono* without reference to any law. The few pertinent awards that I found were, with very few exceptions, either from International Chamber of Commerce (ICC) arbitration or from *ad hoc* arbitration with European arbitrators of academic background.

The total number of international commercial arbitration cases handled worldwide is difficult to guess. It may be noted, however, that the ICC—which is just one of several major institutions administering such cases—currently has about 500 new cases per year. In addition to such institutional arbitration, there are many *ad hoc* arbitral proceedings that do not appear on any statistics. Judging from the data available, the total number per year is likely to be several thousand, not counting the many run-of-the-mill commodity quality arbitrations, which are handled by the various international trade associations swiftly and without much legal brouhaha.

Since arbitral awards are not normally published, the number of undetected cases is unknown. However, as proponents of the *lex mercatoria* have been combing the field for such awards for decades and with access to the archives of many arbitral institutions, the number of undetected cases is likely to be rather low. For the purpose of this chapter, I partly updated my list based on a sample of publications between 1989 and 1999. I put the results in the following two tables.[5] The first table contains 34 awards that are based exclusively on a non-national legal standard. The second one contains 20 awards that are based on such a standard in combination with a national law. Together, these 54 awards highlight several intriguing and often overlooked aspects.

First, more than one-fourth of these awards concern so-called state contracts, that is, transactions between (typically developing or communist) states or state

---

[4] I omit in this chapter the awards of the Iran–US Claims Tribunal, which has a special legal regime based on a treaty between Iran and the USA: see Hanessian, 1989: 309.

[5] The tables are not meant to be conclusive. Some entries are doubtful, some published awards are bound to have escaped notice, and some awards are difficult to categorise. The idea behind this incomplete exercise is simply to provide a rough picture.

Table 6.1: Exclusive Use of a Non-national Legal Standard[a]

	Choice of NNLS[b] by the parties	Amiable composition[c] together with explicit choice of NNLS	Implicit choice of NNLS by the parties	Choice of lex mercatoria by the arbitrators	Same, based on amiable composition	TOTAL
Private business transactions	• ICC 1375/65[d] • ICC 6378/91		• ICC 1569/70 • ICC 1859/73 • ICC 4840/86	• ICC 2291/75 • ICC 2375/75 • *Banque du Proche-Orient v. Foucherolle* 1978 • ICC 3131/79 (*Pabalk v. Norsolor*) • ICC 5065/86 • ICC 5321/87 • ICC 5953/89 *Valenciana v. Primary Coal* • ICC 7331/94[e] • ICC 8365/96 • ICC 9246/96	• *Mechema v. Troisem* 1977 • ICC 3540/80 • ICC 3267/79/84	18
State contracts[f]	• *Petroleum Devel. Ltd. v. Abu Dhabi* 1951 • *Elf v. NIOC* 1982	• ICC 3327/81	• *Ruler of Qatar v. IMOC* 1953 • *Sapphire v. NIOC* 1963	• ICC 3572/80 (*DST v. Rakoil*) • ICC 4338/84 • ICC 5030/92 • ICC 8261/96		9
n/a	• ICC 1776/70 • ICC 1890/72 • ICC 3321/79	• Unspec. award 1966 concern. oil business • Unspec. award 1970 between two oil co.s	• ICC 1641/69		• ICC 1850/72	7
TOTAL	7	3	6	14	4	34

Table 6.2: Combination of a National Legal System with a Non-national Legal Standard

	Based on a choice of law by the parties		Based on other reasons[g]	TOTAL
	Choice of (principles of) public international law	Choice of trade usage and/or general principles of law		
Private business transactions[h]		• ICC 5904/89 • ICC 4761/84/87[i] • Eurotunnel case[j]	• ICC 1404/67 • ICC 1402/67 • ICC 1512/72 • ICC 4489/84 • ICC 5314/88 • ICC 8385/95	9
State contracts	• BP v. Libya 1973 • Topco v. Libya 1977 • Liamco v. Libya 1977	• ICC 3380/80 • Kuwait v. Aminoil 1982	• Lena Goldfields v. Soviet Union 1930 • Saudi Arabia v. Aramco 1958 • ICC 3896/82/85 (Framatome v. AEOI)	8
n/a		• ICC 5331[k]	• ICC 1472/68 • ICC 2478/74	3
TOTAL	3	6	11	20

organisations and foreign multinationals, mainly concerning oil exploitation. A seminal decision of 1951 concerned such a contract between the Sheik of Abu Dhabi and Petroleum Development Ltd.[6] The British arbitrator was obviously put off by the idea of applying the Abu Dhabi law of that time. He opted instead for a "modern law of nature"—the "principles rooted in good sense and common practice of the generality of civilised nations"—and simply applied English law (see Dasser, 1989: 180–2).

My point here is that if one talks about *lex mercatoria* as an independent international business law, one cannot take such state contracts of the 1950s and 1960s as examples. They form a separate category under various aspects, not least because of their distinct—and often explicitly stated—touch of public international law, which places them somewhat outside the reach of private national laws anyway. However, at a closer look, Professor Goldman's (1964) seminal paper on the *lex mercatoria* refers exclusively to such awards, including the Abu Dhabi case.

Secondly, in six additional awards, the arbitrators were empowered to decide as *amiables compositeurs*, that is, based on equity without any regard to substantive legal rules.[7] Any reference to the *lex mercatoria* in such decisions is less than revolutionary even under traditional legal thinking. Once we are within the

---

[6] (1951) 18 International Law Reports 144.

[7] For a discussion of the *amiable composition* and its relationship with the *lex mercatoria*, see Dasser (1989, 142–55).

Notes to Table 6.1 and 6.2

[a] Source of awards published before 1989: Dasser (1989). Sources of later awards (unless otherwise indicated): Jarvin, Derains, and Arnaldez (1994); Arnaldez, Derains, and Hascher (1997); yearly reports of ICC awards in *Journal de droit int.* (Clunet); Yearbook Commercial Arbitration (YbCA). Not taken into account are awards based on the Unidroit Principles of International Commercial Contracts of 1994.

[b] Non-national legal standard, such as general principles of law/commerce/international law. The term "*lex mercatoria*" was not used in any of these cases. The parties generally referred to general principles and (sometimes) custom, partly with reference to public international law principles.

[c] Explicit authorization of the arbitrators to base their decision on equity instead of on any specific law.

[d] The last two digits of the ICC award number indicate the year in which the award was rendered.

[e] In the end, the tribunal applied the Vienna Sales Convention, which allegedly "reflected" the "general principles of international business."

[f] Contracts between a state or a state enterprise and a foreign private company.

[g] Generally excluded are: (a) awards that merely refer to the arbitrators' generally acknowledged duty to take into account relevant trade usages, such as under Art. 17 (2) ICC Rules of Arbitration (1998); and (b) awards based on the common legal principles of two national legal systems (for such cases, see for example, Gaillard 1999, 214, 215–16).

[h] Including transactions with companies from developing countries.

[i] The contract referred to Libyan law exclusively, but the parties mitigated this choice of law during the procedure by common consent.

[j] Choice by the parties of the principles common to English and French law and, failing that, the principles of international commercial law as they have been applied by national and international tribunals (see Gaillard, 1999: 215).

[k] Gaillard (1999); *Journal de droit int.* (Clunet) 1995, 23.

framework of the amiable composition, the arbitrators can refer to any rule they want, whether or not it is a traditional legal rule, a non-national legal or merely a moral one. They may also refer to no rule at all.

Thirdly, several awards refer to some kind of public international rule, such as general principles of law recognised by (public!) international tribunals. This applies mainly (but not exclusively) to state contracts, as may be expected, since state contracts traditionally hover in the twilight zone between private and public international law. Yet, such awards mostly have little to do with a *lex mercatoria* understood as common rules and principles applied by private commercial enterprises in their daily business.

Fourthly, only seven awards are based on an explicit and exclusive choice by the parties of something comparable to a *lex mercatoria*, such as "*les principes généraux du droit naturel et de la justice*", "principles of law and custom in force throughout the civilized world", or "general principles of law applicable in Northern Europe" (see Dasser, 1989: 180 ff.), although one may rightly object that general principles of law are simply the lowest common denominator of national laws and have nothing to do conceptually with a *lex mercatoria*. In fact, I am not aware of any contract that contains an explicit reference to the *lex mercatoria*, such as "this agreement is subject to the *lex mercatoria*". Normally, the parties either choose a national law in the traditional manner, or, if they cannot agree on a specific national law, they leave open the question of the applicable law. It is in these latter cases that arbitrators tend to use their freedom in favour of a non-national legal standard for various reasons. Thus, it was mainly the arbitral tribunals themselves, consisting of internationally trained lawyers, that decided to skip national laws in favour of the *lex mercatoria*—or, in a few cases, persuaded the parties to agree on the *lex mercatoria* during the procedure in order to relieve the tribunal and the parties' own counsel from cumbersome and expensive legal research.

Fifthly, some of these awards are the kind of desperate or even freak decisions that just happen, but cannot be generalised—hard cases make bad law. Finally, and surprisingly, a closer look shows that most of the awards do not really apply international trade usage, that is, rules created *by* merchants, but some general principle of law which is more an amalgamation of national laws or a fancy word for the arbitrator's subjective sense of justice. In other words, I found very few traces of a *lex mercatoria* in its original sense.

This makes it very difficult to set up lists of actual rules of the *lex mercatoria*. The few lists proposed so far contain a mere 20 to 70 rules, often with some very doubtful entries.[8] Of course, these lists do not include trade usages that are far too particularised—both territorially and sectorially—to be included in lists of universally applicable rules. Still, this lack of readily available rules prevents

---

[8]   See Berger (1996: 217 ff.) (68 rules); Mustill (1987: 174–7) (20 rules). See also van Houtte (1995: 27–8); Fouchard, Gaillard and Goldman (1996: 830 ff.). For the new list see http://www.tldb.de.

businesspeople (and ordinary lawyers) from feeling comfortable with the *lex mercatoria*.

The fact that there turned out to be a couple of awards based on a non-national legal standard is one thing. Another thing is whether those awards are of any economic value. For this reason, I continued the research for my thesis by asking the question whether such awards were binding and enforceable (see Dasser, 1989: 267–384).

Generally speaking, arbitral awards are not binding and enforceable simply on their own—although this was postulated in the wild young days of *lex-mercatorism*[9]—except under very specific circumstances.[10] Generally, an award needs at least some support by a state power in order to be effective. This support is subject to two kinds of control: first, in the form of a (mostly very limited) appeal at the place where the award was rendered; and, secondly, in the form of recognition and enforcement procedures in another country, if the need for such an enforcement arises. While the first step is usually subject to individual state arbitration laws, which are now more and more influenced by the 1985 UNCITRAL Model Law of International Commercial Arbitration (UNCITRAL Model Law), the second is normally subject to the universally recognised 1958 New York Convention Concerning Recognition and Enforcement of Foreign Arbitral Awards (NYC).

My conclusion was that such awards could already at the end of the 1980s be assumed to be binding and enforceable in most of the important jurisdictions, including Switzerland, although there were only very few court decisions (see Dasser, 1989: 347–9, 383–4). France acted as a trailblazer with its liberal arbitration regime in its new Civil Procedure Code of 1981. This regime, which was held to embrace the revolutionary French *lex mercatoria* doctrine, served as an example for both the Dutch and the Swiss revisions of 1986 and 1989, respectively.

In the meantime, several important national laws have been revised, including German and English law. The revisions typically restricted the scope of review of arbitral awards by state courts even further. In spite of this growing openness of national arbitration laws, I have not noticed any major increase in the frequency of awards based on the *lex mercatoria* up-to-date. This is especially true in view of the substantially increased number of published awards,

---

[9] See the references in Dasser (1989, 352).

[10] E.g., awards rendered under the auspices of the International Centre for Settlement of Investment Disputes between States and Nationals of Other States (ICSID) are not subject to national rules on setting-aside or enforcement (1965 Washington Convention on the Settlement of Investment Disputes, Arts. 52–54). Some awards may also be autonomously enforced in case of close-knit business circles. However, it is unclear to what extent such business circles still exist today and would function in litigious moments without the backup of state power looming behind the loser.

although the *lex mercatoria* is now more often discussed in awards thanks to the growing familiarity with the term among the parties' counsel.

CONSEQUENCES

In sum, what I discovered in the late 1980s still appears to be valid today. First, at least in arbitral practice, a *lex mercatoria* as something akin to an independent legal order does exist, but plays a marginal role. Secondly, most relevant national legal systems do not second-guess an arbitrator's application of a non-national legal standard. No purist legal theory can discuss that fact away. International arbitration is allowed to live its own life within an officially protected zone. Of course, this zone is limited by notions of public policy (for example, concerning competition laws), but this is a general conflict-of-law problem that concerns not just the application of a *lex mercatoria*, but any legal system, national or non-national (see Dasser, 1996).

Thus, parties can choose a non-national legal system as the law applicable to their contract if they wish—provided that they combine this clause with arbitration. Whether it is wise to do so, is a completely different question. My experience in practice is that up to now it has *generally* been not wise, and that parties almost never even consider choosing a vague *lex mercatoria* as the applicable law. There are exceptions in desperate situations that call for desperate measures.

Anyway, I notice that cases in court are increasingly decided on the factual level, not on the legal level. If in the adjudicator's view one party wronged the other party, it will normally lose the case no matter which law may or may not apply. This observation probably mirrors the one by Dezalay and Garth (1996: 34–42, 85–99) that the *lex mercatoria* is linked to the "grand old men" of arbitration, who are gradually being replaced by American-style "technocrats". While the first enjoy academic discussions of legal theories, the latter focus on the facts and technicalities of a case.

The question remains what rules actually comprise the *lex mercatoria* as an autonomous legal order. Klaus Peter Berger of the University of Munster, Germany, focuses much of his work on exactly that question. In March 1998, he founded an institute called CENTRAL, Centre for Transnational Law, that is devoted to research on the *lex mercatoria*.[11] CENTRAL is currently undertaking an extensive field study on arbitral and transactional practices concerning the use of the *lex mercatoria* as a legal order.[12]

CONCLUSIONS

Some years ago, I wrote an article entitled "Lex Mercatoria: Tool of the Practitioners or Toy of the Academics?" (Dasser, 1991). I still believe that the *lex*

---

[11] See http://www.uni-muenster.de/Jura.iwr/central.
[12] Now online at http://www.tldb.de (Transnational Law Database).

mercatoria is a fascinating toy. However, for businesspeople and their lawyers it is largely irrelevant, apart from the humble (but very important) trade usages. But then, as I tried to explain, the latter are completely different and should be called by their traditional name in order to avoid misunderstandings.

What remains of the *lex mercatoria*, which aspired to become a universal substantive law of global commerce, may indeed be a mere method of adjudication, as Filip De Ly proposes in his chapter in this volume (see also Gaillard, 1999: 215). However, such a method is again something completely different. It is well established that arbitrators normally enjoy even larger discretion than state judges for lack of an effective appeal procedure, and that they often do not hesitate to take advantage of their freedom to do whatever they deem to be the right thing. In practice, the consequence is a broad range of awards that have very little in common and may not deserve a common label.

REFERENCES

Arnaldez, Jean-Jacques, Derains, Yves, and Hascher, Dominique (compilers) (1997), *Collection of ICC Arbitral Awards, 1991–1995: Recueil des sentences arbitrales de la CCI, 1991–1995* (Paris: ICC Pub.).

Berger, Klaus Peter. (1996), *Formalisierte oder "schleichende" Kodifizierung des transnationalen Wirtschaftsrechts: zu de methodischen und praktischen Grundlagen der lex mercatoria* (Berlin; New York: de Gruyter) (published in English as *The Creeping Codification of the Lex Mercatoria* (The Hague; Boston: Kluwer Law International, (1999).)

Berman, Harold J., and Dasser, Felix J. (1998), "The 'New' Law Merchant and the 'Old': Sources, Content, and Legitimacy" in T. E. Carbonneau (ed.), *Lex Mercatoria and Arbitration: A Discussion of the New Law Merchant* (rev. edn., Yonkers, NY: Juris; Cambridge, Mass.: Kluwer Law International).

Carbonneau, Thomas E. (ed.) (1998), in *Lex Mercatoria and Arbitration: A Discussion of the New Law Merchant* (rev. edn., Yonkers, NY: Juris; Cambridge, Mass.: Kluwer Law International).

Dasser, Felix. (1989), *Internationale Schiedsgerichte und lex mercatoria: rechtsvergleichender Beitrag zur Diskussion über ein nicht-staatliches Handelsrecht* (Zurich: Schulthess).

—— (1991), "Lex Mercatoria: Werkzeug der Praktiker oder Spielzeug der Lehre?", *Schweizerische Zeitschrift für internationales und europäisches Recht* 1; 299–323.

—— (1996), "Neue Tendenzen im Internationalen Kartellprivatrecht der Schweiz", *Aktuelle Juristische Praxis* 5; 950–7.

Dezalay, Yves, and Garth, Bryant G. (1996), *Dealing in Virtue, International Commercial Arbitration and the Construction of a Transnational Legal Order* (Chicago, Ill.: University of Chicago Press).

Fouchard, Philippe, Gaillard, Emmanuel, and Goldman, Berthold (1996), *Traité de l'arbitrage commercial international* (Paris: Litec).

Gaillard, Emmanuel (1999), "Use of General Principles of International Law in International Long-Term Contracts", *International Business Lawyer* 27; 214–24.

Goldman, Berthold (1964), "Frontières du droit et 'lex mercatoria'", *Archives de philosophie du droit* 9; 177–92.

Goode, Roy (1997), "Usage and Its Reception in Transnational Commercial Law", *International Comparative Law Quarterly* 46; 1–36.

Hanessian, Grant (1989), "General Principles of Law in the Iran–U.S. Claims Tribunal", *Columbia Journal of Transnational Law* 27; 309–52.

Jarvin, Sigvard, Derains, Yves, and Arnaldez, Jean-Jacques (compilers) (1994), *Collection of ICC Arbitral Awards, 1986–1990: Recueil des sentences arbitrales de la CCI, 1986–1990* (Paris: ICC Pub.).

Lagarde, Paul (1982), "Approche critique de la lex mercatoria" in P. Fouchard, P. Kahn and A. Lyon-Caen (eds.), *Le droit des relations économiques internationales: etudes offertes à Berthold Goldman* (Paris: Librairies Techniques).

Mustill, Michael (1987), "The New *Lex Mercatoria*: The First Twenty-five Years" in M. Bos and I. Brownlie (eds.), *Liber Amicorum for the Rt. Hon. Lord Wilberforce* (Oxford: Clarendon Press).

Paulsson, Jan (1990), "La *lex mercatoria* dans l'arbitrage C.C.I.", *Revue de l'arbitrage*, 55–100.

Van Houtte, Hans (1995), *The Law of International Trade* (London: Sweet & Maxwell).

7

Global Markets, New Games, New Rules: The Challenge of International Private Governance

FRANCO FURGER

Abstract

The processes of economic globalisation have led to a renewed interest in the question of the social regulation of economic activities. Unfortunately, these debates are often informed by metaphorical—and ultimately sterile—views of markets and economic activities. In particular, it is rarely acknowledged that markets often display a considerable self-governance capacity. In this chapter, I discuss how private governance and decentralised law can emerge in a variety of settings. I rely on the theory of repeated games, on network theory and economic sociology to account for the emergence and evolution of rules outside the legal domain. I develop a typology of private systems of governance and I use this typology to formulate predictions about the credibility and robustness of these arrangements. In the second part of the chapter, based on this theoretical framework, I examine three prototypical cases of private governance at the international level: global electronic commerce, standard-developing organisations, and "informational regulation". The discussion shows that while the availability of raw information remains a critical factor for sustaining these arrangements, their long-term viability may depend upon the existence of cross-cutting ties among the various constituencies involved. Absent such ties, the likelihood that these arrangements will disintegrate is significant. The discussion shows that conflicts among constituencies are not necessarily detrimental. In some cases, a disagreement over the interpretation of data and information can trigger the establishment of cross-cutting ties among opposing constituencies, thus significantly increasing the chances that these constituencies will eventually be able to reach a consensus.

Imagine a wondrous new machine, strong and supple, a machine that reaps as it destroys. It is huge and mobile, something like the machines of modern agriculture but vastly more complicated and powerful. Think of this awesome machine running over open terrain and ignoring familiar boundaries. It plows across fields and fencerows with a fierce momentum that is exhilarating to behold and also frightening. As it goes, the machine throws off enormous mows of wealth and bounty while it leaves behind great furrows of wreckage. Now imagine that there are skillful hands on board, but no one is at the wheel. In fact, this machine has no wheel nor any internal governor to control the speed and direction [Greider, 1997: 11].

INTRODUCTION: THE LIMITS OF METAPHORS IN PUBLIC POLICY

T HE QUOTATION, TAKEN from a recently published book by a well-known American journalist, neatly illustrates the diffuse anxiety generated by the much-debated processes of economic globalisation. Greider's message is clear: economic globalisation has got out of control, and political institutions seem unable (or unwilling) to assert any degree of control over an economic process that generates as much good as it produces considerable harm.

Globalisation has led to a renewed interest in the relationship between economic and political institutions—in the question of the social regulation of economic activities. Often, these discussions are informed by two mutually exclusive accounts of economic globalisation. According to one view, nation-states are losing their ability to regulate international trade and financial flows. Such a diminished regulatory capacity is usually viewed as one of the main sources of social and environmental disruptions in developing countries, while at the same time producing unemployment and social unrest in industrialized nations (Greider, 1997; Rodrik, 1997; Dawkins, 1994). In this view, democratically elected national governments are ceding their power to large multinational corporations whose top management is accountable only to shareholders. On the other end of the spectrum we find advocates of the free market who emphasise the economic benefits of global trade to the participating nations, especially to the developing nations, while at the same time ignoreing or downright dismissing its potential negative impact (Micklethwait and Wooldridge, 2000; Krugman, 1997).

To be sure, current debates about economic globalisation are considerably more sophisticated than the preceding discussion suggests. Nevertheless, they share with these two positions what may be called a Manichean view of economic activities. Such a view usually assumes that it is possible, both at the conceptual and empirical levels, to distinguish unambiguously between economic activities and the legal system.[1] According to this view, economic exchange is anomic, economic activities are guided by exclusively naked economic self-interest and devoid of any moral concerns. The anomic nature of economic exchange provides the theoretical and moral foundations for adopt-

---

[1] For the purpose of the present discussion, legal rules are responsible for "orderly" competition among economic actors, and for protecting the citizens against the worst effects generated by these activities.

ing and implementing legal rules. These rules embody the public interest and establish a "framework" within which economic actors are allowed to operate.

I submit that this analytical distinction is based on a metaphorical and increasingly misleading characterisation of economic activities.[2] It is informed by a conception of economic exchange as an "ideal gas", as a domain of social interaction characterised by a large number of decision makers blindly pursuing their narrowly defined self-interest. The sharp distinction between the economic and the public domains is also responsible for the sterility of current debates about globalisation and for the lack of viable political responses to the challenges posed by economic globalisation.

In this chapter, I develop the view that markets are neither blind machines without internal steering capacity, nor anomic social settings. If a metaphor must be used, then perhaps this: markets resemble crystalline structures. The way in which atoms are positioned with respect to one another gives rise to crystalline structures with specific physical characteristics. It is precisely the existence of social structures within markets and between markets and other social domains that forms the basis for a market's governance capacity. For the purpose of the present discussion, social structures consist of networks of personal and professional ties as well as the norms, standards and practices shared by the economic actors that comprise these social networks.

The assumption that markets do have an internal steering capacity is incompatible with the traditional, sharp distinction between "community" and "society". As I show in this chapter, economic activities may display "communal" traits. Accordingly, a more appropriate way to characterise the environmental and social harm caused by processes of economic globalisation is the notions of "fractured polity".

It has been argued that there is nothing mysterious about the emergence of self-governance structures. This phenomenon—so say the critics—can easily be understood as the outcome of political struggles over the proper role of government in human affairs. Accordingly, self-governance is merely a reflection of a broader effort to devolve and dilute the power of the nation-state. The reality is far more complex. Self-governance can hardly be considered an epiphenomenon of conservative politics. The empirical evidence shows that devolution of regulatory power can hardly be considered an adequate explanation for the emergence of industrial codes in the United States. In the environmental and labour policy, one would be hard pressed to identify significant cases of devolution—at least in the United States. The threat of regulation or increased

---

[2] Metaphors are powerful tools for making sense of our world. Metaphorical thinking shapes to a considerable extent an individual's perceptions. By their very nature, metaphors can operate as social filters, focusing individuals' perceptions on certain features of their social environment while deflecting the attention from others (Lakof and Johnson, 1983). Scholars are not immune to the power of metaphors. Some sociologists and historians of science have argued that metaphors are in fact a key aspect of doing physics and many other scientific disciplines. Central concepts such as "field", "wave" and "particle" are the result of metaphorical thinking and everyday life experience (Freudenthal, 1986).

monitoring and compliance efforts seems at first to provide a better explanation for these efforts. A closer examination shows that the adoption of these programmes has rarely if ever been motivated by an explicit regulatory threat. A perceived loss of legitimacy in the eyes of the general public can often be identified as the initial trigger. On the other end, the increased interest of several large non-governmental organisations (NGOs) in partnerships with the private sector originates in dissolution and frustration with negotiating multilateral agreements. Corporate downsizing has also contributed to enabling these partnerships, as laid-off mid-level managers have often found new challenges in large public interest groups (Murphy and Bendell, 1997: 1–8).

The term "community" suggests a "relational" view of modern markets. I believe that a relational approach to market analysis is better suited to understanding many examples of private international governance. While traditional approaches to market analysis are forced to characterise these examples as a rare and ultimately irrelevant empirical curiosity, a relational approach to the same phenomenon can provide a robust framework for explaining their emergence and for conceptualising their evolution.[3]

To a statist model of law and order self-governance theoretically challenging. There are several reasons for this. First, self-governance amounts to assuming that rules and quasi-legal standards can emerge outside the shadow of the law. Secondly, it also amounts to assuming that the existence of such quasi-legal standards does not depend upon mechanisms of law enforcement backed by the state. Thirdly, self-governance seems to suggest that regulatory power in modern societies—broadly defined—is not the monopoly of the state. In this sense, one could also say that modern societies display a multiplicity of "governance structures". Finally, self-governance makes it possible to envisage forms of governance that transcend national borders—the global Bukowina discussed by Teubner (Teubner, 1997).

In this chapter, I lay out a sociological account of self-governance not as an alternative to the rational actor paradigm but as an extension of this model. There is no need to choose between "over-socialised" models of human action as those traditionally advocated by sociologists and "under-socialised" approaches preferred by economists (Granovetter, 1985). Accordingly, in the next section I show that game theory provides several important insights. Game theory demonstrates that rational actors embedded in networks of personal ties can easily sustain rules and norms. In addition, it shows that sustaining such rules depends critically upon the availability of information about each participant's conduct. Finally, it demonstrates that lack of critical information may prompt the participants to address these information problems by implementing specific institutional arrangements.

---

[3] A relational account of market institutions is not entirely new. Scholars such as Emile Durkheim and Max Weber pointed to what economic sociologists have dubbed the social embeddedness of economic action (Granovetter, 1985, 1992; Granovetter and Swedberg, 1992; Swedberg, 1997; Uzzi, 1996, 1997; Burt 1992). Some preliminary thoughts on a "relational sociology" can be found in Emirbayer (1997).

I complement game theory with network analysis to show that self-governance is not limited to small groups confined to geographically limited areas. While network analysis has become a technical academic discipline, it was originally advocated as a promising theoretical framework to bridge the gap between micro- and macro-sociological analysis (Granovetter, 1973; Giddens, 1984). The discussion shows that network structure rather than sheer group size has an identifiable impact on the capacity of individuals and organisations to sustain rules and norms.

In the remainder of the chapter I rely on this hybrid theoretical framework to examine three distinct cases: a case of global electronic commerce (auctions on the Internet), the role of standard-developing organisations, and an example of what is known as "information regulation". The discussion of these three cases puts the role of raw information as a causal explanation of the emergence of self-regulatory arrangements in perspective. While the availability of information remains a critical factor, I argue that the emergence and efficiency of self-governing institutional arrangements may depend upon resolving what some sociologists of science refer to as "interpretative flexibility" (Collins, 1992). Without some degree of consensus among the various constituencies comprising a self-regulatory arrangement, information is of little help in creating and maintaining structures of self-governance. Finally, I show that interpretative flexibility is not always detrimental. In some cases, conflicts over the reliability and the significance of empirical evidence can prompt the formation of ties among opposing constituencies, thus significantly increasing the chances that these constituencies will eventually be able to reach a consensus.

THE EMERGENCE OF RULES AND INSTITUTIONS AMONG RATIONAL ACTORS

A Typology of Private Systems of Governance

In this section, I show that the theory of non-co-operative games provides a useful theoretical framework for the empirical analysis of private governance.[4] Private governance is defined as follows: It consists of a business community broadly defined, that is, a set of firms competing with one another or simply member of the same industry, one or more constituencies, and possibly what I refer to as a "bridging institution" (an institutional arrangement or an organisation that mediate between private interests and their constituencies). The term bridging institution does not designate a specific type of organisation. Rather, it points to the societal role played by a variety of organisations. Perhaps the most important example of bridging institution is the state

---

[4] See Kreps (1990) and Fudenberg and Tirole (1995) for an introduction to game theory.

(legislative and executive branches). But, as our discussion should demonstrate, many other organisations may on occasion take on the role of a bridging institution. For example, a trade group responsible for managing an environmental management programme over time may come to be seen by all constituencies as a credible bridging institution. Many other private organisations have a long history of mediating between private and public interests. In the USA, standard-developing organisations such as the American Fire Protection Association (building codes) and the American Society for Testing and Materials (ASTM) have long played such a role. Consumer organisations such as the Consumers Union have a time-honoured tradition of mediating between manufacturers and consumers by evaluating product safety and quality.

Furthermore, private governance is characterised by the absence of the state as a source of influence or coercion. Rather, the pressure and influence are associated with the various constituencies. The notion of "constituency" is broader than the more popular notion of "stakeholders". One obvious constituency is the state, but the state is hardly the only, and in many cases not even the most important, source of social pressure. Constituencies such as trade associations, large industrial customers, standard-developing organisations or auditing firms can hardly be described as stakeholders. Constituency is not simply synonymous with customer, either, although in some cases customers must indeed be considered one important constituency. A constituency consists of all the individuals and organisations that may have a significant negative impact on the economic performance of a firm.[5] A negative economic impact can take different forms, from losing business because of consumers' boycotts, to a damaged long-standing relationship with a large customer, to a ruined reputation caused by demonstrations by environmental and citizens' groups whose actions have received considerable press coverage and finally to less favourable contractual conditions imposed by a financial institution.

The preceding discussion has demonstrated how the concept of constituency may be used to characterise different instances of international (and national) private governance. "Constituency" is however only one of two relevant elements of a private system of governance. There seems to be a fundamental difference between the negotiations conducted by a firm's management with a group of activists at the local level and the response of the same management to the attempt of an international NGO to discredit a firm through a well-orchestrated media campaign. In both cases, one could say that the relevant "constituency" is an environmental group. However, in the former case, repeated face-to-face interactions form the basis for the firm's response to the concerns expressed by its

---

[5] The notion of constituency is not too different from the term "task environment" commonly used in the public administration literature (Scott, 1987). In this chapter I will use the former term, as it better conveys the political nature of the expectations that may be placed upon an industrial organisation.

local constituency. In the latter case, no face-to-face interactions take place, and no personal ties exist between management and the NGO. The interaction between the firm and its constituency is mediated in the sense that it takes place mainly through the news media. The NGO brings pressure upon the firm through the media of mass communication such as consumer magazines, newspapers, television and the Internet. The firm may respond in a similar way, through a well-orchestrated public relations campaign. While in the former case the parties involved may well be described as a polity, in the latter case no cross-cutting ties exist among the parties involved.

The second key dimension captures the nature of the interactions between the various constituencies and the target of their action, typically a firm or an industry. These interactions can take place face-to-face (unmediated), or they can be mediated, typically through means of mass communication. The distinction between mediated and unmediated interactions is not too dissimilar from Giddens' twin concepts of social and system integration (Giddens, 1984: 64–8), two concepts I will be using throughout the chapter.

The central question to be pursued in this section and throughout the chapter is to what extent private governance can succeed in addressing problems of collective action, i.e. at producing various public goods. The public goods under consideration range from adopting a set of legal requirements to improving environmental quality and protecting public safety. To pursue this question, I rely both on non-cooperative game theory and on economic sociology. Non-cooperative game theory is relevant for several reasons. By making collective action the subject of inquiry, it underlines the non-obvious nature of producing a public good. It sheds light on the motives and mechanisms that enable a possibly large number of rational actors to solve problems of collective action despite strong incentives to do otherwise (Hechter, 1987).

The fact that game theory characterises individual motives and the range of possible informal sanctions in a primitive way does not limit its relevance. If it is possible to demonstrate that purely rational individuals or organisations can solve a problem of collective action, it is plausible to conclude that the same public good will indeed be produced under less restrictive conditions, i.e. when the actors involved are not exclusively rational and self-interested.

Another important reason for relying—at least initially—on non-cooperative game theory resides in the ability of this mathematical tool accurately to model widely different and possibly complex strategic interactions. In this, it shares with economic sociology a considerable attention for structural details as key determinants of collective action. This point has forcefully been made by Elinor Ostrom when she pointed out that policy-making in general and government activism in particular are too often informed by metaphorical characterisations of rather complex social settings (Ostrom, 1990: 1–28). Typical examples include the well-known "tragedy of the commons", introduced by Hardin to explain environmental degradation (Hardin, 1968) and the "Prisoner-Dilemma" often invoked to account for self-defeating social outcomes.

Armed with this mathematical tool, the social scientist can abstract from the minutiae of case study analysis and pursue a few key questions. One such key question has just been introduced: How can problems of collective actions be solved in the absence of a legal system backed by the state? Several related questions follow. Does the number of participating individual or organisational actors matter? Is geographical dispersion an issue? What mechanisms of social regulation other than state enforcement may prevent free-riding behaviour? In the remainder of this section, I use non-cooperative game theory and economic sociology as tools for examining these questions in a systematic way. I illustrate how game theory and network analysis can be used to move the analysis from a metaphorical account to a more realistic description of a relatively simple case.

The first case under consideration is the enforcement of contractual obligations within a business community, the adoption of the institutions necessary to adjudicate contractual disputes and to enforce judicial decisions. This is an example of the provision of a public good in the absence of state intervention. A business community represents a case of private governance consisting of a bridging institution and of business interests only. In this case, no external constituency is affected by these trade activities. Accordingly, no constituency is exercising pressure or influence on this business community. While the traders involved still face a problem of collective action, no genuine public good is involved.

In a second step, I focus on what I consider the most interesting case of international private governance, on industries providing a public good in response to pressures applied by one or more constituencies. Typically, the public good produced by these industries consists of several, usually rather generic requirements aimed at establishing a common framework for managing environmental and safety problems and/or dealing with labour concerns.

Sustaining Contractual Obligations within Business Communities

At the core of the following discussion is a situation in which the members of a business community depend upon enacting and sustaining common legal standards for conducting their business in the absence of an external legislative body and of an enforcing agency. The legal literature has occasionally discussed this question under the label of "decentralised law-making". Cooter, for example, has pointed out that business communities can under certain circumstances develop well-established, informal business norms, and uses this observation to develop an alternative approach to adjudication (Cooter, 1996). The relevance of business self-governance is not limited to contract law and dispute resolution. The adoption of common technical standards within industries characterised by fast technological change provides another relevant example of the endogenous provision of public and club goods. In this section, I provide an illustration of how game theory can be used to discuss this question. In a first step, I discuss the simplest business community. In subsequent steps and gradually generalise the results obtained to increasingly more realistic situations.

Consider first a business community consisting of only two traders. The trading activities involve the fulfilment of some mutual obligations. Fulfilling these obligations may be time-consuming or costly. If both traders fulfil their obligations and behave honestly an exchange will take place to their mutual benefit. However, each trader would be better off if the other partner held up his part of the contract, while she neglected her obligations. Obviously, if both partners decide to violate their mutual agreement, the transaction will fall apart, and neither partner will reap any benefits. This type of strategic situation has attracted enormous scholarly attention, and is commonly known as the Prisoner-Dilemma game (PD game). See Figure 7.1 for a short discussion of this strategic situation.

The one-shot PD game has often been used to illustrate the "tragedy of the commons" (Hardin, 1968) and the failures of collective action (Olson, 1965). Applied to our situation, the message conveyed by a one-shot PD game is clear: without third party enforcement, economic exchange is unlikely to occur and government intervention is called for. This kind of reasoning can easily be applied to a wide range of social interactions in which the collective outcome that does not reflect their own best interest.

Even in this highly simplified example, tragedies and failures are neither the only possible outcome nor a necessary result. To understand why this may be so, I now turn to the case where the traders face each other not only once, but many times. In a repeated PD game, the incentive structure changes dramatically.

In a repeated PD game, the traders evaluate the payoffs they expect to receive, not only in their first round, but in future exchanges as well. The logic for upholding contractual obligations is straightforward. Both players may be expected to behave professionally and honestly in the current round if they plan on doing business with one another in the future, that is, if they place a high enough value on the payoffs from future trades. In this case, the sum of discounted payoffs from future interactions may well exceed the payoff from behaving dishonestly in the current round. Under certain circumstances, it may be in the best interest of both traders to fulfil their contractual obligations in every round of the game. The resulting equilibrium solution is a Nash equilibrium, as neither player has an incentive to deviate from the equilibrium path.

Repeated games provide a strong rationale for assuming that rules can indeed be sustained without external intervention. However, the relevance of this result would be quite limited if it were limited to two-person PD games. Fortunately, it can be shown that rules can be sustained in any other type of repeated two-person games. In addition, this result holds not only for two-person repeated games, but also for any n-person game (Fudenberg and Maskin, 1986). These conclusions are valid for infinite horizon games with discounting (participants

The one-shot Prisoner-Dilemma Game:

   Each player can choose to fulfill (s1 res. t1) or to neglect his obligations (s2 res. t2). Each pairs of figures in parenthesis represent the (net) benefits to each player for every combination of individual choices. The payoff to trader 1 is represented by the figure on the left, and payoff to trader 2 by the number to the right.

Trader 2

		t1	t2
Trader 1	s1	(5,5)	(−3,8)
	s2	(8,−3)	(0,0)

The game is played only once, and the players must make their choice without knowing their opponent's choice. Under these circumstances, what course of action can these players be expected to take? For trader 1, strategy s2 is always superior to s1 (8>5, 0>−3): no matter what trader 2 will do, trader 1 will be better off by choosing s2. s2 is said to strictly dominate s1. From the point of view of trader 2, t2 strictly dominates t1 (8>5, 0>−3): no matter what trader 1 will do, she will be better off by choosing t2. As a result, the players will end up with payoffs (0,0), i.e. with the pair of choices (s2, t2). In plain English, this means that under the present circumstances, these players are very unlikely to do business with each other.

   The solution (s2, t2) is a Nash equilibrium: Neither player has an incentive to change his strategy, as such a change would make them worse off. In equilibrium, if trader 1 changes his strategy from s2 to s1, he will face a payoff of −3. The same argument applies to trader 2. In sum, each trader's choice is a best reply to his adversary's choice.

   Although (s2, t2) is a Nash equilibrium, as neither one of the two traders will regret his or her choice, a more efficient solution exists. However, in this case the Pareto-efficient solution (s1, t1) is **not** a Nash equilibrium. Inspection of the payoffs shows that if the traders choose (s1, t1), they have an incentive to deviate from this choice. (s1, t1) are not mutually best responses. In plain English—despite their mutual interest in choosing the superior pair of strategy (s1, t1), rationality compels both traders to adopt the inferior solution (s2,t2).

Figure 7.1

The repeated Prisoner-Dilemma game:

One version of the repeated PD-game assumes that the game is repeated ad infinitum. Each trader discounts future payoffs at a rate α $(0 \,''\, \alpha < 1)$. The discounted value of the payoffs stream for player j is defined as $\sum\limits_{i=1}^{\infty} \alpha^{i-1} u_j(i) = \dfrac{u_i(i)}{1-\alpha}$, where α is the discount rate $(0 \,''\, \alpha < 1)$ and $u_j(i)$ is the payoff received by player j during round i.

Alternatively, the repeated PD-game can consist of a finite but undetermined number of rounds. If q is the likelihood that the game will be played one more time, the expected cumulated payoff is defined as:

$$\sum_{i=1}^{\infty} q^{i-1} u_j(i) = \frac{u_i(i)}{1-q}.$$

Consider the following numerical illustration. Players are not allowed to communicate after each round, but they can announce their strategic choices before beginning playing. Player 1 announces she will play s1 as long as player 2 plays t1. If player 2 ever plays t2, player 1 will play s2 forever after. Player 2 realizes that if he plays t2 now, he will receive a payoff of 8, and of 0 afterwards. His discounted value for violating contractual requirements is 8. By contrast, his discounted value for behaving honestly is $\dfrac{5}{1-\alpha}$. If player 2 doesn't discount future payoffs too much, he will have an incentive to fulfill his obligations with player 1. For any $\alpha > \dfrac{3}{8}$ player 2 is very likely to play t1 if player 1 plays s1. For $\alpha > \dfrac{3}{8}$, these two strategies are now a Nash equilibrium. Each is a best reply to the other, i.e. the players have no incentive to deviate from their choice, i.e. they are both a Nash equilibrium and they are Pareto-efficient.

Figure 7.2

play forever), and for finite but undetermined horizon (participants play for a limited number of rounds, but do not know in advance for how many rounds), and are commonly known as the folk theorem: in repeated games, any feasible solution of the stage game can be sustained as a Nash equilibrium.

In sum, the ability of a group of rational actors to sustain a common rule in the presence of strong incentives to do otherwise is by no means limited to simple strategic interactions of marginal relevance. The folk theorem indicates that repeated interactions should indeed be considered a key element of private governance. The relevance of repeated interactions as a way to achieve a mutually beneficial outcome has amply been demonstrated by Robert Axelrod in his now classic *Evolution of Cooperation* (Axelrod, 1984).

Business Communities and the Challenge of Self Governance

Despite its generality, the relevance of the folk theorem up to this point remains limited. N-person repeated games are a poor model of any economic exchange among the members of a business community. Typically, in n-person repeated games every participant plays against all other players, and players do not change over time. By contrast, economic exchange usually takes place between two players only. Obviously, every player conducts business with several other members of his business community, but rarely with all. Finally, the trading population may change over time, as new players enter the market, while other may leave. In more technical terms, this situation may be described as a series of matching games (Kamecke, 1989; Ellison, 1994). In each round of the game, every trader is matched with another trader according to a matching rule. Under these circumstances, can trust and honest behaviour be sustained among traders, and what kind of matching rule may sustain this behaviour?

In a world of economic exchange characterised by a potentially high number of traders, it is not self-evident whether a trader will have an incentive to behave honestly. Generally speaking, the larger the business community, the less likely it is that any two traders will repeatedly do business with each other. As a result, some traders may conclude that defecting in the present round will not reduce their future payoffs. Unless other mechanisms of social regulation can be identified, one cannot avoid the conclusion that under these circumstances, common rules are not likely to be sustained.

Violations of rules and standards may be sanctioned not by the party who experienced them but by a third party. Thus, a trader considering violating some common rule must take into account the possibility that another trade partner may sanction his or her decision. In this case, common rules are not sustained through reciprocity. Rather, they are the result of a communal effort, hence the characterisation of this situation as "community enforcement" (Kandori, 1992).

The sociology of the professions provides some illustrations. It is well known that standards of professional ethics within legal firms and in hospitals are routinely upheld by "peers". For example, senior lawyers and medical doctors routinely observe and reprimand the conduct of their colleagues if it is deemed incompatible with the ethical standards of their profession (Carlin, 1966: 96–118; Freidson, 1970: 137–57).

This intuitive description hides significant technical problems. The viability of "community enforcement" depends critically upon assuming that third parties will indeed sanction deviant behaviour. However, sanctioning a violation is itself associated with costs. It is therefore critical that sanctioning is not too costly for third parties. Thus, one may wonder whether a third party will be willing to assume the cost of punishing a violator for the sake of the common good. Experience suggests that individuals are indeed willing to sanction deviant behaviour as long as the associated costs are small. Mathematical economists have shown that this is indeed the case. This result is independent of the population size and the matching rule (Okuno-Fujiwara and Postlewaite, 1995; Kandori, 1992; Okuno-Fujiwara, Postlewaite and Suzumura, 1990).

Social Regulation and Informational Needs

The viability of the self-regulatory mechanism described in the preceding section depends upon a business community meeting a very restrictive assumption. "Community enforcement" is possible only if players can respond optimally to their opponent's choice in every round of the game. This presupposes that all players have a perfect knowledge of each other's trade history (for the purpose of this discussion, information is perfect if player A is fully informed about the trade history of player B). In other words, individual behaviour is public information.

This is obviously a very restrictive condition. The trade history of every player is likely to be public information only in small groups, and within geographically limited areas. In larger populations, or in geographically dispersed groups, information about the trade history of other players may not be public. Usually, players will be informed only about their own trade history, and to some extent about the trade history of the players with whom they trade most often, but certainly not about the trade history of every other player.

The need for detailed information can be considerably reduced if the members of a business community develop a reputation for trustworthiness and honest behaviour. Reputation in this context is defined as an attribute ascribed to a trader by other members of the business community. Ascription is based on observed past behaviour. If player A observes that in the course of playing against B, B generally sticks to her strategy, in the eyes of A B becomes trustworthy (Mailath and Samuelson, 1998; Raub and Weesie, 1990; Wilson, 1985; Kreps *et al.*, 1982; Kreps and Wilson, 1982). Clearly, for B to have a reputation in the sociological sense of this term, many other group members must view her as trustworthy. Assuming that this is indeed the case, B's reputation becomes valuable.

It is not difficult to see why a good reputation is a valuable economic asset. A player with a good reputation has an incentive to live up to his or her reputation and not to behave opportunistically. Taking advantage of another player's good faith may bring higher short-term payoffs, but it also destroys one's good reputation not only in the eyes of the current player, but in the eyes of other business partners. As a result, the costs of behaving opportunistically in the short term may significantly outweigh the benefits (see Milgrom, North and Weingast, 1990: 6–8, for a detailed discussion).

A good reputation eliminates some of the problems involved in occasional economic exchanges, that is, in exchanges among traders not familiar with one another. In these cases, a good reputation becomes a surrogate for a long-term relation. It is a certification of good conduct that eliminates the need for gathering detailed personal information. A reputation mechanism may also be characterised as an example of system integration.

An individual's reputation significantly reduces but does not entirely eliminate the information needs of a business community. In particular, it is unclear how an individual's reputation may develop, and how this information is made available to the members of the community. Obviously, an individual's reputation, especially in a large group, cannot be considered public information. In addition, for individuals to have an incentive to conform to their reputation, information about instances of deviant behaviour must also be readily available to all community members. In the absence of specific mechanisms of information gathering and distribution it is difficult to see how a business community may be able to sustain its own rules.

BEYOND GAME THEORY: THE SOCIAL FOUNDATIONS OF ECONOMIC ACTION

Introduction

In the recent past, economic historians have argued that formal institutional arrangements may be adopted by a business community in response to the deficiencies of informal reputation mechanisms. In this view, these arrangements are adopted not so much to replace informal reputation mechanisms, but to complement and reinforce them. Perhaps not surprisingly, two recurrent "problems" solved by these formalised institutional arrangements is the gathering and distribution of information about violations of contractual obligations. At the centre of these works are institutional arrangements adopted by business communities in the absence of national legal systems in the Middle Ages. Illustrations of this argument have been provided for the Champagne Fairs (Milgrom, North, and Weingast, 1990), for the Maghribi traders (Greif, 1989, 1993), and for the merchant guilds (Greif, Milgrom, and Weingast, 1994). It is well known that during that period of time commercial activities in Europe were not protected by the rule of law, traders were exposed to the whims of local and national despots, and were unable to seek redress in court. Yet, trade began to flourish well before nations and national legal systems emerged. This is a particularly relevant situation, as contemporary processes of economic globalisation face a similar challenge.

Let us briefly consider the Champagne Fairs. This is a particularly relevant example, as it focuses on the Law Merchant and on the institution of private judges in the twelfth and thirteenth centuries. The authors of this study demonstrate that this institution "solves" several interconnected problems (Milgrom, North, and Weingast, 1990: 10–11): Traders must be adequately informed, so that they can "punish" (i.e., boycott) traders who have behaved dishonestly in the past. Traders must also have an incentive to sanction these transgressions. Without specific incentives, it may not be in a trader's best interest to boycott another trader, as such a choice is costly. Finally, victims of fraud must have an incentive to report the instance, even though this step may generate additional costs. Milgrom and his colleagues demonstrate that the institution of the private judges does indeed support honest behaviour among the traders as a Nash equilibrium. In less technical terms, such a system of adjudication is indeed capable of maintaining honest behaviour among traders even in the case of a large number of traders, and of occasional transactions.

The sophistication of the models developed by these economists, combined with their ability to explain widely different patterns of economic exchange, should compel sociologists and political scientists to take the underlying theoretical argument seriously. Simplified to the extreme, these works seem to suggest that the adoption by a business community of formal institutional arrangements in the absence of national legal systems can be explained as a response to the many deficiencies of an informal reputation system. Thus, one may be inclined to conclude that game theory can easily explain the emergence of private governance.

Such a conclusion would be premature. The models developed by Milgrom and his colleagues do an excellent job of demonstrating that the institution of the private judges can indeed sustain honest behaviour among traders in the context of a quite realistic model of global trade activities. But they do not show that these institutional arrangements were adopted in response to rampant dishonest behaviour among traders. Nor do they demonstrate that a reputation system existed and that it had failed for lack of appropriate public information. The authors simply assume that a reputation system had failed, and that traders were facing significant information problems. But since the authors do not explain how a reputation system may emerge and be maintained, it is impossible to determine whether such a system had failed. In fairness, Milgrom and his colleagues are careful not to postulate a causal relationship between the (assumed) inefficiency of the informal reputation mechanism and the emergence of formal institutions.

Demonstrating a causal connection between failure of an informal reputation system and the adoption of a formal institutional arrangement ultimately calls for an explanation of how social regulation based exclusively on a reputation mechanism operates, how it ensures that the relevant information is distributed and under what circumstances it may fail. For example, one needs to explain how traders learn that a reputation mechanism has failed in the first place, as opposed to selected individuals experiencing an occasional breach of contract. Reaching this conclusion requires efficient information exchange among traders. But failing to exchange information is precisely the reason the informal reputation system is failing. Clearly, to explain the transition from an informal reputation mechanism to a formal institutional arrangement theoretical refinements are needed.

The economic literature never examines exactly how an informal reputation mechanism may fail. The usual answer to this question is "group size". With increasing group size, the public observability of individual trade records quickly deteriorates. As a result, traders are unable to select an optimal response in every round of the game. They may erroneously punish another trader, or they may trade with a player who should have been punished. But it is not difficult to demonstrate that group size—measured by the number of group members—does a poor job of explaining why a business community may be induced to adopt a formal institutional arrangement. In the next section I show that relying on group size as a measure of informational failure may be misleading. I then propose an alternative framework to account for the failure of informal reputation mechanisms.

Group Size, Information Diffusion and Institutions

The economic literature does not explicitly define the concept of group. More often than not a group is implicitly equated to a small number of individuals who have frequent face-to-face interactions. A group in this sense is simply a small, tightly knit community, in which everybody literally knows everybody else. Conversely, in large groups not everybody will know everybody else. In such groups, it becomes exceedingly difficult for any group member to obtain accurate information about a member's past trade record or reputation.

Such a definition of group is not only intuitive, it is also tautological: Informal reputation mechanisms are predicted to fail in large groups, but large groups are defined in terms of inefficient reputation mechanisms. The limits of this definition of group can be demonstrated by the two examples: information diffusion in the international marine industry, and the diamond trade in New York City. The international marine industry—in terms of its size and the global nature of its operations—can hardly be considered small. Yet, during his interviews with marine underwriters, shipowners, consultants and other industry representatives the author (Furger, 1997) was repeatedly told that the international marine industry is a "small world". For example, an industry representative mentioned that an instance of collusion between a shipyard and a shipowner in Singapore would be common knowledge in London within a week. Anecdotal evidence suggests that information can indeed spread very quickly within this industry. Or consider the case of the diamond trade in the New York Jewish community. A striking feature of this trade is the practice among traders of lending diamonds to one another for examination without ever drafting a contract, relying solely on the traders' reputations and on relationship of mutual trusts (Ben-Porath, 1980; Coleman, 1988).

The first example demonstrates that information can circulate fairly efficiently even within very large groups and over very large distances. Efficient information exchange can be explained in part by the industry structure. To this day London is one of the most important centres of the international marine industry. All leading industry and professionals associations have either their headquarters or branch offices in London. In addition, the most widely circulated trade publications such as the *Lloyd's List* are published in London. Not surprisingly, this community is concentrated in the City, its offices are within walking distance of one another, and industry representatives informally exchange views and information on a daily basis in pubs and restaurants (see Furger, 1997, for a discussion of this example). The second example demonstrates the effectiveness of an individual's reputation and of informal sanctioning mechanisms as a means of private governance as opposed to third-party enforcement of, contractual obligations.

It appears that group size is not a good explanation for the transition from an informal reputation system to a fully developed, formalised institutional arrangement. Clearly, a better conceptualisation of group and community is needed. I propose to describe a group in terms of the structure of the relationships among the group members. In the remainder of this section I show that relational considerations and network analysis provide a robust theoretical foundation for explaining transitions from informal to formal institutional arrangements.

A group can be defined in the following way: an individual is considered a member of a group if he or she entertains direct or indirect ties with all other members of the group. Being member of a group in this sense does not require that an individual is familiar with every other member of the group. An indirect connection is sufficient. A group can then be described by means of a matrix. A relationship between any two individuals j and i is denoted as an "x" in the corresponding location. This qualitative description can be refined in several ways. For example, directionality in personal relationships can be introduced, relationships can be characterised as "strong" or "weak", and so forth.

Network analysis (Wasserman, 1994; Scott, 1991; Granovetter, 1973) provides the conceptual and technical means to determine to what extent information can be circulated among the members of a community even though the community—measured by its size—may be considered too large to support an informal mechanism of information diffusion.

For example, if two individuals are connected with one another by a significant number of paths, they are more likely to recognise distorted or intentionally manipulated information. In addition, the shorter the average length of these paths, the quicker information will diffuse from one individual to the next. Furthermore, "critical paths" may exist in the sense that a group may depend upon two individuals to assure social cohesion. In this case, these individuals are connected through what Granovetter called a "weak tie" (Granovetter, 1973). Clearly, these network attributes play a critical role in enabling or limiting information diffusion and social cohesion. More importantly, measures of information diffusion and social cohesion as outlined in this section are only weakly related to group size. Thus, these measures allow the possibility that smaller but weakly interconnected groups (i.e., groups with a small number of paths or longer paths) may be less compelled to adopt formal institutional arrangements than larger groups characterised by a higher degree of interconnectedness. In the latter case, it is conceivable that the group shows a different degree of interconnectedness, that is, it may eventually break down into several smaller groups (see Figure 7.3).

	Pl. 1	Pl. 2	Pl. 3	Pl. 4	Pl. 5
Pl. 1		x			x
Pl. 2	x		x		
Pl. 3		x		x	
Pl. 4			x		x
Pl. 5		x		x	

Figure 7.3

There are still other factors that may trigger the adoption of a formalised institutional arrangement. For example, some individuals in the group may be considered more "central" than others, in the sense that they have a larger number of ties to other community members, and can therefore either ensure the reliable diffusion of information or they can distort it. If more than one such individual exists within a group, some group members may receive contradictory bits and pieces of information. Sharply divergent assessments of an individual's reputation can generate substantial inefficiencies and ultimately prompt a group to adopt a more formal institutional structure.[6] In sum, a network analysis of group structure provides several important clues to why relatively small groups may not adopt a formal institutional arrangement, while larger business communities can sustain endogenous rules by relying on informal mechanisms of social regulation.

---

[6] Some preliminary work has been conducted by Ronald Burt (Burt, 1998, 1999). He has shown that the emergence of trust does indeed depend crucially on the structure of the network.

PRIVATE GOVERNANCE AND THE PROVISION OF PUBLIC GOODS

A Conceptual Framework

The discussion so far has been focused exclusively on governance within members of a business community, that is, on cases of quasi-legal norms and private institutions created by and enforced for the benefit of a community of traders. In all these cases the legal issues under consideration remain confined to the private sector. By contrast, the examples discussed in the remainder of this section involve significant negative externalities that may impact on one or more constituencies. By definition, these constituencies are not involved in the business transactions that generate the externalities. Externalities may range from the risks to consumers and customers of producing and handling paints and coatings, to the depletion of fisheries and the unsustainable harvest of rare timber in the tropical forests, among others. These genuine public concerns have given rise to intriguing new forms of international governance (Bendell, 2000; Reinicke and Deng, 2000; Smith, Naim, and Naim, 2000; Cutler, Haufler, and Porter, 1999; Teubner, 1997).

Even though these arrangements differ considerably from each other in terms of their governance structures, their mandate and the constituencies involved, they all share a few distinctive features. First, national governments do not directly participate in them, or play only a marginal role. Secondly, they all rely on a formalised governing structure that mediates between the business interests and their constituencies. These governing bodies may be described as instances of a bridging institution as I have defined it above. Thus, these private systems of governance consist of three main elements: the source of one or more externalities, usually a firm or an entire industry, one or more constituencies affected by these externalities, and a bridging institution mediating between private interests and public concerns.

The introduction of externalities and constituencies make it necessary to develop a slightly different account of the provision of public goods. Business self-regulation can be explained as traders adopt adjudication and enforcing mechanisms as a result of conducting business with one another. It is precisely because the traders are members of a business community integrated both through longstanding business relationships and through a reputation mechanism that a public good such as a legal system can emerge. In the presence of externalities and multiple constituencies, one needs to explain the motives that may lead an industry to provide a genuine public good in response to the demands of one or more constituencies. Since—initially at least—no cross-cutting ties exist between a business community and its (often vocal) constituencies, one could say that we are facing a case of a "fractured polity".

The notion of fractured polity should not be taken to mean the absence of any kind of interactions between business interests and their constituencies. "Fractured" in this case indicates that no cross-cutting ties exist between business leaders and their constituencies. The business interests and their constituencies "interact" in a mediated way. Citizens and environmental groups apply pressure on an industry by launching information campaigns, by alerting the news media, by writing letters and more recently by flooding top executives with e-mails. These actions may have two distinct goals. They may be aimed at damaging the public image of a firm, or they are designed to negatively affect revenues. Business for its part usually responds to these actions with elaborate public relations campaigns. Obviously, such mediated interactions are a poor substitute for face-to-face communication. Nevertheless, they are the means by which constituencies influence the industrial members' perceived costs and benefits of doing business as usual.

Industrial Self-Regulation

Industrial self-regulation represents a situation in which the relationship between constituencies and the bridging organisation is mediated, whereas interactions between the bridging organisation and industrial firms is direct.

There are currently several examples of industries that have taken an active stance in response to external pressures. Typically, an industry's response consists in introducing several, broadly defined requirements aimed at improving the environmental and safety record of its industrial members. Over time, the often generic and ambiguous meaning of these requirements is translated into more specific and detailed expectations through the adoption of "best practices", made available by industry leaders and freely distributed to all industrial members.

Instances of industrial self-regulation—"communitarian regulation" as Rees (1997) has dubbed it—include the Responsible Care programme by the Chemical Manufacturers Association (Nash and Ehrenfeld, 1997), the Coating Care initiative by the National Paint and Coating Association, and the Apparel Industry Partnership (Golodner, 1997). Not surprisingly, industries with an international orientation such as the textile industry are increasingly interested in environmental, safety and health codes as means of creating an even playing field. Domestic programmes of self-regulation such as those adopted by the National Association of Chemical Recyclers and the American Chemical Distributors may be expected to evolve along a similar path.

An important reason for developing an environmental programme is a legitimacy crisis, prompted by a highly visible industrial accident or by the industry reputation for harbouring egregious violators of environmental laws. A legitimacy crisis usually translates in all industry members experiencing a deterioration of their public image, independently of their environmental record.

A legitimacy crisis presents an industry with a difficult collective action problem: restoring the public image of an entire industry amounts to providing a public good. Providing this public good requires the participation of all industry members. At the same time, a member can easily free-ride on the efforts of other firms. Yet, an increasing number of industries have been fairly successful at improving their public image by adopting sophisticated programmes of environmental and safety management.

Conventional explanations, adoption decisions based on the size of an industry or its geographical dispersion are unconvincing: there does not seem to be a relationship between industry size, geographical dispersion and the provision of public goods. A more promising explanation lies in the differential impact of external pressure on some industry members. Just as a trader may be exposed to retaliation by his peers for not meeting his contractual obligations, an industrial firm with a poor environmental record may be exposed to considerable pressure by other industry members concerned about the negative consequences of a poor environmental record. And as in the case of business self-regulation, the pressure to improve a firm's environmental performance may originate with the firm's industrial customers. But unlike business self-regulation, a poor performer may face pressure from other sources, as well. For example, it may be challenged by local activists, by large environmental groups and by the media. An often underestimated source of pressure is direct competitors who believe—often rightly—that poor environmental performance gives a competitor an unfair competitive edge. Typically, a few large firms with considerable expertise in successfully managing environmental and safety problems face a multitude of smaller and small firms with limited expertise and even more limited financial resources. Under these circumstances, the industry leaders may come to the conclusion that the best way to restore their industry public image is to work with their trade association to develop a set of common environmental and safety standards, to be adopted and implemented by the entire industry.

There is significant anecdotal evidence that this description fits at least two such programmes, the American Chemistry Council's Responsible Care programme and Coating Care, developed by the American Paint and Coating Association. However, the evidence available does not illuminate the process by which tensions between leading firms and poor performers may eventually translate into the adoption of an industry-wide environmental management programme, and what factors may prevent an industry from addressing this problem of collective action. At an intuitive level, one can speculate that an industry's ability to resolve internal tensions may depend to a considerable degree on the existence of ties among top executives and on the efficient diffusion of relevant information across the industry. Support for this intuition is provided by recent work in economic sociology. Mark Granovetter has argued that successes and failures of collective action can best be explained by focusing on network structures. He introduces three ideal types of networks, the highly coupled, the weakly coupled and the decoupled network (Granovetter, 2000: 17–22):

- A highly decoupled structure consists of almost entirely disconnected networks of strong ties. The absence of cross-cutting ties will make it very difficult for such a social group to address collective action problems.
- A weakly coupled structure has several crosscutting ties linking two or more highly clustered networks. Individuals straddling across networks, make it possible for these social groups to successfully manage problems of collective action.
- Finally, highly coupled network structures can be expected to manage collective action problems more easily.

The decision to adopt a programme of self-regulation can then be analysed in terms of network structures within a given industry. This is a complex exercise that cannot be pursued in this chapter. See Furger (2000) for an elaboration of this argument. The analysis is fundamentally more difficult because, unlike the case of business self-regulation, industrial members seem to lack obvious means to apply significant sanctions to peers unwilling to improve their environmental records. In addition, it is unlikely that a trade association will assume a strong policing role. Trade associations are usually notin a position to impose specific, monetary sanctions on violators. Antitrust laws are partly responsible for this situation. Legal constraints however are not decisive. A more important limitation is the very limited authority a trade association has to take on a formal policing role. In addition, it is not immediately clear whether information about poor performers or free riders can efficiently circulate among all the parties involved.

Scholars have often concluded that industrial self-regulation is very unlikely to be effective. These authors invariably fail to realise that formal sanctions are but one form of social regulation, and that both industrial peers and trade association representatives may resort to a variety of informal, less visible sanctions to compel an industry member to improve its environmental record. While the relevance of informal sanctions in the case of industrial self-regulation has never been investigated, there is significant evidence that informal sanctions in modern societies remain as important as they were in rural societies (Braithwaite, 1993, 1989).

Business–NGO Collaborations

A second, important case is represented by what has been dubbed "business–NGO collaborations" (Bendell, 1998; Murphy and Bendell, 1997). In this case, industrial interests and their constituencies participate in the design and implementation process in a direct, more or less democratic way. Negotiations between business and NGOs representatives take place face-to-face. Over time such repeated interactions give way to fairly stable cross-cutting ties among the various constituencies that once formed a fractured polity.

As for programmes of industrial self-regulation, the adoption and implementation of these initiatives can only partially be explained in terms of a legitimation crisis, consumer boycotts and bad press. All these factors may well be necessary, but hardly a sufficient, condition. They are not the cause of such a complex negotiation process. Unlike cases of industrial self-regulation, business–NGO collaborations have attracted the attention of practitioners, and less from academics. As a result, the available literature is rich but mainly descriptive and does not shed much light on the underlying sociological and institutional factors that may account for the implementation of such unusual co-operative agreements. This is somewhat ironic, as this particular approach to international self-governance seems indeed quite promising.

Business–NGO collaborations are in part the result of a strategic reorientation of large NGOs. Over the last few years, many NGOs have targeted large industrial corporations directly rather than trying to influence national governments through the legislative process (Keck and Sikkink, 1998). This reorientation in part reflects practical considerations. In some cases, it may be far more effective to focus on one specific corporation rather than on a plethora of national governments. But the change is not simply pragmatic. As Murphy and Bendell point out, large NGOs are increasingly managed by executives with considerable private sector experience. These managers are much more inclined than their predecessors to collaborate with the private sector. Often, they bring with them an extensive network of very valuable professional ties. Furthermore, information technologies in general and the Internet in particular have helped tremendously the traditionally fragmented and dispersed NGO universe to build powerful international coalitions. Finally, it is worth noting that some of these collaborative efforts are rooted in deep frustration by some leading environmental groups with the complexity and the excruciatingly slow pace of international multilateral negotiations.

A, prototypical example of business–NGO collaboration is the so-called 1995 Group formed to implement sustainable standards of timber harvesting in southern countries. It consists of timber companies, furniture manufacturers, retail stores, consumer and environmental advocates. This group was later institutionalised in what is now the Forest Stewardship Council (FSC). FSC designs standards of sustainable timber harvesting, and accredits organisations responsible for certifying forests managed in a sustainable way (Bendell and Murphy, 2000: 70).

A second example of a business–NGO collaboration is the Marine Stewardship Council (MSC). In 1996 WWF-International launched a partnership with Unilever Corporation, the world's largest buyer of frozen fish, to provide economic incentives for the seafood industry to adopt practices of sustainable fishing. These efforts eventually translated into what is now known as Marine Stewardship Council (MSC). The MSC constituency is not as broad as the FSC constituency. The FSC tried from the beginning to be as inclusive as possible. FSC is a membership organisation that represents a broad range of interest in the forestry industry. As a result, the implementation of the FSC's vision has proceeded at a glacial speed. By contrast the MSC was created as a strategic alliance between Unilever and WWF. The MSC is not a membership organisation, and it is less inclusive than the FSC. MSC seems more concerned about achieving its stated goals than by proceeding in what its constituency may perceive as a legitimate way. Not surprisingly, some constituencies such as fishermen's unions in Canada and the South have been very suspicious of these efforts.

Other relevant examples of business–NGO alliances exist. The Fairtrade Foundation, a coalition of international development, consumer and fair trade organisations, launched a pilot project in 1997 in cooperation with British companies aimed at developing appropriate codes of conduct in dealing with their southern suppliers. A similar initiative, the Ethical Trading Initiative (ETI), with a broader mandate and with government financing was launched in early 1998.

A final example of a business–NGO alliance is provided by the CERES initiative (Coalition for Environmentally Responsible Economies). This initiative is noteworthy not because of its impact on its industrial members (large industrial US manufacturers in a variety of industries), which to the best of my knowledge is limited, but because it includes unions and financial institutions. Finally, it is worth noting that business–NGO alliances are not exclusively focused on environmental issues. The Fair Labor Foundation, another example of a business–NGO alliance, focuses on labour standards in the textile industry.

Standard-developing Organisations

A well-established type of international private governance is the standard-developing organisation (SDO). While SDOs certainly do not represent a new phenomenon, scholars have been slow to recognise that in many industrialised countries SDOs have a time-honoured history of playing an active role in public policy. In addition to standard-developing, SDOs may perform a variety of other activities such as conducting tests of parts, components, products and systems, and providing auditing and certification services. Classification societies in the international marine industry are a particularly interesting example of SDOs (Furger, 1997). These organisations are not only responsible for developing standards of safety for all major parts and components and for the vessel structure; they also ensure compliance with these standards by periodically surveying ships on behalf of regulators and insurance companies. Other relevant examples of SDOs include technical organisations such as the Factory Mutual and the Underwriters Lab. Their names are suggestive of their history: originally founded by the insurance industry to assess a variety of industrial risks, they later became independent operators.

Certain instances of SDOs provide an illustration of a governance structure in which a bridging institution interacts with the industrial firms and their constituencies exclusively in a mediated way. The basis of interaction in this case is represented by test results, labels, certificates, audits, and so forth. Consider for example the Insurance Institute of Highway Safety, funded by the US insurance industry. This little-known organisation is responsible for conducting crash and component tests on new vehicles on behalf of the insurance industry. While in the past this information has been used exclusively by insurance companies to induce car manufacturers to improve the safety of their vehicles, the results of crash tests are now available on the Internet and can be used by prospective buyers to inform their buying decisions. Other relevant examples include product testing by the consumers' unions and rating agencies in the financial sector. In all these cases, the SDO fulfils its role as a bridging institution by disseminating relevant information among producers and consumers alike.

The test results published by the Institute of Highway Safety and other similar organisations is an excellent example of what has been called "informational regulation" (Kleindorfer and Orts, 1998). In essence, informational regulation provides the public with the means for making choices that reflect their beliefs, preferences and concerns. The possibility of relying on information as a regulatory tool is intriguing, especially at the international level. In many regards, information is the only means available to the public to bring pressure upon recalcitrant firms operating in countries with low environmental and safety standards, or in nations with limited resources to enforce existing laws and regulations.

An apparent success story is the EPA Toxic Release Inventory programme. Established as part of the Emergency Planning and Community Right-to-know Act of 1986 (EPCRA), the Toxic Release Inventory (TRI) requires industrial facilities to monitor and report the production of approximately 650 hazardous chemicals (as at 1999). I discuss this case below. A second example of informational regulation used to improve environmental standards is PROPER (Program for Pollution Control, Evaluation and Rating), initiated five years ago by BAPEDAL, the Indonesian environmental protection agency (World Bank, 1999: 57–79). In this case, the regulatory agency itself plays the role of bridging institution. According to representatives of the World Bank, this programme is currently being implemented in other developing countries.

Other Forms of Private Governance

In addition to the three types of private governance just discussed, there exist several other, less obvious cases of private governance. For example, large industrial customers may on occasion become a bridging institution. In this case, a (typically smaller) firm may implement an environmental management system as a condition for sustaining a long-term business relationship. Large industrial firms are motivated to take these steps largely out of concern for their public image. For example, Ford currently expects (but does not officially require) all its suppliers to be ISO14000 certified. Nike has faced considerable criticism for dealing with suppliers deemed to operate in unacceptable ways by Western consumer groups. Another relevant example is provided by the E3 programme (Encouraging Environmental Excellence). This programme, developed by the American Textile Manufacturers Institute, requires its industrial members to co-operate with their suppliers in an effort to reduce the upstream environmental impacts (ATMI, 1998).

Another unusual example of private governance is provided by the financial sector. Financial institutions, especially European and Japanese banks, have developed considerable interest in sustainability as part of their core business activities (Ganzi and DeVries, 1998). So have many European insurance companies. While the usage of these environmental screening and management tools is now justified mostly on business grounds, they were originally introduced in response to criticism by some vocal environmental groups. Just as large, highly visible corporations concerned for their public image exercised considerable pressure on their suppliers to improve their environmental records, so have leading banks and insurance companies leaned on their customers to avoid the negative consequences of a bad publicity.

In some cases, systems of private governance can be nested. For example, in 1995 UNEP launched an "insurance initiative".[7] Insurance companies participating in this initiative are required to adopt and implement several requirements aimed at improving the sustainability of their own operations. More importantly, the programme requires the participating companies to incorporate sustainability criteria (however defined) in their core business practices. Many leading European insurance companies have subscribed to this programme. Not surprisingly, many of the participating insurance companies had already taken steps in a similar direction. Conceivably, the UNEP initiative may strengthen the most innovative insurance companies by establishing a set of common standards recognised and adopted by the entire industry. The creation of such a framework could, in time, mitigate if not eliminate concerns about free riding among participating insurance companies.

International Private Governance: Preliminary Conclusions and Open Questions

The preceding discussion has shown that international private governance is not just an abstract possibility, it is an increasingly important reality. One could also say that we are facing the emergence of new forms of polity, closely associated with the creation of new public arenas and populated by a variety of new political constituencies. These public arenas differ considerably from more

---

[7] In 1992 UNEP launched a similar initiative for the banking sector.

traditional forms of public space: wholly detached from any sense of territoriality, not easily recognisable by the non-initiated, yet potentially open to external participation, and perhaps also exposed to manipulations.

The possibility of "mediated governance" is an important one, for obvious reasons: International governance is not territorial and cuts across numerous traditional administrative and political boundaries. It is hard to image how private governance could emerge at the international scale without relying on mediated political processes: private interests and their constituencies can hardly be expected to be embedded in extensive networks of personal and professional ties, as they often are at the national and regional level. Such mediated systems of private governance are exposed to one significant threat: In a world in which information becomes a crucial resource, the incentives to manipulate and distort information for political purposes must be taken very seriously. Criminal intent apart, one needs to consider carefully how and what information is gathered. Anyone familiar with the Internet can testify to the fact that in the information age it has become exceedingly easy to fabricate, distort and manipulate information.

It is certainly possible to anticipate that repeated distortions, abuses and manipulation will eventually lead to the demise of mediated systems of private governance. On the other hand, one could easily imagine that such distortions may actually trigger a public debate among the affected constituencies about acceptable ways to convey relevant information to the public. Political conflicts can produce important and unexpected by-products, such as new cross-cutting ties, new rules and new approaches to governance. For example, they could lead to the creation of cross-cutting ties among private interests and their constituencies. This is a crucial point worth emphasising. Without such cross-cutting ties—weak-links in Granovetter's terminology—there is little chance that private interests and their constituencies will be able to find mutually satisfactory solutions to extant political conflicts. It is precisely the creation of such weak links that can transform a mediated system of private governance into an international polity that actually deserves this label.

The alternative to this scenario is familiar. The private interests and their constituencies will remain locked in a political struggle conducted exclusively through mediated interactions (i.e., in the absence of cross-cutting ties). In this case, political solutions are not found through sound discourse. They are the outcome of public relations battles conducted in the media and on the Internet and characterised by a systematic misrepresentation of the opponent's positions. Under these circumstances, compromising political attitudes will be weeded out on each side in favour of hardened and increasingly irreconcilable, dogmatic positions.

But just how effective and legitimate are forms of international private governance largely based on system integration? In the remainder of this chapter, I examine this issue by discussing three cases of international private governance.

The first case may be considered a "baseline" case. It bears considerable similarity to the case of the medieval trade, but it is firmly grounded in the twenty-first century. It is an example of mediated self-governance for which legal guarantees exist but cannot easily be enforced: auctions and procurement (consumer-to-consumer and business to-business) on the Internet. The relevance of this case can hardly be overestimated. Auctions are quickly moving from being a favourite tool of exchange for private households ("electronic yard sales") to a global means of procurement and bidding for everything from coal to heavy equipment and medical devices. The institutions implemented by these auction houses seem at first to support the view that the adoption of formalised institutional arrangements can indeed be described as an effort to improve upon inefficient reputation mechanisms and to facilitate the distribution of relevant information among a large number of market participants. In this case, the system of governance consists of a fairly homogenous business community—a community of traders—whose dealings are shaped by the rules and regulations established by the auction house.

The second case focuses on standard-setting organisations and their role as bridging institutions between private interests and a variety of distinct constituencies, such as customers, local communities and citizen groups. The discussion shows that these organisations provide much more than just raw information to a variety of constituencies. It also shows that the evolution from an informal reputation mechanism to a full-blown mediated system of governance is not as straightforward or even inevitable as the discussion of private judges in the Champagne Fairs may suggest. The term "standard-setting organisation" is used in the broadest possible way to include traditional standard-developing organisations and other organisations that have begun to play a similar role.

The third and final case examines a prototypical example of informational regulation, that is, of mediated governance. This discussion comes to a somewhat paradoxical conclusion. For informational regulation to operate as an efficient reputation mechanism (i.e., as a credible means of mediated governance), a considerable amount of preliminary negotiation and face-to-face interactions among the constituencies involved is necessary. In other words, the efficiency of mediated governance depends to a significant extent upon establishing cross-cutting ties among the constituencies involved. Conversely, the political conflicts surrounding inefficient informational regulation (i.e., information provision not universally recognised as credible and fair) may lead to the creation of several cross-cutting ties among the various constituencies.

PUBLIC INFORMATION, INSTITUTIONS AND SOCIAL EMBEDDEDNESS

eBay: Electronic Communities Built and Maintained on Reputation

eBay is an Internet-based firm that enables traders to participate in auctions on a global scale. It may be considered a prototypical example of a global business community in which business and personal relationships are rare, and trade is sustained largely by a reputation mechanism. eBay is relevant to the present discussion because it provides an opportunity to assess the effectiveness of a reputation mechanism as the primary means for dealing with the challenges of collective action posed by a very large business community.

eBay is a non-trivial example of electronic commerce at the global scale. As such, it faces similar challenges as the medieval traders did in the twelfth century: How can auctions be sustained over time if the traders for all practical purposes are often unable to enforce mutual contractual obligations? Without a strong assurance that contractual obligation will be met, a business community such as eBay integrated almost exclusively through systemic means could hardly be sustained. eBay is not an isolated case. Auction sites have become quite popular on the Internet as means to buy and sell both used and new goods. Examples include Auction Central, Auction Sales and Yahoo auctions. The relevance of the eBay experience is not limited to auctions. A number of entrepreneurs have recognised that creating trust and helping companies establish a reputation for trustworthiness may be profitable activities. For example, GeoTrust's mission is to provide buyers and sellers with instant access to a participant's "trust profile" in an online transaction (see GeoTrust's website). And while industry portals such as E-Steel (worldwide suppliers of steel products), and DirectAg (farming industry) have been created mainly as a way for reducing search and procurement costs for industry members, it is easy to predict that the commercial viability of these enterprises will depend crucially upon institutionalising social mechanisms for sustaining trust among their customers.

The possibility of fraud and abuses on auction sites is real. Consider the following message posted by a man believed to have used online auctions to sell stuffed animals that were never delivered:

> Ha ha ha ha ha, all you people are really quite ridiculous. You make a deal via e-mail, never see the person, never speak with the person and then get upset when you get ripped off. You must be a bunch of morons. I really hope, for my sake, that you all disregard the posting and continue as usual [Cooper, 1999].

Instances of abuse and fraud are however rare. Despite the large volume of daily transactions conducted on eBay, the firm's representatives claim that eBay averages only 27 complaints of fraud per million auctions (Bloomberg News, 1999; Leibovich, 1999). In 1999, the trading volume on eBay had reached over 9.5 million transactions per quarter.

One of the most interesting aspects of eBay's response to the challenge raised by fraud and legal uncertainty is an elaborate reputation mechanism. Buyers are encouraged to rate every transaction by providing positive or negative feedback. The feedback is mainly a reflection of the sellers' responsiveness to deliver the goods. A positive feedback translates into a positive point, negative feedback bring the seller a negative point. eBay keeps track of positive and negative tallies separately.[8] Sellers have no control over their scores. However, they have the right to hide them. eBay also provides a mechanism of dispute resolution as well as insurance coverage and escrow services. Finally, eBay asks—but does not require—traders to identify themselves by providing detailed credit card information.

In addition to auctions, eBay has established a variety of discussion forums. In these forums, eBay users have the opportunity to discuss matters of interest. According to journalistic sources, these discussion forums have been extremely helpful in building a strong sense of community among traders. Participants use this opportunity not only to exchange views about quality and value of goods. They also discuss issues pertaining to the honesty and trustworthiness of other traders and debate what constitute acceptable rules of conduct and normal practices.

This centralised exchange system, combined with the scores voluntarily provided by the buyers, solves a very complex information problem: How can every potential buyer be kept informed about the trading history of every potential seller? As I have shown above, it is possible to envisage an institutional arrangement that dramatically reduces the searching costs to potential buyers of assessing the reputation of unknown, prospective sellers, and to create incentives for sellers to meet their contractual obligations. Interestingly, buyers in this case do not have a strong incentive to provide feedback, especially positive feedback. They do not face sanctions by the business community for not providing feedback. Yet, it appears that most buyers do provide feedback, often solicited by the sellers.

As no emperical analysis of exchange practices on eBay is available, it is impossible to determine the specific impact that the reputation system has on traders' behaviour. In particular, it is unclear whether occasional sellers (i.e., sellers with no interest in future transactions) are more prone than frequent sellers to fraudulent action. And one should not ignore the fact that for transactions taking place within a country, buyers can still rely on external law enforcement to uphold their contractual obligations or to settle disputes.[9] Nevertheless, it is remarkable that such a system of exchange exists in the first place, and that contractual obligations seem to be upheld largely without relying on law enforcement.

Despite its technological complexity, eBay is a rather simple example of a business community integrated through systemic means, that is, it is largely dependent upon a reputation mechanism for its viability. The relationship between the trade history and the reputation of individual traders is unambiguous, the scores are rarely in dispute, and the relevant information is public and

---

[8] Note that this reputation system is exposed to manipulation. eBay cannot entirely prevent the co-ordinated action of a clique of traders aimed at discrediting or artificially inflating the reputation of another trader. According to newspaper reports, eBay is addressing these issues.

[9] Note that in countries as large as the USA, the cost of using the legal system may well exceed its benefits. This is likely to be the case for small-value transactions conducted over large distances.

perfectly observable. Under these circumstances, it is possible to envisage a large business community whose members conduct business with one another exclusively on the basis of their reputation. But just how relevant is this experience to other cases of private governance? The case of standard-developing organisations—discussed in the next section—demonstrates, that information gathering and information dissemination must indeed be considered necessary elements of an efficient system of private governance. However, this case also shows that mere information gathering and dissemination cannot guarantee efficiency.

Private Standard-developing Organisations as Bridging Institutions

In the preceding example, I have examined the case of a business community that relies on a reputation mechanism as a means of system integration (i.e., to sustain efficient trade and uphold contractual obligations). This example seems at first to support the view that private institutional arrangements are indeed adopted by large business communities in response to the shortcomings of informal reputation mechanisms. In this section I argue that this account of collective action is valid only under rather restrictive conditions.

Consider first the case of eBay. Reputation scores are an important source of information to buyers, but in many cases, they do not necessarily suggest whether a prospective seller should be considered trustworthy. In the absence of some shared rules, how can a buyer determine whether a prospective seller is indeed trustworthy? How many positive points are sufficient to reassure a buyer about a seller's honesty? And what if the prospective seller has both a high positive score and several negative points? Does it matter that the prospective seller received negative feedback early on, that is, can his negative points be discounted? As this brief discussion demonstrates, there are hardly any natural rules to help a buyer determine whether a prospective seller can be trusted. The discussion forums provide a partial solution to this problem: they enable buyers to "negotiate" the meaning of positive and negative points by exchanging their experience with specific buyers. In short, discussion forums allow buyers to make sense of an ambiguous and messy empirical reality.

It appears that even a seemingly straightforward reputation mechanism such as the one implemented on eBay cannot entirely operate without assuming that a "good reputation" is ultimately the outcome of a social negotiation among the traders. Without a common understanding of what constitutes a good or bad reputation, reputation scores are of limited help as a social device to improve the efficiency of trade. Or, to put in another way, an unambiguous individual reputation can be inferred from an individual's positive and negative scores only if the community members rely on common evaluative rules. In sum, the efficiency of a reputation mechanism depends—somewhat paradoxically—on social negotiations and communicative action.

The importance of rules of thumb and interpretative schemes as tools for making sense of a messy, ambiguous or even contradictory empirical reality becomes clearer in the case of standard-setting organisations. In this second case, we are facing a system of private governance consisting of manufacturers, their customers and a standard-developing organisation. The relevant constituency in this case consists of a possibly very large number of customers. Interactions between manufacturers and customers are entirely mediated in the sense that no personal ties exist between manufacturers and their customers, or between the standard-developing organisation and its own constituencies (i.e., industrial firms and customers). The products under consideration may be harmful to the buyers. Relevant examples include electrical appliances, power tools, cars, toys and food and hygienic products among others.

The relevance of standard-developing organisations at the international level can hardly be overestimated. In the United States alone there are literally hundreds of SDOs whose standards affect public safety and health. For example, the Society of Automotive Engineers is the second largest standard-setting organisation with 4,200 standards and the US Pharmacopoeia ranks third with 2,900 standards (Cheit, 1990: 7). Born as national organisations, over time many SDOs have been recognised as authoritative sources of technical expertise at the international level.[10]

SDOs represent a significant departure from the case of business self-governance, SDOs exemplify a case of private interests playing a significant role in public affairs. One can say that SDOs are engaged in the production of a public good. The prototypical situation to be discussed in this section can be described as follows. An industry consisting of several, directly competing manufacturers produces a good for a mass market that may be harmful to the consumers, or can negatively affect their health. The manufacturers are aware of this possibility, and so is the public. Furthermore, no legal standards of safety or of due care exist. Under these circumstances, will the manufacturers choose to adopt adequate standards of safety? More generally, can these manufacturers be expected to produce a public good in the absence of legal coercion? Ever since Mancur Olsson published his now classic *Logic of Collection Action* in 1965, the answer to this question seems obvious. A closer examination shows that the situation is less straightforward than it seems.

Each competing manufacturer faces the following basic options: either he makes an unsafe product at a lower cost by reducing safety standards, or he manufactures a safer product, at a higher cost. In the former case, he expects to lose market shares to less scrupulous competitors. Consumers for their part are unable to determine *a priori* whether a product is safe or not, that is, whether the product they are buying has been designed according to strict or not so strict safety

---

[10] Despite their significant role as private regulators, standard-developing organisations have attracted little scholarly attention. Relevant exceptions are Yilmaz (1998), Krislov (1997), Sykes (1995) and Cheit (1990).

standards. In other words, information about the safety of the product is largely private, and consumers cannot directly observe the quality of the product.

We can describe this situation as a repeated game. Each manufacturer plays a finite but undetermined number of rounds. Each round represents a possible transaction with a consumer. A consumer may or may not make a buying decision. Furthermore, every transaction takes place with a different customer. This means that repeated interactions between a manufacturer and its customers are excluded. Thus, business relationships cannot be forged, and anonymous market transactions are the only type of interaction between manufacturers and consumers. Under these circumstances, a manufacturer may be able to reap higher profits in the short term by selling lower quality products. However, this move will most likely destroy his reputation (assuming the product will indeed fail). Repeated product failures in turn are likely to undermine the manufacturer's ability to do business with other customers in the future (Kreps, 1990: 531–3). So one can predict that a manufacturer with a reasonably long planning horizon will indeed adopt higher safety standards. This situation is not too different from our discussion of "community enforcement" above. The manufacturer has a strong incentive to produce a public good precisely because if he does not, he can expect to be punished by other consumers who will avoid doing business with him.

For the manufacturer to opt for a safer design, three conditions must be met. First, consumers must be aware of the product safety record, i.e. the product safety record must be publicly available. Secondly, the manufacturer must be aware that the consumers are indeed informed about his safety record. Thirdly, customers must be able to establish a causal, unambiguous link between product failures and design criteria. In other words, consumers must be able to determine that a product failure can be attributed to poor design. These are rather demanding requirements, not likely to be met in reality. As a result, customers may have considerable difficulties ascertaining whether a product failure is the result of poor safety standards or is the consequence of inadequate use, or else it must be considered an instance of poor manufacturing.

Making such a determination usually requires technical expertise not available to an average consumer. Scientific and technical uncertainties may enable the manufacturer to assert that the product has been designed by following the highest safety standards, and that a fatality must be viewed as a rare case of poor manufacturing. Consumers for their part have no way to know whether the manufacturer is telling the truth. As the product may come be seen as not safe, future customers may simply avoid buying the product, and the market for this product will fall apart.

Manufacturers anticipating these problems may respond by establishing a set of common design and manufacturing standards. As part of these efforts, they may create a separate organisation focused exclusively on designing standards, and testing and certifying the industry products—in short, a standard-developing organisation. Standard-developing organisations may be regarded as yet another example of a social institution that solves several related problems (of inform-ational and of other nature). By certifying that a product has been safely designed and manufactured, they eliminate the need for consumers to monitor its safety record, thus greatly reducing the need for information gathering and information evaluation. In this sense, standard-developing organisations provide what could be labelled "interpretative relief". In addition, they simplify considerably the search for the causes of product failures. They also eliminate—to a large extent—free riding. Finally, their technical and scientific expertise combined with their independence assure the credibility and trustworthiness of the standard-developing process and of their test results. In sum, SDOs are key to the endogen-ous production of a public good. In the terminology developed above, they pro-vide an illustration of a private system of governance predicated almost entirely on mediated interactions.

Standard-developing organisations may operate as a bridging institution in a variety of contexts. Between manufacturers and consumers in specific product markets (as in the case of the American Meat Institute or the American Bakers' Association), between two industrial sectors (for example, the American Concrete Institute operates at the interface between the concrete and the construction industry) or else between the public at large and a variety of related industries (the American Association of Mechanical Engineers illustrates this point).

The history of standard-developing organisations in the USA seems to indicate that the private sector cannot be expected always to develop its own bodies of governance to deal with problems of collective action. It is no coincid-ence that the codes developed by the National Fire Protection Association, a US standard-setting organisation widely considered the *de facto* worldwide developer of fire safety codes, was created at the turn of this century by the insurance industry in response to fire hazards in crowded urban areas. Organisations such as the Underwriters Labs (UL), the Factory Mutual, and the Insurance Institute of Highway Safety were also created by US insurance industry.[11] On the other hand, several standard-developing organisations have indeed been created by their industry. A case in point is the Meat Institute, an organisation with strong ties to the meat producing industry. This seems to suggest that an industry cannot be expected to solve efficiently problems of collective action. To put it in other words, even acute information problems do not automatically induce an industry to respond to these challenges by adopting a suitable institutional arrangements. The reasons for this situation are complex and cannot be examined here. See Furger, 2000, for some initial thoughts on this issue.

One key feature of this particular of type private system of governance is that one constituency, the customers, can "vote with their wallet". Although

---

[11] While the UL and the American Fire Protection Association are now largely independent of the insurance industry, both the Institute of Highway Safety and Factory Mutual have strong ties to the insurance sector. The Institute of Highway Safety in particular is fully funded by the insurance industry.

mediated, the relationship between manufacturers and their constomers is strong: poor product design translates immediately in loss of revenue. Such a strong and proportionate economic feedback may not always be present. This is often the case when it is very difficult to demonstrate a causal link between the adoption of the standard and intended outcomes. The situation is made even worse when the standard is aimed at several constituencies, only one of which are actual customers. In such a case, while reputational concerns may indeed lead to the adoption of the standard, it is almost impossible to demonstrate that such a standard actually addresses the problems it was designed to solve.

Consider for example the case of labour codes such as SA 8000 and of environmental standards such as EMAS and ISO 14000. These codes can hardly be compared to traditional product standards, as they apply to production processes, plant or entire organisations. Typically, they consist of several elements. ISO14000 for example requires a firm—among other things—first to identify all environmental impacts, then to prioritise them, and finally to adopt policies to eliminate the most important ones. However, the standard is non-prescriptive in that it does not require the firm to achieve any specific environmental goals. It is an elaborate framework to help a firm manage its environmental impacts in a systematic way.

The complex and open nature of these standards prevents an SDO from conducting rigorous tests. Certification then is based on—possibly extensive—audits. The shift from testing to auditing introduces a host of new difficulties. Of particular importance in this context is the observation that audits simply assure compliance to (mostly) procedural standards. They are largely decoupled from "outcomes". As a result, it is quite possible that firms certified to the same standard display widely different levels of safety and environmental performance. This issue may or may not be an important problem, but it certainly increases the importance of the auditors' independence and the auditors' professional ethics. And on both counts, one may have reasons to be somewhat sceptical, as the auditor's services are paid for by the firm subject to the audit. While this issue has not yet received much attention in current debates about environmental management systems such as ISO14000 or EMAS, there is considerable evidence that under certain circumstances it does indeed undermine the credibility of these standards (Furger, 1997).

So far concerns about professionalism and conflicts of interest have not defined the relationship between adopters of these standards and their constituencies. Rather, it is mutual disinterest. One could also say that no well-defined constituency has yet to emerge.[12] It is precisely the uncertainty surrounding the relationship between standard implementation and environmental

---

[12] There are some noteworthy exceptions. ISO, a leading international standard-developing organisations, has been criticised by several environmental groups for excluding public interest organisations from fully participating in the development of the ISO14000 series of environmental management standards (Krut and Gleckman, 1998).

performance that accounts for the lack of interactions between business interests and their constituencies. This ambiguity is unlikely to be eliminated as long
as no cross-cutting ties exist between the private sector and its constituencies.[13]

The lack of cross-cutting ties and of a sustained dialogue over the role of these
standards at the national and international level has another important consequence: auditing firms do not have an incentive to develop a reputation for high-
quality auditing procedures and for high standards of professional ethics. Under
these circumstances, it becomes largely irrelevant whether an auditing firm conducts a strict audit or is lenient with poorly performing firms. In sum, the system of private governance under consideration may well turn out to be very
inefficient. Economic inefficiency suggests that the institutional arrangement
under consideration does not allow industrial firms to determine whether their
decision to adopt and implement a system of environmental and safety management can be justified on economic grounds, and does not allow customers
and other constituencies such as private citizens and NGOs to decide whether
the adoption of these standards should somehow be rewarded or should rather
be discredited as an ineffective approach to environmental and safety management.

In this section, I have discussed the motives and mechanisms underlying an
industry's efforts at solving problems of collective action. I have also shown that
these efforts may translate into highly inefficient institutional arrangements characterised essentially by what may be called a fractured polity. A defining trait of
such polities is the absence of cross-cutting ties: one or more key constituencies,
such as environmental or labour groups, does not entertain any ties with the network of decision-makers involved in developing the standards. In the next section, I show that the lack of cross-cutting ties between the adopters of a standard
and their constituencies is not only a source of inefficiency, it may also lead to
conflicts over the means of system integration (i.e., over the specifics of reputation
mechanisms). The discussion shows that conflicts are a double-edged sword. In
some cases they generate "creative destruction" and lead to improvements in the
credibility of a reputation mechanism. In addition they can lead to establishing
cross-cutting ties between industry and its constituencies where those were
absent. But they can also undermine the efficiency of a system of private governance by generating several, mutually incompatible reputation mechanisms.

Scorecard: Restoring Fractured Polities

In this section, I focus on the Toxic Release Inventory (TRI) as a prominent
illustration of information used to improve the environmental performance of

---

[13] Note that there are no incentives for industrial firms to eliminate ambiguity. Poorly performing firms have a strong incentive to avoid measuring performance. On the other hand, well
performing firms do have an incentive to avoid discrediting the standard's reputation. Why these
firms rarely take a leading role remains unclear.

an industry. Providing information about the potential risks from industrial facilities to residential communities in the USA was the aim of the Emergency Planning and Community Right-to-know Act of 1986 (EPCRA). A first step in this direction was made with the implementation of the Toxic Release Inventory (TRI). Under the provisions of TRI, EPA identified and established annual reporting requirements for approximately 650 hazardous chemicals (as of 1999).

In 1998, the Environmental Defense Fund, a leading US environmental group, decided to make the TRI data broadly available to the public by publishing them in easily understandable form on the Internet. The project, called Scorecard, is probably the most advanced experiment in what some scholars have called informational regulation (Kleindorfer and Orts, 1998).[14] Currently, Scorecard is based on 1996 TRI data, and is derived from the reports of over 21,500 manufacturing and federal facilities. Visitors to Scorecard can obtain quantitative information about a variety of pollutants produced in their neighbourhood. Scorecard provides two basic types of information: a measure of environmental impact, generally in pounds, and environmental impact rankings, which a user can access in different ways (at the zip code, state level, by facility). According to EDF, in its first day of operation, Scorecard received over a million hits.

TRI is a prominent, but by no means the only, example of information regulation. In Britain, Friends of the Earth, a national environmental group, has implemented a similar approach. An analogous effort has been initiated by the Indonesian environmental agency (BAPEDAL). BAPEDAL has recently finished conducting a pilot project in which it used information about environmental performance on a plant-by-plant basis to create incentives for firms to improve their compliance record (World Bank, 1999: 57–79). A somewhat different case of information regulation is provided by the "Global Reporting Initiative" (GRI). GRI is an example of an international movement aimed at developing a coherent framework for measuring environmental performance. The initiative is supported by many environmental groups, social investment funds and a multinational corporations. More focused efforts, again developed by the private sectors, exist as well. For example, the Sustainable Investment Research International Group (SiRi), a new consortium of corporate social research firms, has recently been created to provide socially responsible investors with information on multinational corporations' social and environmental track records.

Informational regulation can be described as an effort at forging what may be considered international polities by integrating—at first only by means of information in a standardised form—a variety of hitherto disconnected constituencies.[15] In some cases, as for TRI, it is more accurate to describe this effort

---

[14] The database can be accessed on the World Wide Web at http://www.scorecard.org.

[15] Technically speaking, a fractured polity can be identified by the existence of what economists call negative external effects (Baumol and Oates, 1988). In his now classic paper on the "Problem of Social Costs", Ronald Coase (1960) argued that one of the reasons parties affected by negative externalities do not engage in direct negotiations are high transaction costs. In this chapter, I have focus on another reason for this state of affair, the lack of information among the affected parties about the negative external effect itself.

as an attempt at restoring fractured polities. In the former case, no cross-cutting ties existed between the private interests and their constituencies, in the latter case such ties may have existed at an earlier point in time. In the case of Scorecard, we are facing a situation characterised by a multitude of new or restored polities. Typically, these polities consist of a chemical plant and the citizens living in the neighbourhoods surrounding the plant. Incidentally, this description fits accurately the Indonesian case, as well.

The broad availability of relevant environmental information creates a strategic situation in which a chemical plant suddenly concerned about the impact of its environmental record on its constituencies. Perhaps more accurately, public disclosure creates a strong incentive for a firm to determine who exactly its constituency is, and how best to respond to demands triggered by this constituency. The use of the term polity is meant to convey precisely this: economic actors may recognise that their constituency is broader than simply their most important customers, and may include organisations or individuals not connected with them by a business relation. In sum, public information enables the creation of systemically integrated polities as no cross-cutting ties at least initially between business interests and their constituencies .

The assumptions motivating Scorecard are clear enough. EDF hopes that by making a wide variety of environmentally-related information on a plant-by-plant basis publicly available, firms will have an incentive to compare each other's performance, and citizens will be able to enter into a direct dialogue with poorly performing facilities to achieve significant environmental improvements. EDF then may be described as another instance of a bridging institution between industry and one of its key constituencies, the communities surrounding industrial facilities. And like other instances of a bridging institution EDF may be expected to play an important, albiet passive role in restoring fractured polities.

Scorecard may be characterised as yet another example of a private institutional arrangement that relies on public information to facilitate the provision of a public good. Perhaps more accurately, Scorecard facilitates the provision of a variety of public goods, one or more for every new or restored polity across the country. By making information about TRI data broadly available, each industrial firm will develop a specific reputation for its environmental performance firmly grounded in its environmental record. Accordingly, poorly performing plants facing hard questions from their constituencies will have a strong incentive to improve their record. Unfortunately, this characterisation is overly simplistic. It represents only one of several possible evolutionary paths, and it is based on several, rather restrictive assumptions. Consider the notion of "environmental performance". Even a cursory examination of the literature on environmental performance shows that there is no consensus on how best to conceptualise environmental performance (National Academy of Engineering, 1999). In the case of Scorecard, environmental performance is reflected in a multi-dimensional pollution record. A neighbourhood is often a receptacle of several hazardous substances, not just one. How a multiplicity of environmental records can be aggregated into a single indicator of environmental performance remains a hot subject of debate. As a result, comparing the environmental performance of industrial plants remains a very difficult exercise. A second, related, question concerns the threats to human health. Reliable toxicity measures are available only for a very limited number of hazardous substances. Moreover, toxicity can be measured in more than one way. Perhaps more importantly, even when the toxic releases from a plant may reasonably be considered a potential risk to public health, it is unclear whether the surrounding population is actually exposed to this risk. In sum, there are good reasons to believe that an industrial facility and its constituency will not agree on what exactly constitutes good environmental performance, let alone how the plant compares to other facilities across the country.

Of all the examples discussed in this chapter, Scorecard offers the clearest illustration of the proposition that an institutional arrangement based solely on information gathering and information provision may not solve the problems of collective action it was designed to address. In the absence of a common under-standing on what constitute good or bad environmental performance, and on how to measure health risks posed by toxic releases, industrial plants across the nation may be confronted with a cacophony of contradictory demands that will stifle any attempt at improving environmental performance.

The most tangible evidence of the ambiguous and contentious nature of the information provided by Scorecard has recently been provided by the American Chemistry Council (ACC), formerly Chemical Manufacturers Association. ACC has criticised the EDF initiative for not providing adequate contextual information, and for relying on a universal toxicity metric (Sissel, 1998a, 1998b). In ACC's view, such a universal metric is unable to take the unique nature of many chemical plants into account, thus distorting the true environmental record of these plants. This view resonates with some ACC members as firms are implementing more precise measures of environmental performance and comparing their performance to direct competitors, and not to the entire industry. Both ACC and representatives of leading chemical companies have pointed out that a universal metric ignores relevant, plant-specific factors, and does not address the issue of commensurability, i.e. which industrial facilities can in fact be meaningfully be compared in terms of their environmental performance.

Lack of attention for context-specific factors could indeed lead to the emergence of a distorted reputation mechanism. Aware of this possibility, ACC has begun implementing a web-based information system that complements Scorecard with additional, plant-specific information (Sissel, 1998a). Whether the ACC information system will actually help citizens make more informed decisions or whether it will contribute to increasing confusion remains to be seen. Interestingly, since the establishment of the TRI in 1986, reported toxic releases have dramatically decreased. While some scholars have pointed to this fact as evidence for the effectiveness of this programme, it is unclear to what extent these remarkable improvements can be attributed to TRI.

Independently of whether Scorecard has succeeded in improving environmental performance, one could argue that it has been at least partially successful in restoring "fractured polities" or at creating new "constituencies" at the local level. In other words, making TRI data available to local communities across America seems to be at least a partially effective way of triggering a dialogue between local communities and industrial facilities (see Rich, Conn and Owens, 1993, for an analysis of the impact of TRI on local communities). In the terminology used in this chapter, one can say that TRI has contributed to establishing critical cross-cutting ties between business interests and their disconnected constituencies. Perhaps more important, it appears that Scorecard has succeeded at initiating a dialogue between a major national environmental group and a leading trade association. Whether this dialogue will evolve into a common understanding of how environmental performance can and should be measured remains to be seen. The fact that ambiguity of and conflict over the interpretation of environmental performance records so far has not degenerated into thinly disguised attempts at discrediting each other's credibility is reason for optimism.

In sum, Scorecard may be regarded as one example of an institutional arrangement that seems on its way to finding a productive response to the uncertainties and conflicts created by the (misguided) assumptions informing its very adoption. That a key aspect of this response is the establishment of cross-cutting ties among industry representatives, local communities, environmental groups, and government officials should come as no surprise.

CONCLUSION

The preceding discussion has shown that international private governance is both empirically relevant and theoretically challenging: empirically relevant because the cases of private governance are too numerous to be dismissed as a marginal phenomenon; theoretically challenging because they suggest the possibility that constellations of private actors can under certain conditions provide a variety of public goods and sustain rules, norms and standards without or with minimal intervention by nation-states. The chapter also suggests that traditional notions of community and polity are becoming increasingly anachronistic and inaccurate. A community may extend well beyond private households and small groups to include an eclectic mix of representatives of public interest organisations, of business firms and of private citizens. The public character of these communities and the political nature of their interactions justify characterising them as new forms of polity, often not bound to specific territories, focused on a relatively narrow set of issues, and integrated as much through cross-cutting ties as by means of new information technologies.

It is no exaggeration to say that many of the cases discussed in this chapter could be characterised as "colonisation of the system by the life world," or of "reverse colonisation". Reverse colonisation is challenging to traditional notions of civil society. In part, this is due to inadequate but deeply entrenched metaphorical views of markets and economic activities. A relational account of private governance allows for the possibility that civil society can indeed emerge at the intersection of markets, government bureaucracies and NGOs. Not surprisingly, this view has been put forward by scholars who have been studying business–NGO collaborations at the national and international level (Bendell, 1998; Murphy and Bendell, 1997).

The chapter also suggests that these institutional arrangements may not always be effective. Newly created rules and standards may not necessarily progress towards becoming well-understood, binding requirements among various constituencies. Stagnation and lack of credibility can indeed become constitutive attributes of some private systems of governance. One key element that seems to account for stagnation or failure is the lack of cross-cutting ties between private interests and their constituencies. However, more empirical research is needed to assess the relevance of cross-cutting ties on the ability of private governance to produce both effective and legitimate outcomes.

Assessing the effectiveness of these new forms of governance is a difficult task. There is no doubt that many of these arrangements would be considered failures if compared to well-established national regulatory systems. On the other hand, nations and national legal systems are the outcome of centuries of social and cultural evolution, while the arrangements discussed in this chapter have been in existence for a few years only. The fact that many of these arrangements have emerged in response to the failures of nation-states to establish binding international norms seems to suggest that nations may not be intrinsically better positioned to respond to the challenges of international governance.

The chapter shows that information technologies are likely to play an increasingly important role in restoring fractured polities and in increasing legitimacy. It is no coincidence that many arrangements characterised by constructive dialogue between private interests and their constituencies were preceded by protest actions, boycotts, mass protests, often enabled by new information technologies. Somewhat paradoxically, information technologies, unlike more traditional news media, may prove very effective in helping establishing institutionalised networks of personal and professional ties among the members of different constituencies.

Not discussed in this chapter but critical to the credibility of these arrangements is the possibility that similar arrangements of private governance may compete with one another for influence and prestige. The devastating consequences of such competitive practices have been documented in at least one case (Furger, 1997). In this area, national regulators could play an important role by providing legitimacy to private arrangements deemed credible and trustworthy and by discrediting arrangements not meeting basic expectations.

Finally, it should be pointed out that competition among different self-regulatory arrangements is not unwelcome. It provides an important check against the accumulation of power by private organisations and unelected officials. In this sense, nation-states should actually welcome some degree of competition. In addition, competition may help determine which forms of international private governance may be considered effective and legitimate. Just as federally organised nations have benefited from the wealth of political experimentation at the state and regional level, we should welcome the multiplicity of private initiatives as a badly needed source of social experimentation and innovation in the international political arena.

REFERENCES

Baumol, William J. and Oates, Wallace E. (1988), *The Theory of Environmental Policy* (2nd edn., Cambridge: Cambridge University Press).
Bendell, Jem (1998), "Citizens Cane? Relations between Business and Civil Society", Paper presented at ISTR 3rd International Conference, Geneva, 8–11 July.
Ben-Porath, Yoram (1980), "The F-Connection: Families, Friends and Firms and the Organization of Exchange", *Population and Development Review* 6; 1–30.
Bloomberg News (1999), "eBay Moves to Protect Online Auction Users from Fraud", *New York Times*, 16 January.
Braithwaite, John (1989), *Crime, Shame and Reintegration* (Melbourne: Oxford University Press).
—— (1993), "Shame and Modernity", *British Journal of Criminology* 33 (1); 1–18.
Burt, Ronald S. (1998)j, "Private Games are too Dangerous", (mimeo, Chicago, Ill.: University of Chicago).
—— (1999), "Trust and Gossip on the Path to Equilibrium", (mimeo, Chicago, Ill.: University of Chicago).
Carlin, Jerome E. (1966), *Lawyers' Ethics. A Survey of the New York City Bar* (New York: Sage).
Cheit, Ross E. (1990), *Setting Safety Standards. Regulation in the Public and Private Sectors* (Berkeley, Cal.: University of California Press).
Coase, Ronald H. (1960), "The Problem of Social Cost", *Journal of Law and Economics* 3; 1–44.
Collins, Harry M. (1992), *Changing Order: Replication and Induction in Scientific Practice* (Chicago, Ill.: University of Chicago Press).
Cooper, Michael (1999), "Beanie Baby Scams and Identity Thefts", *The New York Times*, 22 September.
Cooter, Robert D. (1996), "Decentralized Law for a Complex Economy: The Structural Approach to Adjudicating the New Law Merchant", *University of Pennsylvania Law Review* 144; 1643–96.
Court, Randolph H., and Atkinson, Robert D. (1999), "On-Line Privacy Standards: The Case for a Limited Federal Role In a Self-Regulatory Regime (Washington, DC: Progressive Policy Institute).

Cutler, A. Claire, Haufler, Virginia and Porter, Tony (eds.) (1999), *Private Authority and International Affairs* (New York: State University of New York Press).

Dawkins, Kristin (1994), *NAFTA, GATT & the World Trade Organization: The Emerging New World Order* (Westfield, NJ: Openn Media).

Durkheim, Emile (1992 (1957)), *Professional Ethics and Civic Moral* (London: Routledge).

Ellison, Glenn (1994), "Cooperation in the Prisoner's Dilemma with Anonymous Random Matching", *Review of Economic Studies* 61; 567–88.

Freidson, Eliot (1970), *Profession of Medicine: A Study of the Sociology of Applied Knowledge* (New York: Harper & Row).

Freudenthal, Gideon (1986), *Atom and Individual in the Age of Newton: On the Genesis of the Mechanistic World View* (Dordrecht: Kluwer Academic Publishers).

Fudenberg, Drew, and Maskin, Eric (1986), "The Folk Theorem in Repeated Games with Discounting or with Incomplete Information", *Econometrica* 54; 533–54.

—— and Tirole, Jean (1995), *Game Theory* (Cambridge, Mass.: MIT Press).

Furger, Franco (1997), "Accountability and Self-Governance Systems: The Case of the Maritime Industry", *Law & Policy* 19; 445–76.

—— (1999), "Institutional Stability and Institutional Change: Empirical Evidence and Theoretical Implications", paper presented at the 1999 Academy of Management Meeting, Chicago, 6–12 August.

Ganzi, John, and DeVries, Anne (1998), *Corporate Environmental Performance as a Factor in Financial Industry Decisions: Status Report* (Washington, DC: Office of Cooperative Environmental Management, US EPA).

Giddens, Anthony (1984), *The Constitution of Society Outline of the Theory of Structuration* (Cambridge: Polity Press).

Golodner, Linda F. (1997), "Apparel Industry Code of Conduct: A Consumer Perspective on Social Responsibility", paper presented at the Notre Dame Center for Ethics and Religious Values in Business.

Granovetter, Mark S. (1973), "The Strength of Weak Ties", *American Journal of Sociology* 78; 1360–80.

—— (1985), "Economic Action and Social Structure: The Problem of Embeddedness", *American Journal of Sociology* 91; 481–511.

—— (1992), "Economic Institutions as Social Constructions: A Framework for Analysis", *Acta Sociologica* 35; 3–11.

—— and Swedberg, Richard (1992), *The Sociology of Economic Life* (Boulder, Colo.: Westview Press).

Greider, William (1997), *One World, Ready or Not. The Manic Logic of Global Capitalism* (New York: Simon & Schuster).

Greif, Avner (1989), "Reputation and Coalitions in Medieval Trade: Evidence on the Maghribi Traders", *Journal of Economic History* 49; 857–82.

—— (1993), "Contract Enforceability and Economic Institutions in Early Trade: the Maghribi Traders' Coalition", *American Economic Review* 83; 525–48.

—— Milgrom, Paul R., and Weingast, Barry R. (1994), "Coordination, Commitment, and Enforcement: The Case of the Merchant Guild", *Journal of Economic History* 102; 745–76.

Hardin, Russell (1968), "The Tragedy of the Commons", *Science* 162; 1243–8.

Hechter, Michael (1987), *Principles of Group Solidarity* (Berkeley, Cal.: University of California Press).

Kamecke, Ulrich (1989), "Non-cooperative Matching Games", *International Journal of Game Theory* 18; 423–31.

Kandori, Michihiro (1992), "Social Norms and Community Enforcement", *Review of Economic Studies* 59; 63–80.

Keck, Margaret, and Sikkink, Kathryn (1998), *Activists Beyond Borders: Advocacy Networks in International Politics* (Ithaca, NY: Cornell University Press).

Kleindorfer, Paul R., and Orts, Eric W. (1998), "Informational Regulation of Environmental Risks", *Risk Analysis* 18; 155ff.

Kreps, David M. (1990), *A Course in Microeconomic Theory* (Princeton, NJ: Princeton University Press).

—— *et al.* (1982), "Rational Cooperation in the Finitely Repeated Prisoners' Dilemma", *Journal of Economic Theory* 27; 245–52.

—— and Wilson, Robert (1982), "Reputation and Imperfect Information", *Journal of Economic Theory* 27; 253–79.

Krislov, Samuel (1997), *How Nations Choose Product Standards and Standards Change Nations* (Pittsburgh, PA: University of Pittsburgh Press).

Krugman, Paul (1997), "In Praise of Cheap Labor. Bad Jobs at Bad Wages are Better than No Jobs at All", *Slate Magazine*, 20 March. Available at http://Slate.msn.com/Dismal/97–03–20/Dismal.asp

Krut, Riva, and Gleckman, Harris (1998), *ISO 14001: A Missed Opportunity for Sustainable Global Industrial Development* (London: Earthscan Publications).

Lakoff, George, and Johnson, Mark (1983), *Metaphors We Live By* (Chicago, Ill.: University of Chicago Press).

Leibovich, Mark (1999), "eBay, 'Cyburbia's' New Subdivision, Stokes Boom", *The Washington Post*, 31 January.

Mailath, George J., and Samuelson, Larry (1998), "Your Reputation is Who You're Not, Not Who You'd Like to Be", CARESS Working Paper 98–11.

Mathews, Jessica T. (1997), "Power Shift", *Foreign Affairs* 76; 50–66.

Micklethwait, John, and Wooldridge, Adrian (2000), *A Future Perfect: the Essentials of Globalization* (New York, NY: Crown Business).

National Academy of Engineering, Committee on Industrial Environmental Performance Metrics (1999), *Industrial Environmental Performance Metrics* (Washington, DC: National Academy Press).

Milgrom, Paul R., North, Douglass C. and Weingast, Barry R. (1990), "The Role of Institutions in the Revival of Trade: The Law Merchant, Private Judges, and the Champagne Fairs", *Economics and Politics* 2; 1–23.

Murphy, David F., and Bendell, Jem (1997), *In the Company of Partners: Business, Environmental Groups and Sustainable Development Post-Rio* (Bristol: The Policy Press).

Nash, Jennifer, and Ehrenfeld, John (1997), "Codes of Environmental Management Practice: Assessing their Potential as a Tool for Change", *Annual Review of Energy & Environment*.

Okuno-Fujiwara, Masahiro, and Postlewaite, Andrew (1995), "Social Norms and Random Matching Games", *Games and Economic Behavior* 9; 79–109.

—— —— and Suzumura, Kotaro (1990), "Strategic Information Revelation", *Review of Economic Studies* 57; 25–47.

Olson, Mancur (1965), *The Logic of Collective Action. Public Goods and the Theory of Groups* (Cambridge, Mass.: Harvard University Press).

Ostrom, Elinor (1990), *Governing the Commons. The Evolution of Institutions for Collective Action* (Cambridge: Cambridge University Press).

Raub, Werner, and Weesie, Jeroen (1990), "Reputation and Efficiency in Social Interactions: An Example of Network Effects", *American Journal of Sociology* 96; 626–54.

Rees, Joseph V. (1997), "Development of Communitarian Regulation in the Chemical Industry", *Law & Policy* 19; 477–528.

Rich, Richard C., Conn, David W., and Owens, William L. (1993), " 'Indirect Regulation' of Environmental Hazards Through the Provision of Information to the Public: The Case of SARA, Title III".

Rodrik, Dani (1997), *Has Globalization Gone Too Far?* (Washington, DC: Institute for International Economics).

Scott, John (1991), *Social Network Analysis: A Handbook* (London: Sage Publications).

Scott, W. Richard (1987), *Organizations : Rational, Natural, and Open Systems* (Englewood Cliffs, NJ: Prentice-Hall).

Sissell, Kara (1998a), "Industry Outreach Enters the Information Age", *Chemical Week* 160; 51–2.

—— (1998b), "CMA Web Site Puts own Spin on Plant Data", *Chemical Week* 160; 2.

Swedberg, Richard (1997), "New Economic Sociology: What Has Been Accomplished, What is Ahead", *Acta Sociologica* 40; 161–82.

Sykes, Alan O. (1995), *Product Standards for Internationally Integrated Goods Markets* (Washington, DC: Brookings Institution).

Teubner, Gunther (1997)," 'Global Bukowina': Legal Pluralismin the World Society", in G. Teubner (ed.), *Global Law without a State* (Aldershot: Dartmouth).

Uzzi, Brian (1996), "Embeddedness and Economic Performance: The Network Effect", *American Sociological Review* 61; 674–98.

—— (1997), "Social Structure and Competition in Interfirm Networks: the Paradox of Embeddedness", *Administrative Science Quarterly* 42; 35–67.

Wasserman, Stanley (1994), *Social Network Analysis: Methods and Applications* (Cambridge: Cambridge University Press).

Wilson, Robert (1985), "Reputations in Games and Markets", in R. Alwin (ed.), *Game-Theoretic Models of Bargaining* (Cambridge University Press: Cambridge).

World Bank (1999), *Greening Industry: New Roles for Communities, Markets, and Governments* (Oxford: Oxford University Press).

Yilmaz, Yesim (1998), "Private Regulation. A Real Alternative for Regulatory Reform", (Washington, DC: Cato Policy Analysis, No. 303).

PART FOUR

The Role of the Legal Profession:
Mega-Lawyers and In-house Counsel

8

Capital Markets: Those Who Can and Cannot Do the Purest Global Law Markets

JOHN FLOOD

Abstract

This paper analyses the probability that multidisciplinary partnerships (MDPs) between law and other types of firms may become major players in the market for worldwide capital growth and development. It argues that a key ingredient for reducing risk and complexity in capital markets work is trust developed among a small number of firms—law firm and investment banks—with extraordinary expertise, experience and enduring relationships. Even if MDPs such as the Big Five accounting firms were to develop these factors at a competitive level, it is unlikely that they will disturb the status quo because of their limited liability, unstable alliances, conflict of interest difficulties, non-uniform standards and organizational characteristics different from those of large law firms.

PROLOGUE

T OWARDS THE END OF the twentieth century three significant events took place in the global legal market that were presaging the globalisation of law. The American Bar Association's commission on multidisciplinary partnerships (MDPs) and fee-sharing between lawyers and non-lawyers recommended that MDPs should be allowed (*The Lawyer*, 1999a: 4; *The Law Society's Gazette*, 1999, 8; Kemeny, 1999a: 11).[1] The Law Society of England and Wales recommended that MDPs should be permitted (Hickman, 1999: 2)[2]

---

[1] At the ABA Annual Meeting in New York in 2000 the House of Delegates, by a 75% to 25% vote, decided to oppose the introduction of MDPs (Williams, 2000: 18).

[2] The Law Society has agreed to speed up its MDP procedures, called Legal Practice Plus. They do not represent fully joined-up MDPs, since they keep the central authority of the firm with the lawyers. *The Lawyer* (2000a) commented: Nick Holt, managing partner at KLegal, welcomes the move. "But it's only part of the proposals, and we want to reach the point of linked partnerships", he says. "I see this as being more relevant to the high-street firm than to the more corporate-orientated practice". One source says the new proposals are akin to the Law Society saying: "We don't mind MDPs so long as we can continue to boss you around".

and, although the Department of Trade and Industry (DTI) thought they should start in 2000, the Law Society expects it will take time before they appear (*The Lawyer*, 1998a: 1). The third event was slightly different: Clifford Chance, the UK's largest law firm, and Rogers & Wells, a well-known New York law firm, decided to merge in the first transatlantic big law firm merger (Barrett, 1999: 3).[3] Two contrary events, but of lesser significance, also occurred. The DTI duplicated the Securities and Exchange Commission's (SEC) ruling that audit firms (i.e., the Big Five), cannot follow Goldman Sachs, the investment bank, and list themselves on the stock market: auditor independence is paramount and could be undermined (*Accountancy Age*, 1999a: 1).[4] Secondly, the Conseil Nationale des Barreux voted to prohibit lawyers from working with, and thus sharing fees with, business consultants, that is, the French bar rejected MDPs (Callister, 1999: 1).[5] Multidisciplinary practice was, therefore, soon to enter the global market for professional services, especially legal services. The magnitude of these changes in the landscape of global lawyering will be of the same order as the transformation of the English landed estates under the hands of Capability Brown.[6]

We are certainly aware that globalisation, as a concept, is coming of age (cf. Held *et al.*, 1999). For example, the 1999 BBC Reith lectures were given by the director of the London School of Economics, and "Third Way guru" to the British prime minister, Anthony Giddens. His lectures, entitled *Runaway World*, attempted to demonstrate how institutions that we have come to take for granted on a local basis—for example, family, education, welfare, culture—are being radically reconstructed in ways that are not always within the clasp of domestic governments or nations. By way of illustration, we could conceive of charitable tax concessions to Canadian ballet companies that could

[3] This has now become a three-way merger with the addition of a German law firm, Pünder Volhard Weber & Axster, but it failed to become a four-way merger with the Australian firm Mallesons Stephen Jaques (Townsend, 1999: 1). Since the announcement of the Clifford Chance–Rogers & Wells merger, there has been a further transatlantic merger, that of Salans Hertzfeld Heilbronn HRK and Christy & Viener (Hoult and Zaki, 1999: 1). In June 2000 there was another full-blown merger between Titmuss Sainer Dechert, London, and Dechert Price & Rhoads, Philadelphia. Before this the two firms had been loosely allied (Tagliabue, 2000: 9). There was an abortive merger attempt between Warner Cranston and Sonnenschein, but Sonnenschein decided to close its London office completely (Farrell, 1999b: 10).

[4] The Big Five have been reprimanded for flouting share ownership regulations. PwC has been admonished by AICPA, the US accounting main professional body, for holding shares in public companies audited by the firm (Michaels, 2000).

[5] The Law Society of Upper Canada has lifted objections to MDPs (*The Lawyer*, 1998b). Victoria, Australia is set to do the same (*The Lawyer*, 1998c), and the New Zealand bar will probably follow suit (NZ Law Society, 1999). The Isle of Man Law Society has voted to relax its rules forbidding MDPs (Blass, 1997). Several European countries explicitly permit MDPs, that is, Germany, Finland, the Netherlands (in part: notaries, patent agents and tax advisors), some cantons in Switzerland (CCBE, 1996). The Netherlands has, however, has determined it will not allow full-scale MDPs, thus precipitating an appeal to the European Court (Laferla, 1999: 22; *Accountancy Age*, 1999b: 3; Swallow, 1999: 2).

[6] Lancelot "Capability" Brown (1716–1783) was a radical landscape gardener who redesigned about 200 large country gardens in England, converting them from the formal French Versailles form to a naturalistic, informal park style.

be equivalent to subsidies under North American Free Trade Area (NAFTA) rules and therefore illegitimate: at some stage it will be impossible *not* to consume genetically modified foods because price differentials between genetically modified food and non-GM products will prevent producers from continuing to use the latter, despite World Trade Organisation rules.

Leaving aside objections to globalisation by such sceptics as Hirst and Thompson (1996), global politics and economy are being driven ineluctably towards a new domain not circumscribed by the usual array of constraints.[7] A combination of governments, especially the USA, the Group of Seven, multinational enterprises, and international governmental organisations (IGOs), sometimes collectively known as the "Washington consensus", are redrawing the global map.[8] Although hyperglobalisers, such as Kenichi Ohmae (1991, 1995), would argue that we are entering the borderless world, it is worth observing, however, that major trade and investment flows are not truly global. The vast bulk of foreign direct investment stock moves between North America, the European Union and Japan (UNCTAD, 1995; Held *et al.*, 1999: 242–55).[9]

What we perceive as globalisation may be interpreted as particular world regions interacting financially in defiance of diurnal rhythms to enhance global capital, which may eventually lead to greater globalisation. Nevertheless, for globalisation to function as a "system" it needs the intermediation and support of institutions to transform the apparent to the real (see Shapiro, 1993). Many of these will be professional service firms similar to accounting firms (for example, PricewaterhouseCoopers), consulting firms (for example, McKinsey), investment banks (Goldman Sachs), and law firms (for example, Clifford Chance), but their interaction can be problematic. Professionals from different groups have diverse cultures and ideologies. In the UK, law and accounting have struggled over status differences for close to two centuries (Abbott, 1988). Yet both are undergoing profound changes that render old ideologies potentially obsolete. Capital growth and development ideally require interaction that is unfettered by hidebound tradition, which is how international capital markets are trying to grow. But each profession has been fighting rearguard actions to prevent others making incursions on its own turf. The use of unauthorised practice rules by state bars in the USA against the Big Five accounting firms is a classic example of turf wars.

Thus at a public level there is a veneer of co-operation while beneath opposition is strong. Unless this suggests that, absent restrictions, the professional world would be a ferment of competitive struggle, one should be aware that certain kinds of work tend to be restricted to small, elite groups, partly as a result

---

[7] I am not particularly concerned with the cultural aspects of globalisation here. See, e.g., Robertson (1992), Flood (1995).

[8] The war against Serbia is a case in point where NATO has attempted to redefine the international law of war, that such wars can be instigated without the sanction of the UN Security Council. See also the role of nongovernmental organisations (Hobe, 1997).

[9] In 1993 World inward FDI stock was greater than $2,000 billion (UNCTAD, 1995).

of tradition and also because of the steep learning curve inherent in the nature of the work. The barriers to entry are usually high. Two types of work, for example, that are buffered this way are international insolvency (see Flood and Skordaki, 1997); and capital markets work. Illustrations given below will highlight the "bespoke approach" of capital markets work: but it merits mentioning the view of the head of investment banking at Goldman Sachs when he says, "[t]he nature of [big mergers and acquisitions] means that there is no template to refer to. It is often the first time, leading to a premium on expertise and experience."[10]

A cardinal point of global commerce is capital markets work. And, naturally, it possesses its own legal practice. Hodgart claims (1999: 6), "[n]o legal service is more globally driven than finance and, within this, capital markets work is the 'purest' global service". Indeed, one could argue that capital markets work is constituting a *jus communis*. To provide some idea of the scale of the work, in 1998 the six largest mergers and acquisitions amounted to over $300 billion and were funded by a combination of equity and debt issues (Hodgart, 1999: 6). Two legal products dominate this field: New York state law and UK law (Flood, 1996).[11] Dignan (1999a) points out that "[i]n a banking transaction, such as the Olivetti and Telecom Italia deal, the senior debt will often come under English law, while the high-yield will go through US law, but the sourcing may come the Continent. Therefore, only those firms with UK, US and European capability will be attractive to clients". The service is global but the products are local.[12] Any major privatisation, for example, will have to include the issue of shares on the New York and London stock exchanges, therefore all documentation will be reviewed and cleared with their respective regulators (see Neate, 1987: 56–94). The fascinating aspect of this is the interaction of the structural developments of professional service firms, their desire for global reach, and the structure of capital markets work, that is, the nexus of organisation and work (Flood, 1996, 1999a).

This story is composed of three parts. I will first discuss the structure of and actors in the capital markets business, attempting to explain what is special about this type of work. Because the number of actors is small and their social density high, I will argue that a key concept for decreasing risk and reducing

[10] The uniqueness of big M&A deals is growing as they get bigger and bigger. In 1999 MCI WorldCom moved to acquire Sprint Corp for $127bn (Rivlin and Silverman, 2000: 9), and in 2000 Vodafone arranged a merger with Mannesmann to create the world's biggest telecom company worth £225bn (Gow, 2000: 32).

[11] This is the reason why in my introductory paragraph the "big events" I refer to are North American and British. Other legal systems are not in the same league as the big two. Some disagree with the notion that New York state law is the dominant American legal force; instead they claim that Delaware law or SEC law is the paradigmatic feature of capital markets work. I am grateful to Rob Rosen for suggesting these alternatives.

[12] Cf. the view of the City of London Law Society in 1989, "[t]he advantages of English law as a 'product' enable solicitors to contribute to this country's balance of payments some £250,000,000 per annum in invisible exports and constitute an important part of the attraction of the City of London as a world financial and insurance centre" (1989: 5).

complexity is high-density trust which encourages compliance among agents (Luhmann, 1979; Bachmann, 1999). If the market is opened up, either the scope of regulation may have to be increased at significant cost for compliance and/or the relationships in the business may become increasingly formalised. Central to the correct functioning of the market is the ability of a small number of law firms and investment banks to provide high levels of expert knowledge within tight time constraints. The law firms require access to the best law graduates (Flood, 1999b) and generally have strong, enduring relationships with large investment banks even though the work is transactional. Secondly, I will examine the nature of MDPs, especially the evolving relationship between lawyers and accountants—the most obvious tie-up in the corporate world. These appear to be the archetypes of a new global professional service firm that ought to be capable of delivering any combination of services anywhere. Thirdly, I attempt to show how MDPs, although apparently repositories of considerable expertise, will not be the most successful vehicle for elite global work such as capital markets. This is not to say that MDPs, or variants of them, will not be able to evolve to take on this work; their relationships with investment banks might evolve a similar concentration to those of elite law firms.

PART I: CAPITAL MARKETS BUSINESS

Corporate finance is crucial to global practice for large law firms. For example, within the City of London the Big Five, or Magic Circle, law firms dominate this field—their market penetration of major corporate and financial institutions is between 25 and 33 per cent, and they have a disproportionate share of FTSE 100 clients (Marks and Griffiths, 1997: 26).[13] In the USA a similarly small number of New York law firms, the Wall Street firms (Barnard, 2000: 1), are consistent repeat players in capital markets work, all of which have a large stock of Fortune 500 companies as regular clients (International Centre for Commercial Law, 1999a, 1999b; see also Silver, 2000).[14] This concentration of expertise is also found in the investment banks, the other side of the equation here, where seven banks tend to dominate this work and all are US based. Hodgart (1999: 6) notes, "three investment banks dominated the global adviser market in 1998, handling $2.23 billion of deals, with the next three banks handling $1.18 billion. Within the US the three leading firms (the same as worldwide) handled $1.2 billion compared with the next three banks with $690 million".

---

[13] The Big Five law firms are Allen & Overy, Clifford Chance, Freshfields, Linklaters, and Slaughter and May (Marks and Griffiths, 1997: 26).

[14] The key US law firms, in no particular order, seem to be Brown & Wood, Simpson Thacher & Bartlett, Weil Gotshal & Manges, Davis Polk & Wardwell, Sullivan & Cromwell, Shearman & Sterling, Cleary Gottlieb Steen & Hamilton, Cravath Swaine & Moore, White & Case, Baker & McKenzie, Fried Frank Harris Shriver & Jacobson, Milbank Tweed Hadley & McCloy, Coudert Brothers, Wachtell Lipton Rosesn & Katz, and Skadden Arps Slate Meagher & Flom.

By 1999 the big three investment banks, Goldman Sachs, Morgan Stanley Dean Witter, and Merrill Lynch, had "each advised on more than $1 trillion in world-wide mergers and acquisitions" (Deogun, 2000: 13). The value of the deals also indicates the rewards to the investment banks and others who participate in capital markets work. At the end of 1999 dozens of managing directors (formerly partners) of Goldman Sachs received $10 million or more in salary (Garfield, 1999: 13). What is clear about this sector is that the critically decisive players are few in number and their networks are densely structured, encouraging repeat-player patterns of activity.[15] Ferguson (1997: 33) spells out the connections:

> A small band of major banks call the shots on the big-ticket equities issues. These are the people to impress for law firms looking to develop market share on these deals. Unfortunately for the pretenders, the banks sit comfortably alongside a similarly small band of law firms. On Wall Street, relationships extend beyond even the eldest partners, and banks and firms share a lineage steeped in the history of New York's development as a financial centre. Some of these old-school ties are part of Wall Street folk law [sic]: Goldman Sachs and Sullivan & Cromwell, Morgan Stanley and Davis Polk & Wardwell.

For example, the relationship between Morgan Stanley and Davis Polk goes back 110 years (Forster, 1997: 37). If we take some of the key investment banks and match them with a sample of their legal advisers the patterns become evident. Table 8.1 illustrates this.[16]

Capital markets work embraces a number of types of activity: for example, privatisations, initial public offerings (IPOs), securitisations, asset and derivative backed issues, and depositary receipt programmes. As I mentioned earlier, New York and English law predominate in these markets. For example, in the Olivetti and Telecom Italia merger, the senior debt came under English law while the high-yield debt went through US law (*The Lawyer*, 1999e). But their competitive edges never remain sharp for long. The complexity of the British Gas issue has been attenuated with the SEC's introduction of Rule 144A,[17] which allows foreign issuers access to American institutions in the USA without

---

[15] I have found only two references to collaboration between investment banks and/or law firms and accounting firms. Linklaters & Alliance were advisers with KPMG to the Mozal SARL (Mozambique) project worth $1.34 billion for a power plant and aluminium facility (IFLR, 1999: 22). Merrill Lynch was part of a consortium with Coopers & Lybrand advised by Skadden Arps for the restructuring and privatisation of the Telephone Organisation of Thailand (Skadden Arps, 1999: 2). Kemeny (1999b: 8) argues, however, that the Big Five are poised to take "a bigger slice of corporate finance deals" whereas "[o]nly a few years ago, it would have been inconceivable for an accountancy firm to be advising on deals of between £20m and £200m. Last year, KPMG advised on 423 deals, while PwC advised on 415, although PwC's deals were worth more in volume."

[16] These samples were derived from LawMoney.com. Within a given year, it is fair to see a preponderance of US law firms involved as legal advisers to the major player investment banks.

[17] The SEC is further revising its rules on cross-border M&As to encourage non-US companies not to exclude US investors because of the difficulty in complying with the former registration requirements (Brown, Bird and Kiernan, 1999).

Table 8.1 Major Investment Banks and Legal Advisers

INVESTMENT BANK	LAW FIRM
Merrill Lynch	Brown & Wood (*New York*) Cravath Swaine & Moore (*New York*) Davis Polk & Wardwell (*New York*) Freshfields (*London*) Skadden Arps (*New York*)
Crédit Suisse First Boston	Allen & Overy (*London*) Clifford Chance (*London*) Cravath Swaine & Moore (*New York*) Davis Polk & Wardwell (*New York*) Shearman & Sterling (*New York*) Simpson Thacher & Bartlett (*New York*) Skadden Arps (*New York*) Weil Gotshal & Manges (*New York*)
Goldman Sachs	Allen & Overy (*London*) Cleary Gottlieb (*New York*) Cravath Swaine & Moore (*New York*) Davis Polk & Wardwell (*New York*) Freshfields (*London*) Sullivan & Cromwell (*New York*)
Morgan Stanley	Brown & Wood (*New York*) Davis Polk & Wardwell (*New York*) Freshfields (*London*) Shearman & Sterling (*New York*) Weil Gotshal & Manges (*New York*)

the burdens of SEC registration (Forster, 1996: 17).[18] This has enabled English law firms to enter the US private placement market, although registered offerings still remain in the US law firms' bailiwick. The growth of the global depositary receipt (GDR) market also shows how competition is spurred. A commentator said:

> In the early days of the GDR equity market, the US firms got hired because they could do the disclosure and depositary agreement under New York law and the UK firms seemed to sense a competitive disadvantage. There were a lot of deals where English firms would write the prospectus with the underwriter. . . . But English lawyers and

[18] Rule 144A entails considerably less due diligence than a registration and incurs less costs. Registration meant many Asian businesses, for example, were averse to coming to the American market (Forster, 1997: 36). SEC Regulation S is the corollary of Rule 144A allowing American investors to buy non-registered stock offshore (Forster, 1996). In the days of the British Gas privatisation, the SEC required the issuers to block any advertising of the stock appearing in the American press (Neate, 1987). With the Internet, this would now be impossible.

Linklaters & Paines in particular wanted to develop the GDR market and to establish a way putting a second certificate in Europe. . . . Linklaters has been developing this market so issuers do not have to use US lawyers. Often even when the US side is small its requirements tend to predominate and a lot of this is trying to say that US investors can invest in Europe . . . It was one way to keep out the US lawyers . . . [Forster, 1996: 22].[19]

That New York law firms have the competitive advantage over UK law firms is put down to them being "exporters of legal technology adapted for local markets by those firms that have the touch which entices a particular client to work with them" (Forster, 1997: 37).[20] A counter arguments says that as the banks become truly global, the US law firms have failed to keep up, which is beginning to loosen traditional ties and open the market for other lawyers.

Two examples of capital markets work will illuminate the role these institutions play. The first is a major international initial public offering (IPO), and the second example involved a large project financing in Russia.

Example 1: Alstom (1998)

In 1998 the largest non-privatisation IPO was a French company, Alstom, amounting to $3.7 billion. Alstom was owned equally by GEC of the UK and Alcatel of France. It had over 400 subsidiaries in over 60 jurisdictions and was registered as a Dutch NV. Among the advisers the global co-ordinators were Goldman Sachs and Crédit Suisse First Boston, and their advisers were Davis Polk & Wardwell and Stibbe Simont Monahan Duhot & Giroux, a "large" French law firm.[21] Acting as counsel to the issuer were Shearman & Sterling and Lovell White Durrant. And, finally, counsel to the selling stockholders were Freshfields and Gide Loyrette Nouel, another "large" French law firm. Before the IPO launched the company's in-house counsel had to take charge of re-organising the company and its various subsidiaries from a Dutch company into a French one. This involved numerous government authorisations, adding to the already complicated and logistically challenging nature of the deal. Preparation for the IPO ran in parallel to the reorganisation and involved French, English, US and international tranches, consisting of a primary offering of shares sold by Alstom and a secondary offering by Alstom's parents. The

---

[19] During 1999, Linklaters advised on deals in excess of $1 trillion. "The firm says its success has been a result of capitalizing on the trend towards globalization and consolidation across a number of industries" (LawMoney.com, 2000).

[20] Another competitive advantage US law firms have over the UK is the level of their hourly billing rates. E.g. the following per partner billing rates from around the world show the differences: Australia, $200–300; Bermuda, $300–450; Hong Kong, $600–700; UK, $375–575; US, $225–450; Vietnam, $75–100 (Lee, 1997: 24). However, some argue that transaction rates are roughly comparable.

[21] In comparison with the large law firms of the USA and the UK, the "large" law firms of mainland Europe are small.

shares were listed in Paris, London and New York and were subject to full regulatory review simultaneously by the SEC in the USA, the London Stock Exchange in the UK, and the COB in France.

The offering involved the issue of American Depositary Receipts, listed in New York, and the first ever UK Depositary Receipts, listed in London. Lovell White Durrant structured the UKDRs and advised Alstom on its employee share offering, which covered some 35 jurisdictions and ran as part of the public offering. Davis Polk & Wardwell led the due diligence, ensuring that the company's diverse material assets and subsidiaries were intact and included in the deal, or at least making sure that fall-back plans were in place if the reorganisation was not completed by the time of the IPO. The firm also advised on the core disclosure document, the adequacy of the disclosure and the underwriting agreement itself.

Just one month before the closing of the IPO, Alstom acquired Cegelec, an electrical contracting and process control business owned by Alcatel which was itself a quarter of the size of the combined issuer. All the work which had been to demonstrate what the group would look like after the reorganisation was redone taking into account the new business. After five months' work the deal was priced to go (IFLR, 1999: 13).[22]

Example 2: Sakhalin II, Russia (1998)

Sakhalin is an island in Arctic Russia with the Piltun-Astokhskoye oil and gas field lying offshore, which may contain as much as the North Sea reserves. This project is Russia's first offshore oil and gas project with an estimated cost of $9 billion. It is also the first project commissioned under Russia's Power Sharing Agreement Law (PSA) of 1996. The legal advisers were Freshfields, for the lenders, and Coudert Brothers, acting as international counsel for the project company. They faced a number of challenges in negotiating the deal, including coping with multiple layers of national and local regulations along with strict environmental laws. As the first offshore project, it had *to develop local laws* as it progressed. A PSA is a direct agreement between the government and investors on a tax regime that the government guarantees to apply to the project for its entire duration. This enables investors to plan costs more accurately and provides security.

A challenge for Sakhalin II was that only 70 per cent of the necessary legislation was in place to support the PSA. Furthermore, the long-term nature of the project means that the project company will have to negotiate contracts to cope with different groups of lenders over time. This may mean lenders submitting documentation to prevent the project company from borrowing in the future.

---

[22] In all, in 1998, Davis Polk & Wardwell advised in five major deals: Alstom (France) $3.7 billion, Swisscom (Switzerland) $6.43 billion, Telefonica (Spain) $2.7 billion, Argentaria (Spain) $2.4 billion, and Salzgitter (Germany) $483 million (IFLR 1999: 7).

Although this was avoided in the first stage of Sakhalin, the project has raised the issue and may use such documentation in its second stage. Finally, the deal was completed in spring amidst a deteriorating Russian economy and falling oil prices. The project company, Sakhalin Energy Investment Company, was sponsored by Mitsui, Marathon, Shell, and Mitsubishi. The lenders were the European Bank for Reconstruction and Development, Overseas Private Investment Corporation (US), and the Export-Import Bank of Japan. The first stage of Sakhalin was funded by sponsor equity of $385 million. A further $348 million in debt is being raised. The project is now in jeopardy because of the Russian financial crisis (IFLR, 1999: 23).

Final Remarks

Capital markets work is risky and subject to the whims of the global economy—Asian economic crises, the "Tequila effect" of the Mexican peso crisis, the Russian economic collapse. It is tightly bounded by deadlines, replete with financial contingency, and extremely demanding of bodies of expert knowledge. Competition between advisers is great. Paul Volcker (1999: 11) noted, "[c]ompetition to 'outperform' is intense". The hostile takeover bid for NatWest bank by the Bank of Scotland demonstrated the need for engaging the most suitable experts (Treanor and Brummer, 1999: 28). NatWest hired Roberto Mendoza, "Wall Street's top defender against hostile bids", to reinforce a defence team that included:

> investment bank Dresdner Kleinwort Benson and McKinsey partner Charles Roxburgh, who was a crucial player in the rescue of the Lloyd's of London insurance market. Mr Roxburgh has the confidence of NatWest chairman Sir David Rowland and his new chief operating officer Ron Sandler, his former right-hand man at Lloyd's of London [Treanor and Brummer, 1999: 28].[23]

The competition Paul Volcker refers to is a combination of factors—the urge for global reach, the desire to make the greatest profits, the need to be the biggest and best—where banks' and law firms' motivations overlap, although they are not truly isomorphic. Law firms are considering the one-stop shop or MDP route (see part II below) and banks wish to be perceived as all-embracing one-stop shops for their clients' ambitions. Not only do we see domestic mergers as the Royal Bank of Scotland acquisition of NatWest, but also increasingly banks look overseas for targets, such as Deutsche Bank's takeover of Bankers Trust

---

[23] McKinsey & Company is a global consulting firm that is usually associated with the hyper-globalisation perspective of globalisation (see Ohmae, 1991: 1995). Ohmae is the senior Tokyo partner for McKinsey. It undertakes considerable research on financial institutions and publishes many books and reports that have caught the popular imagination and helped create the mythological aspects of globalisation, e.g., Rosenthal and Ocampo (1988), Bleeke and Ernst (1992), Casserley (1992), and Bryan with Farrell (1996). This chapter, however, concentrates on the Big Five accounting firms.

(*The Lawyer*, 1999e). Banks want to do both advisory and loan work. Volcker's conception of competition is further intensified when we realise that, as demonstrated above, the big cross-border deals involve the big three of Goldman Sachs, Merrill Lynch and Morgan Stanley. The concentration of market power raises cost of entry for both banks and law firms outside the "magic circle".

One result has been a capacity and willingness to reach out for more exotic, potentially high-yielding investments. The private sectors of emerging economies, with their strong growth potential, have become prime targets. Perhaps the crucial factor here is that the law firms, and the investment banks, are devising the financial and legal maps of the world as they do the work. They are not merely responding to a set of problems that need answers; they are generating the questions and then finding solutions, which at best will always be partial (cf. Tomasic *et al.*, 1996). The institutions, IGOs, investment banks and law firms, through capital markets work, are creating a *global political economy* for the future that will be the engine of their aims for global capital. Because the game is high-risk and, of course, high-yield, there is a reluctance among the players to grant roles to novices and outsiders, which maintains the environment of the game as a hermetically sealed unit, and the rewards of the game are distributed among the few. This serves to suggest that in capital markets work lawyers enjoy a high degree of autonomy that enables them to create and to innovate solutions.[24] It affords them high professional status.

PART II: MULTIDISCIPLINARY PARTNERSHIPS

What happens to the Big Five accounting firms has long mattered to the legal profession but probably never as much as now; the news from the accounting world is news of change, of something happening, of preparations and plans—perhaps of going to war? The Big Five have always characterised themselves as global institutions. Law would be the last component to be added in a strategy of global delivery of professional services.

The Big Five have reorganised. KPMG replaced its traditional regional structure with a nationally run business-sectoral service as part of an ambitious overhaul of its UK practice.[25] Already KPMG has incorporated its audit arm. PricewaterhouseCoopers (PwC) and Ernst & Young have heavily invested in the creation of a Jersey Limited Liability Partnership (LLP) and have already applied for judicial review of the Inland Revenue's ruling that they would be treated as companies if they registered offshore to limit their liability (cf. Sawin, 1999: 20).

---

[24] I am grateful to Martin Shapiro for suggesting this hypothesis.

[25] KLegal, the legal arm of KPMG, is now undergoing a similar restructuring, splitting into 6 groups comprising consumer markets, financial services, infrastructure and government, industrial markets, owner-managed businesses and information, communications and entertainment (*The Lawyer*, 2000a).

The Big Five have set up firms to operate as their legal arms in the UK. Their experiences on the continent convinced, if not pushed, them to offer legal services in the UK. The associated law firm is a method successfully tried and tested, in Paris and other European capitals. Paris has been particularly important to the Big Five in planning their overall strategies for law firms around the world. Accountants' law firms occupy no fewer than six out of the top nine places by size in France and their fee income totals more than £200 million (Cannon, 1997: 28). The recent history of the Big Five shows that Arthur Andersen was the first, with the establishment of Garrett & Co as a two-partner firm in the summer of 1993. Arnheim & Co was set up by PwC in March 1996. Ernst & Young were widely expected to be the third Big Five firm to set up a legal practice, only to be overtaken by Cooper & Lybrand's (now part of PwC) setting up of Tite & Lewis, a firm fronted by two ex-Stephenson Harwood partners. Deloitte & Touche, with an extensive legal network in several European capital cities, has now opened its law arm. KPMG, with law firms dotted around Europe, the largest being Fidal in France, launched KLegal, which will be a *de facto* MDP (Farrell, 1999a: 3), which it accomplished by poaching lawyers from Arnheim, Tite & Lewis (Quick, 1999: 8).[26] It will not be a stand-alone firm, although it "will have a separate entrance to comply with Law Society regulations" (Farrell, 1999a: 3).[27]

The Big Five's law firms have expanded rapidly. Once established, the accounting law firms have grown beyond recognition. Both Garrett & Co and Arnheim & Co started as greenfield ventures. Yet, after two years, Garrett & Co had 30 partners and 50 assistant solicitors in five UK offices (London, Reading, Birmingham, Leeds and Manchester) and had launched a major advertising campaign to recruit London assistants of talent. Garrett & Co made a further leap forward by acquiring Glasgow-based Dorman Jeffrey & Co, a 14-partner practice with substantial expertise in the insolvency field. Outside the UK Andersen's Spanish legal arm merged with Madrid's largest law firm, J&A Garrigues, to form a practice of over 500 lawyers (Darnhill, 1997: 40). The effect of these mergers was to alter the status of accounting firm lawyers from tax advisers to lawyers *per se*: "[a]ccording to one Spanish lawyer: 'It was a matter of perception. They were not seen as lawyers'" (Cannon, 1997: 27). Arthur Andersen has now more than 1,700 commercial lawyers in worldwide network (see Table 8.2). Arnheim & Co was started by a 35-year old corporate finance ex-Hammond Suddards partner, with plans to have 10 lawyers on board by the end of 1996, which it did, and 50 lawyers within four years, which it has exceeded. Unlike the small practices set up by Arthur Andersen and Price

---

[26] KPMG has now formed a "strategic alliance" with a large US law firm, Morrison & Foerster, to provide tax advice. This appears to be the first big alliance—to deal with tax issues—between a Big Five accounting firms and a US law firm. PwC is also searching for a US law firm partner (Dignan, 1999b: 7).

[27] One City lawyer has commented on the move: "It's almost a fallback option to be doing a start-up. They are really starting two or three years behind the game" (Farrell, 1999: 3).

Waterhouse, Coopers & Lybrand, as it then was, chose to "hit the ground running". Their firm, Tite & Lewis, immediately slotted into the lower end of City firms with a fee income projected at around £5 million in the first year. Arnheim & Co, Tite & Lewis merged under PwC, but Tite & Lewis soon moved to Ernst & Young (Kemeny, 2000: 10). The PwC chairman's open invitation to City law firms to join PwC in building a legal arm of 3,000 business lawyers in the major centres of the world has given rise to wild speculations of things to come.[28] The first move in this direction has been to incorporate all PwC's law firms under a single brand, "Landwell", which is innocuous in any language, to make the biggest Big Five legal arm yet (Farrell, 1999c: 2). All of these manœuvres have generated a push to create global law firms attached to the Big Five. And the result of these developments is that the Big Five's law firms are now firmly located in the top 50 worldwide law firms. Table 8.2 shows their rankings and size.

Table 8.2 Ranking and Size of Big Five Accounting Law Firms Compared with Law Firms

NAME	TOTAL NUMBER OF LAWYERS	RANK IN IFLR TOP 50 LAW FIRMS*
Clifford Chance/Rogers & Wells/Pünder (London)	2518	1
Baker & McKenzie (Chicago)	2432	2
Landwell (PwC) •	1735	3
Arthur Andersen Legal Services •	1718	4
Skadden Arps Slate Meagher & Flom (New York)	1366	5
Jones Day Reavis & Pogue (Cleveland)	1353	6
KPMG •	1264	7
Sidley & Austin (Chicago)	872	15
Ernst & Young •	954	16
White & Case (New York)	922	17
Blake Dawson Waldron (Sydney)	716	29
Deloitte Touche •	691	30
Fulbright & Jaworski LLP (Houston)	675	31

• represents accounting firms
*IFLR: International Financial Law Review

[28] There are constant rumours around the City of London that X law firm is about to merge with Y of the Big Five.

While statutory prohibition was removed by the Courts and Legal Services Act 1990, it is still technically impossible for accountants to enter into partnerships with solicitors. And there remains ambivalence over the idea (see also Chambers and Parnham, 1996). A survey of finance directors (FDs) (*Accountancy Age*, 1999) found that:

> only 33% of FDs of small and medium-sized businesses . . . said they would hire a lawyer from the same firm that does their audit. Of the 51% who opposed mixed practices, most believed that they would compromise an auditor's duty to offer independent advice . . . [A] respondent, who asked to remain anonymous, said: "I might want to confide my most business secrets to my lawyer. I wouldn't let my auditor in on the act until I had covered my bases".

However, a survey commissioned by the *Financial Times* found that "more than half of the UK and US's big corporate buyers of legal services are willing to use a firm that combines lawyers and accountants" (*The Lawyer*, 1999b: 7).

While MDPs appear to offer economies of scale that should be attractive to producers of business professional services, consumers are unclear about the advantages. Moreover, both the SEC and the DTI have voiced reservations about the threats to independence of auditors by these sorts of interlocks. These reservations have met with support from the New York City Bar Association and the Pennsylvania Bar Association, who agree and disagree respectively with the ABA's proposals on MDPs (*The Lawyer*, 1999c: 7). The Law Society in its consultation paper raised the spectre of conflicts of interest between the lawyer's attorney–client privilege and the auditor's duty to disclose (Law Society, 1998: 18). In fact, this is the recurring theme of opposition against MDPs (e.g., Marson, 1999: 17; Wolfram, 1999; cf. Mullerat, 2000). The plans of the Big Five rest on the provision of legal services across national boundaries, and this strategy has, in the last couple of years, been directed by the most senior management in the Big Five. As the global legal supremo at the former Coopers & Lybrand commented, "London was important for us in order to have an English law capability in the network of [European] offices. Now this is done, we expect to be able to accelerate our progress in integration and service offerings" (Chambers and Parnham, 1996: 18). While the managing partner of Garrett & Co suggested that it was only a matter of time before the Big Five accountancy networks dominated international legal services.

Thirty years ago, accountants were primarily involved in auditing and accounting. Step by step, they have moved into tax, management, consultancy, human resources, information technology and corporate finance. It now appears to be the turn of legal services before the accountant's evolution into a full service professional adviser is complete. Auditing has long been a problematic core activity for the accounting profession. It is of course restricted from outside competition (as a registered and regulated professional activity) but it is nowhere as profitable as other activities and in addition carries huge liability exposure. Auditing's main value is very much as a springboard for offering other ancillary services to the captive auditing client base. However, this in itself can be problematic; for example, Andersen Worldwide was in the process of sorting out the very public problem of electing its new chief executive. The election had been made impossible by the open hostility shown by Arthur Andersen towards the candidate put forward by Andersen Consulting and the other way round. Ironically, the consulting arm of Andersen Worldwide generated more profits in 1996 than the auditing–accounting sector ($4.9 billion compared to $4.6 billion). The two have now divorced.

Accounting firms consist of component parts in varying stages of development. It is generally agreed that the audit side is mature and so is tax. Consulting is also becoming mature whereas corporate finance and law are still young. The legal services market is particularly attractive because of its size (twice that of the tax market) and its close fit with other areas of practice such as tax, corporate finance work and general corporate law. Furthermore, accounting firms count on their capability to offer legal services themselves as a defence against the competition of growing tax departments of City firms such as Clifford Chance. By adding general legal services to their list of offerings, the Big Five can prepare to meet the challenge of the big City firms in the tax area and their practice of tagging general legal services on to specialist tax advice.

The legal capacity sought by the Big Five can come only from City law firms. In a general environment of expansion, even euphoria, and demand for business legal services, accounting law firms have joined City firms and US firms with a UK presence in the battle to attract suitable lawyers at all levels. This does indicate that the strategies of law firms and accounting firms are diverging. As the European co-ordinator for PwC (and ex-Pinsent & Curtis London managing partner) suggested: "they [the top City firms] are going the same route as us and there is only room for a certain number of players". The recent merger fever among solicitors' firms supports this idea of diverging strategies along the theme of expansion. Also, in the last couple of years there has been a significant change in the extent to which the top City law firms have increased their dominance over other firms, leading to what is known as the "Super Group" of the Big Five (Marks and Griffiths, 1997).

The accounting model for growth, consolidation and geographical coverage appears to have been accepted as the main paradigm of professional practice development. Like accountants, City law firms appear to have recognised that professional services can only follow their clients and what the clients look for is reliable service in many different jurisdictions (cf. Flood, 1996; cf. Silver, 2000). As the UK market for legal services is rather small and static, there is nowhere to expand but overseas. This suits the clients (as long as they do not get asked to meet the cost of expansion) as much as the lawyers and the accountants. Less than that would be sufficient as the basis for building a special relationship.

Lawyers and accountants are striking their different bargains out of their special relationship in accounting legal firms. For the accounting profession the setting up of a legal arm means the opportunity to maximise the work their auditing client base is put to; to gain access to new types of services; to compete more effectively with other accounting firms but also with City firms (over services already provided by both) and US law firms that currently represent the only other alternative to a truly global practice (cf. Barrett, 1999; Silver, 2000). For the legal profession the main bargain is geographical as well as service and client expansion (undreamed of even among the Super Group of the Big Five) as well as protection. Any alliance with a Big Five firm offers formidable protection against other competition either from within the legal profession (nationally and internationally) or other firms of accountants.

But are lawyers ready to contemplate that they may be finished as a result of their special relationship with accountants? The differences in professional cultures and practices are often exaggerated in that respect. In the legal press, accounting firms are presented as more commercial than law firms and with little admiration or time for individualism (people that work for Arthur Andersen have been nicknamed "Androids"). Along the same lines, partners just do not matter as they are all paid on performance (interestingly, City law firms have in fact been agonising over whether to adopt accounting career and pay structures). Accountants are also said to work less hard. A newly qualified solicitor—used to working long City hours—was told at her second interview with one of the accounting law firms that the accountants (who live on the floor above the lawyers) descend on the lawyers after eight o'clock in the evening to see who is still working—this being a sure sign that the lawyers concerned lack effective working practices. So far, the omens are not good. Arthur Andersen's attempted takeover of Wilde Sapte, a 300-year-old City law firm, ended in public humiliation for the law firm when it was spurned by its suitor for carrying too much deadweight in its partnership (Flood, 1998: 16). However, we should recall that Andersen has taken over Scotland's largest law firm, Dundas & Wilson, and that of Spain, now J & A Garrigues Andersen y Cia (Cannon, 1997: 25; Marcos, 2000).

PART III: BRINGING IT TOGETHER

It is no surprise that the number of players in capital markets work is small. The key variables are size, reputation and status. Law firms, for example, must be able to devote large numbers of staff to critical time-bound projects. When ING bought the liquidated Barings merchant bank, the law firm of Slaughter and May had one weekend to do the work (banks are sensitive creatures when put into play this way): they immediately put 30 lawyers on the project (Fay, 1996). Moreover, these firms must be capable of attracting the best-qualified lawyers to work for them. Remuneration and types and scale of work generated provide magnets for staff.[29]

---

[29] The extent to which remuneration is a key magnet compared to the bonuses and share options offered by investment banks and dot coms is questionable. It is difficult for law firms, whether American or British, to match these institutions.

The next variable is reputation. It is significant because markets for expert knowledge tend to be small and sustained through relatively stable memberships or networks of ties. These memberships are socially structured and depend on developing trust and order (Granovetter, 1985; Baker, 1990; Webb and Nicolson, 2000). Reputation, therefore, plays a considerable role, as Leifer (1985: 443) indicates: "[a] small and identifiable group of producers, attached to brands, develop stable and distinct reputations among consumers and hold onto stable market (volume) shares. The reputations are not arbitrarily distributed across producers, but are often tied to market share". This is very much the situation with the magic circles of investment banks and law firms, for example, Goldman Sachs and Sullivan & Cromwell. It is virtually impossible for an outsider to breach these barriers. Those that have managed it have done so by indirect means.[30]

One further element is implicated in the configuration of these professional markets, namely, the effect of status as perceived by producers and consumers. Since reputations are unevenly and unequally distributed, perceived differences in quality frequently result in high-status producers receiving more customers than low-status producers, despite the quality of service rendered. Likewise, the business flows to them with minimal or no costs of advertising (Podolny, 1993). Furthermore, these producers feel it is *infra dignatatem* to market or to advertise. Slaughter and May has no marketing department, instead depends on its history and word of mouth: "[o]n the whole, the approach of the firm is to present ourselves in an understated way, and to say that we don't believe in big glossy brochures" (Farrell, 1999d: 29). The Big Five accounting firms, however, spend enormous sums on developing global brands (MacKay, 2000: 20).

The interaction between size, reputation and status means markets like capital markets are difficult to enter and price is the least crucial determinant in selecting a professional service firm.[31] The connections between status and quality are, however, at best fuzzy, since they depend upon incomplete signals about their nature from producers, buyers and interested third parties. There are also time lags in the signalling process (White, 1981). The embeddedness of social relations within markets helps to facilitate the distribution of signals, but consumers, for example, large corporations, are usually risk-averse and will require substantial proof of quality standards (Podolny, 1993: 838).

The result of these processes is that a small coterie of investment banks and law firms develops that then consolidates and reproduces itself. Their modes of working and their social positions are recognisable to, and consonant with, each other and result in close proximity in both social and economic spheres of activity. This enables them to establish relationships of trust that reduce the complexity inherent in globalisation to relatively nominal levels: that is, the moral

---

[30] Skadden Arps, which is now a player in capital markets, established its reputation initially through hostile takeover work (Caplan, 1993).

[31] E.g., the market for auditing services among large corporations is dominated by the Big Five accounting firms which possess the numbers of auditors and cost structure that enable them to undertake, say, the auditing of Ford. See Han (1994).

and epistemic communities produced by their interactions facilitate chaos diminution (Luhmann, 1979). In a world of emerging markets, crisis-ridden economies, the ability to trust, to know who one is dealing with, is essential and it engages the participants in a common cause: to establish a common global patterning for types of work like capital markets (cf. Fukuyama, 1995). To sustain success in capital markets work necessitates continuing modes of excluding outsiders, to preserve the club. With the shared understandings that emerge from a tightly formed relationship it is likely that the normative order constructed around the work becomes encoded in the participants' institutional personae. They, themselves, are the creators and guarantors of the stability of the normative order for capital markets work. The banks and their attendant law firms, in conjunction with international governmental organisations, are embedding their norms in the structures of the countries' legal systems and economies. Because there are only two legal systems at play, English and New York, resistance is virtually impossible, as some far eastern countries have discovered.[32]

Can MDPs become the future vehicles for capital markets work? At present, the Big Five accounting firms are on the periphery of this field. They have been attempting to break into corporate finance, but with minimal effectiveness. If they are successful in attracting large numbers of City, and other, lawyers into their fold, they will be seen to be offering "seamless global service" (Cannon, 1997: 25). Thus far, their main success has been in attracting junior and medium-ranking lawyers.

MDPs appear to be potential vehicles for a whole range of corporate finance work having a global reach far in excess of that of any law firm, provided they can accumulate the expertise from other institutions. However, the transatlantic law firm merger seems to have the potential for expanding law firms' hold over capital markets work. The head of legal and compliance at ING Barings said:

> I'd like to see two major UK firms get into bed with each other then merge with a US firm—Allen & Overy and Freshfields maybe, with Davis Polk or Cravath . . . Then the sparks would really fly. There is a limit to how much UK firms can grow organically and retain respectability; they have to go for quality. For firms of this kind to join with each other would really terrify the rest [Ferguson, 1997: 35].

This is the stark choice facing the big law firms. Their size and the levels of remuneration they can offer are potentially severe obstacles for them, since they cannot match the investment banks and dot coms. The attractiveness of partnership is no longer as strong as it was once was; it is not a secure matching of individual and institution. Either is now able to jettison the other without fuss. Stasis is not an option for law firms, but where they go next to capitalise on their advantages is unclear.

[32] The relaxation of SEC disclosure requirements has now prompted corporates in the Far East to enter the US capital markets.

MDPs have downsides. The questions of standards of quality are relevant—most of the Big Five are agglomerations of franchises, local partnerships, alliances, with overarching global, senior partnerships that dominate. Uniform standards throughout the organisation are difficult, if not impossible, to maintain. Law firms are better able to achieve this, making them more appealing to financial institutions that provide capital markets work which must "take for granted" the quality standards of their advisers. Finally, this raises the problem of how MDPs would overcome the present arrangements of referral based on the critical elements of trust, reputation and status. As diffuse global organisations, they are not structured in ways that enable them to break into the capital markets work. They have not generated sufficient cultural and social capital to become members of a small and exclusive club that creates enormous rewards for its members.

There are problems with limited liability, especially if the Big Five incorporate offshore (for example, in Jersey): accounting firms (and, query, MDPs) cannot travel the Goldman Sachs route and therefore offer the scale of rewards accruing to investment bankers, for example, $10 million this year. And investment banks are already attracting lawyers from private practice. Alliances are not always stable: Arnheim, PwC's original legal head, pointed out, "[b]ig five firms risk giving away their client base if the alliance does not work. In opportunity cost terms, if this arrangement had not worked, PwC would not have burnt its bridges with other law firms" (Cannon, 1997: 27). There are serious conflict of interest difficulties: the *Prince Jefri* case against KPMG demonstrated the courts are reluctant to accept Chinese Walls as long-term solutions to conflicts.[33]

The range of potential conflicts is increasing as regulators take a more proactive role with professional advisors. This is especially marked in the case of the SEC and accounting firms. The SEC has been cracking down on the ownership of shares by managers of accounting firms in their audit clients (*Accountancy Age*, 2000: 1). Further regulatory incursion has occurred with PwC being ordered by the SEC, after it introduced new independence quality controls for auditors, to fire its head of transaction services, a UK partner based in London, because his brother-in-law was the financial controller of audit client, Reuters (Kemeny, 2000: 8). The SEC has considerable extraterritorial clout that could endanger the global ambitions of the mega-professional service firm. And despite opposition from the Big Five and a hostile Congress, the SEC has managed to impose some limits on the range of consultancy work large accountancy firms can undertake for audit clients (Perry, 2000: 4). If these big firms find themselves conflicted out of global business, the cost would be huge. The basic dilemma is as follows: "[i]f a firm audits a company's accounts it has a duty to disclose. If the same firm is a legal adviser to the company it has a duty to protect the client" (Cannon, 1997:

---

[33] *Prince Jefri Bolkiah* v. *KPMG* (HL) 1998 <http://www.parliament.the-stationery-office. co.uk/pa/ld199899/ldjudgmt/jd.../prince01.htm>.

28). The examples of capital markets work above illuminate the potential for conflict of this type, especially where issues of due diligence are involved.

More subtly, there are the cultural factors that militate against the success of MDPs as capital market vehicles. Any law firm that marries a Big Five accounting firm will be absorbed completely: it can never be a marriage of equals. The Big Five are too big compared to the global law firms. This is one of the reasons we begin to see the transatlantic law firm merger moves beginning. When Clifford Chance originally formed, it was the senior partner's aim to be able to merge with a big accounting firm on equal terms (Flood, 1996). Now that such a merger is no longer feasible, law firms themselves must find alternatives to build economies of scale in the global market.[34] Apart from size, the culture of the organisations is different, with accounting firms arranged more bureaucratically and hierarchically than law firms. Although law firms are, of necessity, becoming corporatised themselves, especially as they grow larger and larger, they have yet to travel as far as accounting firms. Yet there is, perhaps, a movement towards convergence; if so, it is still indeterminate.

REFERENCES

Accountancy Age (1999a), "KPMG Float Barred: Blow to Partner Windfall Hopes as DTI Toes US Line", <http://webserv.vnunet.com/www_user/plsq1/pkg_vnu_search_mo.right_frame?p_story=81765.>.

—— (1999b), "Multidisciplinary Practices: European Court of Justice to Rule on the Future of MDPs", *Accountancy Age,* 2 September; 3.

Bachmann, Reinhard (1999), "Trust, Power and Control in Trans-Organizational Relations", paper presented SASE Conference, July, Madison, Wisc.

Baker, Wayne E. (1990), "Market Networks and Corporate Behavior", *American Journal of Sociology* 96; 589–625.

Barnard, David (2000), "Paper on Large Law Firms", unpublished paper for New York/London Colloquium, December.

Barrett, Paul M. (1999), "Law Merger Points to International Trend: U.S.–British Linkup May Spark Similar Deals", *The Wall Street Journal Europe*, 25 May; 3.

Blass, Tom (1997), "Manx Law Society Votes for MDPs to Stall Foreign Incursions", *Legal Business* July/August; 17.

Bleeke, Joel, and Ernst, David (1992), *Collaborating to Compete: Using Strategic Alliances and Acquisitions in a Global Marketplace* (New York: John Wiley).

Brown, Meredith M., Bird, Paul S., and Kiernan, James A. (1999), "SEC Rules on Cross-Border Offers and Rights Offerings", *International Financial Law Review,* December; 22.

Bryan, Lowell, with Farrell, Diana (1996), *Market Unbound: Unleashing Global Capitalism* (New York: John Wiley).

Callister, Fiona (1999), "French Bar Rejects Full Blown MDPs", *The Lawyer,* 12 April; 1.

---

[34] Interestingly, when a large law firm in Sydney, Australia, rejected a merger proposal from a big accounting firm, a quarter of the firm's partners left in protest (*The Lawyer*, 1999c).

Cannon, Phillipa (1997), "International Practice: The Big Six Move In", *International Financial Law Review*, November; 25.

Caplan, Lincoln (1993), *Skadden: Power, Money, and the Rise of a Legal Empire* (New York: Farrar Strauss Giroux).

Casserley, Dominic (1992), *Facing Up to the Risks: How Financial Institutions Can Survive and Prosper* (New York: Harper Business).

CCBE (1996), Declaration on Multidisciplinary Partnerships.

Chambers, Michael, and Parnham, Richard (1996), "Accountants in the Legal Market: Has the Strategy Failed?", *Commercial Lawyer*, February; 17.

City of London Law Society (1989), *The Work and Organisation of the Legal Profession: A Response to the Government's Green Paper* (London: City of London Law Society).

Darnhill, Andrew (1997), "MDPs: Ignore Them at Your Peril", *Accountancy*, August; 40.

Deogun, Nikhil (2000), "Top 3 Firms for Deals Set $1 Trillion Mark", *Wall Street Journal Europe*, 3 January; 13, 23.

Dignan, Chris (1999a), "Are UK Firms Ready for Global Banking?", *The Lawyer Online*. <http://www.thelawyer.co.uk/TLglobalbank.html>.

—— (1999b), "KPMG Forges Link with Top 25 US Law Practice", *The Lawyer* 7, 9 August.

Farrell, Sean (1999a), "KPMG Launches Law Firm Ahead of MDP Approval", *The Lawyer*, 3 May; 3.

—— (1999b), "Was Sonnenscheins' a Flawed Strategy?" *The Lawyer*, 11 October; 10.

—— (1999c), "PwC Plans Total Integration of Legal Network", *The Lawyer*, 6 September; 2.

—— (1999d), "Brand and Deliver?", *The Lawyer*, 15 February; 20.

Fay, Stephen (1996), *The Collapse of Barings* (London: Richard Cohen Books).

Ferguson, Nick (1997), "What the Client Demands", *International Financial Law Review*, December; 33–5.

Flood, John (1995), "The Cultures of Globalization: Professional Restructuring for the International Market" in Y. Dezalay and D. Sugarman (eds.), *Professional Competition and Professional Power: Lawyers, Accountants and the Social Construction of Markets* (London: Routledge).

—— (1996), "Megalawyering in the Global Order: The Cultural, Social and Economic Transformation of Global Legal Practice", *International Journal of the Legal Profession* 3; 169.

—— (1997), "Normative Bricolage: Informal Rule-Making by Accountants and Lawyers in Mega-Insolvencies" in G. Teubner (ed.), *Global Law Without a State* (Aldershot: Ashgate/Dartmouth).

—— (1998), "Fatal Attraction: A Tale of a Failed MDP", paper presented to RPPU, Law Society, July. London.

—— (1999a), "Professionals Organizing Professionals: Comparing the Logic of United States and United Kingdom Law Practice" in D. Brock, M. Powell and C. R. Hinings (eds.), *Restructuring the Professional Organization: Accounting, Health Care and Law* (London: Routledge).

—— (1999b), "Legal Education, Globalization, and the New Imperialism" in F. Cownie (ed.), *The Law School: Global Issues, Local Questions* (Aldershot: Ashgate/Dartmouth).

Forster, Richard (1996), "Davis Polk & Wardwell Leads the World's Equity Advisers", *International Financial Law Review*, September; 17–25.

Forster, Richard (1997), "New York Firms Seek the World's Business", *International Financial Law Review*, December; 36–9.

Fukuyama, Francis (1995), *Trust: The Social Virtues and the Creation of Prosperity* (London: Hamish Hamilton).

Garfield, Andrew (1999), "High-Flying Goldman Sees Wage Bill Double to $8.7bn.", *Independent*, 22 December; 13.

Gow, David (2000), "Now Vodafone Wants Net Alliances", *Guardian*, 5 February; 32.

Granovetter, Mark (1985) "Economic Action and Social Structure: The Problem of Embeddedness", *American Journal of Sociology* 91; 481.

Held, David, McGrew, Anthony, Goldblatt, David, and Perraton, Jonathan (1999) Global Transformations: Politics, Economics and Culture (Cambridge: Polity Press).

Hickman, Lucy (1999), "LawSoc Votes for MDPs After 10-year Wait", *The Lawyer*, 18 October; 2.

Hirst, Paul, and Thompson, Grahame (1996), *Globalisation in Question* (Oxford: Polity Press).

Hobe, Stephan (1997), "Global Challenges to Statehood: The Increasingly Important Role of Nongovernmental Organizations", *Indiana Journal of Global Studies* 5; 191.

Hodgart, Alan (1999), "Introduction", in *IFLR Review of the Year: Capital Markets Forum 1999* (London: Euromoney).

Hoult, Philip, and Zaki, Sara (1999), "Warner Cranston and US Firm Sonnenschein in Merger Link", *Legal Week*, 30 September; 1.

International Centre for Commercial Law (1999a), "Capital Markets and Securitization—Debt and Equities—New York", <http://www.icclaw.com/us500/edit/ny6.htm>.

—— (1999b), "Capital Markets and Securitization—IPOs—New York", <http://www.icclaw.com/us500/edit/ny7.htm>.

Kemeny, Lucinda (1999a), "US Bar Association Endorses MDPs", *Accountancy Age*, 17 June; 11.

—— (1999b), "Corporate Finance: The Next Frontier", *Accountancy Age*, 13 May; 8.

—— (2000), "Accountants vs Lawyers in Battle for Legal Supremacy", *Sunday Times*, 17 October; 10.

Laferla, Alison (1999), "Brewing Up a Storm in Benelux", *The Lawyer*, 2 August; 22.

LawMoney.com. (2000), "Linklaters Hits the $1 Trillion Mark", <http://www.law-money.com/homepage/Display_Story/Previewstory.asp?StoryNum=3626>.

Law Society (1998), *Multi-Disciplinary Practices: Why? . . . Why not?* (London: Law Society).

Law Society's Gazette, The (1999), "US Report Recommends MDPs". *The Law Society's Gazette*, 9 June; 8.

Lawyer, The (1998a), "Law Society Aims to Have MDPs Operating by 2000", <http://www.the-lawyer.co.uk/cgi-bin/W3Vnewlib/MO=3/UI=?CT=NEWS&SC=&RI=0000082208.htm>.

—— (1998b), "MDPs Get Cautious Approval from Law Society in Canada", <http://www.the-lawyer.co.uk/cgi-bin/W3Vnewlib/MO=3/UI=?CT=INTER-NAT&SC=&RI=0000075012.htm>.

—— (1998c), "Australian State Gives Green Light to MDPs", <http://www.the-lawyer.co.uk/cgi-bin/W3Vnewlib/ MO=3/UI=?CT=INTERNAT&SC=&RI=0000069450.htm>.

—— (1999a), "US Bar Set to Drop Multidisciplinary Partnership Ban", *The Lawyer*, 7 June; 4.

—— (1999b), "Law Forums Discuss MDP Challenges", *The Lawyer*, 13 September; 7.

—— (1999c), "Penn Bar Opposes MDP Plans", *The Lawyer*, 9 August; 7.

—— (1999d), "Partners Quit Sydney Firm in MDP Row", <http://www.the-lawyer.co.uk/cgi-bin/W3Vnewlib/ MO=3/UI=?CT=NEWS&SC=&RI=0000085661.htm>.

—— (1999e), "Are UK Firms Ready for Global Banking?", <http://www.the-lawyer.co.uk/Tlglobalbank.html>.

—— (2000a), "Law Society to Push MDPs Through Early", <http://www.the-lawyer.co.uk/cgi-bin/W3Vnewlib/MO=3/UI=?CT=NEWS&SC=&RI=0000162779.htm>.

—— (2000b), "KLegal Apes KPMG's Sector-Based Teams", <http://www.the-lawyer.co.uk/cgi-bin/W3Vnewlib/MO=3/UI=?CT=NEWS&SC=&RI=0000162927.htm>.

Lee, Paul (1997), "Setting the Law Firm Standard", *International Financial Law Review*; 16.

Leifer, Eric M. (1985), "Markets as Mechanisms: Using a Role Structure", *Social Forces* 64; 442.

Luhmann, Niklas (1979), *Trust and Power* (Chichester: John Wiley).

MacKay, Elizabeth (2000), "One Size Will Not Always Fit", *Accountancy Age*, 17 February; 20.

Marcos, Francisco (2000), "The Storm Over Our Heads: The Rendering of Legal Services by Audit Firms in Spain", *International Journal of the Legal Profession* 7; 7.

Marks, Sarah, and Griffiths, Catrin (1997), "The Wannabes", *Legal Business*, July/August; 26.

Marson, Brian (1999), "Viewpoint: MDPs Offer the Chance to Diversify", *The Lawyer*, 1 February; 17.

Michaels, Adrian (2000), "US Regulator Orders Sweeping Controls on Auditors", <http://www.ft.com/hippocampus/q33ad7a.htm>.

Mullerat, Ramón (2000), "The Multidisciplinary Practice of Law in Europe", paper presented to 2000 ABA Mid-Year Meeting, Dallas, Texas.

Neate, F. W. (ed.) (1987), *The Developing Global Securities Market* (London: Graham & Trotman and International Bar Association).

New Zealand Law Society (1999), "MDP Options Paper Released", <http://www.nz-lawsoc.org.nz/lawtalk/mdpsum.htm>.

Ohmae, Kenichi (1991), *The Borderless World* (London: Fontana).

—— (1995), *The End of the Nation State* (New York: The Free Press).

Perry, Michelle (2000), "SEC Wins Audit War", *Accountancy Age*, 23 November; 4.

Podolny, Joel M. (1993), "A Status-based Model of Market Competition", *American Journal of Sociology* 98; 829.

Quick, Chris (1999), "Stepping Over the Legal Boundary", *Accountancy Age*, 13 May; 8.

Rivlin, Richard, and Silverman, Gary (2000), "M&A Records on Both Sides of the Atlantic", *Financial Times*, 1 January; 9.

Robertson, Roland (1992), *Globalization: Social Theory and Global Culture* (London: Sage).

Rosenthal, Jim, and Ocampo, Juan (1988), *Securitization of Credit* (New York: John Wiley).

Sawin, Witold (1999), "LLPs—A Legislative Muddle", *Accountancy Age*, 17 June; 20.

Shapiro, Martin (1993), "The Globalization of Law", *Indiana Journal of Global Legal Studies 1*; <http://www.law.indiana.edu/glsj/vol1/shapiro.html>.

Silver, Carole (2000), "Globalization and the U.S. Market in Legal Services—Shifting Identities", *Law and Policy in International Business 31*; 1093.

Skadden, Arps (1999), "Privatizations", <http://www.sasmf.com/onefirm/experience/privatization.html>.

Swallow, Matheu (1999), "PwC and Andersens to Challenge MDP Ban", *The Lawyer*, 23 August; 2.

Tagliabue, John (2000), "Global Links Reshape Law Landscape", *International Herald Tribune*, 5–6 August; 9.

Teubner, Gunther (1998), "Legal Irritants: Good Faith in British Law or How Unifying Law Ends Up in New Divergences", *Modern Law Review* 61; 11.

Townsend, Abigail (1999), "CC Calls off Mallesons Talks", *The Lawyer*, 26 July; 1.

Treanor, Jill, and Brummer, Alex (1999), "Defence Team Hires Big Gun", *Guardian*, 23 October; 28.

UNCTAD (1994), *World Investment Report 1995: Transnational Corporations and Competitiveness* (New York: United Nations).

Webb, Julian, and Nicolson, Donald (2000), "Institutionalising Trust: Ethics and the Responsive Regulation of the Legal Profession", *Legal Ethics*; 2.

White, Harrison C. (1981), "Where Do Markets Come From?", *American Journal of Sociology* 87; 517.

Williams, Tony (2000), "Comment", *International Financial Law Review*, August; 18.

Wolfram, Charles W. (1999), "Multidisciplinary Partnerships in the Law Practice of European and American Lawyers" in J. J. Barcelo, and R. C. Cramton (eds.), *Lawyers' Practice & Ideals: A Comparative View* (Boston: Kluwer Law International).

9

The Role of Global Law Firms in Constructing or Obstructing a Transitional Regime of Labour Law

HARRY ARTHURS*

Abstract

Some business transactions are more global than others; so too the normative systems by which they are governed. This study examines a deviant type of transaction—employment relations in transnational companies—and proposes that a number of forces tend to reinforce its local character. While a lex mercatoria *may be emerging, even a* jus humanitatus, *few observers detect evidence of an inchoate* lex laboris. *Global law firms are important agents of this localising tendency. Despite their documented contribution to the creation of a system of transnational law in other contexts, interviews with some 40 lawyers in seven countries revealed an almost unanimous view that labour law was not only local in fact, but inevitably and properly so. Nonetheless, it is clear that the political economy of globalisation has affected the labour strategies of transnational corporations, the content and administration of local labour law and the moral economy of legal practice in the field.*

INTRODUCTION

The Legal Culture of Global Business Transactions

T O SUGGEST THAT there is something called "the legal culture of global business transactions" is to invite debate on a series of dubious propositions: that "legal" is a useful descriptor, that there is a unified—presumably global—legal "culture", that the "global" can be distinguished from the domestic or national legal culture, and that all "business transactions" can

* I should like to acknowledge the financial support of the Social Sciences and Humanities Research Council of Canada, and the invaluable assistance of Robert Kreklewich, Raziel Zisman, Angela Long and Nadia Flaim.

be treated alike. By examining the activities and beliefs of labour lawyers who act for transnational corporations, I hope to contribute to that debate.

To begin tritely, law does not produce and reproduce itself. Few scholars would suggest that the law of business transactions is made exclusively by or for those transactions, that it has nothing to do with the complex and volatile environment—with the polity, society, culture and economy—in which those transactions occur. As I have argued elsewhere, three powerful forces—analytically distinct but mutually supportive—have shaped that environment: globalisation, to be sure, but also neo-liberal policies and a revolution in production, transportation and information technology. These forces have wrought profound changes in legal institutions, public administration and the legal profession (Arthurs and Kreklewich, 1996; Arthurs, 1996a, 1997c), in corporate functions and structures (Arthurs, 2000), in employment relations (Arthurs, 1996b, 1997a, 1998c, 1998d), in the social and economic structures of local communities (Sassen, 1994, 1998), in the physical environment (Dolzer, 1998), in virtually everything. However, it is not possible to disaggregate globalisation effects from the others.

Moreover, as Santos reminds us, globalisation is not a single phenomenon, but many—"globalized localisms" and "localized globalisms"—which manifest themselves in different ways in different sites and circumstances (Santos, 1995). In such an environment, the search for a single, unified legal culture can only be viewed as quixotic. After all, if legal pluralism has taught us anything, it is that even domestic legal systems encompass a multiplicity of state and non-state legal fields, each with its own norms, institutions, processes and cultures (Griffiths, 1986; Merry, 1988), and that we ought to focus on internormativity, rather than assume coherence (Belley, 1996). Indeed, investigation of legal cultures in various contexts has often produced similar conclusions (Gessner, 1994; Plett and Menschievitz, 1991; Ogliati, 1995; Friedman, 1994). Finally, the concept of business transactions needs to be problematised. I will do this by examining a deviant species of that *genus*—employment relations in transnational companies. Some business transactions, we shall see, are more global than others; so too the normative systems by which they are governed.

The Legal Culture of Transnational Labour and Employment Relations

Essentially, then, as part of a broader inquiry into what normative systems regulate employment relations in transnational enterprises, my more specific concern is to discover what role global law firms play in constructing those normative systems.

In this formulation, the question implicates especially the work of scholars who have explored the role of law firms, consulting firms and corporate cadres in producing the *congeries* of legal regimes which support global business transactions (Garth, 1985; Trubek *et al.*, 1994; Dezalay and Sugarman, 1995; Dezalay and Garth, 1996; Flood, 1996; Teubner, 1997). Such regimes include the complex regulations of the WTO, international conventions on civil aviation and copyright, the trading rules of the great stock and currency exchanges, the arcane and specialised rituals of the International Bank for Clearances and the diamond trade, the constitutional protocols of the EU and NAFTA, the governance structures and networks of transnational corporations, and the contracts, compromises and arbitral jurisprudence which give shape and definition to global business transactions. In the creation and administration of these regimes, as noted, the great transnational law firms and consulting firms have played a leading role, as advisors and negotiators for governments, business, international agencies and social movements, as strategists, lobbyists and intermediaries, as advocates and arbitrators, and especially as architects of regimes of private ordering and authors of the documents which express them. However, as I will attempt to demonstrate, these firms have not played the same facilitative and creative role in constructing a global regime of labour law. In apparent contrast to the law of commercial contracts, intellectual property, banking and insolvency, the law of employment and industrial relations remains resolutely local in character.

This in itself is not an idiosyncratic conclusion. It represents the consensus of virtually all observers, whether of the global economy (Santos, 1995; Boyer, 1995) or of its principal regions (von Maydell, 1993; Teague, 1993; Ojeda-Aviles, 1993; Baldry, 1994; Sciarra, 1998; Streeck, 1995; Wedderburn, 1996).[1] However, it does seem odd that no overarching regime of labour law exists to regulate various aspects of employment in transnational labour markets. Labour, as an important factor of production, is one of the variables captured by the principle of comparative advantage, the *leitmotif* of globalisation. Labour, as a class or movement, professes—if it does not actually practise—principles of international solidarity. And individual employees—those with certain kinds of talents, skills and knowledge—commute physically and electronically from one country to another, providing technical, professional and managerial services to their transnational employers, quite indifferent to local labour markets, laws or customs.

Moreover, there is a long history of attempts to regulate employment relations beyond the juridical space of particular states. Some of the earliest international conventions dealt with labour—child labour, slave labour, labour at risk on the seas and in dangerous occupations[2]—and from its inception in 1919, the ILO has worked to secure adherence to internationally accepted norms of

---

[1] But see *contra* Guery (1992), Bercusson (1995).

[2] See e.g. Declaration Relative to the Universal Abolition of the Slave Trade (1815) (signed by eight European powers at the Congress of Vienna); Berne Conventions of 1906 (world's first two multilateral labour conventions); C.5 Minimum Age (Industry) Convention, 1919, ILO (First Session, International Labor Conference, Washington); C.6 Night Work of Young Persons (Industry) Convention, 1919, ILO (First Session, International Labor Conference, Washington); C.7 Minimum Age (Sea) Convention, 1920, ILO (Second Session, International Labor Conference, Geneva).

employment. But still we have no system of transnational labour law. Despite almost 200 Conventions and an equal number of "recommendations", despite scores of reports emanating from investigative committees, despite the eloquent remonstrations of its Governing Body, the ILO has not managed to construct an effective juridical regime of employment law or industrial relations. The EU— otherwise almost manic in its regulatory exertions—has been uncharacteristically diffident in the realm of individual and especially collective labour law; one observer suggests that at best it has moved recently from a "non-regulatory" to a "pre-regulatory" posture (Sciarra, 1995). And NAFTA—a powerful engine of hemispheric integration—has developed an elaborate evasive strategy to avoid even the appearance of intruding on the domestic labour practices of its member states (McGuiness, 1994; Cook, 1994; Robinson, 1994).

Nor, finally, should national sovereignty be regarded as an insuperable obstacle to the creation of a transnational labour law regime. States can and do agree to subordinate their domestic legal regimes to global arrangements when it suits their purposes. They bind themselves—perhaps irrevocably—to international standards in fields such as human rights (Keith, 1997) and comprehensively amend their own laws to conform to treaty commitments,[3] even to the point of permanently disabling their own regulatory functions (Schneiderman, 1996). They willingly harmonise their laws with those of their trading partners in order to facilitate business transactions (Bennett, 1991; Hoberg, 1991) or foreign investment (Rotstein, 1993; Horton, 1993). In countless, subtle ways they align their national legal values, norms, institutions and cultures more closely with those of the global hegemon (Arthurs, 1997b), not least by colluding or acquiescing in the creation of legal regimes by various non-state, transnational actors.

The resulting transnational legal regimes are often hybrids: they occasionally emerge in national forums and draw sustenance from state law; they are sometimes promulgated or promoted by international agencies; often, they thrive in the shadow of formal institutions. But their most salient characteristic is that they are ultimately generated by transnational corporations (Teubner, 1997), their law firms and consultants (Dezalay and Garth, 1996), and other non-state actors operating in the global economy including standards organisations (Salter, 1988, 1993), sectoral and professional bodies (Arthurs, 1999), nongovernmental organisations (NGOs), social movements and advocacy groups (Santos, 1995; Merry, 1997; Trubek *et al.*, 1998). As a contribution to the project of global governance, the proliferation of such regimes might seem desirable, even inevitable. It is certainly substantial: some observers contend that a new *lex mercatoria* already governs transnational business transactions (Trubek *et al.*, 1994; Dezalay and Sugarman, 1995; Dezalay and Garth, 1996; Teubner, 1997); others even detect the appearance of a new *jus humanitatus* governing our common environmental and cultural heritage (Santos, 1995). But

---

[3] See e.g. Act to Implement the North American Free Trade Agreement, Stat. Canada 1993, c.44.

no knowledgeable observer claims that these non-state actors—otherwise so productive and prolific—are creating a new *lex laboris*.

Why not?

The short answer is that many states which compete for their "fair share" of opportunities in the global economy do so on the basis of lower labour standards. They reckon that introduction of transnational labour standards would force them to revise their own standards upwards, thus depriving them of their comparative advantage. Moreover, even if they wished to hold locally-based employers to worldwide labour standards, states cannot easily overcome the technical difficulties of extraterritorial regulation (Stone, 1995). The slightly longer answer is that transnational corporations do not wish to construct a new global regime of labour law. In general, they prefer to be able to shop among local labour regimes, resorting to transnational employment norms only when compelled to do so by public pressure (Compa and Hinchcliffe-Daricarrère, 1995), market forces (Baker and Mackenzie, 1998) or managerial convenience (Nielsen, 1999). The longest answer—though not necessarily the most cogent one—is that the principal architects of other non-state transnational regimes, lawyers and consultants, have no incentive to be similarly creative in labour matters. They have little to gain from inventing a new transnational labour regime when doing so risks a potential confrontation with the state, the displeasure of clients and the devaluation of their own professional capital. Nonetheless, by describing how labour lawyers locate themselves in relation to the legal culture of transnational business transactions, I hope to make some important points about both globalisation and lawyering.

THE ROLE OF LAWYERS IN LABOUR LAW

As Bourdieu contends in arguing for attention to the "legal field" (Bourdieu, 1987), as Teubner and his colleagues have tried to show with their studies of autopoeisis in the global sphere, in transnational corporations and in work-places (Teubner, 1994, 1997), as Garth, Dezalay, Sugarman and Flood have demonstrated in their work on professional labour markets (Dezalay and Sugarman, 1995; Dezalay and Garth, 1996; Flood, 1996), social fields and their normative systems are, to a large extent, constituted by co-operation and competition among strategically-located actors. The labour lawyers interviewed for this study certainly fit that description. They help to articulate the relationships between the global and local economies, between the expectations of their clients and the requirements of the national legal system, between the national legal system and substate normative systems generated within and amongst other social fields, including specific economic sectors and enterprises and, not least, between capital and labour. Moreover, when they represent transnational corporations they compete and collaborate in the legal field with a variety of other friendly professionals—public officials, consultants, local and head office

managers—and confront an array of potentially unfriendly professionals—officials of unions and social movements, journalists and politicians.

According to the literature, these strategic mediations, these formative
encounters, ought to make lawyers as important contributors to a global legal
culture of labour law as they have been to domestic labour law. Thus, if we want
to comprehend their global contribution, or its lack, we must first understand
the nature of their contribution to domestic labour law. McBarnet suggests, in
a different sociolegal vernacular, that lawyers use the "tools" of legal form and
ideology to work the "raw material" of law to serve their "dominant client":
capital (McBarnet, 1984). This indeed is what labour lawyers have done for
much of the last 200 years. Most of them have worked skilfully and industri-
ously on the raw material of the law to fashion doctrines and remedies on behalf
of employers in order to suppress unions and deprive workers of their legal protections and moral entitlements both in the workplace and, often, as citizens.
Naturally, there were exceptions: an oppositional minority of lawyers acting for
"non-dominant clients"—workers, workers' organisations and government
regulatory agencies—tried to use law to alleviate the harshness and unfairness
of industrial capitalism. But by and large labour lawyers were—in an ideological and highly partisan sense—employers' lawyers.

This changed to some extent with the political enfranchisement of workers,
growing revulsion against "sweated labour", the growing acceptance of collective bargaining, the emergence of new legal structures of labour market regulation and especially the post-war "fordist compromise" which incorporated
workers and their unions into the capitalist system in exchange for the enhance-
ment of their legal, social and economic rights. These developments, beginning
in the early years of the twentieth century, expanded the state's role in labour
law and transformed the legal field of labour law in most advanced economies.

However, the extent and form of transformation varied greatly. Responding
to pre-war precedents, both positive and negative, most Western European
countries adopted social market or social democratic policies during the post-
war period, with highly centralised collective bargaining systems, corporatist
determination of labour market policies and an extensive emphasis on security
and benefits for workers. The United States took a different route, with highly
decentralised collective bargaining, unregulated or poorly regulated labour
markets and a modest menu of benefits for workers, provided primarily by
employers rather than the state.

These divergent public policy experiences were reflected in different legal cultures and patterns of labour law practice. In the United States, the legal activism
of the New Deal in the mid-1930s (Irons, 1982) was soon succeeded by a period
of "deradicalisation" (Klare, 1978), and then by an anodyne era of "industrial
pluralism" with its emphasis on private norm generation and dispute resolution
(Stone, 1981; Barenberg, 1993). In terms of labour law practice, the tendency
was towards "normalisation"—a decline in highly adversarial and ideological
behaviours, enhanced adherence to a model of dispassionate professionalism,

growing legal sophistication, and an increased emphasis on the role of labour lawyers on both sides of the equation as managers of conflict and architects of compromise. But this tendency has been reversed over the past 20 years or so. Under the pressure of technological change, the flexibilisation of production, deregulation of the labour market, intensified globalisation and juridification, the power of the American labour movement has declined considerably, and the meagre protections of state law have become yet more sparse. The result has been a change in labour law practice: capital is ascendant; accommodation with unions and government regulators is off the agenda in many industries; management lawyers are once again hammering fiercely at the "raw material of the law" to reduce its effectiveness (Weiler, 1990) and like other successful artisans who have brought about technological change, as we shall see, they may have made themselves dispensable.

American labour relations, labour law and labour law practice are notorious for their "exceptionalism", although they have to some extent been reproduced in a few countries which have consciously borrowed American labour market policies and imitated or imported American patterns of legal and corporate practice. But unique American legal concepts and arrangements in the field of business law have been secreted in the interstices of corporate practice, only to emerge ultimately as Santos' "globalised localisms", as the dominant influence on the putative "legal culture of global business transactions". Is the same turning out to be true in the labour field?

LABOUR LAWYERS IN THE GLOBAL ECONOMY: AN EMPIRICAL STUDY

The Lawyers

In search of an answer to that question, I interviewed 40 lawyers in seven countries[4] who ought to be knowledgeable about the possible emergence of a system of transnational labour law, the provenance of such a system, its effects on employers and employees, and its relationship to domestic regimes of labour law. All interviewees were labour law specialists; almost all acted exclusively for transnational and domestic corporations and executives; two acted only for unions and workers; and two acted for both labour and management.

Of course, their responses are not the last word on the subject.[5] My sample may have been too small and insufficiently random; lawyers are not trained

[4] Interviews were conducted in the United Kingdom, France, Belgium, the Netherlands, Mexico, the United States and Canada between May 1996 and December 1998. No Asian, Eastern European or South American lawyers were interviewed; conceivably they might have a different perspective on the intrusion of western labour law norms.

[5] Each interview lasted 1½ to two hours. Almost all interviews were conducted in English, other than a few in French or Spanish; and all were taped and/or recorded in writing. All respondents were given assurances of confidentiality, which is why I have not identified individual respondents, their firms or clients.

sociological observers; their testimony is subject to the normal distortions of professional ideology, discourse and self-interest; and the pressure of their daily practice predisposes them to take a case-by-case view of events, rather than a systemic, long-term view. And, it might be argued, they are not necessarily the right people to ask about transnational law; only a scholarly minority would likely recognise the shaping influence on domestic law of international or foreign influences. However, given such potential distortions in their testimony, I did not simply ask these labour lawyers what they thought about the possible existence, source, content or consequences of a global regime of labour law. Rather, I tried to elicit revealing details about their professional formation and careers, the tasks they perform, the nature of their clientele, the fora in which they work, the sources of law and other norms which they invoke, their relationships with colleagues, clients, state officials and adversaries. To summarise their views: none felt that there was a new *lex laboris* in the making. On the contrary, when asked the question directly, all respondents strongly asserted that domestic law—not transnational norms— governed labour and employment relations in his or her country. These views were not contradicted by their detailed accounts of the work they actually did, of the arguments and advice they provided to clients and of the legal sources they drew upon. Nor, for that matter, is there much scholarly evidence that transnational law has shaped domestic law: rather the contrary. Much of what passes for transnational law was no more than an export version of "best practice" in Western Europe and the United States, a source of great controversy in the ILO at the height of the cold war (Cox, 1977). And leading scholars insist that more than most types of law, labour law is nonexportable (Kahn-Freund, 1976).

There are some obvious reasons why labour law has failed to acquire a transnational dimension similar to that of other fields of business law. Reciprocity is the paradigm around which commercial relations are organised; unequal power characterises the relations between employer and employed. Business disputes and contracts occur between firms; labour disputes and contracts occur within firms. State law may be somewhat peripheral to most conventional business arrangements; it is even more so to employment relations. Powerful corporations have the financial resources to invoke state labour law when it favours them, the political influence to change it when it does not, or *in extremis* the economic power to ignore it; workers seldom have any of these. For all of these reasons, employment norms—derived from power, defined by contract, embedded in custom, mutable in practice—tend to be firm-specific, even workplace-specific (Arthurs, 1985, 1998c). No wonder, then, that many of my respondents were bemused by the suggestion that they may be important actors in shaping labour law regimes—domestic or transnational.

The Influence of Transnational Professional Contacts and Culture

Virtually all respondents had ample exposure to foreign—principally American—legal influences. As noted, they acted for (or, in a few cases, against) foreign transnationals doing business in the country where they practised. Most of the European and American (but not Canadian or Mexican) respondents also represented domestic transnationals doing business abroad. Most were members of transnational law firms or alliances of law firms, or maintained informal relationships with and received referrals from them. About a third of the European and Mexican lawyers were actually members of foreign-based law firms, in some cases working alongside American or British colleagues. About one-quarter of the Europeans and Mexicans had received academic training in, or practical exposure to, a foreign legal system, especially that of the United States. And of course, the Canadian lawyers practised under a labour law regime which was closely modelled on American legislation, and is influenced on an ongoing basis by American jurisprudence and academic literature. In short, if there were such a thing as a transnational legal culture, then these lawyers would be deeply involved in it.

However, if they are, they do not seem to know or believe they are. Few respondents were prepared to acknowledge that their professional formation, practical exposure, working relationships or clientele influenced their understanding of or response to legal issues. They generally reported receiving little substantive direction on legal matters from foreign colleagues; few of them worked closely or directly with lawyers based abroad; and only a few had more than sporadic contact even with their clients' foreign-based in-house counsel. Generally, they worked on a day-to-day basis directly with local corporate management and only occasionally dealt with head office management or with lawyers representing the same corporation in other countries. Only the Canadians—who reported the highest incidence of close contact with foreign lawyers and executives—were inclined to agree that their participation in a transnational legal field had given them a critical perspective on their own system or prompted them to "borrow" specific legal doctrines or strategies from foreign partners, contacts in practice or professional literature. (Ironically, those European and Mexican lawyers who acknowledged that they had been influenced by their contact with foreign law, lawyers and clients focused mostly on how they had reorganised their law practice to conform to an Anglo-American model.)

The Direct Application of International Legal Norms

None of the respondents believed that international legal norms had much effect on their advice to clients or in litigation. Their explanations varied. Some felt that national norms were higher than those decreed internationally, so there was no need to have recourse to the latter. Others believed that labour lawyers know very little about international law in general and international labour standards in particular. Only a very few respondents, for example, acknowledged ever having raised or being directly confronted with a legal argument based on an ILO convention. As one said dismissively, "the ILO is not visible over the horizon". None acknowledged having encountered the non-binding "codes of conduct" for MNCs operating abroad, which have been promulgated by the OECD, the ILO and the EU and adopted by many transnational corporations.

Virtually all respondents believed that labour law would remain national law in the near-term. Amongst the Europeans a few—but only a few—did regard EU directives as having a significant impact, but only on a short list of collective and individual labour law issues. Several also acknowledged that in the distant future there might be greater convergence of national systems under the influence of these directives, especially in regard to redundancies, the treatment of employees in corporate mergers, and European Works Councils. In the NAFTA countries, respondents obviously acknowledged the existence of a transnational labour law regime—the North American Agreement on Labor Cooperation (the NAALC)—but they generally tended to discount its juridical and practical significance. Several respondents had actually been involved in one or more of the dozen high-profile NAALC complaints initiated to that point, but even they denied that that regime was an important source of new labour law. Rather, they tended to regard the NAALC complaints as merely the continuation of politics by other means. It must be said, however, that several thoughtful Mexican and Canadian respondents did regard free trade under NAFTA as a catalyst for the restructuring of the national economy, politics and public policy and thus—in the end—of the existing regime of industrial relations and labour law.

The Indirect Influence of Transnational Legal Norms

Of course, at a high level of generality, most developed (and many developing) countries choose to commit themselves (if not always to adhere) to decent minimum labour standards, to acknowledge the right of workers to organise and bargain collectively and to prohibit the exploitation of vulnerable workers. In public policy debates or legislative projects, they may sometimes reference international norms, as well as the labour laws and policies of their neighbours or trading partners. And enterprising advocates may express in the vernacular of domestic labour law arguments which are actually derived from transnational labour regimes or foreign labour law systems. But neither the tendency of advanced economies to adjust their labour laws to prevailing Fordist (and now neo-liberal) understandings at about the same time, nor the occasional magpie display by clever lawyers of borrowed legal trinkets, is strong evidence of the emergence of a distinctive labour law of transnational business, a global field of labour law, or a transnational juridical system with widely accepted labour law concepts, rules, institutions or practices.

The Influence of Transnational Corporate Clients

If a regime of global labour law is not being created by lawyers and other professional actors in the transnational legal field, is it being created elsewhere by less obvious actors? Specifically, to what extent can we identify traces of such a global regime imbricated within the managerial and production processes of transnational corporations, slowly given shape and substance by human resources and industrial relations managers, unions and individual workers?

Some studies suggest that transnational companies exhibit national characteristics associated with their country of origin or the country in which their head office is located (Jackson, 1993; UNCTAD, 1994; Kustin and Jones, 1995; Bartlett and Ghosal, 1998). However, these characteristics are most likely to be manifest in relation to overall corporate strategies and governance structures (Kriger and Rich, 1987; Gillies and Morra, 1996) and arguably, by extension, to the primary agents of those strategies—elite executives, technical experts and professionals posted abroad (Trompenaars, 1992).

However, at the level of general human resources or industrial relations policies and practices, the picture seems different. While one series of empirical studies seems to point to "a broad yet tentative convergence" of patterns of workplace relations across national boundaries within a given transnational company, under specified conditions (Frenkel, 1994; Frenkel and Royal, 1997, 1998) more broadly-based analyses seem to point to the variability of certain "transnational channels of influence" across companies (Coller and Marginson, 1998). Thus, many studies stress variations within and amongst transnational corporations reflecting differences based on countries of origin, management philosophy, national and regional mandates and markets, sectoral factors, level of employee and other considerations (Morrison, Ricks, and Roth, 1991; Lorenz, 1992; Hoffman, 1994; Ferner, 1994; Sölvell and Zander, 1995; Ferner, 1997; Pauley and Reich, 1997), even within elements of the same firm (Milkman, 1991; Streeck, 1994; Drache, 1994) and its extended corporate family (Ghoshal and Bartlett, 1990). Inter- and intrafirm variability is a particular feature of the structures of collective bargaining which, predictably, are regarded by most employers and governments as unsuited for, if not actually illicit in, the global economy (Enderwick, 1984; UNCTAD, 1994; Lucio and Weston, 1994; Boyer, 1995; Freeman, 1995). And specifically, TNC responses to labour law in general appear to be heterogeneous, complex and poorly documented (Florkowski and Nath, 1993).

On the whole, it seems, transnational corporations—which tend to think globally in most respects—seem to act locally when they deal with workers. But this is not an invariable rule: when local labour standards are less favourable to their off-shore employees than conditions in the home country, a TNC will naturally take advantage of the local *status quo*; but when they are more favourable, it will argue that local operations must be made "competitive" and local labour standards brought into line with a supposed global norm.

In a backhanded fashion, the lawyers interviewed confirmed the existence of this contradiction. They said, for example, that dealing with transnational clients presented special challenges, which differed from those of dealing with domestic clients. A very common account of relations with their US-based transnational clients centred on the necessity of "educating" these clients who generally arrived in a new host country with established human resources policies but no knowledge of local law or industrial relations practices. As one Canadian respondent put it, "much of my work involves cooling the jets of American clients". In Canada and Europe, where labour standards and union support are generally higher than in the United States, many American corporations expressed a determination to operate abroad as they did at home—without unions, without employment contracts, without a repertoire of employment benefits; and many expressed initial indignation at the need to modify their employment practices. According to many respondents, American firms are often surprised to encounter the greater employment security and job-related benefits enjoyed by European and Canadian workers. Or, to take a different example, Japanese, and to some extent European, firms are sometimes taken aback by the emphasis which their North American legal advisors place on the need to address issues of workplace discrimination, harassment, safety and health.

Confronted with a tension between national employment standards and those which foreign transnationals sought to introduce, many respondents apparently tried to "domesticate" their clients, to persuade them to modify both their expectations and their behaviour to conform to local law and practice. In the normal course, they stated, they would be domesticating local management, rather than officials from the corporate head office in another country.

Respondents reported varying degrees of success with this approach. Some Canadian lawyers reported that their US clients were impatient, even incredulous, when told that particular approaches developed within the American context could not be applied in neighbouring Canada—a somewhat odd reaction since Canadian and American employment laws are far more similar than the legal systems of any other two countries studied. In some cases, Canadian respondents reported that they were able to develop innovative strategies which allowed their clients to adhere to their own internal policies and to operate, in effect, without regard to Canadian law, while running minimal risks of being found in violation. European lawyers, on the other hand, seemed to encounter somewhat less difficulty in dealing with their American clients. The explanation, according to European respondents, was that labour costs were usually a relatively modest factor in the decision to do business in a particular country. As a result, clients more easily agreed to comply with local requirements for job security and benefits. This explanation must be qualified in the case of the United Kingdom, which during the 1980s deregulated its labour market in a successful attempt to become an attractive gateway to Europe for American, Korean and Japanese transnationals.

Thus we see diverse tendencies within transnational corporations as they react to local labour standards derived from state law and industrial relations practice. Sometimes, TNCs comply scrupulously with local regulations, even in jurisdictions with high standards. For example, in the case of corporate restructuring, mergers and acquisitions in Europe, failure to address employment-related issues might jeopardise the whole transaction. However, they sometimes comply only in the formal sense. For example, some Mexican respondents claim to have made their clients understand that the costs of complying with apparently onerous local constitutional and statutory requirements were in fact relatively trivial, and that they could operate in Mexico pretty much unencumbered by what looked like considerable regulatory constraints. One way or another, though, local compliance seems to be the rule and the introduction of a global regime the exception.

But there are exceptions. In a few instances, lawyers do seem to be constructing something resembling transnational labour law or even worldwide corporate employment norms. For example, several respondents had been asked to adapt a corporation-wide employee handbook to local conditions, to vet standard contracts used to define the employment terms of peripatetic executives or to draft codes of employment practice to which off-shore subsidiaries and suppliers would be required to conform. And in the latter instance, as one respondent frankly noted, legal advice was sometimes sought for negative, not positive, reasons: clients feared that the failure of senior executives to perform due diligence by taking steps to prevent sexual harassment or promote safety standards might not only adversely affect their careers; it might lead to their being found civilly or criminally liable. For the most part, then, initiatives to move forward with explicit transnational strategies originated with the clients themselves, rather than their legal advisors. But not always: several respondents who practised in the same large transnational law firm reported that labour law practitioners in that firm met periodically to co-ordinate the advice they tendered to clients whom they represented in multiple jurisdictions.

Finally, most respondents agreed that the corporation, rather than the lawyer, not only initiated the underlying corporate strategy and made the final decision on adherence, non-adherence or nominal adherence to local labour law, but actively directed and orchestrated the activities of its legal representatives in various countries. For example, in the case of Europe-wide mergers and acquisitions, one respondent reported, while clients might ask a particular law firm to take the lead in bringing together the necessary legal services to deal with employment issues in each country affected, they would be just as likely to use their own legal or human relations departments to co-ordinate teams in different jurisdictions. This underlines the tendency of transnational corporations to see themselves as primary authors of their own internal employment "law", often either ignoring their outside lawyers altogether or merely asking them to vet policy statements, contracts or operating manuals which were formulated internally.

Other Influences

This study has concentrated on management-side lawyers. Only four respondents acted for unions or individual rank-and-file workers, while about one-quarter acted on occasion for executives as well as corporations. Thus, the study does not directly take into account the contribution made to legal culture by a completely different group of lawyers—those who represent governments, international agencies, unions, social movements and other transnational advocacy groups in legal or political fora. However, the significance of that omission should not be overestimated. While some international union structures do exist (Bendiner, 1987) and while *ad hoc* transnational union co-operation is not unknown (Cook and Katz, 1994; Bercusson, 1997; Trubek *et al.*, 1999), none of the respondents reported having personally encountered much evidence of it and none foresaw the likelihood of it becoming a common occurrence, even in Europe. On the other hand, as is well known, transnational corporations have been successfully attacked by social movements (including unions) for specific abuses such as child labour, unsafe working conditions and other exploitative labour practices. Campaigns by these movements have led to consumer boycotts, political criticism and threats to ban goods produced in substandard conditions from the market-place. Moreover, social movements and NGOs—and their lawyers—have been actively promoting the adoption of global labour standards. Apart from occasional tactical victories, however, they do not have much so far to show for their efforts.

True, UN covenants and ILO conventions protecting labour rights are binding in international law, but only upon states which have ratified them,[6] not upon employers. True, there have been proposals to strengthen international protection for workers by conditioning participation in trade regimes upon compliance with labour rights, but these have so far not succeeded. True, international bodies—the ILO, the EU, the OECD—have promulgated non-binding codes of conduct by which transnational corporations might commit themselves to observe basic labour rights such as freedom of association and the right to a living wage and safe working conditions, but these establish no enforcement procedures. True, significant numbers of transnationals and their sectoral

---

[6] Only Mexico has ratified most ILO conventions and gives them direct domestic effect; all the other countries require implementing legislation—a particular problem in Canada where the federal government makes and ratifies most treaties, while the provinces have primary jurisdiction in labour matters; the USA has not ratified most of the important conventions while the UK has actually resigned from several it had previously ratified.

organisations have recently adopted voluntary codes of labour standards (Rubin, 1995; Compa and Hinchcliffe-Darricarère, 1995; OECD, 1998), but these do not yet appear to influence the day-to-day formulation and administration of human resources or industrial relations policies, and perhaps they never will (Arthurs 2001).

Thus, it seems likely that the testimony of lawyers who work on behalf of workers to limit the power of transnationals would not differ much from that of my management respondents: they too would acknowledge that no *lex laboris* is likely to emerge in the near future. Indeed, the few labour side lawyers I talked to said as much.

Conclusion

To sum up, to the extent that transnational regimes of labour law have developed, transnational corporations rather than their lawyers appear to be their primary architects. The role of lawyers, at most, is to help to create favourable conditions for these regimes by mediating between the employment practices and policies of their foreign-based, transnational clients, and the national legal systems in which they function. As we will see next, however, "mediating" does not simply mean modifying the behaviour of the client; it has definite consequences for law and lawyers.

THE EFFECTS OF GLOBALISATION ON NATIONAL LABOUR LAW

Given that 40 experienced labour lawyers could detect nothing resembling a distinctive transnational legal culture of employment relations, I asked respondents whether globalisation was affecting national labour law in some way. Their answers are revealing.

The Dominant Influence on Labour Law of National Politics, Industrial Relations and Legal Culture

Most respondents who commented on the point stressed that local labour law was profoundly influenced by national cultural, social and political history—Mrs. Thatcher's assault on union power in the United Kingdom, the revolutionary and republican tradition in Mexico and France, the post-war experience of communal and confessional solidarity in Holland and Belgium. This point seemed to have had least salience in Canada which, of course, adopted US-style labour legislation in the 1940s, and has experienced a pervasive American corporate presence for a century or more (Arthurs, 1996b). Canadian respondents did, however, cling to the national myth that Canada is (for now, at least) a kinder and gentler society than the neighbouring hegemon.

Many respondents also believed that special characteristics of their national legal tradition presented a formidable obstacle to the importation of foreign or transnational labour law or procedures citing, for example, the discursive nature of Anglo-American legal drafting, the comprehensive and highly prescriptive nature of the French Civil Code and labour codes, and the constitutionalisation of labour rights in Mexico. Furthermore, the tacit assumptions of each industrial relations system were perceived as virtually precluding penetration by outside influences. Thus, Mexican lawyers clearly help their clients by steering them through the channels connecting the state, the governing party and the PRI unions; Canadian lawyers know they have to deal with the realities of branch plant management; French lawyers are sensitive to the risk of social and political turmoil if established worker rights are significantly impaired; and Dutch lawyers are sensitive to the need for their small country to maintain a social consensus in order to adjust successfully to an inevitable process of regional and global economic integration. For all of these reasons, most respondents—except for Canadians—tended to claim there had not been, nor would there ever likely be, successful importation into their countries of the labour law arrangements and employment practices which transnational corporations had developed in their home countries. However, despite the belief of most respondents in the inviolability of their national labour systems, those systems are clearly changing

Globalisation and the Legal Culture of Industrial Relations

Significant legal changes had occurred, or were in process, in the industrial relations systems of almost all countries where interviews were conducted. The American labour movement and collective bargaining system had been in decline over a lengthy period, with at best scant prospects for a near-term recovery (Hacker, 1999). The UK had just gone through a prolonged period of Conservative rule during which the power of trade unions was effectively destroyed, and the labour market was radically deregulated (Hepple, 1995). In Holland, several long-established labour market institutions were being overhauled or abandoned as the result of changes in employer practice, trade union policies, or the interpretation of state law by public officials (Van Peijpe, 1998). In Mexico, several projects of fundamental labour law reform seemed to be moving forward, in tandem with the general restructuring of the state and its governing party, the PRI; if implemented, these reforms would end the monopoly of the official trade union movement, encourage the growth and militancy of the new, independent unions, and normalise a system of arm's length labour-management relations (Bierma, 1998; Payne, 1998). In France, a proposed restructuring of labour market institutions was generating considerable controversy and unrest at the time the interviews were conducted. These reforms were not in fact implemented, and with the election of the Jospin government, the agenda changed; however, it remains to be seen whether, and to what extent, France will ultimately deregulate its labour market (EIRO, 1997, 1998). Finally, in Canada important legislative and administrative changes in labour law had been introduced in several provinces to create a more "business friendly" environment by deregulating the labour market and weakening the statutory regime of collective bargaining, much as has happened in the United States (Burkett, 1998).

Thus, it is clear that globalisation—with technology and neo-liberalism—actually *is* reshaping national labour law. Different national systems are responding with different degrees of urgency and through different modalities, but all seem to be moving generally in the direction of deregulated labour markets, disempowered unions, insecure job tenure and flexible, non-standard terms of employment. As one respondent stated, "the internationalization of problems has to end with the internationalization of law". But while the decline of workers' legal rights under neo-liberalism operates in the domain of state law, the enhanced ability of employers to dictate new workplace norms is located primarily in the domain of private ordering. The shift in corporate practice and procedure, in corporate treatment of employees and unions, reflects a shift in the balance of power between employers and workers which has been brought about not so much by new laws as by new technologies, delivery systems, management structures and, of course, globalisation.

Lawyers are seldom directly involved. Unlike the law of global business transactions, the new workplace norms are not primarily the result of changes in international standards or national labour law, or even in the professional *praxis* of employment contracts or labour negotiations. Nor can they be detected through close observation of the legal field as it is conventionally understood. In fact, legal forms and practices may remain unchanged even as the reality of conditions in the workplace is transformed. The new normative reality of employment in the global economy may originate in explicit human resource policies promulgated by TNCs and their subsidiaries; more commonly, it is merely experienced by workers as the after-shock of corporate pricing and production strategies designed to cut costs and boost flexibility and efficiency. Of course, states have some relationship to these corporate policies and strategies: they may impose discipline on workers who resist them, allow the machinery of labour market regulation to run down and rust, or even make futile efforts to cajole or threaten employers intent on exercising their power abusively. But in general neither state labour law nor the activity of labour lawyers can be seen as major factors in the new norms of employment relations, the new laws of work, which have been emerging within global enterprises.

THE EFFECT OF GLOBALISATION ON LABOUR LAWYERS

This is not to suggest that labour lawyers themselves remained unaffected by globalisation. In two crucial respects, at least, globalisation is an important factor in their professional lives.

The Moral Economy of Normative Mediation

As suggested earlier, what labour lawyers do most crucially is to mediate amongst global and local economic interests, between the conflicting interests of management and labour, between their clients' economic interests and state law, between state law and non-state normative systems. In performing these mediative functions, especially between different legal regimes, labour lawyers—as one respondent put it—sometimes perform like "fleas and wasps". They contribute to the cross-pollination of normative systems, using their exposure to the human resources policies and practices of domestic and foreign corporate clients to transmit innovations and best practices from one to another, thus helping to disseminate new workplace regimes as they evolve under pressure of the global economy. Similarly, lawyers—especially those who have worked or studied abroad—can in principle mediate amongst divergent state systems. They may use their knowledge of several systems to facilitate harmonisation or convergence of state law within trade blocs, or to promote the adoption of explicit transnational norms under the auspices of the ILO, the EU, the NAALC or some other agency. Several respondents—not all with the most obvious credentials—reported participating in such activities.

However, another aspect of "mediation" is more problematic. Both in Europe and in North America, "mediation" sometimes takes the form of active lobbying to align domestic law with the interests of transnationals, by reducing barriers to globalisation and by promoting flexibilisation and the reduction of statutory protections and benefits. In effect, governments are persuaded to repeal or amend legislation, or change administrative practice, or otherwise to favour employer over employee interests. Some respondents—in Mexico and Canada, for example—justified such initiatives as part of a long-delayed and much-needed effort to liberalise the local economy and deregulate the labour market—ultimately, they contended, for the good of all, including workers. However, Canadian and Mexican workers seem unlikely to be grateful for this particular form of mediation.

Still, the picture is complex. Some respondents who acted exclusively or primarily for employers, claimed to favour equitable regimes of state law and corporate practice which respect workers' interests as well those of their clients. Thus, some English respondents spoke critically of the anti-union excesses of the Thatcher era and looked forward to a rebalancing of state labour law; some respondents in Belgium, Holland and France indicated that despite their professional contribution to globalisation and neo-liberal policies, they remained personally committed to existing social democratic or social market policies; and several North American respondents expressed their commitment to regimes which ensured decent treatment of workers, on both principled and practical grounds.

Thus, as lawyers mediate between corporate, worker and state interests, they sometimes experience contradictions amongst their personal values, their economic interests and their professional obligations. For example, while none of the Mexican respondents acknowledged being involved in such practices themselves, all reported that "disreputable" labour lawyers arrange for spurious "protection agreements" to be signed between transnationals and compliant unions, to the prejudice of workers. Likewise, several Canadian lawyers reported that they had worked just within the letter, if not the spirit, of local law to achieve a "union-free environment" for transnational clients, and that they knew of other lawyers who were not quite so fastidious.

What might be called the moral economy of normative mediation obviously troubled many, if not most, respondents. They often stressed that they would not act for clients who wanted them to do things which violated the law or offended their professional or personal ethics. Indeed, several said that they had declined to act for clients who refused to accept their advice to comply with local law and industrial relations norms, and that they had invited obdurate clients to secure an opinion from another law firm confirming that a particular legal interpretation was the correct one. Two or three reported, with evident satisfaction, that transnational clients who had ignored their advice had later experienced labour conflict and legal difficulties. Respondents of this persuasion were, it seems, willing even at some risk to themselves to try to persuade foreign transnational clients to adjust their corporate practices to local state policies, rather than the reverse.

Labour Lawyers in the Political Economy of the Legal Profession

Relative to legal specialists dealing with other aspects of transnational business law, labour lawyers seem to occupy a peripheral role within the profession. That role, however, seems to vary from country to country.

Several US respondents suggested that the large, transnational Wall St. law firms—the putative architects of global legal regimes—have largely ceased to practise traditional labour law. In part the issue is demand: as union membership and power have dwindled in the past 20–30 years, fewer clients need the services of lawyers specialising in collective bargaining. In part it is supply: labour law practice cannot generate revenues comparable to other specialties or sufficient to pay the high salaries and overheads of Wall St. firms. Whatever the explanation, it seems that even transnational clients are being served more cheaply and expertly in the United States by niche firms of labour law specialists, by "regional" counsel located near their production facilities and especially by in-house legal staff.

On the other hand, globalisation and other economic changes have generated lucrative new practice opportunities in what is now called employment law: entertainment and sports law; executive contracts, group pension and insurance contracts; and high profile civil and criminal litigation resulting from allegations of discrimination and harassment. These new fields of practice certainly affect actors in the global economy, especially privileged actors, but it is by no means clear that they involve a new transnational legal culture. On the contrary, for Wall St. firms at least, they generally involve the application of US law either to US-based corporations or to foreign corporations operating in the USA. Such issues raise some problems of extraterritoriality—if, for example, a US corporation commits discrimination abroad (Stone, 1995; Starr, 1996)—but otherwise do not seem to be producing anything resembling a global regime of law.[7]

There are some exceptions to this picture. As mentioned earlier, at least one large US-based global law firm in fact offers labour law advice to TNCs through most of its domestic and foreign offices. These offices attempt to serve clients in multiple locations, facilitate firm-wide consultation and co-operation on clients' labour problems, and provide global strategic and legal advice on labour and employment law issues. But even lawyers in this firm, in several jurisdictions, insisted on the quintessentially local character of their labour law practice. For European firms, the picture is somewhat different, perhaps because the public policy environment is different. Several large law firms, cross-border networks of mid-sized firms, and the legal departments of major accounting/consulting firms seem to pursue a somewhat more ambitious approach to transnational labour law issues, although they too claimed to be advising essentially on local law, except for the few important labour issues which have been addressed by EU directives.[8] In none of these cases, however, could it be said that labour law was a major focus of the firm's work.

Canada and Mexico—both recipients of considerable foreign direct investment, both hosts to many branch plants—also provide interesting insights into the role of labour law practice in the global economy. The Canadian case is rather closer to the European. Most large law firms do have labour departments, although several sizeable specialist labour law practices have also developed. As in Europe, the Canadian respondents generally provide advice on local law to local management, although some report an increasing incidence of direct involvement with US-based executives and, as noted, increasing client pressures to conform to US law and practice. The Mexican case is somewhat unusual in that several of the leading labour law practices are small firms built around two generations of family members. While some of the larger law firms also have labour law departments, these family firms do a considerable amount of labour

---

[7] A possible exception relates to attempts to create transnational standardised (or at least comparable) compensation packages for the peripatetic executive and professional cadres of transnational firms. Anecdotal evidence provided during the interviews suggests that this issue is being addressed by means of contractual strategies, with dispute resolution dealt with according to "choice of law" provisions, rather than by means of arbitration, as in the case of other international contracts.

[8] See e.g., Council Directive 75/129/EEC (collective redundancies); Council Directive 77/187/EEC (employee rights in the event of transfers of undertakings or businesses); Council Directives 79/7/EEC, 86/378/EEC 86/613/EEC (equal treatment of women and men); Council Directive 94/45/EC (European Works Councils).

law on behalf of TNCs which engage them directly, or are referred by Mexican corporate law firms which do not practise labour law. Respondents emphasised the relational character of labour law practice in Mexico, which includes making connections for foreign clients with "responsible" trade unions and helping them navigate the unique institutions of the Mexican labour law system. Conceivably, this relational dimension of practice explains the tendency to practice labour law in small family firms.

By and large, then, we can say that labour law practice—even on behalf of transnational corporations—does not entail the prestige, rewards and potential influence associated with transnational practice in fields such as insolvency, intellectual property, mergers and acquisitions or contract. Perhaps this marginal position in the political economy of the profession is an artifact of labour law's association with local, rather than transnational, law practice and institutions; perhaps it is simply a projection of the low esteem in which this field of practice is held domestically (Dezalay, 1986; Bourdieu, 1987); perhaps it is a recognition of the tendency of corporations to manage their own labour law problems without the help of the great Cravathist law firms. Whatever the explanation, the marginal role of labour law practice tends to reinforce the impression that labour lawyers are not in fact engaged in the project of constructing a new regime of transnational labour law, a new *lex laboris*.

CONCLUSION

There is a good case for arguing that economic globalisation—especially in its local manifestations—is reinforced by what I have elsewhere described as "globalisation of the mind" (Arthurs, 1997b), the embrace by strategic, knowledge-based elites in business, government, the professions, academe, and the media of a new set of values, processes, institutions and practices, of a new paradigm of governance. To this extent, I align myself with scholars who stress that the social field of law is constituted through the agency of professional elites, especially lawyers. But my study of labour lawyers moves me to propose a significant *caveat*: lawyers are not the primary actors and they do not act autonomously. Lawyers, rather, derive their influence from, and align their objectives with, the dominant forces in the society, economy and polity that they inhabit. For current purposes, those forces are epitomised by transnational corporations, the principal proponents and beneficiaries of globalisation, which neither need law nor are constrained by law in their dealings with workers. Thus, as McBarnet suggests, in this context at least, we see lawyers not so much using law as a tool to fundamentally alter social relations as working upon the malleable material of law to make it conform to the new realities of the global economy.

REFERENCES

Arthurs, Harry (1985), "The Law of the Shop: The Debate over Industrial Pluralism", *Current Legal Problems* 38; 83–116.
—— (1996a), "Lawyering in Canada in the 21ˢᵗ Century", *Windsor Yearbook of Access to Justice* 15; 202–25.
—— (1996b), "Labour Law without the State?", *University of Toronto Law Journal* 46; 1–45.
—— (1997a), "Labour Law and Industrial Relations in the Global Economy", *Industrial Law Journal* 18; 571–87.
—— (1997b), "Globalization of the Mind: Canadian Elites and the Restructuring of Legal Fields", *Canadian Journal of Law and Society* 12; 219–46.
—— (1997c), "Mechanical Arts and Merchandise: Canadian Public Administration in the New Economy", *McGill Law Journal* 42; 29–61.
—— (1998a), "The Political Economy of Canadian Legal Education", *Journal of Law and Society* 25; 14–32.
—— (1998b), "A Collective Labour Law for the Global Economy?" in C. Engles and M. Weiss (eds.), *Labor Law and Industrial Relations at the Turn of the Century: Liber Amicorum in Honour of Roger Blanpain* (The Hague; London; Boston: Kluwer).
—— (1998c), "Landscape and Memory: Labour Law, Legal Pluralism and Globalization" in T. Wilthagen (ed.), *Advancing Theory in Labour Law in a Global Context* (Amsterdam: North Holland Press).
—— (1999), "A Global Code of Ethics for the Transnational Legal Field?", *Legal Ethics* 2; 21–31.
—— (2000). "The Hollowing Out of Corporate Canada" in J. Jenson and B. de Sousa Santos (eds.), *Globalizing Institutions: Case Studies in Social Regulation and Innovation* (Aldershot: Ashgate Publishing).
—— (2001). "Private Ordering and Workers' Rights in the Global Economy: Corporate Codes of Conduct as a Regime of Workplace Regulation" in J. Conaghan, K. Klare and M. Fischl (eds.), *Transformative Labor Law in the Era of Global-ization*.
Arthurs, Harry, and Kreklewich, Robert (1996), "Law, Legal Institutions, and the Legal Profession in the New Economy", *Osgoode Hall Law Journal* 34; 1–60.
Baker and Mackenzie (1998), "New Developments in Global Equity Compensation", *The Global Employer* 3 (2); 30.
Baldry, Christopher (1994), "Convergence in Europe—A Matter of Perspective?", *Industrial Relations Journal* 25 (2); 96–109.
Barenberg, Mark (1993) "The Political Economy of the Wagner Act: Power, Symbol, and Workplace Cooperation", *Harvard Law Review* 106; 1379–1496.
Bartlett, Christopher, and Ghosal, Sumantra (1998), *Managing Across Borders* (Boston, Mass.: Harvard Business School Press).
Belley, Jean-Guy (1996), *Soluble Law: Québecois Contributions to the Study of Internormativity* (French version published as *Le Droit Soluble.*) (Paris: n.p.).
Bendiner, Burton (1987), *International Labor Affairs—The World Trade Unions and the Multinational Companies* (Oxford: Clarendon Press).
Bennett, Colin (1991), "How States Utilize Foreign Evidence", *Journal of Public Policy* 11; 31–53.

Bercusson, Brian (1995), "The Conceptualization of European Labour Law", *Industrial Law Journal* 24 (1); 3–18.

—— (1997), "Globalizing Labour Law: Transnational Private Regulation and Countervailing Actors in European Labour Law" in G. Teubner (ed.), *Global Law Without a State* (Gateshead).

Bierma, Paige (1998), "Work in Progress", *Business Mexico* 8 (2); 8–12.

Bourdieu, Pierre (1987), "The Force of Law: Toward a Sociology of the Juridical Field", *Hastings Law Journal* 38; 805–53.

Boyer, Robert (1995), "The Future of Unions: Is the Anglo–Saxon Model a Fatality, or Will Contrasting National Trajectories Persist?", *British Journal of Industrial Relations* 33 (4); 545–56.

Burkett, Kevin (1998), "The Politicization of the Ontario Labour Relations Framework in the 1990s", *Canadian Labor and Employment Law Journal* 6; 161–84.

Coller, Xavier, and Marginson, Paul (1998), "Transnational Management Influence Over Changing Employment Practice: A Case From the Food Industry", *Industrial Relations Journal* 29 (1); 4–17.

Compa, Lance, and Hinchcliffe–Darricarrère, Tashia (1995), "Enforcing International Labor Rights through Corporate Codes of Conduct", *Columbia Journal of Transnational Law* 33 (3); 663–89.

Cook, Maria Lorena (1994), "Regional Integration and Transnational Labor Strategies Under NAFTA" in M. Cook and H. Katz (eds.), *Regional Integration and Industrial Relations in North America* (Ithaca, NY: ILR Press).

—— and Katz, Harry (eds) (1994), *Regional Integration and Industrial Relations in North America* (Ithaca, NY: ILR Press).

Cox, Robert (1977), "Labour and Hegemony", *International Organization* 31 (3); 385–424.

Dezalay, Yves (1986), "From Mediation to Pure Law: Practice and Scholarly Representation within the Legal Sphere", *International Journal of the Sociology of Law* 14; 89–107.

Dezalay, Yves, and Garth, Bryant (1996), *Dealing in Virtue: International Commercial Arbitration and the Construction of a Transnational Legal Order* (Chicago, Ill.: University of Chicago Press).

—— and Sugarman, David (eds.) (1995), *Profession Competition and Professional Power: Lawyers, Accountants and the Social Construction of Markets* (London; New York: Routledge).

Dolzer, Rudolf (1998), "Global Environmental Issues: The Genuine Area of Globalization", *Journal of Transnational Law and Policy* 7; 157–79.

Drache, Daniel (1994), "Lean Production in Japanese Auto Transplants in Canada", *Canadian Business Economics* 2 (3); 45–59.

EIRO (1997), "Annual Review for France", <www.eiro.eurofound.ie/1997/12/features/FR9712198F.html>.

—— (1998), *Annual Review for France*, <www.eiro.eurofound.ie/1998/12/features/FR9812152F.html>.

Enderwick, Peter (1984), "The Labour Utilization Practices of Multinationals and Obstacles to Multinational Collective Bargaining", *Journal of Industrial Relations* 26; 345–64.

Ferner, Anthony (1994), "Multinational Companies and Human Resource Management: An Overview of Research Issues", *Human Resource Management Journal* 4 (1); 79–102.

Ferner, Anthony (1997), "Country of Origin Effects and HRM in Multinational Companies", *Human Resource Management Journal* 7 (1); 19–37.

Flood, John (1996), "Mega-lawyering in the Global Order—The Cultural, Social and Economic Transformation of Global Legal Practice", *International Journal of the Legal Profession* 3; 169–214.

Florkowski, Gary, and Nath, Raghu (1993), "MNC Responses to the Legal Environment of International Human Resource Management", *International Journal of Human Resource Management* 4 (2); 305–24.

Freeman, Richard (1995), "The Future of Unions in Decentralized Collective Bargaining Systems; US and UK Unionism in an Era of Crisis", *British Journal of Industrial Relations* 33 (4); 519–36.

Frenkel, Stephen (1994), "Patterns of Workplace Relations in the Global Corporation: Toward Convergence?" in K. Belanger, P. Edwards and L. Haiven (eds.), *Workplace Industrial Relations and the Global Challenge* (Ithaca, NY: ILR Press).

—— and Royal, Carol (1997), "Globalization and Employment Relations", *Research in the Sociology of Work* 6; 3–41.

—— and —— (1998), "Corporate–Subsidiary Relations, Local Contexts and Workplace Change in Global Corporations", *Relations Industrielles-Industrial Relations* 53 (1); 154–82.

Friedman, Lawrence (1994), "Is There a Modern Legal Culture?", *Ratio Juris* 7 (2); 117–31.

Garth, Bryant (1985), "Transnational Legal Practice and Professional Ideology", *Michigan Yearbook of International Legal Studies* 7; 3–21.

Gessner, Volkmar (1994), "Global Interaction and Legal Cultures", *Ratio Juris* 7 (2); 132–45.

Ghoshal, Sumantra, and Bartlett, Christopher (1990), "The Multinational Corporation as an Interorganizational Network", *Academy of Management Review* 15 (4); 603–25.

Gillies, James, and Morra, Daniela (1996), "Stakeholders and Shareholders in a Global World", *Policy Options* 17 (10); 32–5.

Griffiths, John (1986), "What is Legal Pluralism?", *Journal of Legal Pluralism* 24; 1–55.

Guery, Gabriel (1992), "European Collective Bargaining and the Maastricht Treaty", *International Labor Review* 131 (4–5); 581–99.

Hacker, Andrew (1999), "Who's Sticking to the Union? Review of S. Aronowitz From the Ashes of the Old: American Labor and America's Future", *New York Review of Books* 46 (3); 45.

Hepple, Bob (1995), "The Future of Labour Law", *Industrial Law Journal* 24 (4); 303–22.

Hoberg, George (1991), "Sleeping with the Elephant: the American Influence on Canadian Environmental Legislation", *Journal of Public Policy* 11; 107–31.

Hoffman, Richard (1994), "Generic Strategies for Subsidiaries of Multinational Corporations", *Journal of Management Studies* 6 (1); 69–87.

Horton, Jennifer (1993), "Pharmaceuticals, Patents and Bill C–91: The Historical Perspective", *Canadian Intellectual Property Review* 10; 145–58.

Irons, Peter (1982), *The New Deal Lawyers* (Princeton, NJ: Princeton University Press).

Jackson, Terrance (1993), *Organizational Behaviour in International Management* (Oxford: Butterworth, Heineman).

Kahn–Freund, Otto (1976), *Selected Writings* (London: Stevens).

Keith, Kenneth (1997), "Sovereignty: A Legal Perspective" in G. A. Wood and L. S. Leland (eds.), *States and Sovereignty: Is the State in Retreat?* (Dunedin: University of Otago Press).

Klare, Karl (1978), "Judicial Deradicalization of the Wagner Act and the Origins of Modern Legal Consciousness 1937–1941", *Minnesota Law Review* 62; 265–339.

Kriger, Mark, and Rich, Patrick (1987), "Strategic Governance: How and Why MNCs are Using Boards of Directors in Foreign Subsidiaries", *Columbia Journal of International Business* 22 (4); 39–46.

Kustin, Richard, and Jones, Robert (1995), "The Influence of Corporate Headquarters on Leadership Styles in Japanese and US Subsidiaries", *Leadership and Organization Development Journal* 16 (5); 11–15.

Lorenz, Edward (1992), "Trust in the Flexible Firm: International Comparisons", *Industrial Relations* 31 (3); 455–72.

Lucio, Miguel Martinez, and Weston, Syd (1994), "New Management Practices in a Multinational Corporation: The Restructuring of Worker Representation and Rights?", *Industrial Relations Journal* 25 (2); 110–21.

McBarnet, Doreen (1984), "Law and Capital: The Role of Legal Form and Legal Actors", *International Journal of Sociology of Law* 12; 231–38.

McGuiness, Michael (1994), "The Protection of Labor Rights in North America: a Commentary on the North American Agreement on Labor Cooperation", *Stanford Journal of International Law* 30; 579–96.

Merry, Sally (1988), "Legal Pluralism", *Law and Society Review* 22; 869–96.

—— (1997), "Global Human Rights and Local Social Movements in a Legally Plural World", *Canadian Journal of Law and Society* 12; 247–71.

Milkman, Ruth (1991), *Japan's California Factories: Labor Relations and Economic Globalization* (Los Angeles, Cal.: Institute of Industrial Relations, University of California).

Morrison, Allen, Ricks, David, and Roth, Kendall (1991), "Globalization versus Regionalization: Which Way for the Multinational?", *Organizational Dynamics* 19; 17–30.

Muchlinski, Peter (1997), "Global Bukowina Examined: Viewing the Multinational Enterprise as a Transnational Law-making Community" in G. Teubner (ed.), *Global Law Without a State* (Gateshead).

Nielsen, Laura–Beth (1999), "Paying Workers or Paying Lawyers: Employee Termination Practices in the United States and Canada", *Law and Policy* 21 (3); 247–82.

OECD (1998), *Corporate Codes of Conduct—An Inventory, Report of the Working Party of the Trade Committee*, TD/TC/WP(98)74 (Paris: OECD).

Ogliati, Vittorio (1995), "Process and Policy of Legal Professionalization in Europe: The Deconstruction of a Normative Order" in Y. Dezalay and D. Sugarman (eds.), *Profession Competition and Professional Power: Lawyers, Accountants and the Social Construction of Markets* (London; New York: Routledge).

Ojeda–Aviles, Antonio (1993), "European Collective Bargaining: A Triumph of the Will?", *International Journal of Comparative Labor Law and Industrial Relations* 9 (4); 279–96.

Pauly, Louis, and Reich, Simon (1997), "National Structures and Multinational Corporate Behaviour: Enduring Differences in the Age of Globalization", *International Organization* 51; 1–30.

Payne, Douglas (1998), "Mexican Labor: Cracks in the Monolith", *Dissent* 45 (1); 23–8.

Plett, Konstanze, and Meschievitz, Catherine (eds.) (1991), *Beyond Disputing: Exploring Legal Culture in Five European Countries* (Baden-Baden: Nomos Verlagsgesellschaft).

Robinson, Ian (1994), "NAFTA, Social Unionism and Labour Movement Power in Canada and the United States", *Relations Industrielles-Industrial Relations* 49; 657–94.

Rotstein, Abraham (1993), "Intellectual Property and the Canada–US Free Trade Agreements: The Case of Pharmaceuticals", *Intellectual Property Journal* 8; 121–37.

Rubin, Seymour (1995), "Transnational Corporations and International Codes of Conduct: A Study of the Relationship Between International Legal Cooperation and Economic Development", *American University Journal of International Law and Policy* 10 (4); 1275–89.

Salter, Liora (1988), *Mandated Science: Science and Scientists in the Making of Standards* (Boston, Mass.: Kluwer Academic).

—— (1993), "The Housework of Capitalism: Standardization in the Communications and Information Technology Sectors", *International Journal of Political Economy* 23; 105–31.

Santos, Boaventura de Sousa (1995), *Towards a New Common Sense: Law, Science and Politics in the Paradigmatic Transition* (New York: Routledge).

Sassen, Saskia (1994), *Cities in a World Economy* (Cal.: Pine Forge Press).

—— (1998), *Globalization and its Discontents* (New York: New Press).

Schneiderman, David (1996), "NAFTA's Takings Rule: American Constitutionalism Comes to Canada", *University of Toronto Law Journal* 46; 499–537.

Sciarra, Silvana (1995), "Social Values and the Multiple Sources of European Labour Law", *European Law Journal* 1; 60–83.

—— (1998), "How Global is Labour Law? The Perspective of Social Rights in the European Union" in T. Wilthagen (ed.), *Advancing Theory in Labour Law in a Global Context* (Amsterdam: North Holland Press).

Sölvell, Orjan, and Zander, Ivo (1995), "Organization of the Dynamic Multinational Enterprise.", *International Studies of Management and Organization* 25; 17–38.

Starr, Michael (1996), "Who's the Boss? The Globalization of US Employment Law", *Business Lawyer* 51; 635–52.

Stone, Katherine van Wezel (1981), "The Post-War Paradigm in American Labor Law", *Yale Law Journal* 90; 1509–80.

—— (1995), "Labor and the Global Economy: Four Approaches to Transnational Labor Regulation", *Michigan Journal of International Law* 16 (4); 987–1028.

Streeck, Wolfgang (1994), *Social Institutions and Economic Performance: Studies of Industrial Relations in Advanced Capitalist Economies* (London: Sage Publications).

—— (1995), "Neo-Voluntarism: A New European Social Policy Regime", *European Law Journal* 1; 31–59.

Teague, Paul (1993), "Between Convergence and Divergence: Possibilities for European Community System of Labor Market Regulation", *International Labor Review* 132 (3); 391–407.

Teubner, Gunther (1994), "Company Interest—the Public Interest of the Enterprise 'in Itself'" in R. Rogowski and T. Wilthagen (eds.), *Reflexive Labor Law—Studies in Industrial Relations and Employment Regulation* (Boston, Mass.: Kluwer).

—— (ed.) (1997), *Global Law Without a State* (Aldershot: Dartmouth Publishing Co.).

Trompenaars, Frederik (1992), *Riding the Waves of Culture* (London: Nicholas Brealey).

Trubek, David, *et al.* (1994), "Global Restructuring and the Law: Studies of the Internationalization of Legal Fields and the Creation of Transnational Areas", *Case Western Reserve Journal of International Law* 44 (2); 407–98.

—— (1999), "Transnational Regimes and Advocacy: A Cure for Globalization", Working Paper Series on Political Economy of Legal Change 4 (Madison, Wisc.: Global Studies Program, International Institute, University of Wisconsin).

Van Peijpe, Taco (1998), "Employment Protection Under Strain (Sweden, Denmark, The Netherlands)", *Bulletin of Comparative Labor Relations* 33; 125–49.

von Maydell, Bernd (1993), "The Impact of the EEC on Labor Law", *Chicago–Kent Law Review* 68; 1401–20.

Wedderburn, Kenneth William (1997), "Consultation and Collective Bargaining in Europe: Success or Ideology?", *Industrial Law Journal* 26; 1–34.

Weiler, Paul (1990), *Governing the Workplace* (Cambridge, Mass.: Harvard University Press).

10

Oil Lawyers and the Globalisation of the Venezuelan Oil Industry

ROGELIO PÉREZ PERDOMO*

Abstract

Petróleos de Venezuela SA (PDVSA), the Venezuelan state oil monopoly, became a multinational in the 1980s and the leading force in the opening of national oil business to foreign enterprises in the 1990s. This article analyses the type of law activities that regulated these changes with special emphasis on the role of PDVSA's lawyers. The research approach is qualitative. The main research instruments were documentation and in-depth interviews of lawyers that qualified as the core group: PDVSA's internal lawyers. Other lawyers and professionals related to the oil business were interviewed to complete the picture.

O IL IS A very important product for Venezuela. The country is among the main exporters and its reserves are among the largest worldwide. Most Venezuelans are aware of the decisiveness of oil for Venezuelan economy. Prices are reported on the front pages of the leading newspapers and most people know the importance of rising or declining prices for the national economy.

Many Venezuelan scholars and writers have put oil in the centre of their thinking and research. There are abundant writings on oil from different perspectives (Baptista and Mommer, 1987; Pérez Schael, 1993). Oil politics and policies have generated important books (Betancourt, 1967; Urbaneja, 1991). There are novels and stories about life in the oil fields. We even have a sophisticated book on the effect of the oil boom of 1974–5 on cities not related at all to the oil business (Briceño León, 1990). Several foreign scholars interested in Venezuela have put oil at the top of their research (McBeth, 1983; Karl, 1997).

ISEA, Caracas. First, I would like to thank the lawyers that gave me interviews but whose anonymity I promised to preserve. Elena Granell and C. Baena, my colleagues in IESA, oriented me on the oil business and on PDVSA corporate culture. Y. Dezalay, Volkmar Gessner, M. Shapiro and Ibrahim Shihata made very valuable comments and suggestions on a first, uncompleted draft. N. Lejter made my english comprehensible and obliged me to clarify my thinking. I am most grateful to them all. I am particularly grateful to J. H. Merryman for his careful reading and comments.

Surprisingly enough, legal literature on oil is relatively poor and nothing has been written on oil lawyers, even if some of them have been quite important for the legal and the political systems.

We should point out the very special place of PDVSA in the political system. Since the 1980s, Venezuela has been living in difficult times. Generally, the state and the political system have been demonised. The state central apparatus as well as many state enterprises are considered inefficient and corrupt. Once considered one of the most prosperous and stable democracies in Latin America, Venezuela has become unstable and a theatre for very frequent corruption scandals. Statist policies followed in the 1960s and 1970s are now considered mistaken and held responsible for the increasing economic difficulties and poverty. Other people are against the market-oriented policies but criticise corruption in the state and state enterprises. In this panorama, PDVSA, the most important state enterprise, is treated as the great exception. It is considered highly efficient and no important corruption scandal has tarnished its image.

This chapter is on PDVSA's lawyers, but before talking about them we will describe briefly the nature of the Venezuelan oil business and the meaning of its globalisation.

THE OIL BUSINESS IN VENEZUELA

Venezuela has a rather long history dealing with oil. Oil was known by the Indians and used by the Spanish conquerors, but its central role dates back to the early twentieth century. By 1926, oil became the country's most important single export, and by mid-century Venezuela was the biggest oil exporter in the world. For the first and longest part of this history, the oil business was in the hands of powerful multinationals, especially Shell and Exxon. Historians have described the increasing control of the business by the national government and Venezuelan managers (McBeth, 1983; Machado de Acedo, 1990; Espinasa, 1996). By the end of the period, in 1975, Venezuelan managers controlled most activities of the oil industry and the multinational subsidiaries (Quiroz Corradi, 1996). The state heavily increased taxes and tightly controlled the multinationals' oil activities.

In 1960 the Venezuelan government announced a new oil policy: no more contracts with multinationals (*concesiones*), the creation of the Corporación Venezolana del Petróleo (or state oil enterprise) and creation of OPEC, jointly with the main Arab producers. In 1975, Venezuela nationalised all oil activities: exploration, production and commercialisation (*Ley que Reserva al Estado la Industria y el Comercio de los Hidrocarburos*, 08–20–75) and created Petróleos de Venezuela, SA (PDVSA), the national holding for all oil activities.

The nationalisation of oil business was not a traumatic process. As it was announced long in advance and negotiated with the multinationals, it came as no surprise. Well-trained people from the Venezuelan subsidiaries were kept in prominent roles in new enterprises that looked very much like the old ones. Shell-Venezuela became Maraven and Creole (Exxon) became Lagoven. All other enterprises, including Venezuelan public and private ones, were finally consolidated in Corpoven. Research and development and educational facilities were put together in new institutions, and the structure was rationalised. The important fact for this chapter is that the oil business was kept quite separate from politics and the state and professional careers in the oil business were respected.

Very soon, nationalist oil policies showed their limits. Venezuela was an important exporter forced to compete against the powerful transnational oil companies (the Seven Sisters). The country had to invest heavily in research and development and the acquisition of refineries and distribution facilities in the world. This policy started in the early 1980s and was called the *internacionalización*. PDVSA became a transnational itself. Today, PDVSA owns Citgo and 50 per cent of Unoven (in association with Unocal) in the United States. In Europe, PDVSA owns 50 per cent of Ruhr Öl (in association with the German Veba Öl) and 50 per cent of Nynäs (in association with the Finnish Neste Oy). Map 10.1 shows the international system of PDVSA's refineries in the world. Furthermore, commercial operations and facilities for the business are still broader. PDVSA sells products worldwide.

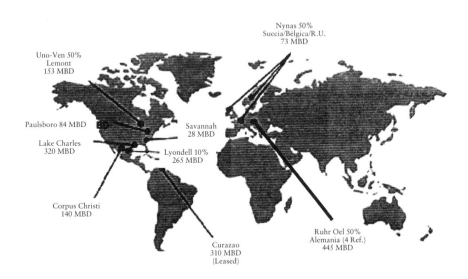

Map 10.1 PDVSA's international system of refineries

NOTE: MBD= Daily capacity of refination in thousands of barrels. Percentages indicate PDVSA's participation. SOURCE: Debates IESA, vol 2, no. 2, Oct-Dec. 1996.

PDVSA is not only the largest Venezuelan enterprise, it is also the most prestigious. It has about 50,000 direct employees and its business statistics are staggering. It ranks 66th in the Fortune (3 August 1998) list of the most important enterprises in the world. Within the oil industry it ranks eighth in revenues and third in profits as percentage of revenues in 1997. Its position is rising: in 1994 it was classified as number 113 in the general list and number 13 in petroleum refining. PDVSA sold US$37,140 millions in 1997 (Petróleos de Venezuela SA, Informe Anual, 1997: 63).

PDVSA has a very strong corporate culture and the "oil people" are proud of their organisation. Even if they are Venezuelan and a part of the Venezuelan public sector, they like to point out that they have their own traditions and they consider themselves to be completely different from Venezuelan public bureaucrats or even private managers or entrepreneurs. They consider themselves—and most people agree—efficient and honest. They are extremely punctual, while most people in Venezuela are quite flexible when time is involved. Much of this culture comes from the transnational oil corporations that were in the country from the early twentieth century until nationalisation in 1975. It is a quite conservative culture. The oil enterprises care for their employees, train them and give them benefits. A career in the oil industry is usually for life: the average employee has 11 years in the organisation. The people in the oil industry are very proud of the meritocracy that controls promotions. On the other hand, some observers point to the existence of paternalism and a very autocratic managerial style. There is a premium on loyalty, not on innovation. Criticisms, as well as mistakes, are not forgotten.

As PDVSA became a prominent international business player, Venezuela had to open itself to foreign investments in oil as well as in other areas of economic activities. Internationalisation was only an initial step in much broader changes in the Venezuelan oil business. The country has an enormous reserve in the Orinoco belt. This oil is heavy and extra-heavy. It comes mixed with metals and requires new and specific technologies for its exploitation. On the other hand, many oil fields in other areas, exploited for many years, became low performance areas. New technologies were required to upgrade wells. Last, but not least, to keep itself among the world top producers, Venezuela required large investments in new exploration and exploitation. These huge technical and financial resources were beyond the capacities of the country and the association with foreign capital abroad naturally led to foreign investment in the country.

The new oil policy was called the *apertura petrolera* (a translation would be "open door"). To have an idea of how diverse the investors are and where they come from, Table 10.1 gives a list of new fields, the enterprises that are investing in them and their country of origin. This is an example of only one round in the *apertura*, the *convenios operativos*, not of all new private investments on Venezuelan oil.

Table 10.2 shows the short list of winners in another round, the *ganancias compartidas*, or shared profits. These are bigger business. There is diversity

Table 10.1 Operational Agreements

Field	Consortium	Country
Kaki	Inelectra-Arco-Polar	Venezuela-USA
Casma-Anaco	Cosa-Cartera de Inversiones-Phoenix	Venezuela
Maúlpa	Inelectra-Arco-Polar	Venezuela-USA
Mata	Pivensa- PBE Trading	Venezuela
Acema	Corepli- Pérez Companc	Venezuela- Argentina
Intercampo	China National Petroleum Co	China
La Concepción	Pérez Companc-William Int	Argentina-USA
B2X–68/79	Penzoil-Cartera de Inversiones-Eccopek-Nimir	USA-Venezuela
Mene Grande	Repsol	Spain
LL652	Chevron-Phillips-Statoil-Arco	USA-Norway-USA
Ambrosio	Phillips	USA
Dación	China National Petroleum Co	China
La Vela-Costa Afuera	Lasmo	UK
B2X–70/80	Phillips-Arco	USA
Cabimas	PanCandian-Penzoil	Canada-USA
Onado	Preusacc	Germany
Colón	Tecpetrol-Corex-CMS Nomeco-Wascana	Arg-USA-Fran-Can
DZO	Occidental	USA
Boscán	Chevron	USA
Urdaneta Oeste	Shell	UK-NL
Falcón Este	Samson-Petrolago-Ingenieria 50-VPI	USA-Venz
Quiamara-La Ceiba	Astra-SI. Petrol-Tecpetrol-Ampolex	Arg-Australia-Chile
Jusepin	Total-Amoco	France-USA
Quiriquire	Maxus-BP-Otepi	Arg-UK-Venz
Pedernales	BP	UK
Uracoa-Bompal	Benton-Vincler	USA-Venz
Oritupano Leona	Perez Companc-Norcen-Servicios Corod	Arg-Can-Venz
Guárico Oriental	Teikoku Oil	Japan
Sanvi Guere	Teikoku Oil	Japan
Gurárico Occidental	Mosbacher	USA

Source: PDVSA.

but the element we want to emphasise is the importance of involved corporations.

The *apertura* implied changes in PDVSA known as *reestructuración* (restructuring). The core of the oil industry is now a single enterprise (PDVSA Petróleo y Gas) with three business units: exploration and production, manufacture and marketing and services. It is a far more flexible organisation. The central idea was to get ready for a far more competitive environment and the project is to

Table 10.2 Results of Round under Shared Profits Contracts

Area	Consortium	Country
La Ceiba	Mobil, Veba Oel, Nippon	US, Germany, Japan
Golfo de Paris-Oeste	Conoco	US
Guanare	Elf Aquitaine, Conoco	France, US
Golfo de Paria -Este	Enron, Inelectra	US, Venezuela
Guarapiche	British Petroleum	UK
San Carlos	Pérez Companc	Argentina
Punta Pescador	Amoco	US
Punta Centro	KK&E, Norcen, Benton	US, Canada

Source: PDVSA.

change the corporate culture, to stimulate innovation and creativity. As an oil executive puts it:

> The previous model was not working well and needed change. We had the maturity to address the problem . . . The pattern that made us successful in the past would not do for the future . . . When we compare ourselves with other parts of the world we realize we are not as good as we thought . . . Restructuring was carefully planned some years ago, but it was at the beginning of this year that was implemented . . . We are making a big effort to teach people what globalization means . . . Restructuring means creating the environment to support a new way of doing things, stimulate initiative, self-management and customer focus. It means management change and people change [Granell de Aldaz, 1999].

LEGAL SERVICES FOR THE OIL BUSINESSES

Oil investments are huge, amounting to many millions of dollars. Any new investment requires careful preparation, protracted negotiations and conflict management. Lawyers have always been important for the oil business and their importance has increased with the *apertura*. Let us start by describing the traditional situation and then discuss the recent changes.

Venezuela has had lawyers and law studies since the early eighteenth century. In the nineteenth and early twentieth centuries, lawyers were part of the political and intellectual elite. By 1926, when oil became important in the economy, the population was 3 million and there were 540 lawyers (Pérez Perdomo, 1981: 144). Legal education follows closely the Civil Law tradition. Venezuelan lawyers intervened from the beginnings of the oil business, on the side both of the foreign enterprises and the Venezuelan government, the two contracting parties in the early times. Among the important Venezuelan oil lawyers was Juan B. Bance (1865–1965). He was an important lawyer and university professor. By the turn of the century he was the lawyer of New York & Bermúdez Company, a very controversial enterprise exploiting a natural asphalt lake in the Eastern part of Venezuela (Harwicht Vallenilla, 1991) that got involved in revolutions and lawsuits. In the 1920s, Bance created the first modern law firm in Venezuela, the Escritorio Bance y Valladares, and was active as a lawyer until the 1940s. He was a lawyer for the Caribbean Petroleum Company and other oil enterprises.

Lawyers were important in smoothing the relations between the oil companies and the Venezuelan government and society. A letter from Mr Holman to Mr Linan, both from Standard Oil, beautifully describes this role in December, 1939. The letter is about Dr Alejandro Pietri and he reproduces it in a book of memories (Pietri, 1945: 375):

> I want to say that with absolutely no exception, all of us have tremendous respect for Dr. Pietri, not only because of his superior legalistic ability, but also because of his business acumen, his general knowledge of the oil business, his outstanding qualifications as a Venezuelan citizen, and his very gentlemanly characteristics. We are fully appreciative of the work he has done in the past on general legal problems, as well as the more important business problems. Considering the size of our business in Venezuela, we have had relatively few lawsuits and we feel Dr. Pietri deserves a good share of credit for this. We also feel that he has made worthwhile contributions toward good relations with the Venezuelan Government and people. While we were educating the "Doc" in the oil business, he was busy educating us in the Venezuelan point of view, this interchange being mutually helpful. We are cognizant of the fact Dr. Pietri has remained aloof from politics in Venezuela in spite of flattering offers from time to time . . . All this means, of course, that he has made very worthwhile contributions (no doubt at times sacrificing momentary personal interests) to the success of our Venezuelan activities in the past and assuming our relations can remain the same, he will contribute even more in the future.

Other lawyers of the mid-twentieth century, like René Lepervanche and Manuel Reyna, were extremely important, representing the legal interests of the oil companies and also lobbying cabinet ministers to improve the often acrimonious relations between the oil companies and the Venezuelan government.

By the 1960s the main oil enterprises had established *consultorías jurídicas* (in-house lawyers) and were regular clients of main law firms. Among these firms, Mendoza, Palacios, Páez Pumar, Acedo, Borjas y Asociados, a succesor of Bance and Valladares, worked for Shell (see Perez Perdomo, 1981: 394, for an interview with Carlos Mendoza, a lawyer in the Bance firm and founder of Mendoza-Palacios). Our oldest interviewee was a lawyer for this firm who handled tax cases for Shell from 1953 on. He became legal counsel and director of Shell in 1963, in place of a Dutch lawyer (Interview 8).

Interviewee 1 graduated as a lawyer in 1964 and immediately started working as a lawyer in the *Consultoría Jurídica* of Shell of Venezuela. A career pattern had already been established by then:

> I began working in the oil industry in 1964, and from the beginning I was pressured to undertake graduate studies. I was somewhat late in doing so, since I first had to learn English. In 1969, the company provided financial support that enabled me to complete

a Master's degree in comparative law . . . The consultoría jurídica [in-house counsel office] had two sections. The national section was the largest, staffed by Venezuelan lawyers, and in charge of a variety of national issues. At Shell, it consisted of some 20 lawyers: 7 or 8 in Caracas and the rest in the states of Falcón and Zulia, the regions where most operations were taking place. In the national section, the scope of issues addressed was quite diverse: fishermen and farmer complaints, labour issues, and a diverse array of contracts. Indeed, a wide variety of themes. The lawyers who worked in the field had to work quickly, as issues emerged. Issues of greater importance, which required further examination, were addressed in Caracas. The international section of the in-house counsel office was considerably smaller, involving some three lawyers. In the past, one or two lawyers had been foreigners, but when I joined the office all were Venezuelan. Issues addressed there included international trade, technology, engineering contracts, international transportation, among others. For instance, I was in charge of leading the group that negotiated the establishment of a refinery in the Dominican Republic [Interview 1].

This interview stresses the structure of a *consultoría jurídica* in an oil multinational in 1960s Venezuela. The largest number of lawyers was located in the oil fields. Legal needs arise there, such as claims from neighbours affected by the oil exploitation, or contract or labour conflicts. Lawyers manage the claims from the beginning, as a way to avoid litigation or a bad business environment. Did nationalisation change this order of things? Not initially. As Interviewee 1 puts it:

> On Friday I was a lawyer in a foreign multinational, and on Monday I was in a public national enterprise, but my desk was the same and the business on my desk was exactly the same. Only the logo that accompanied my name changed.

This soft transition was carefully planned. The Venezuelan political elite did not want to destroy the machinery that was working well and was the main source of government income. Soon, however, new needs emerged. The former multinational subsidiaries were no longer competing among themselves and had to create new co-ordination mechanisms.

As we have seen, the international department was very small. When an important international issue arose, headquarters lawyers were called in. Should the need arise, they consulted external law firms with experience in international business and conflicts. After nationalisation, this resource was no longer available.

In the new structure, PDVSA became a holding company that took the place of the headquarters. Initially, PDVSA's role was to cushion the change and to manage contacts with the political world. In this task, lawyer-scholar-politician A. Aguilar Mawsdley, the first chief PDVSA lawyer, had a very important role. Soon, however, PDVSA had to take on the proper functions of a holding company. The main co-ordination mechanism was a committee integrated by the *filiales'* (subsidiaries') main legal advisors and the top PDVSA lawyers. This committee distributed work, because it was inefficient to duplicate the same common tasks in every enterprise. The international expertise was concentrated in PDVSA and the special enterprises that dealt with specific international matters.

The big change was in 1998. When Maraven, Lagoven and Corpoven disappeared, most lawyers went to *PDV Servicios*, one of the business units of the corporation. Only the headquarters and specialised enterprises kept their *consultorías jurídicas*. The basic result was the creation of a law firm within the corporation. Lawyers are concentrated in one building and work very much as a law firm. Some lawyers work permanently or temporarily within another unit. The hierarchy has been flattened. Lawyers are assigned to projects. Usually, a lawyer is the head of the legal team for one project and a member of other legal teams. Hierarchy is less visible. In addition, the new policy involves a more discreet use of external law firms, and a more intensive use both of internal lawyers and individual specialists.

The total number of lawyers in legal functions is 140. This is a large number if compared with legal departments in Belgian industrial enterprises (Van Houtte, 1999), but it is not especially large if we compare with American (Liggio, 1997) or French (Boigeol, 2000) enterprises. It is smaller than in Venezuela's main financial enterprises. It is important to point out that Venezuela has a long tradition of in-house counsel and that the number of lawyers working as in-house counsel are more numerous than lawyers working in big law firms.

Among PDVSA's lawyers there is a lot of functional specialisation. The lawyers that work in oil exploitations are general practitioners. They give general advice and manage the usual conflicts. When they find a complex problem, they report it to Caracas. There, most lawyers have a sub-disciplinary specialisation. They are tax, labour, contracts, litigation and international lawyers. There is even a small unit on legislative intelligence. PDVSA has no criminal lawyers, but has two contracted lawyers that usually give advice or attend cases when they arise.

Direct contact with foreign law firms started quite early. In 1976, PDVSA entered into an arrangement with Sherman-Sterling of New York. This is a general law firm with experience in international business. Nonetheless, as my interviewee put it, it was selected because it had no dealings with the oil multinationals and it was important to avoid any conflict of interest. Sherman-Sterling had an important international network that was very useful for PDVSA at the beginnings. Soon afterwards, PDVSA developed its own network: "we started to shop in boutiques" (Interview 1).

THE CAREER OF OIL LAWYERS

The career pattern of lawyers within the oil industry did change with nationalisation policies. There are two ways of entry. One is the recruitment of a young lawyer, fresh out of law school or with postgraduate courses in a foreign country.

Even if there is no explicit policy, graduation in the Universidad Católica Andrés Bello—whose law school is the most prestigious and elitist—or Universidad Central de Venezuela, is a plus. At a certain point Lagoven established as a policy actively to recruit the best UCAB alumni. It should come, then, as no surprise that most oil lawyers are UCAB or UCV alumni. The exception is Maracaibo: most lawyers there come from the prestigious local university (Universidad del Zulia).

Hiring practices seem quite meritocratic. As we found in the interviews, the use of an open advertisement in the newspapers is common. The enterprise chooses among competing candidates. In one case a lawyer used a network, but networks served mostly information purposes. For hiring, the careful consideration of the *curriculum vitae* and interviews are used extensively. In addition, periodic performance evaluation is part of PDVSA's corporate culture.

Managers integrate lawyers into the business and the life of the organisation as a whole. Lawyers know they should know more than law. As soon as they are hired, they are sent to the fields and start working in committees that deal with different aspects of the business. Another interviewee made these comments about this experience:

> An "internship" in the oil fields was and is a company policy. Currently they run introductory courses, which did not exist before, where new employees become acquainted with the structure of the company and its activities. However, nothing is as valuable as direct, hands-on experience. It is crucial to understand and to live what the company does, and to gain the trust of the people. For instance, production facilities and refineries are marked by highly differentiated cultures. People in production are concentrated on their jobs and are not diplomatic, they will not hesitate in doing anything. Refinery people are far more cautious, and are willing to examine all sides of a given problem. They are focused more on the industrial dimension.
>
> We did a bit of everything in the [oil] fields. We attended the meetings of the people in operations, and slowly we learned the language and the problems of the business. We would get involved in negotiations with suppliers, contracts, labour issues. We even helped write letters with piquete, that is, letters that addressed delicate matters. We dealt with a good number of labour and traffic cases. We did not however deal with criminal cases, those were submitted to outside lawyers [Interview 2].

The pattern might vary according to the needs of the business. Interviewee 7 asked to be sent to the fields (because he and his wife wanted to live in a small community), but he was needed in Caracas and stayed there.

The second way of entrance is as an experienced and qualified lawyer. The third interviewee was a lawyer with eight years' experience in the Instituto de Comercio Exterior where he attained the position of chief lawyer (*consultor jurídico*). He then pursued LLM studies in Pennsylvania. On his return, he had a commitment to work at the Institute that had sponsored the fellowship, but there was much political uncertainty involving the Institute. He told a friend he was looking for a job and this friend knew Maraven was looking for a qualified lawyer. He was interviewed and hired. He has been an oil lawyer for 15 years. Our fourth interviewee worked for seven years at the *Comisión Nacional de*

Valores (Securities and Exchange Commission). He left this position for an important accounting firm. He felt he was learning nothing there, and after a year he started looking for another job. He saw an advertisement in the newspaper. The enterprise that was looking for a lawyer was not identified. It was Corpoven which wanted a lawyer with experience in economic matters; he felt he was the type of lawyer the enterprise was looking for. He got the job in 1981.

Our fifth interviewee followed a very similar pattern. She graduated in 1985 from Universidad Central de Venezuela, carried out postgraduate studies on tax law, and worked in an accounting firm and in a small legal firm before becoming a lawyer in Lagoven in 1991. She saw an advertisement in the newspaper, and was interviewed and hired:

> In the interview, I inquired about their policy to send lawyers to study abroad, and told them I was strongly interested in that possibility. That was indeed my dream. I had been accepted at Harvard when I had obtained my undergraduate degree, but the economic situation, together with changes in the policy involving government scholarships, made it impossible for me to take advantage of that opportunity. They said they were inclined to send me abroad, but that first I had to work at the company for several years. I was finally able to leave in 1993. I was not accepted at Harvard then, but I did get accepted at NYU, where I obtained a Master's degree in comparative law. Actually, one learns American law rather than comparative law, but the programme was very good and I have found it very useful.

Our ninth interviewee, a graduate from Universidad Santa María in 1972, got a doctoral degree from Paris I with a dissertation on oil nationalisations. She worked first for OPEC and from 1978 for the Ministerio de Energía y Minas, the oil regulator. She became an expert on negotiations and in 1980 was hired by Lagoven after several interviews. Her fluency in English, French and German helped her a lot:

> The beginnings in the job are not easy. As the fourth interviewee puts it, the [oil] industry has an enormously challenging environment. You must interact with a lot of people in the business, engineers, finance experts. You have to learn their language and to learn how the oil business works.

One of the features of PDVSA culture is that you have to work in teams, and the lawyers have to be involved in the business from the beginning:

> You cannot say no and you have to find the proper legal way to get what the business requires, but strictly the legal way, no shortcuts [Interview 4].

These tensions explain that a number of lawyers leave the organisation quite early. Salaries and benefits are quite high by Venezuelan standards, but lawyers mostly interested in law and unwilling to venture into business and technical matters have to leave. They are not necessarily fired. They just stay in the type of job that requires only legal skills and have no way to go up in the corporate ladder. People who prefer a more individualistic way to work or are more adventurous tend to leave too. Most lawyers who leave join a law firm or establish an individual practice. The fifth interviewee, the woman-lawyer who was hired in 1991, left in 1996 for BP. As she was the first interviewed woman-lawyer, I asked her about possible gender discrimination and her reasons for leaving:

> In Lagoven-Caracas, we were seven women-lawyers (out of 17 lawyers), and in the corporation as a whole we were 12 (out of 46). I never felt open discrimination. I believe that in all my years at Lagoven, I only heard one sexist remark. I never felt badly. Of course, it was a machista environment, one knew that, but it was nothing compared with the machismo I found at BP . . . In Lagoven it's hard to tell how discrimination was carried out. I believe its origin was that friendships and connections would start in drinking sessions, which usually took place on Friday evenings until the early hours of Saturday. They would get drunk together and become great friends. Of course, at the time of a promotion, friendship counts. One may not be interested in those connections, and one has no obligation in that regard, but there is a price to pay. I decided to leave because a man, who was less qualified, and who had less merit, was promoted instead of me. They put him above me. Also, the opportunity emerged at BP, where the salary was better and where I was offered a higher position in the hierarchical structure. However, it was not money that made me leave. Money is not my motivation.

Interviewee 9 confirmed the perception of hidden discrimination. She found her work in Maraven rather dull, but frequently was "borrowed" by other oil subsidiaries for advice on technological negotiations, her area of specialisation. At a certain point she did not feel appreciated by her supervisor. She thinks her supervisor was conservative and probably disliked her as an outspoken woman and because of her innovative character. She left and has had a distinguished career both in government and private practice. She continues to advise the oil industry but as a private practitioner.

When lawyers are young, PDVSA is rather generous in providing opportunities for training. Participation in postgraduate studies in law, most of them at the UCV, in law executive courses provided by UCAB in many provincial cities, or in executive courses at IESA, is encouraged. The LL.M, or a joint degree in business and law, in a prestigious American university is the elephant kill for a young and promising PDVSA lawyer. In this case PDVSA used to provide complete financial support. The subsidiary or filial could make the difference too. The fourth interviewee, who made his oil career in Corpoven, did not get any pressure for postgraduate studies in the USA and did not know of any Corpoven lawyer that received such a benefit. On the contrary, lawyers from Maraven and Lagoven (Shell and Exxon before the nationalisation) felt this pressure. Most recently, the opportunities to go abroad have been restricted for economic reasons.

Interviewed lawyers expressed high job satisfaction. Even interviewee 5, who left Lagoven, is quite positive:

> It was a wonderful experience . . . I had the opportunity to participate in huge international negotiations, involving hundreds of thousands of dollars. After being involved in such negotiations, everything else seems unimportant. Imagine, a kid interacting with lawyers from the most prestigious international law firms. I appreciated very much that they trusted me, they trusted my ability [Interview 5].

I obtained a very similar answer from Interviewee 7.

After a number of years in their careers, lawyers tend to stay, but they can find it very difficult to go up to top legal jobs. They may find opportunities in other corporate endeavours. Interviewee 2 found the career prospects in the legal department, after 18 years in it, very limited, and he was able to get an important position in another department. He finds the pattern rather usual:

> I know at least 20 high executives that started their career in *jurídico* and that at a certain point in their careers left for another department [Interview 2].

A career in PDVSA is professionally prestigious. One of the features of Venezuelan legal profession is the importance of in-house counsel. The prestige of the in-house counsel depends on the enterprise and PDVSA is clearly the most important enterprise in the country. But the prestige of PDVSA's lawyers is limited to the professional circles mostly because the enterprise requires the complete dedication. Lawyers are very busy and, in addition, the corporate culture would not easily tolerate a professional who is very active in the academy, in politics or even in the Colegio de Abogados, the professional law association. The combination of lawyer-scholar or lawyer-politician, frequent among elite lawyers, is most unusual within PDVSA, especially in the second half of last century.

Our interviewees insisted they were asked to have a business-oriented attitude. They have to know about the oil business and get acquainted with the activities of the firm. They have to participate in the business design from the beginning. And, as our fourth interviewee explained:

> we are here (in PDVSA) not to say no. We are here to indicate how a deal is legally possible and how it could be done without cutting corners or suggesting any doubtful manoeuvre.

External lawyers consulted for this research have a good opinion of PDVSA's internal lawyers. Nevertheless, they see most of them as too interested in business issues, and not enough in legal issues. Internal lawyers complained that the external ones are exclusively interested in legal matters:

> Sometimes they come with an 18-page opinion that we have to throw in the garbage can because they do not understand the oil business [Interview 5].

Within the corporation, lawyers do not play a leading role. As interviewee 4 said, "[t]his is an enterprise of engineers". CEO Luis Giusti, an engineer, led the *apertura*, according to my first interviewee. Nevertheless, PDVSA's culture is one of teamwork, and lawyers are important in the teams. He said:

> A feature of our corporate culture is teamwork. The lawyer's role in the team is to guarantee we will not have trouble with the course we decide to take. The lawyer is not to be consulted after we have a problem. The lawyers follow and accompany the business deal from the beginning. We participate constantly [Interviewee 4].

This has been the case for nationalisation, internationalisation and *apertura*.

CONFLICT PREVENTION AND *APERTURA*

Venezuela is a highly legalised but not a litigious country. The number of lawyers (law graduates) has increased very quickly in the last 20 years (76 per 100,000 inhabitants in 1971, 223 in 1995). The number of registered documents has increased faster. On the other hand, the number of courts and litigation rates are decreasing in relative terms, except for labour disputes (Pérez Perdomo, 1996). These facts allow the hypothesis that the number of Venezuelan lawyers working in government or as in-house counsel is larger than that working in private practice.

Most lawyers in PDVSA work in conflict prevention: studying the legality of new ventures, helping in the design of business contracts, negotiating, drafting documents and so on. All these activities could be classified as conflict prevention. All serious Venezuelan enterprises give much importance to this task, as most enterprises elsewhere (Van Houtte, 1999; Spangler, 1986), but in Venezuela there is the additional motive of a very inefficient and even corrupt judiciary (Pérez Perdomo, 1996).

Globalisation has increased the number and importance of international contracts and has required a clearer business orientation. Both interviewees 1 and 4 explained lawyers' "bureaucratisation" in the 1970s and 1980s, as a consequence of being a state enterprise and being a monopoly. The internationalisation in the 1980s, the feverish activities of *apertura* and the presence of competitors have increased the need to be efficient and flexible. The number and variety of contracts with foreign enterprises have grown exponentially.

I asked if there were frequent or difficult cultural conflicts dealing with foreign lawyers. The most common answer was negative, but there seem to be two problems. One was the habit of some foreign lawyers of talking directly to the business managers. "This is easy to solve. We have to show them who we are" (Interview 3). On more technical matters, the most difficult task is to get acquainted with the contracting style of common law (Interview 7).

In oil business language, *apertura* is the second step on the way to globalisation. The first step was *internacionalización*, PDVSA's investments in the US and Europe. *Apertura* refers to foreign investments in Venezuela for oil exploration, production and commercialisation. For the Venezuelan oil industry this implies competitive or collaborative relations with foreign enterprises. Our interest is to explore the business relation patterns and the role of lawyers in them.

Internationalisation involved only PDVSA's top lawyers. They mostly worked with the foreign firms that advise PDVSA in important acquisition efforts in foreign countries. The many other lawyers were not used in the design of the business. Afterwards, if a firm owned by PDVSA in a foreign country has a conflict or any other legal problem, the lawyers in charge are foreign lawyers. Only when the problem is important and concerns international relations are

PDVSA's headquarter lawyers involved and eventually there are further consultations with international law firms and legal specialists.

The *apertura* has a different nature. Both the interviewees and the literature point out the different *rondas* (phases or rounds). The first *ronda* concerns the Orinoco oil belt *(faja petrolífera del Orinoco)*. The belt is an enormous reservoir of heavy and extra-heavy oil that requires new and sophisticated techno-logies for extraction and production. Few corporations had the technological capacity to work in the area. Once these firms are located (outsourced), there is negotiation. In Venezuelan legal terminology the agreement is a *contrato de servicio*. It is in legal and economic terms quite complex, but is a rather simple business: the service enterprise promises performance, PDVSA evaluates the activities and results, and pays for the services.

Another *ronda* consists of contracts for the reactivation of mature fields. These fields have been exploited for many years and their production is declining. New technologies allow for reactivation. Again, only a few organisations have the technology. They are called and get a service contract. Each type of contract is prepared very carefully. They are long and detailed contracts, very much in the style of common law.

The third *ronda* is called "shared risk contracts for exploration and exploitation". They constitute a radical departure from old nationalist policies, since foreign oil companies are invited to act in the country not as contracted enterprises for specific purposes but as PDVSA's competitors or associates. In fact they are both, because the business engineering is quite complex. The departure was possible because the Venezuelan oil legislation (the *Ley que Reserva al Estado . . .* Article 5) allowed foreign investment under special circumstances and if Congress approved the contracts. When PDVSA and the government decided that oil should be open to foreign investors, the first task was to study the legality of the different types of possible contracts.

The preparation of contracts was a delicate task. In addition to legality, it was necessary to design an attractive business both for Venezuela and for the investors. There was a lot of research involved, studying the different possible modalities of business and contracts. Foreign lawyers with great experience in the oil business were consulted from the beginning. Here is a brief description of the process of contracting, in the words of the leading Venezuelan lawyer involved:

> After a careful study of the business, we prepared, with the support of our advisers, an initial tender protocol, where the several aspects of the contract were addressed. We took this document for discussion with those corporations that were potentially interested. They made observations and suggestions. With this new material we revised our original document, and we decided how to make an offer that would be attractive for potential investors and favorable for the nation as well. It was then that we prepared the final tender protocol. This document is a contrato de adhesión, which allowed no further negotiation. Those firms that were interested took part in an auction, and the several participating firms offered advantages in the form of bonuses. Then we would take the best offer.

The contract has two main parts: for exploration, the risk is entirely on the investors' shoulders. They have a set period for the exploration, and are obliged to perform a certain amount of activities and hire a minimum number of Venezuelan personnel. A joint venture will be established for exploitation. PDVSA can choose between 1 and 35 per cent of the shares.

A very important aspect of the contracts of both internationalisation and *apertura* is the rules on conflict prevention and management. The contracts themselves are important instruments of legal certainty, as they establish very detailed obligations for both sides. Contracts are long, detailed and casuistic. They are written in English, with no translation into Spanish. I had the opportunity to take a look at some of them, and to ask questions. Interviewee 7 explained that international contracts were, following the Common Law style, longer than most businesspeople are used to. For a national contract, for example, a reference to *caso fortuito* or *fuerza mayor* can make useless the long list of cases that appear in the Common Law contracts. Some contracts have technical annexes that make them hundreds of pages long.

The clauses on applicable law and conflict management are very important. They are more or less standard, according to the subject-matter of the contract. Contracts on exploration and exploitation of oil in Venezuela have a clause designating Venezuelan law in case of disagreement. Contracts for selling oil or derivative products mostly use Venezuelan law, but the terms of the contracts are adapted from international regulations. The chartering of ships uses English maritime law. Large engineering contracts in Venezuela, usually with international enterprises, use Venezuelan law. For technological services, it depends on the strength of the foreign firm. If Venezuelan law is not accepted, usually the parties may agree on New York law. For contracts of financing or financial advice, New York law is most used. For asset purchase agreements, New York law is generally highly regarded. For association agreements, Delaware law is preferred.

For businesspeople, more important than applicable law is the clause about who will decide the conflict. The usual clause provides for consultation and negotiation mechanisms and, in case of persistent differences, arbitration according to the rules of the International Chamber of Commerce of Paris, or New York. Usually there are three arbitrators, one chosen by each party, and the third by the two other arbitrators. In case of disagreement, the Chamber of Commerce would choose the arbitrator. Most arbitration clauses are short, but in some cases business partners prefer lengthy clauses, mostly because they are used to them.

The search for legal certainty is crucial to these issues. Foreign investors are not comfortable with Venezuelan legislation and Venezuelan courts. Given PDVSA's importance, and the Venezuelan sensibility on oil matters, they are probably right. Our third interviewee explained the perception of Venezuelan lawyers and the preference for New York law:

A lawyer in the international department must speak English very well. Negotiations always take place in English. We must be thoroughly familiar with international law, and especially American law, since the majority of our contracts are subject to New York law. We are quite familiar with those laws, and we also have good advisers . . . Our businesses with the Netherlands Antilles are numerous, and Dutch law is very similar to Venezuelan law, but we have faced very unpleasant surprises in Curacao, because of some of the interpretations of local courts. It does not seem right to me to have an important contract subject to a law that I am not comfortable with. However, we do not always use New York law. In maritime matters, we use British law. The British developed good maritime law, very thorough and trustworthy.

From the legal point of view, the *apertura* process can be considered success-ful. First of all the contracts passed the difficult test of congressional approval with the support of a solid political majority. On the other hand, many corpor-ations from different countries participated in the bidding. Tables 10.1 and 10.2 show the winners and their great diversity. In Venezuela, criticism has been sub-dued. Political criticism came, predictably, only from the ultra-nationalists or left wing critics of denationalisation. A group of critics went to the Supreme Court and alleged the unconstitutionality of the Act of Congress authorising the *apertura* contracts. They attacked the arbitration clause and the controlling powers of PDVSA (instead of Ministerio de Energía y Minas). The Supreme Court did not take immediate action and the case was allowed to die. But no criticism was made of the transparency of the process, and no political scandal has resulted.

The definitive test was the change of government in February 1999. President Chávez was very critical of PDVSA and its policies as a candidate, and even as an elected President. He chose as Ministro de Energía y Minas a leading left-wing critic of *apertura* (Rodríguez Araque, 1996). Nevertheless, when the gov-ernment settled down, investors were reassured and no major changes on internationalisation and apertura have been announced or are being planned.

CONFLICT AND LITIGATION

The ultimate test of knowing whether contractual and institutional arrange-ments have been successful is the number of conflicts. We will always have the problem of half empty-half full perception, because it is impossible to know the number of avoided conflicts. Given the number of contracts, the number of cases that go to arbitration or to courts is minimal. Yet, lawyers in the litigation department perceive that PDVSA is involved in too many conflicts. They think that everybody wants to litigate with PDVSA: it is the deepest pocket in the country and there is the lure of a successful case that can make you rich. But they are aware of the fact that there are few international conflicts.

Interviewee 6 provided very precise figures to sustain the perception that everybody in Venezuela litigates against the enterprise. There were 713 active cases on 31 December 1998. 168 were initiated in that year. PDVSA is acting as a plaintiff in 38 cases and is claiming a total of 1,732 million bolivars. They are mostly cases of failure to comply with contractual obligations as well as some important bankruptcies. In 675 cases PDVSA is acting as defendant. Three quarters of these cases are labour claims. The economic importance of these cases is small. There are 59 civil or commercial lawsuits, for larger amounts, totalling 394,324 million bolivars. This is two thirds of the total amount claimed. Tax and administrative cases are important too: 78 totalling 167,493 millions, or one quarter of claims. Unfortunately, we lack comparative figures with other oil corporations.

If we analyse the figures, the fact is that the amount of litigation is quite low for a corporation of the size of PDVSA. The only odd figures are labour cases. PDVSA's reputation is that of a good, though strict, boss. The explanation is that Venezuela's labour legislation promoted litigation. People who are fired have a strong incentive to claim unjustified dismissal. If they lose the case, they receive in any case a fixed amount plus indexation for inflation. In the worst case, it is a better alternative than to put money in a savings account. In the country as a whole, labour cases have gone up while civil and commercial cases are very stable in absolute numbers (Pérez Perdomo, 1995).

Our interviewees explained civil or commercial cases against PDVSA in terms of greed. There are people who think that a judicial claim could be an instrument for further negotiation in cases of damage caused by oil production or industrial exploitation. Interviewee 6 explained that PDVSA's lawyers are very careful: if the case is strong they never yield one inch, and they usually win their cases. It is worthwhile to point out that most are tort cases. Contracts seem to be successfully doing the job of conflict prevention.

Tax cases are brought by the tax administration (Seniat) against PDVSA, a state enterprise. This can happen because different state units are quite independent, and Seniat officials have incentives to make claims with little cost to them.

That PDVSA court lawyers think there is much litigation is easily explained: individually, they have a lot of work. An independent observer might have a different opinion about the amount of litigation because he is looking at a larger picture. Unfortunately we cannot compare PDVSA's experience with other large corporations.

Corporate lawyers produced a picture of international conflicts (Interviews 3, 4 and 7) as quite frequent. Negotiation is the most common way to handle conflicts. Usually there is pre-established mechanism for negotiation. In the shared risk contracts of *apertura*, there are *comités de control*, with representative from both sides. The committees' meetings are quite frequent. At least one committee meets every month (Interview 4). No conflict has gone to arbitration in relation to *apertura* contracts. In other cases negotiations fail and the conflicts go to arbitration. PDVSA has eight active cases (as of June 1999). Engineering contracts have given rise to one or two cases that are in arbitration. Delays in the arrival of ships are quite frequent and can be quite costly. It is important to establish responsibility. Arbitration is considered quite expensive, and generally the parties try to solve the case by negotiation.

PDVSA has only a few cases in foreign courts, mostly tort cases. One of these cases is about a ship that damaged port facilities; another case involves contractors working for PDVSA in the USA, who spilled hydrochloric acid. The interviewees were quite familiar with the cases and explained their technical aspects, even though foreign law firms are in charge of these cases.

CONCLUSIONS

The history of the Venezuelan oil business could be presented as "from transnationals to transnationals" (Quiroz Corradi, 1996). At the beginning of this century the foreign transnationals came to Venezuela to exploit oil. In the last 20 years, PDVSA has become a transnational itself. Lawyers have played a quite important role in this history, and their importance has increased substantially. Early Venezuelan oil lawyers eased the relations of foreign enterprises with the Venezuelan government and society. They were, in a sense, local lawyers. Current oil lawyers—or at least some of them—help in the design of international deals and are involved in international litigation in addition to the more traditional domestic matters. Oil lawyers, and especially Venezuelan lawyers, have become more important for their business.

There is no doubt that oil lawyers have provided legal certainty for oil businesses. The very success of oil businesses and the relative lack of conflicts within the industry or with non-oil business and regulators could be pointed out as the ultimate proof. Lawyers have generated legal certainty through participation in business planning and negotiating and drafting contracts. We agree with the more general remarks of Gessner (1998) on this point. The lawyers concerned are, in the first place, in-house counsel. Both national and foreign external lawyers are called in when need arises. The in-house counsel regulate the use of external lawyers.

Some oil lawyers felt the legislative, judicial and scholarly poverty with regard to oil matters was a personal or group failure. Oil lawyers could have been more active in lobbying legislators or producing knowledge in order to build a more coherent body of oil law and oil related taxation. Legal doctrine could have clarified matters and increased legal certainty. These remarks of oil lawyers have to be understood within a tradition in which scholarly research frequently goes together with law practice. The explanation they give for what they consider their failures is the intensity of their activities as oil lawyers.

It is clear that not all PDVSA's lawyers have become globalised or are required to understand foreign law or the English language. Such knowledge is strictly necessary only for those in the international field. However, the knowledge of foreign law is important in order to advance in one's professional and corporate career, as is familiarity with business and with national law. To be too international, or to be too national, is criticised. As interview 7 put it: "important businesses are not exclusively national or international. They are mixed up and lawyers have to wear both hats".

Present-day top Venezuelan oil lawyers are incomparably more important for their business than their forebears. A plausible explanation is PDVSA's global importance. As in-house counsel are very much used and are very important in Venezuela, one might hypothesise that they are more important in PDVSA than in other oil multinationals.

Reliance on lawyers and contracts for the creation of legal certainty is not exclusive to oil lawyers. In general terms businesses in Venezuela rely on them far more than on informal deals or courts. The very role of lawyers and the purpose of contracts are to avoid unnecessary conflicts and litigation. When conflicts cannot be avoided and negotiation fails, a third party intermediary is necessary. This third parties appointed in the contracts are arbitrators, but the arbitration cases are few compared with the enormous amount of contracts and operations (Pérez Perdomo, 1996).

The Venezuelan judiciary is considered highly unpredictable, inefficient and even corrupt. The people most aware of the situation are Venezuelan lawyers themselves (Pérez Perdomo, 1996). It is not a surprise that international contracts chose arbitration. Arbitration is considered highly reliable because the arbitrators are few, well known and prestigious (Dezalay and Garth, 1996), but they are also considered too expensive. This is the reason arbitration is avoided whenever possible.

Oil lawyers do not use a corpus of international law applicable to the international oil business. There is no reference to *lex mercatoria*, *lex petrolia*, or to any other international general legal standard in the contracts. Interviewed lawyers suggested that the expression "general principles of international business" is too imprecise to be useful. Some international guidelines or conventions (such as the Vienna Convention on International Sale of Goods) are usually incorporated in the contracts. Reference is made to a specific national law. When Venezuelan law is not acceptable or familiar to the other party, foreign law is used as neutral ground. The New York law of contracts and English maritime law are the ones most used. Interviewees felt these were good laws. My hypothesis is that this is not because they are ethically or aesthetically better, but because they are known, predictable and reasonably complete.

We have not found *guanxi* to be an important aspect of oil business. On the contrary, we have found an extremely legalised environment. Even in PDVSA's policies on contracting and hiring, we have found a visible preoccupation for using transparent procedures and much attention to law and contracts. Of course, some *guanxi* is inevitable. I have to confess I used *guanxi* to get the interviews. I expect to have more *guanxi* in PDVSA, but I am sure my *guanxi* would not be of any use in getting a contract or business deal.

REFERENCES

Baptista, Asdrúbal, and Mommer, B. (1987), *El petróleo en el pensamiento económico venezolano* (Caracas: Ediciones IESA).

Boscán de Ruesta, Isabel, Moreno León, J. I., Sánchez, S., Galdos, J., Anzola, O. and Brewer-Carías, A. (1997), *La apertura petrolera* (Caracas: Fundación Estudios de Derecho Administrativo).

Betancourt, Rómulo (1967), *Venezuela, política y petróleo* (2nd edn., Caracas: Senderos).

Briceño-León, Roberto (1990), *Los efectos perversos del petróleo* (Caracas: Fondo Editorial Acta Científica Venezolana, Consorcio de Ediciones Capriles).

Boigeol, Anne (2000), "La montee des juristes en France", unpublished paper, on file with the author.

Dezalay, Yves, and Garth, B. (1996), *Dealing in Virtue: Internaational Commercial Arbitration and the Construction of a Transnational Legal Order* (Chicago, Ill.: University of Chicago Press).

—— (1997), "Law, Lawyers and Social Capital: 'Rule of Law' versus Relational Capitalism", *Social and Legal Studies* 6 (1).

Espinasa, Ramón (1996), "El negocio petrolero: De enclave foráneo a industria nacional", *Debates IESA* 2 (2).

Gessner, Volkmar (1998), "Globalization and Legal Certainty" in V. Gessner and A. C. Budak (eds.), *Emerging Legal Certainty: Empirical Studies on the Globalization of Law* (Aldershot: Dartmouth).

Granell de Aldaz, Elena (1999), "Globalization and Cultural Change: Are Venezuelan Managers Ready?" IESA, paper in 1999 HRSP Research Symposium Building corporations through people in the midst of major economic and cultural shifts (June), (Ithaca, NY: Cornell University).

Harwicht Vallenilla, Nikita (1991), *Asfalto y revolución: La New York & Bermudez Company* (Caracas: Monte Ávila).

Karl, Terry Lynn (1997), *The Paradox of Plenty: Oil Booms and Petro-States* (Berkeley, Cal.: University of California Press).

Liggio, Carl D. (1997), "The Changing Role of Corporate Counsel", *Emory Law Journal* 46 (3).

Machado de Acedo, Clemy (1990), *La reforma de la Ley de Hidrocarburos de 1943: Un impulso hacia la modernización* (Caracas: OESE).

Naím, Moisés (Director del Proyecto) (1989), *Las empresas venezolanas: su gerencia* (Caracas: Ediciones IESA).

Pérez Perdomo, Rogelio (1981), *Los abogados en Venezuela* (Caracas: Monte Ávila Editores).

—— (1984), "La investigación jurídica en Venezuela contemporánea", in H. Vessuri (ed.), *Ciencia académica en la Venezuela moderna. Historia reciente y perspectiva de las disciplinas científicas* (Caracas: Fondo Editorial de Acta Científica).

—— (1996), "De la justicia y otros demonios" in M. E. Boza and R. Pérez Perdomo (ed.), *Seguridad jurídica y competitividad* (Caracas: Ediciones IESA).

Pérez Schael, María Sol (1993), *Petróleo, cultura y poder en Venezuela* (Caracas: Monte Ávila).

Pietri, Alejandro (1945), *De la vida estudiantil y profesional* (Caracas: Tipografía Americana).

Quiroz Corradi, Alberto (1995), "De las transnacionales a las transnacionales: La historia petrolera vista por un gerente", *Debates IESA* 2 (2).

Rodríguez Araque, Alí (1996), "La reapertura petrolera o el futuro del pasado", *Debates IESA* 2 (2).

Spangler, Eve (1986), *Lawyers for Hire: Salaried Professionals at Work* (New Haven, Conn.: Yale University Press).

Urbaneja, Diego Bautista (1991), *Pueblo y petróleo en la política venezolana del siglo XX* (Caracas: Cepet).

Van Houtte, Jean (1999), "Law in the World of Business: Lawyers in Large Industrial Enterprises", *International Journal of the Legal Profession* 6 (1).

PART FIVE

The Role of Business Networks: Relationism and *Guanxi*

11

Social Logic as Business Logic: Guanxi, *Trustworthiness, and the Embeddedness of Chinese Business Practices*

WAI-KEUNG CHUNG AND GARY G. HAMILTON

Abstract

This chapter explores the nature of Chinese business practices by looking at their social foundations. We argue that the use of an inter-subjective logic based on the norms of social relationships provides an institutional foundation for economic transactions in Chinese business settings. The logic of social relationships—or what we call guanxi *logic—is embedded in daily practices of the Chinese business community. Rather than making economic decisions less "economic", relational rules embedded in* guanxi *places interpersonal business transactions within a prescriptive framework, thereby increasing the calculability of economic outcomes. Guanxi logic is, therefore, a socially meaningful way to enhance economic rationality. Although relational rules play a role in Chinese economic practices similar to that of a legal framework in Western economic practices, the results are quite different. Whereas Western legal norms depersonalise market activity, Chinese relational rules personalise transactions, making them part of the interpersonal social matrix of daily life.*

WHAT IS *GUANXI*?

THE FIRST STEP in our discussion is to clarify the meaning of *guanxi*. In the Chinese language, *guanxi* carries several different connotations.[1] In the most general sense, *guanxi* simply means "relationship". Any social

---

[1] *Guanxi* has been translated into English in different ways. They include social relationship, social connection, personal relationship, particularistic relationship and personal tie. *Guanxi* certainly is about relationship or connection, but none of those translation conveys the idea of how people are related or connected in a Chinese context. Since the cultural meaning of *guanxi* is more than what can be represented by the term "relationship" or "connection", we prefer not to translate it.

relationship—for example, the relationship between parents and children or between teachers and students—can be identified by the term *guanxi*. In this sense, the word does not carry any necessary connotations about how those relationships work.

The second usage carries the more specific meaning that most Chinese associate with the word. *Guanxi* identifies a subset of relationships that work according to the norms of reciprocity. Parent/child or teacher/student relationships are hierarchical and not, strictly speaking, based on the expectations of reciprocation. However, a broad range of relationships in everyday life are less formally structured and less hierarchical in nature, and a great many of these relationships are defined normatively by the principle of reciprocity. So important are these relationships in Chinese society that some scholars (e.g., King, 1991; Fei, 1992) claim that *guanxi* is a fundamental organisational principle of Chinese society, ranking in importance with familial piety (*xiao*). "To a significant degree", said Ambrose King (1991: 79), "the cultural dynamic of *guanxi* building is a source of vitality in Chinese society".

A third and decidedly pejorative connotation of *guanxi* has emerged in contemporary Mainland China. This third meaning refers to "the use of someone's authority to obtain political or economic benefits by unethical person(s)" (*Xinci Xinyu Cidan*, 1989: 92). *Guanxi* or *guanxixue* represents a way to bypass laws and regulations through personal connections with state officials or with people who control scarce resources. Different from the second meaning, *guanxi* here refers to "a system that depends on the institutional structure of society rather than on culture" (Guthrie, 1998: 255). Most studies that are related to economic reforms in China discuss *guanxi* in this sense (e.g., Agelasto, 1996; Davies *et al.*, 1995; Hsing, 1997; Xin and Pearce, 1996; Yang, 1994).[2] In this chapter, we will focus primarily on the second usage of the term *guanxi*, with some discussion in the conclusion on the third meaning of the term.[3]

In a concise way, then, the second meaning of *guanxi* implies the following characteristics:

(1) The relationship between two persons is situational and informal, in the sense that both parties to the relationship have discretion over how the relationship is defined.[4]

(2) Once both parties agree to a relationship, there is an assumption that the principle of reciprocity will be observed. When there is a *guanxi* between

---

[2] There are also studies that look at *guanxi* in a more general sense. There is a literature that focuses on whether *guanxi* or networks matter in marketing. Luo (1997), e.g., studies how foreign-invested enterprises benefit from an extensive *guanxi* network by creating more efficient marketing performance. Others include Davies *et al.* (1995), Abramson and Ai (1997). See also Bian (1997) for a focus on the relationship between job-seeking and *guanxi* in China.

[3] Seemingly oblivious to the nuances of the term, many studies do not distinguish the differences between these two usages.

[4] Sometimes *guanxi* can be used to refer to relationships between groups or organisations, but they are connected mainly through personal ties.

two persons, a favour granted from one side will be returned, at least in principle, by the other side.

(3) The promise of reciprocity rests on the personal trust (*xinyong*) that exists between the two persons. Additional feelings of mutual trustworthiness develop as each act of reciprocity is realised.

(4) The feelings of personal trust are normatively displayed through expressions of *ganqing*, that is human emotions and affection.

(5) The development of *guanxi* usually refers to a relatively long-term and stable relationship, or at least one that is expected to be long-lived.[5]

(6) In order for the relationship to remain effective, *guanxi* has to be "cultivated" after it is established.

(7) *Guanxi* is not an all-or-nothing concept. *Guanxi* can be of various degrees of strength and stability.

(8) *Guanxi* is a selective attachment. By definition, one cannot have a *guanxi* relationship with everyone.

What is important to *guanxi* is the recognition of a mutual commitment. The *guanxi* logic will be launched and the relationship will be proceeded only when *both* sides are interested in further development of the *guanxi*. Therefore, when people say they have good *guanxi* with another person, they mean that they have known the other person for a relatively long time and that they have helped each other before. Also, they know that the other person is willing to do them a favour if there is a need, a favour that may not be available to everyone. If such a favour is given, then the other has an obligation to reciprocate at some point in the future.

A THREE-DIMENSIONAL VIEW OF *GUANXI*

The rules of reciprocity structure *guanxi* relationships. From an individual's point of view, selectivity and the management are the all-important aspects of having social relationships outside the close circle of family members. To understand how *guanxi* works, it is essential to understand the processes of selecting and managing these social relationships.

A widely accepted conception is that *guanxi* is most easily established between people with "a commonality of shared identification" (Jacobs, 1979: 243). People with a common background, such as people from the same kin group, native place, school, occupation, or even surname, will find it easier to establish a reciprocal bond. A shared background, which we might think of as a foundation for developing *guanxi*, cannot guarantee that a 'stable' *guanxi* can be developed. There is, however, a rather imprecise rule of thumb about which "categories of social relations" (Landa, 1994)[6] are the most likely to produce

---

[5] Almost by definition, short-term relationships cannot be *guanxi*. Accordingly, it is redundant to say "long-term *guanxi*".

[6] See also Tsui and Farh (1997: 60), who propose the same idea, and suggest that *guanxi* bases "are major determinants of the strength or closeness of interpersonal relationships in China".

long-lasting relationships. In principle, for instance, one's cousin is supposed to be more important than someone with the same surname; people who attended the same school may be considered to be "closer" than people who share the same occupation. This difference in the ranking of categories, however, makes a difference only in the initial stages of *guanxi* formation. One's kinsman does not necessarily have a "better" *guanxi* with you than someone from your workplace. If shared attributes were the key factors determining *guanxi*, then it would not take so long or so much careful attention to create good *guanxi* connections. Although some form of shared attribute may be a precondition for the establishment of *guanxi*, that attribute gives no indication of the actual degree of closeness within a particular *guanxi* relationship. In the end, all such rules of thumb are situation-specific and applied on a case-by-case basis.

The closeness of a *guanxi* relationship between two persons depends not as much on the social category of sameness as on the perceived qualities that each sees in the other. To explain how people assess the nature and the degree of closeness of their own *guanxi* relationships, we should look at three analytically distinctive dimensions: normative, instrumental and affective. A close *guanxi* can exist or be developed for different reasons. Two persons can be close because they are bound by obligations, or because they have strong affection for each other, or because they are instrumentally related to each other. Most of the time, there is a combination of the above three dimensions. To determine the nature, strength and stability of a *guanxi*, we should, therefore, look at the *combined* magnitude of these three dimensions.

Normative Dimension

Guanxi often develops because two individuals are tied to each through some kind of prescriptive relationship. In colloquial terms, such prescriptive non-nuclear family relationships are routinely categorised as being either relatives or friends (*qinqi pengyou*). It is important to recognise that one's family and one's relatives are carefully distinguished categories, each of which has many subcategories. Family here refers to the family members who are under the same *fang* (i.e., the same branch of a larger family) and not family in some loose sense. Family relationships are not *guanxi* relationships. One cannot say, for instance, that one "has *guanxi*" with one's father or that one need to "*la guanxi*" (pull connections) with one's brother. Family members are "close" (*qin*), their relationships are not normatively defined by reciprocity or strictly instrumental interests, but rather by filial piety (*xiao*) and required interpersonal responsibilities, which are normatively defined by generation, gender, and seniority (Baker, 1979). These same family principles apply to a lesser degree to one's interactions with relatives outside one's immediate branch of the family, and even less yet to friends and colleagues. More distant relatives, therefore, are potentially open for establishing a *guanxi* relationship.

Within each of these broad categories of relatives and friends, there are many subcategories.[7] China's eminent social scientist, Fei Xiaotong (1992), describes these differential categories as the primary organisational features of Chinese society. All types of social activities are structured through these differential categories of relationships. In principle, individuals relate to each category of people with a distinctive set of norms and obligations.[8] The sets of social relationships that each individual maintains form a matrix of personal relationships. The degree of interpersonal "closeness" is, in part, a function of the categorical norms and obligations that link two people together. For instance, relationships between oneself and one's relatives are determined normatively according to the nature of their relatedness within the lineage structure.[9] One's immediate uncle, for instance, is closer than one's wife's uncle, and one's cousin is closer than one's cousin's wife. In terms of normative expectations, one would be more obliged to take care of a paternal than an affinal uncle. Here, exchanges of favour between relatives are based on obligation and not on instrumental calculation. One *should* help when the social norms oblige one to do so. Categories of relationships among relatives are, therefore, hierarchical in terms of closeness and extent of obligation, and the norms of reciprocity are sometimes reinforced and sometime compromised by the norms of family responsibility. As many writers point out, Chinese are often reluctant to enter into *guanxi* relationships with relatives because family obligations may override instrumental needs.

Friends, however, are normatively not as close as relatives, and therefore often make better candidates for a *guanxi* relationship. Normative expectations still structure the relations among friends,[10] but the expectations that govern these relationships are less restrictive. Among friends, there are fewer required obligations, and so there is a better opportunity to negotiate a relationship that is mutually satisfying and advantageous to both parties. The relationships between *qinren* (family and relatives) have the strongest normative constraints

[7] *Qinqi Pengyou* (relatives and friends), as an expression in everyday use, portrays the social world beyond the family of typical Chinese. In Chinese rural life, for example, this expression is further subdivided. There will be a relatively distinct category for fellow villagers (*xiangqin*) which is in between relatives and friends. But at the same time we can still put it into the non-relative category (i.e., as friends) (Kipnis, 1997: 25–6).

[8] Fei's (1992) idea of *chaxugeju* (differential mode of association) suggests that the Chinese relate to each other according to the category of social relationship.

[9] Hwang (1987) only put family relationships as expressive or emotional relationships and has neglected their normative base. In fact, the normative aspect may be more crucial in shaping the relationships within the family than the emotional aspect. You may not like your family members but you have to conform, by and large, to the normative obligations assigned by external social norms. As Hwang also acknowledged, conflicts within Chinese families are not uncommon. To suggest that family relationships should be classified as ties that "render an individual's feelings of affection, warmth, safety, and attachment" overemphasises the emotional base of the family relationships. Family ties are better viewed as strongly prescriptive obligations that can be shaped and further strengthened by both affection and instrumental considerations.

[10] *Zhong* (faithfulness), *cheng* (sincerity) and *xin* (trustworthiness) are the normative expectations defining the ties between friends. Hwang (1987: 954) describes these principles as a part of *renqing*, as "a set of social norms by which one has to abide in order to get along well with other people in Chinese society".

and obligations, those between *shuren* (familiar persons) have fewer, but still significant, constraints and finally those between *shenren* (strangers) have only the most general constraints and no specific obligations at all.[11]

The normative dimension of *guanxi* refers to the normative expectations that are embedded in the relationship linking two people. The closer the relationship is, the more a sense of moral obligation becomes. *Guanxi* relationships balance obligation and sanction, on the one hand, and flexibility and instrumentality, on the other hand. When the normative dimension is too strong, flexibility and instrumentality diminish. When the normative dimension is too weak, obligations and collective sanctions will be too few to ensure reciprocity over the long term. The process of creating a reliable network of relatives and friends always involves the careful balancing of normative constraints and instrumental flexibility.

Instrumental Dimension

People need to cultivate a network of relatives and friends because they have the potential of providing access to material and ideal resources that are or may become available. An exchange of favours, in this case, is based on rational calculation of cost and benefits. How instrumentally and mutually important the relationship is to the two persons will determine how close the *guanxi* is or may become. *Guanxi,* however, does not exist when a relationship is purely instrumental. A purely instrumental relationship is usually one shot (or short-term) and unstable (Hwang, 1987). To turn an instrumental into a *guanxi* relationship (i.e. a relatively long-term and stable relationship) either the normative or the affective dimension has to be strengthened (or most of the time, both). When one interacts with someone categorically defined as a stranger, the normative constraints are few or non-existent, and the affective level is minimal. The major consideration governing such interactions will be instrumental. For instance, when Chinese interact with non-Chinese, there is a perception that "foreigners" do not recognise the norms of Chinese society, and hence "respectful instrumentality" is the appropriate form of interaction with them.

Affective Dimension

One can develop close *guanxi* relations with another person solely because an affective bond forms between the two persons.[12] As Fei (1992) notes, such affective ties are usually gender specific. Men normatively form such ties with

---

[11] Social obligation that acts as normative constraint between strangers is minimal among Chinese, simply because obligations are expected only from those who have particular relationships with you. See Hwang (1987: 951–2).

[12] An extreme scenario would be *yijianrugu* (like old friend at first sight).

other men and women with other women. These ties are decidedly emotional. Maybe one likes the other person's personality, or maybe the two share similar world-views, tastes or habits. Whatever the personal reasons, the two individuals want to keep a relationship going, and so the two actively engage in reciprocity. The greater the degree of affection (*ganqing*), the more reciprocity is practised, and the more reciprocity is practised, the closer and more emotion filled the relationship becomes.

These three dimensions are only analytical distinctions. In reality, one's specific *guanxi* with another person simultaneously combines normative expectations, interests and a sense of mutual affection. What favours are offered and exchanged is determined by balancing the normative obligations, instrumental calculations, and affection.[13] If all three are aligned in the same direction, the magnitude will be strong and the relationship will be relatively stable. Each dimension reinforces the others, so that a more stable and long-term *guanxi* can be established. Affection or *ganqing*, however, would have to be considered as the *sine qua non* of any *guanxi* relationship, for without emotional sincerity the chances for long-term reciprocity are diminished.[14] A relationship which is both instrumental and affective is certainly better, i.e. stronger and more stable, than a relationship with only one of them. A stronger *ganqing* can always produce a stronger *guanxi*. If one wants to cultivate *guanxi*, one must cultivate *ganqing*, which is in some respects the easiest of the three dimensions to increase. When the social positions of both parties (the normative dimension) and the utility of the relationships (the instrumental dimension) are relatively fixed, then increasing the intensity of the affective dimension is a way to have closer *guanxi*.[15]

The three dimensions, however, do not necessarily run in the same direction. One has moral obligations to one's cousin, but one does not necessarily like or want to do business with him or her. People are often closely connected to others with whom they have no blood relationship. It is not uncommon for mutual admiration between two friends to be so strong that each would be willing to do almost anything for the other with very little instrumental calculation. Inconsistency among the three dimensions, therefore, does not prevent the development of a *guanxi* relationship. It is the case, however, that a *guanxi* with

---

[13] Fei's scheme of social relationships is basically normative (see Fei, 1992: chaps. 4–6). He sees Chinese social relationships as relationships defined by differential moral expectations. His scheme understates the emotional and instrumental components. Hwang (1987), on the other hand, neglects the normative aspect of the social relationships and emphasises only the expressive and the instrumental components. Even though *guanxi* is supposed to be the combined consideration of the three components on the same level, it may not "appear" to be so in some situations. In business *guanxi*, for example, the normative and affective dimensions will always be emphasised in an explicit way. The instrumental consideration, which actually is the essential part, will always remain as implicit (Chen, 1990).

[14] Kipnis (1997: 23) even suggests that *guanxi* and *ganqing* "are often interchangeable". *Guanxi*, as a term, seems to refer more to the material aspects, while *ganqing* seems to be more about the human feelings involved. But at the same time, "[g]uanxi involve human feelings and *ganqing* involves material obligation". They are two sides of the same coin.

[15] Gift giving, invitations to banquets, showing concern, visiting when the other is sick, and so forth, are the cultural "tactic" to be used to increase the affection between the two parties.

dimensions going in different directions will be weaker than if they are all aligned.

Although inconsistency in the dimensions of *guanxi* does not necessarily lead to conflict, sometimes it does. A typical and widely reported scenario (DeGlopper, 1972; Fei, 1992; Hwang, 1987; King, 1991) in which inconsistency does lead to conflict occurs when one desires a more instrumental calculation than is permitted by norms or affection. Transactions between buyers and sellers become uneasy when personal factors are involved. Sellers want to get a better price than they are able to get when they sell to a relative or friend. Buyers want to choose a better product than they are able to do when they buy from a relative or friend. In these cases, one may try to avoid intermixing *guanxi* and business in some contexts.

Using these three dimensions of *guanxi* logic, Chinese place people with whom they are interacting into categorical frames, such as *jiaren* (family members), *shuren* (familiar person) and *mosheren* (stranger), or *zijiren* (one of us, insider) and *wairen* (outsider). The classifications, however, are always elastic. The relationship between two persons can always change, whenever there is a qualitative or quantitative change in one or more of the dimensions. The person involved can be "upgraded" from *wairen* to *zijiren* (or be "downgraded") or even go from *shuren* to *jiaren*, as commonly occurs with fictive kinship ties, such as when two individuals " become brothers" or "become sisters". Because the different combinations of the three dimensions lead to different behavioural orientations, there is a great complexity and infinite variety in the way *guanxi* logic is applied in everyday life. Moreover, to the people interacting in daily life, there is always ambiguity in how people fit into the categorical matrix of Chinese society. As Fei (1992) notes, however, ambiguity is the very essence of this Chinese mode of association. All classifications are necessarily elastic and allow changes and constant subjective, contextual reinterpretations.

THE INDETERMINATE LOGIC OF *GUANXI*

The basic operative logic of *guanxi* is the logic of reciprocity. A long-term and stable *guanxi* should be a relationship of mutual benefit in the long run. This mutual benefit is realised through "a serialized balanced reciprocity of obligations and favors" (Yao, 1987: 92). The balancing of reciprocity, however, is not formulaic and predetermined. First, there is no specification on *when* one should return a favour. Owing someone a favour only obligates one to return it a later time, but at no particular time in the future. In fact, returning a favour too fast will likely be interpreted as not wanting to develop the relationship into a long term one.

Secondly, the *actual* amount of exchange for each time can be flexible, even though the overall mutual exchange of benefit should be more or less equal, or at least both sides should feel that way. The return of a favour will not always be of equal value. Often the norm is to return a larger favour than the one received earlier (Fei, 1992: 124). Also, giving favour to another without asking for any in return in the short run can strengthen *guanxi*. In this sense, one can "store" potential returns from the others and in order to access to favours at some time in the future when there is a need. The exchange is, therefore, not a balanced ledger between debtor and creditor. In principle, favours should equal out in the long run, but at any one point in time they will be out of balance.[16] People actually feel better when others owe them favours (*qian renqing*), rather than the reverse.

Thirdly, not only is the amount of exchange not defined, but also the kind of favour for the exchange is intentionally left open. *Renqing,* a personal favour in an abstract form,[17] is considered to be the medium of exchange. Every time you do someone a favour, the favour will be considered as a *renqing*. The content of *renqing*, however, is not defined, and so a *renqing* can be anything that can be exchanged. Frequently, the items exchanged are of a very different nature. For instance, one side may lend money and the other side may help one's daughter get into a good school. There is, literally, no way to quantify the favour in order to find out whether they are of equal value. Indeed, the whole point of *renqing* is its indeterminate nature: open-ended, flexible, oriented towards a future that is unknown and unknowable. What is important is a continuing cultivation of the *guanxi* bond in the present, so that one is assured of help, whatever that help might be and whenever it is needed.

Fourthly, there is no well-defined (or objective) standard on *how much* one should give in return for an earlier favour. With a *guanxi*, you are supposed to return a favour, but the amount to be returned is a calculation based on a weighing of the three dimensions of *guanxi*. If you are expected to return a favour, the nature of the favour will first be determined by what is normatively appropriate, such as the amount of money in the red pouch that one gives at the wedding for one's cousin's daughter (Yan, 1996). The next consideration will be the degree of affection mutually recognised between the two individuals. The extent to which one likes the other person has an effect on the magnitude and kind of favour one returns. Finally, one instrumentally calculates the amount that one can afford to return. A good *guanxi* partner understands that the other might want to reciprocate at a higher level than he or she is actually able to do.

The logic of *guanxi* is governed by the logic of reciprocity. This logic is necessarily fuzzy. The exchange is supposed to be unspecified, and therefore a favour is flexible in the timing, amount, and content.[18] Both sides of a *guanxi*

[16] If one side is always getting more or is taking advantage of the other side, this *guanxi* will be unstable and cannot be maintained for too long. But, in a life-long relationship, whether the exchange is equal or not is not a major concern.

[17] *Renqing* literally means "human's feelings". It is in fact considered to be a human (with feelings) only if you are kind enough to do favour to the others. You have no "human touch" if you refuse to do someone a favour.

[18] By contrast, if Chinese are dealing with strangers with whom they have no *guanxi*, every exchange will consist of "haggling over every ounce" (*jinjinjijiao*).

relationship accept and encourage this indeterminacy, because both know *guanxi* is ongoing and long-term. In this sense, *guanxi* is more a process than a condition. If mutual commitment is assured through friendship and trust, then the exchange will be continuous and constantly "re-created" (Kipnis, 1997: 25). Indeterminacy and trust go hand in hand. Ideally, *guanxi* relationships are aimed more at future uncertainties than at present needs. Such relationships have to be developed through an on-going process. If one returns a *renqing* abruptly and quickly, one is indicating that the relationship should not be extended into the future. The accounting of *renqing* is only balanced and clear when one or both sides of the exchange relationship no longer want the relationship. Even death does not necessarily end a *guanxi* relationship. After one of the two parties dies, the children of the deceased may, depending on the circumstances, feel obliged to carry on the *renqing* of the parent.

GUANXI AND BUSINESS TRANSACTIONS

As a social phenomenon, *guanxi* implies a society that is structured primarily in terms of social relationships. In fact, a number of sociologists of Chinese society, most prominently Fei Xiaotong (1992), have made an important contrast between the organisational dimensions of Western and Chinese societies. Western societies, on the one hand, are structured through organisational boundaries and organisational identities; even the family is a type of organisation. Although relationships may have affective aspects, they are still defined in legal terms, so that members of a family (for example, wives and children) have the legal rights according to their status, as well as general legal rights as citizens. By contrast, Chinese societies are organised through the medium of categorical social relationships, which provides the structural matrix within which Chinese cognitively structure all aspects of their daily life. The categories of relationships are a more significant organisational feature of Chinese society than group boundaries.

Given the pervasiveness and taken-for-granted quality of this differential mode of association, *guanxi* for Chinese implies a general orientation to how social relationships ought to be developed outside the family. Accordingly, Chinese often prefer interaction (or social exchange) with people with whom they already have some kind of social connection. At any one point in time, these social connections create a social network in which one's future is potentially vested. The network formed by one's numerous *guanxi* thus becomes one's framework for personal social and economic mobility. This framework represents a "preference scheme", a ranking of those with whom one has vested interests and commitments to interact and with whom he or she is willing to apply (in various degrees) the logic of reciprocity.

It is in this distinctive socially constructed world of social relationships that economic activity is embedded. As a number of studies have shown, Chinese businessmen prefer to use *guanxi* as a primary medium for business relationships (e.g., Chen, 1994, 1998; DeGlopper, 1972; Greenhalgh, 1988; Hamilton, 1996; Kao, 1993; Redding, 1990; Hwang, 1987; Weidenbaum, 1996).[19] Among Chinese, as among Westerners, the activity of buying and selling (*maimai*) is about maximising gains and realising instrumental interests. *Guanxi* involves instrumental calculations, as well as considerations of long- and short-term interests. Conducting business according to the logic of *guanxi*, therefore, implies no trace of irrationality or of doing something out of the ordinary. Moreover, for Chinese to do business with each other in any other way, even the Western way through laws and contracts, might seem irrational and extraordinary. Therefore, as in Western societies, in Chinese societies, doing business runs according to the same rules as living an every-day existence.

It is not surprising, therefore, that Chinese like to do business with other people who understand the same rules as they do. Because *guanxi* is built on the rules of reciprocity, the rules can only be enforced within a network of people who understand and who are morally obligated to follow the rules. In this context, everyone linked together through interpersonal networks observes the actions of everyone else, and thus everyone shares the same rules and, collectively or individually, can sanction those who do not live up to their obligations. Except at the margins, therefore, *guanxi* networks normally do not incorporate strangers. If one is doing business with someone with whom one has *guanxi*, rather than an anonymous person in the market-place, one can expect transactional relationships to be conducted according to the rules of *guanxi*.

We can further conceptualise the context of business in Chinese societies by means of game theory, most clearly with Robert Axlerod's well-known demonstrations (1984) about the outcomes of the "prisoner's dilemma" game. He shows that the most successful solution to an iterated game in which one can choose either to maximise one's gain at the expense of another or to co-operate and share gains is always co-operation. We can think of *guanxi* as a clearly developed inter-subjective set of "tit-for-tat" rules that greatly enhance the level of co-operation in Chinese society. The logic of co-operation is similar to that

---

[19] *Guanxi* is also important for business transactions in Mainland China, but in a rather different sense. In Mainland China, *guanxi* has been considered as an institutional substitute in many arenas, including the business sector. When social and economic resources cannot be obtained through regular institutional framework, *guanxi* or personal connection will become a substitute channel. *Guanxi* here is still "personal". The main difference, however, is that it has become more instrumental and utilitarian during the reform era (Gold, 1985). Even though the normative and affective components are still essential for the existence of *guanxi*, the instrumental component is a lot more important for *guanxi* to be activated. In order to benefit from your *guanxi*, i.e., to get what you want, you have to be prepared for a more immediate return of benefits to the other side. *Guanxi*, in Mainland China, does not refer to the personal relationships *per se* anymore, but refers more to the *use* of such personal relationships to pursue instrumental goals. It becomes more specific and materialistic. Favour exchange is mostly based on immediate benefit calculation. Gift exchange, which used to be a practice to maintain a good *guanxi*, for example, is now, to an extent, a means of pursuing political and economic interests (Yan, 1996; Yang, 1994). *Guanxi* that is largely based on materialistic exchange is less guided by social norms, is more costly to maintain, is less stable, and lasts for a shorter term than *guanxi* that is based on an affective bonds.

found in a great many locations (Axlerod, 1984). Where the Chinese may differ from other societies is the extent to which these "tit-for-tat" rules provide the institutional foundation for everyday interaction.

Conceptualised in this way, *guanxi* is not so much a cultural logic as it is a structural system of repeated interactions based on ongoing, more or less equal exchanges of favours. The daily practice of *guanxi* in all Chinese societies creates an institutional base for ongoing business activity. For most businesses, only some transactions occur among *guanxi* partners. If a particular transaction is between *guanxi* partners, then the economic calculation needs to include long-term, as well as short-term dimensions. If long-term calculations applies in a specific instance, then one would expect one's transactional partner to be willing to offer favours if needed, to be flexible and considerate, and to be oriented to long-term mutual benefits of both partners.

Long-term business relationships are cultivated in the same way as long-term social relationships, according to the three dimensions described above. Developing the *ganqing* component of relationships,[20] for example, is a way to strengthen them, shifting the underlying calculations from the short to the long term. If one finds a business partner who is good (for example, a subcontractor), one would try to develop the relationship *socially* in order to maintain it over future good and bad times. Such a relationship is, foremost, a business relationship (DeGlopper, 1972), but the process of making the relationship long-term requires that the relationship be maintained by using a social logic as well as a business one. Being joined in a long-term relationship makes profit-making co-operative and mutually beneficial, and converts individual enterprises into a collective venture.

Guanxi in business is an iterated process and not a condition of being. It works like the lubricant for a machine. A manufacturer who needs a subcontractor will look for one among his friends or even his friends' friends. He may prefer to find a subcontractor from someone whom he knows directly or through his network of connections. His final selection, however, would not be based solely, or even primarily, on the closeness of *guanxi*. *Guanxi* cannot make things work; it only make things work *better*. If a machine itself is not working, a lubricant will be of no use. One would not subcontract to one's best friend if that friend could not promise a reasonable price, if not the cheapest; or produce goods of an acceptable quality (Zheng and Liu, 1995). If the relationship is not beneficial, regardless of whether the transaction partner is a relative or not, one would de-emphasise the social component of the relationship and perhaps even cut both the instrumental and social ties. Moreover, to

---

[20] Whether *ganqing* is the most important dimension is situational. Chen (1994), for example, suggests that the combined effect of *ganqing* and instrumental calculation may depend on one's social and economic status or strength. *Ganqing* is considered to be relevant *only* when both sides of the *guanxi* are relatively equal in social status and economic strength. In business *guanxi*, if one's status and strength are similar to those whom you try to "connect", affection may weigh more than instrumental calculations. If their status and strength are not equivalent, then instrumental calculation will dominate. Affection, even if present, will be devalued in this case.

continue with an economic relationship that is well known not to be beneficial will raise questions among one's friends and colleagues about how trustworthy one is in the long run.

In Chinese societies, therefore, business activities include a social dimension. This social dimension does not make an economic decision less "economic". Rather, the social logic adds another level and more complexity to economic calculation. One's economic success depends not only on the competitiveness of one's products, although that is certainly important; but also on how good one's *guanxi* is with others and to what extent one is viewed as a worthy *guanxi* partner. In Chinese economies, business reputation means a lot. By supplementing business relationships with social logic, "non-economic relations are transformed into those having material significance" (Yao, 1987: 97).

In normative terms, Chinese businesspeople prefer personal dealings to impersonal ones, long-term relationships to short-term ones. This normative orientation differs from that of Western economies. Western market institutions assume atomistic actors, impersonal dealings and profit maximisation, even though a good many market participants may do otherwise. In fact, at the level of individuals, Westerners and Chinese may not be so far apart. At a minimum, we should not exaggerate the differences. Many of the most successful Chinese entrepreneurs would likely want to move toward more impersonal/contractual transactions, and thereby avoid the many requests for increasing *guanxi* that comes with business success. And many Western entrepreneurs find personal and informal transactions beneficial and practise them regularly. The differences between Chinese and Western business contexts increase at the institutional and normative levels. Regardless of individual desires, the institutional and inter-subjective foundations of the economies differ dramatically. The transactional matrix in Chinese economies is personalised through the shared use of reciprocity as a normative standard. Equally, the framework of business in Western economies rests on contract and the de-personalised nature of corporate law. These institutional differences lead to differences in economic outcomes, as we will now explain.

THE INSTITUTIONAL CONTEXT OF INTERFIRM NETWORKS

The use of *guanxi* among Chinese businesspeople spawns the formation of interfirm networks. Quite a number of writers (Kao, 1993; Redding, 1990; Hamilton, 1996) have discussed this propensity towards networking in Chinese economies and believe it to be one of the main reasons Chinese entrepreneurs have been so successful in recent years. In the past decade, Western business networks have also proliferated, as has the scholarly discussions about how networking works in Western business contexts. By contrasting the networking of firms in the Chinese and Western contexts, we can further illustrate the differences between economic organisation and economic outcomes based on those differences.

In Western economies, inter-firm co-operation has become a commonplace strategy by which firms enhance their competitive advantage through making purposeful contractual alliances with other firms. Scholars (Oliver, 1990; Powell, 1990; Podolny and Page, 1998) observing such alliances see network forms of organisation as a kind of governance structure that differ from intra-firm hierarchies, on the one hand, and co-ordination through contracts based on impersonal market transactions, on the other hand.[21] Network forms of govern-ance introduce a level of flexibility not found in either hierarchy or market. In times of rapid economic change, the inability to foresee and thus to limit risks makes interfirm alliances an effective way to manage opportunities for growth, while each firm simultaneously concentrates on its core competencies. Since contracts between partners in an alliance cannot possibly foresee all contingen-cies that may arise in the future, interfirm networks also require non-contractual dimensions, such as trust and the willingness to co-operate. Podolny and Page (1998) see this willingness to co-operate and the ethic of trust as the defining ele-ments of inter-firm networks, characteristics that distinguishes them from mar-ket and hierarchical forms of economic organisation.[22] In fact, achieving mutual trust, rather than exercising direct control, is now seen to be the preferred way to monitor inter-firm exchanges, a recognition that has now generated a sizable organisational literature about how to create the necessary trust to form a last-ing alliance (Das and Teng, 1998; Doney *et al.*, 1998; Lane and Bachmann, 1996; Lewicki *et al.*, 1998; Lyons and Mehta, 1997; Nooteboom, 1997; Zaheer *et al.*, 1998).

Judging from these accounts, it appears that both Western firms and Chinese firms extensively use interfirm networks to enhance their businesses, and both rely on mutual trust as the way to monitor co-operative ventures. A closer look, however, reveals substantial differences. In the first place, the networks them-selves are quite different. In a Western context, interfirm alliances connect firms, whereas in a Chinese context, *guanxi* connects people, which in turn may or may not connect firms. Secondly, the institutional foundations on which alliances are based also differ. Western business alliances rest, in the last instance, on the contractual agreement firms reach and the legal framework on which the contracts are based. *Guanxi* relationships, in the last instance, rest on mutual trust, individual reputation, and the inter-subjectively based normative order in which *guanxi* relationships are embedded. Thirdly, trust between the two cases rests on very different grounds. In a Western business environment, trust is separate from the contractual basis of the alliance. Trust is generated over time through long-term interaction, and may additionally have inter-personal dimensions. For instance, as long as there is no legal violation, a breach

---

[21] Powell and Smith-Doerr (1994) list at least four types of network-based collaborations where each pursues different kinds of co-operation. Oliver (1990), on the other hand, suggests six types of interorganisational relations.

[22] Transaction cost economics, for example, most of the time suggests that trust is a redundant concept (Nooteboom *et al.* 1997; Williamson, 1993).

of trust may incur few or no sanctions from other firms linked in a network. In the Chinese environment, however, trust is a normative and an essential part of a relationship. Without trust, there is no meaningful relationship, and a breach of trust, if serious enough, would lead to ostracism from the network and lost of reputation.

For these reasons, trust among Western businesspeople is more difficult to generate and maintain, but less problematic than among Chinese business-people. Trust is more difficult to generate and maintain among Western busi-nesspeople because it is a product of localised interaction between firms instead of an aspect of a generalised normative order, as it is in Chinese societies. For Western contexts, as Powell and Smith-Doerr (1994: 390) said, "the level of co-operation increases with each agreement between the same partners and indi-vidual partners become more skilled at learning through alliances". Trust is generated by interaction, but is not institutionally monitored, so that breaches of trust can be effectively sanctioned. The only way effectively to monitor inter-firm co-operation and to reduce the risk of opportunism is through adding a legal layer to the relationship (Arrighetti *et al.*, 1997; Das and Teng, 1998; Lane and Bachmann, 1996; Luhmann, 1979; Zucker, 1986). The omnipresence of law in the West pushes all relationships, even the most affective ones, into a legal framework, a fact making network forms of organisation ultimately dependent on legal controls. Networks in the Western context, therefore, represents instru-mental connections either that are institutionalised through formal means or that remain as informal relationships without a stable institutional foundation that can used to sanction violators (Dean *et al.*, 1997). Trust in Western soci-eties, therefore, is not as problematic as it is in Chinese societies because people always fall back on the laws, which results in trust being ephemeral and situa-tional, instead of stable and normative.

By contrast, in the Chinese context, trust is relatively easy to generate and maintain, but remains problematic. Interpersonal trust is easy to generate because the normative rules for doing so are widespread and strongly prescrip-tive. Breaches of interpersonal trust become violations of general rules that everyone can sanction. Therefore, trust-bearing relationship are supported by a moral community that sees the practice of *guanxi* logic and trust as "normal", as "expected" social practices that are the very foundation of social life.

In Chinese societies, from an individual's point of view, trust is a problematic feature of everyday social life. Just as in the Western societies, where violations of the law are commonplace and sanctionable, in Chinese societies, breaches of trust are also commonplace and sanctionable to some degree. The ubiquity of *guanxi* as everyday practice, even as the way of demonstrating one's human-ness,[23] makes trustworthiness a primary quality of people, a quality that people learn how to cultivate in themselves (at least for purpose of social presentation)

---

[23] The phrase *zuoren* (acting as person) has the distinctly social meaning suggests that a person is capable of entering into sincere relationships with others. Such a person is not selfish.

and to evaluate in others. From an individual's point of view, trust is necessarily generated, maintained and sanctioned within the small group of people with whom one has relationships. For Western societies, laws are universally applicable. Laws provide generalised institutional foundations for groups that may vary tremendously in size and function. By contrast, in Chinese societies, although the norms are general to the society, *guanxi* and trust are actualised only small groups. Even though *guanxi*-based networks can be quite extensive, connecting weak ties (friends of friends) into a strongly cohesive network, they remain interpersonal in character.

Because of these institutional differences between Chinese and Western societies, we can conceptualise interfirm linkages in the Western business settings as "strong-firm networks". The firm is the core, the institutionally solid foundation, and the ties to other firms are generally weak and situational. In the Chinese context, however, networks, may be thought of as "strong-tie networks", where the firms are less important than the network they constitute (Redding, 1991). The firms, in the form of actual business ventures, may come and go, but relationships persist over time. For example, in the last two decades, the composition of Taiwan's manufactured exports has constantly changed, as world demand and profits from production shifted dramatically. In one period of change, Taiwan's footwear industry moved to Mainland China. Back in Taiwan, the same people who were once making shoes reconstituted their networks to make other products, the most unusual of which was helicopters (Kao and Hamilton, 1999). Firms may change, but the relationships continue and are capable of being reconstructed for other purposes.

Strong-firm networks that exist in Western economies are capable of anything that individual firms may be capable of. Boeing, for instance, once was a vertically integrated firm making commercial and military aeroplanes. Now Boeing has become a very complex global network of independent and subsidiary firms that still make aeroplanes. Networks are a means to recreate greater efficiencies. By contrast, strong-tie networks in Chinese economies are capable of doing activities beyond what any single firm could do. Co-operation is the essential element of the activities. For example, the so-called "satellite-assembly systems" are standard ways to produce products in Taiwan. Products manufactured by such networks range widely from bicycles to computers. Based on orders from overseas buyers, a network of entrepreneurs divides the manufacturing process into discrete steps that can be allocated to a network of firms. Each firm in the network produces a part or parts of the final product. All parts are assembled at central sites and the final product is shipped to the buyer. As products change the actual composition of firms in a network also changes. Because relationships are personal, and therefore multidimensional, sometimes one person is a primary manufacturer and next time the same person is loaning capital to someone else taking the lead role.

CONCLUSION: THE CHINESE WAY OF DOING BUSINESS IN A
GLOBAL ECONOMY

In the preceding discussion, we have contrasted Western laws and Chinese inter-personal norms as if they were mutually exclusive phenomena. In the global economy that has developed in the last half of the twentieth century, it is clear that Western laws and Chinese interpersonal norms coexist. Chinese entre-preneurs are global businesspeople. They vary greatly in terms of their "Chineseness" (Wang, 1999) and in terms of whether they are able and willing to do business with other Chinese by using the logic of *guanxi*. The key question is, therefore, to what extent are global laws governing commercial transactions supplanting Chinese ways of doing business? Based on our own research in Taiwan and the Mainland, the answer is surprisingly straightforward.

A global legal framework and local Chinese norms for doing business sup-plement more than conflict with each other. The real conflict between laws and *guanxi* is found on the Chinese Mainland. This is the third meaning of *guanxi* that we alluded to in the introduction. We should understand this type of *guanxi*, however, not as an extension of the patterns we have discussed in this chapter, but rather as a corruption of them. The widespread collusion between Chinese entrepreneurs and state officials is being attacked by high-level politi-cians, not only because it is illegal according to Mainland law, but also because it undermines the moral foundation for "normal" interactions among business-people and between businesspeople and state officials. The observations (Guthrie, 1998, 1999) that this collusion is declining as Chinese businesses become more globally integrated and competitive is certainly correct, but it does not mean that Chinese businesspeople are beginning to interact with each other strictly in legal terms. Quite the contrary is true. In Chinese society *guanxi* has always applied, and continues to apply to relatively small groups of people linked together in reciprocal networks. Until recently, there were not many options about how to interact with people, whether Chinese or not, who were not part of one's own network. Global legal framework introduces a set of regulatory institutions that can apply to those with whom one is not otherwise connected.

These global laws will certainly help shape Chinese economic institutions. Firms are incorporated legally. Corporations listed on local stock exchanges use Western accounting practices, as they are required to do. Environment laws, labour laws and product-liability laws are all taking effect, and are changing the way Chinese business is being done. But this globalising legal framework adds an institutional environment in which *guanxi* logic works even better than before. Now distant relationships can be monitored through laws, while close relation-ships can be personal and based on trust and reciprocation. For instance, many Taiwanese entrepreneurs are eager to develop joint ventures with American and European firms, as is common in sub-contract manufacturing. Such entrepreneurs would not think of using *guanxi* logic to make the deal, and in fact they normally insist on a legally binding contract. Once they have the agreement, however, the same entrepreneurs will put together a production network consisting of independent Chinese-owned firms without a legally binding contract among any of the Chinese participants. Legal logic binds the first agreement and *guanxi* logic binds the second, and together both sets of agreements enhance the control and flexibility of the Chinese entrepreneurs in their effort to make money (Kao and Hamilton, 2000).

It is our conclusion, therefore, that global law enhances the ability of Chinese entrepreneurs and their firms to be players in the global economy. Their very success in the global economy paradoxically, however, enhances their use of *guanxi* logic among their close colleagues. The success of a great many Chinese entrepreneurs in Taiwan, Hong Kong, Mainland China, as well as Southeast Asia, rests on their ability to put together flexible networks and to engage in high-risk ventures. The learned process of building these networks and making them so flexible and so efficient accentuates the social foundation on which they are founded. The use of *guanxi* is an essential aspect of the long-term calculations that form the institutional foundations of these networks.

Therefore, legal rules and *guanxi* logic work hand-in-glove to make Chinese entrepreneurs the formidable businesspeople they have become. The interpersonal and processural nature of Chinese networks makes them highly adaptable to different economic conditions. When these processes are embedded in an economic environment structured through legal institutions, then the levels of economic risks are further reduced and predictability increased. If our thesis is correct, the spread of global legal institutions will set the stage for further advances in the global success of Chinese economies, a success that will continue to be based on the Chinese ability to put together interpersonal networks based on reciprocation—*guanxi* networks.

REFERENCES

Abramson, Neil R., and Ai, Janet X. (1997), "Using *Guanxi*-Style Buyer–Seller Relationships in China: Reducing Uncertainty and Improving Performance Outcomes", *The International Executive* 39 (6); 765–804.
Agelasto, M. (1996), "Cellularism, *Guanxiwang*, and Corruption: A Microcosmic View from Within a Chinese Educational Danwei", *Crime Law and Social Change* 25 (3); 265–88.
Arrighetti, Alessandro, Bachmann, Reinhard, and Deakin, Simon (1997), "Contract Law, Social Norms and Inter-firm Cooperation", *Cambridge Journal of Economics* 21; 171–95.
Axelrod, Robert (1984), *The Evolution of Cooperation* (New York: Basic Books).
Baker, Hugh (1979), *Chinese Family and Kinship* (New York: Columbia University Press).
Baker, W. E. (1990), "Market Networks and Corporate Behavior", *American Journal of Sociology* 96; 589–625.

Barney, J. B., and Hansen, M. H. (1994), "Trustworthiness as a Source of Competitive Advantage", *Strategic Management Journal* 15; 175–90.

Bian, Y. J. (1997), "Bringing Strong Ties Back In: Indirect Ties, Network Bridges, and Job Searches in China", *American Sociological Review* 62 (3); 336–85.

Chen, Chieh-hsuan (1994), *Xieli Wangluo yu Shenhuo Jiegou. Taiwan Zhongxiao Qiye de Shehui Jinji Fenxi* (Cooperative Network and the Structure of Daily Life), (Taipei: Lianjin Publishing Company).

——— (1998), *Taiwan Chanye de Shehuixue Yanjiu* (The Sociological Study of Taiwan's Industry) (Taipei: Lianjun Publishing Company).

Chen, Xuewen. (1997), *Mingqing Shiqi Shangyeshu ji Shangrenshu zhi Yanjiu* (A Study of the Ming Qing Commerce Manual and Merchant Manual) (Taipei: Hungye Wenhua).

Charny, D. (1990), "Nonlegal Sanctions in Commercial Relationships", *Harvard Law Review* 104; 373–467.

Cohen, Myron (1976), *House United, House Divided. The Chinese Family in Taiwan* (New York: Columbia University Press).

Das, T. K., and Teng, Bing-sheng (1998), "Between Trust and Control: Developing Confidence in Partner Cooperation in Alliances", *Academy of Management Review* 23 (3); 491–512.

Davies, H., Leung, Thomas, Luk, K. P. T., Sherriff, K., and Wong, Y. (1995), "The Benefits of '*Guanxi*': The Value of Relationships in Developing the Chinese Market", *Industrial Marketing Management* 24; 207–14.

Dean, John, Holmes, Scott, and Smith, Sharyn (1997), "Understanding Business Networks: Evidence from the Manufacturing and Service Sectors in Australia", *Journal of Small Business Management* 35 (1); 78–84.

DeGlopper, Donald R. (1972), "Doing Business in Lukang" in W. E. Willmott (ed.), *Economic Organization in Chinese Society* (Stanford, Cal.: Stanford University Press).

DiMaggio, Paul J., and Louch, H. (1998), "Socially Embedded Consumer Transactions: For What Kinds of Purchases Do People Most Often Use Networks?", *American Sociological Review* 63 (5); 619–37.

Doney, P. M., *et al.* (1998), "Understanding the Influence of National Culture on the Development of Trust", *Academy of Management Review* 23 (3); 601–20.

Dore, Ronald 1983), "Goodwill and the Spirit of Market Capitalism", *British Journal of Sociology* 34; 459–82.

Edwards, Clive T. (1997), "Japanese Interfirm Networks: Exploring the Seminal Sources of Their Success", *Journal of Management Studies* 34 (4); 489–510.

Faure, David, and Pang, Anthony (1996), "The Power and Limit of the Private Contract in Ming-Qing China and Today" in L. Douw and P. Post (eds.), *South China: State, Culture and Social Change During the 20th Century* (Amsterdam: Koninklijke Nederlandse Akademie van Wetenschappen).

Fei, Xiaotong (1992 (1947)), *From the Soil. The Foundations of Chinese Society* (trans. Gary G. Hamilton and Wang Zheng, Berkeley, Cal.: University of California Press).

Gerlach, Michael L. (1992), *Alliance Capitalism: The Social Organization of Japanese Business* (Berkeley, Cal.: University of California Press).

Gold, Thomas (1985), "After Comradeship: Personal Relations in China Since the Cultural Revolution", *China Quarterly* 104; 657–75.

Granovetter, Mark (1985), "Economic Action and Social Structure: The Problem of Embeddedness", *American Journal of Sociology* 91; 481–510.

Granovetter, Mark (1992), "Problems of Explanation in Economic Sociology" in N. Nohria and R. G. Eccles (eds.), *Network and Organization. Structure, Form and Action* (Cambridge, Mass.: Harvard Business School Press).

Greenhalgh, Susan (1988), "Families and Networks in Taiwan's Economic Development" in E. Winckler and S. Greenhalgh (eds.), *Contending Approaches to the Political Economy of Taiwan* (Armonk, NY: M. E. Sharpe).

Gulati, Ranjay (1998), "Alliances and Networks", *Strategic Management Journal* 19; 293–317.

Hagen, James M. (1998), "Trust in Japanese Interfirm Relations: Institutional Sanctions Matter", *Academy of Management Review* 23 (3); 589–600.

Hamilton, Gary G. (1994)m "Civilizations and the Organization of Economics" in N. J. Smelser and R. Swedberg (eds.), *The Handbook of Economic Sociology* (Princeton, NJ: Princeton University Press).

—— (ed.) (1996), *Asian Business Networks* (New York: Walter de Gruyter).

Hansen, Valerie (1995), *Negotiating Daily Life in Traditional China. How Ordinary People Used Contracts 600–1400* (New Haven, Conn.: Yale University Press).

Hsing, You-Tien (1997), "Building *Guanxi* Across the Straits: Taiwanese Capital and Local Chinese Bureaucrats" in A. Ong and D. Nonini (eds.), *Ungrounded Empires. The Cultural Politics of Modern Chinese Transnationalism* (New York: Routledge).

Hwang, Kwang-kuo (1987), "Face and Favor: The Chinese Power Game", *American Journal of Sociology* 92; 944–74.

Jacobs, Bruce J. (1979), "A Preliminary Model of Particularistic in Chinese Political Alliances: '*Renqing*' and '*Guanxi*' in a Rural Taiwanese Township", *China Quarterly* 78; 237–73.

Kao, Cheng-Shu and Gary G. Hamilton (2000), "Reflexive Manufacturing: Taiwan's Integration in the Global Economy", *International Studies Review* 3(1); 1–19.

Kao, John (1993), "The Worldwide Web of Chinese Business", *Harvard Business Review* (March-April); 24–35.

King, Ambrose Yeo-chi (1991), "*Kuan-hsi* and Network Building: A Sociological Interpretation", *Daedalus* 120 (2); 109–26.

Kipnis, Andrew B. (1997), *Producing Guanxi. Sentiment, Self, and Subculture in a North China Village* (Durham, NC: Duke University Press).

Kollock, P. (1994), "The Emergence of Exchange Structures: An Experimental Study of Uncertainty, Commitment, and Trust", *American Journal of Sociology* 100; 313–45.

Landa, Janet Tai (1994), *Trust, Ethnicity, and Identity. Beyond the New Institutional Economic of Ethnic Trading Networks, Contract Law, and Gift-Exchange* (Ann Arbor, Mich.: The University of Michigan Press).

Lane, Christel, and Bachmann, Reinhard (1996), "The Social Constitution of Trust: Supplier Relations in Britain and Germany", *Organization Studies* 17 (3); 365–95.

Leung, T. K. P., Wong, Y. H., and Wong, Syson (1996), "A Study of Hong Kong Businessmen's Perceptions of the Role '*Guanxi*' in the People's Republic of China", *Journal of Business Ethics* 15; 749–58.

Lewicki, Roy J., Mcallister, Daniel J., and Bies, Robert J. (1998), "Trust and Distrust: New Relationships and Realities", *Academy of Management Review* 23 (3); 438–58.

Lewis, D. J., and Weigert. A. (1985), "Trust as a Social Reality", *Social Forces* 63; 967–85.

Lufrano, Richard John (1997), *Honorable Merchants. Commerce and Self-Cultivation in Late Imperial China* (Honolulu, Hawaii: University of Hawaii Press).

Luhmann, N. (1979), *Trust and Power* (Chichester: Wiley).

Luo, Yadong (1997), "*Guanxi* and Performance of Foreign-invested Enterprises in China: An Empirical Inquiry", *Management International Review* 37; 51–70.

Lyons, Bruce, and Mehta, Judith (1997), "Contracts, Opportunism and Trust: Self-interest and Social Orientation", *Cambridge Journal of Economics* 21; 239–57.

McElderry, Andrea (1997), "Doing Business with Strangers: Guarantors as an Extension of Personal Ties in Chinese Business" in K. G. Lieberthal *et al.* (eds.), *Constructing China. The Interaction of Culture and Economics* (Ann Arbor, Mich.: Center for Chinese Studies, University of Michigan).

Mellinger, G. D. (1956), "Interpersonal Trust as a Factor in Communication", *Journal of Abnormal Social Psychology* 52; 304–9.

Menkhoff, T. (1993)m *Trade Routes, Trust and Trading Networks—Chinese Small Enterprises in Singapore* (Saarbrücken; Fort Lauderdale, Flo.: Verlag Breitenbach Publishers).

Nooteboom, Bart, Berger, Hans, and Noorderhaven, Niels G. (1997), "Effects of Trust and Governance on Relational Risk", *Academy of Management Journal* 40 (2); 308–38.

Oliver, Amalya L., and Ebers, Mark (1998), "Networking Network Studies: An Analysis of Conceptual Configurations in the Study of Inter-organizational Relationships", *Organization Studies* 19 (4); 549–83.

Oliver, Christine (1990), "Determinants of Interorganizational Relationships: Integration and Future Directions", *Academy of Management Review* 15 (2); 241–65.

Paniccia, Ivana (1998), "One, a Hundred, Thousands of Industrial Districts. Organizational Variety in Local Networks of Small and Medium-Sized Enterprises", *Organization Studies* 9:4; 667–99.

Podolny, Joel M., and Page, Karen L. (1998), "Network Forms of Organization", *Annual Review in Sociology* 24; 57–76.

Powell, Walter W., and Smith-Doerr, L. (1994), "Networks and Economic Life" in N. J. Smelser and R. Swedberg (eds.), *The Handbook of Economic Sociology* (Princeton, NJ: Princeton University Press).

Putman, Robert (1993), *Making Democracy Work: Civic Traditions in Modern Italy* (Princeton, NJ: Princeton University Press).

Redding, S. G. (1990), *The Spirit of Chinese Capitalism* (Berlin: Walter de Gruyter).

Sako, M. (1992), *Prices, Quality and Trust* (Cambridge: Cambridge University Press).

Tsang, Eric W. K. (1998), "Can *Guanxi* be a Source of Sustained Competitive Advantage for Doing Business in China?", *Academy of Management Executive* 12 (2); 64–72.

Tong, Chee Kiong, and Kee, Yong Pit (1998), "*Guanxi* Bases, *Xinyong* and Chinese Business Networks", *British Journal of Sociology* 49 (1); 75–96.

Uzzi, Brian (1996), "The Sources and Consequences of Embeddedness for the Economic Performance of Organizations: The Network Effect", *American Sociological Review* 61; 674–98.

—— (1997), "Social Structure and Competition in Interfirm Networks: The Paradox of Embeddedness", *Administrative Science Quarterly* 42; 35–67.

Watson, Rubbie S. (1985), *Inequality Among Brothers. Class and Kinship in South China* (Cambridge: Cambridge University Press).

Weidenbaum, Murray (1996), "The Chinese Family Business Enterprise", *California Management Review* 38 (4); 141–56.

Williamson, Oliver E. (1975), *Markets and Hierarchies: Analysis and Antitrust Implications* (New York: Free Press).

Williamson, Oliver E. (1993), "Calculativeness, Trust, and Economic Organization", *Journal of Law and Economics* 36; 453–86.

Wang Gungwu (1999), "Chineseness: The Dilemmas of Pace and Practice" in G. G. Hamilton (ed.), *Cosmopolitan Capitalists: Hong Kong and the Chinese Diaspora at the End of the Twentieth Century* (Seattle, Wash.: University of Washington Press).

Xin, Katherine R., and Pearce, Jone L. (1996), "*Guanxi*: Connections as Substitutes for Formal Institutional Support", *Academy of Management Journal* 39 (6); 1641–58.

Xinci Xinyu Cidan (New Phases New Words Dictionary) (1989), (Beijing: *Yuwen Chubanshe*).

Yan, Yunxiang (1996), *The Flow of Gifts. Reciprocity and Social Networks and a Chinese Village* (Stanford, Cal.: Stanford University Press).

Yang, Mayfair M. H. (1994*), Gifts Favors & Banquets. The Art of Social Relationships in China* (Ithaca, NY: Cornell University Press).

Yamagishi, Toshio, Cook, Karen S., and Watabe, Motoki (1998), "Uncertainty, Trust, and Commitment Formation in the United States and Japan", *American Journal of Sociology* 104 (1); 165–94.

Yeung, Henry Wai-chung (1997), "Business Networks and Transnational Corporations: A Study of Hong Kong Firms in the ASEAN Region", *Economic Geography* 73 (1); 1–25.

Zaheer, Akbar, McEvily, Bill, and Perrone, Vincenzo (1998), "Does Trust Matter? Exploring the Effects of Interorganizational and Interpersonal Trust on Performance", *Organization Science* 9 (2); 141–59.

Zheng, Boxun, and Yijun, Liu (1995), "Righteousness Versus Profit and the Transaction Process between Enterprises: A Case Study Analysis of Taiwan's Interorganizational Network" ("Jili zhi Bian yu Qiyi Jian de Jiaoyi Lichang: Taiwan Zhuzhi Jian Wangluo de Gean Fengxi"), *Bentu Xinlixue Yanjiu* 4; 2–41.

Zhou, Yu (1996), "Inter-firm Linkages, Ethnic Networks, and Territorial Agglomeration: Chinese Computer Firms in Los Angeles", *Papers in Regional Science* 75 (3); 265–91.

Zucker, Lynne G. (1986), "Production of Trust: Institutional Sources of Economic Structure, 1840–1920", *Research in Organizational Behavior* 8; 53–111.

12

Coasean Foundations of a Unified Theory of Western and Chinese Contractual Practices and Economic Organisations

JANET TAI LANDA*

Abstract

It is not easy for western economists or western businessmen to understand the Chinese way of doing business because the Chinese do not rely on formal contracts but place great emphasis on the importance of guanxi *(personal relationships/connections) and trust in their business dealings with fellow-Chinese. Because of this difference in contractual practice, it has long been recognised by western businessmen that doing business with the Chinese in China and elsewhere in the overseas Chinese diaspora is difficult. This paper shows that it is possible to understand the Chinese preference for informal or extra-legal* guanxi *way of doing business, manifesting in Chinese particularistic modes of economic organisation, such as an ethnically homogeneous middleman group (EHMG)/trading network, as an efficient system of contracting under conditions of contract-uncertainty. I do this by developing a unified theory of western and Chinese contractual practices and modes of economic organisation resting on Coasean transaction-cost foundations. My theory of the EHMG (1978, 1981) establishes links with Oliver Williamson's (1975, 1985) "Markets, Hierarchies" approach to economic organisation by extending it to "Markets, Hierarchies, and Ethnic Trading Networks" research program. I also show that my theory of the EHMG, when stripped of its Coasean transaction-cost and rational choice*

* Earlier versions of the chapter were presented at the American Economic Association (AEA) annual meetings in New Orleans 4–7 January 1997, and at the "Contracting for Joint Ventures in China" Conference at the University of Pittsburgh in May 1997. I wish to thank Gary Hamilton, the discussant of my paper at the AEA meetings in New Orleans, for his helpful comments. I also wish to thank Richard Appelbaum for helpful comments in the preparation of this latest version of the chapter.

foundations, is essentially the same as sociologist Granovetter's (1985) socio-logical embeddness approach to social networks. Finally, I develop some hypotheses for promoting international East–West transactions.

INTRODUCTION

I T IS NOT easy for western economists or western businessmen to understand the Chinese way of doing business because the Chinese do not rely on for-mal contracts but place great emphasis on the importance of *guanxi* (per-sonal relationships/connections) and trust in their business dealings with fellow-Chinese.[1] Because of this difference in contractual practice, it has long been recognised by western investors that doing business with the Chinese in China (People's Republic of China) and elsewhere in the overseas Chinese diaspora (Hong Kong, Taiwan, Vietnam, Singapore, Malaysia, and Indonesia) is difficult. This is because to many western economists and investors:

> A modern legal system as practiced in a Western developed economy is sometimes considered essential for the proper functioning of a market economy: The non-Western legal system in China is considered deficient . . . [because] under Chinese law a contract is enforced partly by an informal social relationship known as "guanxi". Guanxi plays an important role in insuring that a contract is honored [Chow, 1997: 322].

This chapter will show that it is possible to understand the Chinese preference for informal or extra-legal *guanxi* way of doing business, manifesting in Asian–Chinese particularistic modes of economic organisation, as an efficient system of contracting under conditions of contract-uncertainty. I will do this by developing a unified theory of Western and Chinese contractual practices and modes of economic organisation resting on Coasean–transaction cost founda-tions.

In an assessment of the influence of his seminal 1937 article "The Nature of the Firm", which laid the foundations of transaction cost economics, Coase (1988: 34–5) said that the article was ignored for over 30 years. It was only in the 1970s and 1980s that there was a renewed interest in his paper by a growing

---

[1] In a headline entitled "Friendship, Trust, and the Chinese Way of Doing Business", the *Straits Times Weekly Overseas Edition* (24 August 1991, 13) reported that the first and biggest gathering of overseas Chinese businessmen—800 overseas delegates from 30 countries—had attended a three-day "World Chinese Entrepreneurs Convention" in Singapore. Noting that the main purpose of the convention was to enable overseas Chinese entrepreneurs from different parts of the world to meet with each other in order to establish "business deals and social ties", the article states that "[d]oing business the Chinese way, especially if it were to culminate in a successful deal, has always been more effective if it is done in an informal atmosphere with someone you trust as a friend. Even for other delegates with no strong historical bonds, it was enough that one shared the same surname, or spoke the same dialect with an otherwise near stranger. The handshakes, the karaoke sessions and the customary 10-course dinners have in their unobtrusive ways, strengthened friendship and established trust." The delegates spoke of the need to promote "Confucian values as a means to understand thrift, hard work and group cohesion".

number of economists, particularly those trying to explain aspects of the organisation of industry, for example, in Williamson's (1975, 1985) work on vertically-integrated firms. The importance of that article, in Coase's view, was the "explicit introduction of the concept of transaction costs into economic analysis" (1988: 34) to explain the existence of the institution of the firm. Coase also attributed the renewed interest in his 1937 article to the immediate success of his 1960 paper, "The Problem of Social Cost", which also incorporated the concept of transaction costs to explain the way in which the legal system could affect the performance of the economic system. Coase (1988, 35) went on to say that he did not know:

> at what point it became apparent to me that the whole of economic theory would be transformed by incorporating transaction costs into the analysis—probably this was a gradual process. . . . How far other economists now share my view of the significance of transaction costs for economic theory I do not know. But there is no question that, starting in the 1970s, a number of economists began to explain the adoption of various business practices (including the emergence of the firm) as a response to the existence of transaction costs.

Unknown to Coase in 1988, he would win the Nobel Prize in Economics in 1991; these two articles were cited for his winning the award. Also unknown to Coase was the great impact of his 1937 paper on my work on the transaction cost implications of social norms (the Confucian code of ethics) embedded in Chinese economic organisations—such as Chinese family firms and Chinese trading networks—for co-ordinating the interdependent activities of economic actors within firms and across markets. My work on Chinese economic organisations—Chinese family firms (Landa, 1978: chap. 2; Landa and Salaff, 1980) and ethnic trading networks (Landa, 1978; 1981: chap. 5)—was part of a larger study explaining why overseas Chinese were so successful as middlemen-entrepreneurs in Southeast Asia (1978, 1999).

This chapter is an attempt to show in what ways my work on Chinese contractual practices and economic organisations rested on Coasean foundations, even though it went beyond traditional transaction cost economics—New Institutional Economics (NIE) to incorporate key concepts in sociology and in anthropology. The chapter is divided into five parts. Part I reviews key aspects of Coase's theory of the firm. Part II discusses my theory of contract law, which is an extension of Coase's theory of the firm to the contractual relations between firms in western economies with well-developed legal infrastructure. Part III discusses my theory of the ethnically homogeneous middleman group (EHMG)/ethnic trading network, and is an extension of my theory of contract law to less-developed or developing economies in which the legal framework for enforcement of contracts is not well developed. In my theory of ethnic trading networks, one can still see clear traces of the influence of Coase's, 1937 paper, even though certain key concepts are drawn from sociology and anthropology. Part IV discusses my theory of ethnic networks and how it provides a conceptual link between the "embeddedness–social networks" approach of economic sociology with the Coase–Williamson "markets–hierarchies" paradigm. The result is an extended "markets–hierarchies–ethnic networks" NIE unified paradigm of western and Chinese contractual practices and economic organisations. Part V suggests some testable hypotheses that flow from my theory of ethnic trading networks, hypotheses which have important policy implications for understanding institutional arrangements that facilitate global business transactions.

COASE'S THEORY OF THE FIRM (1937)

In neoclassical economics there are only decentralised markets where the price mechanism co-ordinate the activities of economic agents who conduct transactions directly with each other. In 1937, Coase published his paper "The Nature of the Firm", in which he posed a puzzle: if all transactions are co-ordinated by the price or market mechanism why do we observe the existence of the institution of the "firm" in the real world? Why are "firms" necessary? And why outside the firm:

> price movements direct production, which is co-ordinated through a series of exchange transactions on the market. Within a firm, these market transactions are eliminated and in place of complicated market structure with exchange transactions is substituted the entrepreneur–coordinator, who directs production. It is clear that these are alternative methods of co-ordinating production [Coase, 1937, reprinted in Stigler and Boulding, 1953: 333].

Coase set out to answer this question by introducing the concept of transaction costs explicitly into economic analysis. Coase argued that there are costs of using the price mechanism to organise production. These costs include: (a) the costs of discovering what the relevant prices are; and (b) the costs of contract negotiation for each exchange transaction that takes place in the market. Coase concentrated on contract negotiation costs. He argued that if the price mechanism is used, a factor of production would have to negotiate a number of contracts separately with each of the factors with whom he is co-operating; these costs could be greatly reduced by organising a firm. By organising a firm, the entrepreneur–co-ordinator substitutes a series of contracts for only one employer–employee contract. Not only does the entrepreneur–co-ordinator economise on transaction costs by reducing the number of separate contracts he must enter into, but also there is no need to specify in detail the various contractual obligations with each of the factors he is co-operating with. According to Coase, the defining characteristic of the employer–employee contract is that:

> for a certain remuneration (which may be fixed of fluctuation) [the employee] agrees to obey the direction of an entrepreneur within certain limits. The essence of the contract is that it should only state the limits to the powers of the entrepreneur. Within

these limits, he can therefore direct the other factors of production [Coase, 1937, reprinted in Stigler and Boulding, 1953: 333].

The firm emerges when the entrepreneur, rather than the price mechanism, has the authority to direct the activities of employees, within certain limits; this discretion is not found in contracts between economic actors where the mutual contractual obligations are spelled out explicitly. Where a long-term contract is called for, a firm may emerge to reduce such contracting costs by organising a firm. He summed up his theory of the firm by saying that: "the operation of the market cost something and by forming an organisation and allowing some authority (an 'entrepreneur') to direct the resources, certain marketing costs are saved" (Coase, 1937, reprinted in Stigler and Boulding, 1953: 333).

Coase then turned his attention to the question of the limits to the size of the firm. He argued that the firm will tend to expand until the costs of organising an extra transaction within the firm becomes equal to the costs of carrying out the same transaction through the market. Coase also addressed the question of when a firm will choose vertical integration, which is when transactions which were previously carried out between entrepreneurs are now organised within one firm. Finally, Coase addressed the question of when a single-product firm will expand into a multi-product firm. He asked us to imagine a town in which there are series of industries, A, B and C, located around a central point in a series of von Thunen rings. Assume that the entrepreneur starts from the central point within the innermost ring, A. As he extends his activities in product A, the cost of organising increases until it becomes equal to that of a different product, B; thus as the firm expands it will, from that point on, include both products A and B.

LANDA'S THEORY OF CONTRACT LAW (1976)

Coase's contribution in his 1937 paper is to explain the firm as a non-market form of economic organisation that is alternative to the price mechanism in co-ordinating the activities of production. So the "firm" and the "market", in Coase's paradigm, are alternative co-ordinating mechanisms. What is missing in this Coasean scenario, however, is the role of the state in enforcing contracts between firms. Since all market transactions involve contracts, and contracts in advanced western capitalist economies are enforced by the state, a theory of contract law is also necessary to explain the role of contract law in co-ordinating the activities between firms. Landa (1976; reprinted in Landa, 1994: chap. 1) provided such a theory of contract law, using a transaction cost/property rights–public choice approach, part of the New Institutional Economics (NIE) to explain the emergence of contract law in an exchange economy, characterised by specialisation and division of labour among producers, middlemen and final consumers.

In my chapter, the focus on transaction costs is shifted from contract negotiation costs to the costs of breach and the costs of enforcing contracts. My chapter on contract law rethinks the concept of market relations between firms in terms of legally binding contractual relations, in which the rules of the game (contract law) are enforced by the state. I showed that the game is played very differently if there is or if there is no external enforcement of the agreements between players in the market. Not only did I shift the emphasis from market relations to contractual relations, I also shifted my emphasis to the role of specialised traders (merchants) that link producers and consumers together. In this sense, my theory of contract law and the theory of EHMG/ethnic trading networks (next section) is not merely a simple extension of the Coasean theory of the firm—in that Coase's theory of the firm is a theory of production—while my emphasis on the role of contract law and ethnic trading networks is a theory of exchange.[2]

Imagine there are three traders, A, B and C, in which B is assumed to be the middleman. Assume that B has located a supplier, A, and has negotiated a contract with her. Imagine the following terms of the contract. Trader A promises to transfer to B rights to the ownership of a specified quantity and quality of a specified commodity and promises to deliver the goods to B at a specified future date, t+1. (Note that when market exchange involves a contract, the goods to be exchanged are rights to ownership of goods, and not exchange of goods themselves.) In consideration of A's promise, B promises to transfer to A rights to the ownership of a specified sum of money (say, $100) and promises to pay that sum to A at a specified future date, t+2. Once the terms of the contract are mutually agreed upon and the contract is signed, a legally binding contract emerges; a person who breaches a contract will be required to compensate monetary damages to the plaintiff when the latter sues him in court. Trader B is now the owner of a "claim to A's goods contract" (Cg) against A. Expecting to receive the goods from A at a specified future date, t+1, B now sells forward his Cg to C at a higher price. Trader B promises to deliver goods to C at a specified future date, t+1 in exchange for C's promise to pay a specified sum of money (say, $110) to B at t+2. As soon as B has made the contract with C, B becomes the profit-seeking middleman who buys low and sells high in order to reap his profits. More precisely, B has a set of expectations—to receive goods from A at t+1, deliver goods to C at t+1, and receive payment from C at t+2—out of which arise B's expectations of future profits ($10). If all three traders honour their contracts, then all the traders' plans and expectations are fulfilled. The legally binding contract plays an important role in co-ordinating the interdependent activities of all three traders, linked by market transactions/contracts.

To appreciate the role of the state in enforcing contracts, let us assume a market economy without a state to enforce contracts, i.e., a market economy

---

[2] Thanks to Gary Hamilton for pointing this out to me at the AEA Conference in New Orleans in January 1997.

characterised by Hobbesian anarchy—contract uncertainty. In such a market economy, any trader can break a contract whenever it is profitable to do so. Let us assume that A, after signing a contract with B, gets a better offer from another middleman (say, $105). With no constraints on contractual behaviour, A would be better off by breaking the contract with B and recontracting with the other middleman. Assuming that B has made no private provisions against A's breach of contract to deliver the goods, B will be forced to break his contract to deliver goods to C. As a consequence, B's profit expectations will be disappointed because C will not pay him the $110 as originally promised. Trader A's breach of contract has imposed social costs or externality on B: middleman B is the victim of an "exchange externality".

Since B cannot go to court to recover monetary damages, hence allowing him to internalise the exchange externality, B must make private provisions to protect his contracts. Trader B can choose one or more of the several methods for the private protection of contracts:

(1) B can search for information regarding A's reputation prior to entering into a contract with her; however, B must incur information costs;
(2) B can personalise exchange relations by trading only with those traders that B can trust; however, B must incur the opportunity costs of excluding outsiders from trade (see Section III):
(3) B might try using the "discipline of continuous dealings" to mitigate against breach; however, this method by itself is not sufficient to constrain a trader from breach of contract;
(4) B can extend credit and threaten the withdrawal of credit; however, B must take on a money-lending function and hence face the risk of loan default;
(5) B can hold commodity inventories as buffers; however, B must incur storage costs;
(6) B can hold cash balances which allow him to adjust quickly to A's breach by going into the market to buy goods from another supplier so as to deliver the goods to C; however, this increases the information costs of finding a new supplier;
(7) B can pool and spread risks of breach by buying from many suppliers instead of from only one supplier, A; however, this increases the costs of contract negotiation;
(8) B can integrate vertically backward to the source of supply; however, B must incur costs of intrafirm co-ordination, and this also may not be a feasible solution for B if he is short of capital.

Thus, each one of the private solutions for the protection of contracts generates its own transaction costs. To minimise the transaction costs of private protection of contracts, traders can form a merchant guild, with guild rules of the game constraining traders from breach. But as the trading population expands in size, it becomes less efficient for traders to rely on the guild solution for the protection of contracts; the state becomes a more efficient contract enforcer.

Once the state emerges to enforce contracts, all exchange externalities are internalised since a trader now has to weigh the benefits of breach with the costs of breach (in the form of paying monetary damages).[3] Occasionally, a trader might still engage in "efficient breach" (Goetz and Scott, 1977), in that the breaching party can compensate the victim of breach but still be made better off by breaching. However, contract law, by assigning liability for breach of contract to the breaching party, introduces an element of inertia into the trader's choice calculus: once a trader signs a contract, she has a strong incentive to honour it. Thus, the role of the state in enforcing contracts, according to my theory of contract law, is that the state economise on the transaction costs of private protection of contracts and hence allow traders to shift some of the scarce resources to trade rather than the protection of contracts. The state, through its role in protecting contracts, "may be viewed as a super-coordinator of inter-firm transactions creating a super-vertically integrated firm, which is which is, in reality, a well-functioning and efficient exchange economy"(Landa, 1976: 917; reprinted in Landa, 1994: 63).

LANDA'S (1981) THEORY OF THE ETHNICALLY HOMOGENEOUS CHINESE MIDDLEMAN GROUP (EHMG)/ETHNIC TRADING GROUPS

My theory of the EHMG is based on fieldwork on Hokkien–Chinese rubber traders in Singapore and West Malaysia (see Landa, 1978: chaps. 3, 4). From the fieldwork, I found that:

(a) Chinese middlemen provided all the basic infrastructure required for successful middleman–entrepreneurship (i.e., they enforce contracts among themselves, provide credit and information to each other, and reduce the risks of bankruptcy). In short, Chinese middleman–entrepreneurs functioned like the "N-entrepreneurs" in Leibenstein's (1968) theory of entrepreneurship, by providing "gap-filling" and "input-completing" functions in underdeveloped economies characterised by lack of infrastructure;

(b) the Chinese middleman group involved in the marketing of smallholders' rubber was dominated by a close-knit group of Hokkien–Chinese, consisting of five clans names: Tan, Lee, Lim, Gan, and Ng; and

(c) the Hokkien–Chinese middlemen had developed a system of discriminatory classification of all potential trading partners into seven categories, based on Confucian code of ethics.

The fieldwork, the subsequent analysis of data, and the findings revealed that:

---

[3] See Landa (1987) for a more sophisticated theory of contract law which takes account of: (a) the foreseeability doctrine of *Hadley* v. *Baxendale* with respect to the recovery of lost profits; and (b) the distinction between fungible and unique goods in contract remedies for breach.

Chinese middlemen were not just a random collection of Chinese traders. Rather, they were linked together in complex networks of particularistic exchange relations to form an ethnically homogeneous middleman group (EHMG). But the real significance of the visible, surface structure of the EHMG lies in its underlying deep structure: the invisible codes of ethics, embedded in the personalized exchange relations among the members of the EHMG, which function as constraints against breach of contract and hence facilitate exchange among Chinese middlemen. The EHMG thus reveals itself to be low-cost club-like institutional arrangement, serving as an alternative to contract law and the vertically integrated firm, which emerged to economize on contract-enforcement and information costs in an environment where the legal infrastructure was not well-developed [Landa, 1981; reprinted in Landa, 1994: 101–2].

I then developed my theory of the EHMG. I argued that under conditions of contract uncertainty, with positive transaction costs of breach and enforcement costs, a rational trader will not indiscriminately enter into impersonal exchange relations with anonymous traders:

> At any particular point in time, an individual is embedded in a "social structure" with rules of the game that serve to constrain his behavior. Hence a rational trader will enter into particularistic exchange relations with traders bound by institutional constraints whom he knows to be trustworthy and reliable in honoring contracts [Landa, 1981; reprinted in Landa, 1994: 103].

The rational trader (Ego) will arm himself with a "calculus of relations" (Fortes, 1969), which allows the trader to rank all potential traders in a market according to a small number of categories corresponding to different grades of traders, in descending order of trustworthiness in honouring contracts. In the multiethnic plural societies of Southeast Asia, Confucian codes of ethics help Ego to establish seven categories of trading partners. The system of discriminatory rankings of trading partners can be represented by the use of von Thunen series of seven concentric circles to depict differences in grades of trading partners, with the best grade (most trustworthy trader) located at the centre. Differences in grades of trading partners correspond with the degree of social distance; close kinsmen being the closest in social distance to Ego is ranked by Ego to fall into the best grade.

Consider Ego, located at the centre of a series of von Thunen concentric rings. How does he choose his network of trading partners? Obviously, Ego will choose the least cost-trading network. Ego will choose all his trading partners from ring 1 before moving on to ring 2; as Ego extends the size of his trading network, his trading network will become more heterogeneous, with a different mix of trustworthy trading partners. At the major ethnic boundary, separating Chinese from non-Chinese, there is a sharp kink in transaction costs; this sharp kink is the major reason Chinese middlemen belong to an ethnically homogeneous group. For those Chinese middlemen who must cross the major ethnic boundary, in order to obtain supplies from non-Chinese smallholders, cash transactions were used to mitigate against the costs of breach of contract. I arrived at the theoretical conclusion that:

The importance of Ego's subjective calculus of relations in determining the objective optimal "mix" of trading partners therefore depends upon the number of members in the constituent concentric circles, the degree of heterogeneity of the population, and a balancing off, at the margin between transaction costs of including outsiders and the opportunity costs of exclusion outsiders. The outcome of Ego's discriminatory choice of trading partners is the formation of a particularistic trading network comprised of members who share the same (Confucian) code of ethics. Given a non-decomposable middleman economy, the structural effect of many individual Chinese middlemen's discriminatory choice is the formation of the EHMG [Landa, 1981; reprinted in Landa, 1994: 106–7].

I explicitly showed how the EHMG emerged from individual rational trader's discriminatory choice of trading partners: "Ego (v1) chooses his trading partners, v2 and v3, on a kinship or ethnic basis; v2 and v3, in turn, choose their trading partners on the same particularistic basis; then the result is the emergence of the EHMG" (Landa, 1981; reprinted in Landa, 1994: 107). In this way, I had provided what sociologists called the "micro-macro link" in sociology: the link between individual rational choice of his trading partners and the emergence of the macro phenomenon of the EHMG. I also discussed how the Confucian code of ethics provided not only the rules of the game for Chinese middlemen-entrepreneurs, but also provided the basis for the subjective classification by Chinese middlemen of all potential trading partners into seven categories. The limits of Confucian ethics marked off the boundary separating Chinese from outsiders: Confucian ethics, in overseas Chinese society, prescribe differences in the patterns of mutual aid obligations between people with varying degrees of social distance within a well-defined social structure—near kinsmen, distant kinsmen, fellow villagers, and fellow Hokkiens:

> Kinship relations, in which social distance is at a minimum, are strong ties that involve the severest degree of constraint in dealings among kinsmen. Kinship relations are the irreducible jural and moral relations, and kinsmen are thus the most reliable people with whom to trade. Because of differences in the degree of behaviorial constraint, each of the five categories of members occupies a special place within the overall social structure of the Hokkien ethnic community. This implies that different behavioral patterns can be predicted for each category of members corresponding to their location in the social structure. The most orderly or reliable pattern of contractual behavior is predicted for close kinsmen and the least reliable or most disorderly behavior is predicted for fellow Hokkiens. This then forms the basis for Ego's internal differentiation of Hokkien traders into five different categories of traders [Landa, 1981; reprinted in Landa, 1994: 109].

The limits of Confucian ethics form the basis for Ego's classification of Chinese and non-Chinese traders; hence resulting in a discriminatory ranking of seven grades of traders.[4] Only recently did I realise that my theory of EHMG,

---

[4] Recently I came across the work of Chinese sociologist Fie Xiaotong (1992), who described the basic characteristic of traditional Chinese society in terms of the concept of "*chaxugeju*" (differential mode of association): each individual is at the centre of a series of widening concentric circles of

developed in 1981, which has a theory of traders developing a subjective system of classification of all potential trading partners, is linked to the cognitive–anthropological approach of Mary Douglas (1985).[5] Other aspects of my theory of ethnic trading networks included: (a) the role of non-price signals such as ethnicity in helping Ego easily to identify a potential trading partner and slot him into one of the subjective categories of grades of trading partners, without having to search for information about the trustworthiness of a potential trading partners; and (b) how the particularistic networks of exchange economise on actual costs of search for information about the degree of trustworthiness of Ego's potential trading partner, for example:

> members of Ego's own ethnic community, being "insiders" are perceived to be more trustworthy than "outsiders." Information acquired from insiders is therefore considered by Ego to be more reliable hence he can economize on the quantity of information he collects [Landa, 1981; reprinted in Landa, 1994: 111].

Just as Coase extended his analysis of the firm from a one-product firm to a multi-product firm, so my theory of ethnic trading networks examined the transaction cost implications of a heterogeneous middleman group. I concluded that a rational trader will try to confine his ethnic trading network to members of a homogeneous middleman group as much as possible, in order to economise on the costs of breach of contract and the costs of contract enforcement in an environment where the legal framework is underdeveloped and where information costs are high. In summary, even though my theory of ethnic trading networks included important sociological concepts such as "social structure", "social distance", and social norms/codes of ethics, it is clear that my theory rests squarely on Coasean transaction cost foundations.

THEORY OF EHMG: LINKS WITH THE "MARKETS-HIERARCHIES",
"EMBEDDEDNESS/SOCIAL NETWORKS" RESEARCH PROGRAMMES

Oliver Williamson (1975, 1985) has done a great deal to promote transaction cost economics. His analysis of the institution of the vertically-integrated firm is an important extension of Coase's theory of the firm. Williamson shifted his emphasis to the *ex post* contractual problem of exchange and argued that asset specificity of a contracting firm allows a contracting partner to act opportunistically to the detriment of the contracting firm. Vertical integration, a private ordering governance structure, thus emerges to cope with the problem of contracting across markets where contractual relations could be costly under

networks of overlapping kin and social relationships. Confucian ethics supply both objective structural framework and the cognitive foundations for such a system of ranking and classification. Fei's analysis made me very aware of how overseas Chinese in Southeast Asia have adapted the traditional Chinese social structure to the social structure of the host country to which they emigrated.

[5] For a survey of my work on trust and informal institutions, including the cognitive foundations of institutions, see Landa (1996).

conditions of bounded rationality, asset specificity and opportunism. My theory of ethnic trading networks also is a theory of private ordering type of governance structure to cope with the problem of opportunism, specifically breach of contract where the legal framework for enforcement is not well-developed; hence relying on the state to enforce contracts by traders is costly. Instead of choosing vertical integration, Chinese middlemen in developing economies choose to particularise exchange relations as a way of economising on transaction costs under conditions of contract uncertainty.

My theory of ethnic trading networks (Landa, 1981) is also related to sociologist Granovetter's (1985) "embeddedness" approach to social networks. Granovetter's article began with a critique of the economists' "methodological individualism" approach to the study of economic man in general, and in particular against Williamson's "markets-hierarchy" approach to the study of methods of co-ordinating economic activities. Specifically, Granovetter criticised economists for adopting an "undersocialised" rational choice view of the economic man, an atomised man who has no social ties with others. Taking account of the fact that in the real world economic relations are often embedded in social relations, Granovetter argued that mutual trust exists to mitigate against malfeasance or opportunistic behaviour of members embedded in such networks. Thus, social networks may function to co-ordinate inter-firm transactions under conditions in which Williamson would predict the emergence of vertically integrated firms. Granovetter advocated a research programme for the development of the "new economic sociology" (see also Swedberg, 1991; Smelser and Swedberg, 1994), different from the "old economic sociology" and from neoclassical economics, that will incorporate the embeddedness approach as its core.[6]

Looking back at my theory of ethnic trading networks (Landa, 1981), it is clear that when the theory is stripped of both its Coasean transaction costs foundations as well as its rational choice foundations, my theory is, in essence, the same as Granovetter's (1985) embeddness–social network approach. But his theory of social networks is incomplete because his theory cannot explain the emergence of trust embedded in personalistic social networks; Granovetter simply assumed the existence of trust embedded in personalistic exchange networks. As Frieland and Alford (1991: 252–3) put it:

> Mark Granovetter stress that both market exchange and bureaucratic hierarchy are embedded in social relations which affect their action (Granovetter, 1985). But how these relationships affect exchange and hierarchy is still ambiguous. In the essay he points out that these relations may hinder or facilitate the operation of the structure. . . . However, social networks per se do not have any content and as such do not entail interests, values, motives, beliefs . . . [and] without content, that is, the distinctive categories, beliefs, and motives, created by a specific institutional logic—it

---

[6] For some of the sociological literature using the "embeddedness–social network" approach in analysing Chinese and other East Asian forms of economic organisation, see the collection of papers in Hamilton (1996). See also the collection of papers in Fruin (1998).

will be impossible to explain what kinds of social relations have what kind of effect on the behavior of organizations and individuals. That content can best be understood by situating those social relations within a particular context. Otherwise, the "embeddedness" approach can easily be assimilated to a rational individualist perspective . . . or to the functionalism of the new institutional economics wherein social relations are derived, just like hierarchy through the limits of exchange. Without the content, of these social relationships, we are unable to understand what trust—so central to these discussions—actually means.

My theory of ethnic trading networks shows that it is, indeed, possible to assimilate the sociological embeddedness approach to a rational choice approach resting on Coasean transaction cost/NIE foundations. My theory of EHMG thus provides a conceptual link between the embeddedness–social network approach of economic sociology, and Coase–Williamson's "markets-hierarchies" NIE analysis of alternative forms of western economic organisations. The result is an extended "markets–hierarchies–ethnic networks" unified theory of western and Chinese contractual practices and economic organisations resting on Coasean transaction cost foundations.

IMPLICATIONS OF A THEORY OF EHMG FOR FORMULATING SOME (TESTABLE) HYPOTHESES

The following (six) hypotheses flow from my theory of EHMG/ethnic trading networks; hypotheses 2, 3, 4 and 5 are especially relevant for research on the kinds of institutional arrangements which will facilitate global economic transactions:

(1) The function of the EHMG as an efficient network form of economic organisation for contract enforcement under conditions of contract-uncertainty may become increasingly redundant as the nation–state plays an increasingly important role in the creation and enforcement of contract law in developing economies (Landa, 1981; Landa, 1998). Even then, the EHMG may still play an important role in an advanced capitalist economy with well-developed legal infrastructure when members of an EHMG can enforce contracts more efficiently than resorting to the law courts. A good example of this is the diamond trade in New York city which is dominated by a close-knit group of Hassidic Jews (Landa, 1988). The diamond trade involves a great deal of trust and the close-knit trading community of Hassidic Jews was able to dominate this trade because the Jews had a long history of enforcing contracts within the Jewish diaspora of Medieval Europe.

(2) With globalisation of economic transactions, and the growing economic importance of East Asia, ethnic trading networks/EHMG will become even more important in international and regional trade. Thus I agree with Appelbaum's (1998) analysis that Chinese/East Asian forms of network

organisation will be increasingly important, not only because of the importance of trust and *guanxi* in enforcing contracts emphasised in this chapter, but also because of an additional reason not mentioned in my work, i.e., that such network organisations, with their emphasis on informal relations, are a flexible type of economic organisation highly adaptable to the needs of global buyer-driven commodity chains (Appelbaum, 1998; Gereffi, 1994). Hence, network organisations are more efficient than the rigid state-enforced contractual relations between firms.[7]

(3) Western companies contracting for joint ventures in China will be more successful in doing business in China if they have an ethnic Chinese joint venture partner, with extensive connections with Chinese officials and other Chinese businessmen. This is especially important in China (PRC) in transition to a market economy where many local-level Chinese cadres are entrenched in strategic "gatekeeping" roles in the granting of quotas, permits, licences, etc. (see Appelbaum, 1998; Landa, 1998). Here trust embedded in particularistic networks unfortunately can be exploited for the purposes of unproductive rent-seeking activities on the part of cadres (Landa, 1998), giving rise to bribery and corruption.[8]

(4) In joint venture contracts between Western and Chinese partners, detailed and elaborate terms of contract are more likely compared with joint venture contracts between Chinese joint venture partners. This reflects the formal contractual system favoured by Western companies and their hired big Western law firms when negotiating with Chinese partners. Chinese joint venture partners, on the other hand, are likely to have simpler, less elaborate contracts, relying more on the trust and goodwill of the partners in dealing with problems that might arise.

(5) Western manufacturers wishing to have access to supplies from Chinese factories would be more successful if they used the service of a Chinese firm to act as its agent; the Western firm signs a legally binding contract with its agent. The agent works through a Chinese factory, which in turn establishes a network of Chinese subcontractors linked by particularistic ties. These informal networks, based on trust, make the Chinese network of subcontractors highly flexible and adaptive to changing market conditions, especially important in buyer-driven commodity chains (see Appelbaum, 1998).[9]

---

[7] Thanks to Richard Appelbaum for pointing this out to me (e-mail correspondence, 7 January 1999).

[8] In Landa (1998), I made an analytical distinction between gift-giving among members of a EHMG as investment in trust, and gift-giving used as bribes in unproductive rent-seeking activity.

[9] Karen Lee wrote an essay for me in 1998 on aspects of Asian business network. She provided a case study of her Hong Kong based firm, which acts as an agent or middleman between an American company and a Hong Kong hand-knitting factory. The Hong Kong factory, in turn, subcontracts the major process—hand-knitting—to kinsmen, clansmen and those living in Chio-Chow in China; there are no formal contracts signed between the Hong Kong factory and its network of subcontractors in Chio-Chow. Trust is very important in assuring timely delivery of products. For a game-theoretic analysis of the principal–agent relationship in the context of Asian business networks, see Huang and Landa (1999).

(6) In joint venture contracts between Chinese partners, it is likely that partnerships are formed along dialect lines. These include, for instance, joint venture contracts formed between Cantonese-speaking Hong Kong partners with partners from Guangdong province, joint venture contracts formed between Hokkien-speaking Taiwanese partners and partners in Fujian province, and joint venture contracts formed between Hokkien-speaking Singapore partners and partners in Fujian province. This is due not only to common dialect but also to the Chinese sense of belonging to their "native place", and hence the greater the degree of trust toward partners from their native place.

REFERENCES

Appelbaum, Richard P. (1998), "The Future of Law in a Global Economy", *Social & Legal Studies* 7 (2); 171–92.

Coase, R. A. (1937), "The Nature of the Firm", reprinted in G. Stigler and K. E. Boulding (eds.), *Readings in Price Theory* (Chicago, Ill.: Richard D. Irwin, 1952).

—— (1960), "The Problem of Social Cos", *Journal of Law & Economics* 3; 1–44.

Chow, Gregory C. (1997), "Challenges of China's Economic System for Economic Theory", *American Economic Review*, American Economic Association Papers and Proceeding, May.

Fei, Xiaotong (1992), *From the Soil: The Foundations of Chinese Society* (trans. Gary G. Hamilton and Wang Zheng, Berkeley, Cal.: University of California Press).

Fortes, Myer (1969), *Kinship and the Social Order: The Legacy of Lewis Henry Morgan* (Chicago, Ill.: Aldine).

Friedland, Roger, and Alford, Robert R. (1991), "Bringing Society Back In: Symbols, Practices, and Institutional Contradictions" in W. W. Powell and P. J. Di Maggio (eds.), *The New Institutionalism in Organizational Analysis* (Chicago, Ill.: The University of Chicago Press).

Fruin, W. Mark (ed.) (1998), *Networks, Markets, and the Pacific Rim: Studies in Strategy* (Oxford: Oxford University Press).

Gereffi, Gary, and Korenieweicz, Miguel (ed.) (1994), *Commodity Chains and Global Capitalism* (Westport, Conn.: Greenwood Press).

Goetz, Charles J., and Scott, Robert E. (1977), "Liquidated Damages, Penalties, and the Just Compensation Principle: Some Notes on an Enforcement Model and a Theory of Efficient Breach", *Columbia Law Review* 77; 554–94.

Granovetter, Mark (1985), "Economic Action and Social Structure: The Problem of Embeddedness", *American Journal of Sociology* 91; 481–510.

Hamilton, Gary G. (ed.) (1996), *Asian Business Networks* (Berlin: Walter de Gruyter).

Huang, Peter H., and Landa, Janet T. (1999), "Asian Business Networks and Forms of Economic Organization: A Psychological Game-Theoretic Approach", paper presented at the University of Maryland IRIS Center Conference on "Collective Action and Corruption in Emerging Economies" (14 May), Washington, DC.

Leibenstein, Harvey (1968), "Entrepreneurship and Development", *American Economic Review* 58; 72–83.

Landa, Janet T. (1976), "An Exchange Economy with Legally Binding Contract: A Public Choice Approach", *Journal of Economic Issues* 10 (4); 905–22.

—— (1978), "The Economics of the Ethnically Homogeneous Chinese Middleman Group: A Property Rights-Public Choice Approach", unpublished Ph.D. dissertation, VPI & SU.

—— (1981), "A Theory of the Ethnically Homogeneous Middleman Group: An Institutional Alternative to Contract Law", *Journal of Legal Studies* 10 (2); 349–62.

—— (1987), "Hadley v. Baxendale and the Expansion of the Middleman Economy", *Journal of Legal Studies* 16; 455–70.

—— (1988), "Underground Economies: Generic or Sui Generis?" in J. Jenkins (ed.), *Beyond the Informal Sector: Including the Excluded in Developing Countries* (San Francisco, Cal.: Institute for Contemporary Studies).

—— (1994), *Trust, Ethnicity, and Identity: Beyond The New Institutional Economics of Contract Law, Ethnic Trading Networks and Gift-Exchange* (Ann Arbor, Mich.: University of Michigan Press).

—— (1996), "Doing the Economics of Trust and Informal Institutions" in S. G. Medema and W. Samuels (eds.), *Foundations of Research in Economics: How Do Economists Do Economics?* (Cheltenham, Brookfield, Vermont: Edward Elgar Publishing Ltd).

—— (1998), "The Co-evolution of Markets, Entrepreneurship, Laws, and Institutions in China's Economy in Transition: A New Institutional Economics Perspective", *University of British Columbia Law Review* 32 (2); 391–421.

—— (1999), "The Law and Bioeconomics of Ethnic Cooperation and Conflict in Plural Societies of Southeast Asia: A Theory of Chinese Merchant Success", *Journal of Bioeconomics* 1(3); 269–84.

—— and Salaff, Janet (1980), "The Socioeconomic Functions of Kinship and Ethnic Networks in the Growth of a Chinese Family Firm in Singapore: A Transactions Costs Approach", unpublished manuscript.

Smelser, Neil J., and Swedberg, Richard (1994), "The Sociological Perspective on the Economy", in N. J. Smelser and R. Swedberg (eds.), *The Handbook of Economic Sociology* (Princeton, NJ: Princeton University Press, and Russell Sage Foundation).

Swedberg, Richard (1991), "Major Traditions of Economic Sociology", *Annual Review of Sociology* 17; 251–76.

Williamson, Oliver E. (1975), *Markets and Hierarchies: Analysis of Antitrust Implications* (New York: The Free Press).

—— (1985), *The Economic Institutions of Capitalism: Firms, Markets, Relational Contracting* (New York: The Free Press).

13

Understanding Chinese Legal and Business Norms: A Comment on Janet Tai Landa's Chapter

JOHN K. M. OHNESORGE*

Abstract

This chapter elaborates on Conference comments offered in response to Professor Tai Landa's "Coasean Foundations of a Unified Theory of Western and Chinese Contractual Practices and Economic Organisations". The second part presents an overview of Tai Landa's chapter, focusing on her theory of contract law and the Ethnically Homogeneous Middleman Group (EHMG). The third part provides an overview of scholarship on commercial law and legality in traditional China, designed to suggest that the concept of "Confucian ethics", which forms a central part of Tai Landa's theory of the EHMG, must include a more nuanced view of legality if it is to be used to describe the set of social norms and values concerning commercial behaviour that actually held in pre-modern China. The fourth part questions the use of the term "rules of the game" to describe the role of law, and non-legal normative systems, in structuring behaviour. Tai Landa and many "new institutionalist" scholars rely on this metaphor, but the metaphor often serves to end enquiry, as if there were simply one way that rules interact with the actual playing of a game, rather than acknowledging and exploring the many various ways in which rule structures interact with the playing of a game. The final part of the chapter explores Tai Landa's vision of the EHMG and its relationship to background legal and political orders, arguing that the EHMG is more dependent upon a background power structure, either of law or of politics, than Tai Landa's model suggests.

---

* My thanks to Bill Alford and Zang Dongsheng for comments and suggestions.

INTRODUCTION

PROFESSOR JANET TAI Landa's contribution to this volume demonstrates the extraordinary value of interdisciplinary approaches when we set out to study a concrete phenomenon, such as contracting behaviour among businesspeople. Although different disciplines may share so little at the level of theory that they seem to speak in different languages, when specific issues or institutions are being studied, especially in a comparative context, the contributions of views derived from radically different theoretical starting points can be crucial to full understanding. The comments that follow, then, are offered in the spirit of applying this principle to Tai Landa's chapter. Words on the page take on a life of their own, particularly when read by someone of another discipline. The issues that Tai Landa's chapter raised in the mind of this reader may not be what she expected, though it is hoped that they are relevant to her argument. Rather than addressing Tai Landa's arguments as a fellow economist or law and economics *aficionado* might, these comments are organised around the themes of Chinese legal and commercial culture (Part III), the understanding of law and social norms as "rules of the game" (Part IV), and relationships between ethnic minority trading groups and background legal and political orders (Part V). First, however, a summary of her arguments will be offered in Part II.

TAI LANDA'S THEORY OF CONTRACT LAW AND THE LOGIC OF THE ETHNICALLY HOMOGENEOUS MIDDLEMAN GROUP (EHMG)

In Part I of her chapter, Tai Landa provides a brief summary of Ronald Coase's use of transaction cost analysis to explain the emergence of the business firm as an alternative to the market for organising production. According to Tai Landa, Coase focused on the transaction costs that would arise if complex, long-term productive activities were to be organised through the use of individual contracts between autonomous market actors. Coase's emphasis, then, was on the costs of *negotiating* the immense number of contracts that such a mode of productive organisation would require, and in such *negotiation* costs he located the impetus for the organisation of production within firms embodying entrepreneur–employee relations of authority. Tai Landa presents this sketch of Coase's work in order to demonstrate how her own theory of contract law, presented in Part II of the chapter, builds upon but also departs from Coase's work. Whereas Coase invoked transaction costs of contract negotiation to explain the firm, she invoked transaction costs of contract *enforcement* to explain the emergence of state-enforced contract law. In particular, she focused her attention on the role of contract law in facilitating exchange between merchants, rather than continuing Coase's focus on the organisation of production. For her, the essence of contract law is state *enforcement* of contractual commitments, which arises to reduce or pre-empt the costs contracting parties would have to incur privately to enforce contractual obligations, or otherwise to protect themselves against strategic behaviour by their trading partners.

In Part III of her chapter, Tai Landa presents her theory of the Ethnically Homogeneous Middleman Group (EHMG), exemplified by the Hokkien-Chinese traders who controlled the trade in rubber in West Malaysia and Singapore. Again the objective is to explain the existence of a social phenomenon using transaction cost analysis, but here what is sought to be explained is not contract law, but rather a social structure, the EHMG, that performed the functions that Tai Landa sees state-enforced contract law as performing in developed societies. But the EHMG was not made up simply of atomistic rational maximisers who happened to share an ethnic origin; rather, it was a code of ethics shared by members of the relevant ethnic group, in this case "Confucian ethics", that facilitated both the formation and the continued functioning of the EHMG. Confucian ethics provided the "rules of the game" for the Chinese traders who controlled the distribution of rubber after its harvest by ethnic Malay smallholders, and also provided the basis for varying levels of treatment accorded to those with whom the EHMG members traded. Malays, who occupied only the lowest level of the distribution pyramid, the harvesting of rubber sap, did not share these "Confucian ethics" and thus, according to Tai Landa, for the Chinese to deal with them in the atmosphere of contractual uncertainty that characterised West Malaysia and Singapore gave rise to potentially higher transaction costs in terms of contract enforcement. For Tai Landa, this explains why the Chinese refused to deal with Malays on terms as favourable as those they accorded one another: "[f]or those Chinese middlemen who must cross the major ethnic boundary, in order to obtain supplies from non-Chinese smallholders, cash transactions were used to mitigate against the costs of breach of contract" (p. 355).

In Part IV of her chapter, Tai Landa compares her own work to that of sociologist Mark Granovetter on "embeddedness", the insight that market exchanges in fact often take place between economic actors who are not the atomistic individuals of microeconomics, but who are tied together in social networks that facilitate trust, and mitigate against strategic behaviour. Tai Landa sees her work as advancing beyond Granovetter's in that she claims to be able to explain the emergence of the trust-facilitating structure, the EHMG, whereas Granovetter simply assumed its existence (p. 358). She claims to be able to "assimilate the sociological embeddedness approach to a rational choice approach resting on Coasean transaction cost/NIE ['New Institutional Economics'] foundations" (p. 359). Part V of her chapter concludes with a brief discussion of some possible implications of her theory, as well as some prescriptions for modes of doing business in China.

EVALUATING AND RE-EVALUATING
CHINA'S COMMERCIAL TRADITION AND LAW

These initial comments were prompted by Tai Landa's opening emphasis on the great gap between China and the West in terms of reliance on detailed, enforceable contracts (p. 347), and her claim that it is "Confucian ethics", something that sounds positively antithetical to law, that provide the "rules of the game" for traders within the EHMG (p. 356). Although her vision of Chinese legal culture is made clear mostly by the lack of attention the subject receives, her characterisation is an important part of her overall argument, which places her within an intellectual lineage that is worth exploring.

In the manner of lawyers marshalling evidence to support a legal argument, historians, social theorists and even less savoury characters have long used characterisations of China's legal culture as ammunition in a range of battles, real and theoretical. In the nineteenth century the British, Americans and other imperial powers demanding trading rights pointed to inadequacies in the Chinese system of justice, including the apparent absence of a sphere of private, non-penal commercial law, to help justify the treaty ports and extraterritorial jurisdiction they established in China, as they did in Japan, Egypt and other parts of the world.[1] The picture of Chinese legality propagated in the West at that time, though based in part on experience in Canton (Guangzhou) and elsewhere, was obviously not based on any comprehensive analysis of Chinese formal law or legal practice and, equally obviously, was highly useful to the project of treaty port imperialism. This does not prove the picture inaccurate, but should stand as a kind of cautionary note to comparative lawyers of the potential implications of denigrating the legal orders of weaker societies, whether those orders are described as primitive and barbarous, or as rife with contractual uncertainly and high transaction costs. A current example of this problem is the International Monetary Fund representative who travels to Russia to investigate the legal environment for business there, then relies overwhelmingly on the public pronouncements of the American Chamber of Commerce and other organisations of foreign investors (Buckberg, 1997). The legitimacy of the conclusions that result from such a research approach suffers dramatically from the fact that they can hardly be separated from the interests of those who supply the data, even if the conclusions contain important elements of truth. Tai Landa's work seems in no way tainted by such an affinity, but her chapter nonetheless would have benefited from a more thorough explication of the actual environment for contract enforcement in Malaysia and Singapore at the time when her research was done. Presumably such environment included both positive legal and socio-cultural norms, and it would be

---

[1] The literature on foreign concessions, extraterritorial jurisdiction and other aspects of the "unequal treaty" system in China is voluminous. A useful overview from an international law perspective is Bau (1921: 85–323).

helpful to know whether the Chinese rubber traders actually understood this normative environment and, if so, in what respects they found it wanting.

Although Tai Landa invokes the "chaos" of the surrounding legal environment to explain the EHMG, in current globalisation rhetoric the threat of chaos is more often deployed to justify than to clarify. For example, we have actually had an "international financial architecture" for decades, but it consisted largely of national regulatory regimes, administered by national authorities. The relaxation of these regimes has been both a cause and a result of the globalisation of finance, but the extent to which they have been systematically dismantled is strangely neglected when people start searching for means to regulate the anarchy created by unrestrained flows of short-term capital. Likewise the WTO, and each new round of global trade talks, is justified by invoking the chaos of politics, parochialism and protectionism that are sure to tip the global trade bicycle if it is not kept moving forward by another burst of diplomatic and international bureaucratic activity. The "world trading system" that this activity maintains is clearly crucial to the existence of actual trade flows, but global trade is probably much less fragile than the guardians of the system fear.

In quite a different context from those seeking justifications for extraterritoriality, Weber, as part of his studies on comparative religious systems and their relation to capitalism, invoked a vision of China's legal tradition as an example of the effect of a lack of formally rational law and adjudication on an otherwise industrious and potentially prosperous society.[2] Given the state of China's economy at the time Weber wrote, China did not raise for Weber the so-called "England problem",[3] though China's relative backwardness in industrial capitalism might well have been attributed to causes other than its legal system. Now, however, after years of rapid economic growth and industrialisation in China, and after the rapid industrialisation of Japan, Taiwan and South Korea during decades when their legal and administrative systems varied considerably from Weberian formal rationality (see Ohnesorge, forthcoming; Upham, 1987; Winn, 1994), it may be time to add the "Asia problem" to the "England problem", even if one accepts Weber's thesis about the historical affinity between industrial capitalism and formal, rational legality in the Continental European context. As will be discussed more fully below, more recent scholarship questions the accuracy of Weber's basic claims about "Kadi justice" in China,[4] but even if Weber misunderstood the nature of legality in traditional China it would be unfair to lay the blame entirely on him, as his picture of law and commerce in China shares much with the views of the Chinese informants who have so influenced Western views of imperial China. With some exceptions, even Chinese scholars highly trained in modern law have tended to conflate Confucian

---

[2] Weber's argument concerning the relationship between traditional Chinese law and the development of capitalism can be found in Weber (1968a: 100–4).

[3] Referring to the fact that industrial capitalism developed initially in England, despite the relative lack of formality in the English legal system by comparison to those on the Continent.

[4] See nn. 13–18 and accompanying text below.

normative ideology with historical reality when addressing law in imperial China (see e.g. Wu, 1932).

The resulting view of late imperial Chinese legality has several basic components addressing, *inter alia*, (i) the "rights consciousness" of the population, (ii) the phenomenology of decision-making by the magistrate, and (iii) the instrumental use of law by the ruler. Central to "rights consciousness" discussions is the idea that Chinese did not have it—that in commerce, for example, written contracts, when used at all, were always less important than relationships based on particularistic ties, and that when disputes arose the preferred method of settlement was mediation conducted well away from any representative of state power.[5] Adjudication of disputes by the magistrate is seen as evidence of an utter breakdown in the private relationship, and potentially a disaster for all involved.[6] The magistrate was available to adjudicate property and other typically private disputes not, as a court in the West, as a public good available for the benefit of private parties. The adjudicatory function of the magistrate is presented instead as a sort of pressure valve to release social tensions arising out of private disputes. When this thesis is presented in purely political terms, emphasis is laid on the fact that the position of magistrate combined judicial and administrative/regulatory roles, and that what was demanded of the magistrate, and what therefore guided his behaviour, was the maintenance of order in his district, rather than the protection of individual rights according to law.[7] A philosophical component that is sometimes added emphasises that the Chinese world view posited a continuum between the human and cosmic orders such that a failure to redress violations of society's moral and ethical (Confucian) norms would constitute a threat to cosmic harmony and order (Bodde and Morris, 1967: 43). In either case, though, the legal work of the magistrate is seen as essentially administrative, an act of governance only tangentially concerned with the vindication of private interests.

While these two aspects of the standard learning on traditional Chinese law have obvious conservative, or statist, implications, the third lesson could be interpreted as an attempt to limit the potential for arbitrariness by the ruler in a system lacking much in the way of institutional constraints on imperial prerogative. The traditional Confucian disdain for the Legalists[8] and their methods,

---

[5] Fairbank and Goldman (1998, 185): "[s]ince formal law mainly served the interests of the state, private of civil law remained only informally developed in this legal system, Resolution of conflicts among the people was therefore achieved through various customary and nonofficial channels".

[6] *Ibid.*, at 183: "[t]he people generally avoided litigation in the magistrate's court, where plaintiffs as well as defendants could be interrogated with prescribed forms of torture and everyone would have to pay fees to the yamen underlings".

[7] See, e.g., Van der Sprenkel (1977 reprint: 70): "[i]n what would be a civil suit in English law, the magistrate would have little interest in doing justice as between the parties, except in so far as it was more likely that a just decision would lead to peace and harmony in the neighbourhood. The legal system subserved administrative ends."

[8] The terms "Legalists" (*fa jia*) describes a school of writers on governance who eschewed Confucianism's emphasis on morality and instead emphasised the primacy of positive penal law. For an excellent discussion of Legalist thought, see Schwartz (1985: 321–49).

despite the oft-noted intertwining of the two traditions in actual imperial governance, can be seen as an attempt, sustained over centuries, to warn the ruler against the dangers of using law in a purely instrumental fashion, a kind of institutionalised check on royal prerogative based not on power but on rhetoric. Confucianism's rhetoric of informality, harmony, and paternalism, rather than rights vindication, in deciding disputes between individuals might be understood as functioning to legitimise a level of discretion on the part of the individual magistrate that would make it difficult for an ambitious emperor to transform basic social life through positive law. The fact that succeeding emperors expressed allegiance to the Code adopted by their respective dynasties, and that the Code of the Tang dynasty (618–907) supplied the form for all subsequent imperial Chinese Codes, suggests that stability, continuity, and non-arbitrariness were valued within traditional Chinese legality, though not, at least formally, for their role in protecting individual rights, or for providing a predictable environment for private commercial action.

Since the 1970s there has been a flowering of interest in traditional Chinese law and its relation to commerce and to private "rights consciousness", as a result of which a much more nuanced picture of imperial Chinese legality is now emerging.[9] While some of this scholarship seems again animated by wider aims, in particular a desire to disprove the Weberian thesis and the indigenous Chinese assumptions that fed it (in particular, P. Huang, 1996), this work has significantly raised the standard for scholarship on traditional Chinese law through its orientation towards social history, and its use of primary materials such as actual contract documents of various kinds, or archival records of disputes adjudicated by magistrates in late imperial China. The following passage from a general social history of eighteenth century China, though emphasising customary over state law, reflects more recent scholarship:

> [C]ustomary law evolved outside the formal legal system to expedite economic (and social) transactions. Legal developments also reflected an increasing need to do business with strangers. Reliance on written contracts for the purchase and mortgaging of land, purchase of commodities and people, and hiring of wage laborers become commonplace in the Qing period. Most eloquently, private (so-called white) contracts supplemented (and soon outnumbered) the red (that is, stamped) official versions registered for a fee with the local yamen. Business partnerships in mining, shipping, commerce, and agriculture could be formalized and protected through this increasingly vigorous and effective system of contract law [Naquin and Rawski, 1987: 102].

The picture of late imperial Chinese commercial life that is emerging recognises a much greater role for contractual formality and for law-like commercial norms than was previously the case, though the role of the state in adjudicating disputes is still hotly contested.

---

[9] Works of several authors focusing on late imperial and early modern China are collected in a volume edited by Bernhardt and Huang (1994). Other important works on this period are Allee (1994); Brockman (1980); and Buxbaum (1971). Important works dealing with earlier periods include Scogin (1990), and Hansen (1995).

Other scholars meanwhile have been collecting, studying and sometimes translating into Western languages the so-called "magistrate's handbooks" that were prepared to assist imperial Chinese magistrates in performing their various duties, including deciding disputes and enforcing the law (see e.g. L. Huang, 1984). Although such handbooks are in a sense secondary to actual decision records as historical evidence of legal practice, they are an important window into the mentality and the role-expectations of those who adjudicated disputes. Given the limited possibilities for obtaining review of magistrates' decisions in matters we would handle through civil and commercial law (*xishi*, or "trivial matters"), and the fact that imperial Chinese law was not written with the creation and protection of private rights as its stated objective, an understanding of what the magistrates thought they were doing is crucial to understanding the relationship between law and private interests in traditional China. Although much archival material apparently remains untouched (Park and Antony, 1993), and although there will certainly be disagreements over interpretation of the primary materials, especially perhaps between lawyers and non-lawyers,[10] one hopes that the days are past when some aphorism of Confucius could be cited in a description of legal reality in late-imperial China.

A third body of scholarship perhaps relevant to Tai Landa's argument has called for a re-examination of the political role of trade and commerce in imperial China, inspired in part by Habermas' writings on the role of the public sphere in European history.[11] This literature again addresses a particular argument, this time Weber's claim that Chinese cities, and the merchant groups that dominated trade there, were qualitatively different from their counterparts in pre-modern Europe, and that this was key to the course of China's legal, political and economic development (Weber, 1968a: 13–20; Weber, 1968b: 1226–31). Another growing body of research focuses on the history of Chinese business and business practices in the late imperial and early modern eras, and by looking at particular industries has provided a much more complete view of the nascent bourgeoisie of late nineteenth and early twentieth century China (see e.g. Cochran, 1980). Finally, even Weber's attempt to invoke as an explanatory variable a sharp contrast between Western and Chinese accounting practices[12] has been seriously challenged.[13]

---

[10] E.g., Philip Huang's attempt to reconstruct out of the prohibitions and punishments that make up the Qing Code a set of positive norms that effectively bound magistrate decision-making in disputes over private economic matters may strike lawyers as oddly formalistic, given the extent of debate within modern jurisprudence over the degree to which our own judges are actually bound by the existing legal materials, which would have to be considered more plausibly binding than the Qing Code.

[11] Important works applying this approach are Rowe (1984) and Rowe (1989). The approach itself is discussed in Rowe (1990) and Wakeman (1993).

[12] Weber (1968a: 243): "[in China] there was no genuine, technically valuable system of commercial correspondence, accounting, or bookkeeping".

[13] Gardella (1992). Despite these attacks on various aspects of Weber's analysis of China, his basic picture has staunch defenders. See, e.g., Fairbank and Goldman (1998: 185–6): "[t]his nondevelopment of Chinese law along lines familiar to the West was plainly related to the nondevelopment of

The potential implications of all this for Tai Landa's chapter are several. First, although Tai Landa makes only passing reference to Chinese commercial law culture in her chapter (p. 347), it is the kind of reference that these days would be greeted with a fair amount of scepticism not only by legal historians, but by a broad range of scholars interested in Chinese law.[14] Any supportable ideal type of law's role in the economic history of the West would clearly differ from law's role in Chinese society, imperial or modern, but it is also quite apparent that the role of law in Chinese life has been systematically underestimated, both in Chinese and in Western scholarship (Alford, 1997), and that temptations, both willful and inadvertent, to preserve these distortions remain today. From constitutional law arguments against universal human rights, to administrative law arguments explaining or justifying bureaucratic informality and discretion, to arguments made in the business context against detailed negotiation and memorialisation of contract terms, claims about the unimportance of law and rights consciousness in the Chinese tradition, even if correct on one level, are easily instrumentalised. Stylised accounts of traditional cultural norms and practices are invoked strategically to legitimate modern conditions that often have little to do with traditional society, and those who benefit from this have little incentive to characterise the cultural tradition accurately. Self-reporting on Confucian ethics and morality can be notoriously unreliable in this respect as, not surprisingly, it tends to be those on top, whether in government or in business, who are most eager to portray traditional tendencies toward hierarchy and paternalism as still widely accepted among modern East Asian populations.

The recent scholarship on Chinese law and commerce also raises the difficulty of deciding what in the way of indigenous Chinese commercial and business practices the rubber traders brought with it, culturally speaking, to Southeast Asia, and what developed there as a result of rational responses to local environmental conditions. Tai Landa convincingly distances herself from the doctrinaire "methodological individualism" of some rational actor explanations of spontaneous norm emergence, but the actual content of the indigenous cultural equipment of the Chinese traders remains a crucial question. For example, the "native-place" banks, commercial guilds and trading organisations discussed by Gary Hamilton operate on a norm of discrimination against outsiders that Tai Landa argues emerged in Malaysia as a rational response to contractual uncertainty and transaction costs in dealing with the ethnic Malays (p. 355). All the Chinese rubber traders brought with them, in her vision, was a system of "Confucian ethics"; the rest of the exclusionary EHMG system evolved in

---

capitalism and an independent business class in old China. There was no idea of the corporation as a legal individual. Big firms were family affairs. Business relations were not cold impersonal matters governed by the general principles of the law and of contract in a world apart from home and family. Business was a segment of the whole web of friendship, kinship obligations, and personal relations that supported Chinese life. . . . *The Chinese state and society . . . had become inured to counterproductive attitudes, goals, and practices that would impede modernization*" (emphasis added).

[14] See, e.g., Naquin and Rawski (1987), and accompanying text.

Southeast Asia as a result of rational decisions by individual Chinese merchants in response to the environment. In this story, discriminatory business practices favouring other Chinese over Malays, such as "cash only" dealing with Malays, were just rational responses to the "sharp kink in transaction costs" (p. 355) that purportedly occurred at the ethnic boundary.

It seems that at least two other possible explanations for the Chinese discrimination against the Malays should be considered however. The first, referred to above, is the possibility that the ethnic in-group trading patterns of the Hokkien-Chinese rubber traders were part of the cultural apparatus they brought with them from China, and that they were part of Chinese *commercial* culture, having little or no connection with "Confucian ethics". In other words, the Hokkien rubber traders, by organising themselves into a network according to kinship and native-place ties, were behaving in Southeast Asia in much the same manner as "native-place" banks and commercial guilds operated in China itself. Known as *huiguan* in Qing China, these organisations:

> provided a meeting ground, lodging, financial assistance, and storage facilities . . . For merchants and artisans, the *huiguan* also provided a mechanism for regulating trade. Regional specialisation was premised on the idea of comparative advantage, but became a device for a vast interlocking network of small monopolies. The *huiguan* helped maintain such monopolies by preventing competition from within the trade and by negotiating on behalf of the group with the state or other merchants. . . . [M]en from a few clusters of counties in Shanxi, Anhui, and Fujian (and later Zhejiang and Guangdong) penetrated and took control of major markets in key commodities [Naquin and Rawski, 1987: 48].

The fact that such organisations were so prevalent within China itself, where everyone shared the same Confucian ethics, suggests that the logic of the EHMG may not be based on anything so fundamental or clear-cut as differing ethical systems.

A second, and less optimistic, view would be that their discriminatory practices *vis-à-vis* the Malays may instead have been the result of non-rational attitudes of ethnic Chinese towards other races, particularly Southeast Asians, that had nothing to do with either Chinese commercial culture or with Confucian ethics. Chinese racial stereotyping has a long historical pedigree, and it is at least arguable that discriminatory trading practices based thereon would have persisted in Malaysia and Singapore, even if irrational, unless they proved radically inefficient. This view leaves the racial attitudes of the Chinese unexplained, but it squares with the discussant's own experience that racial and ethnic divides persist in East Asia, and elsewhere, under circumstances that render them distinctly irrational from an economic perspective. A logical implication of Tai Landa's account would be that racial discrimination in economic relations would wither away in the absence of an economic rationale, if race were no longer a useful "non-price signal" in her terms (p. 357). This economically deterministic stance has in fact been adopted by those opposed to antidiscrimination legislation in the

USA,[15] but the dynamics of racial biases and the discrimination that results therefrom are poorly captured by this sort of base-superstructure analysis.

Finally, because the existing literature on Chinese and indeed East Asian law generally has been so prone to stereotyping along Confucian lines, we should be careful even when some currently observed phenomenon in fact does correspond to the stereotyped image. As Tai Landa noted in her discussion of her chapter, she does not focus on *guanxi* as something uniquely Chinese, but as a label for a set of phenomena known in many societies. It could be added that several modern East Asian societies have suffered under governments that fluctuated between authoritarianism and totalitarianism. Under such conditions a reliance on private networks and informal contacts in conducting one's private life, and in one's relations with the state, is probably likely to emerge anywhere. Perhaps this was the very reason for the comparatively heavy reliance on social ties rather than formal legal relations in traditional China and other parts of East Asia, but the modern persistence of these practices might be based at least in part on a coincidental congruence in structures of authority, rather than being a cultural holdover, something "Chinese".

Applying this to the legal environment in which international trade and business are carried out, Tai Landa offers an important reminder that businesspeople from any culture are likely to develop non-state norms and systems of dispute resolution if the external environment so demands, but also that what any particular group develops will reflect the particularism of its culture. While we might agree, then, that Western domination in the development of the governance structures of international business is likely to result in outcomes that reflect Western cultural preoccupations I would add that non-Western cultures, in this case the Chinese, are not necessarily as antithetical to law and legalised business relations as we have been led to believe.

LAW (+ SOCIAL NORMS) AS "RULES OF THE GAME"

This second set of comments addresses Tai Landa's assimilation of contract law (p. 352), guild rules (p. 353), Confucian ethics (p. 356) and the non-legal norm

---

[15] See e.g. Epstein (1995: 175–6): "[t]he antidiscrimination laws ignore the power of the market to deal with the most invidious forms of discrimination. . . . [T]he employer who sacrifices economic welfare for personal prejudice will pay for her preferences on the bottom line. By forgoing superior labor in order to hire inferior workers, she will sacrifice resources to indulge consumption choices, and will be at a systematic disadvantage relative to employers whose economic motivations are more rational." A point of interest is that, at least in the employment discrimination context, Epstein believes that the market will not take care of irrational discrimination if the group discriminated against has no option but to take its business elsewhere, and that therefore the preferred solution in the US context is increased competition among employers: *ibid.*, at 176–7. Although like Tai Landa he finds efficiency arguments justifying discriminatory behaviour among closely-knit groups: *ibid.*, at 177–8, one might ask whether Epstein's preference for competition would lead him to approve of regulatory action against the Chinese rubber merchants, either to break their control of distribution, or to prohibit their discriminatory dealing.

structure within the Chinese EHMG (p. 355) to the "rules of the game". There seems little point in objecting to the use of such simplifying concepts or categories generally: it seems inevitable that we rely on such devices for understanding the world, whether in scholarship or in everyday life. This practice presents problems, however, one of the most serious being that the simplifying concept or image being invoked may actually describe a range of various phenomena, thus allowing different audiences to hear and accept a common metaphor, while in fact holding quite varied understandings. Tai Landa's chapter raises a particular metaphor, "rules of the game", that seems to be invoked more and more frequently in the broader social science literature to describe not only law, but also non-legal norm systems (see e.g. North, 1990: 4–5). I do not want to argue here against the use of the metaphor *per se*, but instead to offer a refinement based on a certain scepticism about rules and rule application, as well as practical commercial law experience.[16]

To say that law is like the rules of a game would be most meaningful if "game" described a single type of activity, in which rules played a single, clear role. In fact it does not. There are games like chess, in which the rules not only define the game in general, but also tightly define any particular move that a player can make. No move can be made in chess if not in conformity with the rules, and there really are no "judgement calls" because the rules themselves are entirely rule-like, and subject to simple, mechanical application. It is impossible to play chess unless one knows essentially all the rules, and it is likewise impossible to imagine situations in which breaches of the rules would be allowed to pass without objection. Notably, chess requires no umpire or referee, because if one does not know and follow the rules exactly, one is not playing the game.

To say that law and commercial activity, or any area of social life, interact in the way that the rules of chess interact with the playing of that game is not plausible as a descriptive matter,[17] but chess is not the only sort of game, and perhaps the "rules of the game" metaphor can still be useful if we broaden our understanding of games to include sports and their governance. In sports, like in chess, the rules obviously matter: soccer is not basketball because the rules are different. But when we think about how sports are actually played, and about how conflicts that arise during the course of play are settled, it becomes apparent that rules in a sport do not function like rules in chess. First, in applying even the clearest rules of a sport, such as the rule that the ball must remain within the playing area, factual disputes are inevitable. This is not possible in chess, but is endemic in sports, and in commercial activity. Secondly, there are important rules, such as soccer's rule on tackling an opposing player, the enforcement of

---

[16] For another comparison of legal rules and games, including chess, see Posner (1990: 49–51).

[17] Of course that does not mean that it must be rejected as a normative project if the materials making up any particular legal field, such as administrative law, could possibly be made to conform to such a vision. For example, Hayek's (1960) view of public law shares something of the chess rules model, though he is concerned primarily that government be constrained by a chess-like set of rules, thus creating a stable environment within which individual planning can take place.

which leaves the official with broad discretion. Officials "manage" the course of play by manipulating several sources of slack arising from: (i) the language of rules that are in the form of standards; (ii) from the fact that events occur once, and leave no record for *ex post* review; (iii) from the fact that the official has total discretion over whether to intervene, unlike a judge who has more limited discretion to refuse to hear a case; and (iv) from the non-reviewability of referee decisions. Consistency in applying these rules/standards is certainly desired, but we also expect referees to apply them more or less strictly even within a particular match, depending upon the state of play.

This sports metaphor is also far from adequate for understanding generally the relationship between formal law and commercial activity,[18] but is raised mainly to show how rules can play radically different roles depending upon the game that is being played. One comparison that may be important from a commercial law perspective, however, is that players of a sport, like actors in the market, can play the game with a knowledge of only the broad, definitional rules, but without knowing the intricacies of many of the particular rules. And, given that many rules are written as standards, knowledge of the "rule" itself is really secondary during the course of play. Players of a sport are actually not concerned with the rules, but are engaged in a goal-oriented activity like the pursuit of profit in business. In trying to win the game they may ask how hard they can tackle an opponent without receiving a yellow card, and this corresponds nicely to Holmes' famous image of the "bad man" and his interest in predictions about judicial outcomes rather than rule explication.[19] In that essay Holmes went further, actually defining law as "[t]he prophecies of what the courts will do in fact" (Holmes, 1897: 461), but a more practically useful definition might be that offered in response by Roscoe Pound, that "[t]he law is not made up of predictions. Instead it is made up of bases of prediction" (Pound, 1937: 3, 11). At least for matters falling within the jurisdiction of the common law Pound did not locate these bases of prediction within a set of authoritative rules, but within a system of law which was "essentially a taught tradition of ideals, method, doctrines, and principles" (Pound, 1937: 8).

If we look at law in this way it becomes clear that it can be misleading to picture real-world market participants as opportunistically deciding whether or not to breach clear obligations created by determinate contract terms and fixed rules. In advance parties may ask for legal advice about the consequences of a proposed course of action, but what they often get from their lawyers is a complicated set of predictions and probabilities that must take into account both the likely interpretations of law, where law includes rules, standards and

---

[18] The image of a referee "managing" the course of a sporting contest might be a useful one for understanding the judicial role in certain types of cases, for example, current antitrust actions in the USA against Microsoft concerning the Windows operating system.

[19] "[I]f we take the view of our friend the bad man we shall find that he does not care two straws for the axioms or deductions, but that he does want to know what the Massachusetts or English courts are likely to do in fact" (Holmes 1897: 460–1).

less determinate materials, as well as various possible interpretations of the facts. Contract language can be conceived of as private "rule of the game" that parties create between themselves, but it also will be subject to varying interpretations as it interacts with legal rules and standards, and with interpretations of fact. There certainly are situations in which "players" consciously decide to break the rules or their contractual commitments in certain situations, as in Tai Landa's example of a sale-resale where a movement in the market price may give the middleman an opportunity to profit from a strategic breach (p. 352). But in commercial life that scenario seems most relevant to sales of bulk, fungible commodities for which there are active markets, which is just one particular area within the vast sphere of activities treated by contract law. In many other commercial endeavours, parties seem to act in pursuit of their perceived business interests, with only a loose understanding of whether such action constitutes a breach of the rules, or the contract. In many such situations "breach" is a conclusion reached by the court, *ex post*, and in many cases the decision will never be reached. Sports umpires often have unreviewable authority to let the game proceed, presumably on the decision that no breach occurred, but possibly also because they feel that the breach was technical rather than substantial. Commercial life is rife with similarly undecided issues, as parties will always be influenced by commercial concerns, concerns over the cost of resorting to the legal system, and so on. In some sense the most important fact is that there is a body to rule authoritatively on disputes in order that the game may proceed.

As we move away from state law into the realm of social norms not recognised as law, the "rules of the game" metaphor may be more plausible if we think neither of chess nor of a sport with a referee, but instead of a "pick-up" game, a game played with no designated referee. Again the rules/norms matter in that they define the game in its broad outlines, but the relationship between norms and action is even less chess-like, as parties playing the game are often willing and able to play in relative ignorance of the game's "legal" intricacies. Perhaps most thought provoking for purposes of understanding the relationship between social norms and social action, however, would be to try to construct a typology of dispute resolution in a pick-up game. An action, like a soccer tackle, is taken, and it is entirely up to the aggrieved party to raise a complaint that a norm has been violated. For various reasons, however, many potential breaches will remain uncalled. One problem may be that the relevant norm takes the form of a standard, and with no authoritative adjudicator to render final judgment, the prospect of group deliberation over whether a tackle was "too rough" could seem a waste of time considering the relatively low payoff even if a favourable judgment is obtained. Parties may also feel social pressure not to interrupt the game by raising claims of foul (a procedural norm against vigorous enforcement of substantive norms), they may find private retribution more satisfying than public "adjudication", or they may decide not to cry foul for fear of reprisal/escalation by the other party. In short, while social norm structures may contain rules, substantive or procedural, that we can identify and study as "rules of the game", for participants the "game" may take place with only a rough, general agreement on the rules, within a procedural system unequipped to rule authoritatively on alleged norm violations, and under circumstances in which practical concerns such as retaliation loom large.

When a player in a pick-up game does complain about a breach, his or her complaint becomes the concern of the whole group (if it is intended to force a ruling rather than just being expressive) because there is no designated authority who can simply rule and allow the game to proceed. One common scenario is that play will stop, there will be a period of rather inconclusive discussion— recitation of the rules, argument over the facts—and then the game will begin again without any authoritative adjudication of right and wrong, breach or no breach. The ball may be given to the complaining side, or the alleged offender may offer a quick though not necessarily heartfelt apology, but often the discussion itself serves as a substitute for an authoritative decision, and the antagonists eventually compromise, or the majority moves to drop the issue and return to the game. A disappointed disputant has essentially two choices: to accept the decision, or not to play at all. Here there is not even a need to reach a definitive determination as to breach.

The point of this pick-up game metaphor is that while shared cultural/social norms facilitate the game, indeed it would be impossible without them, it is not necessary that such norms be clearly articulated, or that they be subject to authoritative adjudication in the event of a dispute. With social norms, even more than with legal norms, there is likely to be both a lack of knowledge and a level of rule indeterminacy at play, with different sides able to invoke conflicting norms in the event of a dispute. The fact that the game eventually continues is no proof that the group somehow enforced a particular substantive norm, even if one or more fairly clear norms were potentially applicable. It may be that the disputing parties were pressured to resolve their dispute so that the game could continue, without a substantive norm ever being selected and applied. If we want to apply the "rules of the game" metaphor to social norms and their functioning, perhaps this is the sort of game we should have in mind.

One benefit of the pick-up game metaphor is that it actually seems to fit better with the highly flexible nature of Chinese commercial networks, one of the themes stressed in conference discussions of Tai Landa's chapter. Such flexibility seems inconsistent with any understanding of the EHMG as providing highly rule-like substantive contract norms and a formal system of group adjudication mandated to produce a final authoritative decision through application of a particular substantive rule or rules. There may be said to be EHMG norms favouring or even mandating flexibility, compromise, or reciprocity where problems in contract performance arise, but such would be relatively un-rule-like norms, going to the dispute resolution process rather than to the substance of commercial activity. Tai Landa stresses the importance of a reciprocity norm within the EHMG, but her image of contract law in developed societies, and of

"Confucian ethics" within the EHMG, seems very much centred around the prohibition of strategic breaching of clear, fixed contractual obligations. In fact, a norm favouring reciprocity in solving disputes that arise would seem to cut against strict enforcement of substantive legal or contractual norms that one normally deals with in contract law.

One way to make sense of this apparent contradiction between rule-like norms and strictly enforced contracts, on the one hand, and the oft-noted flexibility of Chinese business networks like the EHMG, on the other, might be to open up for scrutiny the content of the contracts in question. Those who work with sales law tend to assume that if there is a written contract it should almost by definition specify basic terms such as quantity, quality, price, shipment, or perhaps other performance terms that create an environment of fairly clear rights and obligations for the parties. A contract that contained only a list of standards ("a reasonable quantity", "reasonable quantity", "market price", "best efforts") would hardly be considered a contract, despite the fact that judicial doctrines might allow a court to find a contract and supply missing terms if it chose to do so. But if the contracts between the Chinese rubber merchants did contain detailed performance terms it seems implausible to think that such contracts were rarely breached, as Tai Landa suggests (p. 354). Exact contract terms in that sort of trade must certainly be breached regularly, simply due to the nature of trade. Shipments will be late, goods will be damaged in shipment, incorrect quantities will be shipped, payments will be late, and so forth. If, on the other hand, the contract terms were in fact standard-like, or if rules governing dispute settlement were not right-enforcing, but oriented more toward procedures for reciprocity, co-operation and accommodation of unexpected difficulties, then what would it mean to say that they were strictly enforced? Perhaps only that a trader who refused to be sufficiently flexible when the rest of the group thought it appropriate, perhaps even by clinging too tightly to favourable contract terms, might eventually be excluded from the group.

The foregoing discussion has crudely outlined three very different images of rules and social action that all might fall within the general "rules of the game" metaphor: chess, a sports contest with a referee, and a "pick-up" match. The intent has not been to replace Tai Landa's metaphor with another, but rather to interrogate her own metaphor to prompt more focused thinking about the many various ways rules, legal and social, actually function in the games they govern. An attempt has also been made to highlight the difference between substantive rules of contract performance, and the procedural rules and practices which address how disputes are resolved. Both types apparently are subsumed within "Confucian ethics" in her chapter, but it would be helpful to know whether these ethics included specific norms about contract performance, or more general norms such as "reciprocity", which are more related to dispute settlement, and to some extent cut against the idea of strict enforcement of substantive norms and aggressive vindication of contractual rights.

One implication of this for understanding developments in the international sphere is that even as international governance appears increasingly legalised, relying upon legal language, legally trained staff, and institutions that look like courts, the role that legal rules actually play will remain an important empirical question. Lawyers are generally not equipped with the analytical tools to explore this issue, and history suggests that legal academics who study and write about emerging legal regimes such as the UN Sale of Goods Convention have too often participated in their creation, and build careers premised on the idea that the regime they created matters, and will function as they imagined.

PROPERTY, POLITICS AND THE PREREQUISITES OF
"SPONTANEOUS" NORMS

Tai Landa presents her model as useful for understanding the emergence of the EHMG under conditions of contractual uncertainty and transaction costs of contract enforcement, and contrasts such conditions with the condition of developed economies (p. 358). But it is clear that such a dichotomy does not really exist: legal uncertainty and enforcement costs are present in any economy, with the difference being one of degree rather than kind. If we accept this as true, then we should expect homogenous groups of all kinds to engage in the sort of in-group exchange behaviour characteristic of Tai Landa's rubber traders. This in turn raises interesting questions of law and politics.

First, given the noted tendency towards circularity in rational actor/transaction cost analysis (if we assume actors are rational it is hard to imagine any social construction being anything but rationally based, and thus subject to rational actor explanation), there is a danger that observed behaviour that is in fact non- or irrational will be assumed to be rational. Why do members of an in-group such as the EHMG hesitate or refuse to deal with outsiders? Do they all have actual knowledge of the untrustworthiness of the outsiders, or are they acting out of prejudice? If they do not have actual knowledge can we also explain, and hence justify, that ignorance on the basis of rationality? In other words, do insiders decide on the basis of a rational calculation that it would be too costly to obtain actual knowledge, so that it is rational to rely on stereotypes? That provides a neat justification for discriminatory behaviour lacking a basis in actual experience, but it seems to assume that individuals have knowledge in advance allowing them to weigh the costs and benefits of obtaining actual knowledge. How does one who decides not to expend the effort to obtain actual knowledge evaluate whether that decision is rational? Reliance on stereotypes is certainly easy, but whether it is efficient depends upon an accurate evaluation of taking an alternative course, and that is precisely what is unavailable to one relying on stereotypes rather than actual knowledge.

Secondly, the idea of a legal vacuum within which social norms evolve is misleading at best, and can result in a de-politicised justification at worst. Malaysia and Singapore in the late 1960s were not a legal vacuum, a Hobbesian state of nature, yet in Tai Landa's chapter we are given no sense of what the actual legal situation was. The Chinese traders' basic property rights were certainly being protected from the majority Malays, and from other Chinese, and the question remains how this was effected. Was it by law? Politics? The property that the Chinese traders were buying and selling was protected from theft and expropriation, but we do not know whether this occurred through the legal system, or through a non-legal arrangement with the political authority, as occurred so often in Southeast Asia.

If we accept that there is no pre-legal, non-political state of nature, in 1960s Malaysia or anywhere else, it opens up further questions of the "rationality" of in-group economic behaviour across various actual historical environments. "Rationality" is not used here in any technical sense, but in a wider sense of what constitutes a sustainable institution at a particular time and place. In a true state of nature a minority group would likely not be able to maintain a system of discriminatory dealings with the majority at the same time that it enjoyed an elevated economic status. In a state of nature then, the rational course, in this non-technical sense, might be to achieve a much deeper integration with the majority, and with other ethnic groups. What allows an ethnic in-group to maintain a system of economic discrimination is, in fact, either a particularistic political arrangement between that group and the ruler, or a functioning legal system that both protects private property and does not prohibit discrimination in economic relations based on race or ethnicity. Furthermore, if the political system is democratic it must be liberal in the sense of protecting private property and economic discrimination from regulation by the majority. A comparison with the so-called "Granger" laws enacted by several Midwestern American states in the 1860s is instructive here. Midwestern farmers and merchants, situated like the Malay rubber collectors at the bottom of a distribution system beyond their control, were able to effect legislative change to regulate rate setting by the railways on which they had to ship their goods. If Malaysia had been a state of nature the majority Malays would not have needed to do this, but Malaysia was not the state of nature, it was a governed society. In a governed society the majority Malays would presumably have been able to bring about legal change in their favour unless the government were undemocratic and not responsive to majority demands, or unless it were a liberal democracy in which the right to discriminate in private economic transactions was protected from majority regulation. Arguably, then, Tai Landa's model works best to explain the emergence of the EHMG in an environment of only limited uncertainty, not in an environment lacking coercive authority maintaining order, or in an environment in which the majority could impose a norm of non-discrimination on the minority traders. Perhaps it would go too far to argue that a functioning liberal legal order is actually a prerequisite to the functioning of the EHMG, but when the state of nature actually is approximated in the modern world, as it was recently in Indonesia, and as it is periodically in America's inner cities, it becomes clear how dependant ethnic minority businesspeople are on law and the state, and what at one point seemed rational can tragically become unsustainable in practical terms.

The EHMG existed as a closed but highly effective organisation for its members, but to do so depended upon a certain relationship with the greater society that must be studied for a full understanding of the EHMG. In many ways international business exists in the same way, operating in the shadows not only of law, but also of politics and power.

CONCLUSION

Lawyers and legal academics have tended to operate in decidedly non-scientific professional culture, where political and normative arguments can be set aside, but not usually excluded for long. Tai Landa has sought to provide lawyers with a theory of contract law and of the EHMG, but to some extent that may be like trying to provide botanists with a theory of "plant". Plants can be categorised and their properties studied quite fruitfully without a theory of their origins. Do plants exist because the rest of the environment required something to perform the functions that plants perform? Perhaps, but for botanists that may not be a pressing question, and the vast majority of lawyers likewise have not devoted a great deal of intellectual energy to questions like why contract law exists. If they did, I suspect that they would display another non-scientific attitude: a willingness to accept multi-causal explanations lacking the parsimony of theory so valued in fields like economics. This would probably be true of non-legal normative systems such those within EHMGs as well: lawyers can readily accept that they matter, and that their effects can be studied, without worrying too much about where they came from.

At this stage in our thinking about the legal culture of international business I would argue positively for more "botany" and less searching for unified theory.[20] International business encompasses many discrete areas of endeavour—manufacturing investment, infrastructure investment, provision of services, trade in goods, trade in technology, shipping and transport, international capital markets—and we need to study and understand their particular legal cultures first, if our claims for a general legal culture of international business are to be well grounded. There are far too many "games" for us to talk sensibly about the "rules of the game" in international business, and in her intense anthropological focus on the EHMG Professor Tai Landa provides a useful example of how research might usefully proceed.

---

[20] I am prepared to accept that I may owe botanists an apology, so long as my point on this is clear.

REFERENCES

Alford, William P. (1997), "Law, Law, What Law? Why Western Scholars of Chinese History and Society Have Not Had More to Say about Its Law", *Modern China* 23; 398–419.

Allee, Mark A. (1994), *Law and Local Society in Late Imperial China: Northern Taiwan in the Nineteenth Century* (Stanford, Cal.: Stanford University Press).

Bau, Mingchien Joshua (1921), *The Foreign Relations of China: A History and a Survey* (New York: Fleming H. Revell Co).

Bernhardt, Kathryn, and Huang, Philip C. C. (eds.) (1994), *Civil Law in Qing and Republican China* (Stanford, Cal.: Stanford University Press).

Bodde, Derk, and Morris, Clarence (1967), *Law in Imperial China* (Philadelphia, Penn.: University of Pennsylvania Press).

Brockman, Rosser H. (1980), "Commercial Contract Law in Late Nineteenth-Century Taiwan" in J. A. Cohen *et al.* (eds.), *Essays on China's Legal Tradition* (Princeton, NJ: Princeton University Press).

Buckberg, Elaine (1997), "Legal and Institutional Obstacles to Growth and Business in Russia", IMF paper on Policy Analysis and Assessment PPAA/97/8 (Washington, DC: International Monetary Fund).

Buxbaum, David C. (1971), "Some Aspects of Civil Procedure and Practice at the Trial Level in Tanshui and Hsinchu from 1789 to 1895", *Journal of Asian Studies* 30; 255–79.

Cochran, Sherman (1980), *Big Business in China: Sino-Foreign Rivalry in the Cigarette Industry, 1890–1930* (Cambridge, Mass.: Harvard University Press).

Epstein, Richard A. (1995), *Simple Rules for a Complex World* (Cambridge, Mass.: Harvard University Press).

Fairbank, John King, and Goldman, Merle (1998), *China: A New History* (enlarged edn., Cambridge, Mass.: Belknap Press of Harvard University Press).

Gardella, Robert (1992), "Squaring Accounts: Commercial Bookkeeping Methods and Capitalist Rationalism in Late Qing and Republican China", *Journal of Asian Studies* 51; 317–39.

Hansen, Valerie (1995), *Negotiating Daily Life in Traditional China: How Ordinary People Used Contracts, 600–1400* (New Haven, Conn.: Yale University Press).

Hayek, Friedrich A. (1960), *The Constitution of Liberty* (London: Routledge & Kegan Paul).

Holmes, Oliver Wendell (1897), "The Path of the Law", *Harvard Law Review* 10; 457–78.

Huang, Liu-hung (1984), *A Complete Book Concerning Happiness and Benevolence: A Manual for Local Magistrates in Seventeenth-Century China* (trans. Djang Chu, Tucson, Ariz.: University of Arizona Press).

Huang, Philip C. C. (1996), *Civil Justice in China: Representation and Practice in the Qing* (Stanford, Cal.: Stanford University Press).

Naquin, Susan, and Rawski, Evelyn S. (1987), *Chinese Society in the Eighteenth Century* (New Haven, Conn.: Yale University Press).

North, Douglass C. (1990), *Institutions, Institutional Change and Economic Performance* (Cambridge: Cambridge University Press).

Ohnesorge, John K. M. (2001), "The Rule of Law, Economic Development, and the Developmental States of Northeast Asia" in C. Antons (ed.), *Law and Development in East and Southeast Asia* (Richmond, Surrey: Curzon Press).

Park, Nancy, and Antony, Robert (1993), "Archival Research in Qing Legal History", *Late Imperial China* 14; 93–129.

Posner, Richard A. (1990), *The Problems of Jurisprudence* (Cambridge, Mass.: Harvard University Press).

Pound, Roscoe (1937), "What is the Common Law?" in *The Future of the Common Law* (Cambridge, Mass.: Harvard University Press).

Rowe, William T. (1984), *Hankow: Commerce and Society in a Chinese City, 1796–1889* (Stanford, Cal.: Stanford University Press).

—— (1989), *Hankow: Conflict and Community in a Chinese City: 1796–1895* (Stanford, Cal.: Stanford University Press).

—— (1990), "The Public Sphere in Modern China", *Modern China* 16; 309–29.

Schwartz, Benjamin I. (1985), *The World of Thought in Ancient China* (Cambridge, Mass.: Belknap Press of Harvard University Press).

Scogin, Hugh T., Jr. (1990), "Between Heaven and Man: Contract and the State in Han Dynasty China", *Southern California Law Review* 63; 1325–1404.

Upham, Frank K. (1987), *Law and Social Change in Postwar Japan* (Cambridge, Mass.: Harvard University Press).

Van der Sprenkel, Sybille (1977 Reprint (1962)), *Legal Institutions in Manchu China: A Sociological Analysis* (London: Althone; New York: Humanities Press).

Wakeman, Frederic Jr. (1993), "The Civil Society and Public Sphere Debate: Western Reflections on Chinese Political Culture", *Modern China* 19; 108–38.

Weber, Max (1968a), *The Religion of China* (trans. Hans H. Gerth (paperback ed.), Glencoe: Free Press).

—— (1968b), *Economy and Society* (vol. 3., ed. Guenther Roth and Claus Wittich, Berkeley, Cal.: University of California Press).

Winn, Jane Kaufmann (1994), "Relational Practices and the Marginalization of Law: Informal Financial Practices of Small Businesses in Taiwan", *Law & Society Review* 28; 193–232.

Wu, John C. H. (1932), "The Struggle Between Government of Laws and Government of Men in the History of China", *China Law Review* 5; 53–71.

14

A Brief Note on Guanxi

TAI-LOK LUI

Abstract

This chapter is about guanxi *and economic exchange. While sharing many researchers' enthusiasm about the promises of a sociology of* guanxi, *the author is sceptical of the practice of reifying* guanxi, *that is defining* guanxi *merely as the functional outcome of the use of personal network and social relation in economic exchange. Indeed, the incorporation of the concept of* guanxi *into economic analysis has brought with it a hollowing out of our understanding of the richer and deeper social meanings of social relations in* guanxi. *Based upon a review of the existing literature on* guanxi *and Chinese business, the author shows the promises and limitations of the concept of* guanxi *to our understanding of contemporary business transactions.*

INTRODUCTION

THE GROWTH OF a sociological literature on *guanxi* in economic exchange (broadly defined as sociological studies of the relevance of personal and social relation to economic transaction) in recent years is an outcome of the changing agenda of the study of economy and society. First, the rise of the newly industrialised economies in East Asia has drawn journalists' as well as academics' attention to the way of doing business and the institutional configuration of business networking in the region. It is observed that personal connections, business networking, trust and goodwill are important concepts for our understanding of the success of business organisations and their economies in East Asia (see e.g. Dore, 1983; East Asia Analytical Unit, 1995; Fruin, 1998; Greenhalgh, 1988; Hamilton, 1991, 1997; King, 1996; Redding, 1990; Weidenbaum and Hughes, 1996). Secondly, closely related to the growing research interests in flexible production, subcontracting, inter-firm linkages, network organisation and industrial district, the studies of goodwill, trust, networking and co-operation (topics which have long been unduly neglected in our sociological understanding of economic action and transaction) in Asian business are expected to have broader theoretical implications for the building of a new economic sociology. In short, a sociological analysis of *guanxi* promises to unravel the dynamics of the East Asian economies and to unpack the governance mechanism based upon social network and trust.

This chapter is about *guanxi* and economic exchange. While sharing many researchers' enthusiasm about the promises of a sociology of *guanxi*, I am sceptical of the practice of reifying *guanxi*, that is defining *guanxi* merely as the functional outcome of the use of personal network and social relation in economic exchange. Indeed, the incorporation of the concept of *guanxi* into economic analysis has brought with it a hollowing out of our understanding of the richer and deeper social meanings of social relations in *guanxi*. Not only does this functionalist interpretation fail to grapple with the underlying social processes and richer contents of *guanxi*, it also misleads us to assume that *guanxi* would necessarily give us the desired outcomes (for example, the spread of business networking and the function of being a lubricant in an environment of institutional uncertainty). Such a functionalist perspective of *guanxi* begs many questions about why and how *guanxi* actually works (and sometimes backfires). In fact, as I shall argue in this chapter, *guanxi* can be sticky and is therefore rather problematic in dealing with conflicts. Although it is quite true that *guanxi* networking often emerges in a social context wherein the legal infrastructure is relatively underdeveloped, it is a rather different thing to say that *guanxi* is a substitute of the legal regulatory framework for economic exchange.

PROMISES AND PROBLEMS

Similar to Williamson's critique of the notion of calculative trust the economistic understanding of *guanxi*, perceiving *guanxi* as a functional substitute for more institutionalised and bureaucratic mechanisms governing economic transaction, is in my view "a contradiction in terms" (Williamson, 1993: 463). To argue that *guanxi* is grounded on economic interests and rational calculation, and is instrumental and calculative in character, and thus is widely practised in some modern economies, will not have anything new to add to the economic approach to organisation studies. Like the concept of trust, the usage of *guanxi* should be more restrictive, "be reserved for noncalculative personal relations" (*ibid.*, 486). The excesses of reinstating the rational and calculative basis of *guanxi* in the current discussion have made the term itself redundant. The suggestion that *guanxi* is rational, instrumental and efficient has the implication of underlining its viability as an alternative mechanism of economic exchange. However, when *guanxi* is taken as just another mechanism for economic transaction, it loses its original, special meanings.

The gist of Williamson's critique of the notion of "calculative trust" is simply that the economic approach itself is able to accommodate those complex issues brought up in the literature on trust. This can be done by sticking closely to the principles of economising and calculativeness. By extending the farsightedness of the economic agent or allowing for more sophisticated calculation in repeated exchanges, the issue of trust (and in our case, the idea of *guanxi*)—what appears to be exposing oneself to other people's opportunistic behaviour or a risky relationship—can be worked out in a manner not very different from other rationally calculated actions. From the sociological perspective, I argue (being critical of Williamson's economistic criticism of the idea of "calculative trust") that the central problem of the economistic understanding of *guanxi* lies in the failure to address the complexity and dynamism of social relations in economic life. The promise of the research on *guanxi* is to unravel the impacts of social relations, through networking and interactions, on economic exchange. The emphasis is, in particular, placed on the contextual character of social interactions. A functionalist and economic understanding of trust simply begs the questions of *why* and *how* economic exchange based upon personal and social ties is viable (Lui, 1998). The same criticism is applicable to the economic understanding of *guanxi*.

THE LIMITATIONS OF A RATIONAL-INSTRUMENTALIST ANALYSIS OF TRUST-BASED TRANSACTION

Among many researchers trying to appropriate sociological discussion of social relations and contextual factors into a rational-instrumentalist and economising framework, Landa's construction of a theory the ethnically homogeneous middleman group (EHMG) (1994; also see 1996 and 1999) is perhaps one of the most rigorous attempts in the current discussion. In her analysis of the role of Chinese middlemen in the facilitation of exchange and transaction in Southeast Asia, Landa (1994: 102, 103 and 108) is not shy to put her analysis in functionalist expression:

> The EHMG thus reveals itself to be a low cost clublike institutional arrangement, serving as an alternative to contract law and the vertically integrated firm, which emerged to economize on contract enforcement and information costs in an environment where the legal infrastructure was not well developed. . . . In order to choose a particularistic network of trading partners that will minimize the out-of-pocket costs of protection of contracts, a rational trader will equip himself with a "calculus of relations". . . . The code of ethics, embedded in kinship/ethnic networks, functions to deter Ego's trading partner from breach of contract and hence may be seen as the functional equivalent of the Law of merchant or modern law of contract.

However, the above treatments of a "calculus of relations" are far from satisfactory. The idea of networking as social lubricant simply cannot explain why in one case personal relations facilitate economic transaction and not in another. It bypasses most of the criticisms of particularism and does not address the issue concerning the abuse and dysfunctions of using personal relations in economic exchange. In this vein, it ignores the "mixture of vigilance and vulnerability" (Sabel, 1991: 33) in trust-based transaction. The failure of appreciating the criticisms of traditionalism, personalism and particularism (say, by those proponents of modernisation theory) will lead us to a one-sided view of the advantages offered by trust-based transaction, without reflecting seriously how nepotism, favouritism and other related problems are cultivated in organisations which place much emphasis on personal relations. Furthermore, it still conceives economic transaction as exchange between atomised actors and thus fails to understand how economic action is actually embedded in social relations and is affected by such contextual factors (cf. Granovetter, 1985). Such analysis of personal connections in economic transaction gives *post hoc* explanation at best and can be tautological—when social relations work, they constitute the lubricant of economic exchange, and when they do not work, they do not.[1]

Problems concerning an instrumentalist and functionalist approach to the issue of trust-based transaction are succinctly summarised by Arrow in his recent remarks on the application of economic methodology to social topics (Swedberg, 1990: 137):

> In a rational type of analysis it will be said that it is profitable to be trustworthy. So I will be trustworthy because it is profitable to me. But you can't very easily establish trust on a basis like that. If your basis is rational decision and your underlying motive is self-interest, then you can betray your trust at any point when it is profitable and in your interest to do so. Therefore other people can't trust you. For there to be trust, there has to be a social structure which is based on motives different from immediate opportunism.[2]

Without further elaborating on the problems of an instrumentalist and calculative appropriation of the concept of trust and *guanxi*, it should be adequate to say that the existing literature still fails to unravel the complexities of social relations in economic exchange. The instrumentalist and calculative conceptions necessarily entail a functionalist analysis of trust-based transaction, and thus further abstracting trust and *guanxi* from the social context and social relations. And in this abstraction process, we would easily fall back into the atomistic conception of economic agent and in consequence fail to unpack the effects of contextual factors on economic action.

---

[1] The failure to see the social processes underlying the classification of socio-economic relations is evident in the work of Landa (1994). Despite the fact that she has noted how trust is confined to social groups within ethnic boundary, given her functionalist orientation she is not interested in looking into how malfeasance and conflict may arise within the same ethnic community. Nor has she been interested in knowing how pre-existing social relations are selectively manipulated and how new personal relations can be constructed into *guanxi* networks. Her recent dialogue with sociological analysis of network and trust (1999) does not really help to deal with this inadequacy.

[2] However, it should also be noted that towards the end of his remarks on "a rational type of analysis" of trust, functionalism slips back into Arrow's discussion. After suggesting that trust arises from a social structure "which is based on motives different from immediate opportunism", he went on to say that an alternative would be "perhaps based on something for which your social status is a guarantee and which functions as a kind of commitment" (Swedberg, 1990: 137).

A leading question in the sociological literature on Chinese business behaviour is about the strategic manœuvre of social relations and networks for doing business (Chan and Chiang, 1994; Chen, 1994 and 1995; DeGlopper, 1972 and 1995; Greenhalgh, 1988; Hamilton, 1991 and 1996; Hsiao, 1992; Ka, 1993; King, 1996; Mackie, 1992; Numazaki, 1992; Redding, 1990, Silin, 1972; Wong, 1988). Most of these studies (see particularly Chen, 1994, for a rigorous discussion of this issue) underline the instrumental and rational basis of *ganqing* (emotional feelings), *renqing* (personal tie of affect and obligation) and *guanxi* (personal connections).[3] Also, there is evidence showing that the Chinese are well aware of the fragility and vulnerability of *guanxi* even when working with persons who are known to be reliable and trustworthy. One way to handle this problem is to develop safeguards against uncertainty and opportunism. Lui's (1994: 85–90) study of the social organisation of industrial outwork in contemporary Hong Kong shows that the Chinese manufacturers often combine various forms of informal work for production instead of becoming dependent on particular subcontractors, internal contractors or outworkers. The manufacturers are well on the alert against the balance of bargaining power between subcontractors, internal contractors and outworkers on the one side, and themselves on the other. To combine various forms of informal work (such as using both subcontractors and home-based outworkers to handle rush orders) for production allows them to enhance production flexibility as well as safeguarding against subcontractors or outworkers who fail to meet their tight schedules. Also, this strategy would give the manufacturers more room for manœuvre to deal with these flexible producers. Indeed, the more interesting issue in the study of the Chinese way of doing business and handling trust is *how* they manage the "vigilance and vulnerability" of trust-based exchange, and not whether they emphasise *guanxi* or otherwise.

Trust is a "history-dependent process" (Meyerson, Weick and Kramer, 1996: 184). Ethnographic studies of Chinese business also show that Chinese businessmen are very careful in assessing the trustworthiness and reliability of the person they are dealing with. In Silin's study of business and credit in a Hong Kong wholesale market, *xingyong* (trustworthiness) is a quality that has been repeatedly emphasised by the respondents (Silin, 1972). Silin observes that "[t]rading partners are selected primarily on the basis of reliability. This emphasis on performance arises from the importance in the operation of the market. One selects as partners people in whom one has the greatest personal confidence and who have proven their reliability in previous association" (Silin, 1972: 337–9).

DeGlopper's study of Lukang, Taiwan, also confirms the importance attributed to *xingyong* (Deglopper, 1972 and 1995). It is noted that *xingyong* is "predicated

---

[3] Translations of these Chinese terms are based on Yang (1994).

on performance in business. It is not given or ascribed. Nobody has good [*xingy-ong*] just because his surname is Lin or Chen. . . . An unpleasant man who pays all his bills on time will have better [*xingyong*] than a good fellow who can't meet his obligations" (Deglopper, 1972: 304). Very often, Chinese businessmen have in their mind a record of the business performance of their trading partners (for an illustration see Chao, 1993: 83). Trust is developed over repeated transactions. And assessment and evaluation are essential processes in the evolution of trust-based exchange.

The concept of *guanxi* is important to our understanding of trust-based exchange among Chinese businessmen. *Guanxi* and networking are important components of Chinese business behaviour. As I have noted earlier, most observers of Chinese business behaviour are well aware that the use of *guanxi* in business networking is strategic. It is the use of social relations and networks for business interests. However, it is equally important to note that most stud-ies have also demonstrated the limits of *guanxi* and networking. Chinese eco-nomic culture is a combination of trust and distrust. Trust is confined to certain social circles—primarily family and kinship groups, but people from the same ethnic or dialect group (place of origin) and close friends can also be included. People outside these restricted circles are often distrusted (Fukuyama, 1995: 75; Redding, 1990: 66; Wong, 1988). The essence of Chinese *guanxi* actually is about the drawing up of a social boundary. Fei's discussion of *chaxugeju* (the differential mode of association) and the vivid description of such mode of asso-ciation similar to "the concentric circles formed when a stone is thrown into a lake" (Fei, 1992: 63) best capture the meanings of defining *guanxi* and drawing up a "map of social relations" with lines and contours expressing boundary and distance in social networking. Indeed, when drawing up the "map" of *guanxi* network, one is trying to delineate social relations in terms of variation in social distance. The structure of a *guanxi* network is "highly stratified in terms of dis-tance of kinship and friendship" (Yan, 1996: 224). The important question to ask is not only that whether one belongs to a *guanxi* network or not, but also that concerning one's position in that network.

The boundary of such social relations can be flexible and elastic (King, 1994: 115). Sometimes, it is confined to the circle of kin. But it can also be extended to distant relatives, people from the same place of origin, schoolmates and friends. The boundary of a familial group can also be redefined, and extended to cover quasi-kinship ties and to serve utilitarian purposes (Lau, 1981). In short, the process of drawing the "map of social relations" is crucial to our understanding of the strategic manœuvre of social networking. In the process of drawing up such a "map of social relations", the Chinese define the boundary within which trust can be extended.

However, even among people within the *guanxi* boundary, "mutual confid-ence cannot be taken for granted" (Menkhoff, 1994: 117). *Guanxi* is an outcome of a deliberate effort of defining an economic relation. It is an element of the Chinese repertoire (a list of recognised modes of economic exchange within that culture) of economic action, which serves to define an economic relation (Davis, 1992: chap. 3). It is one of the many classificatory schemes of economic action within the Chinese culture. Transaction among related persons is not by defini-tion a trust-based exchange. Trust in *guanxi* is an outcome of social interaction, with both sides of the parties engaged in economic exchange coming to recog-nise that their transaction is now framed in terms of trust. The term trust is, dif-ferently put, a "tool kit" (cf. Swidler, 1986) within the Chinese culture that people can draw upon to define an economic relation and the proper ways of conducting economic transactions among trusted partners. From this perspec-tive, *guanxi* is emotional, moral as well as instrumental.[4] The important point to note here is that Chinese businessmen would not unconditionally or casually extend the boundary of *guanxi* and trust-based transaction to any person they know of. As remarked earlier, there is an attempt to assess the trustworthiness of business partners. Nor would they define any economic transaction with known persons (say, people from the same ethnic origin) as trust-based exchange. These observations suggest that one's reputation within the Chinese business community is an achievement and not an ascription (based upon eth-nicity or kinship ties) (DeGlopper, 1995: 206). It is exactly because of such a con-ception of personal network and trust that the Chinese would talk about *la guanxi* (to call on personal connections for help). By *la guanxi*, we mean "to establish or strengthen relations with others when no preestablished relation exists between them, or where a preestablished relation is remote" (King, 1994: 116). What is pertinent here is that such a practice of 'pulling personal connec-tions', very often through the introduction of an intermediary (*zhongjianren*), who can be a mutual friend of the parties in business or a well known figure within a business community, indicates the arbitrariness of *guanxi* and the related trust-based exchange. Through personal introduction, trust can be extended to a business partner who, without a reference from the intermediary, is likely to be treated as a stranger and whose business transaction would be conducted in an entirely different manner. That is, by building social connec-tions, one can seek the opportunity of re-classifying a business transaction from a formal and impersonal business deal into one that is framed as a trust-based exchange.

In this manner, the business transaction is no longer an exchange between two anonymous business agents, but is embedded in the social network of a par-ticular (business, ethnic or local) community. The *zhongjianren* is the person who risks his/her reputation to secure the trust between the two business par-ties. As DeGlopper (1995: 206) observes in Lukang, "[a]ll transactions take place before an audience or chorus of [*nei-hang-ren*], who continually observe and comment on each other's doings". The business transaction is no longer a pri-vate exchange carried out in a anonymous market-place, but rather a social

---

[4] The issue concerning the unity of human feelings and instrumentality is best handled by Chen (1994) and Kipnis (1997).

event which is made visible and the participating agents are held responsible for the actual handling of the event in a proper way.

But the more important point is that such a socially classified trust relationship is consequential (Davis, 1992). The classification imposes constraints on the way a trust-based exchange is conducted. Particularly, moral constraints, expressed in the form of an informally constructed code of ethics, are introduced to define behaviour in conducting the transaction. For example, trust-based co-operation is unlikely to be terminated abruptly. *Guanxi* is expected to be maintained and spread over a series of transactions, especially through intensive personal interactions. The moral constraint on trust-based exchange is best shown in the handling of conflict among contracting partners. In a study of flexible production in textile factories in a district called He-mei (near Taichung, Taiwan), Chao (1993: 56–60 and 83–8) shows that even in a situation of conflict (because the subcontractors are not able to meet the quality requirements or not capable of working flexibly to fit in with the schedule of the core firm), the core factory owner still needs to maintain a friendly front and finds a compromise with his subcontractors.

One example is that a subcontractor fails to deliver the required quality and the core firm owner is subsequently asked by his buyer for a price reduction (Chao, 1993: 55–6). The core firm owner asks for compensation but, at the same time, assists his subcontractors by taking care of the supply of raw materials. The difficult situation encountered by the core firm owner is that, on the one hand, he is well aware that his subcontractors are not as reliable as he has expected and thus conflict may still arise in future co-operation and, on the other, he will be seen by other people in the same *guanxi* network to be unkind and overly formal if he immediately terminates his economic transaction with them. The key word is "tolerance" in the handling of such an unhappy incident. Economic rationality and instrumentality are pertinent but one is not expected to draw on such considerations in handling a trust-based business collaboration. The framing of a business transaction in terms of trust and *guanxi* will restrict the use of calculative and instrumental reasoning in dealing with conflicts and arguments. Until the subcontractors have gone beyond a certain limit of tolerated behaviour, and thus in the eyes of other people in the same *guanxi* network they have exploited a trust relation, the core firm owner is morally restrained from taking drastic action against incompetence.

Another example is also the failure of a subcontractor in delivering quality products (Chao, 1993: 84–5). The core firm owner says that there is a limit in tolerating substandard products. But in the termination of collaboration, the relation between the core firm owner and his subcontractor is still framed in moral terms. As put by the core firm owner (Chao, 1993: 85):

> The subcontractors only make a small profit from their work. When there is quality problem and they are asked for compensation, . . . they simply cannot cope with the problem. Recently I have problem with my subcontractor. It is a real headache. And I decide not to receive his call. . . . I do not want to destroy our relation by "tearing off

our faces". I, therefore, try to avoid him. But I expect that things may change after December. If we really cannot continue to collaborate, I will seriously consider a change of partner. *Qing-gan* [emotional feelings] is one thing. But I have to survive and there are no reasons why I have to suffer for his failure to produce quality products. This is impossible. And there are no points for me to ask for small compensations. This will not be effective. So I talk to my subcontractors and say if they cannot accept my requirements or have difficulties in handling my work, voice out and tell me. If they really cannot make it, then they should quit.

The core firm owner has to give "face" to his incompetent subcontractor and to allow the latter to withdraw from the collaboration. Should it be just another transaction in an anonymous market, the owner would have terminated the collaboration right away. Since this is a trust-based transaction, morals are important in determining the behaviour of the business partners.

Without quoting more examples, it should be clear that trust is consequential because it frames the interactions among the contracting parties. After classifying a relation as trust-based exchange, the contracting parties are expected to behave in accordance with the moral prescriptions.

It is interesting to observe that the Chinese are well aware of the negative consequences of the mismanagement of personal connections and trust. King (1994: 121) notes that "[t]o engage in [*renqing*] or to establish [*guanxi*] with others usually means a heavy social investment. Once one is inside the [*renqingwang*] (network of *renqing*) or [*guanxiwang*] (network of *guanxi*), . . . [h]e is, in this case, socially obliged to respond to any request for help from others. as such, the individual will lose autonomy and freedom".

In other words, because of the moral and emotional tones of trust and *guanxi*, a Chinese businessman is likely to find that, in some circumstances, the strategy of social networking may backfire. The mismanagement of trust and personal connections will significantly restrict the room for manœuvre and, more importantly, introduce particularistic and personal concerns to business strategising. Chinese businessmen are wary of the exploitation of trust and personal connections in business transactions (also see DeGlopper, 1972: 321–33). There is a certain limit to the use of *guanxi* and the related trust-based exchange in the operation of business. A businessman with a reputation of overdrawing personal connections or being too lenient towards the exploitation of such connections by his/her business partners (i.e., the practice of favouritism) will not be well received by others in the same business community. In this regard, the Chinese have a compartmentalisation strategy (King, 1994: 123) to separate the functional requirements of business transaction from the personal and particularistic elements in social life. Up to a point then Chinese businessmen would draw upon their own cultural resources—for instance, the saying of "*shu huan shu, lu huan lu*" (money is money, *guanxi* is *guanxi*)—to redefine the business relation and adopt a "business-is-business" approach to the business transaction (also see King, 1994: 123; DeGlopper, 1972: 323). The adoption of this compartmentalisation strategy is a response to the moral and emotional constraints imposed by the notions of trust and personal connections evoked in the process of an economic exchange.

What I intend to illustrate from the above discussion is that *guanxi* can be fruitfully analysed in the light of the repertoire of economic action. It is a classificatory scheme with moral implications for constraining the instrumental drives in economic exchange (also see Callon, 1998). It is through the mutual sustenance of such a frame of trust and *guanxi* that malfeasance is deterred in transaction. And it is through the mutual consensus of developing a trust relation that the contextual effects of social relation will be pertinent to conditioning economic action. But I have also noted that the management of trust-based exchange is by no means an easy task. *Guanxi* can be exploited by one side of the business transaction. Our discussion of Chinese business behaviour shows how Chinese businessmen manage this problem. Particularly, I underline the moral constraints in the process of managing trust-based exchange. From the start of classifying a transaction as trust-based exchange to the termination of such a relationship, the handling of the business relation is shaped by the moral atmosphere of a social network. To follow this line of thinking, the central issue for discussion is not about whether *guanxi* is instrumental or otherwise but how mutual trust is based upon *guanxi* constructed in the process of economic exchange. What we need to know is *how* a trust relation is sustained, *how* *guanxi* is used to resolve conflicts, the *threshold of tolerance* in that kind of relation, and *how* a trust-based exchange is terminated.

CONCLUSION: WHAT *GUANXI* IS NOT ABOUT

Guanxi is about interpersonal ties and social relations. But the essence of *guanxi* is not reducible to either interpersonal networking or social relations. To use the term *guanxi* interchangeably with any other description depicting the use of interpersonal ties for securing material and non-material advantage, a sign of a functionalist understanding of *guanxi*, would be de-contextualising *guanxi*. The practice of *guanxi* is embedded in specific social, cultural and institutional settings. As well put by Hamilton and Wang (1992: 22), within a *guanxi* network:

> each [interpersonal] tie is, simultaneously, both normatively defined and strictly personal. Each tie is normative in the sense that it consists of an explicit category of social relationship that requires specific, prescribed "ritual" (*li*) behavior. The tie is strictly personal in the sense that the specific prescribed actions needed to maintain the link based on norms of reciprocity and are defined as personal obligations on the part of each individual, particularly the subordinate in the dyadic relationship. . . .

Guanxi is more than the sum of interpersonal ties. It consists of networks as well as the normative and institutional settings governing how individuals behave within such networks of social relations. *Guanxi* works in a society in which considerations of order, and not laws, predominate; and in this context, "order means . . . that each person must uphold the moral obligations of his or her network ties" (*ibid.*: 24). The idea of social obligation is central to the Chinese understanding of *guanxi*:

> Order in this kind of society depends primarily on people's obedience to their principal social obligations. Therefore, the social obligations for every category of relationship must be spelled out, the people must be taught about those obligations, and "correction" must be meted out for any failure to learn. The unit of control is dyadic relationship, and not the individual, as is the case with a rule of law. Therefore, the entire network of people joined through a set of relationships is implicated in any one person's failure to perform appropriately. As Fei points out, control in this system is a shared responsibility . . . (*ibid.*).

How social obligations should be honoured is not only described in classics of Confucian texts, but also institutionalised in family and clan rules (Fei, 1998) as well as rules and regulations of surname and native place associations. *Guanxi* becomes not an abstract idea but firmly embedded in the everyday life in Chinese communities. Migration and movement of people and economic activities do not undermine *guanxi*. Rather, the idea of *guanxi* is spread to overseas Chinese communities via the Chinese diasporas:

> In Chinese migrant communities around the world, these [business] networks were institutionalized as sworn brotherhood, surname, and native place associations. These associations called upon a variety of symbols, such as ritual oaths and bonds of kinship based on distant, mythical ancestors, to legitimize themselves and create lines of trust and control among their members. In turn, the very institutionalization of these symbols reinforced their significance as concrete concerns shaping the lives and culture of migrants. Through such associations migrants maintained links to news from their villages, funneled money and influence back home, had their bones shipped back after they died, and met with fellow migrants who provided mutual aid and mutual pressure to maintain village morality and live up to village standards of success [McKeown, 1999: 320].

In this way, *guanxi* is both a kind of tacit knowledge and institutionalised. How one should behave in a *guanxi* network is never spelled out in black and white. Yet, through cultural learning, people come to know what is expected from them in a relation defined as *guanxi*. It is important to point out that this does not imply a culturalist argument in the sense that the Chinese follow the cultural norms as normative ideals. In fact, as shown in the above paragraph, the idea of *guanxi* is firmly embedded in various practices of community life (such as those of native place associations). The expectations and tacit rules governing interpersonal relations become institutionalised as common practices among members of the communities.

My emphasis is that the term *guanxi* is intended to mean something more than merely the strategic use of interpersonal ties for obtaining material and non-material advantages. If *guanxi* is so narrowly defined, then it can be, for example, *blat* in Russia (see Ledeneva, 1998) and any other strategic use of social relations for the advancement of personal interests. The practice of decontextualising *guanxi,* as one finds in the functionalist interpretation of the term, would make it very difficult to understand why and how social relations can be more effectively used both for smoothing out transaction and guarding against opportunistic behaviour in Chinese communities. While it is quite right to say that *guanxi* would become more predominant in an environment of contract uncertainty (Landa, 1999), it is another thing to argue that *guanxi* constitutes a governance structure capable of replacing contract and other legal regulations. In fact, as I have argued in the earlier section that *guanxi* is emotional and moral. Whereas it works quite effectively in easing tensions and preventing opportunistic moves in pre-transactional stages, *guanxi* is relatively problematic in dealing with conflicts. Indeed, *guanxi* has a certain quality of stickiness so that once a transaction is defined as a *guanxi* exchange, it is not easy to terminate the business connection. The parties involved are expected to give face to the business partner and to allow for unintended mistakes. In this regard, Appelbaum (1998) is quite right to observe that *guanxi* plays an important part in doing business in global Chinese business communities. However, *guanxi* would not be a replacement of the existing modes of legal regulatory structure for handling global business transaction.

REFERENCES

Appelbaum, Richard P. (1998), "The Future of Law in a Global Economy", *Social and Legal Studies* 7; 171–92.
Callon, Michel. (1998), "Introduction: The Embeddedness of Economic Markets in Economics", in M. Callon (ed.), *The Laws of the Markets* (Oxford: Blackwell).
Chan, K. B., and Chiang. C. (1994), *Stepping Out: The Making of Chinese Entrepreneurs* (Singapore: Prentice Hall).
Chao, W. L. (1993), "An Analysis of Collaborative Production Networks Among Taiwan's SMES: A Case Study of the Textile Industry in He-mei (in Chinese)", unpublished Master's Thesis, Tunghai University.
Chen, Chieh-hsuan (1994), *Cooperative Networks and the Structure of Everyday Life* (in Chinese) (Taipei: Luen Chin Publications).
—— (1995), *Monetary Networks and the Structure of Everyday Life* (in Chinese) (Taipei: Luen Chin Publications).
Coleman, James S. (1990), *Foundations of Social Theory* (Cambridge, Mass.: Harvard University Press).
Davis, John (1992), *Exchange* (Buckingham: Open University Press).
DeGlopper, Donald R. (1972), "Doing Business in Lukang" in W. E. Willmott (ed.), *Economic Organization in Chinese Society* (Stanford, Cal.: Stanford University Press).
—— (1995), *Lukang: Commerce and Community in a Chinese City* (Albany, NY: State University of New York Press).
Dore, R. P. (1983), "Goodwill and the Spirit of Market Capitalism", *British Journal of Sociology* 34; 459–82.

East Asia Analytical Unit (1995), *Overseas Chinese Business Networks in Asia* (Parkes: Department of Foreign Affairs and Trade).

Fei, C. K. (1998), *Family and Clan Regulations in China* (in Chinese) (Shanghai: Shanghai Academy of Social Science Press).

Fei, Xiaotong (1992), *From the Soil: The Foundations of Chinese Society* (Berkeley, Cal.: University of California Press).

Fruin, W. Mark (ed.) (1998), *Networks, Markets, and the Pacific Rim* (New York: Oxford University Press).

Fukuyama, Francis (1995), *Trust* (London: Hamish Hamilton Ltd).

Granovetter, Mark (1985), "Economic Action and Social Structure: The Problem of Embeddedness", *American Journal of Sociology* 91; 481–510.

Greenhalgh, Susan (1988), "Families and Networks in Taiwan's Economic Development" in E. A. Winckler and S. Greenhalgh (eds.), *Contending Approaches to the Political Economy of Taiwan* (Armonk: M. E. Sharpe, Inc).

Hamilton, Gary (ed.) (1991), *Business Networks and Economic Development in East and Southeast Asia* (Hong Kong: Centre of Asian Studies).

—— (1996), "Competition and Organization: a Reexamination of Chinese Business Practices", *Journal of Asian Business* 12; 7–20.

—— (1997), "Organization and Market Processes in Taiwan's Capitalist Economy" in M. Orru, N. W. Biggart and G. Hamilton (eds.), *The Economic Organization of East Asian Capitalism* (Thousand Oaks, NJ: Sage Publications).

—— and Wang, Zheng (1992), "Introduction: Fei Xiaotong and the Beginnings of a Chinese Sociology" in X. Fei (ed.), *From the Soil* (Berkeley, Cal.: University of California Press).

Hsiao, Michael H. H. (1992), "The Entrepreneurial Process of Taiwan's Small-Medium and Big Businessmen" (in Chinese), *The Chinese Journal of Sociology* 16; 107–38.

Ka, C. M. (1993), *Market, Social Networks, and the Production Organization of Small-Scale Industry in Taiwan* (in Chinese) (Taipei: Institute of Ethnology).

King, Ambrose Y. C. (1994), "Kuan-hsi and Network Building: A Sociological Interpretation" in W. Tu (ed.), *The Living Tree: The Changing Meaning of Being Chinese Today* (Stanford, Cal.: Stanford University Press).

—— (1996), "The Transformation of Confucianism in the Post-Confucian Era: The Emergence of Rationalistic Traditionalism in Hong Kong." in W. Tu (ed.), *Confucian Traditions in East Asian Modernity* (Cambridge, Mass.: Harvard University Press).

Kipnis, Andrew B. (1997), *Producing Guanxi* (Durham, NC: Duke University Press).

Landa, Janet Tai (1994), *Trust, Ethnicity, and Identity* (Ann Arbor, Mich.: The University of Michigan Press).

—— (1996), "Doing the Economics of Trust and Informal Institutions" in S. Medema and W. Samuels (eds.), *Foundations of Research in Economics* (Aldershot: Edward Elgar).

—— (1999), "Coasean Foundations of a Unified Theory of Western and Chinese Contractual Practices and Economic Organization", paper presented at the workshop on "The Legal Culture of Global Business Transactions", the International Institute for the Sociology of Law, Oñati, Spain.

Lau, S. K. (1981), "Chinese Familism in an Urban-Industrial Settings: The Case of Hong Kong", *Journal of Marriage and the Family* 43; 977–92.

Lui, Tai-lok (1994), *Waged Work at Home: The Social Organization of Industrial Outwork in Hong Kong* (Aldershot: Avebury).

Lui, Tai-lok (1998), "Trust and Chinese Business Behaviour", *Competition and Change* 3; 335–57.

Mackie, J. A. C. (1992), "Overseas Chinese Entrepreneurship", *Asian Pacific Economic Literature* 6; 41–64.

McKeown, Adam (1999), "Conceptualizing Chinese Diaspora, 1942 to 1949", *The Journal of Asian Studies* 58; 306–37.

Menkhoff, Thomas (1994), "Trade Routes, Trust and Tactics" in H.-D. Evers and H. Sclirader (eds.), *The Moral Economy of Trade* (London: Routledge).

Meyerson, Debra, Weick, K. E., and Kramer, R. M. (1996), "Swift Trust and Temporary Groups" in R. M. Kramer and T. M. Tyler (eds.), *Trust in Organizations* (Thousand Oaks, NJ: Sage Publications).

Numazaki, Ichiro (1992), "Networks and Partnerships", unpublished Ph.D Dissertation, Michigan State University.

Redding, S. Gordon (1990), *The Spirit of Chinese Capitalism* (Berlin: Walter de Gruyter).

Sabel, Charles (1991), "Moebius-Strip Organizations and Open Labor Markets" in P. Bourdieu and J. S. Coleman (eds.), *Social Theory for a Changing Society* (Boulder: Westview Press).

—— (1993), "Studied Trust: Building New Forms of Cooperation in a Volatile Economy" in R. Swedberg (ed.), *Explorations in Economic Sociology* (New York: Russell Sage Foundation).

Silin, Robert H. (1972), "Marketing and Credit in a Hong Kong Wholesale Market" in W. E. Willmott (ed.), *Economic Organization in Chinese Society* (Stanford, Cal.: Stanford University Press).

Swedberg, Richard (1990), *Economics and Sociology* (Princeton, NJ: Princeton University Press).

Swidler, Ann (1986), "Culture in Action", *American Sociological Review* 51; 273–86.

Weidenbaum, Murray, and Hughes, Samuel (1996), *The Bamboo Network* (New York: Martin Kessler Books).

Williamson, Oliver E. (1993), "Calculativeness, Trust, and Economic Organization", *Journal of Law and Economics* 36; 453–86.

Wong, S. L. (1988), *Emigrant Entrepreneurs* (Hong Kong: Oxford University Press).

Yan, Yunxiang (1996), *The Flow of Gifts: Reciprocity and Social Networks in a Chinese Village* (Stanford, Cal.: Stanford University Press).

Yang, Mayfair Mei-hui (1994), *Gifts, Favors and Banquets: The Art of Social Relationships in China* (Ithaca, NY: Cornell University Press).

15

Responding to Comments by
John K. M. Ohnesorge and Tai-lok Lui

JANET TAI LANDA

T HE AIM OF my chapter in this volume is to provide a unifying theoretical
framework, which would explain the empirical realities of two contrasting modes of contracting practices for contract enforcement: the
guanxi (personal ties) used by overseas Chinese merchants in Southeast Asia, in
contrast to the use of contract law preferred by Western businessmen. Given the
aim of my chapter, I am afraid that most of Professor Ohnesorge's comments on
my chapter miss the point. What Ohnesorge has done is to use my chapter as a
springboard to discuss various *empirical* issues of Chinese legal tradition/
Chinese commercial culture in China, as well as the socio-legal environment in
which overseas Chinese merchants operated—issues which by themselves are
important[1]—but not germane to a commentary on my theoretical chapter. I
will, however, respond to two important criticisms.

First, Ohnesorge criticises my chapter by saying that I underestimate the role
of law in Chinese life, imperial or modern. But why should my chapter, which
is a theoretical chapter, concern itself with the empirical issue of the role of law
in Chinese society? Moreover, in a recent paper, McConnaughay (forthcoming
2001), a partner for many years in a law firm located in Toyko and Hong Kong,
emphasised the two contrasting modes of Asian and Western contractual practices in which law plays a minor role in Asian commercial traditions.[2] Thus, I

---

[1] For scholars interested in the details of the socio-legal environment in which Hokkien traders
operated in Singapore and West Malaysia—including the importance of Confucian cultural norms
of mutual aid/reciprocity and the responses of Hokkien Chinese traders to their environment—see
Landa (1978: chap. 3). As to the question of "what kind of indigenous Chinese commercial and
business practices the rubber traders brought with them, culturally speaking, to Southeast Asia",
"and what developed there as a result of rational responses to local environmental conditions"
(Ohnesorge, this volume), see Landa (1978: chap. 2).

[2] McConnaughay says, "the percentage of Asian commercial parties who attribute to law a role
that is comparable to the role of law in Western commercial traditions is miniscule in comparison
to the number of Asian parties whose commercial expectations still are based on relational practices and traditions. . . . After having represented highly sophisticated Asian clients for much of the
twenty years I practised law prior to teaching, I have no doubt about how my clients' commercial

fail to understand why Ohnesorge said that I underestimate the role of law in Chinese society.

Secondly, Ohnesorge said that my attempt (as an economist) to provide a unifying framework is very much like trying to provide botanists with a theory of "plant"; "botanists" here is used by Ohnesorge as a metaphor for "lawyers", and "plants" as a metaphor for "law". His argument is that "[p]lants can be categorised and their properties studied quite fruitfully without a theory of origins". Ohnesorge continues, "[a]t this stage in our thinking about the legal culture of international business I would argue positively for more 'botany' and less searching for unified theory". What he is arguing here is that law should be treated as an autonomous science, disconnected and insulated from neighbouring social sciences. Ohnesorge talks about the need to understand the legal culture in greater detail for each of the many elements that make up trade, and gives a list of those parts saying that: "we need to study and understand their particular legal cultures first". In his view, a unified theory that would explain similar behaviour in all these fields has little merit. What he is saying is that lawyers do not need to know the origins of contract law or the EHMG in order to practise law. Further, he argues that if they did desire to know the origins of contract law, the necessary knowledge would be superficial and anecdotal, or multicausal. In short, he is saying that my unified theory explaining two contrasting contractual modes is irrelevant to the practice of lawyers.

My responses to Ohnesorge's methodological criticism of my chapter are as follows. First, my theory is *not* written specifically for lawyers; it is written for a general social science audience. Ohnesorge, a legal scholar, was assigned by the organisers of the Oñati conference to be the discussant of my paper. Rational choice sociologists, unlike Ohnesorge, would have little difficulty in accepting my unified theoretical framework, which explains the origins and functions not only of contract law, but also of the EHMG.

Secondly, Ohnesorge takes a position that advocates the autonomy of law by insulating his discipline from the insights of other neighbouring social science disciplines. He uses botany as a metaphor for the many disciplines within law, and advocates more specialisation within the discipline of law, and less effort directed toward unification of the different branches of law. Ohnesorge has chosen a bad metaphor for his comparison. First, Darwin revolutionised botany by bringing Malthus' economic ideas into biological thinking. Secondly, biology, with its great diversity of sub-disciplines, underwent a great intellectual transformation between the 1930s and 1940s to achieve an evolutionary synthesis, resulting in modern evolutionary biology, which was part of a larger movement towards unifying the biological sciences. The key word for the process of unification of knowledge is "consilience" (Wilson, 1998); consilience is pursued as an

references and expectations were completely consistent with those I describe in my chapter, despite their obvious capacity to acknowledge and understand the different preferences and expectations typical of commercial actors from Western legal traditions" (e-mail correspondence with the author, 24 Feb. 2001).

ideal by today's biologists. Within the social sciences, economics is by far the most "imperialistic" of the social sciences, expanding into neighbouring disciplinary fields, creating new subdisciplines such as law-and-economics, public choice theory (economics and political science) and most recently "bioeconomics" (the consilience of economics with biology; see Landa and Ghiselin, 1999). In the discipline of law, legal scholar and judge Richard Posner is the strongest proponent of the consilience of law with economics. Ohnesorge, by advocating law as an autonomous discipline, makes it more difficult for legal scholars to understand complex phenomena like East–West international commercial transactions, which are at the same time economic, legal, social and cultural. I believe that much more valuable insights into such a complex multi-faceted system would be achieved through an approach that uses a multi-disciplinary and unifying theoretical framework rather than using one single discipline.

REPONSE TO LUI'S COMMENTS

I am afraid that Professor Lui did not read my chapter or my 1981 paper carefully. First, he cites the 1994 reprint of my 1981 paper instead of the year when the paper was originally published, which gives the uninformed reader the wrong impression that my theory of EHMG was written nine years after the paper by sociologist Granovetter (1985), hence giving the incorrect impression that my work builds upon Granovetter's paper, which is clearly not the case. Secondly, in his haste to challenge the rational choice approach to economic phenomena, Lui misinterprets my chapter and 1981 paper when he writes:

> Furthermore, it still conceives economic transaction as exchange between atomized actors and thus fails to understand how economic action is actually embedded in social relations and is affected by such contextual factors (cf. Granovetter, 1985).

Lui thus believes that my theory of the EHMG depicts the rational agent as the atomistic economic man. This is the "methodological individualism" approach underlying traditional rational choice theory. But, as clearly stated in my chapter in this book, my economic theory of EHMG (Landa, 1981), with trust embedded in ethnic trading networks, is very similar to sociologist Granovetter's (1985) embeddedness approach, in that my rational traders are embedded in a Chinese ethnic community, and within this larger ethnic community, the rational trader makes his choice of trading partners, guided by the Confucian "rules of the game" which provided Hokkien traders with categories of social relationships efficiently to define and rank all potential traders in a market into seven categories. Thus, my theory of Chinese trading networks does *not* depict atomistic individuals operating in a social or environmental vacuum. My theory of the EHMG, stripped of its transaction costs foundations, is in essence the same as sociologist Granovetter's embeddedness approach, which Lui applauds.

Lui also criticised my chapter for my failure in "appreciating the criticisms of traditionalism, personalism, and particularism". However, the purpose of my chapter in this volume was directed at only one aim: to develop a unified economic theory that will explain the contrasting modes of Western and Asian contractual practices. To ask me to discuss other aspects of personalism that are of interest to sociologists is clearly beyond the scope of my project. However, I should note that more than two decades ago, I co-authored a paper with sociologist Janet Salaff that addressed the traditional sociologists' criticisms of personalism and particularlism in economic transactions (see Landa and Salaff, 1980). We rejected these arguments in favour of a new point of view and a new approach (the transaction cost approach) that emphasised the efficiency aspects of particularism in economic transactions.[3] As for the criticism that I neglected to discuss the issues of "abuse and dysfunctions of using personal relations in economic exchange", I co-authored a paper with Yoon on this very issue, using the terminology of "rent-seeking behaviour" in public choice theory rather than the more standard sociologist's terminology of bribery and corruption (see Landa and Yoon, 1999).

REFERENCES

Landa, Janet T., and Ghiselin, Michael (1999), "The Emerging Discipline of Bioeconomics: Aims and Scope of the *Journal of Bioeconomics*", *Journal of Bioeconomics* 1; 5–12.
—— and Salaff, Janet W. (1980), "The Socioeconomic Functions of Kinship and Ethnic Networks in the Growth of a Chinese Family Firm in Singapore: A Transaction Cost Approach", unpublished paper presented at the Structural Analysis Workshop Series, Sociology Department, University of Toronto (8 February).
—— and Yoon, Yong J. (1999), "The Political Economy of Chinese Trading Networks & Korean Chaebols: Profit-seeking vs. Rent-seeking Entrepreneurship", paper presented at the Allied Social Sciences Association meetings in New York (3–5 January).
McConnaughay, Philip H. (2001), "Rethinking the Role of Law and Contracts East-West Commercial Relationships", *Virginia Journal of International Law* 41 (forthcoming).
Wilson, Edward O. (1998), *Consilience: The Unity of Knowledge* (New York: Alfred A. Knopf).

---

[3] The paper, later revised, was submitted to the *American Journal of Sociology*. It was rejected by the referee, who recommended that we should not be using the transaction costs approach—to explain the growth and expansion of the Tan Kah Kee firm, which had relied heavily on (particularistic) kin and ethnic networks for acquiring capital, pooling information, and so forth—but rather a Marxian class-struggle framework instead.

16

Settling Business Disputes with China

JEROME A. COHEN

Abstract

This paper discusses the history and practice of settling business disputes between Chinese and foreign firms from the perspective of an experienced American international lawyer. It summarizes China's post-Mao resort to law as a key instrument of economic development, including its adherence to a wide array of multilateral and bilateral agreements and the somewhat less effective measures to build the legal institutions necessary to transform law from form to instrument. At the contract stage, China-foreign business agreements generally provide for arbitration of disputes not amenable to negotiation. Actual dispute resolution, however, is highly varied depending on factors such as the nationality of the non-Chinese disputant. Extra-legal factors such as the foreign party's political muscle, personal connections, willingness to compromise, use bribery or mobilize publicity augment the legal positions involved. Two case histories are presented showing the value of prosecuting strong legal positions through vigorous efforts directed toward informal administrative channels. Finally, because "local protectionism" is the greatest weakness in China's judicial system, enforcement of dispute awards is problematic and informal settlement is the normally foreign party's best strategy.

INTRODUCTION

IN THE 1980S, most of my work in the People's Republic of China (PRC) concerned making contracts rather than breaking them. From the branch offices of a large American international law firm in Beijing and Hong Kong, I advised Western and Japanese multinational companies about China's legal and business environment, the range of choices available for launching co-operation, the anticipated consequences of each, the most suitable types of documentation, and strategies and tactics for negotiating the documents. I also did a great deal of negotiating and, as the decade wore on, more and more dispute resolution.

In the 1990s, most of my work in China involved the settlement of international business disputes through both informal and formal means. Drawing upon personal experience rather than conventional sociological research, it is this topic that I will introduce here, with an emphasis upon informal means. Perhaps these "Tales from the Trenches" will interest sociologists of law.

Preliminarily, let me state the obvious—that the virtue of my intimate involvement in China matters is undoubtedly accompanied by the vice of loss of perspective. Even worse, because China has been my rice bowl in one way or other for almost 40 years, you may find me a biased observer. During the McCarthy era, when the State of Massachusetts enacted a law requiring every university teacher to take an oath to support the Constitution and the *Boston Globe* asked Harvard's famed constitutional law professor T. R. Powell whether he would do so, he quipped: "Why shouldn't I support the Constitution? It's supported me all my life"!

I should also note that the settlement of international business disputes with China is hardly a new problem for Westerners. The so-called "Canton System" devised by the Chinese Empire in the middle of the eighteenth century seemed an intelligent and even generous bureaucratic response to the civil and criminal-type disputes that from the outset plagued foreign trade with China (see Edwards, 1980: 236, 261). Yet, as the very first American ship to call at Canton discovered in 1784, the Canton System left much to be desired, at least in cases deemed serious enough to warrant judicial handling. Indeed, during the decades immediately preceding the Opium War of 1839, increasing Western—especially English and American—dissatisfaction with the administration of Chinese justice produced a growing clamour not only for reforms in criminal law and procedure but also for a more regularised arrangement for resolving commercial disputes (see Morse, 1960: chaps. 5, 7).

After China's defeat in the Opium War, of course, those Western demands for judicial reform, which cast interesting light on contemporary concerns for the "rule of law" and "human rights" in the PRC, resulted in the imposition upon China, for over a century, of a system of foreign extraterritorial courts (see Willoughby, 1920: 13–28). That system, which shortly thereafter Commodore Perry's "black ships" also foisted on Japan, denied civil as well as criminal jurisdiction to courts of the host country in cases involving disputes between nationals of many other countries and local persons and businesses. Although some Chinese reportedly preferred their disputes to be heard before the foreign rather than the local tribunals, the extraterritorial regime gradually became a despised symbol of imperialist oppression. During the first half of the twentieth century, the drive to rid China of extraterritoriality provided the principal impetus for the country's establishment of a formal Western-style legal system. Thus, China adopted the forms of Western law, not because of any appreciation of their intrinsic value but because that was the price demanded by the imperialist powers for ending extraterritoriality, as had already been done in Japan. This background is important to bear in mind for those who deal with China today, for nationalistic sensitivities persist, as recent events have reminded us.

Before discussing contemporary Sino-foreign dispute resolution, it is necessary to outline its context.

TWENTY YEARS OF LEGAL PROGRESS IN CHINA[1]

In the spring of 1979, the People's Republic of China displayed virtually none of the attributes of a formal legal system. The Soviet-style legal system that had begun to take root in the mid-1950s had long since been abandoned. Legislation actually in use was sparse and unsystematic, and Communist Party decrees were more prominent than government norms. In the previous three decades, outside the Soviet bloc, the PRC had entered into few multilateral conventions and bilateral treaties with domestic legal implications. Legal institutions—the courts, the procuracy, state arbitration tribunals, the legal profession—were a shambles after a 20-year period that began with the Anti-Rightist Movement of 1957–8 and culminated in the Cultural Revolution of 1965–8. Legal education and scholarship were only beginning to revive. Although popular fear and cynicism regarding the administration of justice were widespread, "rights consciousness" was low. Yet many among the articulate classes hoped that the Deng Xiaoping era might offer society greater legal security than Chairman Mao had—suppressing crime, protecting the basic rights of the person and promoting economic development, including co-operation with foreign governments and business.

At the close of 1999, China's progress in constructing a legal system seems impressive, despite glaring deficiencies and continuing obstacles.

Domestic Legislation

The past two decades in the PRC have witnessed one of the greatest legislative floods in world history. Not only at the central level but also at the provincial and local levels, there has been a prodigious effort to promulgate norms to deal with most human activity—civil, commercial, administrative and criminal. The 1982 Constitution has been the most publicised of a host of laws and regulations demonstrating the PRC's return to reliance on law as a major tool of state-building and government organisation. A broad range of contract, corporate, securities, bankruptcy, banking, insurance, accounting, labour, land, tax, patent, trade mark, copyright, environmental, industrial, agricultural, maritime and other legislation has revealed Beijing's post-Mao resort to law as a key

---

[1] This section is a revised version of a talk given at the Harvard Law School Conference on Contemporary Chinese Legal Development, 27 March 1999.

instrument of economic development. China's genuine "great leap forward" in foreign trade and its enormous success in attracting foreign investment and technology since 1979 have been due in no small measure to its systematic enact-ment of a rather complete set of foreign-related business legislation. Nor have Chinese legislators neglected areas as diverse as property, inheritance, the family, the media and the regulation of public order.

To be sure, there are still gaps in legislative coverage, and much of the exist-ing legislation is in need of refinement and of updating required to keep abreast of the rapid pace of economic, social and even political change. PRC legislators are ambitious reformers, always eager to improve their product, as was recently illustrated by the enactment of a Securities Law and a Uniform Contract Law that build upon earlier norms and by revisions to the Constitution, codes of criminal law and procedure and other enactments. And a good deal more law-making is under way in response to urgent pressures, such as the hope for expanded global business transactions and entry into the World Trade Organisation.

International Agreements

The PRC has also made great strides in constructing its legal system by adher-ing to many relevant multilateral international conventions and by erecting an extensive network of bilateral agreements with most foreign governments. For example, in order to facilitate international business co-operation, Beijing has since 1979 joined a bevy of intellectual property conventions, the UN Convention on Contracts for the International Sale of Goods, the New York Convention on the Recognition and Enforcement of Foreign Arbitral Awards, diplomatic and consular conventions and many others that have domestic legal effects, and it has concluded hundreds of bilateral arrangements with other countries, of which consular and trade agreements and tax and mutual protec-tion of investment treaties are only the first to come to mind.

Legal Institutions

A relatively small group of able and dedicated domestic and international law-makers can churn out norms at record-breaking speed, as the Chinese recently have. But enforcing the new norms in China's vast and diverse economic–social–political environment is, of course, a much greater challenge, one that involves millions of legal personnel staffing a range of institutions, both govern-mental and non-governmental.

The courts are the greatest weakness in the PRC legal system today. Although considerable legislation has been adopted concerning the organisation, struc-ture, responsibilities, procedures and ethics of the judicial system and although the Supreme People's Court and the Ministry of Justice have laboured mightily to overcome problems arising from low professional competence, corruption, *guanxi* (social connections) and local protectionism, the lower courts, including some provincial High Courts, must still be considered of questionable reliability. Moreover, despite all of China's recent legal progress, judicial administrators continue to dominate individual judges and Communist Party control over judicial decision-making remains as strong as ever in politically sensitive cases, as the world press reminds us daily, threatening to frustrate the hopes of the leadership as well as the masses for a court system that is perceived to be legitimate at home and abroad (see Cohen, 1997: 793).

Yet the courts in various parts of the country are improving, although the pace and nature of their progress are uneven. The procuracy, however, seems to be lagging behind the courts in its reform programme and tangible achievements, but there are signs of improvement at the central level, and it obviously requires time to translate reformist aspirations into prosecutorial practice. The reform process in the procuracy as well as the courts would be bolstered if both institutions received greater financial support from the Central Government and if the central legal organs used these added resources to gain greater control over personnel and policies of their local subordinates.

The accomplishments of the China International Economic and Trade Arbitration Commission (CIETAC), now the world's busiest arbitration institution, and the China Maritime Arbitration Commission (CMAC) offer hope that the PRC will be capable of establishing courts that are as competent and independent as CIETAC and CMAC tribunals. Although CIETAC, with which I am more familiar as both arbitrator and advocate, ought to adopt further reforms to assure its impartiality, it already enjoys an impressive reputation among some foreign business people as well as Chinese officials. China's domestic arbitration organisations, recently revised to throw off the dead hand of Soviet influence by distancing themselves from the clutches of government, can also be expected to provide increasingly fair and competent adjudication in a broad range of disputes, including those involving foreign and foreign-owned companies (see Cohen and Kearney, 1999). As in other countries, a reputable arbitration system may help to stimulate further judicial reform in China, by offering a competitive alternative and by stimulating demands for more reliable judicial enforcement of arbitration awards.

China's lawyers, non-existent 20 years ago, have made substantial progress and now number over 100,000. They are increasingly well trained by a burgeoning legal education system that has been perhaps the greatest growth industry in recent PRC higher education. Some legally sophisticated specialists in various fields are rising in China's largest cities, on law school faculties as well as in the rapidly expanding law firms. Foreign law schools have also contributed to this achievement through the opportunities they have afforded some promising PRC lawyers, scholars and students. Unfortunately, many PRC lawyers still seem impervious to the ethical precepts embodied in the Lawyers Law, the

Judges Law and other new norms designed to break the hold of corruption over the judicial system. Furthermore, most lawyers are unable or unwilling to represent controversial clients or causes, especially in politically sensitive criminal cases. Those who have sought to undertake such representations despite official and unofficial intimidation—always a minority in every society—deserve our admiration.

An overview of legal institutions should not overlook the dramatic rise of legal expertise in PRC legislative and administrative agencies and in state-owned enterprises (SOEs) and private enterprises. China's legislative progress would not have been possible without the increasingly impressive legal talent acquired by the National People's Congress, the State Council, various ministries and commissions and their local counterparts. Lawyers within the administrative agencies as well as those in the emerging legal departments of SOEs and private companies play an important role in implementing legislation, making contracts and settling disputes.

Procedure

Although the legal procedure of China's millennial imperial system was notorious for its complexity, Chinese have always undervalued the importance of procedure in implementing law and attaining justice. To its credit, the PRC has devoted a great deal of energy to the enactment of civil, arbitral, administrative and criminal procedure legislation, and the provisions in those laws, if faithfully implemented, would do much to endow the administration of justice in the PRC with the attributes of fundamental fairness Americans compendiously describe as "due process of law". Even the Constitution of the Chinese Communist Party requires notice and a hearing to be given prior to the imposition of sanctions upon Party members.

Yet PRC judges, prosecutors, lawyers, government and Party officials and even PRC law professors and scholars—with some distinguished exceptions—have not accorded this body of legislation the respect and attention it deserves. Indeed, I have occasionally been surprised by how little heed reputable legal experts have paid to procedural requirements when participating in actual cases. For example, "doing things the Chinese way" still prevails over rules prohibiting *ex parte* contacts with adjudicators.

Nevertheless, procedural practice is improving in all spheres, and some exciting experiments, such as civil trials based on the adversary system, are under way and may influence future legislation. Moreover, valuable experience is being acquired in implementing legislative innovations such as civil class actions, judicial review of administrative acts and defence lawyer participation in early stages of the criminal process.

Rising Rights Consciousness

As might be expected, rights consciousness appears to be rising in China, although broader, more systematic research will be needed to confirm details of this trend. The causes are many, of course, including the expansion of the middle class, the re-emergence of private property and entrepreneurship, improvements in and greater access to education, the impact of communications and globalisation, the advent of investigative journalism, the stimulus and opportunities created by foreign trade and investment, and increasing popular dissatisfaction with the selective law enforcement, corruption and unfairness of a regime that has aroused expectations of something better. In less than a decade, over 30 million securities accounts have been established on China's new stock exchanges, which Chinese regulators interpret to mean that over 100 million people have become involved with the implications of stock ownership. Over 18 million Chinese are currently employed by foreign-invested enterprises, which often serve as mini-universities in a country that allocates too few resources to higher education. Private home ownership is becoming more feasible, adding to the awareness of property rights. All of such factors lead ordinary Chinese to test official propaganda that holds forth the promise of legal protection.

Moreover, the increasingly effective response of the PRC legal system to those demands is itself heightening rights consciousness and the willingness of other citizens to seek to vindicate their legal rights. Every time a civil suit prevails, an arbitration award is enforced, an accused is acquitted, an illegal administrative act is overturned by the courts or compensation for damages is granted to those who surmount the hurdles presented by the State Compensation Law, others are encouraged to try their luck. And if the system disappoints them, as too often happens, the disappointed—emboldened by the relaxation of controls over the expression of opinion by those who do not present an organised challenge to the regime—are less reluctant than in the past to raise questions and to demand answers.

This is why I believe that, in the long run, if the overall trends and policies of the PRC's past two decades continue, prospects for the protection of those "human rights" emphasised in the West will improve in China as the legal system continues to improve.

But how long is the "long run" likely to be? And what kind of legal system can one expect in the interim? For example, will we witness a consolidation of the present trend toward perfecting one legal system for dealing with most Chinese and the rest of the world while retaining the old-style repressive system for dealing with those characterised, however inaccurately, as seeking to undermine state power? Such a development would demonstrate the continuing vitality of Chairman Mao's famous but specious dictum that, in applying the law, government must distinguish between "internal contradictions among the people" and "contradictions between the enemy and ourselves" and act with unbridled ferocity in the latter case.

Experience first in Japan and more recently in Taiwan and South Korea, the two areas socially most similar to the PRC, suggests that the "long run" should not be consigned to the indefinite, unachievable future, as the advent of true Communism should be. Yet the experience of other East Asian societies also suggests that history cannot be bypassed, either by the National People's Congress or even a unanimous resolution in favour of human rights in China by that most peremptory of legislative bodies, the United States Congress. Realists must recognise the wisdom of the Chinese phrase *xuyao yige guocheng* (literally "everything requires a process", i.e., "Rome wasn't built in a day").

If the growth of a genuine legal system took decades for the relatively small populations of Taiwan and South Korea, surely we cannot expect the process to be completed during the tenure of China's current technocratic leaders, even though they have shown considerable, if imperfect, understanding of the importance of law to China's development.

NEGOTIATING MEANS OF DISPUTE RESOLUTION

Given the context described in the foregoing section, how do sophisticated firms that deal with China cope with dispute resolution? Contract negotiations give them their first opportunity. Most contract disputes, of course, are disposed of by informal discussions between the parties, in China and elsewhere. Therefore, virtually all Sino-foreign contracts call for resolution of disputes by "friendly consultation" between the parties, and some require such discussions as a pre-requisite to either party invoking the assistance of any formal institution to resolve the problem. Occasionally a specific means of consultation is spelled out, for example by stipulating that designated high-ranking representatives of the parties must meet within a given period to consider the matter. Many multi-nationals will resist any compulsory consultation clause unless the duration of the required consultation is limited to a brief period, for fear that the Chinese side will claim that consultation possibilities have not been exhausted and thereby seek to delay resort to formal dispute resolution.

Although China takes pride in the prominence that its legal system and society accord to the mediation (conciliation) of disputes and although a large percentage of international business disputes are in fact settled by the mediation of PRC arbitrators or judges after a dispute has been referred to their institution, most international contracts that I have seen do not require mediation or even refer to it. Occasionally a contract will call for compulsory resort to the Beijing Conciliation Centre (BCC) or some other arrangement for invoking the assistance of a third party in promoting an agreed settlement, and, of course, the parties are free, after a dispute occurs, to refer it to a mediation organisation or an individual mediator. Yet my impression is that mediation independent of an adjudication or arbitration institution does not play a statistically significant role. My own firm's practice has never taken us to the BCC or to any similar arrangement, nor do clients or even Chinese parties generally suggest inserting such a provision in the contract. The BCC is reportedly not very busy, and, as sometime Chairman of the China Conciliation Committee of the American Arbitration Association (AAA), I can testify to the inertness of that facility despite the preparation of rules for Sino-American joint conciliation that track an earlier set of rules prepared by Hamburg for the German-China trade.

Probably most PRC-foreign business contracts, after the obligatory reference to the desirability of "friendly consultation", go on to provide for arbitration as the exclusive formal means of resolving a dispute that does not seem amenable to a harmonious outcome. This is not only because Chinese tend to regard arbitration as more congenial to their traditional preference for informal dispute resolution than courts, but also because of foreigners' mistrust of PRC courts. Moreover, both sides often are attracted by certain practical benefits of arbitration, such as the ability of each to select an arbitrator, the greater assurance of the tribunal's commercial expertise and honesty, the privacy and confidentiality of the proceedings, greater informality and the predictable prospect for a reasonably speedy decision.

There are usually four major questions to be addressed in negotiations relating to the arbitration clause: the site of arbitration, the administering organisation, the rules to be applied and the law that will govern the interpretation of the contract. PRC negotiators plainly prefer to have arbitration in China, usually before CIETAC and under its rules. It is also now possible for disputes between foreign-invested entities that are PRC legal persons and other PRC entities to be handled by the domestic Chinese arbitration organisations now found in some 130 Chinese cities, such as the Beijing Arbitration Commission, which is the busiest of them. Foreigners are understandably wary of these new, little-known domestic organisations, the rules of which are in some respects not as welcoming to foreigners as CIETAC's.

Until recently, it was not practical to have international arbitration in China under other auspices, such as the systems of the International Chamber of Commerce (ICC) or the United Nations Commission on International Trade Law (UNCITRAL), since CIETAC and the domestic arbitration organisations are unwilling to apply the rules of those foreign systems and were also opposed to the formation by others of *ad hoc* arbitral tribunals on Chinese territory. Nor was it clear that Chinese courts would recognise and enforce awards made under such systems in China. A foreign lawyer in Shanghai, however, has just informed me of two recent ICC arbitrations held in China with the expectation the awards will be eligible for enforcement in China as foreign awards under the UN Convention on the Recognition and Enforcement of Foreign Arbitral Awards. One hopes that this expectation will be fulfilled, since the last thing that any foreign company is looking for is another potential obstacle to enforcement of arbitration awards in PRC courts.

As CIETAC has gained in experience and progressively improved its procedures in order to attract foreign patronage, it has gained credibility abroad as well as at home. One big breakthrough came a decade ago when CIETAC began to appoint foreigners to the large panel of experts from which its arbitrators must be chosen, assuring foreign parties that there could be at least one non-PRC arbitrator on their tribunals. An even bigger, albeit unannounced, breakthrough came more recently, when CIETAC began to implement contract clauses providing that the presiding arbitrator must be a non-PRC national, thereby opening up the possibility that only one of the three arbitrators in a given tribunal might be from the PRC. This is a crucial point in offering comfort to foreigners, who otherwise sometimes worry that Chinese arbitrators might be biased against a foreign firm, especially if the Chinese party to the dispute, usually a state-owned enterprise, is part of the foreign trade system, in which many Chinese arbitrators have worked or still work.

Foreigners would be even more inclined to patronise CIETAC if it provided disputants with full information concerning each arbitrator's professional background and affiliations, as other international arbitration organisations do, so as to render meaningful the parties' right to challenge the arbitrator's impartiality. It would also be helpful if the CIETAC rules offered guidance concerning the conduct of the hearing. In the absence of such guidance some PRC arbitrators are tempted to import judicial procedures and legal rigidity into the hearing, even though one of arbitration's virtues is generally thought to be the escape it offers from court technicalities.

Since PRC law permits arbitration of international contract disputes abroad, even in the case of joint venture contracts providing for investment in China, many multinationals still insist on seizing the opportunity. Chinese companies are usually under instructions to negotiate until the final hour to avoid this outcome, but never to lose the deal because of it. PRC negotiators have accepted many foreign sites, arbitration institutions and rules, with ICC, UNCITRAL, the London Court of Arbitration and especially the Stockholm Chamber of Commerce being popular, depending on the national identity of the foreign firm, the nature of the transaction and other factors. Hong Kong, Singapore, Japan and occasionally the AAA also have acceptable organisations. In trade matters, if CIETAC is not acceptable to the foreign side, as a "compromise" the PRC often seeks to agree on arbitration in the country of the defendant, a provision frequently seen, for example, in Sino-Japanese contracts. But many foreign companies also shun such a provision since the case they worry about is the one in which the PRC party will be defendant, and that will be tried before CIETAC, which is what they wish to avoid.

Governing law is not an issue if the transaction involves an investment-type arrangement in China, since PRC legislation requires that Chinese law govern in those circumstances. In other types of transactions the parties are free to bargain. Frequently, however, neither is willing to accept the law of the other's country, they do not agree on that of a third country or some other body of legal principles and, therefore, nothing is stipulated about governing law. In most such cases Chinese negotiators view this situation with equanimity, especially if, as in cases of licensing of technology, import of complete plant or other capital goods, compensation trade, processing or assembly, the bulk of contracted activity is to take place in China. In those circumstances they believe, particularly if any dispute is to be arbitrated or adjudicated in China, that the arbitration panel, applying customary private international law principles, will select Chinese law as having the closest connection to the facts. PRC legislation as interpreted by the Supreme People's Court gives them a substantial basis for confidence in this regard.[2]

If, as sometimes occurs, the parties fail to agree on arrangements for arbitration, serious disputes will inevitably end up in court, usually a Chinese court unless the contract specifies otherwise. When a dispute occurs, unsophisticated parties occasionally are surprised that their failure to deal with dispute resolution in the contract means that they are committed to a court solution unless they can then persuade the other side that arbitration is mutually beneficial, which happens from time to time but not often. International financial contracts, such as loan agreements and guarantees, usually provide for resolution in the courts of the home jurisdiction of the foreign financial institution and sometimes in Chinese courts as well.

ACTUAL DISPUTE RESOLUTION

It is impossible, of course, to give a comprehensive description and analysis here of what has been a long and diverse experience. The subject deserves a book. Moreover, it is preaching to the choir to note the difficulty of formulating accurate generalisations about anything, not least the legal culture of dispute resolution with China, which turns out to be the clash of Chinese legal culture with a range of alien counterparts. How business disputes with the PRC are settled reflects to an important degree who the non-Chinese disputant is. Americans, Europeans, Japanese and non-PRC Chinese each have their own distinctive, if overlapping, approaches, and their PRC hosts have been struggling to adapt to each.

Indeed, the very likelihood that a dispute will occur reflects distinctive cultural approaches. In the 1980s, as Hong Kong and overseas Chinese took the lead in negotiating investment and other complex contracts in China, their projects in the Shenzhen Special Economic Zone and elsewhere in Guangdong Province near Hong Kong spawned an unusual number of serious court disputes, so many that CIETAC, ever alert to expand its business beyond its headquarters in Beijing, promptly established its first branch in Shenzhen.

---

[2] See *Supreme People's Court, Explanation of Several Questions Concerning the Application of the Law on Economic Contracts Involving Foreign Interests*, 19 October 1987.

Investigation revealed that the contracts that gave rise to the disputes often shared two related characteristics. The first was that they often failed to provide for contingencies likely to occur in implementing such transactions. The second was that, when the contracts did provide for anticipated contingencies, they did so in language that was frequently so ambiguous or sloppy that reasonable people could readily reach conflicting interpretations. Those contracts were usually negotiated between PRC representatives and overseas businessmen of Chinese origin who were eager to be among the first to mine the riches of the Motherland and were susceptible to blandishments such as: "[s]ince we are all Chinese and trust each other, there's no need to waste a lot of time negotiating detailed Western-style contracts".

Japanese multinationals, although surprisingly legalistic and cautious in assessing the investment environment in China, have nevertheless often contented themselves with contracts of less than Western-style specificity, largely because skilful Chinese negotiators have played upon not only their shared Confucian-Buddhist heritage but also the tremendous harm to China inflicted by Japanese imperialism. This failure to spell things out in the contract has contributed to many misunderstandings, which PRC negotiators have sometimes attributed to the canny Japanese negotiating style. One leading PRC business official, when asked whether it was easier negotiating contracts with Americans or Japanese, told me that Americans' penchant for detailed documents made it much more difficult to negotiate with them than the Japanese. Trouble with the Japanese came later, my informant claimed, since, when implementing the deal, they would say: "Oh, you want tops to those bottles? Of course, that will be extra"!

Cultural characteristics also come into play with respect to whether and when a dispute will be recognised. Hong Kong and overseas Chinese, and especially Japanese, multinationals, are very reluctant to acknowledge the existence of a serious dispute. The Japanese, hoping that time will reward their patience, are often prepared to take a long time and to employ subtle and indirect responses to a perceived problem rather than directly confront the Chinese at the outset. The major Japanese trading companies, each of which has over 100 joint ventures in China, most of them modest in size, have frequently allowed disputes and dissatisfaction to fester rather than bring matters to a boil and perhaps prejudice their huge trading operations, which far outweigh the significance of their investments. Their preference for informal settlement is stronger than that of most Western companies and, consequently, they are frequently willing to accept less than complete satisfaction of their claims.

Of course, Western as well as Asian companies prefer informal settlement for good practical reasons such as the desire to avoid greater out-of-pocket expenses, diversion of time and other resources and adverse impact on relations between the parties. Many still recall the traditional attitude of PRC trading companies that prevailed until the late 1980s—that any foreign resort to arbitration would be regarded as "a most unfriendly act", with a clear implication that this would adversely affect future business opportunities. In that era, if PRC trading companies thought that the foreign party had a legitimate contract grievance, they would agree to make it up to the foreigner by sweetening the terms of their next contract rather than formally acknowledging the existence of a dispute and an error.

PRC attitudes have softened in this respect during the past decade, as Chinese firms have become more accustomed to global transactions and the need for formal dispute resolution. Actually, in the 1990s Chinese firms have increasingly initiated both arbitration and litigation against foreign contract partners. Moreover, structural changes have eliminated the retaliatory power of the small group of PRC national trading companies that formerly monopolised trade under what was then known as the Ministry of Foreign Trade. Now many other national ministries have organised their own business companies and the economy has become largely decentralised, so that foreigners have to deal with thousands of new PRC entities, freeing foreigners from much of the fear that pursuing a dispute with one such entity might impact on relations with others, especially from the same national organisation.

Obviously, the likelihood that informal efforts will prove successful in settling any international business dispute will depend on a number of factors. Strictly speaking, some of them, such as the foreign party's political muscle, its "*guanxi*" or personal connections, its willingness to compromise or resort to bribery and its ability and willingness to mobilise publicity, may have little to do with the legal merits of the dispute. Yet, the effectiveness of all the above measures, perhaps even including bribery, is enhanced by a strong legal position. Indeed, my own experience in settling disputes, which does not include any exposure to bribery, suggests that the single most important factor is the strength of a party's legal case.

I have settled many contract disputes informally by literally laying down the law—the relevant legislative/regulatory provisions and contract terms—to a PRC administrative official who has responsibility for the project in question and the power to bend the Chinese party to his will. The stronger the legal case, the better the chance of winning.

How does this work in practice? Let me mention a typical contract case from the mid-1980s. A leading Japanese manufacturer had licensed its technology to a PRC enterprise owned by the government of Sichuan Province in China's Southwest. The contract could not have been clearer—there was to be no export of the product made with the licensed technology and no use of the Japanese company's trade mark without the advance, written consent of the licensor. Yet not long after the contract was approved by the provincial government and became effective, my client discovered that the licensee, without the client's consent or even notice to it, was exporting the product to the United States and using the licensor's trade mark. It even had the nerve to establish a US subsidiary that it purported to endow with the exclusive right to sell this product in the USA, where the Japanese company's subsidiary had been selling the product for over 30 years!

My Japanese client, who had ambitious hopes for the China market, was very upset at this first dispute with China and concerned that it might have to invoke formal legal measures to resolve the problem and thereby earn a bad reputation in China. I assured the client that the matter could be disposed of informally because it was clear that the Chinese party had violated the contract. The only problem was to locate the most authoritative decision-maker in the government hierarchy. This proved to be the provincial foreign trade commission that had approved the contract. After its officials met my client, studied the contract and verified the facts, it promptly put an end to the offending conduct, "educated" the Chinese party and restored harmony to the relationship, which has subsequently flourished.

Many disputes with China are, of course, more complicated, and many of these resist informal settlement. Yet, if the law and contract plainly favour the foreign side, it is usually worth a vigorous effort to gain relief via informal administrative channels. Allow me to relate another "war story" to illustrate how successful informal dispute resolution in China requires the co-ordinated mobilisation of a host of pressures.

My client, a small American multinational that had purchased the 50 per cent interest held by another American company in a joint venture in China's rust-belt Liaoning Province, had also purchased an additional 10 per cent from the PRC joint venturer, receiving representations and warranties that the venture was free of debt. When the client subsequently approached a local Chinese bank for a working capital loan to be made to the venture and secured by a mortgage on venture assets, it learned that, contrary to the contractual assurances given by the PRC joint venturer, the Chinese vice chairman/deputy general manager of the venture, without any authorisation from or notice to the venture or the foreign investor, had some months earlier used the venture's corporate seals to borrow one million US dollars in the name of the venture and to mortgage the venture's assets as security. This individual, who had also continued to serve as a leader of the PRC joint venturer, a city-owned enterprise that had exhausted its own credit, had in addition persuaded the local bank not to transmit the proceeds of the loan to the venture's account, but to that of the PRC joint venturer.

When my client discovered the deception and contract violation, it no longer wanted to continue co-operation with the PRC party or even to continue operations in China. Since, in the circumstances, selling its interest to a third party would not be likely to recoup its investment, it asked me to settle the dispute by persuading the PRC party to buy out the client's 60 per cent interest at a price equal to the client's investment. Since the PRC party was actually insolvent, which is why it had originally engaged in the fraudulent conduct in question, the client's request seemed a tall order, one that my law firm colleagues thought we could not fill.

Our only hope was to convince the city government, which had approved both the venture and my client's subsequent entry into the deal and which apparently had knowledge of the PRC party's deception, not only to approve the buy-out but also to pay for it. This required a multi-faceted strategy designed to maximise pressures on the city government.

The first thing I did was obtain a letter from the Chinese Consul General in New York to the Governor of Liaoning Province describing the deception, vouching for my client's standing and goodwill toward China and requesting assistance. Since such letters alone are rarely effective, I then had to activate the Governor's office and the provincial government to give more than lip service to our cause. For this purpose I sought out the US Consul General in the provincial capital of Shenyang. Fortunately he was both sympathetic and close to the Deputy Governor in charge of foreign investment, with whom he had been collaborating in Liaoning's campaign to revive its economy through increased foreign investment. The Deputy Governor gave me and our Consul General a marvellous banquet and assured me that, after I familiarised myself with the PRC joint venturer and the city government involved, the provincial foreign investment commission would prove responsive to my suggestions.

So my next step was to go to the city and open negotiations with the PRC joint venturer and the Deputy Mayor in charge of foreign investment. Before making my first visit to the city, with the assistance of a recent Beijing University law graduate who was serving as a paralegal in our firm's Beijing office, I prepared a memorandum in Chinese demonstrating not only that contract violations and fraud had been committed but also that there was a strong likelihood that both the vice chairman/deputy general manager who represented the PRC joint venturer and his friends at the bank had violated China's criminal law and financial regulations.

Armed with this memorandum but recognising that I was embarking on an uphill fight, I approached my first meeting in the city with more than customary trepidation. As I entered the outskirts, however, I saw a near-miraculous sight. Coming toward me on the road was a long caravan of about 40 large open trucks that was being paraded around the city. Standing in the open part of each, just behind the driver's cab, were four hapless men, each with a signboard labelled "economic criminal" hanging around his neck and each being gripped by the scruff of his neck by a fierce-looking public security officer. The city, it turned out, was in the midst of showing its support for the nationwide "Strike Hard at Criminals" mass movement! Buoyed by this beautiful sight, 15 minutes later I started my long-anticipated meeting by saying to my host, "Mr Mayor, I am delighted to see how determined this city is to stamp out economic crime. Now, let me explain this case to you".

This was a good opener but it took several more visits to soften up the opposition. During those visits I made it clear that we were preparing to use all available legal and governmental channels to win relief. I told them that we were retaining vigorous PRC counsel in a nearby city and made a point of contacting him from the local hotel so that the call might be monitored by the city government. Although the original joint venture contract had an arbitration clause and foreign parties usually prefer this option to going to a local court, when the Chinese side seemed unusually eager to accept arbitration I became suspicious and told them that we were preparing to go to court since they had violated the representations and warranties clause of their contract for transferring a 10 per cent interest and that contract had no arbitration clause. I suspected that both the PRC joint venturer and the city officials feared going to court even on an economic matter since, once in court, the matter could quickly get out of control and lead to a criminal investigation as well. To heighten their concern, I also stated that we were considering whether the case should be submitted to the provincial procuracy for possible investigation. Incidentally, the chief perpetrator of the deception—the vice chairman/deputy general manager of the venture—never made an appearance and was supposedly ill in hospital.

Back in Beijing between visits, I reported the dispute to the relevant Vice Minister of the Ministry of Foreign Trade and Economic Co-operation (MOFTEC) and his staff in order to put additional pressure on the provincial foreign investment commission under their jurisdiction. I also prepared to report the case to the national Procurator General's office if the provincial government should need more prodding.

The result of all these machinations was that the Chinese joint venturer fully acknowledged its contract violation and obligation to buy out my client. The city government did too, and it appeared shaken by the letter of the Chinese Consul General, which the Governor had forwarded to it in order to show that the case was affecting the PRC's foreign relations. Yet, the problem was still how to generate enough pressure to stimulate the city government to make the immediate lump sum $3 million payment that would come close to making my client whole.

That required another trip to the provincial capital, where the US Consul General had arranged a meeting with the head of the foreign investment commission, who opened with a surprisingly hard line, stating that this was really just an ordinary commercial dispute and there was no need to ask government assistance. I knew that this official had recently been in the USA proclaiming the virtues of investing in Liaoning and was currently taking out large advertisements in the foreign press to the same effect. So I asked him, raising my voice for the only time in this entire negotiation, whether he would like to have *The Wall Street Journal, The New York Times* and Hong Kong's *South China Morning Post* reveal the true story of how American investors are treated in Liaoning. At that point, he offered to be helpful in obtaining approval for the city's buy-out on our terms. Publicity is the last refuge of a desperately frustrated foreign investor.

The story came to a happy ending shortly afterward. Although perhaps more colorful than most, it is not atypical. I recently settled two separate disputes in different Chinese provinces for a foreign power company whose contracts were plainly violated by state-owned companies in cahoots with local officials, and the techniques used were similar.

CONCLUDING THOUGHTS

This is the real world of PRC dispute resolution—a rough and tumble, occasionally Wild West, environment. Yet the rule of law is part of the story, even for informal settlements. Pressures are not likely to be effective if the client does not have a persuasive legal case on the merits. Moreover, the existence of functioning formal legal institutions and the ability of the foreign company to resort to them, if necessary, constitute one of the strongest pressures for informal settlement. Although PRC companies and the officials who control them are becoming increasingly sophisticated about formal dispute resolution, most still dearly wish to avoid it.

Further discussion of the realities of PRC dispute resolution, including discussion of experiences with arbitration and adjudication, will have to await a longer study. Yet a few final remarks must be made about those formal processes, as a reminder of their limitations. For example, some foreign-related economic disputes that go to Chinese court become a political football, where legal arguments and action in the courtroom are merely the tip of the iceberg. CIETAC arbitration offers a more stable setting, but, as previously mentioned, some of its procedures need further improvement, and some observers fear the impact of possible off-the-record contacts and of the cosy MOFTEC family atmosphere that prevails.

The greatest problem may not be the obstacles to fair decision-making in arbitration or even adjudication, but what happens if a party wins. Enforcement in PRC courts of both foreign and domestic arbitration awards and court judgments is uncertain, to say the least, whether the would-be enforcer is a foreign company or a Chinese entity from another part of the PRC. "Local protectionism" may be the greatest weakness in the nation's judicial system, and resort to arbitration often merely postpones, but does not avoid, involvement with local courts. The great thing about a successful informal settlement is that, by definition, it provides at least some actual relief to a party whose contract rights have been violated, instead of leaving the "victorious" party with a judgment or award, obtained at much greater cost, that may not be worth the paper on which it is written.

Yet, does pressing administrative officials to give contractual relief, instead of seeking such relief from arbitration or judicial institutions, inhibit the development of China's legal system? Some PRC judges and officials have recently raised the question. Occasionally an official who formerly would give help to foreigners with legal grievances will now refuse to do so, admonishing the foreigner's counsel to make use of the country's evolving legal institutions instead. Some officials also say that they no longer dare to press PRC entities to honour contract obligations because the unhappy Chinese party might bring a legal action against them for damages under the new State Compensation Law, which begins to put teeth into China's constitutional protection of its citizens against officials' arbitrary infringements of their rights. These arguments are sometimes merely excuses of officials who do not want to take responsibility, but some thoughtful officials are quite sincere in voicing them.

To date my response has been to tell them that, whatever the merits of such arguments in theory, the likely result in practice is that my client will go to law, spend $200,000 and two years seeking formal vindication, and then still have to return to the competent official to engineer an effective implementation of its rights. If the lawyer's first duty is to the client, at this stage of China's legal development it seems to me that the lawyer has to continue to press for informal settlement whenever possible.

REFERENCES

Cohen, Jerome A. (1997), "Reforming China's Civil Procedure: Judging The Courts", *American Journal of Comparative Law* 45 (4); 793–804.
—— and Kearney, Adam (1999), "The New Beijing Arbitration Commission" in Freshfields (ed.), *Doing Business in China: People's Republic of China*, (Yonkers, NY: Juris Publishing, Inc.), pt. IV.
Edwards, R. Randle (1980), "Ch'ing Legal Jurisdiction over Foreigners" in J. A. Cohen, R. R. Edwards and F. C. Chen (eds.), *Essays on China's Legal Traditions* (Princeton, NJ: Princeton University Press).
Morse, H. W. (1960), *The International Relations of the Chinese Empire* (Taipei, Taiwan: Books World Co.).
Willoughby, Westel W. (1920), *Foreign Rights and Interests in China* (Baltimore, Mld.: Johns Hopkins Press).

Index

Page numbers of tables are shown in italics.